Dictionary of
BABY NAMES

Dictionary of
BABY NAMES

STRATHEARN

This edition published by
STRATHEARN BOOKS LIMITED
Toronto, Canada

© 2000 Geddes & Grosset, an imprint of Children's Leisure Products Limited,
David Dale House, New Lanark, Scotland

First printed 2000
Reprinted 2001

Cover illustrations by Jane Molineaux, Simon Girling and Associates.
Baby photograph by Dia Max, courtesy of Telegraph Colour Library

ISBN 1 84205 023 0

Printed and bound in Europe

A

Aamor *see* AENOR.

Aaron a masculine first name meaning 'mountaineer, enlightener' (*Hebrew*). In the Old Testament, Aaron, who was an older brother of Moses, became the first High Priest of the Israelites. A contracted diminutive is Arn.

Abán a masculine first name meaning 'little abbot', from *aba*, 'abbot' (*Irish Gaelic*). The anglicised form is Abban.

Abban the anglicised masculine form of ABÁN.

Abbie a feminine diminutive form of ABIGAIL, also used independently.

Abbot or **Abbott** a surname, meaning 'father of the abbey' (*Old English*), used as a masculine first name.

Abby a feminine diminutive form of ABIGAIL, also used independently.

Abdul or **Abdullah** a masculine first name meaning 'servant of Allah' (*Arabic*).

Abe (1) a masculine first name meaning 'father' (*Aramaic*). (2) a masculine diminutive form of ABRAHAM and ABRAM.

Abel a masculine first name meaning 'breath, fickleness, vanity' (*Hebrew*). In the Bible it is the name of the second son of Adam and Eve, who was killed by his brother, Cain.

Abelard a masculine first name meaning 'nobly resolute' (*Germanic*).

Aberah a feminine variant form of AVERAH.

Abiathar a masculine first name meaning 'father of plenty' or 'excellence' (*Hebrew*). In the Old Testament he was a priest and the only survivor of a massacre of the priesthood ordered by King Saul.

Abiel a masculine first name meaning 'father of strength' (*Hebrew*).

Abigail a feminine first name meaning 'my father's joy' or 'hand maid' (*Hebrew*). In the Old Testament Abigail was the woman who brought provisions to David and his followers and who later married David. Diminutive forms are Abbie, Abby and Gail.

5

Abijah a masculine first name meaning 'to whom Jehovah is a father' (*Hebrew*). It is a name often found in the Old Testament, most notably that of a king of Judah who ruled for two years, and that of the second son of Samuel, who, with his brother JOEL, ruled Israel. A diminutive form is Bije.

Abner a masculine first name meaning 'father of light' (*Hebrew*). In the Old Testament Abner was the chief of King Saul's army who declined to fight Goliath.

Abra a feminine first name meaning 'mother of multitudes' (*Hebrew*).

Abraham a masculine first name meaning 'father of a multitude' (*Hebrew*). In the Old Testament Abraham is the first of the patriarchs, and he is regarded as the founder of Israel. He was originally named ABRAM. Abraham Lincoln (1809–65) was the sixteenth President of the United States. Diminutive forms are Abe, Bram, Ham.

Abram a masculine first name meaning 'father of elevation' (*Hebrew*). It was the original name of ABRAHAM. Diminutive forms are Abe, Bram.

Absalom a masculine first name meaning 'my father is peace' (*Hebrew*). In the Old Testament he was the third and favourite son of King David. He killed his half-brother for raping his sister Tamar but was eventually pardoned. He led a rebellion against his father but was defeated by JOAB, who killed him.

Acacia the name of a plant, possibly meaning 'immortality and resurrection' (*Greek*), used as a feminine first name.

Acantha a feminine first name meaning 'thorny, spiny' (*Greek*).

Ace a masculine first name meaning 'unity, unit' (*Latin*).

Achilles a masculine first name that may come from a river name and that of the legendary Greek hero who joined the Greek attack on Troy. He was killed when an arrow from the bow of Paris was guided by Apollo to his heel, his only vulnerable part.

Ackerley a surname, meaning 'from the acre meadow' (*Old English*), used as a masculine first name.

Ackley a surname, meaning 'from the oak tree meadow' (*Old English*), used as a masculine first name.

Ada (1) a feminine diminutive of ADELA or names beginning with Adal, also used independently. (2) a variant form of ADAH. Ada, Countess Lovelace (1815–52), was the only legitimate daughter of Lord Byron and she worked with Charles Babbage, inventor of the Analytical Engine, a forerunner of the computer. The computing language ADA was named in her honour.

Adabel or **Adabela** or **Adabella** feminine variant forms of ADABELLE.

Adabelle a feminine first name meaning 'joyful and beautiful', a combination of ADA and BELLE. Variant forms are Adabel, Adabela and Adabella.

Adah a feminine first name meaning 'ornament' (*Hebrew*). In the Old Testament Adah was one of the two wives of Lamech, the son of Methusalah. A variant form is ADA.

Adair (1) a masculine first name, the root of which is Irish Gaelic *doire*, 'oak wood', and the origin of the name may be 'dweller by the oak wood', or perhaps 'attendant of the oak grove', since the oak was a sacred tree in Celtic lore, tended by the druids. (2) a Scottish masculine form of EDGAR.

Adalard a masculine first name meaning 'noble and brave' (*Germanic*).

Adalia a feminine first name from an early Saxon tribal name, the origin of which is unknown (*Germanic*).

Adam a masculine first name meaning 'man, earth man, red earth' (*Hebrew*). In the Bible Adam was the first man on earth and the father of the human race.

Adamina a feminine form of ADAM (*Latin*).

Adamnan a masculine first name, probably a diminutive form of Adam, 'little Adam' (*Gaelic*). The Gaelic form is both Adhamhán and Adomnán. St Adamnan, a seventh-century abbot of Iona, wrote his famous *Life of St Columba*.

Adar a feminine first name meaning 'fire' (*Hebrew*). As the name in the Jewish calendar for the twelfth month of the Biblical year and the sixth month of the civil year, it is a name sometimes given to girls born in that period.

Addie feminine diminutive of ADELAIDE.

Addison a surname, meaning 'Adam's son', used as a masculine first name (*Old English*).

Adeel a masculine variant form of ADIL.

Adela a feminine first name meaning 'of noble birth; a princess' (*Germanic*). A diminutive form is DELLA.

Adelaide a feminine first name meaning 'of noble birth; a princess' (*Germanic*). A diminutive form is Addie.

Adelbert *see* ALBERT.

Adèle or **Adele** the French feminine form of ADELA, now also used as an English form.

Adelfia a feminine variant form of ADELPHIA.

Adelheid a feminine first name meaning 'noble kind' (*Germanic*). A diminutive form is Heidi.

Adeline or **Adelina** a feminine first name meaning 'of noble birth; a princess' (*Germanic*). A diminutive form is Aline.

Adelpha a feminine variant form of ADELPHIA.

Adelphia a feminine first name meaning 'sisterly, eternal friend of mankind' (*Greek*). Variant forms are Adelfia, Adelpha.

Adeon a masculine first name that has been related to Welsh *adain*, 'wing' (Welsh), although perhaps it is a form of AEDDAN.

Aderyn a feminine first name from *aderyn*, 'bird' (*Welsh*).

Adhnúall (pronounced *a-nooall*) a masculine first name from *adnúall*, 'sweet of sound' (*Irish Gaelic*). In Celtic legend, this was the name of one of the hounds of FIONN macCumhaill.

Adil a masculine first name meaning 'honest' (Arabic). A variant form is Adeel.

Adin a masculine first name meaning 'sensual' (*Hebrew*). In the Old Testament Adin was one of the patriarchal heads of Israel.

Adina a feminine first name meaning 'voluptuous, ripe, mature' (*Hebrew*).

Adlai a masculine first name meaning 'God is just' (*Hebrew*). In the Bible Adlai was the overseer of King David's herds. A more recent bearer of the name was the American lawyer and Democrat politician Adlai Ewing Stevenson (1900–1968) who was twice defeated in the presidential elections.

Adler a masculine first name meaning 'eagle, perceptive one' (*Germanic*).

Adney a masculine first name meaning 'island-dweller' (*Old English*).

Adolf the German masculine form of ADOLPH.

Adolfa or **Adolfina** feminine variant forms of ADOLPHA.

Adolph or **Adolphus** a masculine first name meaning 'noble wolf; noble hero' (*Germanic*). A diminutive form is Dolph.

Adolpha a feminine first name meaning 'noble she-wolf, she who will give her life for her young', the feminine form of Adolf (*Germanic*). Variant forms are Adolfa, Adolfina, Adolphina.

Adolphe the French masculine form of ADOLPH.

Adolphina a variant feminine form of ADOLPHA.

Adon or **Adonai** a masculine first name meaning 'lord', a sacred word for God (*Hebrew*).

Adonia a feminine first name meaning 'beautiful goddess of the resurrection; eternal renewal of youth' (*Greek*).

Adoniram a masculine first name meaning 'lord of height' (*Hebrew*).

Adonis a name meaning 'lord' and that of the Greek god, borrowed from the Phoenicians, who was a favourite of VENUS. William Shakespeare (1654–1616) wrote a poem, *Venus and Adonis* (1593), that tells of the passion of Venus for the youthful Adonis and the killing of the latter by a wild boar.

Adora a feminine first name meaning 'adored and beloved gift' (*Latin*).

Adorabella a feminine first name meaning 'beautiful gift', a combination of ADORA and BELLA.

Adorna a feminine first name meaning 'adorned with jewels' (*Latin*).

Adrian a masculine first name meaning 'of the Adriatic' in Italy (*Latin*). It was the name adopted by several popes, including Adrian IV (Nicholas Breakspear) (*c.*1100–1159), the only English pope (1154–59). Variant forms are Adrien, HADRIAN.

Adrianne a feminine form of ADRIAN.

Adriel a masculine first name meaning 'from God's congregation' (*Hebrew*). In the Old Testament Adriel married Merab, SAUL's oldest daughter, although she had previously been promised to DAVID.

Adrien a masculine variant form of ADRIAN. It is sometimes used as a feminine first name.

Adrienne a feminine form of Adrian. Adrienne Corrie is British actress.

Adwen a masculine first name meaning 'fiery' (*Cornish*), a name related to the Gaelic AED.

Aeb or **Aebh** feminine variant forms of AOBH.

Aebhric (pronounced *ive-rick*) an Irish Gaelic masculine first name of unknown meaning. It was the name of the monk of Erris who wrote down the story of the *Children of Lír*. English forms are Evric, Everett.

Aebill a variant feminine form of AÍBELL.

Aed (pronounced *aigh*) a masculine first name meaning 'fiery one', from *áed*, 'fire' (*Scottish and Irish Gaelic*). A common name among the Gaels, and said to have been the most frequent personal name in early

Ireland. It was so common that most who had the name had a further descriptive name or nickname, like Aed Finn (Gaelic *fionn*, 'fair') or Aed Ruad (Gaelic *ruadh*, 'red'). It was the name given to several high kings of Ireland and a king of the Scots, son of Kenneth MacAlpin. The name is also found as Aedh, Aodh.

Aedammair (pronounced *ay-dammar*) a diminutive and feminine form of AED (*Irish Gaelic*). Traditionally Aedammair was the first Irish nun.

Aedán (pronounced *ay-dann*) a diminutive form of Aed, with the -an suffix (*Scottish and Irish Gaelic*). The Anglicised forms are AIDAN and Edan. An early king of Dalriada was named Aedán, as were twenty-three other saints of the Gaelic Church.

Aeddan a masculine first name derived from *aed*, 'fire' (Welsh). Aeddan was a warrior of the Old Welsh, featuring in the sixth-century poem 'Y Gododdin'.

Aedh a variant masculine form of AED.

Aednat a feminine diminutive form of Aed (*Irish Gaelic*). A variant form is AODHNAIT.

Aefa an anglicised feminine form of AOIFE.

Ael (pronounced *ale*) a masculine first name meaning 'rocky', from *ail*, 'rock' (*Breton*). A name with a similar meaning to Peter.

Aelda or **Aeldra** a feminine variant form of ALDORA.

Aelheran (pronounced *ale-eran*) a masculine first name meaning 'iron-browed', from *ael*, 'brow', and *haearn*, 'iron' (*Welsh*). A saint's name, preserved in Llanaelhaearn in Caernarfonshire.

Aelwen a feminine first name meaning 'fair-browed' (*Welsh*).

Aelwyn a masculine first name meaning 'fair-browed' (*Welsh*), the masculine form of Aelwen.

Aeneas a masculine first name meaning 'commended' (*Greek*). In Virgil's *Aeneid*, Aeneas was a Trojan hero who escaped when Troy was taken and sailed for Italy. After numerous adventures he was driven by a tempest to Carthage where DIDO fell in love with him. On orders from Zeus, however, he sailed for Italy. In the New Testament Aeneas was healed by Peter after suffering paralysis for eight years. A variant form is Eneas.

Aengus *see* ANGUS.

Aenor (pronounced *ay-nor*) a feminine first name from the Breton name Aamor, probably from a root-word meaning 'bright' (*Irish Gaelic*).

Aerfen a feminine first name meaning 'renowned in battle' (*Welsh*). This was the name of an early Welsh goddess, whose cult was linked to the River Dee in North Wales.

Aeron a masculine first name the meaning of which is unclear; but possibly *aeron*, 'berry' (*Welsh*). It is also the name of an early Welsh wargod, derived from the Brythonic *agroná*, 'slaughter'. Some scholars have identified it with the Scottish river name Ayr, but this has also been disputed.

Aeronwen a feminine variant form of AERONWY.

Aeronwy a feminine first name meaning 'the berry stream' (*Welsh*). The name comes from the River Aeron in Ceredigion. A variant form is Aeronwen.

Aethelbert a variant form of ETHELBERT.

Aethelred a variant form of ETHELRED.

Afonso the Portuguese masculine form of ALPHONSO.

Afra a variant feminine form of APHRA.

Africa the name of the continent used as a feminine first name.

Agatha a feminine first name meaning 'good; kind' (*Greek*). St Agatha (202–251) was an early Christian martyr. Dame Agatha Christie (1890–1976) was a prolific writer of detective stories. A diminutive form is Aggie or Aggy.

Agave a feminine first name meaning 'illustrious, famous' (*Greek*). In Greek mythology, Agave was a daughter of CADMUS who was driven mad by the gods because of her ill-treatment of SEMELE.

Aggie or **Aggy** a feminine diminutive form of AGATHA, AGNES.

Agnes a feminine first name meaning 'chaste, pure' (*Greek*). St Agnes was a fourth-century Christian martyr and patron saint of young girls. Agnes was a very popular name in Scotland until the late twentieth century. 'Black Agnes' Randolph, Countess of Dunbar, was a fourteenth-century heroine of the Scottish warsof independence. Diminutive forms are Aggie, Aggy, Agneta, Nessa, Nessie.

Agnès the French feminine form of AGNES.

Agnese the Italian feminine form of AGNES.

Agneta a feminine variant form of AGNES.

Agostino the Italian masculine form of AUGUSTINE.

Agroná *see* AERON.

Agustín the Spanish masculine form of AUGUSTINE.

Ahern a masculine first name meaning 'horse lord, horse owner' (*Irish Gaelic*).

Ahmad or **Ahmed** a masculine first name meaning 'praiseworthier' (*Arabic*). It is one of the names applied to MOHAMMED.

Ahren a masculine first name meaning 'eagle' (*Germanic*).

Aíbell a feminine first name meaning 'radiance', 'spark' (Irish Gaelic). This was the name of an old Irish goddess, later viewed as a fairy queen, with her mound at Craigeevil, near Killaloe in County Clare. She figures in numerous legends. Variant forms of the name are Aebill, Aoibheall; anglicised to Aibinn or Eevin.

Aibinn a feminine anglicised form of AÍBELL.

Aibgréne (pronounced *a-grenya*) a feminine first name meaning 'radiance of the sun', from *grian*, 'sun' (*Irish Gaelic*). The name of a daughter born to Deirdre and Naoise, in the Legend of the Sons of Usna, who married the king of Tir nan Og.

Aibhlinn (pronounced *ave-linn*) a feminine first name, an Irish and Scottish Gaelic form of AVELINE (Norman French), anglicised into EVELYN.

Aibreán (pronounced *ap-reeann*) the Irish Gaelic feminine form of APRIL.

Aidan the anglicised masculine form of AEDÁN. A variant form is Edan. St Aidan (d. 651) was an Irish missionary in Northumbria who founded a monastery on Lindisfarne (Holy Island). Aidan Quinn is an American film actor.

Aideen (1) a feminine form of AED (Irish Gaelic). Aideen was the wife of the legendary warrior Oscar, grandson of Fionn macCumhaill. (2) an anglicised feminine form of Irish ETAIN.

Aife a feminine variant of AOIFE.

Aiken (1) a Scottish male diminutive form of ADAM, shortened to Ad, with the diminutive suffix -kin added. Aiken Drum is the hero of a familiar Scottish nursery song. (2) or **Aitken** the Scottish form of ATKIN, a surname meaning 'son of Adam' (*Old English*), used as a masculine first name.

Ailaw a feminine first name meaning 'melodious' (Welsh).

Ailbe a masculine or feminine variant of AILBHE; Ailbe Grùadbrecc, 'of the freckled cheeks', was wife to Fionn MacCumhaill after Gráinne.

Ailbhe (pronounced *al-veh*) a masculine or feminine first name meaning 'white', from *albho*,'white' (*Irish Gaelic*). Twelve warriors of the Fianna bore this name. AILBE is a variant form.

Ailean a feminine Scots Gaelic form of ALAN.

Aileen an anglicised Scottish feminine form of Gaelic Eibhlinn, Helen (*see* EILEEN). The form Aileen is also used on the Isle of Man.

Ailill (pronounced *al-yill*) a masculine first name probably derived from Gaelic *ail*, 'rock' (Irish Gaelic), although an alternative is 'sprite', as in Old Welsh *ellyll*. An anglicised version is Aleel. It was a well-known name in ancient Ireland; the name of Queen Medb's consort, and numerous other kings and heroes.

Ailis an Irish Gaelic feminine form of ALICE.

Ailsa a feminine first name that comes from Ailsa Craig, the rocky isle off the Ayrshire coast also known as Paddy's Milestone. The name's derivation is probably from the Old Norse proper name Ael, with -ey, 'island'.

Aimée the French feminine form of AMY.

Aindrea a Scottish Gaelic masculine form of ANDREW.

Áine (pronounced *an-yeh*) a feminine first name meaning 'brightness' (*Irish Gaelic*). This was the name of an early fertility goddess, who later was viewed as a fairy queen. There are many legends around her, including her bewitchment of Maurice, Earl of Desmond, who however gained control of her by seizing hold of her cloak. Although often anglicised as Annie or Anne, the names have quite separate sources.

Aingeall (pronounced *an-gheeall*) a feminine first name meaning 'angel' (Irish and Scottish Gaelic). *See also* MELANGELL.

Ainnle (pronounced *ann-leh*) an Irish Gaelic masculine first name the meaning of which is unclear. In Celtic legend, it was the name of one of the three sons of Usna, brother to Naoise, Deirdre's lover. All three were famed warriors.

Ainsley a masculine or feminine variant form of AINSLIE. Ainsley Gotto became famous in an Australian political scandal.

Ainslie a place name, from *Aenes lie*, 'Aene's meadow' or 'meadow of the respected one' (*Old English*), then a surname, now increasingly used as a masculine or feminine first name. A variant form is AINSLEY.

Aisha or **Aishah** a feminine first name meaning 'prospering' (*Arabic*). Variant forms are Asia, Ayisah, Aysha, Ayshia.

Aisleen a feminine or masculine variant of AISLING.

Aisling (pronounced *ash-ling*) a feminine or masculine first name from *aisling*, 'dream' (*Irish and Scots Gaelic*), not used as a personal name until modern times. Variant forms are Aisleen, Aislinn, Ashling.

Aislinn a feminine or masculine variant of AISLING.

Ajay a masculine first name meaning 'unconquerable' (*Sanskrit*).

Akash a masculine first name meaning 'sky' (*Sanskrit*).

Akshar a masculine first name meaning 'not forgotten' (*Sanskrit*).

Al masculine diminutive of ALAN, ALBERT, etc. Al Pacino is an American film actor who came to stardom in *The Godfather* and whose original name was Alberto.

Alain the French masculine form of ALAN.

Alair (pronounced *allar*) a masculine first name meaning 'cheerful', 'vital', from *alair*, 'cheerful' (*Irish Gaelic*).

Alan a masculine first name meaning 'rock-like, steadfast', from *ailinn* 'rock' (Scottish Gaelic). *Ailean nan Sop*, 'Alan of the Straws' is a well-known character in Scottish Highland folk-tales. A popular name in Scotland since the time of the early Stewarts, when Alan FitzWalter, High Steward of Scotland, assumed the surname which was ultimately to be that of the royal line. In his case the name probably came from Brittany, although the root is the same. Other forms are ALLAN, ALLEN. *See* ALUN.

Alanna (1) a feminine first name meaning 'o child', from the Gaelic *a leanbh* (Irish Gaelic). (2) a feminine form of ALAN. Variant forms are Alana, Alannah, Lana.

Alard a masculine variant form of ALLARD.

Alaric a masculine first name meaning 'noble ruler; all-rich' (*Germanic*).

Alarica a feminine variant form of ALARICE.

Alarice feminine form of ALARIC (*Germanic*). Variant forms are Alarica, Alarise.

Alarise a feminine variant form of ALARICE.

Alasdair the Scottish Gaelic masculine form of ALEXANDER. This name was made popular by three kings of Scotland, especially Alexander III (died 1293). Other forms are ALASTAIR, ALISTAIR, ALISTER. Diminutive forms are Al, Aly, Ally.

Alastair a masculine variant form of ALASDAIR. Alastair Stewart was a British TV newscaster.

Alaw a feminine first name meaning 'melodious' (Welsh).

Alban (1) a masculine first name meaning 'Scot' (Scottish Gaelic). The name comes from the Gaelic name for Scotland, Alba. (2) a Welsh masculine first name that comes from St Alban, the Roman soldier who was the first British Christian martyr, in AD 303, and was venerated among the Brythonic tribes. The Latin name is Albanus, from *alba*, 'mountain'. (3) a masculine first name meaning 'white', or of Alba in Italy (*Latin*).

Albanus the Latin masculine form of ALBAN.

Albern a masculine first name meaning 'noble warrior' (*Old English*).

Albert a masculine first name meaning 'all-bright; illustrious' (*Germanic*). Albert the Great (Albertus Magnus) (1206–80) was a Dominican friar, bishop and philosopher and the teacher of St Thomas Aquinas. Albert Brooks is an American film actor and director. Diminutive forms are Al, Bert, Bertie.

Alberta feminine form of ALBERT.

Albin *see* ALBAN.

Albina a feminine first name meaning 'white, very fair' (*Latin*). Variant forms are Albinia, Alvina, Aubina, Aubine.

Albinia a feminine variant form of ALBINA.

Albrecht a German masculine form of ALBERT.

Alcina a feminine first name meaning 'strong-minded one', from a legendary woman who could make gold from stardust (*Greek*).

Alcott the surname, meaning 'old cottage or hut' (*Old English*), used as a masculine first name.

Alcyone a feminine first name that comes from the name of a woman in Greek mythology who drowned herself from grief at her husband's death and who was turned into a kingfisher. Variant forms are Halcyone, Halcyon.

Alda a feminine first name meaning 'wise and rich' (*Germanic*). Variant forms are Eada, Elda.

Alden a surname, meaning 'old or trustworthy friend' (*Old English*), used as a masculine first name.

Alder a surname, meaning 'alder tree' (*Old English*) or 'old, wise and rich' (*Germanic*), used as a masculine first name .

Aldis (1) a surname, meaning 'old house' (*Old English*), used as a masculine first name. (2) a feminine diminutive form of some names beginning with Ald-.

Aldo a masculine first name meaning 'old' (*Germanic*). Aldo Ray (1926–91) was an American film actor. A variant form is ALDOUS.

Aldora a feminine first name meaning 'of noble rank' (*Old English*). Variant forms are Aelda, Aeldra.

Aldous a masculine variant form of ALDO. Aldous Huxley (1894–1963) was an English novelist and essayist whose best-known novel was *Brave New World* (1932).

Aldrich a surname, meaning 'old, wise ruler' (*Old English*), used as a masculine first name.

Aldwin or **Aldwyn** a masculine variant form of ALVIN.

Alec a Scottish masculine diminutive form of ALEXANDER, sometimes used as a name in its own right. Alec Baldwin is an American actor.

Aled the name of a river in Denbighshire (*Welsh*) used as a masculine first name. Aled Jones was a celebrated boy singer. A variant form is Aleid.

Aleda a feminine variant from of ALIDA.

Aleel an anglicised masculine form of AILILL.

Aleid a masculine variant form of ALED.

Aleria a feminine first name meaning 'like an eagle' (*Latin*).

Aleron a masculine first name meaning 'eagle' (*Latin*).

Aleta a feminine variant form of ALIDA.

Alethea a feminine first name meaning 'truth' (*Greek*).

Alex (1) a masculine diminutive of ALEXANDER, now used independently. (2) a feminine diminutive of ALEXANDRA, now used independently. A variant form is Alix.

Alexa feminine diminutive of ALEXANDRA.

Alexander a masculine first name, the anglicised form of *Iskander*, 'defender of men' (*Greek*), made famous by Alexander the Great (*c.*360–330 BC). It was the name adopted by several popes and became a popular name in Scotland, since three of the country's most effective medieval kings bore this name. Diminutive forms are Alec, Alex, Alick, Lex, Sandy. *See also* ALASDAIR.

Alexandra and **Alexandrina** feminine forms of ALEXANDER. Diminutive forms are Alex, Alexa, Lexie, Lexy, Sandie, Sandra, Sandy.

Alexas a masculine variant of Alexis that was used by William Shakespeare (1564–1616) for the character of Cleopatra's duplicitous minister in his play *Antony and Cleopatra*.

Alexia a feminine form of ALEXIS.

Alexina feminine form of ALEXANDER.

Alexis a masculine or feminine first name meaning 'help, defence'

(*Greek*). A variant form is ALEXAS.

Alf or **Alfie** masculine diminutive forms of ALFRED.

Alfonsine feminine form of ALPHONSE (*Germanic*). Variant forms are Alphonsina, Alphonsine, Alphonza.

Alfonso a Spanish and Italian form of ALPHONSO.

Alford a surname, meaning 'old ford' (*Old English*), used as a masculine first name.

Alfred a masculine first name meaning 'good or wise counsellor' (*Germanic*). Alfred Molina is an English actor. Diminutive forms are Alf, Alfie.

Alfreda feminine form of ALFRED. Diminutive forms are Alfie, Allie. Variant forms are Elfreda, Elfreida, Elfrida, Elva, Elga, Freda.

Alger a masculine first name meaning 'elf spear' (*Old English*). Alger Hiss (1904–96) was an American politician who was imprisoned for perjury associated with alleged spying activities.

Algernon a masculine first name meaning 'whiskered' (*Old French*). A diminutive form is Algie, Algy.

Algie or **Algy** a masculine diminutive form of ALGERNON.

Ali a masculine first name meaning 'noble' or 'excellent' (*Arabic*).

Alice or **Alicia** a feminine first name meaning 'of noble birth; a princess' (*Germanic*). William Shakespeare (1564–1616) used the name Alice for the character of the French princess's attendant who acts as interpreter between the princess and King Henry V in his play *King Henry V*. Variant forms are Ailis, Alison, Alys, Alyssa, Eilis. A diminutive form is Allie or Ally.

Alick a masculine diminutive of ALEXANDER, now sometimes used independently as a first name.

Alida (1) a feminine first name meaning 'little bird'; 'small and lithe' (*Latin*). (2) a Hungarian form of ADELAIDE. Variant forms are Aleda, Aleta, Alita. Diminutive forms are Leda, Lita.

Aliénor a French feminine form of ELEANOR.

Alima a feminine first name meaning 'learned in music and dancing' (*Arabic*).

Aline a feminine contraction of ADELINE.

Alison (1) a Scottish feminine form of ALICE and a former diminutive of it now used entirely in its own right. Variant forms are Allison, Alyson and Alysoun. The diminutive form is Allie or Ally. Alison Cockburn wrote a version of *The Flowers of the Forest*. (2) a masculine first name meaning 'son of ALICE'; 'son of a nobleman' (*Old English*).

Alistair a masculine variant form of ALASDAIR.

Alister a masculine variant form of ALASDAIR.

Alita a feminine variant form of ALIDA.

Alix a feminine variant form of ALEX.

Allaid (pronounced *allay*) a masculine first name from the Ossian poems of James Macpherson (1736–96), from *allaid*, 'untamed', 'wild-living' (*Old Scottish Gaelic*).

Allan or **Allen** masculine variant forms of ALAN.

Allard a masculine first name meaning 'noble and brave' (*Old English*). A variant form is Alard.

Allegra a word for 'cheerful' or 'blithe' used as a feminine first name (*Italian*).

Allie a feminine diminutive of ALICE, ALISON.

Allison a feminine variant form of ALISON.

Ally (1) a feminine diminutive of ALICE, ALISON. Ally Sheedy is an American film actress.(2) a masculine diminutive of ALASDAIR. Ally McCoist is a Scottish footballer and presenter.

Alma a feminine first name meaning 'loving, nurturing' (*Latin*). Alma Cogan was an English singer.

Almha (pronounced *al-wah*) a feminine first name from the name of a Celtic goddess associated with strength and healing (*Irish Gaelic*).

Almira a feminine first name meaning 'lofty; a princess' (*Arabic*).

Almo a masculine first name meaning 'noble and famous' (*Old English*).

Aloha a word for 'welcome' used as a feminine first name (*Hawaiian*).

Alonso a Spanish form of ALPHONSO. William Shakespeare (1564–1616) used the name for the king of Naples, the enemy of Prospero, in his play *The Tempest*. A diminutive form is Lonnie.

Alonzo *see* ALPHONSO.

Aloysius a Latin form of LEWIS.

Alpha a masculine or feminine first name meaning 'first one' (*Greek*).

Alpheus a masculine first name meaning 'exchange' (*Hebrew*). In the New Testament Alpheus was the father of James the Less, one of Christ's Apostles.

Alphonse the French masculine form of ALPHONSO.

Alphonsina or **Alphonsine** feminine variant forms of ALFONSINE.

Alphonso or **Alphonsus** a masculine first name meaning 'all-ready; willing' (*Old German*). St Alphonsus Liguori (1696–1787), one of the Doctors of the Roman Catholic Church, was a priest who founded an order of missionary preachers working with the rural poor.

Alphonza a feminine variant form of ALFONSINE.

Alpin a masculine first name of uncertain meaning but possibly 'blond' (*Scottish Gaelic*). Alpin was the father of Kenneth, first king of both the Pictish and Scottish nations.

Alroy a masculine first name meaning 'red-haired' (*Scottish Gaelic*).

Alston a surname, meaning 'old stone' (*Old English*), used as a masculine first name.

Alta a feminine first name meaning 'tall in spirit' (*Latin*).

Althea a feminine first name meaning 'healing' (*Greek*). A diminutive form is Thea.

Altman a masculine first name meaning 'old, wise man' (*Germanic*).

Alton a surname, meaning 'old stream or source' (*Old English*), used as a masculine first name.

Alula a feminine first name meaning 'winged one' (*Latin*) or 'first' (*Arabic*).

Alun the name of a North Wales river, whose origin means 'flowing among rocks', used as a masculine first name. The personal name may be from the river or may go back directly to the root-form *ail*, 'rock'. Alun of Dyfed figures in the *Mabinogion* tales. The name was taken as a bardic name by the nineteenth century Welsh bard John Blackwell. *See also* ALAN.

Alura a feminine first name meaning 'divine counsellor' (*Old English*).

Alva (1) the name of a Scottish town, from Gaelic *ail*, 'rock', *magh*, 'plain' (Scottish Gaelic), used as a feminine first name but probably has also picked up associations with ALMHA. (2) a feminine first name meaning 'white' (*Latin*).

Alvah a masculine first name meaning 'exalted one' (*Hebrew*).

Alvin a masculine first name meaning 'winning all' (*Old English*). A variant form is Aldwin or Aldwyn.

Alvina or **Alvine** a feminine first name meaning 'beloved and noble friend' (*Germanic*). A diminutive form is Vina.

Alwyn the name of the River Alwen in Wales, used as a masculine first name. Its derivation is from *ail*, 'rock', and *wyn*, 'white' (*Welsh*), a reminder of the Welsh song 'David of the White Rock'.

Aly a masculine diminutive form of Alasdair. Aly Bain is a celebrated Shetland fiddle player.

Alys the Welsh feminine form of ALICE.

Alyson or **Alysoun** feminine variant forms of ALISON.

Alyssa a feminine variant form of ALICE or ALICIA.

Alyth a place name, meaning 'steep place', used as a feminine first name.

Alzena a feminine first name meaning 'woman, purveyor of charm and virtue' (*Arabic*).

Amabel a feminine first name meaning 'lovable' (*Latin*). A diminutive form is MABEL.

Amadea the feminine form of AMADEUS.

Amadeus a masculine first name meaning 'lover of God' (*Latin*).

Amado the Spanish form of AMATO.

Amairgein a masculine variant form of AMAIRGIN.

Amairgin (pronounced *a-mar-yin*) a masculine first name meaning 'wondrously born' (*Irish Gaelic*). This name is borne by numerous figures in the early legends of Ireland. Alternative forms include Amairgein and Amargen and the anglicised form is Amorgin.

Amalghaidh the Gaelic masculine form of AULAY.

Amalia (1) a feminine first name meaning 'work' (*Germanic*). (2) an Italian and Greek form of AMELIA.

Amalinda a feminine variant form of AMELINDA.

Amanda a feminine first name meaning 'worthy of love' (*Latin*). Amanda Donohoe is a British-born film actress. Diminutive forms are Manda, Mandy.

Amargen a masculine variant form of AMAIRGIN.

Amariah a masculine first name meaning 'whom Jehovah promised' (*Hebrew*).

Amaryllis a feminine first name meaning 'sparkling' (*Greek*). It became a name for a shepherdess or country girl in pastoral poetry.

Amasa a masculine first name meaning 'a burden' (*Hebrew*). In the Old Testament Amasa was the nephew of King DAVID and the commander of the army of ABSALOM.

Amber the name of a gemstone used as a feminine first name.

Ambert a masculine first name meaning 'shining bright light' (*Germanic*).

Ambrin or **Ambreen** the Arabic word for ambergris used as a feminine first name.

Ambrogio the Italian masculine form of AMBROSE.

Ambrose a masculine first name meaning 'immortal' (*Greek*). The Welsh form is EMRYS and the Latin form Ambrosius. It was the name of St Ambrose of Milan (339–397), one of the Doctors of the Roman Catholic Church, and as such was widely venerated beyond his territory of Lombardy.

Ambrosia or **Ambrosina** feminine variant forms of AMBROSINE.

Ambrosine feminine form of Ambrose. Variant forms are Ambrosia, Ambrosina.

Ambrosius the Latin masculine form of AMBROSE. See also EMRYS.

Amédée the French masculine form of AMADEUS.

Amelia a feminine first name meaning 'busy, energetic' (*Germanic*). A diminutive form is Millie.

Amélie the French feminine form of AMELIA.

Amelinda a feminine first name meaning 'beloved and pretty' (*Spanish*). Variant forms are Amalinda, Amelinde.

Amelinde a feminine variant form of AMELINDA.

Amena a feminine first name meaning 'honest, truthful' (*Gaelic*).

Amerigo an Italian variant form of ENRICO.

Amery a masculine variant form of AMORY.

Amethyst the name of the semiprecious gemstone used as a feminine first name (*Greek*).

Amin a masculine first name meaning 'honest' (*Arabic*).

Amina the feminine form of Amin.

Aminta or **Amintha** or **Aminthe** a feminine first name meaning 'protector', a shepherdess in Greek mythology (*Greek*).

Amit a masculine first name meaning 'limitless' (*Sanskrit*).

Amlodd (pronounced *am-loth*) a masculine first name from Welsh Arthurian legend of uncertain meaning. Amlodd was the grandfather of King Arthur.

Ammon a masculine first name meaning 'hidden' (*Egyptian*).

Amorgin the anglicised masculine form of AMAIRGIN.

Amory a masculine first name meaning 'famous ruler' (*Germanic*). Variant forms are Amery, Emery, Emmery.

Amos a masculine first name meaning 'bearer of a burden' (*Hebrew*). Amos was a Hebrew prophet of the eighth century BC and the first to have a Book of the Bible called after him.

Amy

Amy a feminine first name meaning 'beloved' (*Old French*). Amy Madigan is an American film actress.

Ana a feminine variant form of A\ NU.

Anaïs (pronounced *an-eye-ees*) a feminine first name meaning 'productive' (*Greek*). Anaïs Nin was a French writer.

Anand a masculine first name meaning joy (*Sanskrit*) and the name of a Hindu god.

Ananda or **Anandi** the feminine form of Anand.

Anann a feminine variant form of A\ NU.

Anarawd (pronounced *ana-rodd*) a masculine first name meaning 'most eloquent', from *iawn*, 'most', 'highly', and *huawdl*, 'eloquent' (*Welsh*), as in modern Welsh *hwyl*.

Anastasia a feminine first name meaning 'rising up, resurrection' (*Greek*). Diminutive forms are Stacey, Stacy, Stacie, Stasia.

Anastasius a masculine form of A\ NASTASIA. It was the name adopted by several popes.

Anatholia or **Anatola** feminine forms of Anatole (*Greek*. A variant form is Anatolia.

Anatole a masculine first name meaning 'from the East' (*Greek*).

Anatolia a feminine variant form of A\ NATHOLIA.

Andie a masculine diminutive of A\ NDREW. It is now being used as a feminine first name. Andie MacDowall is an American film actress.

Anderson the surname, meaning 'son of Andrew' (from 'manly') (*Greek*), used as a masculine first name.

Andrasta a feminine first name meaning 'invincible' (*Brythonic*). Andrasta was a goddess of the Celtic tribes in what is now England

André the French masculine form of A\ NDREW, becoming popular as an English-language form.

Andrea a feminine form of A\ NDREAS or A\ NDREW. A variant form is A\ NDRINA; the Italian form of A\ NDREW.

Andreas Greek, Latin, German and Welsh masculine forms of A\ NDREW.

Andrés the Spanish masculine form of A\ NDREW. It was the original name of the Cuban-born American film actor Andy Garcia.

Andrew a masculine first name meaning 'strong; manly; courageous' (*Greek*). It early became a popular name for boys in Scotland because of the cult of the Apostle St Andrew as the nation's patron saint (as well as that of Russia). Many famous people have borne this name including the famous sailors Sir Andrew Barton (died 1511) and Sir Andrew Wood (*c*.1455–1515), and the philanthropic millionaire Andrew Carnegie (1835–1919) who made his fortune in the United States. The variant form ANDRO is occasionally found. Diminutive forms are Andy, Andie, Andy, Dandie, Drew.

Andrewina a variant form of ANDRINA.

Andrina or **Andrine** a female form of ANDREW, popular when it was common for girls to be given a feminised version of their father's name. Another form is Andrewina.

Andro a masculine variant form of ANDREW. Andro Linklater is a British author.

Andy a diminutive form of ANDREW, ANDRES. Andy Garcia is a Cuban-born American film actor.

Aneirin or **Aneurin** (pronounced *an-eye-rin*) a masculine first name, perhaps a Welsh form of the Latin *Honorius*, or alternatively derived from the Welsh root forms *an*, 'very', *eur*, 'golden', with the diminutive ending *-an*. Aneirin was one of the earliest Welsh poets, author of 'Y Gododdin'. Aneurin Bevan, Welsh Labour politician, introduced the National Health Service into Britain in the 1940s. A diminutive form is Nye.

Anemone a feminine first name meaning 'windflower', the name of the garden plant used as a feminine first name (*Greek*).

Angel (1) a feminine diminutive of ANGELA (*Greek*). (2) a masculine form of ANGELA. Thomas Hardy (1840–1928) used the name for his character Angel Clare in his novel *Tess of the D'Urbervilles*.

Angela or **Angelina** a feminine first name meaning 'messenger' (*Greek*).

Angelica a feminine first name meaning 'lovely; angelic' (*Greek*). A variant form is ANJELICA.

Angelo a masculine Italian form of ANGEL. William Shakespeare (1564–1616) used the name for the character of the hypocritical deputy of the Duke of Vienna in his play *Measure for Measure* and for that of a goldsmith in *The Comedy of Errors*.

Angharad (pronounced *ang-harrad*) a feminine first name meaning 'the well-loved one' (*Welsh*). In the seventh century Angharad was the wife of Rhodri Mawr.

Angus a masculine first name meaning 'the unique one' or 'only choice', anglicised from *aon*, 'one' and *gus*, 'strength' (*Scottish Gaelic*). The

Gaelic form is Aonghas, from a Pictish name Oengus. A Pictish king of this name died in AD 761, and his name is preserved in the former county of Angus. The form Oengus also figures in Old Irish literature, notably in the character of Angus Og, the god of youth. A diminutive form is Gus.

Anil a masculine first name meaning 'wind' (*Sanskrit*) and the name of a Hindu god.

Anila the feminine form of ANIL.

Anish a masculine first name meaning 'masterless' (*Sanskrit*).

Anisha the feminine form of ANISH.

Anita the feminine Spanish diminutive of ANN, now used independently as an English-language form. A diminutive form is Nita.

Anjelica a feminine variant form of ANGELICA. Anjelica Huston is an American film actress.

Anluan a masculine first name meaning 'great hound', probably with the sense of great warrior (*Irish Gaelic*).

Ann a feminine first name meaning 'grace' (*Hebrew*). A variant form is HANNAH. A diminutive form is Annie.

Anna the feminine Latin form of ANN. In the New Testament it is the name of a Jewish prophetess who witnessed the presentation of Jesus in the Temple.

Annabel or **Annabelle** or **Annabella** a feminine first name meaning 'lovable' (possibly from AMABEL). Diminutive forms are Bella, Belle. Annabella Sciorra is an American film actress.

Annan a Scottish place name, meaning 'water' or 'waters' (*Scottish Gaelic*), used as a masculine first name.

Anne the French feminine form of ANN now commonly used as an English-language form. St Anne was the mother of the Virgin Mary.

Anneka a feminine Dutch diminutive of ANNA.

Annette a French diminutive of ANN, used as an English-language form. Annette Bening is an American actress and wife of Warren Beatty.

Annie a feminine diminutive form of ANN.

Annika a feminine Swedish diminutive of ANNA.

Annis or **Annice** a medieval feminine diminutive of AGNES.

Annona a feminine variant form of ANONA.

Annunciata a feminine first name from the Italian form of *nuntius*, 'bringer of news', i.e. the angel Gabriel, who delivered the announcement of the Virgin Mary's conception, a name often given to children born on 25 March, Lady Day (*Latin*).

Annwr (pronounced *ann-ur*) a Welsh feminine form of Aneirin. In Arthurian legend, Annwr attempted to seduce Arthur.

Annwyl (pronounced *ann-ul*) a masculine first name meaning 'very dear' (*Welsh*).

Anona a feminine first name meaning 'annual crops', hence the Roman goddess of crops (*Latin*). A variant form is Annona. Diminutive forms are Nonnie, Nona.

Anora a feminine first name meaning 'light, graceful' (*Old English*).

Anscom a masculine first name meaning 'one who dwells in a secret valley', 'a solitary person' (*Old English*).

Anselm or **Ansel** a surname, meaning 'god helmet', i.e. under the protection of God (*Germanic*), used as a masculine first name. St Anselm of Canterbury (1033–1109) was one of the Doctors of the Roman Catholic Church.

Anselma feminine form of Anselm. A variant form is Arselma.

Ansley a surname, meaning 'clearing with a hermitage or solitary dwelling' (*Old English*), used as a masculine first name.

Anson a surname, meaning 'son of Agnes or Anne' (*Old English*), used as a masculine first name.

Anstice a surname, meaning 'resurrected' (*Greek*), used as a masculine first name.

Anthea a feminine first name meaning 'flowery' (*Greek*).

Anthony a masculine variant form of Antony. It is the name of several saints, including St Anthony of Padua (1195–1231), who is the patron saint of the poor, and St Anthony of Thebes (250–340), the founder of Christian monasticism. The diminutive form is Tony.

Antoine the French masculine form of Anthony, now used independently as an English-language form. A variant form is Antwan.

Antoinette feminine diminutive of Antonia, now used as an English-language form. A diminutive form is Toinette.

Anton a German masculine form of Antony, now used as an English-language form. Anton Lesser is an English actor.

Antonia feminine form of Antony. Lady Antonia Fraser is an English historian and biographer. Diminutive forms are Toni, Tonia, Tonie, Tony.

Antoninus a Roman family name meaning 'priceless; praiseworthy' (*Lat-*

in) used as a first name. St Antoninus (1389–1459) was archbishop of Florence and one of the founders of modern theology.

Antonio the Italian and Spanish masculine form of ANTONY. William Shakespeare (1564–1616) used the name for characters in several of his plays, most notably for that of the merchant in *The Merchant of Venice* from whom Shylock demands his pound of flesh and that of the usurping Duke of Milan in *The Tempest*.

Antony a masculine first name meaning 'priceless; praiseworthy' (*Latin*) from the Roman family name ANTONINUS. William Shakespeare (1564–1616) used this form of the name for Mark Antony (Marcus Antonius) in his plays *Julius Caesar* and *Antony and Cleopatra*. A variant form is Anthony. A diminutive form is Tony.

Antwan a masculine variant form of ANTOINE.

Anu (pronounced *an-oo*) a feminine first name meaning 'wealth', 'abundance of riches' (*Irish Gaelic*). In Celtic mythology, the semi-mythical Tuatha Dé Danann were 'the tribe of Anu'. She was a goddess of both good and evil, a figure of great power. Alternative forms are Ana, Anann. The name has no connection with Anne.

Anup a masculine first name meaning 'incomparable' (*Sanskrit*).

Anwell a masculine first name meaning 'beloved' (*Gaelic*).

Anwen a feminine first name meaning 'very beautiful or fair'(*Welsh*).

Anyon a masculine first name meaning 'anvil' (*Gaelic*).

Aobh (pronounced *ave*) a feminine first name meaning 'radiant, attractive', from Old Gaelic *oíb*, 'attractiveness'. In Celtic mythology, Aobh was the mother of the legendary Children of Lir, who were turned into swans. Variant forms of the name are AEB, AEBH.

Aodh a variant masculine form of AED.

Aodhagán (pronounced *ayd-a-gann*) a masculine first name meaning 'little AED'. The root is *aed*, 'fiery' (*Irish Gaelic/Manx*). Aodhagán O Raithile was a notable lyric poet of the seventeenth century. The anglicised form is Egan.

Aodhnait a feminine variant form of AEDNAT.

Aoibheall a feminine variant form of AÍBELL.

Aoibhín (pronounced *aiv-een*) a feminine first name meaning 'shining one' (*Irish Gaelic*). This was the name of numerous Irish princesses. *See also* AOIFE, EAVAN.

Aoife (pronounced *ay-fa*) an ancient feminine first name, stemming from

Old Irish Gaelic *aoibhinn*, 'of radiant beauty'. Nowadays it is often wrongly assumed to be a form of EVE and often anglicised into EVA. In Celtic mythology, Aoife was a Scottish 'Amazon' who bore a son to Cuchulainn, whom the hero was later to unwittingly kill in battle. The name was borne by numerous other women of legend and history. A variant form is Aife. The anglicised form is Aefa.

Aonghas (pronounced *inn-ess*) a masculine first name. The Scots Gaelic masculine form of ANGUS.

Aphra a feminine first name meaning 'dust' (*Hebrew*) or 'woman from Carthage' (*Latin*). Aphra Behn (1640–89) was an English playwright and novelist. A variant form is Afra.

April the name of the month, *Aprilis* (*Latin*), used as a feminine first name.

Ara a feminine first name meaning 'spirit of revenge', and the name of the goddess of destruction and vengeance (*Greek*).

Arabella or **Arabela** a feminine first name meaning 'a fair altar' (*Latin*). Diminutive forms are Bella, Belle.

Araminta a feminine first name meaning 'beautiful, sweet-smelling flower' (*Greek*). A diminutive form is Minta.

Archard a masculine first name meaning 'sacred and powerful' (*Germanic*).

Archer a surname, meaning 'professional or skilled bowman' (*Old English*), used as a masculine first name.

Archibald a masculine first name meaning 'very bold; holy prince' (*Germanic*). In parts of Scotland it was often erroneously identified with Gillespie (*see* GILLEASBUIG). A diminutive form is Archie or Archy. It is also a widely established surname in Scotland and northern England.

Archie or **Archy** a masculine diminutive form of ARCHIBALD. The American writer Don Marquis used the name for archy and mehitabel, his famous cockroach and cat whose stories were written by archy on a typewriter the shift key of which he could not operate.

Ardal a masculine first name meaning 'high valour' (*Irish Gaelic*). Ardal O'Hanlon is an Irish comedian.

Ardán (pronounced *ar-dann*) a masculine first name derived from *ardàn*, 'pride' (*Old Irish Gaelic*). In Celtic mythology, Ardán is the third son of Usna and brother of Naoise, Deirdre's lover. In the tale he is referred to as 'fierce', or 'unyielding': it is certainly a warrior name.

Ardath a feminine first name meaning 'field of flowers' (*Hebrew*). Variant forms are Aridatha, Ardatha.

Arddun (pronounced *arth-un*) a feminine first name meaning 'beautiful one' (*Welsh*).

Ardella or **Ardelle** or **Ardelis** a feminine first name meaning 'enthusiasm, warmth' (*Hebrew*).

Arden (1) a masculine first name meaning 'burning, fiery' (*Latin*). (2) a surname, meaning 'dwelling place' or 'gravel' or 'eagle valley' (*Old English*), used as a masculine first name.

Ardley a masculine first name meaning 'from the domestic meadow' (*Old English*).

Ardolph a masculine first name meaning 'home-loving wolf rover' (*Old English*).

Arduinna a feminine first name, of unknown meaning, of a Gaulish goddess of the Ardennes forest whose symbolic animal was a boar. A hunting goddess, her name has been linked with Greek Diana.

Areta or **Aretha** a feminine first name meaning 'excellently virtuous' (*Greek*). Variant forms are Aretta, Arette, Aretas.

Aretas a feminine variant form of ARETA.

Aretta or **Arette** feminine variant forms of ARETA.

Argante (pronounced *ar-ganta*) a masculine or feminine Old Gaelic or Welsh first name of unknown meaning. It was the name of a Celtic goddess of the underworld.

Argenta or **Argente** or **Argente** a feminine first name meaning 'silver' or 'silvery coloured' (*Latin*).

Argus a masculine first name meaning 'all-seeing, watchful one', from Argus Panoptes, a character from Greek mythology with a hundred eyes all over his body (*Greek*).

Argyle or **Argyll** the Scottish place name, meaning 'land or district of the Gaels' (*Scottish Gaelic*), used as a masculine first name.

Aria the Italian word for 'beautiful melody', from *aer*, 'breeze' (*Latin*), used as a feminine first name.

Ariadne a feminine first name meaning 'very holy' (*Greek*). In Greek mythology, Ariadne was a daughter of the king of Crete who saved Theseus from the labyrinth.

Arianrhod a feminine first name meaning 'silver disc' (*Welsh*). This is the name of a goddess from the *Mabinogion* cycle of tales, associated with the moon, beauty, inspiration and poetry.

Arianna an Italian feminine form of ARIADNE.

Arianne a French feminine form of ARIADNE.

Aric a masculine first name meaning 'sacred ruler' (*Old English*). Diminutive forms are Rick, Rickie, Ricky.

Ariel a masculine first name meaning 'God's lion' (*Hebrew*). In the Old Testament Ariel was one of the men used by Ezra to seek for leaders of the Jewish church. William Shakespeare (1564–1616) used the name for the character of the spirit of the air in *The Tempest*. It is occasionally used as a feminine first name.

Ariella or **Arielle** feminine forms of ARIEL.

Aries a masculine name meaning 'the ram' (*Latin*), the sign of the Zodiac for 21 March to 19 April.

Arjun a masculine first name meaning 'bright' (*Sanskrit*).

Arlan a Cornish masculine first name. It was the name of a legendary early saint of Cornwall, his name perhaps a corruption of Allen or Elwin, also Cornish saints.

Arleen a feminine variant form of ARLENE.

Arlen a masculine first name meaning 'pledge' (*Irish Gaelic*).

Arlene or **Arlena** (1) a Gaulish feminine first name, perhaps from the place name Arles. (2) the feminine form of ARLEN. (3) a feminine variant form of CHARLENE, MARLENE. Variant forms are Arleen, Arlina, Arline, Arlyne.

Arlie or **Arley** or **Arly** a surname, meaning 'eagle wood' (*Old English*), used as a masculine first name.

Arlina or **Arline** or **Arlyne** feminine variant forms of ARLENE.

Armand a French masculine form of HERMAN.

Armel a masculine first name meaning 'stone prince or chief' (*Breton Gaelic*).

Armelle the feminine form of ARMEL.

Armilla a feminine first name meaning 'bracelet' (*Latin*).

Armin a masculine first name meaning 'military man' (*Germanic*).

Armina or **Armine** feminine forms of ARMIN. Variant forms are Erminie, Erminia.

Armstrong a surname, meaning 'strong in the arm' (*Old English*), used as a masculine first name.

Arn (1) a masculine diminutive of ARNOLD, ARNULF. (2) a contraction of AARON.

Arnalda feminine form of ARNOLD (*Germanic*).

Arnall a surname variant form of ARNOLD (*Germanic*) used as a masculine first name.

Arnaud or **Arnaut** French forms of ARNOLD.

Arnatt or **Arnett** surname variant forms of ARNOLD used as masculine first names.

Arne a masculine first name meaning 'eagle' (*Old Norse*). A diminutive form is Arnie.

Arnie a masculine diminutive form of ARNE or ARNOLD.

Arno a masculine diminutive form of ARNOLD, ARNULF.

Arnold a masculine first name meaning 'strong as an eagle' (*Germanic*) or 'eagle meadow' (*Old English*). Arnold Bennett (1867–1931) was an English novelist. Arnold Schwarzenegger is an Austrian-born body-builder and film star. Diminutive forms are Arn, Arnie, Arno, Arny.

Arnott a surname variant form of ARNOLD used as a masculine first name.

Arnulf a masculine first name meaning 'eagle wolf' (*Germanic*). Diminutive forms are Arn, Arno.

Arny a masculine diminutive form of ARNOLD.

Arphad a masculine variant form of ARVAD.

Arselma a feminine variant form of ANSELMA.

Art an Irish Gaelic masculine first name, probably from the same Indo-European root as *arctos*, 'bear' (*Greek*). The bear was celebrated for its strength. In Irish legend, the best-known Art is a somewhat tragic hero, Art Oenfer, 'the lonely', son of CONN of the Hundred Battles and father of CORMAC macAirt.

Artair the Gaelic masculine form of ARTHUR.

Artemas a masculine form of ARTEMIS (*Greek*). In the New Testament Artemas was one of Paul's companions on part of his journeys.

Artemis in Greek mythology the name of the virgin goddess of hunting and the moon, the derivation of which is unknown. The Roman equivalent is DIANA.

Arthen a Welsh masculine first name cognate with Art, it was the name of a local god in Wales and given also to a ninth-century king of Ceredigion.

Arthur a masculine first name that has been linked to *arctos*, 'bear' (*Greek*) but also to a Celtic root form *ar*, 'plough', and to Brythonic *arddhu*, 'very black'. It was the name of the legendary leader of British resistance to the invading Anglo-Saxons. Its earliest appearance is in Welsh documents. The Gaelic form is ARTAIR. In the north of Scotland, it may also be a form of the Old Norse name Ottar.

Arturo the Italian and Spanish masculine forms of ARTHUR.

Arun a masculine first name meaning 'brownish red' (*Sanskrit*).

Aruna the feminine form of ARUN.

Arundel an English place name, meaning 'a valley where nettles grow' (*Old English*), used as a masculine first name.

Arva a feminine first name meaning 'ploughed land, pasture' (*Latin*).

Arvad a masculine first name meaning 'wanderer' (*Hebrew*). A variant form is Arpad.

Arval or **Arvel** a masculine first name meaning 'greatly lamented' (*Latin*).

Arvid a masculine first name meaning 'eagle wood' (*Norse*).

Arvin a masculine first name meaning 'people's friend' (*Germanic*).

Arwel a Welsh masculine first name, the meaning of which is uncertain.

Arwen a variant form of ARWYN.

Arwenna a feminine form of ARWYN.

Arwyn a masculine first name meaning 'muse' (*Welsh*). A variant form is Arwen.

Asa a masculine first name meaning 'healer, physician' (*Hebrew*). In the Old Testament Asa was the third king of Judah after its division into two kingdoms. Asa Briggs is an English historian and writer.

Asaf or **Asaph** (pronounced *ass-af*) a Welsh masculine first name. It was the name of the early Welsh saint who is commemorated in the North Wales bishopric of St Asaph, which is a variant form.

Asahel a masculine first name meaning 'made of God' (*Hebrew*). In the Old Testament Asahel was a nephew of King DAVID.

Asaph (1) a masculine variant form of ASAF. (2) a masculine first name meaning 'a collector' (*Hebrew*). In the Old Testament Asaph was a musician.

Ascot or **Ascott** an English place name and surname, meaning 'eastern cottages' (*Old English*), used as a masculine first name.

Ash a masculine or feminine first name from *aesc*, meaning 'ash tree' (*Old English*). The ash tree was widely worshipped among the Celtic peoples; ash, oak and thorn were a powerful triad. *See also* ROWAN.

Asha a feminine first name meaning 'hope' (*Sanskrit*).

Ashburn a surname, meaning 'stream where the ash trees grow' (*Old English*), used as a masculine first name.

Ashby an English place name, meaning 'ash-tree farmstead' (*Old English*), used as a masculine first name.

Asher a masculine first name meaning 'happy, fortunate' (*Hebrew*). In the Old Testament Asher was the founder of one of the Twelve Tribes of Israel.

Ashford an English place name, meaning 'ford by a clump of ash trees' (*Old English*), used as a masculine first name.

Ashia a feminine first name, possibly derived from Ash or Asia. Ashia Hansen is an English athlete.

Ashley or **Ashleigh** the surname, meaning 'ash wood or glade' (*Old English*), used as a masculine or feminine first name. Ashley Judd is an American actress.

Ashlin a masculine first name meaning 'ash-surrounded pool' (*Old English*).

Ashling a feminine or masculine variant of AISLING.

Ashraf a masculine first name meaning 'nobler' (*Arabic*).

Ashton an English place name, meaning 'ash-tree farmstead' (*Old English*), used as a masculine first name.

Asia a feminine variant form of AISHA.

Aslam a masculine first name meaning 'more sound' (*Arabic*).

Asma a feminine first name meaning 'more important' (*Arabic*).

Asphodel a daffodil-like plant, the origin of whose name is obscure, used as a feminine first name (*Greek*).

Asshur a masculine first name meaning 'martial, warlike' (*Semitic*). In the Old Testament Asshur was a son of Shem and forefather of the Assyrians.

Astra feminine diminutive of ASTRID.

Astrid a feminine first name meaning 'fair god' (*Norse*). A diminutive is Astra.

Atalanta or **Atalante** the name of a mythological character who agreed to marry the man who could outrun her (*Greek*). A variant form is Atlanta.

Atalya a feminine first name meaning 'guardian' (*Spanish*).

Athanasius a masculine first name meaning 'immortal' (*Greek*). St Athanasius of Alexandria (*c*.295–373) was one of the Doctors of the Roman Catholic Church.

Athena or **Ahthene** or **Athenée** a feminine first name from that of the goddess of wisdom in Greek mythology. Her Roman counterpart is MINERVA (*Greek*).

Atherton a surname, meaning 'noble army's place' (*Old English*), used as a masculine first name.

Athol or **Athole** or **Atholl** a place name in the Perthshire district that is now used as a masculine first name. It comes from *ath*, 'ford' (*Scottish Gaelic*) and Fotla, the name of one of the seven sons of the legendary founder of the Picts, Cruithne.

Athracht (pronounced *ath-rach*) a feminine first name from *athrach*, 'change' (*Irish Gaelic*), perhaps describing the change of life from that of an aristocratic girl to that of a female hermit. It was the name of a sixth-century Irish saint.

Atlanta a feminine variant form of ATALANTA.

Atlee or **Atley** or **Atley** a surname, meaning 'at the wood or clearing' (*Old English*), used as a masculine first name.

Atwater or **Atwatter** a surname, meaning 'by the water' (*Old English*), used as a masculine first name.

Atwell a surname, meaning 'at the spring or well of' (*Old English*), used as a masculine first name.

Auberon a masculine first name meaning 'noble bear' (*Germanic*). A variant form is OBERON. A diminutive form is Bron.

Aubin a surname, meaning 'blond one' (*French*), used as a masculine first name.

Aubina a feminine variant form of ALBINA.

Aubrey a masculine first name meaning 'ruler of spirits' (*Germanic*).

Aude (pronounced *awd-a*) (1) a Cornish feminine first name. In the French *Chanson de Roland*, Aude is a Breton princess betrothed to Roland. When Charlemagne wished instead to wed her to his son, she fell dead. (2) the name also exists in Old Norse: Aude 'the Deep-Minded' was the founder of a colony on Iceland in the eleventh century.

Audrey a feminine first name meaning 'noble might' (*Old English*). William Shakespeare (1564–1616) used the name for the character of a country wench in his comedy *As You Like It*.

August (1) the Polish and German masculine form of AUGUSTUS. (2) the eighth month of the year, named after the Roman emperor AUGUSTUS, used as a masculine first name.

Augusta feminine form of AUGUSTUS. Diminutive forms are Gussie, Gusta.

Auguste the French masculine form of AUGUSTUS.

Augustin the German and French masculine forms of AUGUSTINE.

Augustine a masculine first name meaning 'belonging to AUGUSTUS' (*Lat-*

in). A diminutive form is Gus. As the first archbishop of Canterbury, St Augustine (died 604) had great prestige in Britain; it is he rather than St Augustine of Hippo (354–430), one of the Doctors of the Roman Catholic Church, who is commemorated.

Augustus a masculine first name meaning 'exalted; imperial' (*Latin*). It was adopted by Octavius Caesar as his imperial name when he became the first emperor of Rome (27 BC). A diminutive form is Gus.

Aulay a Scottish masculine first name. The Gaelic form is Amalghaidh, a version of Old Norse Olaf. The MacAulay clan claims a Viking origin.

Aura or **Aure** or **Aurea** a feminine first name meaning 'breath of air' (*Latin*). A variant form is Auria.

Aurelia feminine form of AURELIUS.

Aurelius a masculine first name meaning 'golden' (*Latin*).

Auria a feminine variant form of AURA.

Aurora a feminine first name meaning 'morning redness; fresh; brilliant' (*Latin*).

Austell (pronounced *oss-tell*) a Cornish or Breton masculine first name from a saint's name of uncertain origin but perhaps linked with the place name Aust on the Bristol Channel. It is preserved in St Austell in Cornwall and Llanawastl in Wales.

Austin a masculine contraction of AUGUSTINE.

Autumn the name of the season, the origin of which is uncertain, used as a feminine first name.

Ava a feminine first name the origin of which is uncertain, perhaps a Germanic diminutive of names beginning Av-. Ava Gardner (1922–90) was a famous American film star.

Aveline a Norman French feminine first name, the Latin form of which, EVALINA, was used by the English writer Fanny Burney (1752–1840) for the heroine of her eponymous first novel. It evolved into EVELYN and the Irish and Scottish form is AIBHLINN.

Avera or **Averah** a feminine first name meaning 'transgressor' (*Hebrew*). A variant form is Aberah.

Averil or **Averill** a feminine English form of AVRIL.

Avery a surname, derived from ALFRED (*Old English*), used as a masculine first name.

Avice or **Avis** a feminine first name meaning possibly 'bird' (*Latin*).

Avril the French feminine form of APRIL.

Awsten (pronounced *ow-sten*) the Welsh masculine form of Augustine.

Axel a masculine first name meaning 'father of peace' (*Germanic*).

Axton a masculine first name meaning 'stone of the sword fighter' (*Old English*).

Ayisah a feminine variant form of Aisha.

Aylmer a surname, meaning 'noble and famous' (*Old English*), used as a masculine first name.

Aylward a surname, meaning 'noble guardian' (*Old English*), used as a masculine first name.

Aysha or **Ayshia** a feminine variant form of Aisha.

Azaliea or **Azalia** or **Azalee** feminine variant forms of the name of the azalea plant, supposed to prefer dry earth, used as a feminine first name.

Azaria feminine form of Azarias.

Azarias a masculine first name meaning 'helped by God' (*Hebrew*).

Azim a masculine first name meaning 'determined' (*Arabic*).

Azima or **Azimah** the feminine form of Azim.

Azura or **Azure** a feminine first name meaning 'blue as the sky' (*French*).

B

Bab or **Babs** feminine diminutive forms of BARBARA.

Baibín (pronounced *ba-been*) an Irish Gaelic feminine form of BARBARA. Báirbre is a variant form.

Bailey or **Baillie** a surname, meaning 'bailiff or steward' (*Old French*), used as a masculine first name and occasionally as a feminine name. A variant form is Bayley.

Bainbridge a surname, meaning 'bridge over a short river' (*Old English*), used as a masculine first name.

Báirbre a feminine variant form of BAIBÍN.

Baird a Scottish surname, meaning 'minstrel or bard', used as a masculine first name. A variant form is Bard.

Bala a masculine or feminine first name meaning 'infant' (*Sanskrit*).

Baldemar a masculine first name meaning 'bold and famous prince' (*Germanic*).

Baldovin the Italian masculine form of BALDWIN.

Baldric or **Baldrick** a surname, meaning 'princely or bold ruler' (*Germanic*), used as a masculine first name. A variant form is Baudric.

Baldwin a masculine first name meaning 'bold friend' (*Germanic*).

Balfour a surname from a Scottish place name, meaning 'village with pasture' (*Gaelic*), used as a masculine first name.

Ballard a surname, meaning 'bald' (*Old English*, *Old French*), used as a masculine first name.

Balor an Irish Gaelic masculine first name. Balor of the Evil Eye was a king of the Fomorians, early invaders of Ireland, whose baleful eye was never opened except on the field of battle, where it rendered his enemies powerless.

Balthasar or **Balthazar** a masculine first name meaning 'Baal defend the king' (*Babylonian*). In the Bible Balthasar was one of the Magi, the three wise men from the east who paid homage to the infant Jesus, presenting him with gifts. William Shakespeare (1564–1616) used the name for characters in four of his plays, including that of an attendant on Don Pedro in his comedy *Much Ado About Nothing*.

Balu a masculine first name meaning 'young' (*Sanskrit*).

Bambi a variant form of the word for *bambino*, 'child' (*Italian*) used as a feminine first name.

Banba or **Banbha** an Irish Gaelic feminine first name. This very ancient name can also refer to the land of Ireland itself; the original Banba came to be seen as a tutelary goddess of Ireland. *See also* ERIN.

Bancroft a surname, meaning 'bean place' (*Old English*), used as a masculine first name.

Banquo a masculine first name that comes from *ban*, 'white', and *cú*, 'hound' (*Scottish Gaelic*), suggesting a nickname origin. The name is familiar from the character that William Shakespeare (1564–1616) created in his play *Macbeth* for Macbeth's one-time comrade.

Baptist a masculine first name meaning 'a baptiser, purifier' (*Greek*).

Baptista feminine form of BAPTIST.

Baptiste a French masculine form of BAPTIST.

Barbara a feminine first name meaning 'foreign, strange' (*Greek*). The popularity of the story of St Barbara, killed about AD 200 by her father for refusing to renounce Christianity, spread the name. Barbara Hershey is an American film actress. A variant form is BARBRA. Diminutive forms are Bab, Babs, Barb, Barbie.

Barbe a Breton feminine first name and that of a mythical saint who is nevertheless venerated in Brittany, probably as a legacy from an earlier Celtic fire goddess in a similar mode to BRIDGET.

Barbie a feminine diminutive form of BARBARA. It has gained currency by the development of the well-known Barbie doll.

Barbra a feminine variant form of BARBARA that has been popularised by the American singer and actress Barbra Streisand.

Barclay a surname, meaning 'birch wood' (*Old English*), used as a masculine first name. Variant forms are Berkeley, Berkley.

Bard (1) a masculine variant form of BAIRD or BARDOLPH. (3) a masculine or feminine first name from the word for 'poet' or 'singer' in all the Celtic languages. This was an honoured profession in all Celtic communities. *See also* TADG.

Bardolph or **Bardolf** a masculine first name meaning 'bright wolf' (*Germanic*). A diminutive form is Bard.

Barlow a surname, meaning 'barley hill' or 'barley clearing' (*Old English*), used as a masculine first name.

Barnaby or **Barnabas** a masculine first name meaning 'son of consolation and exhortation' (*Hebrew*). A diminutive form is Barney. In the New Testament Barnabas who took part with Paul in missionary activity.

Barnard a masculine variant form of BERNARD. A diminutive form is Barney.

Barnet or **Barnett** a surname, meaning 'land cleared by burning' (*Old English*), used as a masculine first name.

Barney a masculine diminutive form of BARNABY, BARNARD or BERNARD.

Barnum a surname, meaning 'homestead of a warrior' (*Old English*), used as a masculine first name.

Baron the lowest rank of the peerage used as a masculine first name. A variant form is Barron.

Barr a masculine first name meaning 'crest', 'top', perhaps signifying 'supreme' (*Scottish Gaelic*). St Barr is the same person as St Finbarr of Cork; his name is preserved in that of the Scottish island of Barra.

Barratt or **Barrett** a surname, meaning 'commerce' or 'trouble' or 'strife' (*Old French*), used as a masculine first name.

Barrfind (pronounced *barr-finn*) a masculine first name meaning 'fair-haired', 'fair-crested'. The name is a turned-about form of FINBARR.

Barrie a surname, which may have come from a Norman immigrant who gave his name to Barry in Angus but has also been traced back to *bearrach*, 'spear' (*Scottish Gaelic*), used as a masculine first name. The variant form is Barry.

Barron a masculine variant form of BARON.

Barry the masculine variant form of BARRIE. Barry Levinson is an American film director.

Bart a masculine diminutive form of BARTHOLOMEW, BARTLEY, BARTON, BARTRAM.

Barthold a variant form of BERTHOLD.

Bartholomew a masculine first name meaning 'a warlike son' (*Hebrew*). Bartholomew was one of Christ's Apostles. Diminutive forms are Bart, Bat.

Bartley a surname, meaning 'a birch wood or clearing' (*Old English*), used as a masculine first name. A diminutive form is Bart.

Barton the surname, meaning 'farm or farmyard' (*Old English*), used as a masculine first name. A diminutive form is Bart.

Bartram a masculine variant form of BERTRAM.

Barzillai a masculine first name meaning 'man of iron' (*Hebrew*).

Basil a masculine first name meaning 'kingly, royal' (*Greek*). St Basil the Great of Caesarea (329–379) was one of the Doctors of the Roman Catholic Church.

Basile the French masculine form of BASIL.

Basilia feminine form of BASIL.

Basilio the Italian and Spanish masculine form of BASIL.

Bat a masculine diminutive form of BARTHOLOMEW.

Bathilda a feminine first name meaning 'battle commander' (*Germanic*).

Bathilde the French feminine form of BATHILDA.

Bathsheba a feminine first name meaning 'daughter of plenty' (*Hebrew*). In the Old Testament Bathsheba was the wife of Uriah. She committed adultery with David and later married him. She was the mother of Solomon and Jedidiah. Thomas Hardy (1840–1928) used the name for Bathsheba Everdene, the heroine of his novel *Far from the Madding Crowd* (1874).

Batiste the French masculine form of BAPTIST.

Battista the Italian masculine form of BAPTIST.

Baudouin the French masculine form of BALDWIN.

Baudric a masculine variant form of BALDRIC.

Bautista the Spanish masculine form of BAPTIST.

Baxter a surname, meaning 'baker' (*Old English*), used as a masculine first name.

Bayley a masculine variant form of BAILEY.

Bea a feminine diminutive form of BEATRICE, BEATRIX.

Beal or **Beale** or **Beall** a surname variant form of BEAU (*French*) used as a masculine first name.

Beaman (1) a masculine first name meaning 'bee keeper' (*Old English*). (2) a variant form of BEAUMONT (*French*).

Beara (pronounced *bay-ara*) an Irish Gaelic feminine first name, that of a legendary Irish princess.

Bearrach a feminine variant form of BERRACH.

Beata a feminine first name meaning 'blessed, divine one' (*Latin*). A diminutive form is Bea.

Beatha (pronounced *bay-ha*) a feminine first name, probably from *beatha*, 'life' (*Irish Gaelic*). A variant form is Bethan. In old Scotland this was also a male name: Macbeth, eleventh-century king of Scots, means literally 'son of life'.

Beathag a feminine variant form of BETHÓC.

Beatie a feminine diminutive form of BEATRICE.

Beatrice or **Beatrix** a feminine first name meaning 'woman who blesses' (*Latin*). William Shakespeare (1564–1616) used the name for the heroine of his comedy *Much Ado About Nothing*. Diminutive forms are Bea, Beatie, Beaty, Bee, Trix, Trixie. The Welsh form is Betrys.

Beaty a feminine diminutive form of BEATRICE.

Beau (1) a masculine first name meaning 'handsome' (*French*). (2) a diminutive form of BEAUFORT, BEAUMONT. Beau Bridges is an American actor and son of Lloyd Bridges.

Beaufort a surname, meaning 'beautiful stronghold' (*French*), used as a masculine first name. A diminutive form is Beau.

Beaumont a surname, meaning 'beautiful hill' (*French*), used as a masculine first name. A diminutive form is Beau.

Beavan or **Beaven** masculine variant forms of BEVAN.

Bébhionn a feminine variant form of BÉIBHINN.

Bec or **Becca** (1) a feminine first name meaning 'little one', from *beag*, 'little' (*Irish Gaelic*). Bec was a goddess of wisdom. (2) a feminine diminutive of REBECCA.

Beckie or **Becky** feminine diminutive forms of REBECCA.

Becuma an Irish Gaelic feminine first name, from that of the wife of Conn of the Hundred Battles. Becuma loved the king's son, Art, but married Conn for his power.

Beda a feminine first name meaning 'maid of war' (*Old English*).

Bedivere the anglicised masculine form of BEDWYR.

Bedwyr (pronounced *bedd-uwir*) a Welsh masculine first name from that of the knight who was with King Arthur at his death, in the Round Table story of Celtic legend. Its anglicised form is Bedivere.

Bee a feminine diminutive form of BEATRICE.

Béfind a feminine variant form of BÉIBHINN.

Béibhinn (pronounced *bay-vin*) a feminine first name meaning 'fair woman' (*Irish Gaelic*). Related Gaelic forms are Béfind, Bébhionn. This name is found in numerous Gaelic love poems and was also the name of the mother of king Brian Boruma. In an anglicised form as Bevin or Bevan, it has been used as a boy's name. In the form Bhéibhinn, the first sound is 'v' and it has been confused with the unrelated Vivien/Vivian, a Norman-French name from Latin *vivere*, 'to live'.

Bel a masculine variant form of BELENUS.

Belenus or **Belenos** a Gaulish masculine first name, perhaps from a Celtic root word meaning 'bright'. This was the name of one of the chief gods of the pre-Christian Celts. It is found in other forms such as Bel, Belus.

Belinda a feminine first name used by the English architect and dramatist Sir John Vanbrugh (1664–1726) in his play *The Provok'd Wife* (1697). Its origin is uncertain, possibly 'beautiful woman' (*Italian*).

Bella or **Belle** (1) a feminine first name meaning 'beautiful' (*French, Italian*). (2) the feminine diminutive suffix of ANNABELLA, ARABELLA, ISABELLA used as a name in its own right.

Bellamy a surname, meaning 'handsome friend' (*Old French*), used as a masculine first name.

Belus a masculine variant form of BELENUS.

Ben a diminutive form of BENEDICT, BENJAMIN, also used independently as a masculine first name.

Bena a feminine first name meaning 'wise one' (*Hebrew*).

Benedetto the Italian masculine form of BENEDICT.

Benedict or **Benedick** a masculine first name meaning 'blessed' (*Latin*). Benedict was the name adopted by many popes as well as of St Benedict (480–546) who founded the Benedictine monastic order. William Shakespeare (1564–1616) used the form Benedick for the hero of his comedy *Much Ado About Nothing*. A variant form is Bennet. Diminutive forms are Ben, Bennie, Benny.

Benedicta a feminine form of BENEDICT, a contracted form of which is Benita. A diminutive form is Dixie.

Benedikt the German masculine form of BENEDICT.

Benita (1) feminine form of BENITO. (2) a contracted form of BENEDICTA.

Benito a Spanish masculine form of BENEDICT.

Benjamin a masculine first name meaning 'son of the right hand' (*Hebrew*). In the Old Testament he was the youngest son of Jacob and Rachel and patriarch of one of the Twelve Tribes of Israel. Diminutive forms are Ben, Benjie, Bennie, Benny.

Benji or **Benjie** a masculine diminutive form of Benjamin.

Bennet a masculine variant form of Benedict.

Bennie or **Benny** a masculine diminutive form of Benedict, Benjamin.

Benoît the French masculine form of Benedict.

Benson a surname, meaning 'son of Ben', used as a masculine first name.

Bentley a surname from a Yorkshire place name, meaning 'woodland clearing where bent-grass grows' (*Old English*), used as a masculine first name.

Beppe or **Beppo** a diminutive form of Giuseppe, occasionally used independently as a masculine first name.

Berchan a Scottish Gaelic masculine first name and that of a tenth-century holy man who compiled a 'Prophecy' or history of the kingdom of the Picts and Scots.

Berc'hed the Breton feminine form of Bridget.

Berenice a feminine first name meaning 'bringing victory' (*Greek*). A variant form is Bernice. A diminutive form is Bunny.

Beriana a feminine variant form of Buryan.

Berkeley or **Berkley** masculine variant forms of Barclay.

Bernadette feminine form of Bernard. St Bernadette of Lourdes (1844–79) was a French peasant girl who saw a vision of the Virgin Mary telling her of a fresh water spring below the ground. The site in Lourdes is now a place of pilgrimage.

Bernard a masculine first name meaning 'strong or hardy bear' (*Germanic*). St Bernard of Clairvaux (1091–1153) was one of the Doctors of the Roman Catholic Church. A variant form is Barnard. Diminutive forms are Barney, Bernie.

Bernardin a French masculine form of Bernard.

Bernardino an Italian masculine diminutive form of Bernard.

Bernardo a Spanish and Italian masculine form of Bernard. William Shakespeare (1564–1616) used the name for a minor character in his tragedy *Hamlet*. Bernardo Bertolucci is an Italian film director.

Bernhard or **Bernhardt** a German masculine form of Bernard.

Bernice a feminine variant form of Berenice. In the New Testament Bernice was a daughter of King Herod Agrippa I and sister of Drusilla. Bernice Rubens is an English novelist who won the Booker Prize in 1970 for her fourth novel.

Bernie a masculine diminutive form of Bernard.

Berrach an Irish Gaelic feminine first name, the source of which is uncertain. In Celtic mythology, Berrach Breac, 'the freckled', third wife of Fionn macCumhaill, was said to be the most generous woman in Ireland. A variant form is Bearrach.

Bert masculine diminutive forms of ALBERT, BERTRAM, EGBERT, GILBERT, HUBERT, etc.

Berta a German, Italian and Spanish feminine form of BERTHA.

Bertha a feminine first name meaning 'bright; beautiful; famous' (*Germanic*). A diminutive form is Bertie.

Berthe the French feminine form of BERTHA.

Berthilda or **Berthilde** or **Bertilda** or **Bertilde** a feminine first name meaning 'shining maid of war' (*Old English*).

Berthold a masculine first name meaning 'bright ruler' (*Germanic*). Variant forms are Barthold, Bertold, Berthoud. Diminutive forms are Bert, Bertie.

Bertie (1) masculine diminutive forms of ALBERT, BERTRAM, EGBERT, GILBERT, HERBERT, etc. (2) a feminine diminutive form of BERTHA.

Bertold or **Berthoud** masculine variant forms of BERTHOLD.

Bertram a masculine first name meaning 'bright; fair; illustrious' (*Germanic*). William Shakespeare (1564–1616) used the name for one of the main characters in his comedy *All's Well That Ends Well*. A variant form is Bartram. Diminutive forms are Bert, Bertie.

Bertrand the French masculine form of BERTRAM. Bertrand Tavernier is a French film director.

Berwyn a Cornish and Welsh masculine first name. Berwyn was an early Celtic saint whose name is preserved in the Berwyn Range of mountains in North Wales and in Merioneth.

Beryl a feminine first name meaning 'jewel' (*Greek*), the name of the gemstone used as a feminine first name.

Bess or **Bessie** feminine diminutive forms of ELIZABETH.

Bet a feminine diminutive form of ELIZABETH.

Beth a feminine diminutive form of ELIZABETH, BETHANY, now used independently.

Bethan (1) (pronounced *bay-han*) a feminine first name, probably from *beatha*, 'life' (*Irish Gaelic*). A variant form is Beatha. In old Scotland this was also a male name: Macbeth, eleventh-century king of Scots, means literally 'son of life'. (2) a Welsh feminine diminutive form of ELIZABETH or ELIZABETH-ANN, also often used as a name in its own right.

Bethany a place name near Jerusalem, the home of Lazarus in the New Testament and meaning 'house of poverty', used as a feminine first name (*Aramaic*).

Bethóc (pronounced *bay-ock*) a feminine first name that is related to Bethan, from beatha, 'life' (*Scottish Gaelic*). It was the name of the daughter of Somerled, Lord of Argyll. A variant form is Beathag.

Betrys the Welsh feminine form of BEATRICE.

Betsy or **Bette** or **Bettina** or **Betty** feminine diminutive forms of ELIZABETH. Bette Davis (1908–89) was a famous American film actress of the 1930s onwards. Bette Midler is an American singer and film actress.

Beulah a feminine first name meaning 'married' (*Hebrew*).

Beuno (pronounced *by-no*) a Welsh masculine first name, that of a seventh-century Welsh saint whose name is preserved in St Beuno's Well, the subject of a poem by the English poet and Jesuit priest Gerald Manley Hopkins (1844–89).

Bev a feminine diminutive form of BEVERLEY.

Bevan (1) an anglicised form of Béibhinn used as a masculine first name. (2) a surname, meaning 'son of EVAN' (*Welsh*), used as a masculine first name. Variant forms are Beavan, Beaven, Bevin.

Beverley or **Beverly** a place name, meaning 'beaver stream' (*Old English*), used as a masculine or feminine first name. Beverley Nichols was an English journalist. Beverly d'Angelo is an American film actress. A diminutive form is Bev.

Bevin (1) a surname, meaning 'drink wine', used as a masculine first name. (2) a variant form of BEVAN.

Bevis a masculine first name meaning 'bull' (*French*). Bevis of Hampton was a hero of English medieval romance.

Beynon a masculine first name meaning 'son of Einion' (*Welsh*).

Bharat a masculine first name meaning 'being maintained' (*Sanskrit*) and the Hindu name for India.

Bharati the feminine form of BHARAT.

Bhaskar a masculine first name meaning 'sun' (*Sanskrit*).

Bhéibhinn (pronounced *vay-vin*) a feminine variant form of BÉIBHINN.

Bianca the Italian feminine form of BLANCH, now also used independently as an English-language form, inspired by Bianca Jagger, the Nicaraguan-born first wife of the pop singer Mick Jagger. William Shakespeare (1564–1616) used the name for a courtesan in his tragedy *Othello* and the sister of the heroine in *The Taming of the Shrew*. The name was also used for one of the main characters in the popular television soap opera *Eastenders*.

Biddy or **Biddie** a feminine diminutive form of BRIDGET.

Bije a masculine diminutive form of ABIJAH.

Bile (pronounced *bee-la*) a masculine first name meaning 'noble warrior' (*Irish Gaelic/Pictish*). In Irish legend, Bile was a leader of the Milesians, one of the early invading groups. In Scotland he was the father of the Pictish king Bridei, whom St Columba visited.

Bill a masculine diminutive form of WILLIAM.

Billie (1) a masculine diminutive form of WILLIAM. (2) a feminine diminutive form of WILHELMINA.

Billy a masculine diminutive form of WILLIAM.

Bina or **Binah** or **Bine** a feminine first name meaning 'bee' (*Hebrew*).

Bing a surname, meaning 'a hollow' (*Germanic*), used as a masculine first name.

Binnie a feminine diminutive form of SABINA.

Birch a surname, from the birch tree (*Old English*), used as a masculine first name. A variant form is Birk.

Birgit or **Birgitta** the Swedish feminine form of BRIDGET. A diminutive form is BRITT.

Birk a masculine variant form of BIRCH.

Bishop a surname, meaning 'one who worked in a bishop's household' (*Old English*), used as a masculine first name.

Bjork an Icelandic feminine first name made famous by the popularity of the Icelandic pop singer Bjork Gudmunsdottir.

Björn a masculine first name meaning 'bear' (*Old Norse*). Björn Borg is a Swedish tennis champion.

Black a surname, meaning 'dark-complexioned' or 'dark-haired' (*Old English*), used as a masculine first name. A variant form is BLAKE.

Bladud a Brythonic Celtic masculine first name from that of a mythical king from old British tales, allegedly founder of the city of Bath and father of King Lear.

Blair a place name and surname, from *blár*, meaning 'a field', 'battleground' (*Scottish Gaelic*), used as a masculine first name.

Blaise a Breton and Cornish masculine first name that may derive from *blas*, 'taste' (*Breton*). It is preserved in St Blazey in Cornwall, and in

France was the name of the religious philosopher Blaise Pascal (1623–62). A variant form is BLEISE, in Celtic legend the tutor of the magician Myrddyn, 'Merlin'.

Bláithin (pronounced *bla-hin*) a feminine first name meaning 'flower', 'blossom', from *bláth*, 'flower' (*Irish Gaelic*). A name of the same meaning is BLÁTHNAT. *See also* BLODWEN.

Blake a variant form of Black; alternatively, 'pale' or 'fair-complexioned' (*Old English*). Blake Edwards is an American film director and Blake Morrison is an English poet.

Blánaid a variant form of BLÁTHNAT.

Blanca the Spanish feminine form of BLANCH.

Blanch or **Blanche** a feminine first name meaning 'white' (*Germanic*). Blanch of Castille (*c*.1188–1252) was the daughter of Alfonso VIII, king of Castile, and Eleanor, daughter of Henry II of England, and the niece of King John. She married King Louis VIII of France and from her were descended the royal houses of Valois, Bourbon and Orleans as well as Edward III of England.

Blane an Irish and Scottish Gaelic masculine first name from that of St Bláan, whose name is preserved in Scottish towns such as Dunblane and Blanefield.

Blathnáid and **Bláthnaid** variant forms of BLÁTHNAT.

Bláthnat (pronounced *bla-na*) a feminine first name meaning 'little flower' (*Irish Gaelic*). Variant Gaelic forms are Blánaid, Bláthnaid and Bláthnaid. In Celtic mythology, she was the wife of the chieftain Cú Roí and betrayed him to his enemy Cuchulainn. She was killed by Ferchertne, his faithful bard, who clasped her to him and leapt from a clifftop.

Bleddyn (pronounced *bleth-in*) a masculine first name meaning 'wolf-like', from *blaidd*, 'wolf' (*Welsh*). Bleddyn ap Cynfryn was a prince in the eleventh century.

Bleise a masculine variant form of BLAISE. In Celtic legend Bleise was the tutor of the magician Myrddyn, 'Merlin'.

Bliss a surname, meaning 'happiness or joy', used as a feminine first name (*Old English*).

Blodeuedd (pronounced *blod-wedd*) a feminine first name meaning 'flower face' (*Welsh*). In Celtic mythology she was a beautiful woman created by the mages GWYDION and Math to be the wife of the hero Lleu

Llaw Gyffes but who betrays him and is ultimately turned into an owl; the story is in the Mabonogion cycle.

Blodwen a feminine first name meaning 'white flower', from *blodau*, 'flowers', *ven*, 'white' (*Welsh*).

Blossom a feminine first name meaning 'like a flower' (*Old English*). Blossom Dearie is an American singer.

Blyth or **Blythe** a surname, meaning 'cheerful and gentle', used as a masculine or feminine first name (*Old English*). Blythe Danner is an American actress and the mother of the actress Gwyneth Paltrow.

Boas or **Boaz** a masculine first name meaning 'fleetness' (*Hebrew*). In the Old Testament Boaz was a landowner of Bethlehem in Judah.

Bob or **Bobby** a masculine diminutive form of ROBERT.

Bobbie or **Bobby** a feminine diminutive form of ROBERTA, now used independently.

Boniface a masculine first name meaning 'doer of good' (*Latin*). St Boniface (672–745) was an English missionary in Germany. It was also the name adopted by several popes.

Bonita a feminine first name meaning 'pretty' (*Spanish*) or 'good' (*Latin*). A diminutive form is BONNIE.

Bonnie or **Bonny** (1) the Scots adjective *bonnie*, 'pretty', reimported from North America as a feminine first name. In the USA it was made famous or notorious by the girl gangster Bonnie Parker. Bonnie Langford is an English actress. (2) a diminutive form of BONITA.

Booth a surname, meaning 'hut' or 'shed' (*Old Norse*), used as a masculine first name.

Boris a masculine first name meaning 'small' (*Russian*). Boris Karloff (1887–1969) was an English-born film actor known for his roles in horror films. Boris Johnson is an English journalist.

Botolf or **Botolph** a masculine first name meaning 'herald wolf' (*Old English*).

Bourn or **Bourne** masculine variant forms of BURN.

Bowen a surname, meaning 'son of OWEN' (*Welsh*), used as a masculine first name.

Bowie a surname, meaning 'yellow-haired' (*Scottish Gaelic*), used as a masculine first name.

Boyce a surname, meaning 'a wood' (*Old French*), used as a masculine first name.

Boyd a surname, meaning 'light-haired' (*Scots Gaelic*), used as a masculine first name.

Boyne the name of an Irish river, meaning 'white cow' (*Irish Gaelic*), used as a masculine first name.

Brad a masculine diminutive form of BRADLEY, now used independently. Brad Dourif and Brad Pitt are American film actors.

Bradford a place name and surname, meaning 'place at the broad ford' (*Old English*), used as a masculine first name.

Bradley a surname, meaning 'broad clearing' or 'broad wood' (*Old English*), used as a masculine first name. A diminutive form is Brad or Bradd.

Brady an Irish surname, of unknown meaning, used as a masculine first name.

Braham a surname, meaning 'house or meadow with broom bushes', used as a masculine first name.

Bram a masculine diminutive form of ABRAM, ABRAHAM.

Bramwell a surname, meaning 'from the bramble spring' (*Old English*), used as a masculine first name.

Bran a Celtic masculine first name meaning 'raven' or 'crow' (*Gaelic*), the name of a god who was believed to possess powers of life and death. The name occurs in legends of all the Celtic countries.

Brand a masculine first name meaning 'firebrand' (*Old English*).

Brandee or **Brandi** or **Brandie** a variant form of BRANDY.

Brandon (1) a surname, meaning 'broom-covered hill' (*Old English*), used as a masculine first name. (2) a variant form of BRENDAN.

Brandubh (pronounced *bran-doov*) a masculine first name meaning 'black raven' (*Irish /Scottish Gaelic*). It was a name borne by a number of provincial kings. An anglicised form is Branduff.

Branduff the anglicised masculine form of BRANDUBH.

Brandy the name of the alcoholic spirit distilled from grapes used as a feminine first name. A variant form is Brandee, Brandi, Brandie.

Brangaine (pronounced *bran-gy-ana*) an Irish Gaelic feminine form of BRONWEN. In legend, Brangaine was the nurse of Iseult who gave her and Trystan a love potion.

Branwen (1) a feminine first name meaning 'raven-haired beauty' (*Welsh*). (2) a variant form of BRONWEN.

Breanna or **Breanne** a variant form of BRIANA.

Bree a feminine diminutive form of BRIDGET.

Bregeen (pronounced *bregh-een*) an Irish feminine first name meaning 'little BRIDGET'.

Brenda a feminine first name, from *brandr*, meaning 'brand' or 'sword' (*Old Norse*). Brenda Blethyn is an English actress.

Brendan or **Brendon** a masculine first name perhaps derived originally from the Old Gaelic *bran*, 'raven', although a link with Welsh *brenhyn*, 'prince', has also been proposed. This was the name of the energetic and far-travelled St Brendan of Clonfert, 'Brendan the Navigator' (died AD 577), who, according to some, traversed the Atlantic in his coracle. An alternative form is BRANDON.

Brenna a feminine first name meaning 'raven-haired beauty' (*Irish Gaelic*).

Brent a surname, meaning 'a steep place' (*Old English*), used as a masculine first name.

Bret or **Brett** a masculine first name meaning 'a Breton', from Breizh, the Breton name for Brittany. Bret Harte (1836–1902) was an American writer who was for a time the American consul in Glasgow. It is also now used as a feminine first name; Brett Butler is an American comedienne.

Brewster a surname, meaning 'brewer' (*Old English*), used as a masculine first name.

Brian (pronounced *breye–an*, the Gaelic pronunciation is *bree-an*) a masculine first name, possibly Breton in origin, from a root-word *bri*, 'dignity, pride'. It gained great prestige from Brian Boruma, 'of the cattle taxes', high king of Ireland (*c*.941–1014), victor and victim of the Battle of Clontarf, at which Viking rule in Ireland was broken, and progenitor of the O'Briens. Variant forms are Brion and Bryan. The Belfast-born Canadian writer Brian Moore (1921–99) used the Gaelic pronunciation of the name.

Briana or **Brianna** (pronounced *bree-ana*) a feminine form of BRIAN. A variant form is Breanna or Breanne.

Brice a surname, from *ap-Rhys*, 'son of Rhys', 'the burning or ardent one' (*Welsh*), used as a first name. The fifth-century Gaulish St Brice or Bricius was bishop of Tours. A variant form is Bryce.

Bríd (pronounced *breeth*) the original Irish Gaelic form of BRIDGET.

Bride an anglicised form of BRÍD and variant form of BRIDGET. The name appears in Scotland as that of a sixth-century St Bride.

Bridei an original Pictish form of BRUDE.

Bridget a anglicised feminine first name from the Irish BRÍD, a name associated with *brígh*, 'power, virtue' (*Irish Gaelic*) and a name of power in the old Celtic world, when it belonged to a goddess. Assimilated into the Christian tradition, the goddess became a venerated saint; indeed there are sixteen or more St Bridgets, of whom the fifth-century St Bridget of Kildare is the best known. The name has numerous variant forms: Brigid and Brigit are the most frequent, with diminutive forms Biddy, Biddie, Bree (Ireland) and Bridie (Scotland). The Breton name Berc'hed is another form. For centuries it was the most popular girl's name in Ireland, as synonymous with an Irish girl as Patrick was with a boy.

Bridie a Scottish feminine diminutive form of BRIDGET.

Brieuc a Breton masculine variant form of BRIOC.

Brigham a surname, meaning 'homestead by a bridge' (*Old English*), used as a masculine first name. Brigham Young (1801–77). was an American Mormon leader who led the Mormon migration to Utah and founded Salt Lake City.

Brigid a feminine variant form of BRIDGET.

Brigide a Spanish, Italian and French feminine form of BRIDGET.

Brigit a feminine variant form of BRIDGET.

Brigitte a French feminine form of BRIDGET. Brigitte Bardot is a French film actress and animal rights campaigner.

Brioc a Welsh masculine first name and that of the sixth-century St Brioc who is also known in Brittany as St Brieuc.

Brion a masculine variant form of BRIAN.

Briony a feminine variant form of BRYONY.

Brisen (pronounced *bree-sen*) a Welsh feminine first name and the name of a witch from the Arthurian legends.

Britney a feminine first name popular in the USA. Possibly a contracted form of BRITTANY. Britney Spears is an American pop singer.

Britt a feminine diminutive form of BIRGIT, now used independently. Britt Eklund is a Swedish film actress.

Brittany the anglicised name of a French region, meaning 'land of the figured, or tattooed folk', used as a feminine first name.

Brochfael (pronounced *broch-file*) a Welsh masculine first name and that of a legendary king, mentioned in the songs of the minstrel Taliesin.

Brock a surname, meaning 'badger' (*Old English*), used as a masculine first name.

Broderic or **Broderick** a surname, meaning 'son of RODERICK' (*Welsh*), used as a masculine first name. Broderick Crawford (1911–86) was a noted American film actor.

Brodie or **Brody** a surname, meaning 'ditch' (*Scots Gaelic*), used as a masculine first name.

Brógán (pronounced *broh-gawn*) an Irish Gaelic masculine first name of uncertain derivation, this was the name of a number of early holy men, including St Brógán who acted as a scribe for St Patrick.

Bron a masculine diminutive form of AUBERON, OBERON.

Brona and **Bronach** variant feminine forms of BRÓNAGH.

Brónagh (pronounced *broh-na*) a feminine first name meaning 'sorrowing', from *brónach*, 'sorrowful' (*Irish Gaelic*). A Celtic equivalent of the name Dolores. Variant forms are Brona, Bronach.

Brongwyn a feminine variant form of BRONWEN.

Bronwen a feminine first name meaning 'white-breast' from *bron*, 'breast', *ven*, 'white' (*Welsh*). Variant forms are Brongwyn, Bronwyn and Branwen. *See also* BRANGAINE.

Bronwyn a feminine variant form of BRONWEN.

Brook or **Brooke** a surname, meaning 'stream', used as a masculine or feminine first name. Brooke Shields is an American actress. A variant form is Brooks.

Brooklyn the name of an area of New York City used as a masculine or feminine first name.

Brooklynn or **Brooklynne** a feminine form of Brooklyn.

Brooks a variant masculine or feminine form of BROOK.

Bruce a surname from Bruis or Brux in Normandy used as a masculine first name. The founder of the family came from Normandy with William the Conqueror; a descendant in Scotland was granted a lordship by King David I. It became a popular first name from the nineteenth century, especially in Australia. Bruce Lee (1940–73) was an American actor and kung fu expert.

Brude the anglicised masculine form of the Pictish Bruide or Bridei, who was the king of the Picts whom St Columba visted in AD 565.

Bruide one of the original Pictish forms of BRUDE.

Brunella feminine form of BRUNO.

Brunhilda or **Brunhilde** a feminine first name meaning 'warrior maid' (*Germanic*).

Bruno a masculine first name meaning 'brown' (*Germanic*). St Bruno (*c*.1032–1101) was the founder of the Carthusian monastic order. Bruno Kirby is an American film actor.

Bryan a masculine variant form of BRIAN. Bryan Brown is an Australian film actor.

Bryce a masculine variant form of BRICE.

Brychan (pronounced *bree-chan*) a masculine first name meaning 'freckled one' (*Welsh*). It was the name of a fifth-century chief whose name is preserved in Brecon and Castell Brychan, Aberystwyth.

Bryn (pronounced *brinn*) a masculine first name meaning 'hill' (*Welsh*). It is not connected with the name Brian.

Brynmawr a masculine variant form of BRYNMOR.

Brynmor a masculine first name from *bryn*, 'hill', and *mor*, 'great' (*Welsh*). A variant form is Brynmawr.

Bryony the name of a climbing plant used as a feminine first name (*Greek*). A variant form is Briony.

Buan (pronounced *bwan*) a masculine or feminine first name meaning 'lasting', 'enduring' (*Irish Gaelic*).

Buck a masculine first name meaning 'stag; he-goat; a lively young man' (*Old English*).

Buckley a surname, meaning 'stag or he-goat meadow' (*Old English*), used as a masculine first name.

Budd or **Buddy** the informal term for a friend or brother used as a masculine first name.

Buddug the Welsh masculine form of BUDOC.

Budoc a Cornish masculine first name that has the same form as Boudicca and is probably from the same root, *buad*, 'victory'. It is the name of the patron saint of Cornwall; his name is preserved in St Budeaux. The Welsh name Buddug is cognate with Budoc.

Buena a feminine first name meaning 'good' (*Spanish*).

Bunny a feminine diminutive form of BERENICE.

Bunty a feminine diminutive meaning 'lamb', now used as a feminine first name.

Buona a feminine first name meaning 'good' (*Italian*).

Burchard a masculine variant form of BURKHARD.

Burdon a surname, meaning 'castle on a hill or valley with a cowshed' (*Old English*), used as a masculine first name.

Burford a surname, meaning 'ford by a castle' (*Old English*), used as a masculine first name.

Burgess a surname, meaning 'citizen or inhabitant of a borough' (*Old French*), used as a masculine first name.

Burhan a masculine first name meaning 'proof' (*Arabic*).

Burk or **Burke** a surname, meaning 'fort or manor' (*Old French*), used as a masculine first name.

Burkhard a masculine first name meaning 'strong as a castle' (*Germanic*). A variant form is Burchard.

Burl a masculine first name meaning 'cup bearer' (*Old English*). Burl Ives is an American folksinger and actor.

Burleigh or **Burley** a masculine first name meaning 'dweller in the castle by the meadow' (*Old English*).

Burn or **Burne** a surname, meaning 'brook or stream' (*Old English*), used as a masculine first name. Variant forms are Bourn, Bourne, Byrne.

Burnett a surname, meaning 'brown-complexioned' or 'brown-haired' (*Old French*), used as a masculine first name.

Burt a masculine diminutive form of Burton, now used independently. Burt Reynolds is an American film actor.

Burton a surname, meaning 'farmstead of a fortified place' (*Old English*), used as a masculine first name. A diminutive form is Burt.

Buryan a Cornish feminine first name meaning 'gift', probably related to Gaelic *beir*, 'gift'. Buryan or Beriana was a Cornish saint. The name Veryan is probably from the same source.

Buster an informal term of address for a boy or young man, now used as a masculine first name. Buster Keaton (1895–1966) was a famous American silent film comedy actor.

Byrne a masculine variant form of Burn.

Byron a surname, meaning 'at the cowsheds' (*Old English*), used as a masculine first name.

C

Cabhán (pronounced *ca-vann*) the original Irish Gaelic form of CAVAN. It is a name similar in sound to Caoimhín (KEVIN) but unrelated.

Cadan (pronounced *cad-an*) a masculine first name meaning 'wild goose' (*Irish Gaelic*). It was the name of a mythical hero of early legend.

Caddick or **Caddock** a surname, meaning 'decrepit' (*Old French*), used as a masculine first name.

Caddie or **Caddy** a feminine diminutive form of CAROL, CAROLA, CAROLE, CAROLINE, CAROLYN.

Cadell a masculine first name, meaning 'battle spirit', from *cad*, 'battle' (*Welsh*). It was a warrior's name.

Cadence a feminine first name meaning 'rhythmic' (*Latin*).

Cadenza the Italian feminine form of CADENCE.

Cadfael (pronounced *cad-file*) a masculine first name meaning 'battle prince' (*Welsh*). The name has been made famous by the Brother Cadfael stories by Ellis Peters.

Cadmus a masculine first name meaning 'man from the east' (*Greek*). In Greek mythology, he was a Phoenician prince who founded Thebes with five warriors he had created.

Cadog or **Cadoc** a masculine first name from *cad*, 'battle' (*Welsh*). It was used as a warrior's name, but the most famous Cadog (505–570) was a saint whose name is preserved in places such as Llangattock.

Cadogan the anglicised masculine form of CADWGAN.

Cadwaladr a masculine first name meaning 'leader in battle', from *cad*, 'battle'; *gwaladr*, 'leader' (*Welsh*). It was the name of legendary heroes and of the sixth-century prince of Gwynedd, Cadwaladr Fendigaid, 'blessed', who died in Rome in the later seventh century. It is also found in the anglicised form of Cadwallader.

Cadwallader the anglicised masculine form of CADWALADR.

Cadwallon a masculine first name, from *cad*, 'battle', and *gallon*, 'scatterer', 'ruler' (*Welsh*).

Cadwgan (pronounced *cad-o-gan*) a masculine first name deriving from *cad*, 'battle' (*Welsh*). Cadwgan was a tenth-century Welsh chieftain associated with Glamorgan, where there is a hill called Moel Cadwgan. The anglicised form is Cadogan.

Cáel (pronounced *kyle*) a masculine first one meaning 'slender one' (*Irish Gaelic*). In Celtic mythology, he was a hero of the Fianna and lover of Créd.

Cáelfind (pronounced *kyle-finn*) a feminine first name meaning 'slender and fair', from *caol*, 'slender' and *fionn*, 'fair' (*Irish Gaelic*). A variant Gaelic form is CAOILAINN. This name was borne by a number of holy women. The anglicised form is Keelin, Keelan or Ceelin.

Caerwyn (pronounced *carr-win*) a masculine first name meaning 'white fort' (*Welsh*).

Caesar a masculine first name meaning 'long-haired' (*Latin*); the Roman title of 'emperor' used as a masculine first name.

Cahal a masculine variant form of CATHAL.

Cahir the anglicised masculine form of Irish Gaelic CATHAÍR.

Cai *see* CEI

Cailean the Scottish Gaelic masculine form of COLIN.

Cain a masculine first name meaning 'possession' (*Hebrew*). In the Bible it is the name of the first son of Adam and Eve, who killed his younger brother, Abel.

Cainche or **Caince** (pronounced *cann-hya*) a feminine first name meaning 'melody', 'songbird' (*Irish Gaelic*). In Celtic mythology, she was a daughter of FIONN macCumhaill, who bears a son to Fionn's enemy Goll macMorna.

Cairbre (pronounced *carr-bra*) a masculine first name that probably means 'charioteer' (*Irish Gaelic*). In Celtic mythology, the great warriors had their personal charioteers, who were not themselves fighting men. A frequent name in Old Irish sources, it is applied to a high king, Cairbre Lifechair, 'of the Liffey', in the tales of the Fenian Cycle.

Cairenn or **Caireann** (pronounced *carr-enn*) an Irish Gaelic feminine first name perhaps taken into the Celtic languages from the Latin *carina*, 'dear'. It was the name of the mother of the early Irish high king Niall of the Nine Hostages, founder of the Ui Neills. She was not the wife of Niall's father but a concubine, traditionally a slave from Britain. It is sometimes anglicised to Carina and Karen.

Cáit (pronounced *kawt*) a shortened Irish Gaelic feminine form of CAITLÍN.

Caitlín (pronounced *kawt-leen*) an Irish Gaelic feminine form of Norman-French Cateline, a form of Catherine. The anglicised version is Cathleen or Kathleen.

Caius a masculine first name meaning 'rejoice' (*Latin*). A variant form is GAIUS.

Cal (1) a feminine diminutive form of CALANDRA, CALANTHA. (2) a masculine diminutive form of CALUM, CALVIN.

Calandra a feminine first name meaning 'lark' (*Greek*). Diminutive forms are Cal, Callie, Cally.

Calandre the French feminine form of CALANDRA.

Calandria the Spanish feminine form of CALANDRA.

Calantha a feminine first name meaning 'beautiful blossom' (*Greek*). Diminutive forms are Cal, Callie, Cally.

Calanthe the French feminine form of CALANTHA.

Calder a masculine or feminine first name from a Scots Gaelic compound meaning 'stream by the hazels', a location name from several parts of Scotland that has become a surname and an occasional first name.

Caldwell a surname, meaning 'cold spring or stream' (*Old English*), used as a masculine first name.

Cale a masculine diminutive form of CALEB.

Caleb a masculine first name meaning 'a dog' (*Hebrew*). In the Old Testament Caleb was one of the spies dispatched by Moses to spy out Canaan. A diminutive form is Cale.

Caledonia the Roman name for Scotland (*Latin*) used as a feminine first name.

Caley (1) a masculine first name meaning 'thin, slender' (*Irish Gaelic*). (2) a diminutive form of CALUM.

Calgacus a masculine first name said to mean 'sword wielder' (*Latin*). It was the name given by the Roman historian Tacitus (AD *c*.55–*c*.120) to the the commander of the Caledonian tribes at the battle of Mons Graupius, AD 83 and is the oldest recorded name of an inhabitant of what is now Scotland.

Calhoun a surname, meaning 'from the forest' (*Irish Gaelic*), used as a masculine first name.

Calla a feminine first name meaning 'beautiful' (*Greek*).

Callan an anglicised masculine form of the Irish Gaelic C<small>ULANN</small>.

Callie a feminine diminutive form of C<small>ALANDRA</small>, C<small>ALANTHA</small>.

Calliope a feminine first name meaning 'lovely voice' (*Greek*). In Greek mythology Calliope was the muse of poetry.

Callista feminine form of C<small>ALLISTO</small>.

Callisto a masculine first name meaning 'most fair or good' (*Greek*).

Callum a masculine variant form of C<small>ALUM</small>.

Cally (1) a feminine diminutive form of C<small>ALANDRA</small>, C<small>ALANTHA</small>. (2) a masculine diminutive form of C<small>ALUM</small>.

Calum (1) the Scottish Gaelic masculine form of *columba*, the Latin word for 'dove'. (2) a diminutive form of M<small>ALCOLM</small>. A variant form is Callum. Diminutive forms are Cal, Cally, Caley.

Calumina a feminine form of C<small>ALUM</small>.

Calvert a surname, meaning 'calf herd' (*Old English*), used as a masculine first name.

Calvin a masculine first name meaning 'little bald one' (*Latin*). Calvin Klein is an American dress designer. A diminutive form is Cal.

Calvina a feminine form of C<small>ALVIN</small>.

Calvino Italian and Spanish masculine forms of C<small>ALVIN</small>.

Calypso a feminine first name meaning 'concealer' (*Greek*). In Greek mythology, Calypso was the name of the sea nymph who held Odysseus captive for seven years. A variant form is Kalypso.

Cameron a Scottish surname, from *cam*, 'hooked' and *sron*, 'nose' (*Scots Gaelic*), used as a masculine or feminine first name. Originally probably only given to boys whose mothers' maiden name was Cameron, it is now in general use and increasingly given to girls as well, the American actress Cameron Diaz being an example.

Camila the Spanish feminine form of C<small>AMILLA</small>.

Camilla a feminine first name meaning 'votaress, attendant at a sacrifice' (*Latin*).

Camille the French masculine and feminine form of C<small>AMILLA</small>.

Campbell (pronounced *cam-bell*) a Scottish surname, from *cam*, 'crooked', and *beul*, 'mouth' (*Scots Gaelic*) or from *champ*, 'field' and *bel*, 'beautiful' (*French*), used as a masculine first name. Its use as a first name probably began in the same way as Cameron.

Candace a feminine variant form of C<small>ANDICE</small>.

Candie a feminine diminutive form of C<small>ANDICE</small>, C<small>ANDIDA</small>.

Candice a feminine first name, the meaning of which is uncertain but possibly 'brilliantly white' or 'pure and virtuous' (*Latin*). It was the name of an Ethiopian queen.Candice Bergen is an American actress. Variant forms are Candace, Candis.

Candida a feminine first name meaning 'shining white' (*Latin*). George Bernard Shaw (1856–1950) used the name for the eponymous heroine of his play *Candida* (1903). Diminutive forms are Candie, Candy.

Candis a feminine variant form of CANDICE.

Candy (1) a feminine diminutive form of CANDICE, CANDIDA. (2) a name used in its own right, from candy, the American English word for a sweet.

Canice an anglicised masculine form of the Irish Gaelic *Coinneach*, 'KENNETH'. Kilkenny Cathedral is dedicated to St Canice, and shows the same name in a different form: *cill*, 'church', Coinneaich, 'of Kenneth'.

Canute a masculine first name meaning 'knot' (*Old Norse*), the name of a Danish king of England (1016–35). Variant forms are Cnut, Knut.

Caoilainn a variant Irish Gaelic form of CÁELFIND.

Caoilfhinn (pronounced *kyle-finn*) a feminine first name meaning 'slender fair one' from *caol*, 'slender', *fionn*, 'fair' (*Irish Gaelic*). Anglicised forms of the name are Kaylin, Keelan. *See also* CÁELFIND.

Caoimhe *see* KEVA.

Caoimhín *see* KEVIN.

Caomh (pronounced *kave*) a masculine first name, from *caomh*, 'gentle', 'noble' (*Irish Gaelic*). It was the name of an Irish legendary warrior and progenitor of the O'Keeffes.

Cara (1) a feminine first name meaning 'friend' (*Irish Gaelic*). *See also* Cera. (2) a feminine first name meaning 'dear, darling' (*Italian*). A variant form is Carina.

Caractacus *see* CARADOG.

Caradoc the anglicised form of the Welsh CARADOG.

Caradog a masculine first name meaning 'beloved' (*Welsh*). It was the name of an early Welsh chieftain who fought against the Romans in the first century AD. The Romans rendered the name as 'Caractacus'. The Irish form is Cárthach, and an anglicised form is Caradoc. Caer Caradoc (Caradoc's fort) is a hill in Shropshire. A variant form is Cradoc.

Cardew a surname meaning 'black fort' (*Welsh*), used as a masculine first name.

Cardigan see CEREDIG.

Carey (1) a feminine first name from a place and river name Cary that occurs in Somerset and in central Scotland, and may be from the Celtic root *car*, 'dark', which is also the source of Kerry in Ireland. An association may also have grown up with Latin *cara*, 'dear'. The phrase 'Mother Carey's chickens' is from Latin *mata cara*, meaning the Virgin Mary. (2) a variant masculine form of CARY.

Cari a feminine variant form of CERI.

Caridad (pronounced *car-ee-dath*) the Spanish feminine form of CHARITY.

Carina (1) a feminine variant form of CARA. (2) an anglicised feminine form of CAIRENN.

Carissa a feminine first name meaning 'dear one' (*Latin*).

Carl (1) an anglicised German and Swedish masculine form of CHARLES. (2) an anglicised masculine form of Irish Gaelic CERBHALL. (3) a masculine diminutive form of CARLTON, CARLIN, CARLISLE, CARLO, CARLOS.

Carla feminine form of CARL. A variant form is Carlin. Diminutive forms are Carlie, Carley, Carly.

Carleton a masculine variant form of CARLTON.

Carley or **Carly** feminine diminutive forms of CARLA.

Carlie a feminine diminutive form of CARLA, CARLIN.

Carlin a feminine variant form of CARLA. Diminutive forms are Carlie, Carley, Carly.

Carlisle a masculine diminutive form of CARL.

Carlo the Italian masculine form of CHARLES.

Carlos the Spanish masculine form of CHARLES.

Carlotta the Italian feminine form of CHARLOTTE.

Carlton a place name and surname, meaning 'farm of the churls' (a rank of peasant) (*Old English*), used as a masculine first name. Variant forms are Carleton, Charlton, Charleton. A diminutive form is CARL.

Carly a feminine diminutive form of CARLA, CARLIN, now used independently. Carly Simon is an American singer.

Carlyn a feminine variant form of CAROLINE.

Carmel a feminine first name meaning 'garden' (*Hebrew*).

Carmela a Spanish and the Italian feminine forms of CARMEL.

Carmelita a Spanish feminine diminutive form of CARMEL.

Carmen a Spanish feminine form of CARMEL.

Carmichael a Scottish place name and surname, meaning 'fort of

Carnation

MICHAEL', used as a masculine first name.

Carnation the name of a flower, meaning 'flesh colour' (*Latin/French*), used as a feminine first name.

Caro a feminine diminutive form of CAROL, CAROLINE.

Carol (1) a shortened masculine form of Carolus, the Latin form of CHARLES. (2) the feminine form of CHARLES. A variant form is Caryl. Diminutive forms are Caro, Carrie, Caddie.

Carola a feminine variant form of CAROLINE. Diminutive forms are Carrie, Caro, Caddie.

Carole (1) the French feminine form of CAROL. (2) a contracted form of CAROLINE. Diminutive forms are Caro, Carrie, Caddie.

Carolina the Italian and Spanish feminine forms of CAROLINE.

Caroline or **Carolyn** the feminine form of Carolus, the Latin form of CHARLES. Caroline of Brunswick (1768–1821) was the wife of George IV. She was tried for adultery in 1820. A variant form is Carlyn. Diminutive forms are Caro, Carrie, Caddie.

Caron (1) (pronounced *carr-on*) a Welsh masculine first name from the name of a saint, found in the place name Tregaron, in Ceredigion. (2) a feminine variant form of KAREN.

Caronwyn a feminine first name meaning 'beautiful loved one', from *caru*, 'to love', and *gwyn*, 'white, fair' (*Welsh*).

Carr a place name and surname, meaning 'overgrown marshy ground' (*Old Norse*), used as a masculine first name. Variant forms are Karr, Kerr.

Carrie a feminine diminutive form of CAROL, CAROLA, CAROLE, CAROLINE, CAROLYN. Carrie Fisher is an American actress and writer.

Carrick a place name, from *caraig*, 'rock or crag' (*Gaelic*), used as a masculine first name.

Carroll the anglicised masculine form of Irish Gaelic CERBHALL.

Carson a surname, of uncertain meaning but possibly 'marsh dweller' (*Old English*), used as a masculine first name.

Carter a surname, meaning 'a driver or maker of cars' (*Old English*) or 'son of ARTHUR' (*Scots Gaelic*), used as a masculine first name.

Cárthach the Irish masculine form of Welsh CARADOG.

Cartimandua a feminine first name from the Latinised Brythonic name of the first-century AD queen of the Brigantes, in what is now northern England.

Carver (1) a masculine first name meaning 'great rock' (*Cornish Gaelic*). (2) a surname, meaning 'sculptor' (*Old English*), used as a masculine first name.

Carwen (pronounced *carr-wen*) a feminine first name meaning 'white love', from *caru*, 'to love' and *ven*, 'white' (*Welsh*).

Carwyn the masculine form of CARWEN.

Cary a masculine form of CAREY. Cary Elwes is an English actor, son of the artist Dominic Elwes. Cary Grant was the adopted name of Archibald Leach.

Caryl (1) a feminine first name deriving from *caru*, 'to love' (*Welsh*). (2) a feminine variant form of Carol.

Caryn a feminine variant form of KAREN.

Carys a feminine first name meaning 'loved', from *caru*, 'to love' (*Welsh*).

Casey (1) a surname, meaning 'vigilant in war' (*Irish Gaelic*), increasingly being used as a masculine or feminine first name. (2) a place name, Cayce in Kentucky, where the hero Casey Jones was born, used as a masculine first name. (3) a variant feminine form of CASSIE, which is also used independently.

Cashel a place name, meaning 'circular stone fort' (*Irish Gaelic*), used as a masculine first name.

Casimir the English masculine form of KASIMIR.

Caspar or **Casper** the Dutch masculine form of JASPER, now also used as an English-language form. In the Bible Caspar was one of the Magi, the three wise men from the east who paid homage to the infant Jesus, presenting him with gifts.

Cass (1) a feminine diminutive form of CASSANDRA. (2) a masculine diminutive form of CASSIDY, CASSIAN, CASSIUS.

Cassandra a feminine first name meaning 'she who inflames with love' (*Greek*). In Greek mythology, Cassandra was a princess, the daughter of King Priam of Troy and Hecuba, whose prophecies of doom were not believed. Diminutive forms are Cass, Cassie.

Cassia a feminine variant form of KEZIA.

Cassian a masculine first name from the Roman family name CASSIUS.

Cassidy a surname, meaning 'clever' (*Irish Gaelic*), used as a masculine first name. A diminutive form is Cass.

Cassie a feminine diminutive form of CASSANDRA.

Cassius a Roman family name, of uncertain meaning, possibly 'empty' (*Latin*), used as a masculine first name. The American boxer Cassius Marcellus Clay changed his name to Muhammad Ali. A diminutive form is Cass.

Cassivellaunus the Latinised form of a Celtic masculine first name, that of a first-century tribal king of southern Britain who fought against Julius Caesar's invading troops.

Castor a masculine first name meaning 'beaver' (*Greek*). In Greek mythology, Castor was the mortal one of the twins born to Zeus and Leda.

Caswallon a hero of the Welsh *Mabinogion* tales who conquers Britain. The name may be modelled at least in part on CASSIVELLAUNUS.

Catalina the Spanish feminine form of KATHERINE.

Caterina the Italian feminine form of KATHERINE.

Cath a feminine diminutive form of CATHERINE.

Catháir (pronounced *ka-har*) a masculine first name, probably derived from *cath*, 'battle', and meaning 'battle-lord' (*Irish Gaelic*). The anglicised form is Cahir.

Cathal (pronounced *ka-hal*) a masculine first name meaning 'strong battler', from *cath*, 'battle' (*Irish Gaelic*). Cathal Brugha (1874–1922) was a leader of the 1916 Easter Rising and was killed in the Irish Civil War in 1922. A variant form is Cahal.

Cathán (pronounced *ka-hann*) a masculine first name meaning 'warrior', from *cath*, 'battle' (*Irish Gaelic*). The name of a descendant of NIALL of the Nine Hostages, who was the founder of the O'Kanes.

Catharina or **Catharine** or **Catherina** feminine variant forms of CATHERINE.

Cathbad (pronounced *cath-bat*) a masculine first name incorporating the stem *cath*, 'battle' (*Irish Gaelic*). This was the name of a celebrated druid who warned the men of Ulster of the baneful future awaiting the baby DEIRDRE. It has been anglicised to Cuthbert.

Cathella a feminine first name formed from the combination of parts of CATHERINE and ISABELLA. It is very much a Scottish and Irish name.

Catherine the French feminine form of KATHERINE, now used as an English-language form. It is the name of several saints, including the fourth-century martyr St Catherine of Alexandria who was tortured on a spiked wheel, and St Catherine of Siena (1347–80), the patron saint of Italy. Diminutive forms are Cath, Cathie, Cathy.

Cathie or **Cathy** feminine diminutive forms of CATHERINE.

Cathleen an anglicised feminine form of CAITLÍN.

Cato a Roman family name, meaning 'wise one' (*Latin*), used as a masculine first name.

Catrin the Welsh feminine form of KATHERINE, CATRIONA.

Catrine a feminine variant form of CATRIONA.

Catriona the Scottish and Irish Gaelic feminine form of KATHERINE. *Catriona*, the novel by Robert Louis Stevenson (1850–94), sequel to *Kidnapped*, popularised the name. Variant forms are Catrine, Katrine, Katrina, Katriona. Diminutive forms are Riona, TRINA.

Cavan the name of the Irish county, derived from Gaelic *cabhán*, 'grassy hill' or 'grassy hollow', referring to a hilly countryside (*Irish Gaelic*), used as a masculine first name. A variant form is Kavan.

Ceallach a masculine or feminine first name meaning 'bright-headed' (*Irish Gaelic*). Ceallach Cualand was the father of St KENTIGERN, or MUNGO, of Glasgow. An alternative form is Cellach, and the anglicised form is Kelly.

Ceara a variant form of CERA.

Cecil a masculine first name stemming from *seisyllt*, 'sixth' (*Welsh*), which could mean 'sixth child', like Latin Sextus, but its use as a first name seems to come from the fame of the surname Cecil in England, where it is the family name of the marquesses of Salisbury. It was the first name of the English writer and poet laureate C. Day Lewis (104–72), the father of Daniel Day Lewis.

Cecile the French feminine form of CECILY, CECILIA.

Cécile the French masculine form of CECIL.

Cecily or **Cecilia** the feminine form of CECIL. St Cecilia was a third-century Roman martyr who became the patron saint of music. Diminutive forms are Celia, Cis, Cissie, Cissy. A variant form is Cicely.

Cedric a masculine first name adapted by the Scottish writer Sir Walter Scott (1771–1832) for a character in *Ivanhoe* from the Saxon Cerdic, the first king of Wessex. Sir Cedric Hardwicke (1893–1964) was an English actor who appeared in many films.

Ceelin an anglicised feminine form of CÁELFIND.

Cei (pronounced *kay*) a Welsh masculine first name, possibly from the common Latin name Caius, which would have been frequently found in Roman Britain. In Welsh legend, he was a companion to King ARTHUR and steward of his household. It is also found as Cai. His name has been anglicised to Sir KAY in the English Arthurian tales.

Ceinwen (pronounced *kyne-wen*) a feminine first name meaning 'fine white one', from *cein*, 'elegant', 'fine', *ven*, 'white' (*Welsh*). Her name is preserved in St Keyne's Well, near Liskeard.

Ceiriog (pronounced *kye-riog*) a Welsh masculine first name from a river name of North Wales.

Celandine the name of either of two unrelated flowering plants, meaning 'swallow', used as a feminine first name (*Greek*).

Celeste a feminine first name meaning 'heavenly' (*Latin*). Celeste Holm is an American actress.

Celestine (1) a feminine diminutive form of Celeste. (2) a masculine name adopted by several popes, one of whom, Celestine V (1209–96), was the first pope to abdicate.

Celia a feminine first name meaning 'heavenly' (*Latin*), a diminutive form of CECILIA. William Shakespeare (1564–1616) used the name for Rosalind's cousin in his play *As You Like It*.

Céline the French feminine form of SELINA.

Cellach a masculine variant form of CEALLACH.

Cemlyn a place name, meaning 'bending lake', used as a masculine first name.

Cendrillon a feminine first name meaning 'from the ashes', the fairytale heroine (*French*); the anglicised form is CINDERELLA.

Cennydd (pronounced *kennith*) the Welsh masculine form of KENNETH. The Welsh St Cennydd, whose name is cognate with Irish CINÁED, is preserved in Senghennydd in Glamorgan.

Cephas a masculine first name meaning 'a stone' (*Aramaic*).

Cera (pronounced *kee-ra*) an Irish Gaelic feminine first name that goes a long way back in Irish legend to the wife of Nemed, leader of the Nemedians, the third set of invaders of ancient Ireland. It was also borne by three saints. An alternative form is Ceara. It is liable to be confused with CARA.

Cerbhall (pronounced *kerr-wal*) a masculine first name meaning 'brave in battle' (*Irish Gaelic*). It was a name borne by several kings in the Gaelic period, and by the fifth President of the Irish Republic, Cearbhall O Dálaigh. Anglicised forms include Carroll and Carl, athough in this latter form it is likely to be confused with German Carl or Karl.

Ceredig (pronounced *ker-ee-dig*) a masculine first name meaning 'lovable', 'kind one' (*Welsh*). Ceredig was a sixth-century king of the Strathclyde Britons. Ceredigion in Wales is called after another Ceredig, son of the semi-legendary fifth-century king Cynedda. The anglicised form is Cardigan.

Ceri (pronounced *kerri*) a Cornish and Welsh masculine or feminine first name meaning 'loved', from *caru*, 'to love' (*Welsh*). Ceri Richards (1903–77) was a distinguished twentieth-century artist. Feminine variant forms are Cari, Kari. A diminutive form is Cerian.

Cerian a feminine diminutive form of CERI.

Ceridwen (pronounced *ker-idwen*) a feminine first name from *cerdd*, 'poetry', and *ven*, 'white' (Welsh). It was the name of the Welsh poetic muse, mother of the minstrel Taliesin.

Cernunnos (pronounced *ker-nunnos*) a masculine first name meaning 'horned one' (*Gaulish*). He was an important god of the continental Celts, portrayed with the body of a man and the head of a stag.

Cerys (pronounced *kerr-ees*) a feminine first name meaning 'love' (*Welsh*).

César the French masculine form of CAESAR.

Cesare the Italian masculine form of CAESAR.

Cethern or **Cethren** (pronounced *ke-hern*) a masculine first name meaning 'long-lived' (*Irish Gaelic*).

Chad a masculine first name the meaning of which is uncertain, possibly 'warlike, bellicose' (*Old English*). St Chad (died 672) was the first bishop of Lichfield.

Chaim a masculine variant form of HYAM.

Chance (1) the abstract noun for the quality of good fortune used as a masculine first name. (2) a variant form of CHAUNCEY.

Chancellor a surname, meaning 'counsellor or secretary' (*Old French*), used as a masculine first name.

Chancey a masculine variant form of CHAUNCEY.

Chander the masculine form of CHANDRA.

Chandler a surname, meaning 'maker or seller of candles' (*Old French*), used as a masculine first name.

Chandra a feminine first name meaning 'moon brighter than the stars' (*Sanskrit*).

Chanel (pronounced *sha-nelle*) the surname of the French couturier and perfumier Coco Chanel (1883–1971) used as a feminine first name. A variant form is Shanel or Shanelle.

Chantal (pronounced *shawn-tal*) a French place name used as a feminine first name.

Chapman a surname, meaning 'merchant' (*Old English*), used as a masculine first name.

Charis (pronounced *ka-rees*) a feminine first name meaning 'grace' (*Greek*).

Charity the abstract noun for the quality of tolerance or generosity used as a feminine first name. It was a popular Puritan name.

Charlene a relatively modern feminine diminutive form of CHARLES, used as a feminine first name. A variant form is Charline.

Charles a masculine first name meaning 'strong; manly; noble-spirited' from *Carl*, 'man' (*Germanic*). It has long been a popular name and a royal one. Diminutive forms are Charlie, Charley, CHAS, CHUCK.

Charlie or **Charley** masculine and feminine diminutive forms of CHARLES, CHARLOTTE. Charlie Dimmock is a popular TV gardener.

Charline a feminine variant form of CHARLENE.

Charlotte a feminine form of CHARLES (*Germanic*). It was the name of George IV's only legitimate child. Diminutive forms are Charlie, Charley, Lottie.

Charlton or **Charleton** masculine variant forms of CARLTON. Charlton Heston is an American film actor.

Charmian a feminine first name meaning 'little delight' (*Greek*). A modern variant form is CHARMAINE.

Charmaine (1) a feminine diminutive form of the abstract noun for the quality of pleasing or attracting people used as a feminine first name. (2) a variant form of CHARMIAN.

Chas a masculine diminutive form of CHARLES.

Chase a surname, meaning 'hunter' (*Old French*), used as a masculine first name.

Chauncey or **Chaunce** a surname, of uncertain meaning, possibly 'chancellor' (*Old French*), used as a masculine first name. Variant forms are Chance, Chancey.

Chelsea a place name, meaning 'chalk landing place' (*Old English*), used as a feminine first name.

Cher (pronounced *sher*) or **Chérie** or **Cherie** (pronounced *sher-ee*) a feminine first name meaning 'dear, darling' (*French*). Cher is an American singer and actress; Cherie Blair is a barrister and the wife of Prime Minister Tony Blair. Variant forms are Cherry, Sheree, Sheri, Sherrie, Sherry.

Cherry (1) the name of the fruit used as a feminine first name. (2) a form of CHÉRIE. A variant form is CHERYL.

Cheryl (1) a feminine variant form of CHERRY. (2) a combining form of Cherry and BERYL. A variant form is Sheryl.

Chester a place name, meaning 'fortified camp' (*Latin*), used as a masculine first name.

Cheyenne (pronounced *shy-ann*) the name of the North American Indian nation, the meaning of which is uncertain, used as a masculine or feminine first name.

Chiara (pronounced *kee-ara*) the Italian feminine form of CLARA.

Chilton a place name and surname, meaning 'children's farm' (*Old English*), used as a masculine first name.

Chiquita (pronounced *chi-keeta*) a feminine first name meaning 'little one' (*Spanish*).

Chloë or **Chloe** a feminine first name meaning 'a green herb, a young shoot' (*Greek*). In the New Testament Chloe was a woman in whose house there was a correspondant of Paul's. In a Greek pastoral poem of the fourth or fifth century AD, it is the name of a shepherdess loved by Daphnis and became a generic name among poets and romance writers for a rustic maiden.

Chloris a feminine first name meaning 'green' (*Greek*). A variant form is Cloris.

Chris a masculine or feminine diminutive form of CHRISTIAN, CHRISTINE, CHRISTOPHER. Chris O'Donnell is an American film actor.

Chrissie (1) a Scottish feminine diminutive form of CHRISTIANA, CHRISTINE. (2) an Irish masculine diminutive form of CHRISTOPHER.

Christabel a feminine first name formed by the combination of the names CHRISTINE and BELLA made by Samuel Taylor Coleridge (1772–1834) for a poem of this name.

Christian a masculine or feminine first name meaning 'belonging to Christ, a believer in Christ' (*Latin*). John Bunyan (1628–88) used the name for the pilgrim hero of his allegory, *The Pilgrim's Progress* (1678). Christian Slater is an American actor. Diminutive forms are Chris, Christie, Christy.

Christiana the feminine form of Christian. A variant form is Christina.

Christie (1) a surname, meaning 'Christian', used as a masculine first name. (2) a masculine diminutive form of Christian, Christopher. (3) a feminine diminutive form of Christian, Christine. A variant form is Christy.

Christina a feminine variant form of Christiana.

Christine a French feminine form of Christina, now used as an English-language form. Christine Keeler was an English call-girl who helped bring about the downfall of Harold Macmillan's Conservative government in 1963. Diminutive forms are Chris, Chrissie, Christie, Christy, Teenie, Tina.

Christmas a masculine first name meaning 'festival of Christ' (*Old English*). Christmas Humphrys was an eminent English judge.

Christoph the German masculine form of Christopher.

Christopher a masculine first name meaning 'bearing Christ' (*Greek*). St Christopher was a third-century martyr about whom little is known. Until 1969 he was the patron saint of travellers. Christopher Lambert is a French film actor. Diminutive forms are Chris, Christie, Christy, Kester, Kit.

Christy a masculine and feminine variant form of Christie. Christy Brown was an Irish writer who suffered from cerebral palsy and who wrote a best-selling autobiography, *My Left Foot*.

Chrystal a feminine variant form of Crystal.

Chuck a masculine diminutive form of Charles. Chuck Norris is an American film actor.

Churchill a place name and surname, meaning 'church on a hill' (*Old English*), used as a masculine first name.

Ciabhán (pronounced *keea-vann*) a masculine first name meaning 'full-haired' (*Irish Gaelic*). In Irish legend, Ciabhán 'of the flowing locks' was the lover of Clídna, with whom he eloped from the land of the sea-god, Manannan. The anglicised form is Keevan.

Cian a masculine first name meaning 'ancient' (*Irish Gaelic*). Anglicised forms are Kean, Keane.

Ciara (pronounced *keera*) a feminine first name meaning 'dark one', from *ciar*, 'dark' (*Irish Gaelic*). Anglicised forms of the name include Keera, Keira, Kira.

Ciarán or **Ciaran** (pronounced *keer-ann*) a masculine first name meaning 'little dark one', from *ciar*, 'dark' (Irish Gaelic), with the diminutive suffix -an. Among several saints to bear the name, perhaps the most celebrated is the founder of the abbey of Clonmacnoise in AD 547, the year of his death. Anglicised forms include Kieran. *See also* KERR.

Cicely a feminine variant form of CECILIA.

Cilla a feminine diminutive form of PRISCILLA (*French*). Cilla Black is an English singer and TV host.

Cináed (pronounced *kin-aith*) a masculine name borne by kings of the Northern Irish Picts. It has been linked to Gaelic Coinneach, KENNETH, but this link is uncertain.

Cinderella a feminine first name from the anglicised form of CENDRILLON, the fairytale heroine. Diminutive forms are Cindie, Cindy, Ella.

Cindi or **Cindie** or **Cindy** a feminine diminuntive form of CINDERELLA, CYNTHIA, LUCINDA, now often used independently. Cindy Crawford is an American model.

Cinzia (prounced *chint-sia*) the Italian feminine form of CYNTHIA.

Cis or **Cissie** or **Cissy** feminine diminutive forms of CECILY.

Claiborne a masculine variant form of CLAYBORNE. A diminutive form is Clay.

Claire the French feminine form of CLARA, now used widely as an English form.

Clara a feminine first name meaning 'bright, illustrous' (*Latin*). A variant form is CLARE. A diminutive form is Clarrie.

Clarabel or **Clarabella** or **Clarabelle** a feminine first name formed from a combination of CLARA and BELLA or BELLE, meaning 'bright, shining beauty' (*Latin/French*). A variant form is Claribel.

Clare (1) a feminine variant form of CLARA. St Clare (1194–1253) was an Italian saint who, influenced by St Francis of Assissi, founded the order of Minoresses or Poor Clares. In the twentieth century she was made patron saint of television. (2) a surname, meaning 'bright, shining', used as a masculine or feminine first name (*Latin*). In the novel *Lolita* (1955) by Vladimir Nabokov (1899–1977), Clare Quilty is am important male character.

Clarence a masculine first name meaning 'bright, shining' (*Latin*). A diminutive form is Clarrie.

Claribel a feminine variant form of CLARABEL.

Clarice (1) a feminine first name meaning 'fame' (*Latin*). (2) a variant form of CLARA. A variant form is Clarissa.

Clarinda a feminine first name formed from a combination of CLARA and BELINDA or LUCINDA.

Clarissa a feminine variant form of CLARICE. Sir John Vanbrugh (1664–1726) used the name in his play *The Confederacy* (1705), and Samuel Richardson (1689–1761) used it for the eponymous heroine of his epistolary novel *Clarissa Harlowe*, one of the longest novels in the English language.

Clark or **Clarke** a surname, meaning 'cleric, scholar or clerk' (*Old French*), used as a masculine first name. Clark Gable (1901–60) was a famous American film actor of the 1930s and 1940s. The 'earth' name of Superman is Clark Kent. A variant form is Clerk.

Clarrie (1) a feminine diminutive form of CLARA. (2) a masculine diminutive form of CLARENCE.

Claud the English masculine form of CLAUDIUS.

Claude (1) the French masculine form of CLAUD. (2) the French feminine form of Claudia.

Claudette a feminine diminutive form of CLAUDIA. Claudette Colbert (1903–96) was a French-born American film actress of the 1930s and 1940s.

Claudia feminine form of CLAUD. In the New Testament Claudia was a Christian woman in Rome who was mentioned in one of Paul's epistles. Diminutive forms are Claudette, Claudine.

Claudine a diminutive form of CLAUDIA. The French writer Colette (1873–1954) used the name for the heroine for four semi-autobiographical novels.

Claudio the Italian and Spanish masculine form of CLAUD. Claudio Aquaviva (1543–1615) was a general of the Society of Jesus (Jesuits) under whose leadership the order grew rapidly. William Shakespeare (1564–1616) used the name in two of his plays: for a young lord of Florence in *Much Ado About Nothing* and the brother of the heroine, Isabella, in *Measure for Measure*.

Claudius a masculine first name meaning 'lame' (*Latin*); the Dutch and German forms of CLAUD. William Shakespeare (1564–1616) used the name for Hamlet's uncle and stepfather in *Hamlet*.

Claus a masculine variant form of KLAUS.

Clay (1) a surname, meaning 'a dweller in a place with clay soil' (*Old English*), used as a masculine first name. (2) a diminutive form of CLAI-

BORNE, CLAYBORNE, CLAYTON.

Clayborne a surname, meaning 'a dweller in a place with clay soil by a brook' (*Old English*), used as a masculine first name. A variant form is CLAIBORNE. A diminutive form is Clay.

Clayton a place name and surname, meaning 'place in or with good clay' (*Old English*), used as a masculine first name. A diminutive form is Clay.

Cledwyn a masculine first name from a Denbigh river name, although a derivation from *cledd*, 'sword' (*Welsh*) is perhaps more likely for the personal name. Cledwyn Hughes, later Lord Cledwyn, was a prominent political figure in the 1960s and 70s.

Clem (1) a feminine diminutive form of CLEMATIS, CLEMENCE, CLEMENCY, CLEMENTINE, CLEMENTINA. (2) a masculine diminutive form of CLEMENT.

Clematis a feminine first name meaning 'climbing plant' (*Greek*), the name of a climbing plant with white, blue or purple flowers used as a feminine first name. Diminutive forms are Clem, Clemmie.

Clemence a variant form of CLEMENCY.

Clemency the abstract noun for the quality of tempering justice with mercy used as a feminine first name (*Latin*). A variant form is Clemence. Diminutive forms are Clem, Clemmie.

Clement a masculine first name meaning 'mild-tempered, merciful' (*Latin*). It was the name adopted by several popes. A diminutive form is Clem.

Clementine or **Clementina** feminine forms of CLEMENT. Diminutive forms are Clem, Clemmie.

Clemmie a feminine diminutive form of CLEMATIS, CLEMENCY and CLEMENTINE.

Cleo a short form of CLEOPATRA, used as an independent feminine first name.

Cleopatra a feminine first name meaning 'father's glory' (*Greek*). Cleopatra (*c.*69–30 BC) was an Egyptian queen (51–30 BC) noted for her beauty. She was the mistress of Julius Caesar and later had a love affair with Mark Antony, which was dramatised in the play Antony and Cleopatra by William Shakespeare (1564–1616). She killed herself with an asp rather than be captured by Octavian. A diminutive form is Cleo.

Clerk a masculine variant form of CLARK.

Cleveland a place name, meaning 'land of hills' (*Old English*), used as a masculine first name.

Clia a feminine diminutive form of CLIANTHA.

Cliantha a feminine first name meaning 'glory flower' (*Greek*). A diminutive form is Clia.

Clídna a feminine variant form of CLÍODHNA.

Cliff a masculine diminutive form of CLIFFORD, now used independently.

Clifford a surname, meaning 'ford at a cliff' (*Old English*), used as a masculine first name. Clifford Odets (1906–63) was an American playwright. A diminutive form is Cliff.

Clifton a place name, meaning 'place on a cliff' (*Old English*), used as a masculine first name.

Clint a masculine diminutive form of CLINTON, now used independently. Clint Eastwood is a well-known American film actor and director.

Clinton a place name and surname, meaning 'settlement on a hill', used as a masculine first name. A diminutive form is CLINT.

Clio a feminine first name meaning 'glory' (*Greek*).

Clíodhna (pronounced *klee-ona*) an Irish Gaelic feminine first name the origin of which is unclear. In legend she was one of the three daughters of a prince of the sea kingdom of Mannannan who eloped with CIABHÁN, son of the king of Ulster, and was drowned in punishment by a tidal wave. A variant form is Clídna, and the anglicised form is Cliona.

Cliona the anglicised feminine form of CLÍODHNA.

Clive a surname, meaning 'at the cliff' (*Old English*), used as a masculine first name. Clive James is an Australian-born writer and TV host.

Clodagh (pronounced *kloda*) an Irish Gaelic feminine first name, probably from the river name Clóideach, in County Tipperary.

Clorinda a feminine first name formed from a combination of CHLORIS and BELINDA or LUCINDA.

Cloris a feminine variant form of CHLORIS.

Clothilde or **Clotilde** or **Clotilda** a feminine first name meaning 'famous fighting woman' (*Germanic*).

Clover the name of a flowering plant used as a feminine first name (*English*).

Clovis the Old French form of LEWIS. Clovis I (*c*.466–511) was a king of the Franks (481–511).

Clyde the name of a Scottish river, meaning 'cleansing one', used as a masculine first name. The name was taken up outside Scotland as a first name, especially in the USA, and was reimported to Scotland. In America its most notorious holder was the gangster Clyde Barrow, shot dead in 1934.

Cnut a masculine variant form of CANUTE.

Cody a surname used as a masculine or feminine first name.

Coel (pronounced *koil*) a masculine first name meaning 'trust' (*Welsh*). Coel was a king in the British kingdom of Strathclyde; in fact probably the origin of 'Old King Cole'.

Cóilín the Irish Gaelic masculine form of COLIN.

Col a masculine diminutive form of COLIN, COLMÁN, COLUMBA.

Colby a masculine first name meaning 'from the dark country' (*Norse*).

Cole (1) a diminutive form of COLEMAN, COLMÁN, NICHOLAS. (2) a surname, meaning 'swarthy' or 'coal-black' (*Old English*), used as a masculine first name.

Coleman a surname, meaning 'swarthy man' or 'servant of NICHOLAS' (*Old English*), used as a masculine first name.

Colette a feminine diminutive form of NICOLE, now used independently. St Colette (1381–1447) was a member of the Poor Clares and founder of the Colettine Poor Clares. A variant form is Collette.

Colin (1) a Scottish masculine first name from the Gaelic Cailean, 'youth', which has close associations with the Campbell clan, whose chief has the Gaelic title MacCailein Mór, 'son of Great Colin'. (2) an Irish masculine first name from Col, an abbreviation of Gaelic Cóilín. (3) an English masculine diminutive form of NICHOLAS, long used independently.

Colla a masculine first name meaning 'lord' (*Irish Gaelic*). It was a frequent name in early Irish legend. The Clan Donald traces its origins back to Colla Uais, an Irish prince of the fifth century.

Colleen a feminine first name meaning 'girl', from *cailin*, 'girl', 'maiden' (*Irish Gaelic*). The generic word for a girl has been taken up as an individual name.

Collette a feminine variant form of COLETTE.

Collier or **Collyer** a surname, meaning 'charcoal seller or burner' (*Old English*), used as a masculine first name. A variant form is Colyer.

Colm (pronounced *collum*) an Irish Gaelic masculine first name meaning 'dove'. The derivation is from Latin *columba*, 'dove'. The most famous bearer of the name is Columcille, 'dove of the church', the Gaelic name of St Columba, founder of Irish monasteries at Durrow, Kells, and other places, and who, when expelled from Ireland for pride and contumacity, established himself on Iona, where he died in 597, having become the most celebrated missionary saint of Scotland. *See* CALUM.

Colmán (pronounced *collaman*) a masculine first name meaning 'little dove' (*Irish Gaelic*). Many holy men bore this name in Ireland and in Scotland, and it is preserved in many place names. Diminutive forms are Col, Cole.

Colombe the French masculine or feminine form of COLUMBA.

Columba *see* COLM.

Columbanus a masculine first name meaning 'little dove', a Latinised form of COLMÁN. St Columbanus (died AD 615) was one of the missionaries who brought Christianity to central Europe. His hermitage cave near Interlaken in Switzerland can still be visited.

Columbine a feminine first name meaning 'little dove' (*Latin*); the name of a flowering plant used as a feminine first name.

Columcille the Gaelic name, meaning 'dove of the church', of St Columba (*see* COLM). It is the middle name of the American-Australian actor Mel Gibson.

Colyer a masculine variant form of COLLIER.

Comfort the abstract noun for the state of wellbeing or bringer of solace used as a feminine first name, in the Puritan tradition (*Latin/French*).

Comgall or **Comghall** or **Comhghall** (pronounced *cow-al*) an Irish Gaelic masculine first name of uncertain meaning. St Comgall founded the monastery at Bangor, County Down. Cowal in Scotland is named after Comghall, a descendant of the first Dalriadic kings.

Comyn a Scottish masculine surname that may have come from the Old French personal name Comin, used as a first name. The Comyns became a powerful family in medieval Scotland and claimants to the throne. Bruce slew John Comyn in Greyfriars Kirk, Dumfries in 1306.

Con (1) a masculine diminutive form of CONAN, CONNALL, CONNOR, CONRAD. (2) a feminine diminutive form of CONSTANCE, etc.

Conachar a variant masculine form of CONCHOBAR.

Conaire (pronounced *con-yara*) a masculine first name from the root *cú*, 'hound' (*Irish Gaelic*). It was the name of a legendary hero and high king of Ireland.

Conall a masculine first name meaning 'wolfish', from *cú*, which means 'wolf' as well as 'hound' (*Irish Gaelic*). Conall Cearnach, 'victorious', is one of the heroes of the Ulster Cycle of legends. The anglicised form is Connel, or Connell.

Conán (pronounced *con-ann*) or **Conan** a masculine first name from *cú*, 'hound', 'wolf' (*Irish Gaelic*). In the Fenian Cycle of legends, Conán macMorna, one of the Fianna, plays the part of a mischief-maker and boaster.

Concepción a feminine first name meaning 'beginning, conception' (*Spanish*), a reference to the Immaculate Conception of the Virgin Mary. Diminutive forms are Concha, Conchita.

Concepta the Latin feminine form of CONCETTA.

Concetta a feminine first name meaning 'conceptive' (*Italian*), a reference to the Virgin Mary and the Immaculate Conception.

Concha or **Conchita** feminine diminutive forms of CONCEPCIÓN.

Conchobar (pronounced *con-ko-warr*) a masculine first name meaning 'lover of hounds' (*Irish Gaelic*). It was borne most famously by the legendary Conchobar macNessa, king of Ulster and frustrated lover of Deirdre. There are many other stories in which he appears. The name has a variety of forms, including Conchubor, Conchobhar, Conachar, and the anglicised form is Conor or Connor.

Conn a masculine first name the source of which is variously taken as from *cú*, 'hound', 'wolf' (*Irish Gaelic*) or from an Old Gaelic root word implying wisdom. The name is borne by some celebrated figures of antiquity, including Conn Céadcathach, 'of the hundred battles', high king of Ireland and regarded as the progenitor of several noble families in Ireland and Scotland.

Connel or **Connell** the anglicised masculine form of CONALL.

Connla a masculine first name meaning 'little hound' (*Irish Gaelic*). The name of the son of CUCHULAINN and AOIFE, slain in fight by Cuchulainn who did not know who he was.

Connor or **Conor** the anglicised masculine form of Irish Gaelic CONCHOBAR.

Conrad a masculine first name meaning 'able counsellor' (*Germanic*). William Shakespeare (1564–1616) used the name for one of the followers of Don John in his comedy *Much Ado About Nothing*. Lord Byron (1788–1824) used the name for the hero of his poem *The Corsair* (1814). A diminutive form is Con.

Conroy a masculine first name meaning 'wise' (*Gaelic*).

Consolata a feminine first name meaning 'consoling', a reference to the Virgin Mary (*Italian*).

Consolation the abstract noun for the act of consoling or the state of solace used as a feminine first name in the Puritan tradition.

Constance feminine form of CONSTANT. Diminutive forms are Con, Connie. A variant form is Constanta.

Constant a masculine first name meaning 'firm, faithful' (*Latin*). Constant Lambert (1905–51) was an English composer. A diminutive form is Con.

Constanta a feminine variant form of CONSTANCE.

Constantine a masculine first name meaning 'resolute, firm' (*Latin*). Constantine I (280–337) was the first Christian emperor of Rome. Constantinople (modern Istanbul) was founded by him. It was also the name of three Scottish kings.

Constanza the Italian and Spanish feminine forms of CONSTANCE.

Consuela a feminine first name meaning 'consolation' (*Spanish*), a reference to the Virgin Mary.

Consuelo the masculine form of CONSUELA.

Conway the anglicised masculine form of Welsh CONWY.

Conwy (pronounced *konn-wee*) a Welsh masculine first name of modern times from what was originally a river name and later also that of a famous castle. The anglicised form is Conway.

Coop a masculine diminutive form of COOPER.

Cooper a surname, meaning 'barrel maker' (*Old English*), used as a masculine first name. A diminutive form is Coop.

Cora a feminine first name meaning 'maiden' (*Greek*). A variant form is Corinna, Corinne.

Corabella or **Corabelle** a feminine first name meaning 'beautiful maiden', a combination of CORA and BELLA.

Coral the name of the pink marine jewel material used as a feminine first name.

Coralie the French feminine form of CORAL.

Corazón (pronounced *cor-a-thon*) a feminine first name meaning '(sacred) heart' (*Spanish*).

Corbin a surname, meaning 'raven, black-haired' or' raucousness' (*Old French*), used as a masculine first name. Corbin Bernsen is an American actor, one of the stars of the TV series *LA Law*.

Corcoran a surname, meaning 'red- or purple-faced' (*Irish Gaelic*), used as a masculine first name.

Cordelia a feminine first name meaning 'warm-hearted' (*Latin*). Cordelia is the youngest daughter of King Lear in the eponymous play by William Shakespeare (1564–1614).

Corey a surname, meaning 'God peace' (*Irish Gaelic*), used as a masculine first name. A variant form is Cory.

Cori or **Corrie** a feminine form of Corey.

Corin in medieval times a conventional name for a shepherd. William Shakespeare (1564–1616) used the name for that of an old shepherd in his comedy *As You Like It*. Corin Redgrave is an English actor.

Corinna or **Corinne** feminine variant forms of CORA.

Cormac (pronounced *corra-mac*) a masculine first name, probably from *corb*, 'chariot', with *mac*, 'son' (*Irish Gaelic*). A popular name in the Gaelic world. Cormac macAirt was the first high king of Ireland, recorded as having his capital at Tara (third century AD). The hero of many stories, he left a reputation for wisdom and prudence. An anglicised form is Cormack or Cormick.

Cormack or **Cormick** anglicised masculine forms of Irish Gaelic COR-MAC.

Cornelia the feminine form of CORNELIUS.

Cornelius a masculine name the origin of which is uncertain, possibly 'horn-like', a Roman family name. St Cornelius (178–253) was pope for two years. William Shakespeare (1564–1616) used the name for characters in *Cymbeline* and *Hamlet*. Cornelius Vanderbilt (1794–1877) was an American financier, and the name has been used for several of his descendants. A variant form is CORNELL.

Cornell (1) a surname, meaning 'Cornwall' or 'a hill where corn is sold', used as a masculine first name. (2) a variant form of CORNELIUS.

Corona a feminine first name meaning 'crown' (*Latin*).

Corrado the Italian masculine form of CONRAD.

Corwin a masculine first name meaning 'friend of the heart' (*Old French*).

Cory a masculine variant form of COREY.

Cosima the feminine form of COSMO.

Cosimo an Italian masculine form of COSMO. Cosimo de' Medici (1389–1464) was the first of the famous Florentine family to exert cultural influence by his patronage of the arts.

Cosmo a masculine first name meaning 'order, beauty' (*Greek*). Cosmo Gordon Lang, Baron Lang of Lambeth (1864–1945), was Archbishop of Canterbury (1928–45).

Cospatrick a masculine first name meaning 'servant of Patrick'. This name is an anglicised version of *gwas* (*Old Welsh*) 'servant', and Padruig, 'Patrick' (*Irish Gaelic*).

Costanza an Italian feminine form of CONSTANCE.

Courtney a surname, meaning 'short nose' (*Old French*), used as a masculine or feminine first name.

Cradoc a masculine variant form of CARADOC.

Craig a surname meaning 'rock', from *carraig*, 'rock, crag' (*Scottish Gaelic*), used as a masculine first name. Craig Ferguson is a Scottish actor who works in the United States and Craig Raine is an English poet.

Cranley a surname, meaning 'crane clearing, spring or meadow' (*Old English*), used as a masculine first name.

Crawford a place name and surname, meaning 'ford of the crows' (*Old English*), used as a masculine first name.

Créd (pronounced *craith*) an Irish Gaelic feminine first name from the name of a daughter of the king of Kerry, who was wooed and won by CÁEL. After his death in the battle of Ventry, she committed suicide.

Creiddlad and **Creiddylad** variant forms of CREUDDYLAD

Creidne (pronounced *craith-nya*) a feminine first name meaning 'loyal' (*Irish Gaelic*). In Irish legend, Creidne was a female member of the Fianna, the troop of warrior-bards who were bodyguards to various kings and high kings. In Celtic legend, female warriors were by no means unusual.

Creighton a surname, meaning 'rock or cliff place (*Old Welsh*, *Old English*) or 'border settlement' (*Scots Gaelic*), used as a masculine first name.

Crépin the French masculine form of CRISPIN.

Cressa a contracted feminine form of CRESSIDA.

Cressida a feminine first name meaning 'gold' (*Greek*). William Shakespeare (1564–1616) used the name for the faithless heroine of his play about the Trojan War, *Troilus and Cressida*, changing if from the Criseyde form used by Geoffrey Chaucer (*c*.1343–1400) in *Troilus and*

Criseyde, his version of the same story. A contracted form is Cressa.

Creuddylad (pronounced *kry-the-lad*) a feminine first name that is the Welsh form of Cordelia. In the story of *Culhwych ac Olwen*, a maiden of this name is described as the most majestic who ever lived. Other forms are Creiddylad, Crieddlad.

Crimthann or **Criomhthann** (pronounced *creev-thann*) a masculine first name meaning 'fox', implying cleverness (*Irish Gaelic*). Crimthann was a name given to Colum Cille before he entered the church.

Crisiant (pronounced *krees-yant*) a feminine first name derived from *crisial* meaning 'crystal' (*Welsh*).

Crispin or **Crispian** a masculine first name meaning 'having curly hair' (*Latin*). St Crispin and St Crispinian were third-century saints who became the patron saints of shoemakers.

Crispus the German masculine form of CRISPIN. In the New Testament, Crispus was the presiding officer of the synagogue at Corinth who was baptised by Paul.

Cristal a feminine variant form of CRYSTAL.

Cristiano the Italian and Spanish masculine form of CHRISTIAN.

Cristina the Italian, Portuguese and Spanish feminine form of CHRISTINA.

Cristóbal the Spanish masculine form of CHRISTOPHER.

Cristoforo the Italian masculine form of CHRISTOPHER.

Cromwell a place name and surname, meaning 'winding spring' (*Old English*), used as a masculine first name.

Crosbie or **Crosby** a place name and surname, meaning 'farm or village with crosses' (*Old Norse*), used as a masculine first name.

Cruithne (pronounced *kroo-eena*) an Old Gaelic masculine or feminine first name. It was the Gaelic name given to the founder of the Picts, whose seven sons represent the seven provinces of Pictland. It was also used as a female name, as in Cruithne, the daughter of the great smith and weapon-maker Lóchan.

Crystal the name of a very clear brilliant glass used as a feminine first name. Variant forms are Cristal, Chrystal.

Crystyn a feminine first name meaning 'follower of Christ', the Welsh form of CHRISTINA.

Cuchulainn (pronounced *koo-hoolin*) a masculine first name meaning 'hound of Culann' (*Irish Gaelic*). In Celtic mythology, when the boy Setanta killed Culann's hound, he promised to play the part of the dog himself, and took this name accordingly: one of many evidences in Celtic lore of shape-changing between people and animals. The boy went on to become the great hero of the Ulster Cycle of legends.

Cuilean (pronounced *cul-yan*) a masculine first name from *cúilean*, 'whelp' (*Scottish Gaelic*) the name of a tenth-century contender for the kingship of the Picts and Scots, killed in battle against King Indulf.

Culann (Irish Gaelic, male) a masculine first name that is probably formed from the Old Irish Gaelic root word *col*, 'chief'. Known from the Cuchulainn story, this name of a legendary smith, maker of the armour of Conchobhar macNessa, king of Ulster. Its anglicised form is Callan or Cullen.

Culhwych (pronounced *kool-hooh*) a masculine first name that may stem from an Old Welsh root-word meaning 'pig-lord'. It was borne by the hero of the old Welsh legend of *Culhwych ac Olwen*. Culhwych, son of Cilydd, bears a curse from before his birth that can only be ended when he wins the love of OLWEN, daughter of the giant Ysbaddaden.

Cullan (1) a surname, meaning 'Cologne' (*Old French*), used as a masculine first name. (2) a place name, meaning 'at the back of the river' (*Scottish Gaelic*), used as a masculine first name. A variant form is Cullen.

Cullen (1) an anglicised masculine form of the Irish Gaelic CULANN. (2) a variant form of CULLAN.

Culley a surname, meaning 'woodland' (*Scottish Gaelic*), used as a masculine first name.

Cunobelinus *see* CYMBELINE.

Curig a Welsh masculine first name and the name of a Welsh saint whose name is preserved in Capel Curig, Caernarvon, Llangurig, Montgomery, and other places.

Curran a surname, of uncertain meaning, possibly 'resolute hero' (*Irish Gaelic*), used as a masculine first name.

Curt (1) a masculine variant form of KURT. (2) a masculine diminutive form of CURTIS.

Curtis a surname, meaning 'courteous, educated' (*Old French*), used as a masculine first name. William Shakespeare (1564–1616) used the name for a character in his comedy *The Taming of the Shrew*. A diminutive form is Curt.

Cuthbert (1) a masculine first name meaning 'famous bright' (*Old Eng-*

lish). St Cuthbert (634–687) was bishop of the Benedictine abbey of Lindisfarne, from which he evangelised Northumbria. (2) the anglicised masculine form of Irish Gaelic CATHBAD.

Cy a masculine diminutive form of CYRIL, CYRUS.

Cymbeline the anglicised masculine form of Cunobelinus, which is a Latinised form of 'hound of Belenus', from *cú*, 'dog', a name borne by a first-century chieftain of south Britain who resisted the Roman invasion. The character of Cymbeline in the eponymous play by William Shakespeare (1564–1616) bears no relation to the historical figure.

Cynan (pronounced *kee-nan*) a masculine first name meaning 'chief' (*Welsh*) and that of a thirteenth-century Welsh prince, Cynan ap Hywel.

Cynddelw (pronounced *keen-dellow*) a Welsh masculine first name and that of a major twelfth-century poet.

Cynddylan (pronounced *keen-thilann*) a Welsh masculine first name and that of a sixth-century prince of Powys.

Cynedda (pronounced *kee-netha*) a Welsh masculine first name and that of a semi-legendary figure of the fifth century: a king of the Britons of Strathclyde, who established their kingdom also in Gwynedd.

Cynfab (pronounced *keen-fab*) a masculine first name meaning 'first son' (*Welsh*).

Cynfael (pronounced *keen-file*) a masculine first name from *cyn*, 'chief'; *mael*, 'armour' or 'prince' (*Welsh*). It was a warrior name.

Cynfrig (pronounced *keen-frec*) a masculine first name from a river name, incorporating Welsh *cyn*, 'head', 'top' (*Welsh*). Anglicised forms are Kendrick, Kendrew.

Cynog (pronounced *kee-noc*) a Welsh masculine first name and that of a sixth-century saint, whose name is preserved in numerous places, including Llangynog and Ystradgynlais.

Cynon a Welsh masculine first name, probably originally a river name, Afon Cynon, and incorporating Welsh *cynnig*, 'offer', suggesting a river that flowed by a chapel or place of offering (like the Scottish river Orrin) but could also derive from *cú*, 'hound', like many other names. Long in use as a personal name and borne by many Old Welsh heroes.

Cynthia a feminine first name meaning 'belonging to Mount Cynthus' (*Greek*). A diminutive form is Cindie or Cindy.

Cyprian a masculine first name meaning 'from Cyprus', the Mediterranean island (*Greek*). St Cyprian (200–258) was an early Christian theologian and bishop of Carthage.

Cyrano a masculine first name meaning 'from Cyrene', an ancient city of North Africa (*Greek*). Cyrano de Bergerac was a French soldier and writer famed as a duellist and for his large nose celebrated in the play by the French writer Edmond Rostand.

Cyrene or **Cyrena** a feminine first name meaning 'from Cyrene' (*Greek*), an ancient city of North Africa. In Greek mythology, Cyrene was a water nymph loved by Apollo. A variant form is Kyrena.

Cyril a masculine first name meaning 'lordly' (*Greek*). St Cyril of Jerusalem (315–386) was bishop of Jerusalem and a Doctor of the Roman Catholic Church. A diminutive form is Cy.

Cyrill the German masculine form of CYRIL.

Cyrille (1) the French masculine form of CYRIL. (2) feminine form of CYRIL (*French*).

Cyrillus the Danish, Dutch and Swedish masculine forms of CYRIL.

Cyrus a masculine first name meaning 'the sun' (*Persian*). Cyrus II (590–529 BC) founded the Persian Empire. A diminutive form is Cy.

Cytherea a feminine first name meaning 'from Cythera', an island off the southern coast of the Peloponnese, in Greek mythology, home of a cult of Aphrodite (*Greek*).

Cythereia a feminine first name, from CYTHEREA. In Greek mythology, it is an alternative name for Aphrodite.

D

Daffodil the name of the spring plant that yields bright yellow flowers used as a feminine first name (*Dutch/Latin*). A diminutive form is Daffy.

Daffy a feminine diminutive form of DAFFODIL.

Dafydd (pronounced *daf-ith*) a masculine first name, the Welsh form of David. Dafydd ap Gwilym (fourteenth century) is one of Wales's greatest poets. The one-time by-name for a Welshman, 'Taffy', comes from this name, because of its frequency in earlier times. Diminute forms are DEWI, Deian and DAI.

Dag a masculine first name meaning 'day' (*Norse*).

Dagan a masculine first name meaning 'earth', the name of an earth god of the Assyrians and Babylonians (*Semitic*).

Dagmar a feminine first name meaning 'bright day' (*Norse*).

Dahlia the name of the plant with brightly coloured flowers, named after the Swedish botanist Anders Dahl ('dale'), used as a feminine first name.

Dai a Welsh masculine diminutive form of DAVID, formerly a name in its own right, meaning 'shining'.

Daibhidh a masculine first name, a Scottish Gaelic form of David and a name borne by two Scottish kings.

Daimíne (pronounced *daa-win*) an Irish Gaelic masculine first name from *daimhín*, 'little fawn' (*Irish Gaelic*). It is anglicised as Damien or Damian.

Dair a Scottish masculine first name that may hark back to *dar*, 'oak' (*Scottish Gaelic*) or may simply be the latter part of ALASDAIR, originally an abbreviation but turned into a separate name by the association with oak.

Dáire (pronounced *darr-ya*) a masculine first name meaning 'fruitful', 'fertile' (*Irish Gaelic*). A popular name in early Ireland. Dáire macFiachna was the owner of the famous Brown Bull of Cooley.

Dairean

Dairean and **Dáirine** Irish Gaelic feminine forms of DARINA.

Daisy the name of the plant, 'the day's eye' (*Old English*), used as a feminine first name. The American-born writer Henry James (1843–1916) used the name for the pretty but unsophisticated eponymous heroine of his short novel *Daisy Miller* (1878). The American writer F. Scott Fitzgerald (1896–1940) used the name for Daisy Buchanan, the main female character in his novel *The Great Gatsby* (1925).

Dale a surname, meaning 'valley', used as a masculine or feminine first name (*Old English*). Dale Winton is a popular TV game show host.

Daley a masculine and feminine variant of DALY.

Dalilah or **Dalila** feminine variant forms of DELILAH.

Dallas (1) a place name and surname, from *dail*, 'field', *eas*, 'falling stream' (*Scottish Gaelic*), used as a first name. (2) a surname, meaning 'dale house' (*Old English*), used as a masculine first name.

Dalton a surname, meaning 'dale farm' (*Old English*), used as a masculine first name.

Daly a surname, from *dáil*, 'meeting', perhaps with the sense of 'counsellor' (*Irish Gaelic*), used as a masculine or feminine first name. A variant form is Daley.

Dalziel a place name and surname, meaning 'field of the sun gleam' (*Scots Gaelic*), used as a masculine first name.

Damian (1) the French masculine form of DAMON. (2) an anglicised masculine form of Irish Gaelic DAIMÍNE.

Damiano the Italian masculine form of DAMON.

Damien (1) a masculine first name meaning 'taming' (*Greek*). (2) an anglicised masculine form of Irish Gaelic DAIMÍNE.

Damon a masculine first name meaning 'conqueror' (*Greek*).

Dan a masculine diminutive form of DANBY, DANIEL.

Dana (1) (pronounced *daa-na*) an ancient Irish Gaelic feminine first name that comes from a Celtic goddess, originally ANU or Ana, 'the abundant one'. The name later was modified to Danu or Dana. An anglicised form is Don. (2) a surname, of uncertain meaning, possibly 'Danish' (*Old English*), used as a masculine or feminine first name. Dana Andrews (1909–92) was an American film actor who starred in such films as *Laura* (1944) and *The Best Years of Our Lives* (1946). (3) a feminine form of DAN, DANIEL.

Danaë a feminine first name from Greek mythology, that of the mother of

Perseus by Zeus, who came to her as a shower of gold while she was in prison. Diminutive forms are Dannie, Danny.

Danby a place name and surname, meaning 'Danes' settlement', used as a masculine first name (*Old Norse*). A diminutive form is Dan.

Dandie or **Dandy** a Scottish masculine diminutive form of ANDREW.

Daniel a masculine first name meaning 'God is my judge' (*Hebrew*). In the Old Testament it was the name of the second son of David and also of the author of the Book of Daniel, a youth who was taken into the household of Nebuchadnezzar, who was given divine protection when thrown into a den of lions. Daniel Day Lewis is an English actor and the son of C. Day Lewis, poet laureate. Diminutive forms are Dan, Dannie, Danny.

Danielle (1) feminine form of DANIEL. (2) the masculine Italian form of DANIEL.

Dannie or **Danny** (1) a masculine diminutive of DANBY, DANIEL. Danny De Vito is an American film actor and producer. (2) a feminine diminutive of DANAË, DANIELLE.

Dante a masculine first name meaning 'steadfast' (*Latin/Italian*). Dante Alighieri (1265–1321) was an Italian poet, philosopher, soldier and politician whose supreme masterpiece was *La Divina Commedia* (*The Divine Comedy*), an allegorical account of his journey through Hell, Purgatory and Paradise.

Danu *see* DANA.

Daphne a feminine first name meaning 'laurel' (*Greek*). In Greek mythology Daphne was a nymph who was loved by Apollo. She beseeched Zeus to protect her, which he did by turning her into a laurel at the moment Apollo was to about to encircle her in his arms. The laurel is particularly associated with Apollo.

Dara (1) a feminine first name meaning 'oak', from *dar*, 'oak' (*Irish Gaelic*). A variant form is Deri. The oak was a venerated tree in Celtic lore, playing a part in the druidic cult. (2) a feminine first name meaning 'charity' (*Hebrew*).

Darby (1) a variant form of Derby, a surname meaning 'a village where deer are seen' (*Old Norse*), used as a masculine first name. (2) a diminutive form of DERMOT and DIARMAID.

Darcey or **Darci** or **Darcie** a feminine form of DARCY.

Darcy or **D'Arcy** a surname, of Norman French origin, used as a masculine or feminine first name. Its use as a first name in Ireland may be influenced by its assimilation to Gaelic *dorcha*, 'dark'. A feminine variant form is Darcey, Darci or Darcie.

Darell a masculine variant form of DARRELL.

Daria the feminine form of DARIUS.

Darian or **Darien** a masculine variant form of DARREN.

Darina a feminine first name from *dáireann*, 'fruitful' (*Irish Gaelic*). The Gaelic name is Dáirine, with alternative forms Daireann, Doirend, Doirenn. Darina Allen is one of Ireland's best-known cooks.

Dario the Italian masculine form of DARIUS.

Darius a masculine first name meaning 'preserver' (*Persian*). Darius I, 'the Great', (550–486 BC) was king of Persia (522–486 BC) and known for his great building projects.

Darlene or **Darleen** the endearment 'darling' combined with a suffix to form a feminine first name (*Old English*).

Darnell a surname, meaning 'hidden nook' (*Old English*), used as a masculine first name.

Darrell or **Darrel** a surname, meaning 'from Airelle in Normandy', used as a masculine first name. Variant forms are Darell, Darryl, Daryl.

Darrelle feminine form of Darrell.

Darren or **Darin** a surname, of unknown origin, used as a masculine first name. A variant form is Darian, Darien.

Darryl a variant form of DARRELL, also used as a girl's name.

Darshan a masculine first name meaning 'see' (*Sanskrit*).

Darthula an English feminine first name adapted by the Scottish poet James Macpherson (1736–96) from the name DEIRDRE in his Ossian poems.

Darton a surname, meaning 'deer enclosure or forest' (*Old English*), used as a masculine first name.

Daryl a variant form of DARRELL, also used as a girl's name. Daryl Hannah is an American film actress.

Dave a masculine diminutive form of DAVID.

David a masculine first name meaning 'beloved' (*Hebrew*). In the Old Testament, David was the second king of the Hebrews (after Saul), who reigned *c*.1000–960 BC. He united the kingdom of Israel and established the capital at Jerusalem. The Welsh form is DAFYDD and the Scottish Gaelic form DAIBHIDH. Diminutive forms are Dave, Davie, Davy. St

David (*c*.520–600), who was a monk and bishop, is the patron saint of Wales.

Davida a Scottish feminine form of David. A diminutive form is Vida.

Davidde the Italian masculine form of DAVID.

Davide the French masculine form of DAVID.

Davidina a Scottish feminine form of DAVID.

Davie a masculine diminutive form of DAVID.

Davin a masculine variant form of DEVIN.

Davina or **Davinia** a Scottish feminine form of David, but the name could also be linked to *daimhin*, 'fawn' (*Scottish Gaelic*). A diminutive form is Vina.

Davis a surname, meaning 'DAVID's son' (*Old English*), used as a masculine first name.

Davy a masculine diminutive form of DAVID.

Dawn the name of the first part of the day used as a feminine first name.

Deaglán the Irish Gaelic form of DECLAN.

Dean (1) a surname, meaning 'one who lives in a valley' (*Old English*) or 'serving as a dean' (*Old French*), used as a masculine first name. Dean Stockwell is an American film actor. (2) the anglicised form of DINO.

Deana or **Deane** feminine forms of DEAN. Variant forms are Dena, Dene.

Deanna or **Deanne** a feminine variant form of DIANA.

Dearbhail (pronounced *jerval*) a feminine first name meaning 'sincere' (*Irish Gaelic*). The anglicised form is DERVLA.

Dearbhorgaill (pronounced *jer-vor-gil*) an Irish and Scottish Gaelic feminine first name that perhaps stems from the same root as DEARBHAIL. An anglicised form is DEVORGUILLA or DEVORGILLA.

Dearborn a surname, meaning 'deer brook' (*Old English*), used as a masculine first name.

Deasúin the modern Irish Gaelic masculine form of DESMOND.

Deb or **Debbie** or **Debby** feminine diminutive forms of DEBORAH.

Deborah or **Debra** a feminine first name meaning 'bee' (*Hebrew*). In the Old Testament Deborah was a prophet and heroine of Israel who fought the Canaanites. Deborah Kerr is a Scottish-born film actress. Debra Winger is an American film actress. Diminutive forms are Deb, Debbie, Debby.

Dechtire (pronounced *dec-tira*) a feminine first name possibly stemming from *deich*, 'ten' (*Irish Gaelic*). In Celtic mythology, Dechtire, daughter of the druid Cathbad, was the mother of CUCHULLAIN. Variant forms are Deichtine, Deicteir and the anglicised Dectora.

Decima feminine form of DECIMUS.

Decimus a masculine first name meaning 'tenth' (*Latin*).

Declan a masculine first name perhaps stemming from *deagh*, 'good' (*Irish Gaelic*). The Gaelic form is Deaglán. It was the name of a fifth-century Celtic missionary who preceded St Patrick to Ireland.

Dectora the anglicised feminine form of Irish Gaelic DECHTIRE.

Dedrick a masculine first name meaning 'people's ruler' (*Germanic*).

Dedwydd (pronounced *ded-with*) a masculine first name meaning 'blessed one' (*Welsh*).

Dee (1) a feminine first name from a river name in Ireland, Wales, England and Scotland that derives from a root word *dia*, 'goddess' (*Gaelic/Welsh*). (2) or **Deedee** a feminine diminutive form of names beginning with D.

Deepak a masculine first name meaning 'small lamp' (*Sanskrit*). A variant form is Dipak.

Deian a Welsh diminutive form of DAFYDD.

Deichtine and **Deicteir** variant feminine forms of DECHTIRE.

Deiniol a masculine first name possibly meaning 'charming' (*Welsh*). St Deiniol was the founder of abbeys at Bangor, Caernarfon, and Bangor-on-Dee.

Deirdre (pronounced *deer-dra*) an Irish Gaelic feminine first name the source of which is uncertain, but despite its legendary linking with 'sorrows', it is unlikely to be anything to do with grief. It may simply mean 'girl' or 'daughter'. It is the name of the tragic heroine of a great poem from the Ulster Cycle and is widely used in Ireland and Scotland. A variant form is Deirdra.

Delfine a feminine variant form of DELPHINE.

Delia a feminine first name meaning 'woman of Delos' (*Greek*). Delos was one of the sacred places of ancient Greece. Delia Smith is probably Britain's best-known cook.

Delicia a feminine first name meaning 'great delight' (*Latin*).

Delight the abstract noun for great pleasure, satisfaction or joy used as a feminine first name (*Old French*).

Delilah or **Delila** a feminine first name, the meaning of which is uncertain but possibly 'delicate' (*Hebrew*). In the Old Testament Delilah was a

Philistine woman who managed to persuade Samson, who was her lover, to tell her that the secret of his strength was his hair and who betrayed this secret to his enemies. Variant forms are Dalila, Dalilah. A diminutive form is Lila.

Dell (1) a surname, meaning 'one who lives in a hollow', used as a masculine first name. (2) a diminutive form of DELMAR, etc.

Della a diminutive form of ADELA now used independently.

Delma (1) feminine form of DELMAR. (2) a diminutive form of FIDELMA.

Delmar a masculine first name meaning 'of the sea' (*Latin*).

Delores a feminine variant form of DOLORES.

Delphine a feminine first name meaning 'dolphin' (*Latin*). A variant form is Delfine.

Delwyn or **Delwin** a masculine first name meaning 'pretty boy', from *del*, 'pretty' (*Welsh*).

Delyth (pronounced *del-ith*) a feminine first name meaning 'pretty girl', from *del*, 'pretty' (*Welsh*).

Demelza a Cornish place name used as a feminine first name, prompted by the heroine of Winston Graham's *Poldark* novels.

Demetra or **Demetria** a feminine form of DEMETRIUS. A diminutive form is Demi.

Demetrius a masculine first name meaning 'belonging to Demeter, goddess of the harvest, earth mother' (*Greek*). In the New Testament Demetrius was a Christian mentioned by John in a letter. William Shakespeare (1564–1616) used the name for one of the heroes of his comedy *A Midsummer Night's Dream* and for one of the Goth princes in his tragedy *Titus Andronicus*.

Demi a diminutive form of Demetra. Demi Moore is an American film actress.

Dempsey a surname, meaning 'proud descendant' (*Gaelic*), used as a masculine first name.

Dempster a surname, meaning 'judge' (*Old English*), used as a masculine first name, formerly a feminine one.

Den masculine diminutive form of DENIS, DENNIS, DENISON, DENLEY, DENMAN, DENNISON, DENTON, DENVER, DENZEL, DENZELL, DENZIL.

Dena or **Dene** feminine variant forms of DEANA.

Denby a surname, meaning 'Danish settlement' (*Norse*), used as a masculine first name.

Denice

Denice a feminine variant form of DENISE.

Denis a masculine variant form of DENNIS. St Denis was the third-century first bishop of Paris and is the patron of France.

Denise the feminine form of DENIS. A variant form is Denice.

Denison a masculine variant form of DENNISON.

Denley a surname, meaning 'wood or clearing in a valley' (*Old English*), used as a masculine first name.

Denman a surname, meaning 'dweller in a valley' (*Old English*), used as a masculine first name.

Dennis a masculine first name meaning 'belonging to Dionysus, the god of wine' (*Greek*). Dennis Hopper and Dennis Quaid are American film actors. A variant form is DENIS. The Cornish form is DENZIL, the Welsh is DION. Diminutive forms are Den, Denny.

Dennison a masculine first name meaning 'son of DENNIS' (*Old English*). Variant forms are Denison, Tennison, Tennyson.

Denny a diminutive form of DENISE, DENNIS.

Denton a surname, meaning 'valley place' (*Old English*), used as a masculine first name.

Denver a surname, meaning 'Danes' crossing' (*Old English*), used as a masculine first name.

Denzil (1) a Cornish masculine form of the Greek name Dionysius, whose anglicised form is DENNIS. (2) a variant form of DENZEL.

Denzel or **Denzell** a surname, meaning 'stronghold' (*Celtic*), used as a masculine first name. Denzel Washington is an American film actor. A variant form is Denzil.

Deon a masculine variant form of DION.

Deórsa a Scottish Gaelic masculine form of GEORGE. *See also* SEÓRAS.

Derek an English masculine form of THEODORIC. Variant forms are Derrick, Derrik. A diminutive form is DERRY.

Derfel a Welsh masculine first name and a saint's name, preserved at Llandderfel, Merioneth. The is also the name of a prophetic character portrayed in John Cowper Powys's novel *Owen Glendower*.

Deri (1) a masculine first name meaning 'oak-like', from *derw*, 'oak tree' (*Welsh*). The anglicised form is Derry. (2) a feminine variant form of DARA.

Dermot the anglicised masculine form of DIARMAID. A diminutive form is DERRY.

Derrick or **Derrik** masculine variant forms of Derek. A diminutive form is
DERRY.

Derry the anglicised masculine form DERI. (2) a diminutive form of
DEREK, DERRICK, DERRIK, DERMOT, DIARMID.

Derryth a Welsh feminine form of DERI.

Dervla the anglicised feminine form of Dearbhail. Dervla Murphy is an
intrepid and well-known travel writer who usually takes a bicycle on
her travels.

Derwent a place name and surname, meaning 'river that flows through
oak woods' (*Old English*), used as a masculine first name.

Desdemona a feminine first name meaning 'ill-fated' (*Greek*). The name
given by William Shakespeare (1564–1616) to the wife of Othello in
his tragedy of that name.

Desirée a feminine first name meaning 'longed for' (*French*).

Desmond (1) a masculine first name from *deas*, 'south', *Mumu*, 'Munster' (*Irish Gaelic*). It is a territorial name associated especially with the
Fitzgerald family. The modern Gaelic form is Deasúin. (2) a masculine
variant form of ESMOND (*Germanic*).

Deva the Latinised form of the river name DEE, found in England, Ireland,
Wales and Scotland, used as a feminine first name.

Deverell or **Deverill** a surname, meaning 'fertile river bank' (*Celtic*), used
as a masculine first name.

Devin or **Devinn** a surname, meaning 'poet' (*Irish Gaelic*), used as a masculine first name. A variant form is Davin.

Devlin a masculine first name meaning 'fiercely brave' (*Irish Gaelic*).

Devon the name of the English county, meaning 'deep ones' (*Celtic*), used
as a masculine first name.

Devona the feminine form of DEVON.

Devorguilla or **Devorgilla** an anglicised form of Irish and Scottish Gaelic
DEARBHORGAILL. In Irish legend Devorguilla was one of the many wom-
en to fall in love with CUCHULLAIN. Devorguilla Balliol, mother of King
John Balliol of Scotland, founded Balliol College, Oxford, and Sweetheart Abbey in Dumfriesshire.

Dewey a Celtic masculine form of DAVID.

Dewi a Welsh masculine form of DAVID. Dewi Sant, or St David, the patron saint of Wales, died in 588.

De Witt a masculine first name meaning 'fair-haired' (*Flemish*).

Dexter a surname, meaning '(woman) dyer' (*Old English*), used as a masculine first name.

Di a feminine diminutive form of DIANA, DIANE, DIANNE, DINA, DINAH.

Diamond the name of the gem, meaning 'the hardest iron or steel' (*Latin*), used as a masculine first name.

Diana a feminine first name meaning 'goddess' (*Latin*). In Roman mythology Diana was an ancient goddess. In later times she was identified with the Greek Artemis, with whom she had various attributes in common, being the virgin goddess of the moon and of the hunt. The name gained fame in the twentieth century from Diana, Princess of Wales (1961–97), the ex-wife of Charles, Prince of Wales. Diminutive forms are Dee, Di.

Diane or **Dianne** feminine French forms of DIANA. Diane Keaton and Dianne Wiest are American film actresses.

Diarmaid (pronounced *der-mit*) a masculine first name meaning 'he who reverences God', from Gaelic *dia*, 'God' (*Irish/Scottish Gaelic*). The name of many heroes of legend, especially Diarmait úa Duibne, the hero of *The Pursuit of Diarmaid and Gráinne*. The last pagan high king of Ireland was said to be Diarmait macCearbhal (died *c.*568). Variant forms are Diarmuid, Diarmid, Diarmait and Diarmit, and the anglicised form is Dermot. A diminutive form is Derry.

Diarmid, Diarmait, Diarmit and **Diarmuid** variant masculine forms of DIARMAID.

Dick or **Dickie** or **Dickon** masculine diminutive forms of RICHARD.

Dickson a surname, meaning 'son of RICHARD' (*Old English*), used as a masculine first name. A variant form is Dixon.

Dicky a masculine diminutive form of RICHARD.

Dido a feminine first name meaning 'teacher' (*Greek*). In Greek mythology Dido was a princess from Tyre who founded Carthage and became its queen. According to Virgil's *Aeneid*, she fell in love with AENEAS but he left her and she committed suicide. Dido was also known as Elissa.

Diego a Spanish masculine form of JAMES.

Dietrich the German masculine form of DEREK. A diminutive form is Till.

Digby a surname, meaning 'settlement at a ditch' (*Old Norse*), used as a masculine first name.

Dilic (pronounced *dee-lik*) a Cornish feminine first name, perhaps an early saint's name.

Dillon a surname of uncertain meaning, possibly 'destroyer' (*Germanic/ Irish Gaelic*), used as a masculine first name.

Dilly a feminine diminutive form of DILYS. Dilly Kean is a writer and performer.

Dilys a feminine first name meaning 'sincere' (*Welsh*). A diminutive form is DILLY.

Dimitri a Russian masculine form of Demetrius.

Dina (1) feminine form of DINO. (2) a variant form of DINAH.

Dinah a feminine first name meaning 'vindicated' (*Hebrew*). In the Old Testament Dinah was the daughter of Jacob and Leah. A variant form is Dina. A diminutive form is Di.

Dino a masculine diminutive ending, indicating 'little' (*Italian*), now used independently as a first name.

Dion (pronounced *dee-on*) a Welsh masculine form of DENNIS, which comes from Greek DIONYSIUS. William Shakespeare (1564–1616) used the name for that of a Sicilian lord in his play *A Winter's Tale*. A variant form is Deon.

Dione or **Dionne** a feminine first name meaning 'daughter of heaven and earth' (*Greek*). In Greek mythology, Dione was the earliest consort of Zeus and mother of Aphrodite.

Dionysius in Greek mythology, the god of wine. Dionysius is the source of the name DENNIS.

Dipak a masculine variant form of DEEPAK.

Dirk (1) the Dutch masculine form of DEREK. Sir Dirk Bogarde (1920–99) was an English film actor. (2) a diminutive form of THEODORIC.

Dixie a feminine diminutive form of BENEDICTA.

Dixon a masculine variant form of DICKSON.

Dmitri a Russian masculine form of Demetrius. Dmitri Shostakovich (1906–75) was a Russian composer.

Dod and **Doddy** Scottish diminutive forms of GEORGE.

Dodie (1) a feminine diminutive form of DOROTHY. Dodie Smith (1896– 1900) was an English playwright. (2) a Scottish masculine diminutive form of GEORGE.

Dodo a feminine diminutive form of DOROTHY.

Dogmael (pronounced *dog-mile*) a Welsh masculine first name. St Dogmael is a Welsh saint, contemporary with St David.

Doirend and **Doirenn** Irish Gaelic feminine forms of DARINA.

Dolan

Dolan a masculine variant form of DOOLAN.

Dolina (pronounced *dol-eena*) a Scottish feminine form of DONALD, common in Gaelic-speaking areas in the nineteenth and early twentieth centuries, and still in use. *See also* DONALDA.

Doll or **Dolly** a feminine diminutive form of DOROTHY. William Shakespeare (1654–1616) used the name for Doll Tearsheet who appears in his play King Henry IV, Part 2. Dolly Parton is an American country and western singer and film actress.

Dolores a feminine first name meaning 'sorrows' (*Spanish*). A variant form is DELORES. Diminutive forms are Lola, Lolita.

Dolph a masculine diminutive form of ADOLPH. Dolph Lundgren is a Swedish-born film actor who appears in action films.

Dom a masculine diminutive form of DOMINIC.

Domenico the Italian masculine form of DOMINIC. Domenico Barberi (1792–1849) was an Italian prelate who worked as a missionary in England.

Domhnall the Scottish Gaelic form of DONALD.

Domingo the Spanish masculine form of DOMINIC.

Dominic a masculine first name meaning 'belonging to the lord' (*Latin*). St Dominic (1170–1221) was the founder of the Dominican order. Dominic Elwes is an English painter and father of the actor Cary Elwes. A variant form is Dominick. A diminutive form is Dom.

Dominica the feminine form of Dominic.

Dominick a masculine variant form of Dominic.

Dominique the French masculine form of DOMINIC, now used in English as a girl's name.

Don (1) a masculine diminutive form of DONAL, DONALD, DONALL. (2) an anglicised feminine form of DANA.

Donal an Irish masculine form of DONALD. A variant form is Donall. Diminutive forms are Don, Donnie, Donny.

Donald a masculine first name from the Gaelic form Domhnall, from a Celtic root *dubno* or *dumno*, 'great ruler'. Nowadays mostly associated with Scotland and once the most popular boys' name in the Highlands and Islands, it was also a frequently used name in old Ireland and is still used there in the form Donal. Donald Sutherland is a Canadian-born film director. Diminutive forms include Don, Donnie, Donny.

Donalda or **Donaldina** a Scottish feminine form of DONALD, usually given to the daughter of a man named Donald. Other feminine forms are Donaldina, Donella, Dolina.

Donall a masculine variant form of Donal.

Donata feminine form of Donato.

Donato a masculine first name meaning 'gift of God' (*Latin*). Donato Bramante (1444–1514) was an Italian architect and painter.

Donella *see* Donalda.

Donn an Irish and Scottish masculine first name. 'Brown' is the most common meaning attributed to this name, although Old Gaelic *donn* had a number of meanings, including 'lord'.

Donna a feminine first name meaning 'lady' (*Italian*).

Donnchadh the Gaelic masculine form of Duncan. In this form the name was popular in Gaelic Ireland as well as in Scotland.

Donnie or **Donny** masculine diminutive forms of Donal, Donald, Donall.

Donovan a surname, meaning 'dark brown' (*Irish Gaelic*) used as a masculine first name.

Doolan a surname, meaning 'black defiance' (*Irish Gaelic*), used as a masculine first name. A variant form is Dolan.

Dora a feminine diminutive form of Dorothea, Theodora, etc, now used independently. Dora Bryan is an English actress. Diminutive forms are Dorrie, Dorry.

Doran a surname, meaning 'stranger' or 'exile' (*Irish Gaelic*), used as a masculine first name.

Dorcas (1) a feminine first name meaning 'a gazelle' (*Greek*). In the New Testament Dorcas was a Christian woman who lived in Joppa. William Shakespeare (1564–1616) used the name for that of a shepherdess in his play *A Winter's Tale*. (2) an anglicised feminine form of the Gaelic *dorchas*, 'dark'.

Doreen an Irish feminine variant form of Dora.

Dorian a masculine first name meaning 'Dorian man' (*Greek*), one of a Hellenic people who invaded Greece in the 2nd century BC. Its use as a first name was probably invented by Oscar Wilde (1854–1900) for his novel, *The Picture of Dorian Gray*.

Dorinda a feminine first name meaning 'lovely gift' (*Greek*). The English comic dramatist George Farquhar (1678–1707) used the name for the daughter of Lady Bountiful in his play *The Beaux Stratagem* (1707). A diminutive form is Dorrie, Dorry.

Doris a feminine first name meaning 'Dorian woman', one of a Hellenic people who invaded Greece in the second century BC (*Greek*). Doris Day is an American film actress and singer. Diminutive forms are Dorrie, Dorry.

Dorothea a German feminine form of DOROTHEA. George Eliot (1819–80) used the name for the heroine of her novel *Middlemarch* (1871–72). A diminutive form is Thea.

Dorothée a French feminine form of DOROTHEA.

Dorothy a feminine first name meaning 'the gift of God' (*Greek*). The American writer L. Frank Baum (1856–1919) used the name for the heroine of his perennially popular *The Wonderful Wizard of Oz* (1900). Diminutive forms are Dodie, Dodo, Doll, Dolly, Dot, Dottie, Dotty.

Dorrie or **Dorry** feminine diminutive forms of DORA, DORINDA, DORIS.

Dorward a masculine variant form of DURWARD.

Dot and **Dottie** or **Dotty** feminine diminutive forms of DOROTHY.

Doug or **Dougie** a masculine diminutive form of DOUGAL, DOUGLAS.

Dougal or **Dougald** or **Dougall** (pronounced *doo-gal*) a masculine first name meaning 'dark stranger', from Gaelic *dubh*, 'dark', and *gall*, 'stranger' (*Scottish Gaelic*). The Gaels differentiated between the Norwegians, 'fair strangers', and the Danes, 'dark strangers'. This name may have been given to a child with one Norse parent. It is often wrongly assumed to be cognate with Douglas, and the diminutive forms Doug and Dougie are the same in both. Variant forms are Dugal, Dugald.

Douglas (pronounced *dugg-las*) a masculine first name meaning 'dark water' (*Scottish Gaelic/Manx*). This was originally a location name from a place in the Scottish Borders, and the surname was adopted by twelfth-century Flemish immigrants. The name achieved great fame with Sir James Douglas, comrade-in-arms of King Robert I. Diminutive forms are Doug, Dougie.

Douglasina a Scottish feminine form of Douglas.

Dow a surname, meaning 'black' or 'black-haired' (*Scottish Gaelic*), used as a masculine first name.

Dowal the anglicised masculine form of DUNGAL. It is the source of the Galloway surname MacDowall.

Doyle an Irish Gaelic masculine form of DOUGAL.

D'Oyley a surname, meaning 'from Ouilly—rich land' (*Old French*), used as a masculine first name. Richard D'Oyley Carte (1844–1901) was the

English impresario who mounted the comic operas of Sir William S. Gilbert and Sir Arthur Sullivan.

Drake a surname, meaning 'dragon or standard bearer' (*Old English*), used as a masculine first name.

Drew (1) a masculine diminutive form of ANDREW. (2) a surname, meaning 'trusty' (*Germanic*) or 'lover' (*Old French*), used as a masculine first name.

Driscoll or **Driscol** a surname, meaning 'interpreter' (*Irish Gaelic*), used as a masculine first name.

Drostan a variant masculine form of DRUST.

Drostán an Irish Gaelic masculine first name from that of a follower of St Columba and founder of the monastery of Deer in Aberdeenshire.

Druce a surname, meaning 'from Eure or Rieux in France' (*Old French*), or 'sturdy lover' (*Celtic*), used as a masculine first name.

Drudwen a feminine first name meaning 'precious' (*Welsh*).

Drummond a surname, meaning 'ridge', used as a masculine first name.

Drury a surname, meaning 'dear one' (*Old French*), used as a masculine first name.

Drusilla a feminine first name meaning 'with dewy eyes' (*Latin*). In the New Testament Drusilla was the youngest daughter of King Herod Agrippa I and sister of Bernice. Her second husband was Felix, the Roman governor of Caesarea.

Drust a Pictish masculine first name and that of several Pictish kings, including the eighth-century Drust, son of Talorcan. Variant forms are Drustan, Drostan, perhaps commemorated in the hill Trostan in County Antrim.

Drustan (1) a Brythonic Celtic masculine first name that is sometimes taken as an older version of TRYSTAN. (2) a variant form of DRUST.

Dryden a surname, meaning 'dry valley' (*Old English*), used as a masculine first name.

Duane a masculine first name meaning 'dark' (*Irish Gaelic*). Variant forms are Dwane, Dwayne.

Dubh (pronounced *doov*) a feminine first name meaning 'dark one', from Gaelic *dubh*, 'black' (*Irish/Scottish Gaelic*).

Dubthach (pronounced *doo-tach*) a masculine or feminine first name, from Gaelic *dubh*, 'black' (*Irish/Scottish Gaelic*). It is the source of the Irish surname O'Duffy.

Dudley a place name, meaning 'Dudda's clearing' (*Old English*), used as a masculine first name. Dudley Moore is an English-born comedian, pianist and film actor.

Duff an ancient surname, from the stem *dubh*, 'dark' (*Scottish Gaelic*), used as a masculine first name.

Dugal or **Dugald** masculine variant forms of DOUGAL. A diminutive form is Duggie.

Duggie a masculine diminutive form of DOUGAL, DOUGALL, DOUGLAS, DUGAL, DUGALD.

Duke (1) the title of an English aristocrat used as a masculine first name. (2) a diminutive form of MARMADUKE.

Dulcibella a feminine first name meaning 'sweet beautiful' (*Latin*). A diminutive form is Dulcie.

Dulcie a feminine diminutive form of DULCIBELLA also used independently as a first name. Dulcie Gray was a Malaysian-born English stage and film actress

Dunc a masculine diminutive form of DUNCAN.

Duncan a masculine first name whose meaning is 'brown warrior', from *donn*, 'brown', and *cath*, 'warrior' (*Scottish Gaelic*). The Gaelic form is Donnchadh, and in this form the name was popular in Gaelic Ireland as well as in Scotland. The first king of all Scotland (1034–40) was Duncan (*c*.1001–1040). Duncan Bán MacIntyre (1724–1812) was a famous Scottish Gaelic poet. Diminutive forms are Dunc, Dunkie.

Dungal (pronounced *dunn-gal* or *dowall*) a masculine first name meaning 'brown stranger', from *donn*, 'brown', and *gall*, 'stranger' (*Scottish Gaelic*). It is anglicised as Dowal, the source of the Galloway surname MacDowall.

Dunkie a masculine diminutive form of DUNCAN.

Dunlop a surname, meaning 'muddy hill' (*Scottish Gaelic*), used as a masculine first name.

Dunn or **Dunne** a surname, meaning 'dark-skinned' (*Old English*), used as a masculine first name.

Dunstan a masculine first name meaning 'brown hill stone' (*Old English*). St Dunstan (c.909–988) was Archbishop of Canterbury (959–988) and an adviser to the kings of Wessex.

Durand or **Durant** a surname, meaning 'enduring or obstinate' (*Old French*), used as a masculine first name.

Durga a feminine first name meaning 'not accessible' (*Sanskrit*).

Durward a surname, meaning 'doorkeeper or gatekeeper' (*Old English*), used as a masculine first name. A variant form is Dorward.

Durwin a masculine first name meaning 'dear friend' *Old English*). A diminutive form is Durwyn.

Dustin a surname, of uncertain meaning, possibly 'of Dionysus', used as a masculine first name. Dustin Hoffman is an American film actor.

Dwane or **Dwayne** masculine variant forms of DUANE.

Dwight a surname, meaning 'THOR's stone' (*Old Norse*), used as a masculine first name.

Dyan a feminine variant form of DIANE.

Dyfan a masculine first name meaning 'ruler' (*Welsh*).

Dyfri (pronounced *dee-fri*) a Welsh masculine first name and that of an early Welsh saint.

Dylan a masculine first name meaning 'son of the waves' (*Welsh*). In the *Mabinogion* poems, it is the name of a son of Arianrod. Appropriately, it was borne by the poet Dylan Thomas (1914–1953).

Dymphna a feminine first name that may stem from *dán*, 'poetry' (*Irish Gaelic*). It was the name of a seventh-century Irish saint.

E

Eachann (pronounced *yach-ann*) the Scottish Gaelic masculine form of the first name HECTOR. It is a translation rather than a sound adaptation. The derivation of Greek Hector is 'horse lord', and this name stems from Gaelic *each*, 'horse'.

Eachna (pronounced *yach-na*) an Irish Gaelic feminine first name, probably a feminine form of EACHANN. A variant form is Echna.

Eada a feminine variant form of ALDA.

Eadaín a feminine variant form of ETAIN.

Ealasaid (pronounced *yalla-suth*) a feminine first name, the Scottish Gaelic form of ELIZABETH.

Ealga (pronounced *yal-ga*) a feminine first name meaning 'noble, brave' (*Irish Gaelic*).

Eamair a feminine variant form of EMER.

Eamonn or **Eamon** (pronounced *ay-mon*) the Irish Gaelic masculine form of EDMUND. Eamonn an Chnuic, 'of the hill', was a famous outlaw of the seventeenth century in County Tipperary. Eamon de Valera (1882–1975) was the first President of the Irish Republic.

Eanraig the Scottish Gaelic masculine form of HENRY.

Earl or **Earle** an English title, meaning 'nobleman' (*Old English*), used as a masculine first name. Variant forms are Erle, Errol.

Earlene or **Earline** feminine form of EARL. A variant form is Erlene, Erline. Diminutive forms are Earlie, Earley.

Earlie or **Earley** feminine diminutive forms of EARLENE.

Eartha a feminine first name meaning 'of the earth' (*Old English*). A variant form is Ertha.

Easter the name of the Christian festival, used as a feminine first name.

Eaton a surname, meaning 'river or island farm' (*Old English*), used as a masculine first name.

Eavan (pronounced *ay-van*) a feminine first name meaning 'radiant' (*Irish Gaelic*). It is a form of AOIBHINN.

Eb a masculine diminutive form of EBEN, EBENEZER.

Ebba (1) a feminine first name meaning 'wild boar' (*Germanic*). (2) an Old English form of EVE.

Eben a masculine first name meaning 'stone' (*Hebrew*). A diminutive form is Eb.

Ebenezer a masculine first name adopted in the seventeenth century by the Puritans from the name of an Old Testament site, meaning 'stone of help' (*Hebrew*), the scene of two defeats of the Israelites by the Philistines. Two writers used the name for that of a miser: Charles Dickens (1812–70) for Ebenezer Scrooge in *A Christmas Carol* (1843), and Robert Louis Stevenson (1850–94) for the name of David Balfour's grasping uncle in *Kidnapped* (1886). Diminutive forms are Eb, Eben.

Eber an Irish and Scottish Gaelic masculine first name the etymology of which is uncertain. It was the name of the supposed founder of the Scots, great-grandson of Scota, a daughter of the Pharaoh Nectanebo. Another, later, Eber was a son of Míl Espáine (*see* MILES).

Eberhard or **Ebert** German masculine forms of EVERARD.

Ebony the name of the dark hard wood used as a feminine first name.

Echna a feminine variant form of EACHNA.

Echo the name for the physical phenomenon of the reflection of sound or other radiation used as a feminine first name. In Greek mythology it is the name of the nymph who pined away for love of Narcissus.

Ed a masculine diminutive form of EDBERT, EDGAR, EDMUND, EDWARD, EDWIN.

Eda a feminine first name meaning 'prosperity, happiness' (*Old English*).

Edaín a feminine variant form of ETAIN.

Edan an anglicised masculine form of AEDÁN.

Edana feminine form of EDAN.

Edbert a masculine first name meaning 'prosperous; bright' (*Old English*).

Eddie or **Eddy** masculine diminutive forms of EDBERT, EDGAR, EDMUND, EDWARD, EDWIN.

Edel a masculine first name meaning 'noble' (*Germanic*).

Edelmar a masculine first name meaning 'noble, famous' (*Old English*).

Eden (1) a masculine first name meaning 'pleasantness' (*Hebrew*), in the Old Testament the name of the paradise where Adam and Eve lived before they sinned. (2) a surname, meaning 'blessed helmet', used as a masculine first name.

Edgar a masculine first name meaning 'prosperity spear' (*Old English*). William Shakespeare (1564–1616) used the name for that of the legitimate son of the Duke of Gloucester in *King Lear*. Diminutive forms are Ed, Eddie, Eddy, Ned, Neddie, Neddy.

Edie a feminine diminutive form of EDINA, EDITH, EDWINA.

Edina a Scottish feminine variant form of EDWINA.

Edith a feminine first name meaning 'prosperity strife' (*Old English*). Variant forms are Edyth, Edythe. Diminutive forms are Edie, Edy.

Edlyn a feminine first name meaning 'noble maid' (*Old English*).

Edmond the French masculine form of EDMUND.

Edmonda feminine form of EDMUND (*Old English*).

Edmund a masculine first name meaning 'prosperity defender' (*Old English*). St Edmund (1175–1240) was Archbishop of Canterbury (1234–40) and a distinguished scholar. William Shakespeare (1564–1616) used the name for that of the natural son of the Duke of Gloucester determined to oust his legitimate brother EDGAR in *King Lear*.

Edna (1) a feminine first name meaning 'pleasure' (*Hebrew*). (2) an anglicised feminine form of Welsh EITHNA.

Ednyfed (pronounced *ed-niffith*) a Welsh masculine first name and that of a thirteenth-century king of Gwynnedd, but referred to in the poem 'The War Song of Dinas Vawr' by the English poet Thomas Love Peacock (1785–1866) as 'Ednyfed, king of Dyfed'.

Edoardo an Italian masculine form of EDWARD.

Édouard the French masculine form of EDWARD.

Edrea feminine form of EDRIC.

Edric a masculine first name meaning 'wealthy ruler' (*Old English*).

Edryd a masculine first name meaning 'restoration' (*Welsh*).

Edsel a masculine first name meaning 'noble' (*Germanic*).

Eduardo the Italian and Spanish masculine form of EDWARD.

Edwald a masculine first name meaning 'prosperous ruler' (*Old English*).

Edward a masculine first name meaning 'guardian of happiness' (*Old English*). It was the name of several kings of England or Britain, including St Edward the Confessor (*c.* 1003–66, ruled 1042–66) whose death was followed by the short reign of Harold before the Norman conquest of England, Diminutive forms are Ed, Eddie, Eddy, Ned, Ted, Teddy.

Edwardina feminine form of EDWARD.

Edwige the French feminine form of HEDWIG.

Edwin a masculine first name meaning 'prosperity friend' (*Old English*).

Edwina feminine form of EDWIN. Edwina Currie is an English politician and novelist. A variant form is Edina.

Edy a feminine diminutive form of EDITH.

Edyth or **Edythe** feminine variant forms of EDITH.

Eevin a feminine anglicised form of AÍBELL.

Efa the Welsh feminine form of EVE.

Effie a feminine diminutive form of EUPHEMIA.

Egan (1) a surname, meaning 'son of HUGH' (*Irish Gaelic*), used as a masculine first name. (2) anglicised form of Irish Gaelic/Manx AODHAGÁN.

Egbert a masculine first name meaning 'sword bright' (*Germanic*).

Egberta feminine form of EGBERT (*Old English*).

Egidio the Italian and Spanish masculine form of GILES.

Eglantine an alternative name for the wild rose, meaning 'sharp, keen' (*Old French*), used as a feminine first name.

Ehren a masculine first name meaning 'honourable one' (*Germanic*).

Eibhlinn (pronounced *aiv-linn*) a feminine first name that is related to *aoibhlinn*, 'radiance' (*Irish/Scottish Gaelic*) and is the source of this name. In the course of time it has sometimes been taken as related to other names, including EVE and AVELINE. Its most common anglicised version is EILEEN.

Eigra (pronounced *eye-gra*) a feminine first name meaning 'fair maid' (*Welsh*). Eigra was the reputed name of King ARTHUR's mother, found in Sir Thomas Malory's Arthurian tales as Igraine.

Eileen (1) the Irish feminine form of HELEN. A variant form is AILEEN. (2) an anglicised feminine form of EIBHLINN.

Eilidh (pronounced *ay-lee*) the Irish and Scottish Gaelic form of HELEN. A diminutive form is Ellie.

Eilir a masculine first name meaning 'butterfly' (*Welsh*).

Eilis an Irish Gaelic feminine first name that is probably a Gaelicised form of ALICE.

Eiluned a Welsh feminine variant form of LUNED.

Eilwen (pronounced *isle-wen*) a feminine first name meaning 'white-browed' (*Welsh*).

Eimear and **Eimer** feminine variant forms of EMER.

Eimhair a Scottish feminine form of EMER.

Einar a masculine first name meaning 'single warrior' (*Old Norse*).

Einion (pronounced *ine-yon*) a masculine first name meaning 'anvil' (*Welsh*). It is a name often found in Welsh legend and anglicised into Eynon. *See* BEYNON.

Eira (pronounced *eye-ra*) a feminine first name meaning 'snow' (*Welsh*). A variant form is Eirwen, equivalent to 'Snow-white'.

Eire (pronounced *ay-ra*) an Irish Gaelic feminine first name and that of an old Irish goddess which has become synonymous with the country of Ireland.

Eirian (pronounced *eye-reean*) a masculine or feminine first name meaning 'fair, shining' (*Welsh*). A feminine-only form is Eirianwen.

Eirianwen the Welsh feminine form of EIRIAN.

Eiriol (pronounced *eye-reeol*) a feminine first name meaning 'beseeching' (*Welsh*).

Eirlys (pronounced *ire-lis*) a feminine first name meaning 'snowdrop' (*Welsh*).

Eirwen a variant feminine form of EIRA.

Eirys (pronounced *eye-ris*) a feminine first name, the Welsh form of IRIS.

Eithlenn a feminine variant form of EITHNA.

Eithna or **Eithne** (pronounced *eth-na*) an Irish Gaelic feminine first name that was also held by some early Irish saints. It stems from Gaelic *eithne*, 'kernel', implying both fertility and the heart of things. Variant forms are Eithlenn and Enya. There is a Welsh form, Ethni, and it is anglicised as Edna, Ena and Ethna.

Ekata a feminine first name meaning 'unity' (*Sanskrit*).

Elaine (1) a French feminine form of HELEN. (2) an anglicised feminine form of Welsh ELEN. Elaine is the name of 'the lily maid of Astolat' who fell in love with Sir Lancelot in the English Arthurian legend related by Sir Thomas Malory.

Elan a feminine first name from a Welsh river name.

Elda a feminine variant form of ALDA.

Elder a surname, meaning 'senior, elder' (*Old English*), used as a masculine first name.

Eldon a surname, meaning 'Ella's hill' (*Old English*), used as a masculine first name.

Eldora a shortened form of El Dorado, meaning 'the land of gold' (*Spanish*), used as a feminine first name.

Eldred a masculine first name meaning 'terrible' (*Old English*).

Eldrid or **Eldridge** a masculine first name meaning 'wise adviser' (*Old English*).

Eldrida feminine form of ELDRID.

Eleanor or **Eleanore** a feminine variant form of HELEN. Eleanor of Aquitaine (*c.*1122–1204) was the wife of King Louis VII of France (1137–52) and then wife of Henry II (1154–89), bringing with her as her dowry the lands that she possessed in France. Eleanor of Castile (1246–90) was the Spanish-born wife of Edward I. A variant form is Elinor. Diminutive forms are Ella, Nell, Nora.

Eleanora the Italian feminine form of ELEANOR.

Eleazer a masculine variant form of ELIEZER.

Electra a feminine first name meaning 'brilliant' (*Greek*).

Elen a feminine first name meaning 'angel, nymph' (*Welsh*).

Elen a Welsh feminine form of HELEN. Elen was the virgin princess in the *Dream of Macsen Wledig*, a tale of the Roman governor Magnus Maximus who tried to make himself emperor of Rome. An anglicised form is ELAINE.

Elena the Italian and Spanish feminine form of HELEN.

Eleonora the Italian feminine form of ELEANOR.

Eleonore the German feminine form of ELEANOR.

Eléonore a French feminine form of LEONORA.

Eleri a Welsh feminine first name and also a river name from Ceredigion. Eleri was a daughter of the fifth-century chieftain BRYCHAN.

Elfed a masculine first name meaning 'autumn' (*Welsh*).

Elffin a masculine variant form of ELPHIN.

Elfleda a feminine first name meaning 'noble beauty' (*Old English*).

Elfreda a feminine first name meaning 'elf strength' (*Old English*).

Elfreida or **Elfrida** or **Elfrieda** feminine variant forms of ALFREDA.

Elga (1) a feminine first name meaning 'holy' (*Old Norse*). (2) a variant form of OLGA.

Elgan a masculine first name meaning 'bright circle' (*Welsh*).

Eli a masculine first name meaning 'elevated' (*Hebrew*). In the Old Testament Eli was a high priest of Israel and teacher of Samuel. A variant form is Ely.

Elias a masculine variant form of ELIJAH. A diminutive form is ELI.

Elidir or **Elidor** a Welsh masculine first name and that of a legendary handsome boy, loved by the gods. Elidir was the father of Llywarch Hen (sixth century).

Eliezer a masculine first name meaning 'my God is help' (*Hebrew*). In the Old Testament Eliezer was the heir of Abraham. A variant form is Eleazer.

Elihu a masculine first name meaning 'he is my God' (*Hebrew*).

Elijah a masculine first name meaning 'Jehovah is my God' (*Hebrew*). In the Old Testament Elijah was a ninth-century BC Hebrew prophet who denounced the worship of the goddess Baal that had been introduced by King Ahab of Israel and Queen Jezebel. A diminutive form is Lije.

Elin (1) a Welsh feminine diminutive form of ELINOR. (2) a Welsh variant form of HELEN.

Elinor a Welsh feminine variant form of ELEANOR.

Eliot a masculine variant form of ELLIOT.

Elis a Welsh masculine form of ELIAS.

Elisa an Italian feminine diminutive form of ELISABETTA.

Elisabeth a French and German feminine form of ELIZABETH now used as an English-language form. Elisabeth Shue is an American film actress.

Elisabetta an Italian feminine form of ELIZABETH.

Élise a French diminutive form of ELISABETH.

Elisha a masculine first name meaning 'God is salvation' (*Hebrew*). In the Old Testament Elisha was a Hebrew prophet who succeeded ELIJAH.

Elissa an alternative name of DIDO.

Eliza a feminine diminutive form of ELIZABETH.

Elizabeth a feminine first name meaning 'worshiper of God, consecrated to God' (*Hebrew*). It is the name of several English queens, including Queen Elizabeth (1533–1603), the only child of Henry VIII and Anne Boleyn. She succeeded to the English throne after her half-brother, Edward VI, and her half-sister, Mary. Diminutive forms are Bess, Bet, Beth, Betsy, Betty, Eliza, Elsa, Elsie, Libby, Lisa, Liza, Lisbeth, Liz.

Ella a feminine diminutive form of CINDERELLA, ELEANOR, ISABELLA, now used independently.

Ellen a feminine variant form of HELEN.

Ellice feminine form of ELIAS, ELLIS.

Ellie a feminine diminutive form of ALICE, EILIDH.

Elliot or **Elliott** a surname, from a French diminutive form of Elias, used as a masculine first name.

Ellis a surname, a Middle English form of ELIAS, used as a masculine first name.

Ellison a surname, meaning 'son of ELIAS' (*Old English*), used as a masculine first name.

Elma (1) a feminine diminutive form of WILHELMINA. (2) a contracted form of ELIZABETH MARY.

Elmer a masculine first name meaning 'noble; excellent' (*Germanic*).

Elmo a masculine first name meaning 'amiable' (*Greek*).

Elmore a surname, meaning 'river bank with elms' (*Old English*), used as a masculine first name. Elmore Leonard is an acclaimed American crime writer.

Éloise or **Eloisa** a feminine first name meaning 'sound, whole' (*Germanic*). A variant form is Héloïse.

Elphin a Welsh masculine first name that may be from the same root as *albus*, 'white' (*Latin*). The name of a proverbially unlucky lad whose fortune changes when he rescues and becomes foster father to the baby Taliesin. A variant form is Elffin.

Elroy a masculine variant form of LEROY.

Elsa a feminine diminutive form of ALISON, ALICE, ELIZABETH.

Elsie a feminine diminutive form of ALICE, ALISON, ELIZABETH, ELSPETH.

Elspeth or **Elspet** Scottish feminine forms of ELIZABETH. Elspeth Buchan (1738–99) was a Scottish religious fanatic and founder of a religious sect, the Buchanites. Diminutive forms are Eppie, Elsie, Elspie.

Elspie a feminine diminutive form of ELSPETH.

Elton a surname, meaning 'settlement of Ella' (*Old English*), used as a masculine first name. Sir Elton John is an English songwriter and singer.

Eluned a feminine first name meaning 'idol' (*Welsh*). A diminutive form is LYNETTE.

Elva a feminine first name meaning 'friend of the elf' (*Old English*). A variant form is Elvina.

Elvey a surname, meaning 'elf gift' (*Old English*), used as a masculine first name. A variant form is Elvy.

Elvin a surname, meaning 'elf or noble friend' (*Old English*), used as a masculine first name. A variant form is ELWIN.

Elvina a feminine variant form of ELVA.

Elvira a feminine first name meaning 'white' (*Latin*).

Elvis a masculine first name meaning 'wise one' (*Norse*). It gained worldwide popularity as the name of the American singer Elvis Presley (1935–77).

Elvy a masculine variant form of ELVEY.

Elwin a masculine variant form of ELVIN; 'white brow' (*Welsh*). A variant form is Elwyn.

Elwyn a masculine first name meaning 'kind, fair', from *elus*, 'kind', and *gwyn*, 'fair' (*Welsh*).

Ely a masculine diminutive form of ELIAS.

Elystan a Welsh masculine form of Old English ATHELSTAN.

Emanuel a masculine variant form of EMMANUEL.

Emeline (1) a feminine variant form of AMELIA. (2) a diminutive form of EMMA. A variant form is Emmeline.

Emer (pronounced *ay-mer*) an Irish Gaelic feminine first name and that of the wife of the great legendary hero CUCHULLAIN. Variant forms are Eamair, Eimear, Eimer, and, in Scotland, Eamhair. Emer was said to possess all six gifts of womanhood: beauty, chastity, soft voice, clear speech, skill with the needle, and wisdom.

Emerald the name of the green gemstone that is used as a feminine first name.

Emergaid (pronounced *aymer-gatt*) a Manx feminine first name and that of a legendary princess of Man.

Emery a masculine variant form of AMORY.

Emil a masculine first name, from that of a noble Roman family the origin of whose name, Aemilius, is uncertain.

Émile the French masculine form of EMIL.

Emilia the Italian feminine form of EMILY. William Shakespeare (1564–1616) used the name for the friend of Desdemona and wife of the duplicitous Iago in his tragedy *Othello*.

Emilie the German feminine form of EMILY.

Émilie the French feminine form of EMILY.

Emilio the Italian, Spanish and Portuguese masculine form of EMIL. Emilio Estevez is an American film actor.

Emily a feminine name of a noble Roman family the origin of whose name, *Aemilius*, is uncertain.

Emlyn a masculine name the origin of which is uncertain, possibly from EMIL (*Welsh*).

Emm a feminine diminutive form of EMMA.

Emma a feminine first name meaning 'whole, universal' (*Germanic*). Jane Austen (1775–1817) used the name for the heroine of her eponymous novel *Emma* (1816). Emma Thompson is an English actress. Diminutive forms are Emm, Emmie.

Emmanuel a masculine first name meaning 'God with us' (*Hebrew*). In the Old Testament it was the name of the child whose birth was foretold by Isiah and who is identified by Christians with Jesus. Variant forms are Immanuel. A diminutive form is Manny.

Emmanuelle the feminine form of EMMANUEL.

Emmeline a feminine variant form of EMELINE.

Emmery a masculine variant form of AMORY.

Emmet or **Emmett** or **Emmot** or **Emmott** a surname, from a diminutive form of EMMA, used as a masculine first name. M. Emmet Walsh is an American film actor.

Emmie a feminine diminutive form of EMMA.

Emory a masculine variant form of AMORY.

Emrys (pronounced *em-riss*) the Welsh masculine form of AMBROSE (Latin Ambrosius). Emrys Wledig, 'prince', was the Welsh name of Ambrosius Aurelianus, leader of the Britons against the invading Saxons in the fifth century AD. Emrys Hughes was a fiery twentieth-century Labour MP.

Emyr a Welsh masculine first name, possibly a form of HONORIUS. Emyr Llydaw was a sixth-century saint. Emyr Humphreys was a well-known twentieth-century writer.

Ena (1) an anglicised feminine form of EITHNA. (2) an Irish and Scottish feminine suffix that, like INA, may have taken on a life of its own as a girl's name.

Enda a masculine first name derived perhaps from *éan*, 'bird' (*Irish Gaelic*). It is not uncommon for boys' names in Gaelic to end in -a, and St Enda, or Enna, was a sixth-century holy man, founder of a monastery on the Aran Islands.

Endellion a Cornish feminine first name. The original form of the name was Endelient, preserved in St Endellion, a legendary saint of the fifth century who eschewed all food and lived on milk and water.

Eneas a masculine variant form of AENEAS.

Enée the French masculine form of AENEAS.

Enfys a feminine first name meaning 'rainbow' (*Welsh*).

Engelbert a masculine first name meaning 'bright angel' (*Germanic*).

Engelberta or **Engelbertha** or **Engelberthe** feminine forms of ENGELBERT.

Enid a feminine first name from Welsh *enaid*, 'soul' (*Welsh*). It is a name found in the Arthurian legends.

Enna *see* ENDA.

Ennis a masculine first name meaning 'chief one' (*Gaelic*).

Enoch a masculine first name meaning 'dedication' (*Hebrew*). In the Old Testament Enoch was the oldest son of Cain and the father of Methuselah.

Enos a masculine first name meaning 'man' (*Hebrew*).

Enrica the Italian feminine form of HENRIETTA.

Enrichetta the Italian feminine form of HENRIETTA.

Enrico the Italian masculine form of HENRY.

Enrique the Spanish masculine form of HENRY.

Enriqueta the Spanish feminine form of HENRIETTA.

Enya a feminine variant form of EITHNA.

Eocha or **Eochai** or **Eochaid** a variant form of EOCHAIDH.

Eochaidh (pronounced *yoch-ee*) a masculine first name from *each*, 'horse' (*Irish Gaelic*), probably meaning 'horse-master' (*see* EACHANN). A very frequent name in old Irish legends and histories. Eochaidh was the name of an ancient sun-god, said to be the possessor of a single red eye. Eochaidh Airem, 'ploughman', was a legendary high king, earthly lover of the beautiful ETAÍN. The name was also used by the Picts. Variant forms are Eocha, Eochaid, Eochai, Eochy.

Eochy a variant form of EOCHAIDH.

Eoganán (pronounced *yo-hanann*) an Irish and Scottish Gaelic masculine first name stemming from Celtic *eo*, 'yew', so suggestive of tree worship in an earlier period. It was the name of one of the seven sons of Oengus (*see* ANGUS), all of whom were holy men of the sixth century. It is also found as Eogan, Eoghan. Anglicised forms are Eugene and Owen, both unconnected with the Celtic etymology of the name.

Eoghan or **Eogan** a masculine variant form of EOGANÁN.

Eoin (pronounced *yonn*) a masculine first name. An Irish Gaelic form of JOHN. Eoin macSuibhne was a chieftain of Ulster in the early fourteenth century. *See also* IAIN, SEAN.

Eolas (pronounced *yo-las*) a masculine or feminine first name meaning 'knowledge', 'experience' (*Irish Gaelic*).

Eph a masculine diminutive form of EPHRAIM.

Ephraim a masculine first name meaning 'fruitful' (*Hebrew*). In the Old

Testament Ephraim was the younger son of Joseph and grandson of
Jacob. He founded one of the Twelve Tribes of Israel. A diminutive
form is Eph.

Epiphany the name of the Christian festival celebrated on 6 January,
meaning 'revelation' (*Greek*), used as a feminine first name.

Eppie a feminine diminutive form of ELSPETH.

Eranthe a feminine first name meaning 'flower of spring' (*Greek*).

Erasmus a masculine first name meaning 'lovely; worthy of love'
(*Greek*). Diminutive forms are Ras, Rasmus.

Erastus a masculine first name meaning 'beloved' (*Greek*). In the New
Testament Erastus was a Christian who attended Paul on his third missionary tour. Diminutive forms are Ras, Rastus.

Erc a masculine first name from Old Irish Gaelic *earc*, 'speckled'. Erc was
the father of Fergus, Angus and Loarn, first lords of Gaelic Dalriada.
Erc macTelt is recorded as the ultimate ancestor of the Clan Cameron.

Ercol a masculine first name perhaps combining Gaelic *earc*, 'speckled',
and *col*, 'lord' (*Irish Gaelic*), although its resemblance to Greek Hercules has also been noted. It was the name of a Connacht warrior, hum-
bled by CUCHULAINN.

Ercole the Italian masculine form of HERCULES.

Erda a feminine first name meaning 'of the earth' (*Germanic*).

Eric a masculine first name meaning 'rich; brave; powerful' (*Old English*). Eric Roberts is an American film actor. A variant form is Erik.

Erica feminine form of ERIC. A variant form is Erika.

Erich the German masculine form of ERIC.

Erik a masculine variant form of ERIC.

Erika a feminine variant form of ERICA.

Erin or **Eriu** the Irish Gaelic poetic name for Ireland used as a feminine
first name.

Erland a masculine first name meaning 'stranger' (*Old Norse*).

Erle a masculine variant form of EARL.

Erlene a feminine variant form of EARLENE. A diminutive form is Erley,
Erlie.

Erley or **Erlie** a feminine diminutive form of ERLENE, ERLINE.

Erline a feminine variant form of EARLENE. A diminutive form is Erley, Erlie.

Erma a feminine first name meaning 'warrior maid' (*Germanic*).

Erminie or **Erminia** feminine variant forms of ARMINA.

Ern

Ern a masculine diminutive form of ERNEST.

Erna a feminine diminutive form of ERNESTA, ERNESTINE.

Ernan the anglicised masculine form of IARNAN.

Erne (pronounced *er-na*) an Irish Gaelic feminine first name and that of a
legendary princess. It is preserved in Lough Erne.

Ernest a masculine first name meaning 'earnestness' (*Germanic*). Diminutive forms are Ern, Ernie.

Ernesta the feminine form of ERNEST. A diminutive form is Erna.

Ernestine the feminine form of ERNEST. Diminutive forms are Erna, Tina.

Ernesto the Italian and Spanish masculine forms of ERNEST.

Ernie a masculine diminutive form of ERNEST.

Ernst the German masculine form of ERNEST.

Errol a masculine variant form of EARL.

Erskine a place name and surname, meaning 'projecting height' (*Scottish
Gaelic*), used as a masculine first name.

Ertha (1) a Cornish feminine first name and that of an early Celtic saint.
(2) a feminine variant form of EARTHA.

Erwin (1) a masculine first name meaning 'friend of honour' (*Germanic*).
(2) a surname, meaning 'wild-boar friend' (*French*), used as a masculine first name. A variant form is Orwin.

Eryl a masculine first name meaning 'watcher' (*Welsh*).

Esau a masculine first name meaning 'hairy' (*Hebrew*). In the Old Testament Esau was the twin brother of Jacob to whom he sold his birthright.

Esmé a masculine or feminine first name meaning 'beloved' (*French*).

Esmeralda a Spanish feminine form of EMERALD. The French writer Victor Hugo (1802–85) used the name for the heroine of his novel *The
Hunchback of Notre Dame* (1831).

Esmond a masculine first name meaning 'divine protection' (*Old English*).

Ess or **Essie** feminine diminutive forms of ESTHER.

Essyllt a feminine variant form of ISEULT.

Esta a feminine variant form of ESTHER.

Este a masculine first name meaning 'man from the East' (*Italian*).

Estéban the Spanish masculine form of STEPHEN.

Estelle or **Estella** feminine variant forms of STELLA. Charles Dickens
(1812–72) used the form Estella for the heroine of his novel *Great Expectations* (1860–61).

Ester the Italian and Spanish feminine forms of ESTHER.

Esther a feminine first name from the name of the planet Venus (*Persian*). In the Old Testament Esther was a Jewish woman wh became queen of Persia and saved her people from massacere. A variant form is Esta. Diminutive forms are Ess, Essie, Tess, Tessie.

Estrella the Spanish feminine form of ESTELLE.

Etaín or **Etáin** (pronounced *ithoyne*) an Irish Gaelic feminine first name and found in Irish mythology. Etaín was the second wife of MIDIR but was changed into a fly and swallowed by a woman, who then gave birth to a 'new' Etaín who married King EOCHAIDH but was eventually reclaimed by Midir and brought back to the 'Land of Many Colours'. Her name is synonymous with feminine beauty. Alternative forms are Edaín, Eadain. The name is sometimes anglicised to Aideen.

Ethan a masculine first name meaning 'firm' (*Hebrew*). In the Old Testament Ethan was one of four men whose wisdom, although great, was surpassed by Solomon. Ethan Coen is an American film writer and director and brother of Joel Coen, with whom he works.

Ethel a feminine first name meaning 'noble' or 'of noble birth' (*Old English*).

Ethelbert a masculine first name meaning 'noble, bright' (*Old English*). St Ethelbert (*c.* 552–616) was a king of Kent (560–616) who was converted to Christianity by St Augustine. A variant form is Aethelbert.

Ethna an anglicised feminine form of EITHNA.

Ethni a Welsh feminine variant form of EITHNA.

Etienne the French masculine form of STEPHEN.

Etta or **Ettie** feminine diminutive forms of HENRIETTA.

Ettore the Italian masculine form of HECTOR.

Euan a masculine variant form of EWAN.

Eudora a feminine first name meaning 'good gift' (*Greek*).

Eufemia the Italian and Spanish feminine form of EUPHEMIA.

Eugen the German masculine form of EUGENE.

Eugene (1) a masculine first name meaning 'well-born; noble' (*Greek*). A diminutive form is Gene. (2) an anglicised form of EOGANÁN.

Eugène the French masculine form of EUGENE.

Eugenia feminine form of EUGENE. Diminutive forms are Ena, Gene.

Eugénie the French feminine form of EUGENIA.

Eulalie a feminine first name meaning 'fair speech' (*Greek*).

Eunice a feminine first name meaning 'good victory' (*Greek*). In the New Testament Eunice was a Jewish woman who, with her mother, Lois, converted to Christianity. Eunice was the mother of Timothy, who became a disciple of Paul.

Euphemia a feminine first name meaning 'of good report' (*Greek*). Diminutive forms are Fay, Effie, Phamie, Phemie.

Eurfron (pronounced *ire-fronn*) a feminine first name meaning 'golden-breasted', from *aur*, 'gold' (*Welsh*).

Eurig (pronounced *eye-ric*) a masculine first name meaning 'golden', from *aur*, 'gold' (*Welsh*).

Euron (pronounced *eye-ronn*) a feminine first name meaning 'golden one', from *aur*, 'gold' (*Welsh*). This was the name of the beloved of the bard Iolo Morgannwg.

Eurwen a feminine first name meaning 'fair, golden', from *aur*, 'gold', and *ven*, 'white' (*Welsh*).

Eurwyn (pronounced *ire-win*) a masculine first name meaning 'fair, golden' (*Welsh*), a masculine form of EURWEN.

Eusebio a masculine first name meaning 'pious' (*Greek*).

Eustace a masculine first name meaning 'rich' (*Greek*). Diminutive forms are Stacey, Stacy.

Eustacia feminine form of EUSTACE. Diminutive forms are Stacey, Stacie, Stacy.

Eva the German, Italian and Spanish feminine forms of EVE.

Evadne a feminine first name the origin of which is uncertain but possibly meaning 'high-born' (*Greek*).

Evalina the Latin feminine form of AVELINE.

Evan a Welsh masculine form of JOHN.

Evangeline a feminine first name meaning 'of the Gospel' (*Greek*).

Eve a feminine first name meaning 'life' (*Hebrew*). In the Old Testament Eve is the first woman on earth and the wife of Adam from whose rib God created her. Diminutive forms are Eveleen, Evelina, Eveline, Evie.

Eveleen or **Evelina** feminine diminutive forms of EVE.

Eveline a feminine diminutive form of EVA, EVE.

Evelyn a feminine or masculine first name that evolved from the Norman French first name AVELINE into a surname before returning to use as a first name. The Irish and Scottish form is AIBHLINN. Evelyn Waugh was a noted English novelist.

Everard a masculine first name meaning 'strong boar' (*Germanic*).

Everett an English masculine form of AEBHRIC.

Everley a masculine first name meaning 'field of the wild boar' (*Old English*).

Evita Spanish feminine diminutive form of EVA. The name was made famous outside the Spanish-speaking world by the musical *Evita* by Andrew Lloyd-Webber about the life of Eva Peron, the wife of the Argentine dictator.

Evric an English masculine form of AEBHRIC.

Evodia a feminine first name meaning 'good journey' (*Greek*).

Ewan (pronounced *yoo-wan*) (1) an anglicised Scottish masculine first name meaning 'youth' (*Gaelic*). Variant forms include Euan, Ewen, Evan. (2) Irish and Scots Gaelic masculine forms of OWEN. (3) a Scottish masculine form of EUGENE. Ewan MacGregor is a Scottish actor. A variant form is Euan.

Ewart (1) an Old French variant form of EDWARD. (2) a surname, meaning 'herd of ewes' (*Old English*), used as a masculine first name.

Ewen a masculine variant form of EWAN.

Eynon the anglicised masculine form of EINION.

Ezekiel a masculine first name meaning 'strength of God' (*Hebrew*). In the Old Testament Ezekiel was a sixth-century BC priest and prophet who was exiled to Babylon. His prophecies are recorded in the Book of Ezekiel. A diminutive form is Zeke.

Ezra a masculine first name meaning 'help' (*Hebrew*). In the Old Testament Ezra was a fifth-century BC priest whose writings are recorded in the Book of Ezra.

F

Faber or **Fabre** a surname, meaning 'smith' (*Latin*), used as a masculine first name.

Fabia feminine form of FABIO. A variant form is FABIOLA.

Fabian the anglicised masculine form of the Roman family name Fabianus, derived from Fabius, from *faba*, 'bean' (*Latin*). St Fabian (189–200) was a pope (236–250) and martyr. William Shakespeare (1564–1616) used the name for one of the characters in his comedy *Twelfth Night*.

Fabián the Spanish masculine form of FABIAN.

Fabiano the Italian masculine form of FABIAN.

Fabien the French masculine form of FABIAN.

Fabienne feminine form of FABIEN.

Fabio the Italian masculine form of the Roman family name Fabius, from *faba*, 'bean' (*Latin*).

Fabiola a feminine variant form of FABIA. St Fabiola (*c.* 325–399) is said to have founded the first public hospital in western Europe.

Fabrice the French masculine form of the Roman family *Fabricius*, from *faber*, 'smith'.

Fabrizio the Italian masculine form of FABRICE.

Fahimah a feminine first name meaning 'intelligent' (*Arabic*).

Fairfax the surname, meaning 'lovely hair' (*Old English*), used as a masculine first name.

Fairley or **Fairlie** a surname, meaning 'clearing with ferns' (*Old English*), used as a masculine first name.

Faisal a masculine first name meaning 'judge' (*Arabic*). Variant forms are Faysal, Feisal.

Faith the quality of belief or fidelity used as a feminine first name. A diminutive form is FAY or Faye.

Fanchon a feminine diminutive form of FRANÇOISE.

Fand a feminine first name from *fand*, 'tear' (*Old Irish*). It was the name of a beautiful heroine of legend.

Fane a surname, meaning 'glad or eager' (*Old English*), used as a masculine first name.

Fanny a feminine diminutive form of FRANCES, also used independently.

Faolán a masculine first name meaning 'wolf-like', from *faolán*, 'wolf' (*Irish Gaelic*). This was a term of praise rather than denigration. The name was borne by an Irish missionary to Scotland and is preserved in the village name St Fillans.

Farah a feminine first name meaning 'joy' (*Arabic*). A variant form is FARRAH.

Farnall or **Farnell** a surname, meaning 'fern hill' (*Old English*), used as a masculine first name. Variant forms are Fernald, Fernall.

Farquhar (pronounced *farr-char*) a Scottish masculine first name, the anglicised form of Fearchar, from Old Gaelic *ver-car-os*, 'very dear one' (*Old Gaelic*).

Farr a surname, meaning 'bull' (*Old English*), used as a masculine first name.

Farrah a feminine variant form of FARAH. Farrah Fawcett is an American film actress who appeared in the TV series *Charlie's Angels*.

Farrell a masculine first name meaning 'warrior' (*Irish Gaelic*).

Fatima (1) a feminine first name meaning 'motherly' or 'chaste' (*Arabic*). It was the name of the daughter of Mohammed. (2) a feminine first name meaning 'of Fatima' in Portugal (*Portuguese*), used as a feminine first name.

Faustina or **Faustine** a feminine first name meaning 'lucky' (*Latin*).

Favor or **Favour** an abstract noun, meaning 'good will or an act of good will, from *favere*, to protect', used as a feminine first name (*Latin*).

Fawn the name for a young deer or a light greyish-brown colour used as a feminine first name (*Old French*).

Fay or **Faye** (1) a feminine first name meaning 'faith' (*Irish/Scottish Gaelic*) (2) a feminine first name meaning 'witch' or 'wise woman from *fée* (*Old French*) or *fay* (*Norman French*). (3) a feminine diminutive form of Faith. (4) a feminine diminutive form of EUPHEMIA.

Faysal a masculine variant form of FAISAL.

Fearchar the Gaelic masculine form of FARQUHAR.

Féchin or **Féchine** (pronounced *fay-hin*) a masculine first name from *fiach*, 'raven' (*Irish Gaelic*). It was a name borne by numerous early saints. A variant form is Féichin. *See also* FIACHRA.

Fedelm *see* FIDELMA.

Federico an Italian and Spanish masculine form of FREDERICK.

Fedlimid or **Fedelmid** (pronounced *fellimy*) an Irish Gaelic masculine or feminine first name of unclear derivation. It is a name found often in ancient sources, occasionally as a female name. A variant form is Feidhilim or Feidhlimidh. It is anglicised as Felim or Felimy.

Féichin a variant form of FÉCHIN.

Feidhilim or **Feidhlimidh** a feminine variant form of FEDLIMID.

Feisal a masculine variant form of FAISAL.

Felice the Italian masculine form of FELIX.

Felicia feminine form of FELIX.

Felicidad the Spanish feminine form of FELICIA.

Felicie the Italian feminine form of FELICIA.

Felicitas a feminine first name from *felicitas*, 'happiness' (Latin) and also the name of the Roman goddess of good luck.

Felicity a feminine first name meaning 'happiness' (*Latin*).

Felim or **Felimy** the anglicised form of FEDELIMID.

Felipe the Spanish masculine form of PHILIP.

Felix a masculine first name from *felix*, 'happy' (*Latin*). In the New Testament Felix was the Roman governor of Caesarea who kept Paul in prison for two years. His wife was DRUSILLA. The name was adopted by several popes.

Felton a place name and surname, meaning 'place in a field' (*Old English*), used as a masculine first name.

Fenella an anglicised feminine form of FIONNUALA. Sir Walter Scott (1771–1832) used the name for a female character in his novel *Peveril of the Peak* (182). Fenella Fielding is an English actress.

Fenton a place name and surname, meaning 'a place in marshland or fens' (*Old English*), used as a masculine first name.

Ferd a masculine diminutive form of FERDINAND.

Ferdia or **Ferdiad** a masculine first name derived from *fear*, 'man', and *dia*, 'god' (*Irish Gaelic*), but if so it is a pre-Christian god; also from *diad*, 'smoke'. Ferdia or Ferdiad was the brother-in-arms of CUCHULAINN, but Cuchulainn slew him in single combat.

Ferdinand a masculine first name meaning 'peace bold' (*Germanic*).

William Shakespeare (1564–1616) used the name for royal characters in two of his comedies, the king of Navarre in *Love's Labour's Lost* and a prince of Naples in *The Tempest*. Diminutive forms are Ferd, Ferdy.

Ferdinando an Italian masculine form of FERDINAND.

Ferdy a masculine diminutive form of FERDINAND.

Fergal a masculine first name derived from *fearghal*, 'brave' (*Irish Gaelic*). Diminutive forms are Fergie, Fergy.

Fergie (1) a masculine diminutive form of FERGAL, FERGUS, FERGUSON. (2) a feminine diminutive form of FERGUSON as a surname. A variant form is Fergy.

Fergus a masculine first name meaning 'best warrior', from Gaelic *fearr*, 'best', and *gas*, 'warrior' (*Irish Gaelic*), or 'only choice' from an older Celtic root, *ver gustu*; although another possibility is 'virile man'. Fergus was a legendary king of Ulster who was supplanted by CONCHOBHAR and so supported Queen Medb in her famous 'Cattle Raid', and the name was borne by many others, including Fergus Mór macErc, founder of the kingdom of Dalriada in Scotland. Diminutive forms include Fergy, Fergie.

Ferguson or **Fergusson** a surname, meaning 'son of Fergus', used as a masculine first name. Diminutive forms are Fergie, Fergy.

Fergy a masculine variant or feminine form of FERGIE.

Fern the name of the plant used as a feminine first name (*Old English*).

Fernald or **Fernall** masculine variant forms of FARNALL, FARNELL.

Fernand a French masculine form of FERDINAND.

Fernanda feminine form of FERDNAND.

Fernando a Spanish masculine form of FERDINAND.

Ffion a feminine first name from a flower name, 'rose' or 'foxglove finger' (*Welsh*).

Ffraid (pronounced *fryde*) a Welsh feminine form of BRIDE found in numerous place names.

Fiachna a masculine first name from *fiach*, 'raven' (*Irish Gaelic*). This name and FIACHRA are often confused.

Fiachra a masculine first name from *fiach*, 'raven' (*Irish Gaelic*). St Fiachra was a seventh-century Celtic saint whose name is preserved in French in St Fiacre and the *fiacre* or horse-drawn cab.

Fianaid (pronounced *fee-ana*) a feminine first name meaning 'little deer' (*Irish Gaelic*).

Fid a feminine diminutive form of FIDELIA, FIDELIS.

Fidel a Spanish masculine form of FIDELIS.

Fidèle a French masculine form of FIDELIS.

Fidelia a feminine variant form of FIDELIS. A diminutive form is Fid.

Fidelio an Italian masculine form of FIDELIS. The German composer Ludwig von Beethoven (1770–1827) used the name for the title of his only opera, *Fidelio*, in which the heroine, Leonora, pretends to be a boy and calls herself Fidelio in order to rescue her husband from prison.

Fidelis a masculine or feminine first name meaning 'faithful' (*Latin*). A feminine variant form is FIDELIA. A diminutive form is Fid.

Fidelma (1) an Irish feminine first name from Fedelm, the prophetess who warned Queen Medb of the coming rout of her army in the Cattle Raid of Cooley. The name has also been borne by a number of Celtic saints, and athough its origin is obscure, it clearly indicates a person of spiritual force. (2) a feminine first name meaning 'faithful Mary' (*Latin/Irish Gaelic*). Diminutive forms are Fid and Delma.

Fifi a French feminine diminutive form of JOSEPHINE.

Filippo the Italian masculine form of PHILIP.

Filippa the Italian feminine form of PHILIPPA.

Fillan *see* FAOLÁN.

Finán (pronounced *fin-ann*) a Scottish and Irish Gaelic masculine first name and that of several early saints of the Celtic church.

Finbarr or **Finbar** or **Findbarr** a masculine first name whose likely meaning is 'the fair-haired one' from *fionn*, 'white', and *barr*, 'head, crest' (Irish Gaelic). St Finbarr of Cork was widely venerated in the Celtic lands. A variant form is Finnbar or Finnbarr. *See* BARRFIND.

Findlay a masculine variant form of FINLAY.

Finegas a masculine variant form of FINNEGAS.

Finegin a masculine variant form of FINGEIN.

Finella an anglicised feminine form of FIONNUALA.

Fingal a masculine first name meaning 'fair stranger', from *fionn*, 'white, fair', and *gall*, 'stranger' (*Scottish Gaelic*). It was a name given to Norsemen by the Celts. In Scotland, however, it is also a name given to FIONN macCumhaill, at least since the fourteenth century, and perpetuated in 'Fingal's Cave' on the Scottish island of Staffa (although this name was not given to the 'cave of music' until the eighteenth century).

Fingein or **Finghean** or **Fingon** a masculine first name meaning 'wine

birth' (*Irish Gaelic*), a common name in old Irish sources. A variant
form is Finegin. The anglicised form is Finnigan.

Finlay or **Finley** (pronounced *finn-la*) a masculine first name from *fionn*,
'fair', and *laoch*, 'hero', 'warrior' (*Scottish Gaelic*). Finlay Currie
(1878–1968) was a Scottish-born film actor, his best-known part probably being that as the convict Magwitch in the film of *Great Expectations* (1946).A variant form, and the surname from it, is Findlay.

Finn (1) a masculine anglicised form of FIONN. (2) In Northern Scotland, a
Norse name.

Finnabair (pronounced *finna-warr*) a feminine first name meaning 'fair-
browed' (*Irish Gaelic*). In legend it was the name of MEDB's daughter,
lover of Fráech (*see* FRAOCH), who died of grief when he was killed by
CUCHULAINN. The name is related to Welsh GWENHWYFAR.

Finnán a masculine first name meaning 'little fair one', from *fionn*, 'fair',
with the diminutive ending -an (*Irish/Scottish Gaelic*). *See also* FINNI-
AN.

Finnbar or **Finnbarr** a masculine variant form of FINBARR.

Finnbheara (pronounced *finn-waira*) an Irish Gaelic masculine first name
from that of a fairy king of Connaught.

Finnegas a masculine first name from *fionn*, 'fair', and *geas*, 'warrior'
(*Irish Gaelic*). It was the name of the tutor of FIONN macCumhaill.
Finnegas sought to catch the magic salmon of all knowledge, and did
so, but his pupil touched the fish, sucked his finger and acquired the
knowledge. A variant form is Finegas.

Finnian an Irish and Scottish Gaelic masculine first name whose derivation is the same as that of FINNÁN, and the two names have often been
confused. St Finnian of Clonard (sixth century) is the best-known bearer of the name.

Finnigan the anglicised masculine form of FINGEIN.

Finola a feminine variant form of FIONNUALA.

Fintan a masculine first name and one of the many incorporating *fionn*,
'white, fair', the other element being construed both as 'ancient' and as
'fire' (*Irish Gaelic*). There were many St Fintans in the Celtic church,
but it goes back into ancient legend as the name of the salmon of knowledge. In another legend, Fintan macBochra was the only Irishman to
survive Noah's flood.

Fiona a feminine first name that is a relatively modern 'artificial' name, athough very popular. It recalls *fionn*, 'white' (*Gaelic*), a constituent of many names.

Fionn (pronounced fin) a masculine first name meaning 'fair-haired' from 'fair, bright' (*Irish/Scottish Gaelic*). This was the name of one of the greatest figures of Celtic legend, the mighty warrior, wise man and bard FIONN macCumhaill, the leader of the Fianna. The anglicised form is Finn. *See also* FINGAL.

Fionnuala or **Fionola** (pronounced *finn-oola*) a feminine first name that stems from *fionn*, 'white', and *ghuala*, 'shoulders' (*Irish Gaelic*). Fionnuala was one of the four children, and only daughter of king Lír and his wife AOBH, all of whom were transformed by enchantment into swans. A variant formis Finola, and the anglicised form is Fenella or Finella. A diminutive form is NUALA.

Fiske a surname, meaning 'fish' (*Old English*), used as a masculine first name.

Fitch a surname, meaning 'point' (*Old English*), used as a masculine first name.

Fitz (1) a masculine first name meaning 'son' (*Old French*). (2) a diminutive form of names beginning with Fitz-.

Fitzgerald a surname, meaning 'son of Gerald' (*Old French*), used as a masculine first name. A diminutive form is Fitz.

Fitzhugh a surname, meaning 'son of HUGH' (*Old French*), used as a masculine first name. A diminutive form is Fitz.

Fitzpatrick a surname, meaning 'son of Patrick' (*Old French*), used as a masculine first name. A diminutive form is Fitz.

Fitzroy a surname, meaning '(illegitimate) son of the king' (*Old French*), used as a masculine first name. A diminutive form is Fitz.

Flann a masculine or feminine first name meaning 'red' or 'red-haired' (*Irish Gaelic*). This ancient name became famous in the later twentieth century as a pen-name of Brian O'Nolan, who wrote as Flann O'Brien.

Flanna feminine form of FLANN.

Flannan a masculine first name meaning 'red-complexioned' (*Irish Gaelic*).

Flavia a feminine first name meaning 'yellow-haired, golden' (*Latin*).

Flavian or **Flavius** masculine forms of FLAVIA. William Shakespeare (1564–1616) used the name for minor characters in several plays, including *Julius Caesar*.

Fleming a surname, meaning 'man from Flanders' (*Old French*), used as a masculine first name.

Fletcher a surname meaning 'arrow-maker' (*Old French*), used as a masculine first name.

Fleur the French word for 'flower' used as a feminine first name.

Fleurette a feminine first name meaning 'little flower' (*French*).

Flinn a masculine variant form of FLYNN.

Flint a masculine first name meaning 'stream, brook' (*Old English*).

Flo a feminine diminutive form of FLORA, FLORENCE.

Flora a feminine first name meaning 'flower' (*Latin*) and that of the Roman goddess of flowers. It became particularly popular in Scotland through Flora MacDonald (1722–90), who aided Prince Charles Edward Stewart in his escape after the failure of the 1745–46 uprising, making her a heroine even among those who opposed the rising. Diminutive forms are Flo, Florrie, Flossie.

Florence (1) a feminine first name meaning 'blooming; flourishing' (*Latin*). Diminutive forms are Flo, Florrie, Flossie, Floy. (2) in Ireland, a masculine name, evidently stemming from an anglicisation of FURSA, which may have been supposed to be linked to Italian Firenze (the city of Florence). A diminutive form is FLURRY.

Florian and **Florent** masculine forms of FLORA.

Florrie or **Flossie** feminine diminutive forms of FLORA, FLORENCE.

Flower the English word for 'bloom' or 'blossom' used as a feminine first name.

Floy a feminine diminutive form of FLORA, FLORENCE.

Floyd an anglicised masculine variant form of the surname Llwyd, or Lloyd, used as a masculine first name. 'Pretty Boy Floyd' is a popular American folk song.

Flurry a masculine diminutive form of FLORENCE. In the *Irish R.M.* stories by Somerville and Ross, the pen names of Edith Somerville (1858–1949) and her second cousin, Violet Martin (1862–1915), Flurry Knox is a 'gentleman among stableboys and a stableboy among gentlemen'.

Flynn a surname, meaning 'son of the red-haired one' (*Scots Gaelic*), used as a masculine first name. A variant form is Flinn.

Fódla (pronounced *foh-la*) an Irish Gaelic land goddess name, synonymous with Ireland, like ERIN and BANBA. In one tradition these three were sisters.

Forbes

Forbes a place name and surname, meaning 'fields or district', from Old Gaelic *forba*, 'field', used as a masculine first name.

Ford the English word for a crossing place of a river used as a masculine first name.

Forrest or **Forest** a surname, meaning 'forest' (*Old French*), used as a masculine first name. Forest Whitaker is an American actor.

Forrester or **Forster** a surname, meaning 'forester' (*Old French*), used as a masculine first name.

Fortuna a feminine variant form of FORTUNE.

Fortune the word for 'wealth', 'fate' or 'chance' (*Latin*) used as a feminine first name. A variant form is FORTUNA.

Foster a surname, meaning 'forester or cutler' (*Old French*) or 'foster parent' (*Old English*), used as a masculine first name.

Fra a masculine diminutive form of FRANCIS.

Fráech a masculine variant form of FRAOCH.

Fraine a masculine variant form of FRAYN.

Fran a feminine diminutive form of FRANCES.

Franca a feminine diminutive form of FRANCESCA.

Frances the feminine form of FRANCIS. Frances McDormand is an American film actress. Diminutive forms are Fanny, Fran, Francie, Franny.

Francesca the Italian feminine form of FRANCES. A diminutive form is Francheschina.

Francesco the Italian masculine form of FRANCIS. A contracted form is FRANCO.

Francheschina a feminine diminutive form of FRANCESCA.

Francie a feminine diminutive form of FRANCES.

Francine a feminine diminutive form of FRANCES, FRANÇOISE.

Francis a masculine first name meaning 'free' (*Germanic*). It is the name of several saints, most notably St Francis of Assisi (1182–1226), the founder of the Franciscan order. Francis Ford Coppola is an American film director. Diminutive forms are Fra, Frank, Francie.

Francisca the Spanish feminine form of FRANCES.

Francisco the Spanish masculine form of FRANCIS. William Shakespeare (1564–1616) used the name for one of the characters in his comedy *The Tempest*.

Franco a contracted masculine form of FRANCESCO.

François the French masculine form of FRANCIS.

Françoise the French feminine form of FRANCES.

Frank (1) a masculine first name meaning 'Frenchman' (*Old French*). (2) a masculine diminutive form of FRANCIS, FRANKLIN. Diminutive forms are Frankie, Franky.

Frankie a masculine diminutive form of FRANK, FRANKLIN.

Franklin or **Franklen** or **Franklyn** a surname, meaning 'free–holder' (*Old French*), used as a masculine first name. Franklin D. Roosevelt (1882–1945) was the 32nd President of the United States (1933–45). Diminutive forms are Frank, Frankie, Franky.

Franky a masculine diminutive form of FRANK, FRANKLIN.

Frans the Swedish masculine form of FRANCIS.

Franz or **Franziskus** German masculine forms of FRANCIS.

Franziska the German masculine form of FRANCES.

Fraoch (pronounced *fraach*) an Irish and Scottish Gaelic masculine first name meaning 'heath'. Although Heather is today a girls' name, Fraoch was a male warrior. An alternative form is Fráech.

Fraser or **Frasier** a Scottish surname, meaning 'from Frisselle or Fresel in France', possibly from *fraise*, 'strawberry', or *frisel*, 'Frisian' (*Old French*), used as a masculine first name. The American sitcom *Frasier* and the character of Dr Frasier Crane have made the name famous. A variant form is Frazer, Frazier.

Frayn or **Frayne** a surname, meaning 'ash tree' (*Old French*), used as a masculine first name. A variant form is Fraine.

Frazer or **Frazier** masculine variant forms of FRASER.

Frea a feminine variant form of FREYA.

Fred a masculine diminutive and feminine form of FREDERICK, FREDERICA.

Freda (1) a feminine diminutive form of WINIFRED. (2) a variant form of FRIEDA.

Freddie or **Freddy** a masculine diminutive and feminine form of FREDERICK, FREDERICKA.

Frédéric the French masculine form of FREDERICK.

Frederica feminine form of FREDERICK. Diminutive forms are Fred, Freddie, Freddy, Frieda.

Frederick or **Frederic** a masculine first name meaning 'abounding in peace', 'peaceful ruler' (*Germanic*). William Shakespeare (1564–1616) used the name Frederick for the brother of the duke and his usurper in his comedy *As You Like It*. Diminutive forms are Fred, Freddie, Freddy.

Frederika a feminine variant form of FREDERICA. Frederika von Stade is an American opera singer.

Frédérique the French feminine form of FREDERICA.

Fredrik the Swedish masculine form of FREDERICK.

Freeman a surname, meaning 'free man' (*Old English*), used as a masculine first name.

Frewin a surname, meaning 'generous friend' (*Old English*), used as a masculine first name.

Freya or **Freyja** a feminine first name meaning 'lady' (*Norse*) and the name of the Norse goddess of love. Dame Freya Stark (1893–1993) was a British traveller and writer. A varaiant form is Frea.

Frieda (1) a feminine first name meaning 'peace' (*Germanic*). (2) a diminutive form of FREDERICA.

Friede the German feminine form of FRIEDA.

Friederike the German feminine form of FREDERICA. A diminutive form is Fritzi.

Friedrich German masculine forms of FREDERICK. A diminutive form is Fritz.

Fritz a masculine diminutive form of FRIEDRICH, also used independently. Fritz Lang (1890–1976) was an Austrian-born American film director.

Fritzi a feminine diminutive form of FRIEDERIKE.

Fulton a surname, meaning 'muddy place' (*Old English*), used as a masculine first name.

Fulvia a feminine first name meaning 'yellow-haired' (*Latin*).

Fursa an Irish Gaelic masculine first name of uncertain derivation. It was borne by a number of Celtic saints, most notably St Fursa who had ecstatic and terrifying visions, the account of which is said to have inspired Dante to write his *Inferno*. The anglicised form is Fursey. *See* FLORENCE.

Fursey the anglicised masculine form of FURSA.

Fychan (pronounced *fee-han*) the Welsh form of Vaughan.

Fyfe or **Fyffe** a surname, meaning 'from Fife', used as a masculine first name.

G

Gabe masculine diminutive form of GABRIEL.

Gabbie or **Gabby** feminine diminutive forms of GABRIELLE.

Gabrán (pronounced *gaw-ran*) a masculine first name perhaps linked with *gabhar*, 'goat' (*Scottish Gaelic*). It was the name of a Dalriadic king, The name is preserved in the Gowrie district of Angus.

Gabriel a masculine first name meaning 'man of God' (*Hebrew*). In the Bible, Gabriel is one of the archangels who was sent to tell Zachariah of the birth of John the Baptist and Mary of the birth of Jesus. Gabriel Byrne is an Irish actor. A diminutive form is Gabe.

Gabrielle feminine form of GABRIEL. Gabrielle Anwar is an English actress. Diminutive forms are Gabbie, Gabby.

Gaea the Latin feminine form of GAIA.

Gael a feminine first name meaning a Gael; *Gaidheal* is a Gaelic speaker (*Irish/Scottish Gaelic*). This modern name is also seen in the forms Gail, Gayle.

Gaenor a Welsh feminine abbreviated form of GWENHWYFAR. It is also found in the anglicised form of Gaynor.

Gaia a feminine first name meaning 'earth' (*Greek*). In classical mythology, Gaia was the goddess of the earth. The Latin form is GAEA.

Gail a feminine diminutive form of ABIGAIL, now used independently. Variant forms are Gale, Gayle.

Gaius a masculine variant form of CAIUS.

Galatea a feminine first name meaning 'white as milk' (*Greek*). In Roman mythology, Galatea was a statue brought to life by Venus. The story inspired the play *Pygmalion* (1913) by the Irish dramatist George Bernard Shaw (1856–1950).

Gale (1) a feminine variant form of GAIL. (2) a surname, meaning 'jail' (*Old French*), used as a masculine first name.

Galen the anglicised masculine form of the Roman family name Galenus, 'calmer' (*Latin*).

Galia a feminine first name meaning 'wave' (*Hebrew*).

Gallagher a surname, meaning 'foreign helper' (*Irish Gaelic*), used as a masculine first name.

Galloway a place name and surname, meaning 'stranger' (*Scots Gaelic*), used as a masculine first name.

Galton a surname, meaning 'rented farm' (*Old English*), used as a masculine first name.

Galvin (1) a masculine or feminine first name, the source of which has been traced to Gaelic *geal*, 'white', and *fionn*, 'bright' and also to *gealbhan*, 'sparrow' (*Irish Gaelic*). (2) a masculine first name that may be a form of GAWAIN.

Gamaliel a masculine first name meaning 'reward of God' (*Hebrew*). In the Old Testament Gamaliel was one of the chieftains chosen by God to help Moses and Aaron in selecting an army.

Ganesh a masculine first name meaning 'lord of the hosts' (*Sanskrit*) and the name of the Hindu god of prophecy.

Garaidh an Irish masculine form of GARETH.

Gardenia the name of a flowering plant with fragrant flowers, called after Dr Alexander Garden, used as a feminine first name (*New Latin*).

Gareth a Welsh masculine form of GERAINT. In the Arthurian legend of the Round Table, Sir Gareth is the younger brother of Sir Gawaine and Sir Gaheris. His nickname in the English versions was 'Beaumains' or 'fine hands', and the name was once taken to stem from Welsh *gwared*, 'mild, gentle', but this is now not accepted. An Irish form of it is Garaidh and it is now increasingly being used as a feminine form. Diminutive forms are Gary, Garry. A variant masculine form is GARTH.

Garfield a surname, meaning 'triangular piece of open land' (*Old English*), used as a masculine first name. Sir Garfield Sobers is a West Indian cricketer who also uses the diminutive form of GARRY.

Garland (1) the name for a wreath or crown of flowers (*Old French*) used as a feminine first name. (2) a surname, meaning 'a maker of metal garlands' (*Old English*), used as a masculine first name.

Garnaid a masculine variant form of GARTNAIT.

Garnet (1) the name of a deep-red gemstone used as a feminine first name (*Old French*). (2) an anglicised masculine form of GARTNAIT or Garnaid. (3) or **Garnett** a surname, meaning 'pomegranate' (*Old French*), used as a masculine first name.

Garrard a masculine variant form of GERARD.

Garratt a masculine variant form of GERARD.

Garret (1) the anglicised masculine form of Irish Gaelic GEARÓID. (2) or **Garrett** a masculine variant form of GARRARD.

Garrison a surname, meaning 'son of GARRET' (*Old English*), used as a masculine first name. Garrison Keillor is an American writer, speaker and broadcaster.

Garry (1) a Scottish river name and place name, meaning 'rough water', that is sometimes used as a masculine first name. (2) a masculine variant form of GARY.

Garth (1) a surname, meaning 'garden or paddock' (*Old Norse*), used as a masculine first name. (2) a variant form of GARETH.

Gartnait a masculine first name of uncertain derivation. It was a common name in the Pictish kingdom and was preserved in the family of the earls of Huntly. A variant form is Garnaid, and although it could be anglicised as Garnet, there is no etymological connection.

Garton a surname, meaning 'fenced farm' (*Old Norse*), used as a masculine first name.

Garve a place name, meaning 'rough place' (*Scots Gaelic*), used as a masculine first name.

Gary (1) a masculine first name meaning 'spear carrier' (*Germanic*). (2) a diminutive form of GARETH. A variant form is GARRY.

Gaspard the French masculine form of JASPER.

Gaston a masculine first name meaning 'stranger, guest' (*Germanic*); from Gascony (*Old French*).

Gauri a feminine first name meaning 'white' (*Sanskrit*).

Gautier or **Gauthier** French masculine forms of WALTER.

Gavan or **Gavin** an anglicised masculine form of GAWAIN.

Gawain a masculine first name meaning 'white hawk', from *gwalch*, 'falcon', *gwyn*, 'white' (*Welsh*). The Welsh form is Gwalchgwyn, and it is taken to be the same name as GWALCHMAI. Sir Gawain of Malory's Arthurian romance is known in Welsh as *Gwalchmai fab Gwyar*. As the principal knight of King ARTHUR he had great prestige, and the name was adopted in Ireland and Scotland as Gavan, Gavin. His parents, Lot and Morgause, were said to be from Lothian and Orkney (the latter being part of the Pictish kingdom until the ninth-century Viking conquest).

Gay (1) or **Gaye** an English adjective, meaning 'being joyous', used as a feminine first name (*Old French*). (2) a masculine first name meaning 'spear', from Gaelic *gáe*, 'spear' (*Irish Gaelic*). Spears were highly significant weapons among the Celts. (3) an Irish masculine diminutive form of GABRIEL. Gay Byrne is a popular Irish TV chat show host.

Gayle a feminine variant form of GAIL.

Gaylord a surname, meaning 'brisk noble man' (*Old French*), used as a masculine first name.

Gaynor the feminine anglicised form of GAENOR. *See also* GWENHWYFAR.

Gearóid (pronounced *garr-rode*) a masculine first name, the Irish Gaelic form of GERALD. The anglicised form is Garret. The name is closely linked to the Fitzgerald family, notably in the person of the fourteenth century third earl of Desmond, the magic-working Gearóid Iarla, 'Earl Gerald', and in the twentieth century by the Irish statesman Garret Fitzgerald.

Gearóidin (pronounced *garr-roh-din*) an Irish feminine first name, the Gaelic form of GERALDINE, a Norman name familiar in Ireland.

Geena a variant form of GINA. Geena Davis is an American film actress.

Gemma the Italian word for 'gem' used as a feminine first name. A variant form is Jemma.

Gene a masculine diminutive form of EUGENE, now used independently. Gene Hackman is an American film actor.

Geneva a feminine variant form of GENEVIEVE; the name of a Swiss city used as a feminine first name.

Genevieve a feminine first name the meaning of which is uncertain but possibly 'tribe woman' (*Celtic*).

Geneviève the French feminine form of GENEVIEVE.

Geoff a masculine diminutive form of GEOFFREY.

Geoffrey a masculine variant form of JEFFREY. Sir Geoffrey Johnson-Smith is an English politician. A diminutive form is Geoff.

Geordie a Scottish masculine diminutive form of GEORGE.

Georg the German masculine form of GEORGE.

George a masculine first name meaning 'a landholder, husbandman' (*Greek*). St George (died *c*.303) was a Christian martyr who became patron saint of England. The Scottish Gaelic form is Deórsa. Diminutive forms are Dod, Geordie, Georgie, Georgy.

Georges the French masculine form of GEORGE.

Georgia or **Georgiana** a feminine form of GEORGE. A diminutive form is Georgie.

Georgie (1) a masculine diminutive form of GEORGE. (2) a feminine diminutive form of GEORGIA, GEORGIANA, GEORGINA, GEORGINE.

Georgina or **Georgine** a feminine form of GEORGE. A diminutive form is Georgie.

Georgy a masculine diminutive form of GEORGE.

Geraint a Welsh masculine form of the Latin name Gerontius. It was the name of the warlike hero of the Welsh Arthurian tale *Geraint and ENID*. Sir Geraint Evans (1922–92) was a noted Welsh opera baritone.

Gerald a masculine first name meaning 'strong with the spear' (*Germanic*). Diminutive forms are Gerrie, Gerry, Jerry. The Irish form is GEARÓID, anglicised as GARRET. *See also* GIRALDUS.

Geraldine the feminine form of GERALD. The Irish form is GEARÓDIN.

Gerallt the Welsh masculine form of GERALD.

Gerard a masculine first name meaning 'firm spear' (*Old German*). Variant forms are Garrard, Garratt, Gerrard. Diminutive forms are Gerrie, Gerry, Jerry.

Gérard the French masculine form of GERARD. Gérard Depardieu is a French film actor.

Gerardo the Italian masculine form of GERARD.

Géraud a French masculine form of GERALD.

Gerhard the German masculine form of GERARD.

Gerhold a German masculine form of GERALD.

Germain a masculine first name meaning 'brother' (*Latin*). Diminutive forms are Gerrie, Gerry.

Germaine the feminine form of GERMAIN. Germaine Greer is an Australian writer and feminist. A variant form is Jermaine.

Geronimo or **Gerolamo** Italian masculine forms of JEROME.

Gerrard a masculine variant form of GERARD.

Gerrie or **Gerry** masculine diminutive forms of GERALD, GERARD. A feminine diminutive form of GERALDINE.

Gershom or **Gershon** a masculine first name meaning 'a stranger there' (*Hebrew*). In the Old Testament Gershon was one of the three sons of Levi.

Gert or **Gertie** feminine diminutive forms of GERTRUDE.

Gertrude a feminine first name meaning 'spear maiden' (*Germanic*).

William Shakespeare (1564–1616) used the name for the queen of Denmark, Hamlet's mother, in his tragedy *Hamlet*. Diminutive forms are Gert, Gertie, Trudi, Trudy.

Gervais the French masculine form of GERVASE.

Gervaise a masculine variant form of GERVASE.

Gervas the German masculine form of GERVASE.

Gervase or **Gervaise** a masculine first name meaning 'spearman' (*Germanic*). Variant forms are Jarvis, Jervis.

Gervasio the Italian, Portuguese and Spanish masculine form of GERVASE.

Gethin a masculine first name meaning 'dark', from *cethin*, 'dusky, dark' (*Welsh*).

Ghislaine an Old French form of GISELLE.

Giacomo an Italian masculine form of JAMES.

Gian or **Gianni** masculine diminutive forms of GIOVANNI.

Gibson a surname, meaning 'son of GILBERT' (*Old English*), used as a masculine first name.

Gideon a masculine first name meaning 'of a hill' (*Hebrew*). In the Old Testament Gideon was one of the great judges of Israel who also led the Israelites to victory over the Midianites.

Giffard or **Gifford** a surname, meaning 'bloated' (*Old French*) or 'gift' (*Germanic*), used as a masculine first name.

Gigi a French feminine diminutive form of GEORGINE, GILBERTE, VIRGINIE.

Gil (1) a masculine diminutive form of GILBERT, GILCHRIST, GILES. (2) a Spanish form of GILES.

Gilbert a masculine first name meaning 'yellow-bright; famous' (*Germanic*). A diminutive form is Gil.

Gilberta a feminine form of GILBERT. Diminutive forms are Gill, Gillie, Gilly.

Gilberte the French feminine form of GILBERT. A diminutive form is GIGI.

Gilchrist a masculine first name meaning 'servant or follower of Christ', from *gille*, 'follower' (*Scottish Gaelic*). A diminutive form is Gil.

Gilda a feminine first name meaning 'sacrifice' (*Germanic*).

Gildas a Welsh masculine first name and that of an ecclesiastic and historian, a contemporary of St David, said to have been born in the kingdom of Strathclyde, and author of *De Excidio Britanniae*, a description of the Saxon conquest of Britain. The name is found in Brittany as Gueltaz.

Giles a masculine first name that comes from *aigidion*, 'young goat'

(*Greek*), referring to the goatskin mantle of the saint. As the name of the patron of Edinburgh's high kirk, the name has some following in Scotland, where it also gains a Gaelic resonance from its resemblance to Gaelic *gille*, 'boy'. A variant form is Gyles.

Gill a feminine diminutive form of GILBERTA, GILBERTE, GILLIAN.

Gilleasbuig (pronounced *gheel-espic*) a masculine first name meaning 'servant of the bishop', from Gaelic *gille*, 'servant' (*Scottish Gaelic*). In the past it was assumed erroneously to be a Gaelic version of Archibald ('bald' implying a clerical tonsure), resulting in numerous Gilleasbuigs anglicising their names to this instead of the more usual Gillespie.

Gilles the French masculine form of GILES.

Gillespie the anglicised form of GILLEASBUIG.

Gillie a feminine diminutive form of GILBERTA, GILBERTE, GILLIAN.

Gillian feminine form of JULIAN. Diminutive forms are Gill, Gillie, Gilly.

Gillmore a masculine variant form of GILMORE.

Gilly a feminine diminutive form of GILBERTA, GILBERTE, GILLIAN.

Gilmore or **Gilmour** a surname, meaning 'follower of Mary', from *gille*, 'follower', *Mhuire*, 'of Mary' (*Scottish Gaelic*), used as a masculine first name. The name of a priest originally. A variant form is GILLMORE.

Gilroy a surname, meaning 'servant of the red haired one' (*Gaelic*), used as a masculine first name.

Gina a feminine diminutive form of GEORGINA, also used independently. Geena is a variant form.

Ginnie or **Ginny** a feminine diminutive form of VIRGINIA.

Gioacchino the Italian masculine form of JOACHIM.

Giorgio the Italian masculine form of GEORGE.

Giorsail (pronounced *ghee-orrsal*) a feminine first name meaning 'grace' (*Scottish Gaelic*).

Giovanna the Italian feminine form of JANE.

Giovanni the Italian masculine form of JOHN. Giovanni Lorenzo Bernini was a great Italian sculptor and architect of St Peter's Basilica in Rome. Diminutive forms are Gian, Gianni.

Gipsy a feminine variant form of GYPSY.

Giraldo the Italian masculine form of GERALD.

Giraldus the masculine Latin form of GERALD. The ecclesiastic Giraldus Cambrensis (Gerald the Welshman) (*c*.1146–*c*.1223) wrote extensively about life in the Celtic world in his own era and its earlier history.

Giraud or **Girauld** French masculine forms of GERALD.

Girolamo an Italian masculine form of JEROME.

Girvan a place name, meaning 'short river' (*Scots Gaelic*), used as a masculine first name.

Gisela the Dutch and German feminine form of GISELLE.

Gisèle the French feminine form of GISELLE.

Giselle a feminine first name meaning 'promise, pledge' (*Germanic*).

Gita a feminine first name meaning 'song' (*Sanskrit*).

Gitana a feminine first name meaning 'gipsy' (*Spanish*).

Giulio the Italian masculine form of JULIUS.

Giuseppe the Italian masculine form of JOSEPH. A diminutive form is Beppe, Beppo.

Gladwin a surname, meaning 'glad friend' (*Old English*), used as a masculine first name.

Gladys the feminine anglicised Welsh form of GWLADYS.

Glanmor a masculine first name from 'clean or bright', and 'great' (*Welsh*).

Glanvil a masculine diminutive form of GLANVILLE.

Glanville a masculine first name meaning 'dweller on the oak tree estate' (*French*). A diminutive form is Glanvil.

Gleda Old English feminine version of GLADYS.

Glen the surname, from *gleann*, 'mountain valley' (*Scottish Gaelic*), used as a masculine first name. A variant form is GLENN.

Glenda a feminine first name meaning 'good, holy' (*Welsh*). Glenda Jackson is an English actress and MP.

Glendon a masculine first name meaning 'from the fortress in the glen' (*Celtic*).

Glenn a masculine variant form of GLEN, now also used as a feminine first name. Glenn Close is an American actress.

Glenna or **Glenne** a feminine form of GLEN.

Glenys a feminine first name meaning 'holy, fair one', from *glân*, 'pure, holy and fair' (*Welsh*). Glenys Kinnock is an MEP.

Gloria a feminine first name meaning 'glory' (*Latin*).

Glyn a masculine first name meaning 'valley' (*Welsh*). A variant form is GLYNN.

Glynis a Welsh feminine first name, the stem of which may be *glân,* as in GLENYS, or it may be *glyn*, 'valley', indicating 'girl of the valley', and the female form of Glyn.

Glynn a masculine variant form of GLYN.

Goddard a masculine first name meaning 'God strong' (*Old German*).

Godfrey a masculine first name meaning 'God peace' (*Germanic*).

Godiva a feminine first name meaning 'God gift' (*Old English*).

Godwin a masculine first name meaning 'God friend' (*Old English*).

Gofannon a masculine first name meaning 'smith', from *gofan*, 'smith' (*Welsh*). It is the name of a legendary blacksmith.

Golda or **Golde** a feminine first name meaning 'gold' (*Yiddish*).

Goldie an anglised feminine form of GOLDA; 'fair-haired' (*English*). Goldie Hawn is an American film actress and comedienne.

Golding a surname, meaning 'son of gold' (*Old English*), used as a masculine first name.

Goldwin a masculine first name meaning 'gold friend' (*Old English*).

Goll a masculine first name meaning 'one-eyed' (*Irish Gaelic*). The best known bearer of this name in Irish legend is Goll macMorna, opponent of FIONN macCumhaill in his bid to lead the Fianna.

Gomer a masculine first name from the Old Testament. He was grandson of Noah and, in Welsh legend, the progenitor of the Welsh people.

Goodwin a surname, meaning 'good friend' (*Old English*), used as a masculine first name.

Gopal a masculine first name meaning 'protector of cows' (*Sanskrit*).

Gordon a masculine first name that was originally a location name, from *gor dun*, 'hill fort' (*Old Gaelic*), of the Scottish Borders, it became a family name and transferred with the family to Strathbogie in northeast Scotland. Diminutive forms are Gord, Gordie.

Gormflath (pronounced *gorrum-la*) a feminine first name meaning 'illustrious ruler', from Gaelic *gorm*, 'illustrious' (and also 'blue') and *flaith*, 'sovereignty' (*Irish Gaelic*). In legend it is the name of numerous princesses and holy women; the best known is the wife of Brian Ború, a powerful dynastic figure in her own right.

Goronwy a masculine first name that was popularised by Goronwy Owen, the Anglesey bard (1723–1769).

Gottfried the German masculine form of GODFREY. A diminutive form is Götz.

Götz a masculine diminutive form of GOTTFRIED.

Grace a feminine first name meaning 'grace' (*Latin*). A diminutive form is Gracie.

Gracie a feminine diminutive form of GRACE. Dame Gracie Fields (1898–1979) was a popular English singer and entertainer.

Grady a surname, meaning 'noble' (*Irish Gaelic*), used as a masculine first name.

Graeme or **Graham** or **Grahame** (pronounced *graym*) a masculine first name that was originally a place name, either from Grantham in England or from Scots *gray hame*, 'grey house', and then became a surname.

Gráinne (pronounced *grawn-ya*) a feminine first name that may come from *grán*, 'grain' (*Irish Gaelic*), suggesting an ancient fertility goddess; it has also been construed as 'she who terrifies'. A name from Irish legend; its most famous bearer was the Gráinne who was intended for marriage to the elderly FIONN macCumhaill but rebelled and eloped with Diarmaid, his nephew, as told in *The Pursuit of Diairmaid and Gráinne*. It is anglicised as Grania.

Granger a surname, meaning 'farmer or bailiff' (*Old English*), used as a masculine first name.

Grania a feminine anglicised form of GRÁINNE.

Grant a surname, from Old French *grand*, 'tall', of twelfth-century Norman-French immigrants to the Badenoch district of Scotland, now often used as a masculine first name.

Granuaile (pronounced *grawn-walya*) an Irish Gaelic feminine first name from that of Granuaile Mhaol, 'of the cropped hair', the sixteenth-century 'pirate queen' of Connaught, also known as GRÁINNE, or in English form Grace O' Malley.

Granville a masculine first name meaning 'large town' (*Old French*).

Gray a surname, meaning 'grey-haired' (*Old English*), used as a masculine first name. A variant form is Grey.

Greeley a surname, meaning 'pitted' (*Old English*), used as a masculine first name.

Greer a Scottish feminine first name, a shortened form of GRIGOR. Greer Garson is a Northern Irish-born American film star.

Greg a masculine diminutive form of GREGOR, GREGORY.

Grégoire the French masculine form of GREGORY.

Gregor a Scots masculine form of GREGORY. A diminutive form is Greg.

Gregorio the Italian and Spanish masculine form of GREGORY.

Gregory a masculine first name meaning 'watchman', from *gregorius*

(*Latin*). It is a name given prestige by its links with saints and popes. Two of the Doctors of the Roman Catholic Church were called Gregory, St Gregory of Nazianzus (*c*.329–*c*.389) and Pope Gregory I, 'the Great' (*c*.540–604). William Shakespeare (1564–1616) used the name for those of servants in two of his plays, *The Taming of the Shrew* and *Romeo and Juliet*. A diminutive form is Greg.

Gresham a surname, meaning 'grazing meadow' (*Old English*), used as a masculine first name.

Greta a feminine diminutive form of MARGARET. Greta Scacchi is an Anglo-Italian actress.

Gretchen a feminine diminutive form of MARGARET, MARGARETE.

Grete a feminine diminutive form of MARGARETE.

Greville a surname, meaning 'from Gréville in France', used as a masculine first name.

Grey a masculine variant form of GRAY.

Grier a surname, a contracted form of GREGOR, used as a masculine or feminine first name. A variant feminine form is GREER.

Griff a masculine diminutive form of GRIFFIN, GRIFFITH.

Griffin a Latinised masculine form of GRIFFITH. Griffin Richardes was an officer in the household of Catherine of Aragon, queen of Henry VIII. In his play Henry VIII William Shakespeare (1564–1616) calls him Griffith. A diminutive form is Griff.

Griffith an anglicised masculine form of GRUFFYDD. A diminutive form is Griff.

Grigor (1) a masculine first name that stems from Old Gaelic *giric*, 'king's crest' (*Pictish/Scottish Gaelic*). Girig was the name of more than one Pictish king. (2) or **Gregor** a Scottish masculine form of GREGORY. (3) the Welsh masculine form of GREGORY.

Grisel a feminine diminutive form of GRISELDA.

Griselda a feminine first name meaning 'stone heroine' (*Germanic*). A variant form is Grizelda. A diminutive form is Grisel, Grissel.

Grissel a feminine diminutive form of GRISELDA.

Grizel a feminine diminutive form of GRIZELDA.

Grizelda a feminine variant form of Griselda. Diminutive forms are Grizel, Grizzel, ZELDA.

Grizzel a feminine diminutive form of GRIZELDA.

Grover a surname, meaning 'from a grove of trees' (*Old English*), used as a masculine first name. Grover Cleveland (1837–1908) was a Democratic politician and the 22nd and 24th President of the United States.

Gruffydd or **Gruffudd** (pronounced *griffith*) a masculine first name meaning 'powerful chief' (*Welsh*) and a great name from Welsh history. Gruffydd ap Llewellyn was an eleventh-century ruler of Wales. The anglicised form is Griffith.

Gruoch (Pictish, female) a Pictish feminine first name the derivation of which is uncertain. This was the name of Macbeth's queen, herself a woman of royal descent.

Guaire (pronounced *gwarr-ya*) a masculine first name from *guaire*, 'noble', 'proud' (*Irish Gaelic*). Guaire Aidne was a seventh-century king of Connacht.

Gualterio the Spanish masculine form of WALTER.

Gualtier the French masculine form of WALTER.

Gualtieri the Italian masculine form of WALTER.

Gudrun a feminine first name meaning 'war spell, rune' (*Old Norse*).

Gueltaz a Breton masculine form of GILDAS.

Guglielmo the Italian masculine form of WILLIAM.

Guido the German, Italian and Spanish masculine forms of GUY.

Guilbert a French masculine form of GILBERT.

Guillaume the French masculine form of WILLIAM. Guillaume de l'Estoc was one of the legendary twelve paladins who attended on Charlemagne.

Guillermo or **Guillelmo** Spanish masculine forms of WILLIAM.

Guin a masculine diminutive form of GWYN.

Guinevere the earliest feminine anglicised form of GWENHWYFAR.

Gulab A FEMININE FIRST NAME MEANING 'ROSE' (*SANSKRIT*).

Gunhilda or **Gunhilde** a feminine first name meaning 'strife war' (*Old Norse*).

Gunnar the Scandinavian masculine form of GUNTER.

Gunter a masculine first name meaning 'battle warrior' (*Germanic*).

Günther the German masculine form of GUNTER.

Gus a masculine diminutive form of ANGUS, AUGUSTUS, GUSTAV.

Gussie or **Gusta** feminine diminutive forms of AUGUSTA.

Gustav the German and Swedish form of Gustavus.

Gustavus a masculine first name meaning 'staff of the Goths' (*Old Norse*). A diminutive form is Gus.

Gustave the French masculine form of GUSTAVUS.

Guthrie a surname, meaning 'windy' (*Scottish Gaelic*), used as a masculine first name.

Guy a masculine first name meaning 'a leader' (*German-French*). Guy de Bourgogne was one of the legendary twelve paladins who attended on Charlemagne. Sir Walter Scott (1771–1832) used the name for the eponymous hero of his novel *Guy Mannering* (1815).

Guyon a French masculine form of GUY.

Gwalchgwyn a Welsh masculine form of GAWAIN.

Gwalchmai a masculine first name meaning 'falcon of May', from *gwalch*, 'falcon', *mai*, 'May' (*Welsh*). The latter part may alternatively mean 'of the plain', from Gaelic *maigh*. Gwalchmai fab Meilir was a poet of the twelfth century. *See* GAWAIN.

Gwatcyn a Welsh masculine first name, a form of Watkin, 'Little Walter'.

Gwaun a masculine first name meaning 'heath' (Welsh).

Gwen a feminine diminutive form of either GWENHWYFAR or of other names beginning in Gwen-, but also found on its own. From *wen*, 'white, fair' (*Welsh*).

Gwenda a feminine first name meaning 'fair, good' (*Welsh*).

Gwendolen or **Gwendolin** a feminine first name meaning 'blessed, fair' (*Welsh*). Diminutive forms are Gwen, Gwenda, Gwennie. It is often anglicised as Gwendoline.

Gwendoline the anglicised feminine form of GWENDOLEN.

Gwendolyn a feminine variant form of GWENDOLEN.

Gwenfron a feminine first name meaning 'fair-breasted' (*Welsh*).

Gwenhwyfar (pronounced *gwen iff-ar*) a feminine first name that stems from *gwyn*, 'white', and *hwyfar*, 'smooth' (*Welsh*). It was the name of Arthur's queen and is found in many legends. Its earliest anglicised form was Guinevere, but it is much more frequently found as Jennifer. Other forms include Gaynor and the abbreviated Gwen.

Gwenllian (pronounced *gwen-hleean*) a feminine first name meaning 'fair, flaxen-haired' (*Welsh*).

Gwennan a feminine first name meaning 'fair, blessed' (*Welsh*).

Gwennie a feminine diminutive form of either GWENHWYFAR or of other names beginning in Gwen-.

Gwenonwyn a feminine first name meaning 'lily of the valley' (*Welsh*).

Gwenydd (pronounced *gwen-ith*) a feminine first name meaning 'Morning Star' (*Welsh*).

Gwili

Gwili (1) a Welsh river name from Carmarthen used as a masculine first name. (2) a shortened form of GWILYM.

Gwilym or **Gwillym** Welsh masculine forms of WILLIAM.

Gwion a masculine first name from the boyhood name of TALIESIN the minstrel; also subject of the poem 'Gwion Bach'.

Gwladys or **Gwladus** (pronounced *glad-iss*) a feminine first name meaning 'ruler' (*Welsh*). Gwladus Ddu was the daughter of Llywelyn the Great. The anglicised form is Gladys.

Gwydion a Welsh masculine first name from that of a powerful sorcerer, from the *Mabinogion* cycle of legends.

Gwylan a feminine first name meaning 'seagull' (*Welsh*).

Gwyn a masculine first name meaning 'white, blessed' (*Welsh*). Gwyn ap Nudd was a legendary Welsh god, king of the 'Otherworld', Annwn.

Gwyneth a Welsh feminine first name from the name of the old province and modern county of Gwynedd. Gwyneth Paltrow is an American film actress. A variant form is Gwynneth. Diminutive forms are Gwyn, Guin.

Gwynfor a masculine first name meaning 'bright lord', from *gwyn*, 'white', and *ior*, 'lord' (*Welsh*). Gwynfor Evans was for many years leader of Plaid Cymru, the Welsh National Party.

Gwynneth a feminine variant form of GWYNETH.

Gyles a masculine variant form of GILES.

Gypsy the name for a member of a people who live a nomadic life used as a feminine first name. A variant form is GIPSY.

H

Haakon a masculine variant form of HAKON.

Habil the Arabic form of ABEL.

Hackett a surname, meaning 'little woodcutter' (*Old Norse*), used as a masculine first name.

Haddan or **Hadden** or **Haddon** a surname, meaning 'heathery hill' (*Old English*), used as a masculine first name.

Hadley a surname, meaning 'heathery hill or heathery meadow' (*Old English*), used as a masculine first name.

Hadrian a masculine variant form of ADRIAN.

Hafwen a feminine first name meaning 'bright summer', from *haf*, 'summer', and *wen*, 'fair' (*Welsh*).

Hagan or **Hagan** a masculine first name meaning 'young HUGH' (*Irish Gaelic*) or 'thorn bush' or 'thorn fence' (*Germanic*).

Hagar a feminine first name meaning 'flight' (*Hebrew*). In the Old Testament Hagar was the secondary wife of Abraham and the mother of his son Ishmael.

Hagley a surname, meaning 'haw wood or clearing' (*Old English*), used as a masculine first name.

Haidee (1) a feminine first name meaning 'modest', 'honoured' (*Greek*). (2) a variant form of HEIDI.

Haig a surname, meaning 'one who lives in an enclosure' (*Old English*), used as a masculine first name.

Hako a masculine diminutive form of HAKON.

Hakon a masculine first name meaning 'from the exalted race' (*Old Norse*). A variant form is Haakon. A diminutive form is Hako.

Hal a masculine diminutive form of HALBERT, HENRY. In his plays *King Henry IV, Parts 1* and *2*, William Shakespeare (1564–1616) has Sir John Falstaff invariably addressing Prince Henry as Hal.

Halbert a masculine first name meaning 'brilliant hero' (*Old English*). A diminutive form is Hal.

Halcyon

Halcyon or **Halcyone** feminine variant forms of ALCYONE.

Haldan or **Haldane** or **Halden** or **Haldin** a surname, meaning 'half Dane', used as a feminine first name (*Old English*).

Hale a surname, meaning 'from the hall' (*Old English*), used as a masculine first name.

Haley a masculine or feminine variant form of HAYLEY.

Halford a surname, meaning 'from a ford in a hollow' (*Old English*), used as a masculine first name.

Haliwell a masculine variant form of HALLIWELL.

Hall a surname, meaning 'one who lives at a manor house' (*Old English*), used as a masculine first name.

Hallam a surname, meaning 'at the hollow' (*Old English*), or a place name, meaning 'at the rocky place' (*Old Norse*), used as a masculine first name.

Halliwell a surname, meaning 'one who lives by the holy well' (*Old English*), used as a masculine first name. A variant form is Haliwell.

Halstead or **Halsted** a surname, meaning 'from the stronghold' (*Old English*), used as a masculine first name.

Halton a surname, meaning 'from the lookout hill' (*Old English*), used as a masculine first name.

Ham a masculine diminutive form of ABRAHAM.

Hamar a masculine first name meaning 'strong man' (*Old Norse*).

Hamilton a surname, meaning 'farm in broken country' (*Old English*), used as a masculine first name.

Hamish an anglicised masculine form of Gaelic Seumas, JAMES, in its vocative form, A Seamuis.

Hamlet or **Hamlett** a surname, meaning 'little home' (*Germanic*), used as a masculine first name. William Shakespeare (1564–1616) used it as the name of the main protagonist of *Hamlet, Prince of Denmark*.

Hammond a surname, meaning 'belonging to Hamon' (*Old English*), used as a masculine first name.

Hamon a masculine first name meaning 'great protection' (*Old English*).

Hamza or **Hamzah** a masculine first name meaning 'lion' (*Arabic*).

Hana a feminine first name meaning 'happiness' (*Arabic*).

Hanford a surname, meaning 'rocky ford' or 'ford with cocks' (*Old English*), used as a masculine first name.

Hani a masculine first name meaning 'joyful' (*Arabic*).

Hank a masculine diminutive form of HENRY.

Hanley a surname, meaning 'from the high meadow or hill' (*Old English*), used as a masculine first name.

Hannah a feminine first name meaning 'grace' (*Hebrew*). In the Old Testament Hannah was a childless wife of Elkanah who prayed for a son. God answered her prayers and she gave birth to Samuel. A variant form is ANN. A diminutive form is Nana.

Hannibal a masculine first name meaning 'grace of Baal' (*Punic*). Hannibal (247–182 BC) was a Carthaginian general in the Second Punic War. The American writer Thomas Harris used the name for a serial killer, Hannibal Lecter, in a series of novels.

Hans a masculine diminutive form of JOHANN.

Hansel a masculine first name meaning 'gift from God' (*Scandinavian*).

Happy an English adjective, meaning 'feeling, showing or expressing joy', now used as a feminine first name (*Old English*).

Harald a masculine variant form of HAROLD. A diminutive form is Harry.

Haralda a feminine form of HAROLD.

Harbert a masculine variant form of HERBERT.

Harcourt a surname, meaning 'from a fortified court' (*Old French*), or 'falconer's cottage' (*Old English*), used as a masculine first name.

Harden a surname, meaning 'the valley of the hare' (*Old English*), used as a masculine first name.

Hardey or **Hardie** masculine variant forms of HARDY.

Harding a surname, meaning 'brave warrior' (*Old English*), used as a masculine first name.

Hardy a surname, meaning 'bold and daring' (*Germanic*), used as a masculine first name. Variant forms are Hardey, Hardie.

Harford a surname, meaning 'stags' ford' (*Old English*), used as a masculine first name.

Hargrave or **Hargreave** or **Hargreaves** a surname, meaning 'from the hare grove' (*Old English*), used as a masculine first name.

Hari a masculine first name meaning 'yellowish brown' (*Sanskrit*).

Harlan or **Harland** a surname, meaning 'rocky land' (*Old English*), used as a masculine first name.

Harley a surname, meaning 'from the hare meadow or hill' (*Old English*), used as a masculine first name.

Harlow a place name and surname, meaning 'fortified hill' (*Old English*), used as a masculine first name.

Harmony the word for the quality of concord used as a feminine first name.

Harold a masculine first name meaning 'a champion; general of an army' (*Old English*). A variant form is Harald. A diminutive form is Harry.

Haroun an Arabic form of AARON.

Harper a surname, meaning 'harp player or maker' (*Old English*), used as a masculine first name.

Harriet or **Harriot** feminine forms of HARRY. Diminutive forms are Hattie, Hatty.

Harris or **Harrison** a surname, meaning 'son of HAROLD or HARRY', used as a first name (*Old English*). Harrison Ford is an American film actor.

Harry a masculine diminutive form of HARALD, HAROLD, HENRY, also used independently.

Harsha a feminine first name meaning 'happiness' (*Sanskrit*).

Hart a surname, meaning 'hart deer' (*Old English*), used as a masculine first name.

Hartford a place name and surname, meaning 'ford of the deer, or army ford' (*Old English*), used as a masculine first name. A variant form is Hertford.

Hartley a surname, meaning 'clearing with stags' (*Old English*), used as a masculine first name.

Hartmann or **Hartman** a masculine first name meaning 'strong and brave' (*Germanic*).

Hartwell a surname, meaning 'stags' stream' (*Old English*), used as a masculine first name.

Harun an Arabic form of AARON.

Harvey or **Harvie** a surname, meaning 'battle-worthy' (*Breton Gaelic*), used as a masculine first name. Harvey Keitel is an American film actor best known for the film *Reservoir Dogs*. A variant form is Hervey and the French form is Hervé.

Hasan a masculine first name meaning 'fair' or 'good' (*Arabic*). Variant forms are Hassan, Hussain, Hussein.

Haslett a masculine variant form of HAZLETT.

Hassan a masculine variant form of HASAN.

Hastings a place name and surname, meaning 'territory of the violent ones' (*Old English*), used as a masculine first name.

Hattie or **Hatty** a feminine diminutive form of HARRIET.

Havelock a surname, meaning 'sea battle' (*Old Norse*), used as a masculine first name.

Hawley a surname, meaning 'from a hedged meadow' (*Old English*), used as a masculine first name.

Hayden or **Haydon** a surname, meaning 'heather hill or hay hill' (*Old English*), used as a masculine first name.

Hayley a surname, meaning 'hay clearing' (*Old English*), used as a masculine or feminine first name. A variant form is Haley.

Hayward a surname, meaning 'supervisor of enclosures' (*Old English*), used as a masculine first name. A variant form is Heyward.

Haywood a surname, meaning 'fenced forest' (*Old English*), used as a masculine first name. A variant form is Heywood.

Hazel the name of the tree, from *haesel* (*Old English*) used as a feminine first name. The hazel tree is important in Celtic lore and tradition. Its twigs are used as divining rods and it was considered a fairy tree in Ireland and Wales.

Hazlett or **Hazlitt** a surname, meaning 'hazel tree' (*Old English*), used as a masculine first name. A variant form is Haslett.

Heath a surname, meaning 'heathland' (*Old English*), used as a masculine first name.

Heathcliff or **Heathcliffe** a masculine first name meaning 'dweller by the heather cliff' (*Old English*).

Heather the name of a purple or white-flowered plant of the heath family used as a feminine first name. It was first used as a girl's name in the nineteenth century, at a time when plant and flower names were very much in vogue.

Hebe a feminine first name meaning 'young' (*Greek*). In Greek mythology, Hebe was the daughter of Zeus and goddess of youth and spring.

Hector a masculine first name meaning 'holding fast' (*Greek*). In Greek mythology Hector was the eldest son of King Priam of Troy and his wife, Hecuba, and the bravest of the Trojans whose forces he commanded. His exploits are celebrated in the Greek epic poem the *Iliad*, attributed to Homer. He was slain in the Trojan War by the Greek hero Achilles.

Hedda a feminine first name meaning 'war, strife' (*Germanic*).

Hedvig or **Hedwig** a feminine first name meaning 'strife' (*Germanic*).

Hefin a masculine first name meaning 'summery' (*Welsh*).

Heidi a feminine diminutive of ADELHEID. A variant form is Haidee.

Heilyn (pronounced *hye-lin*) a masculine first name meaning 'cup-bearer' (*Welsh*).

Heinrich the German masculine form of HENRY. Diminutive forms are Heinz, Heinze.

Heinz or **Heinze** masculine diminutive forms of HEINRICH.

Helen or **Helena** a feminine first name meaning 'bright one' (*Greek*). In Greek mythology, Helen was the most beuatiful woman of her age and the wife of Menelaus. She eloped to Troy with Paris, an event that brought about the Trojan War. Helen Mirren is a well-known English actress. William Shakespeare (1564–1616) used the form Helena for heroines in two of his plays, *A Midsummer Night's Dream* and *All's Well that Ends Well*. Helena Kennedy is a prominent British barrister and a life peer. The Irish and Scottish Gaelic form is Eilidah. Diminutive forms are Lena, Nell.

Helene the German feminine form of HELEN.

Hélène the French feminine form of HELEN.

Helga a feminine first name meaning 'healthy, happy, holy' (*Old Norse*).

Helge masculine form of HELGA.

Helma a feminine first name meaning 'protection' (*Germanic*).

Héloïse a French feminine variant form of ÉLOISE. Héloïse (c.1101–1164) was the pupil, mistress and wife of the French philosopher and theologian Peter Abelard.

Hema a feminine first name meaning 'golden' (*Sanskrit*).

Hendrik the Dutch masculine form of HENRY.

Henri the French masculine form of HENRY.

Henrietta the feminine form of HENRY. Diminutive forms are Hettie, Hetty, Netta, Nettie.

Henriette the French feminine form of HENRIETTA.

Henry a masculine first name meaning 'the head or chief of a house '(*Germanic*). Diminutive forms are Harry, Hal, Hank.

Hephzibah a feminine first name meaning 'my delight is in her' (*Hebrew*). A diminutive form is Hepsy.

Hepsy a feminine diminutive form of HEPHZIBAH.

Hera a feminine first name meaning 'queen of heaven' (*Greek*). In Greek mythology, Hera was the sister and wife of Zeus. Her counterpart in Roman mythology is JUNO.

Herakles the Greek counterpart of HERCULES.

Herb a masculine diminutive form of HERBERT.

Herbert a masculine first name meaning 'army bright' (*Old English*). A variant form is Harbert. Diminutive forms are Herb, Herbie.

Herbie a masculine diminutive form of HERBERT.

Hercule the French masculine form of HERCULES.

Hercules a masculine first name meaning 'glory of HERA' (the Latin form of the name of Herakles, the Greek hero, son of Zeus and stepson of HERA).

Hergest a Welsh masculine first name from the Radnor place name. *The Red Book of Hergest* is an early (sixth century) source of Welsh verse.

Heribert the German masculine form of HERBERT.

Herman a masculine first name meaning 'warrior' (*Germanic*).

Hermann the German masculine form of HERMAN.

Hermes a masculine name from that of a god in Greek mythology, the messenger of the gods, with winged feet. His counterpart in Roman mythology is MERCURY.

Hermia a feminine first name probably invented by William Shakespeare (1564–1616) who used the name for one of the heroines of his comedy *A Midsummer Night's Dream*.

Hermione a feminine first name derived from that of HERMES. In Greek mythology Hermione was the daughter of the Greek Menelaus and his wife Helen who was nine years old when Helen went to Troy with Paris. William Shakespeare (1564–1616) used the name for the queen of Sicily in his play *The Winter's Tale*. Hermione Gingold (1897–1987) was an English actress.

Hermosa a feminine first name meaning 'beautiful' (*Spanish*).

Hernando a Spanish masculine form of FERDINAND.

Hero a feminine first name of unknown meaning, possibly connected with the name of the Greek goddess Hera and not connected to the noun 'hero'. In Greek mythology Hero was a priestess of Aphrodite who killed herself when her lover, Leander, was drowned swimming the Hellespont to visit her. William Shakespeare (1564–1616) used the name for the wronged cousin of Beatrice in his comedy *Much Ado About Nothing*.

Herrick a surname, meaning 'powerful army' (*Old Norse*), used as a masculine first name.

Herta a feminine first name meaning 'of the earth' (*Old English*). A variant form is Hertha.

Hertford a masculine variant form of HARTFORD.

Hertha a feminine variant form of HERTA.

Hervé a French masculine form of HARVEY.

Hervey a masculine variant form of HARVEY.

Hesketh a surname, meaning 'horse track' (*Old Norse*), used as a masculine first name.

Hester or **Hesther** feminine variant forms of ESTHER.

Hestia a feminine first name meaning 'hearth' (*Greek*). In Greek mythology Hestia was the goddess of family peace.

Hettie or **Hetty** feminine diminutive forms of HENRIETTA.

Heulwen a feminine first name meaning 'sunshine' (*Welsh*).

Hew a Welsh masculine form of HUGH.

Hewett or **Hewit** a surname, meaning 'little HUGH or cleared place' (*Old English*), used as a masculine first name.

Heyward a masculine variant form of HAYWARD.

Heywood a masculine variant form of HAYWOOD.

Hezekiah a masculine first name meaning 'strength of the Lord' (*Hebrew*). In the Old Testament was a king of Judah who undertook reforms.

Hi a masculine diminutive form of HIRAM, HYRAM.

Hibernia the Latin name for Ireland used as a feminine first name.

Hibiscus the marshmallow, the Greek/Latin) name of a brightly flowering plant used as a feminine first name.

Hieronymus the Latin and German masculine forms of JEROME. Hieronymus Bosch (*c*.1450–1516) was a Dutch painter noted for his macabre allegorical paintings of Biblical subjects.

Hilaire the French masculine form of HILARY.

Hilario the Spanish masculine form of HILARY.

Hilary now principally a feminine first name meaning 'cheerful; merry' (*Latin*) but formerly used as a masculine first name. St Hilary of Arles (315–367) was one of the Doctors of the Roman Catholic Church. A variant form is Hillary.

Hilda a feminine first name meaning 'battle maid' (*Germanic*). St Hilda (614–680) was an English nun who founded the abbey of Whitby of which she became the abbess. A variant form is Hylda.

Hildebrand a masculine first name meaning 'battle sword' (*Germanic*).

Hildegard or **Hildegarde** a feminine first name meaning 'strong in battle' (*Germanic*). St Hildegard of Bingen was a composer, poet and mystic.

Hillary a variant form of HILARY.

Hilton a surname, meaning 'from the hill farm' (*Old English*), used as a masculine first name. A variant form is Hylton.

Hippolyta the feminine form of HIPPOLYTUS. In Greek mythology Hippolyta was an alternative name for the queen of the Amazons. William Shakespeare (1564–1616) used the names Theseus and Hippolyta for the Duke and Duchess of Athens in his comedy *A Midsummer Night's Dream*.

Hippolyte the French masculine form of HIPPOLYTUS.

Hippolytus a masculine first name meaning 'allowing horses loose' (*Greek*). In Greek mythology Hippolytus was a son of Theseus and Hippolyta whose stepmother, Phaedra, fell in love with him and made accusations about him to revenge herself for his indifference. After Theseus arranged for Hippolytus's death, Phaedra killed herself. The story forms the basis of the tragedy *Phèdre* (1677) by the French dramatist Jean Racine (1639–99).

Hiram a masculine first name meaning 'brother of the exalted one' (*Hebrew*). In the Old Testament Hiram was a king of Tyre (970–936 BC) who was an ally of David and Solomon. A variant form is Hyram. A diminutive form is Hi.

Hobart a masculine variant form of HUBERT.

Hogan a masculine first name meaning 'youthful' (*Irish Gaelic*).

Holbert or **Holbird** masculine variant forms of HULBERT.

Holbrook a surname, meaning 'brook in the valley', used as a masculine hero of the Napoleonic Wars, Captain Horatio Hornblower, in a series of novels.

Hortensia or **Hortense** a feminine first name meaning 'of the garden' (*Latin*).

Hortensio the masculine form of Hortensia. The name was used by William Shakespeare (1564–1616) for a suitor of BIANCA in *The Taming of the Shrew*.

Horton a surname, meaning 'muddy place' (*Old English*), used as a masculine first name.

Hosea a masculine first name meaning 'salvation' (*Hebrew*). In the Old

Testament it was the name of the Hebrew prophet who wrote the Book of Hosea.

Houghton a surname, meaning 'place in an enclosure' (*Old English*), used as a masculine first name. A variant form is HUTTON.

Houston or **Houstun** a surname, meaning 'HUGH's place' (*Old English*), used as a masculine first name.

Howard a surname, meaning 'mind strong' (*Germanic*), used as a masculine first name. Howard Keel is an American singer and film actor. A diminutive form is Howie.

Howe a surname, meaning 'high one (*Germanic*) or hill (*Old English*) used as a masculine first name.

Howel or **Howell** anglicised masculine forms of HYWEL.

Howie a masculine diminutive form of HOWARD.

Hubert a masculine first name meaning 'mind bright' (*Germanic*). A variant surname form is Hobart. A diminutive form is Bert.

Huberta the feminine form of HUBERT.

Hudson a surname, meaning 'son of little HUGH' (*Old English*), used as a masculine first name.

Hugh (1) a masculine first name meaning 'mind; spirit; soul' (*Danish*). (2) an anglicised form of AED.

Hughina a Scottish feminine first name, a typically Highland name, for a daughter of HUGH.

Hugo the Latin, German, and Spanish masculine form of HUGH.

Hugues the French masculine form of HUGH.

Hulbert or **Hulburd** or **Hulburt** a surname, meaning 'brilliant, gracious' (*Germanic*), used as a masculine first name. Variant forms are Holbert, Holbird.

Hulda or **Huldah** a feminine first name meaning 'weasel' (*Hebrew*). In the Old Testament Huldah was a prophetess who interpreted a message from God for Josiah.

Humbert a masculine first name meaning 'bright warrior' (*Germanic*).

Hump or **Humph** masculine diminutive forms of HUMPHREY.

Humphrey or **Humphry** a masculine first name meaning 'giant peace' (*Old English*). Humphrey Lyttleton is an English jazz musician and radio show host. Diminutive forms are Hump, Humph.

Hunt or **Hunter** a surname, meaning 'hunter' (*Old English*), used as a masculine first name.

Huntingdon a place name and surname, meaning 'hunter's hill' (*Old English*), used as a masculine first name.

Huntington a surname, meaning 'hunter's farm' (*Old English*), used as a masculine first name.

Huntley or **Huntly** a surname, meaning 'hunter's meadow' (*Old English*), used as a masculine first name.

Hurley a masculine first name meaning 'sea tide' (*Gaelic*).

Hurst a surname, meaning 'wooded hill' (*Old English*), used as a masculine first name.

Hussain or **Hussein** a masculine variant form of HASAN.

Hutton a masculine variant form of HOUGHTON.

Huw (pronounced *hyoo*) a Welsh masculine form of HUGH.

Huxley a surname, meaning 'HUGH's meadow' (*Old English*), used as a masculine first name.

Hy a masculine diminutive form of HYAM.

Hyacinth the name of the flower adapted from the name of the hero of Greek mythology whose blood after his killing by Apollo caused a flower to spring up, used as a feminine first name.

Hyam a masculine first name meaning 'man of life' (*Hebrew*). A variant form is Hyman. Diminutive forms are Hi, Hy.

Hyde a surname, meaning 'a hide (a measurement unit) of land' (*Old English*), used as a masculine first name.

Hylda a feminine variant form of HILDA.

Hylton a masculine variant form of HILTON.

Hyman a masculine variant form of HYAM.

Hypatia a feminine first name meaning 'highest' (*Greek*).

Hyram a masculine variant form of HIRAM. Diminutive forms are Hi, Hy.

Hywel (pronounced *how-el*) a masculine first name meaning 'outstanding, eminent' (*Welsh*). Hywel Dda, 'the good', was a tenth-century Welsh king, famous for setting up a system of laws. Anglicised forms are Howel, Howell.

I

Iachimo an Italian masculine form of JAMES. William Shakespeare (1564–1616) used the name for one of the characters in his play *Cymbeline*.

Iacovo an Italian masculine form of JACOB.

Iago a Welsh masculine form of JAMES, from Latin Jacobus. William Shakespeare (1564–1616) used the name for Othello's duplicitous lieutenant in his tragedy *Othello*.

Iain (pronounced *ee-yann*) the Scottish Gaelic masculine form of JOHN. The anglicised version Ian is also very popular.

Ian an anglicised masculine form of IAIN. A variant form is Ion.

Ianthe a feminine first name meaning 'violet flower' (*Greek*). The English poet Walter Savage Landor (1775–1864) used it as a poetic name for his early sweetheart, Sophia Jane Swift, thus setting a fashion that was followed by other poets, including Lord Byron (1788–1824) and Percy Bysshe Shelley (1792–1822).

Ianto a Welsh masculine diminutive form of IFAN.

Iarlaith (pronounced *yarr-la*) a masculine first name from *iarl*, 'knight' (*Irish Gaelic*). It was the name of a fifth-century Irish saint. The anglicised form is Jarlath.

Iarnan (pronounced *yarr-nan*) a masculine first name meaning 'iron man', from *iarann*, 'iron' (*Irish/Scottish Gaelic*), indicating strength and fixity of purpose. St Iarnan was an uncle of St Columba. His name is preserved in Killearnan, on the Black Isle in Scotland. An anglicised form is Ernan.

Ibby a feminine diminutive form of ISABEL.

Ibrahim the Arabic masculine form of ABRAHAM.

Ichabod a masculine first name meaning 'inglorious' (*Hebrew*). In the Old Testament Ichabod was the posthumous son of Phinehas and grandson of Eli.

Ida (1) a feminine first name meaning 'god-like' (*Germanic*). (2) the anglicised feminine form of IDE.

Idabell a feminine first name meaning 'god-like and fair'.

Ide (pronounced *ee-ja*) a feminine first name from *íde*, 'thirst' (*Old Irish Gaelic*), meaning in this case thirst for virtue and knowledge. It was was the name of St Ide. It is anglicised to Ida, though in this form it can also derive from other sources including Greek.

Idonia a feminine first name meaning 'sufficient' (*Latin*).

Idony or **Idonie** a feminine first name from Norse mythology, the name of the keeper of the golden apples of youth.

Idris a masculine first name meaning 'fiery lord' (*Welsh*). Idris Gawr was a legendary figure from around the seventh century, who has given his name to Cader Idris (Idris's Fort), a mountain in Merioneth.

Idwal a masculine first name meaning 'lord of the ramparts', from *iud*, 'lord' (*Welsh*).

Iestyn the Welsh masculine form of JUSTIN.

Ieuan a Welsh masculine form of JOHN. A variant form is Iwan.

Ifan (pronounced *ee-fan*) a Welsh masculine form of John.

Ifor a Welsh masculine form of IVOR.

Igerna a feminine variant form of IGRAINE.

Ignace the French masculine form of IGNATIUS.

Ignacio a Spanish masculine form of IGNATIUS.

Ignatia feminine form of IGNATIUS.

Ignatius a masculine first name, from *ignis*, 'fire' (*Greek*). St Ignatius of Antioch (died *c*.110), on his way to martyrdom in Rome, wrote seven letters that cast light on the early Christian church. St Ignatius of Loyola (1491–1556) was the Spanish founder of the Society of Jesus (Jesuits).

Ignatz or **Ignaz** German masculine forms of IGNATIUS.

Ignazio the Italian masculine form of IGNATIUS.

Igor the Russian masculine form of IVOR.

Igraine a Cornish feminine first name. This was the name of the mother of King ARTHUR. Wife of Gorlois, duke of Cornwall, she conceived Arthur by UTHER Pendragon, whom she married after Gorlois's death in battle. Variants are Igerna, Ygraine, Yguerne. *See* EIGRA.

Ike a masculine diminutive form of ISAAC.

Ilario the Italian masculine form of HILARY.

Ilka a feminine diminutive form of HELEN.

Illtyd (pronounced *il-tood*) a masculine first name from *iud*, 'lord', probably meaning 'lord of all' (*Welsh*) (*see* DONALD). He was a Welsh saint of the fifth century whose name is preserved in Llantwit Major, in Glamorgan.

Ilona a Hungarian feminine form of HELEN. A diminutive form is Ilka.

Ilse a feminine diminutive form of ELISABETH.

Imelda an Italian feminine form of a Germanic name meaning 'universal battle'. Imelda Staunton is an English actress.

Immanuel a masculine variant form of EMMANUEL. A diminutive form is Manny.

Imogen (pronounced *immo-genn*) a feminine first name from *innogen*, 'girl, maiden' (*Celtic*), which probably has the same source as Gaelic *nighean*, 'daughter, girl'. It was used by William Shakespeare (1564–1616) for one of his characters in *Cymbeline* and misspelled by him or his printer. Imogen Stubbs is an English actress.

Imperial a feminine first name meaning 'relating to an emperor' (*Latin*).

Imran a masculine first name meaning 'the family of Imran' (*Arabic*). Imran Khan is a Pakistani cricketer and politician.

Ina a feminine diminutive form of names ending in *-ina*, e.g. GEORGINA, WILHELMINA.

Inderjit a masculine first name meaning 'conqueror of Indra' (*Sanskrit*).

India the name of the South Asian country used as a first name.

Indra a masculine first name of uncertain meaning and that of a Hindu god.

Indulf an ancient Pictish masculine first name and that of more than one Pictish king.

Ineda (pronounced *inn-ida*) a Cornish feminine first name and that of a Celtic saint, possibly confused with St ENDA. The derivation seems to be the same as that of Enda.

Inés or **Inez** Spanish feminine forms of AGNES.

Inga a feminine diminutive form of INGEBORG, INGRID.

Inge (1) a masculine diminutive form of INGEMAR. (2) a feminine diminutive form of INGEBORG, INGRID.

Ingeborg a feminine first name meaning 'fortification of Ing', the god of fertility (Frey) (*Old Norse*). Diminutive forms are Inga, Inge.

Ingemar a masculine first name meaning 'famous son of Ing' (*Old Norse*). A variant form is Ingmar. A diminutive form is Inge.

Inger a feminine variant form of INGRID.

Ingmar a masculine variant form of INGEMAR. Ingmar Bergman is a Swedish film and stage director.

Iphigenia

Ingram a surname, meaning 'raven angel' (*Germanic*) or 'river meadow' (*Old English*), used as a masculine first name.

Ingrid a feminine first name meaning 'maiden of Ing', the god of fertility (Frey) (*Old Norse*). Ingrid Bergman (1915–82) was a famous Swedish film star. A variant form is Inger. A diminutive form is Inga, Inge.

Inigo a Spanish masculine form of IGNATIUS, now used as an English-language form. Inigo Jones (1573–1862) was an English architect and designer who introduced Palladianism into England.

Innes or **Inness** a surname, meaning 'island or meadow-dweller', from Gaelic *inis*, 'island, water-meadow' (*Scottish Gaelic*), occasionally used as a masculine or feminine first name.

Innogen *see* IMOGEN.

Ioan one of the Welsh masculine forms of JOHN.

Iola a feminine variant form of IOLE.

Iolanthe a feminine first name meaning 'violet flower' (*Greek*). The name was used by Sir William S. Gilbert (1836–1911) and Sir Arthur Sullivan (1842–1900) for the name of a fairy who married a mortal in their comic opera satirising the House of Lords and Courts of Chancery.

Iole a feminine first name meaning 'violet' (*Greek*). In Greek mythology Iole was a princess who was promised by her father to anyone who could defeat him in an archery competition. When he was defeated by Hercules, he refused to honour his promise. A variant form is Iola.

Iolo or **Iolyn** a Welsh masculine diminutive form of IORWERTH. Iolo Goch, the bard, was an associate of Owain Glyndwr. Another bard, Iolo Morgannwg (1747–1826) created the *Gorsedd of Bards*.

Ion (1) a masculine variant form of Ian. (2) in Greek mythology the name of the founder of the Ionian race and the eponymous subject of drama by Euripides (418 BC).

Iona a feminine first name from that of the name of the Scottish Hebridean island. It is actually a medieval misreading of the original name, Ioua, perhaps meaning 'island of yews'. Iona Brown is a noted English violinist and conductor.

Ione a feminine first name meaning 'a violet' (*Greek*).

Iorweth a masculine first name meaning 'worthy lord' (*Welsh*). An alternative, usually found as a surname, is Yorath. A diminutive form is IOLO or Iolyn.

Iphigenia a feminine first name meaning 'strong' (*Greek*). In Greek mythology Iphigenia was the daughter of Agamemnon and Clytemnestra who was taken by her father to be sacrificed to the goddess Artemis who saved her and made her a priestess. The story has inspired tragedies by the Greek dramatist Euripides (*c*.480–406 BC), the French dramatist Jean Racine (1639–99) and the German dramatist Johann Wolfgang von Goethe (1749–1832).

Ira a masculine first name meaning 'watchful' (*Hebrew*). In the Old Testament Ira was one of King David's leading officers.

Irene a feminine first name meaning 'peace' (*Greek*). Irene (752–803) was the wife of the Byzantine emperor Leo IV and ruled as guardian of her son, Constantine VI, and later co-emperor with him. She became a saint of the Greek Orthodox Church. A diminutive form is Renie.

Iris a feminine first name meaning 'rainbow' (*Greek*). In Greek mythology Iris was the swift golden-winged messenger of the gods and the personification of the rainbow. Dame Iris Murdoch (1919–99) was an English novelist and philosopher.

Irma a feminine first name meaning 'noble one' (*Germanic*).

Irvine or **Irving** a surname, meaning 'fresh or green river' (*Celtic*), used as a masculine first name.

Irwin a surname, meaning 'friend of boars' (*Old English*), used as a masculine first name. Irwin Shaw (1913–84) was a prolific American playwright and novelist.

Isa (1) a feminine diminutive form of ISABEL. (2) the Arabic name for Jesus.

Isaac a masculine first name meaning 'laughter' (*Hebrew*). In the Old Testament was the only son of Abraham and Sarah and father of Esau and Jacob who became second of the patriarchs of Israel. A variant form is IZAAK. A diminutive form is Ike.

Isabel or **Isabella** Spanish feminine forms of ELIZABETH, now used as separate English-language names. William Shakespeare (1564–1616) used the form Isabella for the heroine of his play *Measure for Measure*. A variant form is Isobel. Diminutive forms are Ibby, Isa, Izzie, Izzy, Tib, Tibbie.

Isabelle the French feminine form of ISABEL.

Isadora a feminine variant form of ISIDORA. Isadora Duncan (1878–1927) was an innovative American dancer and choreographer.

Isaiah a masculine first name meaning 'salvation of Jehovah' (*Hebrew*).

In the Old Testament he was the Hebrew prophet after whom the Book of Isaiah is named.

Iseabail (pronounced *ish-bel*) the Scottish Gaelic feminine form of ISABEL. It is anglicised as Ishbell.

Iseabeal (pronounced *eesh-aval*) the Irish Gaelic feminine form of Isabel, itself a Spanish form of Elizabeth.

Iseult a feminine first name meaning 'fair to look on' (*Cornish/Welsh*). There are two famous Iseults in the Arthurian legends, Iseult of Ireland, the true lover of TRISTAN, and Iseult 'of the White Hands' of Brittany, who deceives him into thinking she is the other. Variant forms are ISOLDE, Isoult, Yseult, Essyllt.

Isham a surname, meaning 'home on the water' (*Old English*), used as a masculine first name.

Ishbel the anglicised feminine form of ISEABAIL.

Ishmael the name in the Old Testament of the first-born son of Abraham, borne by Hagar, his wife Sarah's Egyptian slave whom Sarah gave to him as she thought she was too old to give birth. When Sarah did give birth to Isaac, Hagar and Ishmael were driven into the desert but were saved by God who miraculously created a spring. Ishmael became a notable warrior and the father of twelve sons. The Arabic form is ISMAIL.

Isidor the German masculine form of ISIDORE.

Isidora feminine form of ISIDORE. A variant form is ISADORA.

Isidore a masculine first name meaning 'gift of Isis' (*Greek*). St Isidore of Seville (*c*.560–636) was a Spanish theologian and Father of the Church.

Isidoro an Italian masculine form of ISIDORE.

Isidro Spanish masculine forms of ISIDORE.

Isla (pronounced *eye-la*) a Scottish river name from Perthshire, in use as a feminine first name since the nineteenth century.

Islay (pronounced *eye-la*) the name of an island of the Inner Hebrides. As a Scottish masculine first name it is almost exclusively associated with Clan Campbell.

Ismail the Arabic masculine form of ISHMAEL, son of IBRAHIM. Ismail was a major Muslim prophet.

Isobel a feminine variant form of ISABEL.

Isola a feminine first name meaning 'isolated, alone' (*Latin*).

Isolde or **Isolda** or **Isold** or **Isoult** a feminine variant form of ISEULT. The

German composer Richard Wagner (1813–83) used the form Isolde for the heroine of this opera *Tristan und Isolde*.

Israel a masculine first name meaning 'a soldier of God ruling with the Lord' (*Hebrew*). In the Old Testament it was the name given to Jacob after he wrestled with the angel of the Lord, thus becoming the name given to the Jewish nation descended from him. A diminutive form is Izzy.

Istvan the Hungarian masculine form of STEPHEN.

Ita or **Ite** a feminine first name meaning 'thirst (for truth)' (*Irish Gaelic*).

Ivan the Russian masculine form of JOHN. It was the name of several tsars.

Ivana a feminine form of IVAN.

Ivar a Scottish masculine variant form of IVOR.

Ives a surname, meaning 'son of Ive (yew) (*Germanic*)', used as a masculine first name. Yves St Laurent is a French couturier who popularised the wearing of trousers for women.

Ivo the Old French and Welsh masculine form of YVES. St Ivo of Chartres (1040–1116) was bishop of Chartres.

Ivor a masculine first name from an Old Norse personal name, Ivar, possibly meaning 'yew army' (Old Norse) adopted into Gaelic as Iomhar. A variant Scottish form is Ivar. A Welsh form is Ifor.

Ivy the name of the plant used as a feminine first name (*English*). Dame Ivy Compton-Burnett (1884–1969) was an English novelist.

Iwan a masculine variant form of IEUAN.

Izaak a masculine variant form of ISAAC.

Izzie or **Izzy** masculine and feminine diminutive forms of ISABEL, ISRAEL.

J

Jabal a masculine first name meaning 'guide' (*Hebrew*). In the Old Testament he was a descendant of CAIN.

Jabez a masculine first name meaning 'causing pain' (*Hebrew*).

Jacinta the Spanish feminine form of HYACINTH.

Jacinth a feminine variant form of HYACINTH.

Jack a masculine diminutive form of JOHN, now used independently. Diminutive forms are Jackie, Jacky.

Jackie or **Jacky** (1) a masculine diminutive form of JACK, JOHN. (2) a feminine diminutive form of JACQUELINE.

Jackson a surname, meaning 'son of Jack', used as a masculine first name. Jackson Pollock (1912–56) was an American abstract expressionist painter.

Jacob a masculine first name meaning 'supplanter' (*Hebrew*). In the Old Testament Jacob was the son of Isaac and Rebecca and ancestor of the Israelites. A diminutive form is Jake. *See also* ISRAEL, JAQUES.

Jacoba the feminine form of JACOB.

Jacobo the Spanish masculine form of JACOB.

Jacqueline a feminine diminutive form of JACQUES. Jacqueline du Pre (1945–87) was an English cellist whose career was brought to an end by mutiple sclerosis. A variant form is Jaqueline. A diminutive form is Jackie.

Jacques the French masculine form of JACOB, JAMES.

Jacquetta or **Jacquenetta** a feminine form of JAMES. William Shakespeare (1564–1616) used Jacquenetta for a character in *Love's Labour's Lost*. Jacquetta Hawkes (1910–96) was an eminent English archaeologist.

Jade the name of the light-green semiprecious stone used as a feminine first name.

Jael a feminine first name meaning 'wild she-goat' (*Hebrew*). In the Old Testament Jael was the woman who killed the Canaanite army chief Sisera when he hid in her tent.

Jagger a surname, meaning 'a carter' (*Middle English*), used as a masculine first name.

Jago a Cornish masculine form of JAMES.

Jaikie a Scottish masculine diminutive form of JAMES.

Jaime (1) a Spanish masculine form of JAMES. (2) a feminine variant form of JAMIE.

Jairus a masculine first name meaning 'he will enlighten' (*Hebrew*). In the New Testament Jairus was an officer of the synagogue whose daughter was resurrected by Jesus.

Jake a masculine diminutive form of JACOB, now used independently.

Jakob the German masculine form of JACOB, JAMES.

Jalal a masculine first name meaning 'glory' (*Arabic*).

Jalil a masculine first name meaning 'honoured' (*Arabic*).

Jalila the feminine form of JALAL, JALIL.

Jamal a masculine or feminine first name meaning 'beauty' (*Arabic*).

James a masculine first name from Jacobus, the Latin form of JACOB. It was the name of two of Christ's apostles, James the Great, son of ZEBEDEE, who was beheaded in Palestine in AD 44, and James the Less, son of ALPHAEUS. It has strong Scottish associations, with six Scottish kings bearing the name. Diminutive forms are Jaikie, JAMIE, Jem, Jemmie, Jemmy, Jim, Jimmie and Jimmy. *See also* JAQUES.

Jamesina a Scottish feminine first name and another example of the once common practice of tacking -ina on to a father's name. A diminutive form is INA.

Jamie a Scottish diminutive form of JAMES that has taken off as a masculine or feminine name in its own right. Jamie Lee Curtis is an American actress.

Jan (1) a masculine diminutive form of JOHN. (2) the Dutch form of JOHN. (3) a feminine diminutive form of JANCIS, JANE, JANET, now used independently.

Jancis a feminine first name formed from a combination of JAN and FRANCES. A diminutive form is Jan.

Jane feminine form of JOHN. Variant forms are Janet, Janeta, Janette, Janice, Janine, Jayne, Jean, Joan. Diminutive forms are Jan, Janey, Janie.

Janet or **Janeta** or **Janette** feminine variant forms of JANE. A diminutive form is Jan.

Janey a feminine diminutive form of JANE.

Janice a feminine variant form of JANE.

Janie a feminine diminutive form of JANE.

Janine a feminine variant form of JANEY.

Japheth a masculine first name meaning 'extension' (*Hebrew*). In the Old Testament Japheth was a son of Noah and brother of Shem and Ham who, with his wife, was among the occupants of the ark.

Jaqueline a feminine variant form of JACQUELINE. A diminutive form is Jaqui.

Jaques a form of Jacob or James adopted by William Shakespeare (1564–1616) for a character in his comedy *As You Like It*.

Jaqui a feminine diminutive form of JACQUELINE.

Jared a masculine first name meaning 'servant' (*Hebrew*). In the Old Testament Jared was the father of Enoch and an ancestor of Jesus.

Jarlath the anglicised masculine form of IARLAITH.

Jarvis a surname form of GERVASE used as a masculine first name. A variant form is Jervis.

Jasmine or **Jasmin** the name of the flower used as a feminine first name. Variant forms are Jessamine, Jessamyn, Yasmin, Yasmine.

Jason a masculine first name meaning 'healer' (*Greek*). In Greek mythology, Jason was the hero who led the Argonauts and had many adventures. In the New Testament Jason was a prominent early Christian in Thessalonica.

Jasper a masculine first name meaning 'treasure master' (*Persian*). *See also* CASPAR.

Javan a masculine first name meaning 'clay' (*Hebrew*). In the Old Testament was a son of JAPHETH and grandson of NOAH whose descendants settled the earth after the flood.

Javier a Portuguese and Spanish masculine form of XAVIER.

Jay (1) a surname, meaning 'jay', the bird (*Old French*), used as a masculine first name. The American writer F. Scott Fitzgerald (1896–1940) used the name for Jay Gatsby, the main male character in his novel *The Great Gatsby* (1925). Jay Presson Allen was an American playwright, screen writer and film producer. (2) a masculine and feminine diminutive form for names beginning with J.

Jayne a feminine variant form of JANE.

Jean (1) the French masculine form of JOHN. (2) a Scottish feminine form of JOHN, from Old French Jehane. This was once one of the most frequent girls' names in Scotland. Robert Burns wrote many love poems to his wife, Jean Armour. The diminutive form is Jeanie or Jeannie.

Jeanette or **Jeannette** a feminine diminutive form of JEANNE, now used independently. Jeannette is a variant form.

Jeanie or **Jeannie** a feminine diminutive form of JEAN.

Jeanne the French feminine form of JANE. A diminutive form is Jeanette.

Jeannette a feminine variant form of JEANNETTE.

Jed a masculine diminutive form of JEDIDIAH.

Jedidiah a masculine first name meaning 'beloved of the Lord' (*Hebrew*). In the Old Testament Jedidiah was the second son of David and Bathsheba. A diminutive form is Jed.

Jeff a masculine diminutive form of JEFFREY. Jeff Bridges is an American actor and son of Lloyd Bridges.

Jefferson a surname, meaning 'son of JEFFREY or Geffrey' (*Old English*), used as a masculine first name.

Jeffrey or **Jeffery** a masculine first name meaning 'district or traveller peace' (*Germanic*). Jeffrey Jones is an American film actor. A variant form is GEOFFREY. A diminutive form is Jeff.

Jehuda feminine form of JEHUDI. A variant form is YEHUDA.

Jehudi a masculine first name meaning 'Jewish' (*Hebrew*). A variant form is YEHUDI.

Jem or **Jemmie** or **Jemmy** a masculine diminutive form of JAMES.

Jemima or **Jemimah** a feminine first name meaning 'dove' (*Hebrew*). Diminutive forms are Mima, Mina.

Jemma a feminine variant form of GEMMA.

Jen a feminine diminutive form of JENNIFER.

Jenifer a feminine variant form of JENNIFER.

Jenkin a masculine diminutive form of JOHN, literally 'little John'.

Jenna or **Jenni** or **Jennie** feminine diminutive forms of JANE, JENNIFER, now used independently. A variant form is Jenny.

Jennifer a Cornish feminine form of GWENHWYFAR. Jennifer Jason Leigh is an American film actress. A variant form is Jenifer. Diminutive forms of Jenna, Jennie, Jennie and Jenny.

Jenny a feminine diminutive form of JANE, JENNIFER, now used independently.

Jeremia feminine form of JEREMIAH.

Jeremiah or **Jeremy** a masculine first name meaning 'Jehovah has appointed' (*Hebrew*). In the Old Testament Jeremiah was a prophet who foretold the fall of Judah to Babylon. His prophecies were recorded in the Book of Jeremiah. Jeremy Irons is an English actor. A diminutive form is Jerry.

Jeremias a Spanish masculine form of JEREMY. Jeremias II (1530–95) was a theologian and patriarch of Constantinople (modern Istanbul).

Jermaine a feminine variant form of GERMAINE.

Jerome a masculine first name meaning 'holy name' (*Greek*). St Jerome (*c.*340–420) was one of the Doctors of the Roman Catholic Church. A diminutive form is Jerry.

Jérôme the French masculine form of JEROME.

Jerónimo the Spanish masculine form of JEROME.

Jerry a masculine diminutive form of GERALD, GERARD, JEREMY, JEROME, now used independently.

Jerusha a feminine first name meaning 'possessed; married' (*Hebrew*).

Jervis a masculine variant form of JARVIS.

Jess a feminine diminutive form of JESSICA, JESSIE.

Jessamine or **Jessamyn** feminine variant forms of JASMINE.

Jesse a masculine first name meaning 'wealth' (*Hebrew*). In the Old Testament Jesse was the grandson of Ruth and Boaz and father of King David.

Jessica a feminine first name meaning 'God is looking' (*Hebrew*). William Shakespeare (1564–1616) used the name for Shylock's daughter in *The Merchant of Venice*. Jessica Lange is an American film actress. A diminutive form is Jess.

Jessie or **Jessy** feminine diminutive forms of JANET, now used as names in their own right.

Jesus the Greek masculine form of Joshua. In the New Testament Jesus is the son of God who was born in Bethlehem and grew up in Nazareth and founded Christianity.

Jethro a masculine first name meaning 'superiority' (*Hebrew*). In the Old Testament Jethro was a priest who gave sanctuary to Moses and whose daughter married Moses. Jethro Tull (1674–1741) was an English agriculturalist who invented the seed drill and whose name was adopted by a twentieth-century pop group.

Jewel the name for a precious stone or valuable ornament used as a feminine first name.

Jezebel a feminine first name meaning 'domination' (*Hebrew*). In the Old Testament Jezebel was the wife of AHAB, king of Israel. She encouraged idolatry and disregarded ELIJAH and ELISHA, provoking civil strife.

Jill a feminine diminutive form of GILLIAN, JILLIAN, now used independently.

Jillian feminine form of JULIAN. Diminutive forms are Jill, Jilly.

Jilly a feminine diminutive form of JILLIAN.

Jim or **Jimmie** or **Jimmy** a masculine diminutive form of JAMES.

Jo (1) a masculine diminutive form of JOAB, JOACHIM, JOSEPH. (2) a feminine diminutive form of JOANNA, JOSEPHA, JOSEPHINE. It was used by the American writer Louisa May Alcott (1832–88) for the young tomboyish heroine, Jo March, of her popular novels *Little Women* (1869), *Good Wives* (1871), *Little Men* (1871) and *Jo's Boys* (1886).

Joab a masculine first name meaning 'Jehovah is Father' (*Hebrew*). In the Old Testament Joab was a nephew of DAVID and his military commander. He defeated the rebellion of ABSALOM, David's son and slew Absalom.

Joachim a masculine first name meaning 'God has established' (*Hebrew*). Joachim of Fiore (*c.*1132–1202) was an Italian mystic and philosopher.

Joan a feminine form of JOHN. St Joan of Arc (1412–31) was a French heroine of the Hundred Years' War. Variant forms are Joann, Joanna, Joanne. Diminutive forms are Joanie, Joni.

Joanie a feminine diminutive form of JOAN.

Joan or **Joann** or **Joanna** or **Joanne** feminine variant forms of JOAN. Joanna Trollope is a popular English novelist. Joanne Woodward is an American film actor and wife of Paul Newman. Diminutive forms are Joanie, Joni.

Joaquin the Spanish masculine form of JOACHIM.

Job a masculine first name meaning 'one persecuted' (*Hebrew*). In the Old Testament Job was a patriarch who was tested by God. The story of his suffering is recorded in the Book of Job.

JoBeth a feminine first name formed by a combination of the diminutives of JOSEPHINE and ELIZABETH. JoBeth Williams is an American film actress.

Jobina feminine form of JOB.

Jocasta the name in Greek mythology of a queen of Thebes who unknowingly married her son. Jocasta Innes is an English interior designer.

Jocelyn or **Jocelin** a masculine or feminine first name meaning 'little Goth' (*Germanic*). Diminutive forms are Jos, Joss.

Jock a masculine diminutive form of JOHN. When John was the most popular boys' name, Jock became synonymous with 'Scotsman'. It has a diminutive form of its own, Jockie or Jocky.

Jockie or **Jocky** a masculine diminutive form of JOCK.

Jodie or **Jody** feminine diminutive forms of JUDITH, now used independently. Jodie Foster is an American film actress and director.

Joe a masculine diminutive form of JOSEPH.

Joel a masculine first name meaning 'Jehovah is God' (*Hebrew*). In the Old Testament Joel was a Hebrew prophet whose oracles are recorded in the Book of Joel. Joel Coen is an American film writer and director and brother of Ethan Coen with whom he works.

Joey a masculine diminutive form of JOSEPH.

Johan a Swedish masculine form of JOHN.

Johann a German masculine form of JOHN. A diminutive form is HANS.

Johanna the Latin and German feminine form of JANE.

Johannes a Latin and German masculine form of JOHN.

John a masculine first name meaning 'Jehovah has been gracious' (*Hebrew*). In the New Testament John was the name of one of Christ's Apostles. Three of the Doctors of the Roman Catholic Church are named John – St John Chrysostom of Constantinople (*c*.329–407), St John Bonaventura (*c*.1217–1274) and St John of the Cross (1542–91) – and many popes adopted the name. John (1167–1216) was king of England (1199–1216). John of Gaunt (1340–99), 'the kingmaker', was a son of Edward III and virtual ruler during the latter years of his father's reign and during Richard II's minority. William Shakespeare (1564–1616) used the name for the double-dealing Don John in *Much Ado About Nothing*. Diminutive forms are Jack, Jackie, Jan, Jock, Johnnie, Johnny.

Johnnie or **Johnny** masculine diminutive forms of JOHN. Johnny Depp is an American film actor.

Jolyon a masculine variant form of JULIAN. This form was used by the English playwright and novelist John Galsworthy (1867–1933) for a character in his Forsyte Saga series of novels.

Jon (1) a masculine variant form of JOHN. (2) a diminutive form of JONATHAN. Jon Lovitz is an American film actor.

Jonah or **Jonas** a masculine first name meaning 'dove' (*Hebrew*). In the Old Testament was a Hebrew prophet who was shipwrecked and swallowed by a 'great fish'. The story is recorded in the Book of Jonah.

Jonathan or **Jonathon** a masculine first name meaning 'Jehovah gave' (*Hebrew*). In the Old Testament Jonathan was the eldest son of SAUL and the great friend of DAVID. A diminutive form is Jon.

Joni a feminine diminutive form of JOAN. Joni Mitchell is a Canadian singer.

Jordan a masculine first name meaning 'flowing down' (*Hebrew*) and the name of an important river in the Middle East. Diminutive forms are Jud, Judd.

Jordana feminine form of JORDAN.

Jorge the Spanish masculine form of GEORGE.

Jos (1) a masculine diminutive form of JOSEPH, JOSHUA. (2) a masculine or feminine diminutive form of JOCELYN, JOCELIN.

Joscelin a French masculine or feminine form of JOCELYN.

Josceline feminine form of JOCELYN.

José the Spanish masculine form of JOSEPH. Diminutive forms are Pepe, Pepillo, Pepito.

Josef a German masculine form of JOSEPH.

Josefa feminine form of JOSEF.

Joseph a masculine first name meaning 'God shall add' (*Hebrew*). In the Old Testament Joseph was the eleventh son of Jacob and one of the twelve patriarchs of Israel. In the New Testament Joseph was the husband of Mary, mother of Jesus. Diminutive forms are Jo, Joe, Joey, Jos.

Josepha feminine form of JOSEPH.

Josephine feminine form of JOSEPH. Diminutive forms are Jo, Josie, Phenie.

Josette a French feminine diminutive form of JOSEPHINE, now used independently.

Josh a masculine diminutive form of JOSHUA, now used independently.

Joshua a masculine first name meaning 'Jehovah is salvation' (*Hebrew*). In the Old Testament Joshua was the successor of Moses who defeated the Canaanites, his story being told in the Book of Joshua. A diminutive form is Josh.

Josiah or **Josias** a masculine first name meaning 'Jehovah supports' (*Hebrew*). In the Old Testament Josiah was a king of Judah who initiated reform and the abandonment of idolatry.

Josie a feminine diminutive form of JOSEPHINE.

Joss a masculine or feminine diminutive form of JOCELYN, JOCELIN, JOSCE-LIN.

Joy the name of the feeling of intense happiness used as a feminine first name (*English*).

Joyce a feminine first name meaning 'sportive' (*Latin*).

Juan the Spanish masculine form of JOHN, now used as an English-language form.

Juana the Spanish feminine form of JANE. A diminutive form is Juanita.

Juanita a feminine diminutive form of JUANA.

Jud or **Judd** masculine diminutive forms of JORDAN, also used independently.

Judah a masculine first name meaning 'confession' (*Hebrew*). In the Old Testament Judah was the fourth son of Jacob and Leah one of whose descendants was to be the Messiah. His descendants settled in the area south of Jerusalem, which was named Judah. A diminutive form is JUDE.

Jude a masculine diminutive form of JUDAH. In the New Testament Jude was a follower of Jesus and brother of James. Jude Law is an English actor.

Judie or **Judi** feminine diminutive forms of JUDITH, now used independently.

Judith a feminine first name meaning 'of Judah' (*Hebrew*). In the Old Testament Judith was a Jewish widow who beheaded the Assyrian general Holofernes in order to save her native town. The story is told in the Book of Judith. Diminutive forms are Jodie, Judie, Judy.

Judy a feminine diminutive form of JUDITH, now used independently. Judy Davis is an Australian film actress.

Jules (1) the French masculine form of JULIUS. (2) a diminutive form of JULIAN, JULIUS. (3) a feminine diminutive form of JULIA, JULIANA.

Julia a feminine form of JULIUS. William Shakespeare (1564–1616) used the name for one of the heroines in his comedy *Two Gentlemen of Verona*. Julia Roberts is an American film actress. A variant form is JULIANA. A diminutive form is Julie.

Julian a masculine first name meaning 'sprung from or belonging to Julius' (*Latin*). Julian the Apostate (331–363) was the last Roman emperor (361–363) to oppose Christianity although brought up as a Christian himself. Julian Sands is an English film actor. A variant form is Jolyon.

Juliana a feminine form of Julius.

Julie or **Juliet** feminine diminutive forms of Julia, now used independently. William Shakespeare (1654–1616) used the name for the young daughter of the Capulets who falls in love with Romeo, the young heir of the Montagues, the enemies of the Capulets, in his tragedy *Romeo and Juliet*, which is probably the world's best-known love story. Julie Walters is an English actress.

Julien the French masculine form of Julian.

Julienne feminine form of Julien.

Julieta a Spanish feminine form of Julia.

Juliette the French feminine form of Julia, now used as an English-language form. Juliette Lewis is an American film actress.

Julio a Spanish masculine form of Julius.

Julius a masculine first name meaning 'downy-bearded' (*Greek*). The name was adopted by several popes.

Junaid or **Junayd** a masculine first name meaning 'warrior' (*Arabic*).

June the name of the month used as a feminine first name (*Latin*).

Juno a feminine first name meaning 'queen of heaven' (Latin). In Roman mythology Juno was the equivalent of the Greek Hera.

Justin the English masculine form of Justinus, a Roman family name from Justus (*Latin*). A variant form is Justinian.

Justina or **Justine** feminine forms of Justin.

Justinian or **Justus** masculine variant forms of Justin.

Justus a masculine first name meaning 'fair, just' (*Latin*).

K

Kady an Irish feminine first name perhaps influenced by Katie, but the name could stem from *céadach*, 'first' (*Irish Gaelic*).

Kamal (1) a masculine first name meaning 'pale red' (*Sanskrit*). (2) a masculine first name meaning 'complete' (*Arabic*). A variant form is Kamil.

Kamala the feminine form of Sanskrit KAMAL.

Kamil a variant form of Arabic KAMAL.

Kamila or **Kamilah** the feminine form of Kamil.

Kalantha or **Kalanthe** feminine variant forms of CALANTHA.

Kalypso a feminine variant form of CALYPSO.

Kane a surname, meaning 'warrior' (*Irish Gaelic*), used as a masculine first name.

Kara a feminine variant form of CARA.

Karadoc a Breton masculine form of CARADOG.

Karel (1) the Czech and Dutch masculine form of CHARLES. (2) a Breton feminine form of CAROL.

Karen (1) a Dutch and Scandinavian feminine form of KATHERINE. Variant forms are Caron, Caryn. (2) an anglicised feminine form of CAIRENN.

Kari a feminine variant form of CERI.

Karin a Scandinavian feminine form of KATHERINE.

Karina an anglicised feminine form of CAIRENN.

Karl a German masculine form of CHARLES.

Karla a feminine form of KARL.

Karlotte a German feminine form of CHARLOTTE.

Karol the Polish masculine form of CHARLES.

Karoline a German feminine form of CAROLINE.

Karr a masculine variant form of KERR.

Kashif a masculine first name meaning 'discoverer' (*Arabic*).

Kasia a feminine variant form of KEZIA.

Kasimir a masculine first name meaning 'peace' (*Polish*).

Kaspar the German masculine form of JASPER.

Kate a feminine diminutive form of KATHERINE, also used independently. William Shakespeare (1564–1616) used this diminutive for KATHARINA in *The Taming of the Shrew*.

Katerina a feminine variant form of KATHERINE.

Kath or **Kathie** or **Kathy** feminine diminutive forms of KATHERINE.

Katharina or **Katharine** German feminine forms of KATHERINE. William Shakespeare (1564–1616) used the form Katharina for the heroine of his comedy *The Taming of the Shrew* and Katharine for a character in *Love's Labour's Lost*. A diminutive form is KATRINE.

Katherine a feminine first name meaning 'pure' (*Greek*). Diminutive forms are Kate, Kath, Katie, Katy, Kay, Kit, Kittie.

Kathleen an anglicised feminine form of CAITLÍN. Kathleen Turner is an American actress.

Kathryn an American feminine form of KATHERINE.

Katie a feminine diminutive form of KATHERINE, now independent.

Katinka a Russian feminine form of KATHERINE.

Katrina a feminine variant form of CATRIONA.

Katrine (1) a feminine diminutive form of KATHARINA. (2) a variant form of CATRIONA. (3) the name of a Scottish loch, meaning 'wood of Eriu', used as a feminine first name.

Katriona a feminine variant form of CATRIONA. A variant form is KATRINE.

Katy a feminine diminutive form of KATHERINE, now used independently.

Kavan a masculine variant form of CAVAN.

Kay (1) a masculine first name meaning 'giant' (*Scots Gaelic*). (2) a feminine diminutive form of KATHERINE, or Catherine, now used independently. A variant form is Kaye. (3) an anglicised masculine form of CEI. Sir Kay was the foster-brother and seneschal of King ARTHUR in the English Arthurian legends.

Kaye a feminine variant form of KAY.

Kayleigh or **Kayla** or **Kayley** (1) a feminine first name the derivation of which is uncertain but possibly 'slender' (*Irish Gaelic*). (2) a feminine first named formed from a combination of KAY and LEIGH, or a variant form of KELLY.

Kaylin or **Kayline** an anglicised feminine form of CAOILFHINN.

Kean or **Keane** anglicised masculine forms of CIAN.

Kedar a masculine first name meaning 'powerful' (*Arabic*). In the Old

Testament Kedar was one of the twelve sons of ISHMAEL (ISMAIL) whose descendants formed a tribe in the Arabian Desert.

Keefe a masculine first name meaning 'noble, admirable' (*Irish Gaelic*).

Keegan a surname, meaning 'son of EGAN' (*Irish Gaelic*), used as a masculine first name.

Keelan or **Keelin** an anglicised feminine form of CAOILFHINN.

Keenan a surname, meaning 'little ancient one' (*Irish Gaelic*), used as a masculine first name.

Keera an anglicised feminine form of Irish Gaelic CIARA.

Keeva a feminine variant form of KEVA.

Keevan the anglicised form of Irish Gaelic CIABHÁN.

Keir a surname, meaning 'dark', from *ciar* (*Scottish Gaelic*), used as a masculine first name. A variant form is Kerr. See also CIARÁN, KIERAN.

Keira an anglicised feminine form of Irish Gaelic CIARA.

Keith (pronounced *keeth*) a place name and surname, probably from *coit*, 'wood' (*Scottish Gaelic*), used as a masculine first name, although it has also been associated with Cait, one of the seven sons of CRUITHNE, father of the Picts.

Keld a Danish masculine form of KEITH.

Kelly (1) a surname, the source of which is *cill*, 'church' (*Irish Gaelic*), indicating a special supporter of the church, used as a feminine or masculine first name. (2) the anglicised masculine or feminine form of CEALLACH. Kelly Lynch and Kelly McGillis are American film actresses.

Kelsey a surname, meaning 'victory' (*Old English*), used as a masculine and feminine first name. Kelsey Grammer is an American actor and star of *Frasier*.

Kelvin the name of a Scottish river, whose name stems from Gaelic *caol*, 'narrow', and *abhainn*, 'stream' (*Scottish Gaelic*), used as a masculine first name.

Kemp a surname, meaning 'warrior' (*Old English*) or 'athlete' (*Middle English*), used as a masculine first name.

Ken a masculine diminutive form of KENDAL, KENDALL, KENDELL, KENDRICK, KENELM, KENNARD, KENNEDY, KENNETH.

Kendall or **Kendal** or **Kendell** a surname, meaning 'valley of the holy river' (*Celtic/Old English*), used as a masculine first name. A diminutive form is Ken.

Kendra feminine form of KENDRICK.

Kendrew and **Kendrick** anglicised forms of Welsh CYNFRIG. A variant form is Kenrick. A diminutive form is Ken.

Kenelm a masculine first name meaning 'royal helmet' (*Germanic*). A diminutive form is Ken.

Kennard a surname, meaning 'strong royal' (*Germanic*), used as a masculine first name. A diminutive form is Ken.

Kennedy a surname, originally a nickname, from *ceann*, 'head', *eidhigh*, 'ugly' (*Scottish/Irish Gaelic*), used as a first name. This name is associated with southwest Scotland and Ireland. A diminutive form is Ken.

Kennet a Scandinavian masculine form of KENNETH. Diminutive forms are Ken, Kent.

Kenneth a masculine first name meaning 'handsome', from *coinneach*, 'handsome' (*Scottish Gaelic*). As the name of a Celtic saint, St Kenneth (515–599), and of the first king of the united Picts and Scots, Kenneth MacAlpin (died 858), it had great prestige. Diminutive forms are Ken, Kennie, Kenny.

Kennie or **Kenny** masculine diminutive forms of KENNETH and other names beginning with Ken-.

Kenrick a masculine variant form of KENDRICK.

Kent (1) a surname, meaning 'from the county of Kent' (meaning border), used as a masculine first name. (2) a diminutive form of KENNET, KENTON.

Kentigern a Brythonic masculine first name probably meaning 'of royal descent', from *teyrn*, 'king' (*Welsh*). This was the name of the Celtic missionary who became Glasgow's patron saint. *See also* MUNGO.

Kenton a surname, meaning 'settlement on the river Kenn', or 'royal place' (*Old English*), used as a masculine first name. It features in the long-running radio soap opera, *The Archers*, as the name of one of Phil and Jill's sons, Kenton Archer. Diminutive forms are Ken, Kent.

Kenyon (1) a masculine first name meaning 'white-haired' (*Gaelic*). (2) a surname, meaning 'mound of Ennion' (*Welsh*), used as a masculine first name.

Kermit a masculine first name meaning 'son of DIARMID' (*Irish Gaelic*).

Kern a masculine first name meaning 'dark one' (*Gaelic*).

Kerr (1) a Scottish masculine form of the surname CARR, used as a masculine first name. A variant form is Karr. (2) a variant masculine form of KEIR.

Kerry the name of the Irish county, probably stemming from *ciar*, 'dark', suggesting 'land of the dark (haired) people' (*Irish Gaelic*), now widely used without any direct connection to the area as a feminine or masculine first name.

Kester a masculine diminutive form of CHRISTOPHER.

Keturah a feminine first name meaning 'incense' (*Hebrew*). In the Old Testament Keturah was a wife of Abraham and mother of six sons.

Kev a masculine diminutive form of KEVIN, KEVAN.

Keva an anglicised feminine form of Caoimhe, an old name indicating 'beauty', 'grace' (*Irish Gaelic*). Keeva is an alternative form.

Kevan a masculine variant form of KEVIN.

Keverne an anglicised masculine version of a Cornish form of KEVIN.

Kevin a masculine first name, from Caomhin, 'born handsome' (*Irish Gaelic*), made popular by the story of St Kevin of Glendalough (died around AD 620), celebrated for his chastity and devotion. This name spread from Ireland in the twentieth century to become a popular one throughout the English-speaking world. Kevin Costner and Kevin Kline are American actors. A variant form is Kevan. A diminutive form is Kev.

Kezia or **Keziah** a feminine first name meaning 'the cassia tree' (*Hebrew*). In the Old Testament Keziah was the second of the three daughters of JOB, born after his period of tribulation. Variant forms are Cassia, Kasia. Diminutive forms are Kizzie, Kizzy.

Kiaran a masculine variant form of KIERAN.

Kiera (pronounced *kee-ra*) an Irish feminine first name, a feminine version of KIERAN. *See also* CIARA.

Kieran an anglicised masculine form of CIARÁN, a saint's name, from *ciar*, 'dark', and the diminutive ending -an (*Irish Gaelic*). Other forms are Kiaran, Kiernan, Kieron.

Kiernan a masculine variant form of KIERNAN.

Kieron a masculine variant form of KIERAN.

Kim a feminine diminutive form of KIMBERLEY, also used independently. Kim Bassinger is an American actress.

Kimberley a surname, meaning 'wood clearing', used as a feminine first name (*Old English*). A diminutive form is Kim.

King (1) the title of a monarch or a surname, meaning 'appearance, or serving in a royal household' (*Old English*), used as a masculine first name. (2) a diminutive form of names beginning with King-.

Kingsley a surname, meaning 'king's meadow' (*Old English*), used as a masculine first name. Sir Kingsley Amis (1922–95) was an English novelist.

Kingston a place name and surname, meaning 'king's farm' (*Old English*), used as a masculine first name.

Kinsey a surname, meaning 'royal victor' (*Old English*), used as a masculine first name.

Kira an anglicised feminine form of Irish Gaelic CIARA.

Kirby a surname, meaning 'church village or farm' (*Old Norse*), used as a masculine first name.

Kirk a surname, meaning 'one who lives near a church' (*Old Norse*), used as a masculine first name. The name was adopted by the American actor Kirk Douglas (born Issur Danielovitch).

Kirkwood a surname, meaning 'church wood' (*Old Norse/Old English*), used as a masculine first name.

Kirsten a Scandinavian feminine form of CHRISTINE.

Kirstie a feminine variant form of KIRSTY. Kirstie Alley is an American actress who appeared in the TV sitcom *Cheers*.

Kirstin a Scottish feminine form of CHRISTINE. A diminutive form is Kirstie.

Kirsty a Scottish feminine first name that was originally an abbreviation of CHRISTINA or KIRSTIN but is often now used on its own. Kirsty Wark is a well-known Scottish television presenter. A variant form is Kirstie.

Kish a masculine first name meaning 'a gift' (*Hebrew*). In the Old Testament Kish was (1) a man whose sons married the daughters of his brother, Eleazar, and (2) the great-uncle of Saul.

Kismet the Turkish form of Arabic *qismah* or *qismat*, meaning 'destiny, fate', used as a feminine first name.

Kit (1) a masculine diminutive form of CHRISTOPHER, KRISTOPHER. (2) a feminine diminutive form of KATHERINE.

Kittie or **Kitty** feminine diminutive forms of KATHERINE.

Kizzie or **Kizzy** feminine diminutive forms of KEZIA.

Klara the German feminine form of CLARA.

Klaus a masculine variant form of CLAUS.

Klemens a German masculine form of CLEMENT.

Knight a surname, meaning 'bound to serve a feudal lord as a mounted soldier' (*Old English*), used as a masculine first name.

Knut a masculine variant form of CANUTE.

Konrad a German and Swedish masculine form of CONRAD.

Konstanz the German masculine form of CONSTANT.

Konstanze the German feminine form of CONSTANCE.

Kora a feminine variant form of CORA.

Korah a masculine first name meaning 'baldness' (*Hebrew*). In the Old Testament Korah was (1) a son of Esau and (2) a rebel against the authority of Moses and Aaron.

Kris a masculine diminutive form of KRISTOFFER, KRISTOPHER.

Kristeen a feminine variant form of CHRISTINE.

Kirstel a German feminine form of CHRISTINE.

Kristen the Danish masculine form of CHRISTIAN, now also used in English as a girl's name. A variant form is Kristin.

Kristian a Swedish masculine form of CHRISTIAN.

Kristin a feminine variant form of KRISTEN. Kristin Scott Thomas is an English actress.

Kristina the Swedish feminine form of CHRISTINA.

Kristoffer a Scandinavian masculine form of CHRISTOPHER.

Kristopher a masculine variant form of CHRISTOPHER. Diminutive forms are Kit, Kris.

Kumar a masculine first name meaning 'boy' (*Sanskrit*).

Kumari a feminine first name meaning 'girl' (*Sanskrit*).

Kurt a masculine diminutive form of CONRAD, now used independently. Kurt Russell is an American film actor. A variant form is CURT.

Kyle a masculine or feminine first name from Gaelic *caol*, 'strait' (*Scottish Gaelic*). It is an increasingly popular name, perhaps in modern times seen as a masculine version of Kylie (*see also* GAEL) or Kayleigh. Kyle MacLachlan is an American film actor.

Kylie a feminine first name formed from a combination of KYLE and KELLY. The name was popular in the early 1990s probably because of the success of pop singer and actress Kylie Minogue.

Kyrena a feminine variant form of CYRENA.

L

Laban a masculine first name meaning 'white' (*Hebrew*). In the Old Testament Laban was the father of Leah and Rachel and father-in-law as well as uncle of Jacob.

Labhra or **Labraid** or **Labraidh** (pronounced *lab-rad*) a masculine first name meaning 'speaker' (*Irish Gaelic*). This might indicate one who speaks in assemblies, or a story-teller. Labraid Loingseach, 'seafarer', 'shipman', is a legendary leader and progenitor of the men of Leinster. It is anglicised into Lowry.

Lacey a surname, meaning 'from Lassy in the Calvados region of Normandy', used as a masculine or feminine first name (*Old French*).

Lachlan a masculine first name that originally meant 'man from Scandinavia', Lochlann being the Scottish Gaelic for 'the land of fjords'. The diminutive form is Lachie.

Ladislas a masculine first name meaning 'rule of glory' (*Polish/Latin*).

Láeg an Irish Gaelic masculine first name from Irish legend, Láeg being the name of Cuchulainn's charioteer and friend.

Laetitia a feminine first name meaning 'happiness' (*Latin*). Variant forms are Latisha, Letitia.

Laing a masculine variant form of LANG.

Laird a Scots masculine form of the surname Lord, meaning 'master, landowner' (*Old English*), used as a masculine first name.

Lalage a feminine first name meaning 'chattering' (*Greek-Latin*). Diminutive forms are Lallie, Lally.

Lallie or **Lally** feminine diminutive forms of LALAGE.

Lambert a masculine first name meaning 'illustrious with landed possessions' (*Germanic*). Lambert, Prince de Bruxelles, was one of the legendary twelve paladins who attended on Charlemagne.

Lamberto the Italian masculine form of LAMBERT.

Lamond or **Lamont** a surname, meaning 'law giver' (*Old Norse/Scots Gaelic*), used as a masculine first name.

Lana a feminine variant form of ALANA.

Lance (1) a masculine first name meaning 'land' (*Germanic*). (2) a diminutive form of LANCELOT.

Lancelot a masculine first name meaning 'a little lance' or 'warrior'; or 'a servant' (*French*). Lancelot Andrewes (1555–1626) was an English Anglican theologian and preacher. A variant form is LAUNCELOT. A diminutive form is Lance.

Lander or **Landor** masculine variant forms of the surname LAVENDER.

Lane a surname, meaning 'narrow road, lane' (*Old English*), used as a masculine first name.

Lang a Scottish masculine form of the surname Long, meaning 'tall or long' (*Old English*), used as a masculine first name. A variant form is LAING.

Langford a surname, meaning 'long ford' (*Old English*), used as a masculine first name.

Langley a surname, meaning 'long meadow' (*Old English*), used as a masculine first name.

Lara a feminine diminutive form of LARISSA (*Latin*). Lara Flynn Boyle is an American actress.

Laraine a feminine variant form of LORRAINE, 'the queen' (*Old French*).

Larissa or **Larisa** a feminine first name the meaning of which is uncertain but possibly 'happy as a lark' (*Greek/Russian*). Diminutive forms are Lara, Lissa.

Lark the English word for a bird famed for rising early and for its song Used as a feminine first name.

Larry a masculine diminutive form of LAURENCE, LAWRENCE.

Lars a Scandinavian masculine form of LAURENCE.

Larsen or **Larson** a masculine first name meaning 'son of LARS' (*Scandinavian*).

Lasair a feminine first name meaning 'flame, blaze' (*Irish Gaelic*).

Lascelles a surname, meaning 'hermitage or cell' (*Old French*), used as a masculine first name.

Laszlo the Hungarian masculine form of LADISLAS.

Latham or **Lathom** a surname, meaning 'barns' (*Old Norse*), used as a masculine first name.

Latimer a surname, meaning 'interpreter' (*Old French*), used as a masculine first name.

Latisha a feminine variant form of LAETITIA.

Launcelot a masculine variant form of Lancelot and the one found in Arthurian legend for the name of the most famous of the knights of the Round Table. He is a major figure in *Idylls of the King* by Lord Tennyson (1809–92).

Laura a feminine first name meaning 'laurel, bay tree' (*Latin*). It was the name of a young woman whom the Italian poet Petrarch (1304–74) met in Avignon in 1327 and with whom he fell in love. She became the inspiration for his poetry, and the name has been popular with poets ever since. A diminutive form is Laurie.

Laurabel a feminine first name formed from a combination of LAURA and MABEL.

Laurel a name for the evergreen bay tree used as a feminine first name.

Lauren feminine form of LAURENCE. Lauren Bacall is an American film actress. A variant form is LOREN. A diminutive form is Laurie.

Laurence (1) a masculine first name meaning 'from Laurentium in Italy, place of laurels' (*Latin*). Sir Laurence Olivier (later Lord Olivier) (1907–89) was an eminent English actor and director. A variant form is LAWRENCE. Diminutive forms are Larry, Laurie. (2) a masculine anglicised form of the Irish LORCAN.

Laurens a Dutch masculine form of LAURENCE.

Laurent the French masculine form of LAURENCE.

Lauretta or **Laurette** a French feminine form of LAURA.

Laurie (1) a masculine diminutive form of LAURENCE. It was used by the American writer Louisa May Alcott (1832–88) for the young, rich neighbour of the March family in her popular novels *Little Women* (1869), *Good Wives* (1871), *Little Men* (1871) and *Jo's Boys* (1886). Laurie Lee (1914–97) was an English poet best known for his autobiography, *Cider with Rosie* (1959). (2) a surname form of this used as a masculine first name. Variant forms are LAWRIE, LAWRY. (3) a feminine dimuntive form of LAURA, LAUREN.

Lavender (1) the English name of the plant that bears blue or mauve flowers used as a feminine first name. (2) a surname, meaning 'launderer', used as a feminine first name (*Old French*). A variant form is LANDER.

Laverne a feminine first name meaning 'the alder tree' (*Old French*). Diminutive forms are Verna, Verne.

Lavinia or **Lavina** a feminine first name meaning 'of Latium' in Italy

(*Latin*). William Shakespeare (1564–1616) used the name for the daughter of Titus in his play *Titus Andronicus*.

Lawrence a masculine variant form of LAURENCE. St Lawrence (died 258) was an early Christian martyr. Lawrence Kasdan is an American screen-writer and film director best known for writing the scripts for two of the *Star Wars* films. Diminutive forms are Larry, Lawrie, Lawry.

Lawrie or **Lawry** (1) a masculine diminutive forms of LAWRENCE. (2) a variant form of LAURIE.

Lawson a surname, meaning 'son of LAWRENCE' (*Old English*), used as a masculine first name.

Lawton a surname, meaning 'from the place on the hill' (*Old English*), used as a masculine first name.

Layton a masculine variant form of LEIGHTON.

Lazarus a masculine first name meaning 'destitute of help' (*Hebrew*). In the New Testament was the brother of Martha and Mary and who was raised from the dead by Jesus.

Lea a feminine variant form of LEAH, LEE.

Leah a feminine first name meaning 'languid', or 'wild cow' (*Hebrew*). In the Old Testament Leah was the first wife of Jacob and the elder sister of Rachel, his second wife. Variant forms are Lea, Lee.

Leal or **Leale** a surname, meaning 'loyal, true' (*Old French*), used as a masculine first name.

Leana a feminine variant form of LIANA.

Leander a masculine first name meaning 'lion man' (*Greek*). In Greek mythology it was the name of HERO's lover who drowned in the Helle-spont.

Leandre a French masculine form of LEANDER.

Leandro an Italian masculine form of LEANDER.

Leane a feminine variant form of LEANNE, LIANE.

Leanna a feminine variant form of LIANA.

Leanne a feminine first name formed by a combination of LEE and ANNE. A variant form is Leane.

Leanora or **Leanore** German feminine variant forms of ELEANOR.

Leda a feminine first name meaning 'mother of beauty' (*Greek*). In Greek mythology, Leda was a queen of Sparta who was visited by Zeus (who appeared to her in the form of a swan) and gave birth to Helen.

Lee (1) a surname, meaning 'field or meadow', used as a masculine or feminine first name (*Old English*). Lee Marvin (1924–87) was a noted American film actor. A variant form is Leigh. (2) a feminine variant form of LEAH.

Leif a masculine first name meaning 'beloved one' (*Old Norse*).

Leigh a masculine variant form of LEE.

Leighton a surname, meaning 'herb garden' (*Old English*), used as a masculine first name. A variant form is Layton.

Leila a feminine first name meaning 'night, dark' (*Arabic*). Variant forms are Lela, Lila, Lilah.

Leith a place name, meaning 'moist place' (*Celtic*) or 'grey' (*Scots Gaelic*), used as a masculine first name.

Lela a feminine variant form of LEILA.

Leland a masculine variant form of LEYLAND.

Lem a masculine diminutive form of LEMUEL.

Lemuel a masculine first name meaning 'devoted to God' (*Hebrew*). In the Old Testament Lemuel was a king of ancient times mentioned in the Book of Proverbs. The Anglo-Irish clergyman and writer Jonathan Swift (1667–1745) used the name for the hero of his novel *Gulliver's Travels* (1726). A diminutive form is Lem.

Len a masculine diminutive form of LEONARD, LENNOX, LIONEL.

Lena a feminine diminutive form of HELENA, etc, also used independently.

Lennard a masculine variant form of LEONARD.

Lennie a masculine diminutive form of LEONARD, LENNOX, LIONEL.

Lennox a place name and surname, meaning 'abounding in elm trees' (*Scots Gaelic*), used as a masculine first name.

Lenny a masculine diminutive form of LEONARD, LENNOX, LIONEL. A variant form is Lonnie.

Lenora a feminine variant form of LEONORA.

Leo a masculine first name meaning 'lion' (*Latin*). The name was adopted by several popes. A variant form is LEON.

Leon a masculine variant form of LEO.

Leona a feminine variant form of LEONIE.

Leonard a masculine first name meaning 'lion strong' (*Germanic*). A variant form is Lennard. Diminutive forms are Len, Lennie, Lenny.

Leonarda feminine form of LEONARD.

Leonardo an Italian masculine form of LEONARD. Leonardo da Vinci (1452–1519) was an Italian painter, sculptor, architect and engineer, and the greatest artist of his age. Leonardo di Caprio is a popular American film actor.

Leonhard a German masculine form of LEONARD.

Leonidas a masculine first name meaning 'of a lion' (*Greek*).

Leonie feminine form of LEO, LEON. A variant form is Leona.

Leonora an Italian feminine form of ELEANOR. The German composer Ludwig van Beethoven (1770–1827) used the name for the heroine of his only opera, *Fidelio* (1805). A variant form is Lenora. A diminutive form is Nora.

Leontine or **Leontina** feminine form of LEONTIUS.

Leontius a masculine first name meaning 'of the lion' (*Latin*).

Leontyne a feminine variant form of LEONTINE. Leontyne Price is an eminent American opera singer.

Leopold a masculine first name meaning 'bold for the people' (*Germanic*).

Leopoldina or **Leopoldine** feminine forms of LEOPOLD.

Leopoldo an Italian and Spanish masculine form of LEOPOLD.

Leroy a masculine first name meaning 'the king' (*Old French*). A variant form is Elroy. Diminutive forms are Lee, Roy.

Lesley the usual feminine form of LESLIE.

Leslie a location name and surname from Aberdeenshire, from *lios*, 'enclosure', and *liath*, 'grey' (*Scottish Gaelic*), often used as a first name. Leslie Nielson is a Canadian-born film actor. This is the usual masculine form, but it is acquiring popularity, particularly in North America, as a feminine form. Leslie Caron is a French-born dancer and film actress.

Lester a surname, meaning 'from the Roman site' (*Old English*) (i.e. the present city of Leicester), used as a masculine first name.

Leticia or **Letitia** feminine variant forms of LAETITIA.

Letizia an Italian feminine form of LAETITIA.

Lettice a feminine variant form of LAETITIA. Diminutive forms are Lettie, Letty.

Lettie or **Letty** feminine diminutive forms of LETTICE.

Lev a Russian masculine form of LEO.

Levi a masculine first name meaning 'joined' (*Hebrew*). In the Old Testament Levi was the third son of Jacob and Leah and ancestor of one of the Twelve Tribes of Israel. In the New Testament it was the original name of Matthew, the tax collector who became one of Christ's Apostles.

Lew or **Lewie** masculine diminutive forms of LEWIS.

Lewis (1) a masculine first name meaning 'bold warrior' (*Germanic*). (2) a Scottish masculine first name probably from French 'Louis', although it could be influenced by the name of the Isle of Lewis, which has been derived from Old Norse as *ljoth*, 'people', *hus* 'houses'. On the other hand, no other old personal names come from island names: Barra, for example, received its name from the personal name Barr, and not vice versa. (3) a Welsh masculine form of French Louis. Diminutive forms are Lew, Lewie.

Lex a masculine diminutive form of ALEXANDER.

Lexie or **Lexy** feminine diminutive forms of ALEXANDRA.

Leyland a surname, meaning 'fallow or untilled land' (*Old English*), used as a masculine first name. A variant form is Leland.

Liadain or **Líadan** or **Liadhain** (pronounced *leea-dan*) a feminine first name, probably from *liath*, 'grey' (*Irish Gaelic*). The story of Liadain and her tragic love for the poet Cuírithir foreshadows the later one of Abelard and Héloise.

Liam (pronounced *lee-am*) a masculine shortened form of William and the most usual Irish Gaelic form of William. Liam Neeson is an Irish-born film actor best known for the film *Schindler's List*.

Liana or **Liane** or **Lianna** or **Lianne** a feminine first name meaning 'sun' (*Greek*). Variant forms are Leane, Leana, Leanna.

Libby a feminine diminutive form of ELIZABETH.

Lidia an Italian and Spanish feminine form of LYDIA.

Liese a feminine diminutive form of ELISABETH, now used independently.

Lije a masculine diminutive form of ELIJAH.

Lil a feminine diminutive form of LILIAN, LILY.

Lila (1) a feminine variant form of LEILA. (2) a diminutive form of DELILAH.

Lilac a feminine first name meaning 'bluish' (*Persian*), the English name of the syringa plant with fragrant purple or white flowers used as a feminine first name.

Lilah (1) a feminine variant form of LEILA. (2) a diminutive form of DELILAH.

Lili a feminine variant form of LILIE.

Lilian (1) a feminine diminutive form of ELIZABETH. (2) a variant form of LILY. A variant form is Lillian.

Lilias or **Lillias** Scottish feminine forms of LILIAN.

Lilibet a feminine diminutive form of ELIZABETH.

Lilie a German feminine form of LILY. A variant form is Lili.

Lilith a feminine first name meaning 'of the night' (*Hebrew*).

Lilli a feminine variant form of LILY.

Lillian a feminine variant form of LILIAN.

Lily the name of the flowering plant with showy blossoms used as a feminine first name. A variant form is Lilli. A diminutive form is Lil.

Lin a feminine diminutive form of LINDA.

Lina a feminine diminutive form of SELINA and names ending in -lina, -line.

Lincoln a place name and surname, meaning 'the place by the pool' (*Celtic/Latin*), used as a masculine first name.

Linda a feminine diminutive form of BELINDA, ROSALIND, etc, now used independently. A variant form is Lynda. Diminutive forms are Lin, Lindie, Lindy.

Lindall or **Lindell** a surname, meaning 'valley of lime trees' (*Old English*), used as a masculine first name.

Lindie a feminine diminutive form of LINDA.

Lindley a place name and surname, meaning 'lime tree meadow or flax field' (*Old English*), used as a masculine first name. A variant form is Linley.

Lindsay or **Lindsey** a surname, meaning 'island of Lincoln', perhaps from Lindsey in England, used as a masculine or feminine first name. Lindsay Duncan is an English actress. Lindsay Anderson (1923–94) was a British stage and film director and occasionally an actor. Variant forms are Linsay, Linsey, Linzi, Lyndsay, Lynsay, Lynsey.

Lindy a feminine diminutive form of LINDA.

Linet a Welsh feminine variant form of LUNED.

Linford a surname, meaning 'from the ford of the lime tree or flax field' (*Old English*), used as a masculine first name. Linford Christie is a famous English athlete.

Linley a masculine variant form of LINDLEY.

Linnette a feminine variant form of LYNETTE.

Linsay or **Linsey** a masculine or feminine variant forms of LINDSAY.

Linton a surname, meaning 'flax place' (*Old English*), used as a masculine first name.

Linus a masculine first name meaning 'flaxen-haired' (*Greek*). In the New Testament Linus was a Roman Christian mentioned by Paul in one of his epistles.

Linzi a feminine variant form of LINDSAY.

Lionel a masculine first name meaning 'young lion' (*Latin*). A diminutive form is Len.

Lis a feminine diminutive form of ELISABETH.

Lisa a feminine diminutive form of ELIZABETH, now used independently. A variant form is Liza.

Lisbeth a feminine diminutive form of ELISABETH.

Lisette a feminine diminutive form of LOUISE.

Lisle a surname, meaning 'island' or 'from Lisle in Normandy' (*Old French*), used as a masculine first name. Variant forms are Lyall, Lyle.

Lissa a feminine diminutive form of LARISSA, MELISSA.

Lister a surname, meaning 'dyer' (*Old English*), used as a masculine first name.

Lita a feminine diminutive form of ALIDA.

Litton a place name and surname, meaning 'loud torrent' (*Old English*), used as a masculine first name. A variant form is Lytton.

Livia a feminine variant form of OLIVIA.

Liz a feminine diminutive form of ELIZABETH.

Liza a feminine variant form of LISA.

Lizbeth a feminine diminutive form of ELIZABETH.

Lizzie or **Lizzy** feminine diminutive forms of ELIZABETH.

Llew (pronounced *hloo*) (1) a masculine first name from *lleu*, 'light', 'fair' (*Welsh*). Lleu Llawgyffes, 'of the steady hand', son of ARIANRHOD, is a principal figure in one of the *Mabinogion* tales. (2) the name may nowadays also be seen as a shortened form of LLYWELLYN.

Llewelyn a masculine variant form of LLYWELYN.

Llian a feminine first name meaning 'flaxen' (*Welsh*).

Lloyd the anglicised masculine form of LLWYD. Lloyd Bridges was an American actor and the father of Beau and Jeff Bridges.

Llud (pronounced *hlood*) a Welsh masculine first name and that of a legendary king of the ancient Britons. It is anglicised as Lud.

Llwyd (pronounced *hloowid*) a masculine first name from the Welsh root word meaning 'grey,' or 'holy'. It was a name for a priest. The anglicised form is Lloyd.

Llywarch a Welsh masculine first name and that of a sixth-century king. Llywarch Hen, 'the old', is the subject of an old Welsh poem, 'The Song of Llywarch the Old', lamenting the ills of old age.

Llywelyn (pronounced *hloo-ell-in*) a masculine first name meaning 'leader', from *llyw*, 'lead' (*Welsh*). Llywelyn Fawr, 'the great', Prince of Wales, died in 1240. The name is sometimes found spelt Llewellyn. Diminutive forms are Lyn, Lynn.

Loarn *see* LORN.

Locke a surname, meaning 'enclosure, stronghold' (*Old English*), used as a masculine first name.

Logan a surname, meaning 'little hollow' (*Scottish Gaelic*), used as a masculine first name.

Lois a feminine first name the meaning of which is uncertain but possibly 'good, desirable' (*Greek*). In the New Testament Lois and her daughter, EUNICE, were Jewish women who were converted to Christianity.

Lola a feminine diminutive form of DOLORES, CARLOTTA, now used independently.

Lolita a feminine diminutive of DOLORES. Lolita Davidovich is an American film actress.

Lombard a surname, meaning 'long beard' (*Germanic*), used as a masculine first name.

Lona a feminine diminutive form of MAELONA.

Lonán a masculine first name meaning 'little blackbird', from *lon*, 'blackbird', with the diminutive suffix -an (*Irish Gaelic*).

Lonnie a masculine variant form of LENNY. A diminutive form of ALONSO.

Lonny a masculine diminutive form of ZEBULON.

Lora a Welsh feminine form of LAURA.

Lorcan or **Lorcán** a masculine first name meaning 'fierce in battle', from *lorc*, 'fierce' (*Irish Gaelic*). It is anglicised to Laurence, with which it has no etymological connection; hence the twelfth-century St 'Laurence' O'Toole should properly be St Lorcan.

Lorelei the name of a rock in the River Rhine from where, in German legend, a siren lured boatmen, used as a feminine first name.

Loren a feminine variant form of LAUREN.

Lorenz the German masculine form of LAURENCE.

Lorenzo the Italian and Spanish masculine form of LAURENCE. In *The Merchant of Venice* by William Shakespeare (1564–1616) Lorenzo is the Italian man in love with Jessica, the daughter of Shylock.

Loretta a feminine variant form of LAURETTA.

Loring a surname, meaning 'man from Lorraine' (bold and famous) (*Germanic/Old French*), used as a masculine first name.

Lorn a Scottish Gaelic masculine first name from Loarn, one of the early rulers of the Dalriada Scots, one of the three sons of Erc, whose name is preserved in the Lorn district of Argyll. An alternative form is Lorne.

Lorna a feminine form of Lorn. The name was invented by the English novelist R. D. Blackmore (1825–1900) for the eponymous heroine of his novel *Lorna Doone* (1869).

Lorne a masculine variant form of LORN.

Lorraine a surname meaning 'man from Lorraine' (bold and famous) used as a feminine first name (*Old French*). Lorraine Bracco is an American actress. A variant form is Laraine.

Lot a masculine first name meaning 'a veil, a covering' (*Hebrew*). In the Old Testament Lot was the nephew of Abraham who lived in Sodom. He and his wife and daughters escaped from the city before its destruction but Lot's wife was turned into a pillar of salt for looking back at the city as they fled. The Arabic form is Lut.

Lotario the Italian masculine form of LUTHER.

Lothaire the French masculine form of LUTHER.

Lottie or **Lotty** feminine diminutive forms of CHARLOTTE.

Lotus the English name of a fruit that in Greek mythology was said to induce languour and forgetfulness, used as a feminine first name. The lotus is a Buddhist symbol.

Lou (1) a masculine diminutive form of LOUIS. (2) a feminine diminutive form of LOUISA, LOUISE.

Louella a feminine first name formed by a combination of LOUISE and ELLA.

Louie a masculine diminutive form of LOUIS.

Louis the French masculine form of LEWIS. Diminutive forms are Lou, Louie.

Louisa feminine form of LOUIS.

Louise the French feminine form of LOUISA, now used widely as an English-language form. Diminutive forms are Lisette, Lou.

Lovel or **Lovell** a surname, meaning 'little wolf' (*Old French*), used as a masculine first name. A variant form is Lowell.

Lowell a masculine variant form of LOVEL.

Lowri a Welsh feminine form of LAURA. Lowri Turner is an English TV presenter.

Lowry an anglicised masculine form of Irish Gaelic LABHRA.

Luc the French masculine form of LUKE.

Luca the Italian masculine form of LUKE.

Lucan a place name, meaning 'place of elms' (*Irish Gaelic*), used as a masculine first name.

Lucas a masculine variant form of LUKE.

Luce a feminine diminutive form of LUCY.

Lucia feminine form of LUCIAN.

Lucian a masculine first name meaning 'belonging to or sprung from LUCIUS' (*Latin*). Lucian Freud (b.1922) is an artist best known for his portraits of nudes.

Luciano an Italian masculine form of LUCIAN.

Lucien a French masculine form of LUCIAN.

Lucienne feminine form of LUCIEN.

Lucifer a masculine first name meaning 'light bringer' (*Latin*). In the Old Testament Lucifer was the angel, usually identified with Satan, who led a rebellion against God. It is also the name applied to the planet Venus when it rises in the morning.

Lucilla a feminine diminutive form of LUCIA.

Lucille or **Lucile** French feminine forms of LUCIA, now used as English-language forms.

Lucinda a feminine variant form of LUCIA. A diminutive form is Cindy.

Lucio a Spanish masculine form of LUKE.

Lucius a masculine first name from *lux*, 'light' (*Latin*). In the New Testament Lucius was a man who was with Paul in Corinth. William Shakespeare (1564–1616) used the name in several of his plays.

Lucrèce a French feminine form of LUCRETIA.

Lucretia or **Lucrece** a feminine first name from *lucrum*, 'gain' (*Latin*). In Roman legend Lucretia was the daughter of a prefect of Rome and wife of Tarquinius Collatinus. Her rape by Sextus Tarquinius and her subsequent suicide were said to have led to the establishment of the Roman republic. The story was the subject of his second poem, *The Rape of Lucrece* (1594), by William Shakespeare (1564–1616).

Lucretius the masculine form of LUCRETIA.

Lucrezia the Italian feminine form of LUCRETIA. Lucrezia Borgia (1480–1519) was an Italian noblewoman and a patron of science and the arts.

Lucy a popular feminine form of LUCIA. St Lucy (died *c*.303) was a Sicilian martyr. A diminutive form is Luce.

Lud a masculine anglicised form of Welsh LLUD. Lud was a mythical king of Britain whose name may survive in 'Ludgate', London.

Ludlow a place name, meaning 'hill by the rapid river' (*Old English*), used as a masculine first name.

Ludmila or **Ludmilla** a feminine first name meaning 'of the people' (*Russian*). St Ludmilla (860–921) established Christianity in Bohemia and was martyred.

Ludo a masculine diminutive form of LUDOVIC.

Ludovic or **Ludovick** masculine variant forms of LEWIS. Ludovic Kennedy is a Scottish journalist. A diminutive form is Ludo.

Ludvig a Swedish masculine form of LEWIS.

Ludwig the German masculine form of LEWIS. Ludwig van Beethoven (1770–1827) was a German composer whose works express great emotional intensity and bridge the classical and romantic traditions.

Luella a feminine variant form of LOUELLA.

Lugaid (pronounced *loo-gad*) an Irish masculine first name from Old Gaelic *lug*, 'light', a frequent warrior name in Old Irish sources and going back to the name of a major Celtic god, Lug.

Luigi an Italian masculine form of LEWIS.

Luis a Spanish masculine form of LEWIS.

Luisa an Italian and Spanish feminine form of LOUISA.

Luise the German feminine form of LOUISA. A diminutive form is Lulu.

Lukas a Swedish masculine form of LUKE, LUCAS.

Luke a masculine first name meaning 'of Lucania' in Italy (*Latin*). In the New Testament Luke was a gentile and a doctor and a friend of Paul who is considered to have been the author of the third gospel.

Lulu a feminine diminutive form of LUISE.

Lundy a place name, meaning 'puffin island' (*Old Norse*), used as a masculine first name.

Luned or **Lunet** a feminine first name probably linked to *eilun*, 'idol', 'image' (*Welsh*). The heroine of a medieval Welsh legend, *Owain and Luned*; daughter of the Lord of the Fountain, she assists Owain to defeat him. Also spelt as Eiluned. Other forms are Linet, LYNETTE.

Lut the Arabic form of LOT.

Lutero a Spanish masculine form of LUTHER.

Luther a masculine first name meaning 'illustrious warrior' (*Germanic*).

Lyall a masculine variant form of LISLE.

Lycurgus a masculine first name meaning 'wolf driver' (*Greek*).

Lydia a feminine first name meaning 'of Lydia' in Asia Minor (*Greek*). In the New Testament Lydia was one of the first people to be converted to Christianity by Paul.

Lyle a masculine variant form of LISLE.

Lyn (1) a feminine diminutive form of LYNETTE, LYNSAY. (2) a masculine diminutive form of LLYWELYN.

Lynda a feminine variant form of LINDA. Diminutive forms are Lyn, Lynn, Lynne.

Lynden or **Lyndon** a surname, meaning 'dweller by lime trees', used as a masculine first name. A diminutive form is Lyn.

Lynette an English feminine form of ELUNED or LUNED. (2) a feminine first name formed from a double diminutive, with the French -ette suffix, 'little', ending added to Lyn. Variant forms are Lynnette, Linnette.

Lynn (1) a feminine diminutive form of LYNDA, now used independently. (2) a masculine diminutive form of LLYWELYN.

Lynne a feminine diminutive form of LYNETTE, LYNSAY.

Lynn a surname, meaning 'pool or waterfall' (*Celtic*), used as a masculine first name. Diminutive forms are Lyn, Lin, Linn.

Lynne a feminine diminutive form of LYNDA.

Lynnette a feminine variant form of LYNETTE.

Lyndsay or **Lynsay** or **Lynsey** a masculine or feminine variant form of LINDSAY.

Lyris a feminine first name meaning 'she who plays the harp' (*Greek*).

Lysander a masculine first name meaning 'liberator' (*Greek*). William Shakespeare (1564–1616) used the name for one of the heroes of his comedy *A Midsummer Night's Dream*. A diminutive form is Sandy.

Lysandra feminine form of LYSANDER.

Lyss a masculine diminutive form of ULYSSES.

Lytton a masculine variant form of LITTON. Lytton Strachey (1880–1932) was an English critic and biographer.

M

Maarten a Dutch masculine form of MARTIN.

Mab an Irish Gaelic and Welsh feminine abbreviated form of MEDB or Maeve. It is not connected with Mabel, which is from Old French Amabel.

Mabel feminine diminutive forms of AMABEL, also used independently. A variant form is Maybelle.

Mabelle a French feminine form of MABEL.

Mabon a masculine first name and that of a Celtic god of youth; *maban* is Welsh for 'child'.

Macbeth *see* BETHAN.

Macha (pronounced *ma-ha*) a feminine first name, perhaps from *magh*, 'plain', referring to land (*Irish Gaelic*). It was the name of a goddess and legendary queen.

Mackenzie a surname meaning 'son of Kenneth' (*Scottish Gaelic*), used as a masculine or feminine first name. Perhaps because of the Mackenzie River, it has become a popular first name for girls in Canada.

Madalena the Spanish feminine form of MADELEINE.

Maddalena the Italian feminine form of MADELEINE.

Maddie or **Maddy** feminine diminutive forms of MADELEINE.

Madeleine or **Madeline** a feminine first name meaning from Magdala on the Sea of Galilee (*French*). Madeleine Stone is an American film actress. A variant form is MAGDALENE. Diminutive forms are Maddie, Maddy, Mala. *See also* MARY.

Madge feminine diminutive forms of MARGARET, MARJORY.

Madhbh a variant form of MEDB.

Madison a surname, meaning 'son of MATTHEW or MAUD' (*Old English*), used as a masculine first name.

Madog or **Madoc** a masculine first name from a Welsh root word, *maddeugar*, indicating 'generous', 'forgiving'. Madog was a renowned holy man of the seventh century. Madog ab Owain Gwynedd, a twelfth-century Welsh prince, is reputed to have sailed as far as America. His name is preserved in that of Portmadoc.

Madonna a feminine first name meaning 'my lady', from the title of the Virgin Mary (*Italian*). *See also* DONNA.

Mae a feminine variant form of MAY.

Maebh a variant form of MEDB.

Mael (pronounced *myle*) a masculine first name from *mael*, 'prince' (*Welsh*).

Maelgwyn or **Maelgwn** a masculine first name meaning 'bright prince', from *mael*, 'prince', and *gwyn*, 'bright', 'fair' (*Welsh*). Maelgwyn or Maelgwn Gwynedd was a king who lived during the sixth century.

Maelona a feminine first name meaning 'princess' (*Welsh*). A diminutive form is Lona.

Maeve the anglicised feminine form of MEDB. Maeve Binchy is a popular Irish writer.

Magda German and Scandinavian feminine form of MAGDALENE.

Magdalene or **Magdalen** feminine variant forms of MADELEINE. *See also* MARY.

Magee a surname, meaning 'son of HUGH' (*Irish Gaelic*), used as a masculine first name. A variant form is MCGEE.

Maggie feminine diminutive forms of MARGARET.

Magnolia the name of a tree with showy flowers, named after French botanist Pierre Magnol, used as a feminine first name.

Magnus a masculine first name meaning 'great' (*Latin*). It became a popular name with the Norsemen. Magnus Magnusson is an Icelandic-Scottish journalist and television presenter.

Mahalia a feminine first name meaning 'tenderness' (*Hebrew*). Mahalia Jackson was an American gospel and jazz singer.

Mahomet a masculine variant form of MOHAMMED.

Mai a Welsh feminine form of MAY or Mary.

Maida the name of a place in Calabria in Spain, where a battle was fought in 1806, used as a feminine first name. A diminutive form is Maidie.

Maidie a feminine diminutive form of MAIDA.

Mailli a Cornish and Scottish Gaelic feminine form of MARY. The Scots form is Mallie.

Mair a Welsh feminine forms of MARY.

Máire (pronounced *maur-ya*) an Irish Gaelic feminine form of MARY.

Máiread (pronounced *my-ratt*) an Irish and Scottish Gaelic feminine form of MARGARET.

Mairi (pronounced *mah-ri*) a Scottish Gaelic feminine form of MARY.

Máirin the Irish Gaelic feminine form of MAUREEN.

Máirtín a Scottish and Irish Gaelic form of MARTIN, after St Martin of Tours, who was the teacher of St Ninian and was much esteemed by the Celts.

Mairwen a feminine first name meaning 'fair Mary', from *gwen*, 'bright' (*Welsh*).

Maisie a Scottish diminutive form of either MARJORY or MARY, also found as a name in its own right.

Maitland a surname, meaning 'unproductive land' (*Old French*), used as a masculine first name.

Makepeace a surname, meaning 'peacemaker' (*Old English*), used as a masculine first name.

Mal a masculine diminutive form of MALCOLM.

Mala a feminine diminutive form of MADELEINE.

Malachi a masculine first name meaning 'messenger of Jehovah' (*Hebrew*). In the Old Testament prophet who wrote the Book of Malachi.

Malachy a masculine first name meaning 'follower of St Seachlainn', from Gaelic *maol*, 'follower', 'disciple', and the personal name Seachlainn (*Irish Gaelic*). It has also been suggested the name can be interpreted as 'follower of MADOG'. St Malachy (1094–1148) was archbishop of Armagh and prominent in Gregorian reform in Ireland. The name has a close resemblance to the Hebrew MALACHI.

Malcolm a masculine first name meaning 'servant of Columba', from Gaelic *maol*, 'servant', and Calluim, 'of Columba' (*Scottish Gaelic*). St Columba was venerated throughout Gaeldom, and this name was borne by four Scottish kings. Diminutive forms are CALUM, Mal, Malc, Malkie.

Malise a masculine or feminine first name meaning 'servant of Jesus', from *maol*, 'servant', and *Iosa*, 'of Jesus' (*Scottish Gaelic*). This name is particularly associated with the Ruthven and Graham families. A variant form is Maylise.

Mallie the Scots feminine form of MAILLI.

Mallory a surname, meaning 'unfortunate, luckless' (*Old French*), used as a masculine first name.

Malone a surname, meaning 'follower of St John' (*Irish Gaelic*), used as a masculine first name.

Malvina an invented Gaelic-sounding name from the eighteenth-century *Ossian* poems by the Scottish poet James Macpherson (1736–96)

Malvina a feminine first name meaning 'smooth brow' (*Scots Gaelic*).

Mame or **Mamie** feminine diminutive forms of MARY, now used independently.

Manasseh a masculine first name meaning 'one who causes to forget' (*Hebrew*). In the Old Testament Manasseh was the first-born son of Joseph and grandson of Jacob and progenitor of one of the twelve tribes of Israel.

Manda a feminine diminutive form of AMANDA.

Mandy (1) a feminine diminutive form of AMANDA, MIRANDA, now used as an independent name. (2) a masculine name meaning 'little man' (*German*).

Manette a French feminine form of MARY.

Manfred a masculine first name meaning 'man of peace' (*Germanic*). A diminutive form is Manny.

Manfredi the Italian masculine form of MANFRED.

Manfried a German masculine form of MANFRED.

Manley a surname, meaning 'brave, upright' (*Middle English*), used as a masculine first name.

Manny masculine diminutive forms of EMMANUEL, IMMANUEL, MANFRED.

Manuel the Spanish masculine form of EMMANUEL.

Manuela a feminine first name meaning 'God with us' (*Spanish*).

Manus an Irish Gaelic form of MAGNUS.

Marc (1) a French masculine form of MARK. (2) a variant form of MARCUS.

Marcán a masculine first name from Gaelic *marc*, 'steed' (*Irish Gaelic*). It was a common name in early Irish literature and is anglicised as Mark.

Marcel a French masculine form of MARCELLUS.

Marcela a Spanish feminine form of MARCELLA.

Marcella feminine form of MARCELLUS.

Marcelle a French feminine form of MARCELLA.

Marcello the Italian masculine form of MARCEL.

Marcellus the Latin and Scots Gaelic masculine form of MARK. St Marcellus (died 309) was pope from 308 but he became unpopular for enforcing penances and was banished before his death. William Shakespeare (1564–1616) used the name for a character in *Hamlet*, and it was the middle name of the American boxer Cassius Clay before he changed his name to Muhammad Ali.

Marcelo a Spanish masculine form of MARCEL.

Marcia feminine form of MARCIUS. A variant form is Marsha. Diminutive forms are Marcie, Marcy.

Marcie a feminine diminutive form of MARCIA.

Marcius a masculine variant form of MARK.

Marco the Italian masculine form of MARK.

Marcos the Spanish masculine form of MARK.

Marcus the Latin masculine form of MARK, now used as an English-language form. A variant form is Marc.

Marcy a feminine diminutive form of MARCIA.

Mared a Welsh feminine form of MARGARET.

Mareddyd a Welsh variant form of MEREDUDD. Maredydd ab Hywel Dda was a tenth-century king.

Margaret a feminine first name meaning 'a pearl' (*Greek*). It became a popular name in Scotland. St Margaret of Scotland (*c*.1046–93) was a religiously minded English princess who in 1070 married Malcolm III, 'Canmore', (*c*.1031–93), king of Scotland (1040–93). She introduced English ways into Scotland and in 1072 founded Dunfermline Abbey. She was canonised in 1250. Margaret of Anjou (1430–82) was a French princess and queen of Henry VI of England. She became the leader of the Lancastrians in the Wars of the Roses and was defeated at Tewkesbury by Edward IV in 1471. Diminutive forms are Greta, Madge, Maggie, Margie, May, Meg, Meggie, Meta, Peg.

Margarete the Danish and German feminine form of MARGARET. Diminutive forms are Grete, Gretchen.

Margaretha a Dutch feminine form of MARGARET.

Margarita the Spanish feminine form of MARGARET. A diminutive form is Rita.

Margaux a feminine variant form of MARGOT.

Marge a feminine diminutive form of MARGERY.

Marged a Welsh feminine diminutive form of Margaret.

Margery in the Middle Ages a feminine diminutive form of MARGARET, but is now a name in its own right. A variant form is MARJORIE. A diminutive form is Madge or Marge.

Margherita the Italian feminine form of MARGARET. A diminutive form is Rita.

Margiad a Welsh feminine diminutive form of Margaret.

Margie a feminine diminutive form of MARGARET.

Margo or **Margot** feminine diminutive forms of MARGARET, MARGUERITE, now used independently. A variant form is MARGAUX.

Marguerite the French feminine form of MARGARET. Diminutive forms are Margo, Margot.

Mari an Irish and Welsh feminine form of MARY.

Maria the Latin, Italian, German, and Spanish feminine forms of MARY. William Shakespeare (1564–1616) used the name for characters in *Love's Labour's Lost* and *Twelfth Night*. A diminutive form is Ria.

Mariam the Greek feminine form of MARY.

Marian a French feminine form of MARION.

Mariana or **Marianna** an Italian feminine form of MARIANNE, MARION. William Shakespeare (1564–1616) used the name for the woman spurned by Antonio in his play *Measure for Measure*.

Marianne (1) a French and German feminine form of MARION. (2) a compound of MARY and ANN.

Maribella a feminine first name formed from a combination of MARY and BELLA.

Marie French feminine form of MARY. A diminutive form is Marion.

Marietta feminine diminutive form of MARIA, also used independently.

Marigold the name of the golden flower used as a feminine first name.

Marilyn feminine diminutive form of MARY, also used independently.

Marina a feminine first name meaning 'of the sea' (*Latin*). William Shakespeare (1564–1616) used the name for the daughter of Pericles in his play *Pericles* because she was born at sea.

Mario an Italian form of MARIUS.

Marion (1) a feminine variant form of MARY. (2) a French masculine form of MARY, in compliment to the Virgin Mary.

Marisa a feminine first name meaning 'summit' (*Hebrew*). Marisa Tomei is an American film actress.

Marius a masculine first name meaning 'martial' (*Latin*).

Marjorie or **Marjory** feminine variant forms of MARGERY.

Mark (1) a masculine first name meaning 'a hammer'; 'a male'; 'sprung from Mars' (*Latin*). In the New Testament Mark accompanied Paul on

Markus

his missionary journeys and was author of the second gospel. A variant form is MARCUS. (2) an anglicised masculine form of Irish MARCÁN.

Markus the German and Swedish masculine form of MARK.

Marland a surname, meaning 'lake land' (*Old English*), used as a masculine first name.

Marlene a feminine first name formed from a contraction of Maria Magdalena (*German*).

Marlo a masculine variant form of MARLOW.

Marlon a masculine name of uncertain meaning, possibly 'hawk-like' (*French*).

Marlow a place name and surname, meaning 'land of the former pool' (*Old English*), used as a masculine first name. Variant forms are Marlo, Marlowe.

Marlowe a masculine variant form of MARLOW.

Marmaduke a masculine first name meaning 'follower of MADOG', from *mael*, 'follower' (*Welsh*). A diminutive form is DUKE.

Marmion a surname, meaning 'brat, monkey' (*Old French*), used as a masculine first name.

Marsaili (pronounced *mar-sally*) a Scottish Gaelic feminine form of MARGERY.

Marsden a surname, meaning 'boundary valley' (*Old English*), used as a masculine first name.

Marsh a surname, meaning 'marsh' (*Old English*), used as a masculine first name.

Marsha a feminine variant form of MARCIA.

Marshall a surname, meaning 'horse servant' (*Germanic*), used as a masculine first name. Marshall McLuhan (1911–80) was a Canadian media analyst and author of *The Medium is the Message* (1967).

Marston a surname, meaning 'place by a marsh' (*Old English*), used as a masculine first name.

Marta the Italian, Spanish and Swedish feminine form of MARTHA, now used as an English-language form. A variant form is Martita.

Martha a feminine first name meaning 'lady' (*Hebrew*). In the New Testament was a friend of Jesus and the sister of LAZARUS and MARY. Diminutive forms are Mat, Mattie.

Marthe the French and German feminine form of MARTHA.

Marti a feminine diminutive form of MARTINA, MARTINE.

Martijn a Dutch masculine form of MARTIN.

Martin a masculine first name meaning 'of Mars; warlike' (*Latin*). The name was adopted by several popes. A variant form is Martyn. A diminutive form is Marty.

Martina feminine forms of MARTIN. A diminutive form is Marti.

Martine the French feminine form of MARTINA, now used as an English-language form. A diminutive form is Marti.

Martino an Italian and Spanish masculine form of MARTIN.

Martita a feminine variant form of MARTA. A diminutive form is Tita.

Marty a masculine diminutive form of MARTIN.

Martyn a masculine variant form of MARTIN.

Marvin an anglicised masculine form of Welsh MERFYN.

Marwood a surname, meaning 'bigger or boundary wood' (*Old English*), used as a masculine first name.

Mary a feminine first name meaning 'bitter'; 'their rebellion'; 'star of the sea' (*Hebrew*). In the New Testament Mary was (1) the mother of Jesus, (2) the sister of LAZARUS and MARTHA and a friend of Jesus, and (3) Mary Magdalene, a woman from Galilee from whom Jesus cast out an evil spirit and who was the first to see him after the resurrection. Variant forms are MARION, MIRIAM. The Arabic form is Maryam. Diminutive forms are Mamie, May, Minnie, Mollie, Polly.

Maryam the Arabic form of MARY.

Maryann or **Maryanne** a feminine first name formed from a combination of MARY and ANN or ANNE.

Marylou a feminine first name formed from a combination of MARY and LOUISE.

Massan a Scottish Gaelic masculine first name and the name of a saint, of uncertain origin, preserved in Glen Masan.

Massimiliano the Italian masculine form of MAXIMILIAN.

Mat a masculine diminutive form of MATTHEW. A feminine diminutive form of MARTHA, MATHILDA.

Mateo the Spanish masculine form of MATTHEW.

Mather a surname, meaning 'mower' (*Old English*), used as a masculine first name.

Matheson or **Mathieson** a surname, meaning 'son of MATTHEW', used as a masculine first name.

Mathias a masculine variant form of MATTHIAS.

Mathieu a French masculine form of MATTHEW.

Mathilda a feminine variant form of MATILDA.

Mathilde the French feminine form of MATILDA.

Matilda a feminine first name meaning 'mighty war' (Germanic). A variant form is Mathilda. Diminutive forms are Mat, Mattie, Tilda, Tilly.

Matilde the Italian and Spanish feminine form of MATILDA.

Matt a masculine diminutive form of MATTHEW. Matt Dillon is an American film actor.

Mattaeus a Danish masculine form of MATTHEW.

Matteo the Italian masculine form of MATTHEW.

Matthais a Greek masculine form of MATTHEW.

Matthäus a German masculine form of MATTHEW.

Mattheus a Dutch and Swedish masculine form of MATTHEW.

Matthew a masculine first name meaning 'gift of Jehovah' (*Hebrew*). In the New Testament Matthew (formerly LEVI) was a tax collector who became one of Christ's apostles. Matthew Parris is an English journalist. Diminutive forms are Mat, Matt, Mattie.

Matthias a Latin masculine form of MATTHEW. In the New Testament Matthias was the apostle who was elected to replace Judas Iscariot. A variant form is Mathias.

Matthieu the French masculine form of MATTHEW.

Mattie (1) a feminine diminutive form of MATILDA. (2) a masculine diminutive form of MATTHEW.

Maud or **Maude** a medieval feminine form of MATILDA.

Maughold (pronounced *maw-hald*) a Manx masculine first name from that of a legendary Manx saint who converted from being a pirate to the life of a holy hermit.

Maura an Irish feminine form of MARY.

Maureen (1) an Irish feminine first name meaning 'little Mary'. Originally a diminutive, it has long been a name in its own right. The Gaelic form is Máirín. (2) a feminine anglicised form of MÓIRIN.

Maurice a masculine first name meaning 'Moorish, dark-coloured' (*Latin*). St Maurice (died *c*.286) was a soldier and early martyr. A variant form is MAURUS. A diminutive form is Mo.

Mauricio a Spanish masculine form of MAURICE.

Maurits a Dutch masculine form of MAURICE.

Maurizio an Italian masculine form of MAURICE.

Mauro the Italian masculine form of MAURUS.

Maurus a masculine variant form of MAURICE. St Maurus was a sixth-century Benedictine monk.

Mave a diminutive form of MAVIS.

Mavis an alternative name of the song thrush used as a feminine first name (*English*). A diminutive form is Mave.

Mavourneen or **Mavourna** a feminine first name meaning 'darling little one', from *mo*, 'my', and *mhuirnín*, 'little darling' (*Irish Gaelic*). Originally and still a term of endearment, it has also gone independent as a name.

Max a masculine diminutive form of MAXIMILIAN, MAXWELL, also used as an independent name. A diminutive form is Maxie.

Maxie (1) a masculine diminutive form of MAX, MAXIMILIAN, MAXWELL. (2) a feminine diminutive form of MAXINE.

Maximilian a masculine name meaning 'the greatest', a combination of *Maximus* and *Aemilianus* (*Latin*). Diminutive forms are Max, Maxie.

Maximilien the French masculine form of MAXIMILIAN.

Maxine feminine form of MAX.

Maxwell a surname, meaning 'spring of MAGNUS', used as a masculine first name. A diminutive form is Max. Maxwell Anderson (1888–1959) was an American playwright and screen writer.

May feminine diminutive form of MARGARET, MARY; the name of the month used as a feminine first name. A variant form is Mae. A diminutive form is Minnie.

Maybelle (1) a feminine first name formed by a combination of MAY and BELLE. (2) a variant form of MABEL.

Mayer a surname, meaning 'physician' (*Old French*) or 'farmer' (*Germanic*), used as a masculine first name. Variant forms are Meyer, Myer.

Maylise a feminine variant form of MALISE.

Maynard a surname, meaning 'strong, brave' (*Germanic*), used as a masculine first name.

Mayo a place name, meaning 'plain of the yew tree' (*Irish Gaelic*), used as a masculine first name.

McGee a masculine variant form of MAGEE.

Meave an anglicised feminine form of MEDB.

Medb (pronounced *mave*) a feminine first name meaning 'intoxicating', 'bewitching' (*Irish Gaelic*). The name is probably cognate with Welsh *meddw*, 'drunk'. It was the name of the legendary queen of Connaught who coveted the Brown Bull of Cooley. The legends invest her with magic powers and an intense attraction for men, few of whom however can stand up to her warlike nature. The source of the name is unclear. It has numerous forms, including Madhbh, Maebh, and the anglicised (and most often used) form Maeve. Another anglicised form is Meave.

Meave an anglicised feminine form of MEDB.

Medea a feminine first name meaning 'meditative' (*Greek*). In Greek mythology Medea was the princess who helped Jason obtain the Golden Fleece from her father, the king of Colchis.

Medrawd a Welsh masculine first name and that of the bastard son of King ARTHUR, in the Round Table stories, anglicised as Mordred.

Medwin a surname, meaning 'mead friend' (*Old English*), used as a masculine first name.

Meg or **Meggie** feminine diminutive forms of MARGARET. Meg Ryan and Meg Tilly are American film actresses.

Megan a Welsh diminutive form of MARGARET now used independently.

Mehetabel or **Mehitabel** a feminine first name meaning 'benefited of God' (*Hebrew*). In the Old Testament Mehetabel was the wife of an Edomite king.

Meilyr a masculine first name meaning 'man of iron' (*Welsh*). Meilyr of Caerleon was a twelfth-century wizard. Meilyr Brydydd (1100–1137) was chief bard to Gruffudd ap Cynan.

Meironwen a feminine first name meaning 'white dairymaid' (*Welsh*).

Mel a masculine diminutive form of MELVILLE, MELVIN, MELVYN. Mel Gibson is an American-born Australian film actor and producer.

Melangell a feminine first name meaning 'honey angel' (*Welsh*). It was the name of a saint, preserved in Llanfihangel.

Melanie a feminine first name meaning 'black' (*Greek*). Melanie Griffith is an American film actress.

Melbourne a surname, meaning 'mill stream' (*Old English*), used as a masculine first name.

Melchior a masculine name of uncertain meaning, possibly 'king of light' (*Hebrew*); in the Bible, Melchior was one of the Magi, the three wise men from the east who paid homage to the infant Jesus, presenting him with gifts.

Melchiorre the Italian masculine form of MELCHIOR.

Meleri a Welsh feminine first name. This was the name of St David's grandmother.

Melfyn a masculine first name meaning 'from Carmarthen' (*Welsh*).

Melinda a feminine first name meaning 'honey' (*Greek*) plus the suffix -inda.

Mélisande the French feminine form of MILLICENT. It was the name used by the Belgian poet and dramatist Comte Maurice Maeterlinck (1862–1949) for the heroine of his tragic poem *Pelléas et Mélisande* (1892), which was later (1902) the basis of an opera by the French composer Claude Debussy (1862–1918).

Melissa a feminine first name meaning 'a bee' (*Greek*). A diminutive form is Lissa.

Melle the Breton feminine form of MARY. It also has resonances in *mel*, 'honey'.

Melody a word for tune or tunefulness used as a feminine first name.

Melville or **Melvin** or **Melvyn** a surname, meaning 'Amalo's place' (*Old French*), used as a masculine first name. Melvyn Douglas (1901–81) was an American film and stage actor. A diminutive form is Mel.

Merab the name in the Old Testament of Saul's eldest daughter who was promised to David but who married Adriel.

Mercedes the Spanish feminine form of MERCY (as a plural). Mercedes Ruehl is an American film actress.

Mercer a surname, meaning 'merchant' (*Old French*), used as a masculine first name.

Mercy the quality of forgiveness used as a feminine first name.

Meredith an anglicised form of Welsh MEREDUDD or MAREDDYD used as a masculine or feminine first name.

Meredudd a masculine first name meaning 'great lord' (*Welsh*). A variant form is Mareddyd. Anglicised forms include Merideg, Meriadoc and, most commonly, Meredith.

Merfyn a masculine first name meaning 'eminent matter' (*Welsh*).

Meri a feminine variant form of MERRY.

Meriadoc an anglicised masculine form of Welsh MEREDUDD or MAREDDYD.

Merideg an anglicised masculine form of Welsh MEREDUDD or MAREDDYD.

Meriel a Welsh feminine form of MURIEL. Variant forms are Merle, Meryl.

Merle (1) a feminine first name meaning 'blackbird' (*Old French*). (2) a variant form of MERIEL. Merle Oberon (1911–79) was a Tasmanian-born film actress.

Merlin or **Merlyn** the anglicised masculine form of MYRDDIN. Merlin was the name of a celebrated wizard, first recorded in the *Black Book of Carmarthen* (thirteenth century), but going back to a sixth-century original. In the Arthurian legends he was made the tutor of King ARTHUR. A variant form is Mervyn.

Merri or **Merrie** feminine variant forms of MERRY.

Merrill a surname, meaning 'son of MURIEL' (*Celtic*) or 'pleasant place' (*Old English*), used as a masculine first name. Variant forms are Meryl, Merryll.

Merry (1) the adjective, meaning 'cheerful, mirthful, joyous', used as a feminine first name (*Old English*). (2) a diminutive form of MEREDITH. Variant forms are Meri, Merri, Merrie.

Merryll a masculine variant form of MERRILL.

Merton a surname, meaning 'farmstead by the pool' (*Old English*), used as a masculine first name.

Merfyn a Welsh masculine first name the source of which has not been satisfactorily established. The anglicised form is Mervyn, Mervin or Marvin. Merfyn Frych was a ninth-century king of Gwynedd.

Mervin or **Mervyn** (1) a surname, meaning 'famous friend' (*Old English*), used as a masculine first name. A variant form is Marvin. (2) an anglicised masculine form of MERFYN. (3) a variant form of MERLIN.

Meryl a feminine variant form of MERIEL, MERRILL. Meryl Streep is an American film actress.

Meta a feminine diminutive form of MARGARET.

Meyer a masculine variant form of MAYER.

Mia a feminine diminutive form of MARIA. Mia Farrow is an American film actress.

Micah a masculine first name meaning 'who is like unto Jehovah?' (*Hebrew*). In the Old Testament Micah was a Hebrew prophet of the late eighth century BC.

Michael a masculine first name meaning 'who is like unto God?' (*Hebrew*). In the Bible Michael is one of the seven archangels. Michael Caine is a well-known English actor. Diminutive forms are Mick, Micky, Mike.

Michaela feminine form of MICHAEL.

Michaella the Italian feminine form of MICHAELA.

Michal a feminine form of MICHAEL. In the Old Testament Michal was the younger daughter of Saul who married David.

Micheál (pronounced *mee-hoyl*) the Irish Gaelic masculine form of MICHAEL. It is a popular name in Ireland, with diminutive forms Mick, Micky, Mike, Mikey.

Michel (1) the French masculine form of MICHAEL. (2) a German diminutive of MICHAEL.

Michele the Italian masculine form of MICHAEL.

Michèle or **Michelle** French feminine forms of MICHAELA, now used as English-language forms. Michelle Pfeiffer is an American film actress.

Mick or **Micky** or **Mickey** masculine diminutive forms of MICHAEL, MICHEÁL. Mickey Rourke is an American film actor.

Midir (pronounced *mid-eer*) an Irish Gaelic masculine first name and that of a chief of the Tuatha Dé Danann, the lover of ETAÍN, portrayed as a proud and possessive figure.

Mignon a word, meaning 'sweet, dainty', used as a feminine first name (*French*). A variant form is Mignonette. A diminutive form is Minette.

Mignonette a feminine variant form of MIGNON.

Miguel the Spanish and Portuguese masculine form of MICHAEL.

Mihangel the Welsh masculine form of MICHAEL.

Mikael the Swedish masculine form of MICHAEL.

Mike or **Mikey** a masculine diminutive form of MICHAEL, MICHEÁL.

Mikhail a Russian masculine form of MICHAEL. A diminutive form is Mischa.

Mil a feminine diminutive form of MILDRED, MILLICENT.

Míl *see* MILES.

Milcah a feminine first name meaning 'queen' (*Hebrew*). In the Old Testament Milcah was a niece of Abraham and sister of Lot. She married another uncle, Nahor.

Mildred a feminine first name meaning 'gentle counsel' (*Germanic*). Diminutive forms are Mil, Millie.

Miles a masculine first name meaning 'soldier' from *miles* (*Latin*). It has Irish link with Míl, also known as Míl Espáine, 'of Spain', last of the legendary invader/settlers of Ireland and a source point of numerous family genealogies. A variant form is Myles.

Milford a place name and surname, meaning 'mill ford' (*Old English*), used as a masculine first name.

Miller a surname, meaning 'miller, grinder' (*Old English*), used as a masculine first name. A variant form is Milner.

Millicent a feminine first name meaning 'work and strength' (*Germanic*). A diminutive form is Millie.

Millie feminine diminutive form of AMELIA, EMILIA, MILDRED, MILLICENT.

Millward a masculine variant form of MILWARD.

Milne a surname, meaning 'at the mill' (*Old English*), used as a masculine first name.

Milner a masculine variant form of MILLER.

Milo or **Milon** a masculine or feminine first name meaning 'the Greek Samson' (*Greek*). Milo of Crotona was a famous Greek athlete who is said to have carried four-year-old cow through the stadium at Olympia. Milo Anderson (1912–84) was an American dress designer.

Milt a masculine diminutive form of MILTON.

Milton a surname, meaning 'middle farmstead or mill farm' (*Old English*), used as a masculine first name. A diminutive form is Milt.

Milward a surname, meaning 'mill keeper' (*Old English*), used as a masculine first name. A variant form is Millward.

Mima a feminine diminutive form of JEMIMA.

Mimi an Italian feminine diminutive form of MARIA. The Italian composer Giacomo Puccini (1858–1924) used the name for that of the heroine of his famous opera *La Bohème* (1896). Mimi Rogers is an American film actress.

Mimosa the English name of a tropical shrub with yellow flowers used as a feminine first name.

Mina a feminine diminutive form of JEMIMA.

Minerva a feminine first name meaning 'wise one'. In Roman mythology Minerva was goddess of wisdom and patron of the arts and trades, the counterpart of THE GREEK ATHENA.

Minette a feminine diminutive form of MIGNONETTE.

Minna or **Minne** a feminine first name meaning 'love' (*Germanic*). Diminutive forms of WILHELMINA.

Minnie a feminine diminutive form of MARY, MAY, WILHELMINA.

Minta a feminine diminutive form of ARAMINTA.

Mira a feminine diminutive form of MIRABEL, MIRANDA.

Mirabel or **Mirabelle** a feminine first name meaning 'wonderful' (*Latin*). Diminutive forms are Mira, Myra.

Miranda a feminine first name meaning 'wonderful' (*Latin*). William Shakespeare (1564–1616) used the name for Prospero's daughter in his play *The Tempest*. Miranda Richardson is an English actress. Diminutive forms are Mira, Myra.

Miriam variant feminine form of MARY. In the Old Testament, Miriam was a sister of Moses and Aaron who watched over the infant Moses in his basket.

Mischa a masculine diminutive form of MIKHAIL.

Mitchell a surname form of MICHAEL, a surname, meaning 'big, great' (*Old English*), used as a masculine first name. The diminutive form is Mitch.

Mitzi a German feminine diminutive form of MARIA. Mitzi Gaynor is an American actress and dancer.

Mo a masculine or feminine diminutive form of MAUREEN, MAURICE, MORRIS.

Modest a masculine first name from the Russian form of *modestus*, 'obedient' (*Latin*).

Modesty an English word from *modestus* (*Latin*) for the quality of being shy or humble, used as a feminine first name.

Modred a masculine first name meaning 'counsellor'; in Arthurian legend the knight who killed King Arthur (*Old English*).

Modwen a feminine first name from *morwyn*, 'maiden' (*Welsh*)

Moelwyn a masculine first name from 'white, bare' (*Welsh*).

Mohammed a masculine first name meaning 'praise' (*Arabic*). It was the name taken by Abd Allah (*c.*570–632), the prophet and founder of Islam. Variant forms are Mahomet, Muhammad, Muhammed.

Moina a feminine first name perhaps stemming from *moine*, 'peat, moss': 'girl of the peat-moss' (*Irish/Scottish Gaelic*).

Moingionn a feminine variant form of MONGFHIND.

Moira an anglicised feminine form of Irish MÁIRE, although there is also a place and earldom of the same name in Ulster. Moira Kelly is an American film actress. A variant form is Moyra.

Móirin a feminine diminutive form of Mór often anglicised as MAUREEN.

Mollie or **Molly** feminine diminutive forms of MARY, now used independently.

Moneak an American feminine variant form of MONIQUE.

Mona a feminine first name probably stemming from *muadhnaid*, 'noble'

(*Irish Gaelic*). (2) a Welsh and Manx feminine first name from a name given by the Romans to a wide stretch of the west coast of Britain and its islands. From it comes Mon, the Welsh name of Anglesey. The Isle of Man is also known as Mona's Isle.

Mongfhind or **Mongfhionn** (pronounced *mo-finn*) a feminine first name meaning 'of the long fair hair', from *mong*, 'long hair', and *fionn*, 'fair' (*Irish Gaelic*). It is the name of numerous figures in history and legend, of whom the most prominent is the jealous stepmother of NIALL of the Nine Hostages. A variant form is Moingionn.

Monica a feminine first name the meaning of which is uncertain but possibly 'advising' (*Latin*).

Monika the German feminine form of MONICA.

Monique the French feminine form of MONICA, now also used as an English form. A variant form is Moneak.

Monroe or **Monro** a variant form of MUNRO.

Montague or **Montagu** a surname, meaning 'pointed hill', used as a masculine first name. A diminutive form is Monty.

Montgomery or **Montgomerie** (1) a surname, meaning 'hill of powerful man' (*Old French/Germanic*), used as a masculine first name. (2) an anglicised masculine form of Irish MUIRCHERTACH. A diminutive form is Monty.

Monty a masculine diminutive form of MONTAGUE, MONTGOMERY.

Mór a feminine first name meaning 'tall', 'big', from Gaelic *mór* (*Irish Gaelic*). It may have been used as a subsitute for MÁIRE. Its diminutive form, Móirín, is often anglicised as MAUREEN.

Morag the feminine Scottish Gaelic form of SARAH.

Moray *see* MURRAY.

Mordecai a masculine first name meaning 'man of Marduk' (Babylonian), meaning a person who worshipped the main Babylonian god. In the Old Testament Mordecai was a cousin of Esther who prevented a massacre of the Jews.

Mordred the anglicised masculine form of MEDRAWD.

Morfudd see MORWEN.

Morgan a masculine or feminine first name that traditionally originates with a Celtic war-goddess, still known as The Morrigan, from *mor*, 'great', and *gan*, which may mean either 'sea' or 'queen' (*Irish Gaelic/Welsh*). Many powerful women have borne this name. The name of

Morgan Mwynfawr (seventh century) is preserved in Glamorgan. Although seen also as a boy's name, in the Arthurian romances Morgan le Fay is a witch queen. Morgan Freeman is an American film actor.

Morgana a purely feminine form of MORGAN.

Moriarty an anglicised masculine form of Irish MUIRCHERTACH.

Morien a masculine first name meaning 'sea-born', from *mur*, 'sea' (*Welsh*).

Moritz the German masculine form of MAURICE.

Morley a surname, meaning 'moor meadow' (*Old English*), used as a masculine first name.

Morna an anglicised feminine form of Irish MUIRNE.

Morrice or **Morris** masculine variant forms of MAURICE. A diminutive form is Mo.

Mortimer a surname, meaning 'dead sea' (*Old French*), used as a masculine first name.

Morton a surname, meaning 'farmstead moor' (*Old English*), used as a masculine first name.

Morven (1) a feminine first name that is probably related to MORWEN. (2) a feminine first name from the name of a mountain in Argyll, from Gaelic *mór bhéinn*, 'big mountain' (*Scottish Gaelic*).

Morwen or **Morwena** a feminine first name meaning 'maiden' (*Cornish/Welsh*). An older form is Morfudd, which was the name of the woman loved by the bard DAFYDD ap Gwilym, unfortunately already married to someone else.

Mosè the Italian masculine form of MOSES.

Moses a masculine first name the meaning of which is uncertain, most probably an Egyptian name. In the Old Testament Moses was the Hebrew prophet who led the Israelites out of Egypt to Canaan, the Promised Land. He also gave the Israelites divinely revealed laws. The Arabic form is Musa.

Moyra a feminine variant form of MOIRA.

Muhammad or **Muhammed** a masculine variant form of MOHAMMED.

Muir a Scottish masculine form of the surname Moore, meaning 'moor' (*Old French*), used as a masculine first name.

Muirchertach (pronounced *murr-hertah*) a masculine first name meaning 'seafarer', from Old Gaelic *muir*, 'sea' (*Irish Gaelic*). The name of a legendary high king, and frequently found in literature and records. It is anglicised into Moriarty and Montgomery.

Muirenn

Muirenn or **Muireann** a variant feminine form of MUIRNE.

Muirne (pronounced *moor-na*) a feminine first name whose derivation is probably from Old Gaelic *muir*, 'sea', and means 'sea-bright' (*Irish Gaelic*), as in MURIEL. Muirne Muncháem, 'of the fair neck', was the mother of Fionn macCumhaill. There is a Gaelic diminutive form, Muirneag. Variant forms are Muirenn, Muireann. It is anglicised as Murna, Morna, Myrna.

Mungo a masculine first name possibly from Old Welsh, *mwyn*, 'dear' and *cu*, 'amiable', meaning 'dear friend'. This was a nickname of KENTIGERN, one of the great Celtic saints and patron of Glasgow Cathedral.

Munro or **Munroe** or **Munrow** a Scottish surname of the Easter Ross clan, perhaps originally from Old Gaelic *mon ruadh*, 'red hill', used as a masculine first name. Variant forms are Monro, Monroe.

Murchadh (pronounced *murr-hah*) the Irish Gaelic masculine form of MURDOCH, anglicised to Murrough, as is MURPHY.

Murdo the anglicised masculine form of MURDOCH.

Murdoch a masculine first name meaning 'sea warrior', from *murchaidh*, 'sea warrior' (*Scottish Gaelic*). The Gaelic form is MURCHADH. An alternative anglicised version is Murdo. Had the ambitions of the Albany Stewarts been gratified, Scotland might have had a King Murdoch instead of James I.

Muriel a Scottish and Welsh feminine first name meaning 'sea bright', from Old Gaelic *murgheal*.

Murna an anglicised feminine form of Irish MUIRNE.

Murphy a surname deriving from Gaelic *muir*, 'sea', and *cú*, 'hound' (*Irish Gaelic*), sometimes used as a masculine first name (and sometimes as a feminine, especially in North America). Other forms include MURROUGH.

Murray a surname, a form of Moray, from Old Gaelic *muir*, 'sea', and *ais*, 'edge, border' (*Scottish Gaelic*), used as a masculine first name. Murray Periah is a cellist and conductor.

Murrough the anglicised masculine form of Irish MURCHADH, MURPHY.

Musa the Arabic form of MOSES.

Myer (1) a surname, meaning 'marsh' (*Old Norse*), used as a first name. (2) a variant form of MAYER.

Myfanwy (pronounced *mih-van-wee*) a feminine first name meaning 'my fine one' (*Welsh*).

Myles (1) a masculine variant form of MILES. (2) a masculine first name meaning 'devotee of MARY' (*Irish Gaelic*).

Myra (1) a feminine first name invented by the poet Sir Fulke Greville (1554–1628), possibly as an anagram of MARY, or to mean 'she who weeps or laments' (*Greek*). (2) a feminine diminutive form of MIRABEL, MIRANDA.

Myrddin (pronounced *mirr-thin*) a masculine first name that appears to combine Old Welsh *myr*, 'sea', and *ddin*, 'hill'. It has been anglicised to MERLIN, the name of a celebrated wizard and is preserved in Carmarthen, 'fort of Myrddyn'.

Myrna an anglicised feminine form of Irish MUIRNE.

Myron a masculine first name meaning 'fragrant oil' (*Greek*).

Myrtle the name of the shrub used as a feminine first name. The American writer F. Scott Fitzgerald (1896–1940) used the name for one of the female characters in his novel *The Great Gatsby* (1925).

N

Naamah a feminine first name meaning 'pretty, loved' (*Hebrew*).

Naaman a masculine first name meaning 'pleasant' (*Hebrew*). In the Old Testament Naaman was a grandson of Benjamin who established a family of Israelites.

Nadezhda a feminine first name meaning 'hope' (*Russian*).

Nadia an English, French and Italian feminine form of NADEZHDA.

Nadine a French feminine diminutive form of NADIA.

Nahum a masculine first name meaning 'comforter' (*Hebrew*). In the Old Testament Nahum was an Israelite prophet of the seventh century BC and author of the Book of Nahum.

Naiada a feminine diminutive form of NAIDA.

Naida a feminine first name meaning 'the water nymph' (*Latin*). A diminutive form is NAIADA.

Nairn a masculine first name meaning 'dweller by the alder tree' (*Celtic*).

Nairne a feminine first name meaning 'from the river' (*Gaelic*).

Naísi a masculine variant form of NAOISE.

Nan a feminine diminutive form of AGNES, ANN, NANCY, NANETTE.

Nana a feminine diminutive form of HANNAH.

Nancy a feminine diminutive form of ANN, now used independently. Nancy Travis is an American film actress. Diminutive forms are Nan, Nina.

Nanette a feminine diminutive form of Ann, now used independently. A diminutive form is Nan.

Naoise (pronounced *nay-si*) an Irish masculine first name and that of the eldest of the three sons of Usna and lover of Deirdre in the famous tale from the *Ulster Cycle*. A variant form is Naísi.

Naomh (pronounced *nayve*) a feminine first name from *naomh*, 'saint' (*Irish Gaelic*). The use of this word as a first name is quite modern.

Naomi a feminine first name meaning 'pleasantness' (*Hebrew*). In the Old Testament Naomi was the mother-in-law of RUTH.

Nap a masculine diminutive form of NAPOLEON.

Napaea a feminine diminutive form of NAPEA.

Napea a feminine first name meaning 'girl of the valley' (*Latin*). Diminutive forms are Napaea, Napia.

Naphtali a masculine first name meaning 'my wrestling' (*Hebrew*). In the Old Testament Naphtali was the second son of Jacob and Bilhah, the maidservant of Rachel, Jacob's wife, who gave her to him because of her infertility. Naphtali founded on the of the twelve tribes of Israel.

Napia a feminine diminutive form of Napea.

Napier a surname, meaning 'linen keeper' (*Old French*), used as a masculine first name.

Napoleon a masculine first name meaning 'lion of the forest dell' (*Greek*). A diminutive form is Nap.

Nara a feminine first name meaning 'nearest and dearest' (*English*).

Narda a feminine first name meaning 'fragrant perfume, the lingering essence' (*Latin*).

Nash a surname, meaning 'ash tree' (*Old English*), used as a masculine first name.

Nat a masculine diminutive form of NATHAN, NATHANIEL.

Natal the Spanish masculine form of NOËL.

Natale the Italian masculine form of NOËL.

Natalie a French feminine form of NATALYA now used as an English-language form.

Natalia a Spanish feminine form of NATALYA.

Natalya a feminine first name meaning 'Christmas' (*Latin/Russian*).

Natasha a Russian feminine diminutive form of NATALYA.

Natene a feminine diminutive form of NATHANIA.

Nathan a masculine first name meaning 'gift' (*Hebrew*). In the Old Testament Nathan was (1) a prophet at the court of David and (2) a son of David and Bathsheba. A diminutive form is Nat.

Nathane or **Nathene** feminine diminutive forms of NATHANIA.

Nathanael a masculine first name meaning 'God gave' (*Hebrew*). In the New Testament Nathanael was one of the early disciples of Jesus, often identified with Bartholomew. A variant form is Nathaniel. A diminutive form is Nat.

Nathania a feminine form of NATHANAEL. Diminutive forms are Natene, Nathane, Nathene.

Nathaniel a masculine variant form of NATHANAEL.

Neachtan a masculine variant form of NECTAN.

Neal or **Neale** a masculine variant form of NIALL.

Nebula a feminine first name meaning 'a cloud of mist' (*Latin*).

Nectan or **Nechtan** a Pictish masculine first name that stems from a root-form *nig*, 'to wash', hence 'purified one'. It is an ancient royal name; it was under their king Nectan that the Picts defeated the invading Anglians in AD 685. The Pictish kings had a priestly role. A variant form is Neachtan.

Ned or **Neddie** or **Neddy** masculine (contraction of 'mine Ed') diminutive forms of EDGAR, EDMUND, EDWARD, EDWIN.

Nehemiah a masculine first name meaning 'Jehovah comforts' (*Hebrew*). In the Old Testament Nehemiah was a sixth-century BC leader of the Israelites on the return from the Babylonian captivity. His story is told in the Book of Nehemiah.

Neil or **Neill** a masculine variant form of NIALL.

Nell or **Nellie** or **Nelly** feminine diminutive forms of ELEANOR, ELLEN, HELEN.

Nelson a surname, meaning 'son of NEIL', used as a masculine first name.

Nemo a masculine first name meaning 'grove' (*Greek*).

Nerice or **Nerine** or **Nerissa** a feminine first name meaning 'from the sea' (*Greek*). William Shakespeare (1564–1616) used the name Nerissa for Portia's waiting-maid in his play *The Merchant of Venice*.

Nero a masculine first name meaning 'dark, black-haired' (*Latin*). It was the name of the Roman emperor (AD 37–68) infamous for his cruelty.

Nerys a feminine first name meaning 'lordly', from *ner*, 'lord' (*Welsh*). Nerys Hughes is a well-known Welsh actress.

Nessa (1) a feminine first name meaning 'ungentle' (*Irish Gaelic*). The explanation lies in the traditional story of Nessa, mother of CONCHOBHAR, or Conor, macNessa. Originally called Assa, or 'gentle one', Nessa was so fierce in defence of the kingdom of Ulster that her name was prefixed by *Ní*, meaning 'not'. (2) a feminine diminutive form of AGNES, VANESSA.

Nessie a feminine diminutive form of AGNES.

Nest or **Nesta** a Welsh feminine diminutive form of AGNES.

Nestor a masculine first name meaning 'coming home' (*Greek*). In Greek mythology, Nestor was a leader of the Greeks at the siege of Troy and as such appears in the play *Troilus and Cressida* by William Shakespeare (1564–1616). Nestor Almenedros (1930–92) was a Spanish-born cinematographer and film director.

Netta or **Nettie** feminine diminutive forms of HENRIETTA.

Neven a masculine variant form of NEVIN.

Neville a place name and surname, meaning 'new place' (*Old French*), used as a masculine first name.

Nevin a surname, meaning 'little saint' (*Irish Gaelic*), used as a masculine first name. Variant forms are Nevin, Niven.

Newell a surname, meaning 'new field' (*Old English*), used as a masculine first name.

Newland a surname, meaning 'new land' (*Old English*), used as a masculine first name.

Newlyn the name of a Cornish town, the origin of which is cognate to Gaelic *naomh*, 'holy', and *linne*, 'pool', used as a feminine first name. Nuline is a variant form.

Newman a surname, meaning 'newcomer, new settler' (*Old English*), used as a masculine first name.

Newton a surname, meaning 'new farmstead or village' (*Old English*), used as a masculine first name.

Niall or **Nial** (pronounced nee-al) an Irish and Scottish masculine first name meaning 'champion', from Old Gaelic *nia*, 'champion'. It was common for disputes to be decided by combat between rival champions from either side. Niall Noígiallach, 'of the Nine Hostages', was a celebrated fifth-century high king of Ireland, progenitor of the Ui Néill dynasty. Variant forms include Neil, Neill, Neal, Neale. The English name NIGEL has been associated with Niall but the resemblance is coincidental.

Niamh or **Niam** or **Niav** (pronounced *nee-av*) a feminine first name meaning 'radiant one' (*Irish Gaelic*). Niamh of the golden hair, daughter of the sea-god Manannan, fell in love with Oisin (Ossian) and took him to Tir nan Og.

Niccolò an Italian masculine form of NICHOLAS.

Nichol a masculine variant form of NICOL.

Nicholas a masculine first name meaning 'victory of the people' (*Greek*). St Nicholas was a fourth-century bishop of Myra who became the patron saint of children, merchants, pawnbrokers and sailors as well as of

Russia. He is also strongly associated with Christmas. A variant form is
Nicolas. Diminutive forms are Nick, Nicky.

Nick a masculine diminutive form of Nicholas, Nicol. Nick Nolte is an
American film actor.

Nickson a masculine variant form of Nixon.

Nicky (1) a masculine diminutive form of Nicholas, Nicol. (2) a feminine
diminutive form of Nicole.

Nicodemus a masculine first name meaning 'conqueror of the people'
(*Greek*). In the New Testament Nicodemus was a Pharisee who tried to
defend Jesus against the other Pharisees.

Nicol a Scottish surname form of Nicholas used as a masculine first
name. Nicol Williamson is a Scottish actor. A variant form is Nichol.

Nicola (1) a feminine variant form of Nicole. (2) an Italian masculine
form of Nicholas.

Nicolas a masculine variant form of Nicholas. Nicolas Cage is an American film actor.

Nicole a feminine form of Nicholas. Nicole Kidman is an Australian-born
film actress and wife of Tom Cruise. Variant forms are Nicola,
Nicolette, Colette. Diminutive forms are Nicky, Nikkie.

Nicolette a feminine variant form of Nicole.

Nigel a masculine first name meaning 'black' (*Latin*).

Nigella a femine form of Nigel. Nigella Lawson is an English journalist.

Nikkie a feminine diminutive form of Nicole.

Nikolaus a German masculine form of Nicholas.

Nils a Scandinavian masculine form of Neil.

Nina a feminine diminutive form of Nancy.

Ninette a French feminine diminutive form of Ann.

Ninian a masculine first name from the Old Gaelic personal name Ninidh,
of uncertain derivation. St Ninian (fourth–fifth century) was one of the
fathers of the Celtic Church in Scotland. The modern Gaelic form of the
name is Ringean.

Ninon a French feminine diminutive form of Ann.

Nissie or **Nissy** a feminine diminutive form of Nixie.

Nita a feminine diminutive form of Anita, Juanita.

Niven a masculine variant form of Nevin.

Nixie a feminine first name meaning 'water sprite' (*Germanic*). Diminutive forms are Nissie, Nissy.

Nixon a surname, meaning 'son of NICHOLAS', used as a masculine first name. A variant form is Nickson.

Noah a masculine first name meaning 'rest' (*Hebrew*). In the Old Testament Noah was a Hebrew patriarch who was chosen by God to save himself, his family and a pair of each animal and bird from the Flood by building a ship (Noah's Ark) in which they could float on the water. The Arabic form is Nuh.

Noble a surname, meaning 'noble, famous' (*Old French*), used as a masculine first name.

Noé the French and Spanish masculine form of NOAH.

Noè the Italian masculine form of NOAH.

Noël or **Noel** a masculine or feminine first name meaning 'Christmas' (*French*).

Noëlle or **Noelle** feminine form of NOËL.

Nola a feminine variant form of NUALA.

Nolan a surname, meaning 'son of the champion' (*Irish Gaelic*), used as a masculine first name.

Noll or **Nollie** masculine diminutive forms of OLIVER.

Nominoë (pronounced *nom-in-o-ay*) a masculine first name and that of a ninth-century Breton king who achieved Breton independence from the Frankish empire.

Nona a feminine first name meaning 'ninth' (*Latin*).

Nonnie a feminine diminutive form of ANONA.

Nora or **Norah** a feminine diminutive form of ELEANOR, HONORA, LEONORA, also used independently.

Norbert a masculine first name meaning 'northern hero' (*Germanic*).

Noreen an Irish feminine form of NORA.

Norma a feminine first name meaning 'a rule' (*Latin*), but probably invented as the name of the eponymous heroine of the opera by the Italian composer Vincenzo Bellini (1801–35).

Norman a masculine first name meaning 'northman' (*Germanic*). A diminutive form is Norrie.

Norrie (1) a Scottish surname, stemming from Old Norse *norge*, 'Norway', indicating someone from that land, used as a masculine first name. (2) a masculine diminutive form of NORMAN.

Northcliffe a surname, meaning 'north cliff' (*Old English*), used as a masculine first name.

Norton a surname, meaning 'northern farmstead or village' (*Old English*), used as a masculine first name.

Norval a masculine first name invented by the eighteenth-century writer John Home (1722–1808) in his play *Douglas* (1756), although it has also been found as an old surname, a shortened form of Normanville, from the fourteenth century.

Norville a surname, meaning 'north town' (*Old French*), used as a masculine first name.

Norvin a masculine first name meaning 'northern friend' (*Old English*).

Norward a surname, meaning 'northern guardian' (*Old English*), used as a masculine first name.

Norwell a surname, meaning 'northern stream', used as a masculine first name.

Norwood a surname, meaning 'north wood' (*Old English*), used as a masculine first name.

Nowell an English masculine form of NOËL.

Nuala (pronounced *noola*) a feminine first name that is probably an abbreviated form of FIONNUALA now used independently. Nola is an alternative form.

Nudd (pronounced *nooth*) a masculine first name and that of a legendary Welsh hero, derived perhaps from the Brythonic god-name Nodons.

Nuh the Arabic form of NOAH.

Nuline a feminine variant form of NEWLYN.

Nye a masculine diminutive form of ANEURIN.

Nyree a feminine first name from New Zealand that was brought to the UK by the actress Nyree Dawn Porter.

O

Oakley a surname, meaning 'oak tree meadow' (*Old English*), used as a masculine first name.

Obadiah a masculine first name meaning 'servant of Jehovah' (*Hebrew*). In the Old Testament Obadiah was a Hebrew prophet and author of the Book of Obadiah, the shortest book of the Bible.

Obed a masculine first name meaning 'serving God' (*Hebrew*). In the Old Testament Obed was a descendant of Judah.

Oberon a masculine variant form of AUBERON. William Shakespeare (1564–1616) used the name for the king of the fairies in his comedy *A Midsummer Night's Dream*.

Obert a masculine first name meaning 'wealthy, brilliant' (*Germanic*).

Octavia feminine form of OCTAVIUS. Octavia (died 11 BC) was a Roman widow, the sister of Octavius Caesar (Augustus), who became the wife of Mark Antony in 41 BC. Antony divorced her in 31 BC after meeting Cleopatra. Through her daughters by Antony she was the grandmother of Caligula and the great-grandmother of Nero. She appears in the play *Antony and Cleopatra* by William Shakespeare (1564–1616) and also in *All for Love* (1678) by John Dryden (1631–1700).

Octavian a masculine variant form of OCTAVIUS. The name was used by the German composer Richard Strauss (1864–1949) and his librettist, the Austrian poet and dramatist Hugo von Hofmannsthal (1874–1929) for the young hero of their opera *Der Rosenkavalier* (1211). The role is actually sung by a woman.

Octavie a French feminine form of OCTAVIA.

Octavius a masculine first name meaning 'eighth' (*Latin*). Octavius Caesar (63 BC–AD 14) was a Roman statesman who was adopted by Julius Caesar in 44 BC. He was the brother-in-law of Mark Antony whom he defeated at Actium in 31 BC. Thereafter he became the first emperor of Rome, adopting the name AUGUSTUS. He appears in two plays by William Shakespeare (1564–1616), *Julius Caesar* and *Antony and Cleopatra*. Octavian is a masculine variant form.

Oda a French masculine form of OTTO.

Odd the Norwegian masculine form of OTTO.

Oddo or **Oddone** Italian masculine forms of OTTO.

Oded a masculine first name meaning 'upholder' (*Hebrew*). In the Old Testament Oded is (1) the name of the prophet Azarias and (2) a Samarian prophet who intercepted to save the lives of captives taken from Judah after its defeat by Israel and Syria.

Odelia or **Odelie** feminine variant forms of ODILE.

Odette a feminine diminutive form of ODA.

Odhrán (pronounced *oh-rann*) a masculine first name from *odhra*, 'dark-haired' (*Irish Gaelic*). The name was borne by St Columba's associate and has strong connections with Iona. 'Reilig Odhrain' is the place where many kings and Lords of the Isles were buried.

Odile or **Odille** a feminine first name meaning 'rich, wealthy' (*Germanic*). Variant forms are Odelia, Odelie, Otilie, Ottilie.

Odoardo an Italian masculine form of EDWARD.

Odysseus see ULYSSES.

Oengus *see* ANGUS.

Ofra a feminine variant form of OPHRAH.

Ogden a surname, meaning 'oak valley', used as first name (*Old English*). Ogden Nash (1902–71) was an American humorous poet.

Ogilvie or **Ogilvy** a surname, meaning 'high peak' (*Celtic*), used as a masculine first name.

Oisín *see* OSSIAN.

Olaf or **Olav** a masculine first name meaning 'divine remnant' (*Old Norse*).

Olave (1) a Manx Gaelic masculine form of OLAF, the name of the founder of the Manx kingdom. (2) a feminine variant form of OLIVE or Olivia.

Oleg the Russian masculine form of HELGE.

Olga the Russian feminine form of HELGA. St Olga (*c*.879–969) was a Russian grand-duchess who began the Christianisation of Russia.

Olimpia the Italian feminine form of OLYMPIA.

Olive a feminine first name meaning 'an olive' (*Latin*). Variant forms are Olivia, Olave.

Oliver a masculine first name meaning 'an olive tree' (*Latin*). Oliver and

ROLAND were the most famous of the legendary twelve paladins who attended on Charlemagne. Oliver Cromwell (1599–1658) was an English Puritan statesman and general who was one of the Parliamentary leaders of the English Civil War. Following the execution of King Charles I, he quelled the Royalist forces in Scotland and Ireland and was Lord Protector of the Commonwealth (1653–58). Diminutive forms are Ollie, Olly, Noll, Nollie.

Oliverio the Spanish masculine form of OLIVER.

Olivia a feminine variant form of Olive. William Shakespeare (1654–1616) used the name for 'a lady of great beauty and fortune' in his comedy *Twelfth Night*. A diminutive form is Livia.

Oliviero the Italian masculine form of OLIVER.

Ollie or **Olly** masculine diminutive forms of OLIVER.

Olwen a feminine first name meaning 'white footprint' (*Welsh*). It is the name of the heroine of the legend of 'Culhwych ac Olwen'.

Olympe the French feminine form of OLYMPIA.

Olympia a feminine first name meaning 'heavenly' (*Greek*). Olympia Dukakis is an American actress.

Omar a masculine first name meaning 'first son' (*Arabic*). Omar (died 644) was the second caliph of Islam (634–644). Omar Sharif is an Egyptian film actor and bridge player. A variant form is Umar.

Ona a feminine diminutive form of names ending -ona, for example Fiona.

Onefre a Spanish masculine form of HUMPHREY.

Onefredo an Italian masculine form of HUMPHREY.

Onfroi a French masculine form of HUMPHREY.

Onofrio the Italian masculine form of HUMPHREY.

Onorio the Italian masculine form of HONORIUS.

Oonagh or **Oona** (pronounced *oo-na*) a feminine first name meaning 'the one' (*Irish Gaelic*), a Gaelic form of UNA, the maiden rescued from the dragon in the legend of St George.

Opal the name of the iridescent gemstone used as a feminine first name, precious stone (*Sanskrit*).

Ophelia a feminine first name from *ophis*, 'serpent' (*Greek*). William Shakespeare (1654–1616) used the name for the young and innocent girl in *Hamlet* who is instructed by her father, Polonius, to spurn the eponymous prince's advances.

Ophélie the French feminine form of OPHELIA.

Ophrah or **Ophra** a feminine first name meaning 'fawn' (*Hebrew*). Variant forms are Ofra, Oprah.

Oprah a modern feminine variant of OPHRAH, introduced by the American television presenter Oprah Winfrey.

Oran an anglicised masculine form of ODHRÁN.

Orazio the Italian masculine form of HORACE.

Orchil an Irish Gaelic feminine first name from a mythical name associated with an ancient goddess of twilight.

Oren a masculine first name meaning 'laurel' (*Hebrew*).

Oreste the Italian masculine form of ORESTES.

Orestes a masculine first name meaning 'mountain climber' (*Greek*). In Greek mythology Orestes was the son of Agamemnon, who killed his mother and her lover in revenge for the death of his father.

Orfeo the Italian masculine form of ORPHEUS.

Orfhlaith a feminine variant form of ORLA.

Oriana or **Oriane** a feminine first name meaning 'golden' (*Latin*).

Oriel a feminine first name meaning 'strife' (*Germanic*).

Orin, Orrin an anglicised masculine form of ODHRÁN.

Orion a masculine first name meaning 'son of light' (*Greek*).

Orla or **Orlaith** a feminine first name meaning 'golden girl', from *ór*, 'gold' (*Irish Gaelic*). Other forms are Orlaith, Orfhlaith.

Orlanda feminine form of ORLANDO.

Orlando the Italian masculine form of ROLAND, with OLIVER the most famous of the legendary twelve paladins who attended on Charlemagne. William Shakespeare (1654–1616) used the name for that of the courageous hero of his comedy *As You Like It*. The English writer Virginia Woolf (1882–1941) also used the name for the hero/heroine of her fantastic novel, *Orlando* (1928).

Ormond or **Ormonde** a surname, meaning 'from east Munster' (*Irish Gaelic*), used as a masculine first name.

Orna a feminine first name meaning 'dark-haired' (*Irish Gaelic*), a feminine form of ODHRÁN.

Orpheus a masculine name of uncertain meaning. In Greek mythology, a Orpheus was a poet who sought to retrieve his wife Eurydice from Hades.

Orrin an anglicised masculine form of ODHRÁN.

Orsino a masculine first name meaning 'little bear'. William Shakespeare (1654–1616) used the name for the lovesick duke of Illyria who begins the comedy Twelfth Night with the famous words, 'If music be the food of love, play on.'

Orso a masculine first name meaning 'bear' (*Latin/Italian*).

Orsola the Italian feminine form of Ursula.

Orson a masculine first name meaning 'little bear' (*Latin/Old French*). Orson Welles (1915–85) was an American film actor and director. His most famous film was *Citizen Kane* (1941), which he directed and in which he starred.

Ortensia the Italian feminine form of Hortense.

Orvil or **Orville** a masculine first name meaning 'golden place' (*Old French*).

Orwin a masculine variant form of Erwin.

Osbert a masculine first name meaning 'God-bright' (*Old English*). A diminutive form is Ossie.

Osborn or **Osborne** or **Osbourne** a surname, meaning 'divine bear, or warrior (*Germanic*), used as a masculine first name. A diminutive form is Ossie.

Oscar a masculine first name meaning 'divine spear' (*Germanic*). It was probably taken to Ireland by the Vikings and appears in the later Fenian Cycle of legends as the son of Ossian, and a great poet and warrior. In his Ossianic poems, the Scottish poet James Macpherson (1736–96) was responsible for a new popularity for the name in Europe.

Oskar the German and Scandinavian masculine form of Oscar.

Osmond or **Osmund** a masculine first name meaning 'divine protection' (*Germanic*). St Osmund (died 1099) was a Norman French bishop of Salisbury who completed and consecrated the cathedral there. A diminutive form is Ossie.

Ossian an Irish and Scottish masculine first name from Oisín, 'little deer', from Gaelic *oisean*. Ossian, bard and warrior, son of Fionn macCumhaill, is one of the great figures of Gaelic legend, who, lured by Niamh, spent hundreds of years in Tir nan Og, and emerged as young as he went in, only to age three hundred years and die in the space of a day.

Ossie a masculine diminutive form of Osbert, Osborn, Oscar, Osmond, Oswald.

Osvaldo the Italian masculine form of Oswald.

Oswald a masculine first name meaning 'divine rule' (*Germanic*). St Oswald (*c.*605–641) was an Anglo-Saxon king of Northumbria (633–641) who restored Christianity to the region. William Shakespeare (1654–1616) used the name for Goneril's steward in the tragedy, *King Lear*.

Oswin a masculine first name meaning 'God-friend' (*Old English*).

Otilie a feminine variant form of ODILE.

Otis a surname, meaning 'son of Ote' (*Germanic*), used as a masculine first name.

Ottar *see* ARTHUR.

Ottavia the Italian feminine form of OCTAVIA.

Ottavio the Italian masculine form of OCTAVIUS.

Ottilie a feminine variant form of ODILE.

Otto a masculine name meaning 'rich' (*Germanic*).

Ottone an Italian masculine form of OTTO.

Owain a Welsh masculine form of Eugenius, 'well-born', anglicised as Owen. It is a popular name in old Welsh legends and that of the hero of the thirteenth-century poem 'Owain'. Owain Glyndwr was the last independent prince of Wales (*c.* 1350–*c.* 1416).

Owen (1) an anglicised masculine form of OWAIN. (2) an anglicised masculine form of EOGANÁN.

Oxford a place name, meaning 'ford for oxen' (*Old English*), used as a masculine first name.

Oxton a surname, meaning 'place for keeping oxen' (*Old English*), used as a masculine first name.

Oz or **Ozzie** or **Ozzy** masculine diminutive forms of names beginning with Os-.

P

Pablo the Spanish masculine form of PAUL. Pablo Picasso (1881–1973) was a Spanish painter and sculptor and a highly influential figure in twentieth-century art. He cofounded the Cubist movement.

Paddy (1) a masculine diminutive form of PÁDRAIG, PATRICK. Paddy Ashdown was the leader of the Liberal Democratic Party (1988–99). (2) a feminine diminutive form of PATRICIA.

Pádraig (pronounced *paw-rik*) the Irish Gaelic masculine form of PATRICK. Diminutive forms are Paddy, Pat.

Paget or **Pagett** or **Padget** or **Padgett** a surname, meaning 'young page' (*Old French*), used as a masculine first name.

Paige or **Page** a surname, meaning 'page' (*Old French*), used as a feminine first name.

Palmiro a masculine first name meaning 'palm' (*Latin*).

Palmira feminine form of PALMIRO.

Paloma the Spanish word for 'dove' used as a feminine first name.

Pam a feminine diminutive form of PAMELA.

Pamela a feminine first name invented by the English poet Sir Philip Sidney (1554–86) derived from the Greek work for 'honey'. A diminutive form is Pam.

Pancho a masculine diminutive form of FRANCISCO.

Pandora a feminine first name meaning 'gifted' (*Greek*). In Greek mythology, Pandora was the first woman on earth. The gods gave her a box full of blessings for mankind, which she was told not to open. She did, and they all flew away except hope.

Pansy (1) a feminine first name meaning 'thought' (*French*). (2) the name of the garden flower used as a feminine first name.

Paola the Italian feminine form of PAULA.

Paolo the Italian masculine form of PAUL.

Paris a masculine first name meaning 'torch, firebrand' (Greek). In Greek mythology Paris was the second son of King Priam of Troy and Hecuba whose abduction of Helen, wife of the Greek Menelaus, led to the Trojan War. He appears in *Troilus and Cressida* by William Shakespeare (1654–1616). Shakespeare also used the name for that of a young nobleman who is encouraged to woo Juliet in *Romeo and Juliet*.

Pascal a masculine first name meaning 'of the passover' (*Latin/French*).

Pasquale the Italian masculine form of PASCAL.

Pat (1) a masculine diminutive form of PÁDRAIG, PATRICK. (2) a feminine diminutive form of PATRICIA.

Patience a feminine first name meaning 'patience' (*Latin*).

Patric a masculine variant form of PATRICK.

Patrice (1) the French masculine form of PATRICK. (2) the French feminine form of PATRICIA.

Patricia the feminine form of PATRICK. Diminutive forms are Paddy, Pat, Patsy, Pattie, Patty, Tricia.

Patricio the Spanish masculine form of PATRICK.

Patricius a masculine variant form of PATRICK.

Patrick a masculine first name meaning 'of noble birth, a patrician' from Latin Patricius. St Patrick (*fl.* fifth century) born to a romanised British family on the West coast of Britain, is the great missionary saint of Ireland, and that country's patron saint. The name was so popular in Ireland as for 'Paddy' and 'Irishman' to be synonymous to outsiders. Patrick Bergin is an American actor. A variant form is Patric. The diminutive forms Paddy and Patsy are usually found in Ireland; Pat is more common in Scotland.

Patrizia the Italian feminine form of PATRICIA.

Patrizio the Italian masculine form of PATRICK.

Patrizius the German masculine form of PATRICK.

Patsy a feminine diminutive form of PATRICIA.

Pattie or **Patty** feminine diminutive forms of MARTHA, PATIENCE, PATRICIA.

Paul a masculine first name meaning 'little' (*Latin*). In the New Testament Paul (born Saul of Tarsus) was a Jewish persecutor of Christians who underwent a conversion on the road to Damascus and became the Christianity's leading missionary, making three missionary journeys to Cyprus, Asia Minor, Greece and Palestine. He wrote many of the Epistles. He was executed in Rome *c.*67.

Paula feminine form of PAUL.

Paulette a French feminine form of PAULA.

Paulina or **Pauline** a feminine diminutive forms of PAULA. William Shakespeare (1654–1616) used the form Paulina for one of the characters in his play *A Winter's Tale*.

Pawl the Welsh masculine form of PAUL.

Payne or **Payn** a surname, meaning 'countryman' (*Old French*), used as a masculine first name.

Peace the word for the condition of tranquillity or calm used as a feminine first name.

Peadar an Irish and Scottish Gaelic masculine form of PETER.

Pearl the name of the lustrous white gem used as a feminine first name.

Pedaiah a masculine first name meaning 'Jehovah ransoms' (*Hebrew*).

Pedr a Welsh masculine form of PETER.

Pedro the Portuguese and Spanish masculine form of PETER. William Shakespeare (1654–1616) used the name for Don Pedro, prince of Arragon, in his comedy *Much Ado About Nothing*. Pedro Almodóvar is a Spanish film director.

Peer a Norwegian masculine form of PETER.

Peg a feminine diminutive form of MARGARET.

Pegeen an Irish feminine diminutive form of MARGARET.

Peggie or **Peggy** a feminine diminutive form of MARGARET.

Peleg a masculine first name meaning 'division' (*Hebrew*).

Pelléas *see* MÉLISANDE.

Pen a feminine diminutive form of PENNY.

Penelope a feminine first name meaning 'duck' (*Greek*). In Greek mythology Penelope was the wife of ULYSSES. During his protracted absence it was assumed that he was dead and Penelope was pestered by suitors whom she put off on the pretext that before she could make up her mind she must first finish a shroud that she was weaving. To gain time, she undid by night the work she had done by day. Diminutive forms are Pen, Penny.

Penny feminine diminutive form of PENELOPE, now used independently.

Peony a feminine first name meaning 'healing' (*Greek*), the name of a plant with pink, red, white or yellow flowers used as a feminine first name.

Pepe a masculine diminutive form of JOSÉ.

Pepin a masculine first name meaning 'enduring' (*Germanic*).

Pepillo

Pepillo or **Pepito** masculine diminutive forms of JOSÉ.

Per a Scandinavian masculine form of PETER.

Perceval or **Percival** a masculine first name meaning 'pierce valley' (*Old French*).

Percy a surname, meaning 'from Perci-en-Auge in Normandy' (*Old French*), used as a masculine first name.

Perdita a feminine first name meaning 'lost' (*Latin*). It was invented by William Shakespeare (1564–1616) for a character in his play *The Winter's Tale*.

Peredur a Welsh masculine first name and the name of the hero of the Arthurian romance *Tair Rhamant*, a seventh son who undergoes magical adventures and may be either a precursor of, or derive from, Sir PERCEVAL, knight of the Holy Grail in the English Arthurian tales.

Peregrine a masculine first name meaning 'wanderer' (*Latin*). Peregrine Worsthorne is an English journalist. A diminutive form is Perry.

Peronel a feminine contraction of PETRONEL.

Peronnik a Breton masculine equivalent of PEREDUR.

Perry (1) masculine diminutive form of PEREGRINE, now used in its own right. (2) a surname, meaning 'pear tree' (*Old English*), used as a masculine first name.

Persephone a Greek feminine first name of uncertain meaning. In Greek mythology, Persephone was goddess of the underworld.

Persis a feminine first name meaning 'a Persian woman' (*Greek*). In the New Testament Persis was a Roman Christian friend of PAUL.

Pet a feminine diminutive form of PETULA.

Pete a masculine diminutive form of PETER.

Peter a masculine first name meaning 'rock' (*Latin*). In the New Testament Peter, originally called Simon, was a Galilean fisherman who was called Peter ('rock') by Jesus. He became the leader of the apostles. He is considered by some Christians to be the first pope. Diminutive forms are Pete, Peterkin.

Peterkin a masculine diminutive form of PETER.

Petra feminine form of PETER.

Petrina a feminine diminutive form of PETRA.

Petronel or **Petronella** feminine form of Petronius, a Roman family name (*Latin*).

Petrucio the Italian masculine form of Peter. William Shakespeare (1654–

226

1616) used the name for the main male character in his comedy *The Taming of the Shrew* but anglicised it to 'Petruchio' so that it was pronounced almost correctly.

Petrus a German masculine form of PETER.

Petula a feminine first name meaning 'asking' (*Latin*). A diminutive form is Pet.

Petunia the name of a plant with white, blue or purple flowers used as a feminine first name.

Phamie a feminine diminutive form of EUPHEMIA.

Phebe a feminine variant form of PHOEBE.

Phedra a feminine first name meaning 'bright' (*Greek*).

Phèdre the French feminine form of PHEDRA.

Phelim a masculine first name meaning 'always good' (*Irish*).

Phemie a feminine diminutive form of EUPHEMIA.

Phenie a feminine diminutive form of JOSEPHINE.

Phil (1) a masculine diminutive form of PHILIP, PHILLIP. (2) a feminine diminutive form of PHILIPPA.

Philbert a masculine first name meaning 'very bright' (*Germanic*).

Philemon a masculine first name meaning 'friendly' (*Greek*). In Greek mythology was an elderly peasant who, with his wife, Baucis, entertained Zeus and Hermes in their cottage. In the New Testament Philemon was a wealthy Christian in Asia Minor to whom PAUL wrote a letter concerning Philemon's slave, who had run away and been converted by Paul who told him to return to Philemon.

Philip a masculine first name meaning 'lover of horses' (*Greek*). In the New Testament Philip was (1) one of Christ's apostles and (2) one of the seven deacons appointed to tend the Christians of Jerusalem, and (3) a son of King Herod the Great. A variant form is Phillip. Diminutive forms are Phil, Pip.

Philipp the German masculine form of PHILIP.

Philippa feminine form of PHILIP. Diminutive forms are Phil, Pip, Pippa.

Philippe the French masculine form of PHILIP.

Phillip a masculine variant form of PHILIP. Diminutive forms are Phil, Pip.

Philomena a feminine first name meaning 'love and strength' (*Greek*).

Phineas or **Phinehas** a masculine first name meaning 'serpent's mouth' (*Hebrew*). In the Old Testament Phinehas was a grandson of Aaron who became a priest and warrior.

Phoebe a feminine first name meaning 'moon' (*Greek*). In the New Testament Phoebe was a Roman Christian woman to whom PAUL wrote. William Shakespeare (1654–1616) used the name for a shepherdess in his comedy *As You Like It*. Phoebe Cates is an American film actress. A variant form is Phebe.

Phoenix the name of a legendary Arabian bird that at the end of a certain number of years is consumed by fire but then regenerates itself. It has been used as a masculine first name in the USA.

Phyllida a feminine variant form of PHYLLIS. Phyllida Law is a British actress and the mother of the actress Emma Thompson.

Phyllis a feminine first name meaning 'a green bough' (*Greek*).

Pia feminine form of PIO.

Pierce a surname form of PIERS used as a masculine first name. Pierce Brosnan is an Irish-born film actor.

Pierre the French masculine form of PETER.

Piers a masculine variant form of PETER.

Pierse a surname form of PIERS used as a masculine first name.

Pieter a Dutch masculine form of PETER.

Pietro the Italian masculine form of PETER.

Pilar a feminine first name meaning 'pillar' (*Spanish*), an allusion to the Virgin Mary who appeared to St James the Greater standing on a pillar.

Pio the Italian masculine form of PIUS.

Pip (1) a masculine diminutive form of PHILIP, PHILLIP. (2) a feminine diminutive form of PHILIPPA.

Pippa a feminine diminutive form of PHILIPPA.

Pius a masculine first name meaning 'holy' (*Latin*). It was the name adopted by many popes.

Placido a masculine first name meaning 'peaceful' (*Latin/Spanish*). Placido Domingo is a prominent Mexican-born opera singer and director.

Plato a masculine first name meaning 'broad' (*Greek*). Plato (*c.*427– *c.*347) was an Athenian who, with his teacher, Socrates, and pupil, Aristotle, initiated western philosophy.

Polly feminine diminutive form of MARY, now used independently.

Pollyanna a feminine first name formed from a combination of POLLY and ANNA. The North American writer Eleanor Hodgman Porter created a fictional character, called Pollyanna Whittier, whose optimism has become synonymous with the name.

Pomona a feminine first name meaning 'fruitful' (*Latin*).

Poppy the name of the plant that has a bright red flower used as a feminine first name.

Portia a feminine first name meaning 'gift' (*Latin*). Portia, daughter of Cato Uticensis, was the wife of Marcus Junius Brutus, one of the conspirators against Julius Caesar. She appears in the play *Julius Caesar* by William Shakespeare (1564–1616), who also used the name for the heroine of his play *The Merchant of Venice*.

Powel a masculine first name meaning 'son of Hywel', from *ap*, 'son' (*Welsh*).

Presley a surname, meaning 'priests' meadow', used as a masculine first name.

Prima the feminine form of PRIMO.

Primo a masculine first name meaning 'first born' (*Latin*).

Primrose the name of the yellow spring flower used as a feminine first name.

Prisca see PRISCILLA.

Priscilla a feminine first name derived from *prisca*, 'ancient' (*Latin*). In the New Testament Priscilla and her husband, Aquila, were Roman Christians who helped Paul in his missionary work. Paul called her Prisca. Diminutive forms are Cilla, Prissie.

Prissie a feminine diminutive form of PRISCILLA.

Proinséas (pronounced *phron-shas*) the Irish Gaelic masculine version of FRANCIS.

Prosper a masculine first name meaning 'favourable, fortunate' (*Latin*).

Pròspero the Italian masculine form of PROSPER. William Shakespeare (1654–1616) used the name (without the accent) for the rightful duke of Milan in his play *The Tempest*.

Prudence the word for the quality of caution or circumspection used as a feminine first name (*Latin*). Diminutive forms are Prue, Prudie.

Prudie a feminine diminutive form of PRUDENCE.

Prue a feminine diminutive form of PRUDENCE, PRUNELLA. Prue Leith is an English cook and cookery writer and the chairman of the Royal College of Arts.

Prunella a feminine first name meaning 'plum' (*Latin*). Prunella Scales is an English actress. A diminutive form is Prue.

Psyche a feminine first name meaning 'of the soul' (*Greek*).

Pugh

Pugh a surname, meaning 'son of HUGH' (*Welsh*), used as a masculine first name.

Pwyll or **Pwll** (pronounced *pull*) a masculine first name from *pwll*, 'wisdom', 'prudence' (*Welsh*). Pwll, prince of Dyfed, is the hero of the first 'branch' of the *Mabinogion* tales.

Q

Qabil the Arabic form of CAIN.

Queenie a feminine diminutive form of the word 'queen', 'the supreme woman', used as a feminine first name (*Old English*).

Quenby a surname, meaning 'queen's manor', used as a feminine first name (*Old English*).

Quentin a masculine first name meaning 'fifth' (*Latin*). A variant form is Quinton.

Querida a feminine first name meaning 'beloved', a Spanish term of endearment used as a feminine first name.

Quinta feminine form of QUINTO.

Quinto the Italian masculine form of QUINTUS.

Quintus a masculine first name meaning 'fifth' (*Latin*). William Shakespeare (1654–1616) used the name for a character in his play *Titus Andronicus*.

Quenel or **Quennel** a surname, meaning 'queen war' (*Old English*), used as a masculine first name.

Quigley or **Quigly** a surname, meaning 'untidy' (*Irish Gaelic*), used as a masculine first name.

Quinby a masculine variant form of QUENBY.

Quincy or **Quincey** a surname, meaning 'fifth place' (*Latin/French*), used as a masculine first name.

Quinlan a masculine first name meaning 'well formed' (*Irish Gaelic*).

Quinn a surname, meaning 'wise' (*Irish Gaelic*), used as a masculine first name.

Quinton a masculine variant form of QUENTIN.

R

Rab a masculine diminutive form of ROBERT, occasionally found as a name in its own right.

Raban a masculine first name meaning 'raven' (*Germanic*).

Rabbie a masculine diminutive form of ROBERT.

Rachel a feminine first name meaning 'lamb' (*Hebrew*). In the Old Testament Rachel was the younger sister of Leah and the second and best-loved wife of Jacob. She was the mother of Joseph and Benjamin. A variant form is Rachelle. Diminutive forms are Rae, Ray.

Rachele the Italian feminine form of RACHEL.

Rachelle a feminine variant form of RACHEL.

Radcliffe a surname, meaning 'red cliff' (*Old English*), used as a masculine first name.

Radha (pronounced *ra-ha*) a feminine first name meaning 'far-seeing'. The name is related to *radharc*, 'vision' (*Irish Gaelic*).

Radley a surname, meaning 'red meadow' (*Old English*), used as a masculine first name.

Radnor a place name and surname, meaning 'red slopes' (*Old English*), used as a masculine first name.

Rae (1) a Scottish surname, perhaps from Gaelic *rath*, 'grace', used as a masculine or feminine first name. (2) a feminine diminutive form of RACHEL.

Rafe a variant form of RALPH.

Raffaele or **Raffaello** Italian masculine forms of RAPHAEL.

Rafferty a surname, meaning 'prosperous' (*Irish Gaelic*), used as a masculine first name.

Raghnailt (pronounced *ran-ailt*) the Irish and Scottish Gaelic feminine form of RAGHNALL.

Raghnall (pronounced *ren-ull*) a Scottish Gaelic masculine version of an Old Norse name brought by the Vikings, Rognvaldr, 'power in counsel', the Norse equivalent of REYNOLD or REGINALD. It has numerous anglicised versions, including Ranald, Ronald, Randal.

Raheel or **Raheela** a feminine variant form of RAHIL.

Rahel a German feminine form of RACHEL

Rahil the Arabic form of RACHEL. A variant form is Raheel, Raheela.

Rahim a masculine first name meaning 'merciful, compassionate' (*Arabic*).

Rahima or **Rahimah** the feminine form of RAHIM.

Raibeart the Scottish Gaelic masculine form of ROBERT.

Raimondo the Italian masculine form of RAYMOND.

Raimund the German masculine form of RAYMOND.

Raimundo a Spanish masculine form of RAYMOND.

Rainaldo an Italian masculine form of REGINALD.

Raine a feminine variant form of RAYNE.

Rainier a French masculine form of RAYNER.

Raisa a feminine first name meaning 'tolerant' (*Greek*).

Raleigh a surname, meaning 'red or deer meadow' (*Old English*), used as a masculine first name. Variant forms are Rawley, Rayleigh.

Ralph a masculine first name meaning 'famous wolf or hero' (*Germanic*). Sir Ralph Richardson (1902–83) was an eminent English actor. Variant forms are Rafe, Rolph.

Ram a masculine first name meaning 'height' (*Hebrew*). In the Old Testament Ram was a descendant of Judah.

Ramón a Spanish masculine form of RAYMOND.

Ramona feminine form of RAMÓN.

Ramsden a masculine first name meaning 'ram's valley' (*Old English*).

Ramsay or **Ramsey** a place name and surname, meaning 'wild garlic river island', used as a masculine first name (*Old Norse*).

Ranald an anglicised masculine form of RAGHNALL.

Rand a masculine diminutive form of RANDAL, RANDOLF.

Randal (1) or **Randall** an Old English surname and diminutive form of RANDOLPH used as a masculine first name. A variant form is Ranulf. (2) an anglicised masculine form of RAGHNALL.

Randolf or **Randolph** a masculine first name meaning 'shield-wolf' (*Germanic*). Randolph Scott (1898–1987) was an American star of many Western films. A variant form is Ranulf. Diminutive forms are Rand, Randy.

Randy a masculine diminutive form of RANDOLPH, that is also used independently.

Ranee or **Rani** a feminine first name meaning 'queen' (*Hindi*).

Rankin or **Rankine** a diminutive surname masculine form of RANDOLPH used as a masculine first name.

Ransom a surname, meaning 'son of RAND', used as a masculine first name.

Ranulf a masculine variant form of RANDOLF.

Raoul the French masculine form of RALPH.

Raphael a masculine first name meaning 'the healing of God' (*Hebrew*). In the Bible Raphael is one of the archangels with powers of healing.

Raphaela feminine form of RAPHAEL.

Raquel the Spanish feminine form of RACHEL.

Ras a masculine diminutive form of ERASMUS, ERASTUS.

Rasmus a masculine diminutive form of ERASMUS.

Rastus a masculine diminutive form of ERASTUS.

Raul the Spanish masculine form of RALPH. Raul Julia was a Puerto-Rican born film actor.

Rawley a masculine variant form of RALEIGH.

Rawnsley a surname, meaning 'raven's meadow' (*Old English*), used as a masculine first name.

Ray (1) a masculine diminutive form of RAYMOND, now used independently. Ray Liotta is an American film actor. (2) a feminine diminutive form of RACHEL. A variant form is Rae.

Rayleigh a masculine variant form of RALEIGH.

Raymond or **Raymund** a masculine first name meaning 'wise protection' (*Germanic*). A diminutive form is Ray.

Rayne a surname, meaning 'mighty army', used as a masculine or feminine first name. Variant forms are Raine (feminine), Rayner (masculine).

Rayner a masculine variant form of RAYNE (*Germanic*).

Rea a feminine variant form of RHEA.

Read or **Reade** a surname, meaning 'red headed' (*Old English*), used as a masculine first name. Variant forms are Reed, Reede.

Reading a place name and surname, meaning 'people of the red one', used as a masculine first name. A variant form is Redding.

Reardon a masculine variant form of RIORDAN.

Rebecca or **Rebekah** a feminine first name meaning 'noose' (*Hebrew*). In the Old Testament Rebecca was the wife of Isaac and mother of Esau and Jacob. She connived with Jacob to deprive Esau of his birthright. Dame Rebecca West (1892–1983) was an English writer. Diminutive forms are Beckie, Becky.

Redding a masculine variant form of READING.

Redman (1) a surname, meaning 'red cairn or thatcher' (*Old English*), used as a masculine first name. (2) a variant form of REDMOND.

Redmond a masculine first name meaning 'counsel protection' (*Germanic*). A variant form is Redman.

Reece a surname form of RHYS used as a masculine first name.

Reed or **Reede** masculine variant forms of READ.

Rees the English masculine form of RHYS.

Reeve or **Reeves** a masculine first name meaning 'steward, bailiff' (*Old English*).

Reg a masculine diminutive form of REGINALD.

Regan a feminine first name meaning 'king's consort', from *rí*, 'king', and *gan* 'queen' (*Irish Gaelic*). The name gets a bad reputation in *King Lear* by William Shakespeare (1564–1616). Variant forms are Reagan, Rogan.

Reggie a masculine diminutive form of REGINALD.

Regina a feminine first name meaning 'queen' (*Latin*).

Reginald a masculine first name meaning 'counsel rule' (*Germanic*). Diminutive forms are Reg, Reggie.

Reid a Scottish surname that is also found as a masculine first name, from Scots *reed*, 'red'; also Gaelic *ruadh*, 'red'.

Reilly a surname, meaning 'valiant' (*Irish Gaelic*), used as a masculine first name. A variant form is RILEY.

Reinald an early English masculine form of REGINALD.

Reine a feminine first name meaning 'queen' (*French*).

Reinhard a German masculine form of REYNARD.

Reinhold a Scandinavian masculine form of REGINALD.

Reinold a Dutch masculine form of REGINALD.

Remus a masculine first name meaning 'power' (*Latin*).

Renaldo a Spanish masculine form of REGINALD.

Renata a feminine diminutive form of RENÉE.

Renato an Italian and Spanish masculine form of REGINALD.

Renatus the Latin masculine form of RENÉ.

Renault a French masculine form of REGINALD.

René a masculine first name meaning 'born again' (*French*).

Renée feminine form of RENÉ.

Renfrew a place name and surname, meaning 'point of the torrent' (*Celtic*), used as a masculine first name.

Renie a feminine diminutive form of IRENE.

Rennie or **Renny** a diminutive surname form of Reynold used as a masculine first name.

Renton a surname, meaning 'farmstead of power' (*Old English*), used as a masculine first name.

Reuben a masculine first name meaning 'behold a son' (*Hebrew*). In the Old Testament Reuben was the eldest son of Jacob and Leah and the founder of one of the twelve tribes of Israel. A diminutive form is Rube.

Reuel a masculine first name meaning 'friend of God'.

Reva feminine form of REEVE.

Rex a masculine first name meaning 'king' (*Latin*).

Rexanne (1) a feminine first name formed from a combination of REX and ANNE. (2) a variant form of ROXANNE.

Reynard (1) a masculine first name meaning 'brave advice' (*Germanic*). (2) 'fox' (*French*).

Reynold a masculine first name meaning 'strong rule' (*Germanic*).

Rhea a feminine name of uncertain origin and meaning. In Roman mythology Rhea was the mother of REMUS and Romulus. In Greek mythology she was the mother of several gods, including Zeus. Variant forms are Rea, Rheia.

Rhedyn a feminine first name meaning 'fern' (*Welsh*).

Rheia a feminine variant form of RHEA.

Rheinallt a Welsh masculine form of REYNARD. Rheinallt was a fifteenth-century bard.

Rhian a feminine first name meaning 'fair maid', from *rhiain*, 'maiden' (*Welsh*).

Rhiannon a feminine first name meaning 'fair maiden' (*Welsh*), but as the name of a princess in the *Mabinogion* tales it also has the sense 'moon goddess' from the old British goddess Rigantona. A variant form is Riannon.

Rhianwen a feminine first name meaning 'pure maiden' (*Welsh*).

Rhisiart the Welsh masculine form of RICHARD.

Rhoda a feminine first name meaning 'rose' (*Greek*). In the New Testament Rhoda was a Christian servant in Jerusalem who was the first to hear Peter on his miraculous release from prison.

Rhodri (pronounced *rod-ree*) a masculine first name from a root form *rhod*, 'circle', 'disc' (*Welsh*), indicative of a crown or coronet. Rhodri Mawr, 'the great' was a ninth-century king of Gwynedd.

Rhona a feminine variant form of RONA.

Rhondda a feminine first name meaning 'slender', from *rhon*, 'lance' (*Welsh*), and by extension 'slim'. It is the name of a South Wales town in a narrow valley.

Rhonwen a feminine first name meaning 'fair and slender', from *rhon*, 'lance', and *gwen*, 'fair' (*Welsh*).

Rhydderch a masculine first name from *rhi*, 'king', dyrch, 'great', 'exalted' (*Welsh*). It was the name of a famous king of Strathclyde in the sixth century; the ring found for him in a salmon by St MUNGO is incorporated in the arms of the city of Glasgow.

Rhydwen (pronounced *ridd-wen*) or **Rhydian** (*ridd-eean*) a masculine first name meaning 'white, or blessed, ford' (*Welsh*).

Rhys (pronounced *rees*) a Welsh masculine first name, possibly meaning 'ardour', from that of Rhys ap Gruffudd, a twelfth-century prince of Deheubarth (southern Wales). The anglicised form is Rees.

Ria a German feminine diminutive form of MARIA.

Riannon a feminine variant form of RHIANNON.

Rica a feminine diminutive form of RODERICA.

Ricardo a Spanish masculine form of RICHARD.

Riccardo an Italian masculine form of RICHARD.

Rich a masculine diminutive form of RICHARD, RICHMOND.

Richard a masculine first name meaning 'a strong king; powerful' (*Germanic*). It was the name of three kings of England. Richard I, 'Coeur de Lion' or 'Lion-hearted' (1157–99), who spent only six months of his ten-year reign (1189–99) in England. Richard II (1367–1400) succeeded his grandfather as a child in 1377. His reign was marked by discontent and baronial opposition and he was forced to abdicate in 1399. Richard III (1452–85) was originally the brother of Edward IV who, after Edward's death in 1483, seized his nephews and declared himself their protector. After their mysterious deaths, he assumed the throne. He was defeated and killed at the Battle of Bosworth. Diminutive forms are Dick, Rich, Richey, Richie, Rick, Rickie, Ricky, Ritchie.

Richey or **Richie** a masculine diminutive form of RICHARD, RICHMOND.

Richmond a surname, meaning 'strong hill' (*Old French*), used as a masculine first name. Diminutive forms are Rich, Richey, Richie.

Rick or **Rickie** or **Ricky** masculine diminutive forms of ARIC, RICHARD.

Rider a surname, meaning 'knight, rider' (*Old English*), used as a masculine first name. Sir Rider Haggard (1856–1925) was an English author of adventure stories, the best known being *King Solomon's Mines* (1885).

Ridley a surname, meaning 'cleared meadow' (*Old English*), used as a masculine first name. Ridley Scott is an English-born film director best known for his film *Blade Runner*.

Rigantona *see* RHIANNON.

Rigby a surname, meaning 'farm on a ridge' (*Old English*), used as a masculine first name.

Rigg a surname, meaning 'at the ridge' (*Old English*), used as a masculine first name.

Riley a masculine variant form of REILLY.

Rina a feminine diminutive form of names ending -rina.

Rinaldo an Italian masculine form of REGINALD. Rinaldo was a prominent figure in medieval romance as one of the paladins who attended on Charlemagne. William Shakespeare (1654–1616) used the name for a character in his comedy *All's Well That Ends Well*.

Ring a surname, meaning 'wearing a ring' (*Old English*), used as a masculine first name.

Riona a feminine diminutive form of CATRIONA.

Riordan a surname, meaning 'bard' (*Irish Gaelic*), used as a masculine first name. A variant form is REARDON.

Ripley a place name and surname, meaning 'strip-shaped clearing' (*Old English*), used as a masculine first name.

Rita a feminine diminutive form of MARGARITA, MARGHERITA, used independently. Rita Hayworth (1918–87) was a famous American film star of the 1940s.

Ritchie a diminutive and surname masculine form of RICHARD.

Ritter a masculine first name meaning 'knight or rider' (*Germanic*).

Roald a masculine first name meaning 'famous ruler' (*Old Norse*). Roald

Dahl (1916–90) was a well-known English writer, particularly of books for children.

Rob a masculine diminutive forms of ROBERT. Rob Lowe is an American film actor.

Robat the Welsh masculine form of ROBERT.

Robbie or **Robby** a masculine diminutive form of ROBERT that is now being used as a name in its own right. Robbie Coltrane is a well-known Scottish actor.

Robert a masculine first name meaning 'bright in fame' (*Germanic*). Robert De Niro is a well-known American film actor. Diminutive forms are Bob, Bobby, Rab, Rob, Robbie, Robby, Robin.

Roberta feminine form of ROBERT.

Roberto the Italian and Spanish masculine form of ROBERT.

Robin a masculine diminutive of ROBERT, now used as independent masculine or feminine first name. Robin Hood was a traditional hero of a group of Old English ballads. He was said to have been a generous and gallant outlaw and robber, living a happy life with his merry comrades, 'under the greenwood tree', in more than one forest, but especially Sherwood. The Welsh form is ROBYN.

Robina a feminine form of ROBIN.

Robinson a surname, meaning 'son of ROBERT' (*Old English*), used as a masculine first name.

Robyn the Welsh masculine form of ROBIN. This spelling, outside Wales at least, is often nowadays used as a feminine first name.

Rocco a masculine name of uncertain meaning possibly 'crow' (*Germanic*).

Rochelle a feminine first name meaning 'little rock' (*French*).

Rochester a place name, and surname, meaning 'Roman fort at the bridges' (*Old English*), used as a masculine first name.

Rock a masculine first name meaning 'stone' or 'oak' (*Old English*).

Rocky an English masculine form of ROCCO.

Rod a masculine diminutive form of RODERICK, RODNEY.

Rodden a surname, meaning 'valley of deer' (*Old English*), used as a masculine first name.

Roddy a masculine diminutive form of RODERICK, RODNEY.

Roderica feminine form of RODERICK. A variant form is Rodericka. A diminutive form is Rica.

Roderich

Roderich the German masculine form of RODERICK.

Roderick or **Roderic** a masculine first name from *ruadh*, 'red', and *rí*, 'king' (Scottish Gaelic); the Gaelic form is Ruairidh. It is cognate with Welsh RHYDDERCH, and its diminutive forms include Rod, Roddie, Rory.

Roderick or **Roderic** a masculine first name meaning 'fame powerful' (*Germanic*). Diminutive forms are Rod, Roddy, Rurik.

Rodericka a feminine variant form of RODERICA.

Roderico or **Roderigo** an Italian masculine form of RODERICK. William Shakespeare (1654–1616) used the name for 'a foolish gentleman' in love with Desdemona in his tragedy *Othello*.

Rodger a masculine variant form of ROGER.

Rodney a surname and place name, used as a masculine or feminine first name. A diminutive form is Rod.

Rodolf an Italian and Spanish masculine form of RUDOLPH.

Rodolphe a French masculine form of RUDOLPH.

Rodrigo an Italian and Spanish masculine form of RODERICK.

Rodrigue the French masculine form of RODERICK.

Roger a masculine first name meaning 'famous with the spear' (*Germanic*). A variant form is RODGER.

Rogerio the Spanish masculine form of ROGER.

Rohan a masculine first name meaning 'healing, incense' (*Sanskrit*).

Rohanna feminine form of ROHAN.

Róisín (pronounced *rosh-een*) a feminine first name meaning 'little rose' (*Irish Gaelic*). As Róisin Dubh, 'Dark Rosaleen', from a seventeenth-century Gaelic poem, the name is synonymous with Ireland.

Roland a masculine first name meaning 'fame of the land' (*Germanic*). Roland, also known as ORLANDO, and OLIVER were the most famous of the legendary twelve paladins who attended on Charlemagne. Oliver and Roland once fought for five days without either gaining the advantage. Variant forms are Rolland, Rowland. A diminutive form is Roly.

Rolanda or **Rolande** feminine forms of ROLAND.

Roldán or **Rolando** Spanish masculine forms of ROLAND.

Rolf a contraction of RUDOLF. A variant form is Rollo.

Rolland a masculine variant form of ROLAND.

Rollo a masculine variant form of ROLF.

Rolph a masculine variant form of RALPH.

Roly a masculine diminutive form of ROLAND.

Roma a feminine first name meaning 'a Roman' (*Latin*).

Romeo a masculine first name meaning 'a Roman' (*Latin*), originally referring to a person who had gone on pilgrimage to Rome. William Shakespeare (1654–1616) used the name for the young heir of the Montagues who falls in love with Juliet, the daughter of the Capulets, the enemies of the Montagues, in his tragedy *Romeo and Juliet*, which is probably the world's best-known love story.

Romilly a surname, meaning 'broad clearing' (*Old English*) or 'place of Romilius' (*Old French*), used as a masculine first name.

Romney a place name, meaning 'at the broad river' (*Old English*), used as a masculine first name.

Ròmolo a masculine first name, the Italian form of Romulus, of Etruscan origin and unknown meaning; in Roman legend, Romulus and his brother REMUS founded Rome.

Romy a feminine diminutive form of ROSEMARY.

Ron a masculine diminutive form of RONALD. Ron Silver is an American actor.

Rona a Scottish feminine first name, probably a feminine form of RONAN. There is also the island of Rona, from *hraun-ey*, 'rough island' (*Old Norse*), but as St Ronan lived and died on North Rona, the two names are intertwined. A variant form is Rhona.

Ronald an anglicised masculine form of RAGHNALL. Diminutive forms are Ron, Ronnie, Ronny.

Ronalda feminine form of RONALD. Diminutive forms are Ronnie, Ronny.

Ronan a masculine first name meaning 'little seal'. The likely derivation is *ron*, 'seal', with the diminutive suffix -an (*Scottish Gaelic*). It was the name of several saints.

Ronnie or **Ronny** (1) a masculine diminutive form of RONALD. (2) a feminine diminutive form of RONALDA, VERONICA.

Rooney a masculine first name meaning 'red, red-complexioned' (*Gaelic*).

Rory a masculine first name meaning 'red' (*Irish and Scots Gaelic*).

Rosa a feminine first name meaning 'a rose' (*Latin*). Diminutive forms are Rosetta, Rosie.

Rosabel or **Rosabella** or **Rosabelle** a feminine first named formed by a combination of ROSA and BELLA.

Rosalie or **Rosalia** a feminine first name meaning 'little and blooming rose' (*Latin*).

Rosalind

Rosalind or **Rosaline** a feminine first name meaning 'beautiful as a rose' (*Latin*). William Shakespeare (1654–1616) used the form Rosalind for the heroine of his comedy *As You Like It* and Rosaline for a character in *Love's Labour's Lost*. Rosaline is also an off-stage character in *Romeo and Juliet* with whom Romeo is supposed to be in love. A diminutive form is LINDA.

Rosamund or **Rosamond** (1) a feminine first name meaning 'horse protection, famous protection' (*Germanic*). (2) 'rose of the world' (*Latin*).

Rosanne or **Rosanna** feminine compounds of ROSE and ANNE. Rosanna Arquette is an American actress. A variant form is Roseanne, Roseanna.

Roscoe a surname, meaning 'deer wood' (*Old Norse*), used as a masculine first name. Roscoe Ates (1892–1962) was an American film actor who appeared in many films as a comic character.

Rose the English form of ROSA; the name of the flower used as a feminine first name. St Rose of Lima (1586–1617) was a Peruvian Dominican nun who was the first person in the Western Hemisphere to be canonised. She is the patron saint of South America. Diminutive forms are Rosette, Rosie.

Roseanne or **Roseanna** feminine variant forms of ROSANNE, ROSANNA.

Rosemarie a feminine first name formed by a combination of ROSE and MARIE.

Rosemary the name of the plant associated with remembrance used as a feminine first name. Diminutive forms are Romy, Rosie.

Rosemonde a French feminine form of ROSAMUND.

Rosetta a feminine diminutive form of ROSA.

Rosette a feminine diminutive form of ROSE.

Rosh a masculine first name meaning 'head' (*Hebrew*). In the Old Testament Rosh was a son of Benjamin.

Rosie a feminine diminutive form of ROSA, ROSE, ROSEMARY, now also used independently.

Roslin or **Roslyn** a place name, meaning 'unploughable land by the pool' (*Scots Gaelic*), used as a masculine or feminine first name. A variant form is ROSSLYN.

Rosmunda the Italian feminine form of ROSAMUND.

Ross a place name and surname, meaning 'promontory or 'wood', from *ros* (*Scottish Gaelic*), now widely used as a masculine first name.

Rosslyn a masculine or feminine variant form of ROSLIN.

Rowan (pronounced *rau-an*) a masculine or feminine first name that comes from the rowan tree, *ruadhan*, 'little red one' (*Scottish Gaelic*). In the past rowan berries were a specific against witchcraft, but the spread of the name has been very recent.

Rowe a surname, meaning 'hedgerow' (*Old English*), used as a masculine first name.

Rowell a surname, meaning 'rough hill' (*Old English*), used as a masculine first name.

Rowena a feminine first name, perhaps an anglicised form of Welsh RHONWEN. The name was used by Geoffrey of Monmouth in his *Historia Regum Britanniae* for the daughter of the fifth-century Saxon invader Hengist. The name was used by Sir Walter Scott (1771–1832) for the heroine of his novel *Ivanhoe*.

Rowland a masculine variant form of ROLAND.

Rowley a surname, meaning 'rough meadow' (*Old English*), used as a masculine first name.

Roxanne or **Roxane** a feminine first name meaning 'dawn of day' (*Persian*). A variant form is Rexanne. A diminutive form is Roxie.

Roxburgh a place name and surname, meaning 'rook's fortress' (*Old English*), used as a masculine first name.

Roxie a feminine diminutive of ROXANNE.

Roy (1) a masculine first name from *ruadh*, 'red' (*Scottish Gaelic*). (2) a masculine first name meaning 'king', from *roy* (*Old French*).

Royal (1) a masculine variant form of ROYLE. (2) the adjective meaning 'befitting a monarch, regal', used as a feminine first name.

Royce a surname form of ROSE used as a masculine first name.

Royle a surname, meaning 'rye hill' (*Old English*), used as a masculine first name. A variant form is Royal.

Royston a surname, meaning 'place of Royce' (*Germanic/Old English*), used as a masculine first name.

Ruairidh the Scottish Gaelic masculine form of RODERICK. A diminutive form is Rurik.

Rube a masculine diminutive form of REUBEN.

Rubén a Spanish masculine form of REUBEN.

Ruby the name of the red gemstone used as a feminine first name.

Rudi a German masculine diminutive form of RÜDIGER, RUDOLF.

Rüdiger the German masculine form of ROGER.

Rudolf or **Rudolph** a masculine first name meaning 'famous wolf; hero' (*Germanic*).

Rudyard a masculine first name meaning 'reed enclosure' (*Old English*).

Rufe a masculine diminutive form of Rufus.

Rufus a masculine first name meaning 'red-haired' (*Latin*). In the New Testament Rufus was a son of Simon who was forced to help Jesus' torture stake. A diminutive form is RUFE.

Rugby a place name and surname, meaning 'Hroca's stronghold' (*Old English*), used as a masculine first name.

Ruggiero or **Ruggero** Italian masculine forms of ROGER. Ruggero Raimondo is an Italian opera baritone and actor.

Rupert an anglicized Germanic masculine form of ROBERT.

Ruprecht the German masculine form of ROBERT.

Rurik a masculine diminutive form of RUAIRIDH.

Russ a masculine diminutive form of RUSSELL.

Russell a surname, meaning 'red hair' (*Old French*), used as a masculine first name. A diminutive form is Russ.

Rutger a Dutch masculine form of ROGER. Rutger Hauer is a Dutch film actor, best known for his part in the film *Blade Runner*.

Ruth a feminine first name meaning 'friend' (*Hebrew*). In the Old Testament Ruth was the daughter-in-law of NAOMI who, after the death of her husband, followed Naomi to Bethlehem where she helped support her by gleaning the fields of Boaz, who later married her. Their great-grandson was DAVID. The story is told in the Book of Ruth.

Rutherford a surname, meaning 'cattle ford' (*Old English*), used as a masculine first name.

Rutland a place name, meaning 'Rota's estate' (*Old English*), used as a masculine first name.

Ruy a Spanish masculine form of RODERICK.

Ryan an Irish surname, from an Old Gaelic word meaning 'chief', used as masculine first name. It is an extremely popular first name, helped by the film star Ryan O'Neal.

Rye a masculine first name meaning 'from the riverbank' (*French*).

Rylan or **Ryland** a surname, meaning 'where rye grows' (*Old English*), used as a masculine first name.

S

Saba a feminine Arabic form of SHEBA.

Sabin a shortened masculine form of SABINUS.

Sabina a feminine first name meaning 'Sabine woman' (*Latin*).

Sabine a French and German feminine form of SABINA.

Sabino an Italian masculine form of SABINUS.

Sabinus a masculine first name meaning 'Sabine man' (*Latin*). A shortened form is Sabin.

Sabra a feminine first name meaning 'restful' (*Hebrew*).

Sabrina a feminine name of uncertain meaning, linked to the name of the River Severn (*pre-Celtic*). A variant form is Zabrina.

Sacha a Russian masculine diminutive form of Alexander now used increasingly as a feminine form, with the variant form of Sasha. Sacha Distel is a French singer.

Sadhbh (pronounced *sawv*) an Irish Gaelic feminine first name meaning 'sweetness'. This was the name of the mother of Oisín, 'Ossian', who was turned into a deer.

Sadie a feminine diminutive form of SARA.

Sal a feminine diminutive form of SALLY, SARAH.

Salina a feminine first name meaning 'from the salty place' (*Greek*).

Sally or **Sallie** feminine diminutive forms of SARA, now used independently.

Salome a feminine first name meaning 'peaceful' (*Hebrew*). In the New Testament Salome was a granddaughter of Herod the Great and stepdaughter of Herodias at whose suggestion she beguiled her grandfather by her dancing into giving her the head of John the Baptist.

Salomo a Dutch and German masculine form of SOLOMON.

Salomon the French masculine form of SOLOMON.

Salomone the Italian masculine form of SOLOMON.

Salvador a masculine first name meaning 'Christ the saviour' (*Latin/ Spanish*).

Salvatore the Italian masculine form of SALVADOR.

Salvia a feminine first name meaning 'sage' (*Latin*).

Sam (1) a masculine diminutive form of SAMSON, SAMUEL, now used independently. Sam Neill is a New Zealand-born film actor. (2) a feminine diminutive form of SAMANTHA.

Samantha a feminine first name the meaning of which obscure but possibly 'listener' (*Aramic*) or a compound of SAM and ANTHEA. A diminutive form is Sam.

Sammy a masculine diminutive form of SAMSON, SAMUEL.

Samson or **Sampson** a masculine first name meaning 'like the sun' (*Hebrew*). In the Old Testament Samson was an Israelite warrior who performed great feats of strength against the Philistines until he was betrayed by DELILAH. Samson, Duc de Bourgogne, was one of the legendary twelve paladins who attended on Charlemagne. William Shakespeare (1654–1616) used the form Sampson for a character in *Romeo and Juliet*. A diminutive form is Sam, Sammy.

Samuel a masculine first name meaning 'name of God' or 'heard by God' (*Hebrew*). In the Old Testament Samuel was a Hebrew prophet, priest, judge and military leader who anointed SAUL and then DAVID, the first two kings of the Israelites. The two Books of Samuel chronicle the origin and early history of the ancient Israelites. Samuel L. Jackson is an American film actor. Diminutive forms are Sam, Sammy.

Samuele the Italian masculine form of SAMUEL.

Samuela feminine form of SAMUEL.

Sancha or **Sanchia** feminine variant forms of SANCIA.

Sancho a masculine first name meaning 'holy' (*Spanish*).

Sancia feminine form of SANCHO. Variant forms are Sancha, Sanchia.

Sanders a shortened masculine form of ALEXANDER. A diminutive form is Sandy.

Sandie a feminine diminutive form of ALEXANDRA.

Sandra a feminine diminutive form of ALEXANDRA, now used independently.

Sandy (1) a masculine diminutive form of ALEXANDER, LYSANDER, SANDERS. Once upon a time this name could be used, like Jock, as the synonym for a male Scot. (2) a feminine diminutive form of ALEXANDRA.

Sanford a surname, meaning 'sandy ford' (*Old English*), used as a masculine first name.

Sanson the German masculine form of SAMSON.

Sansón the Spanish masculine form of SAMSON.

Sansone the Italian masculine form of SAMSON.

Santo a masculine first name meaning 'saint' (*Italian*).

Saoirse (pronounced *sair-sha*) an Irish feminine first name meaning 'freedom', which has been used as a personal name from the twentieth century, when Ireland regained its independence.

Sapphire (1) a feminine first name derived from *saphir*, 'beautiful' (*Hebrew*). (2) the name of the blue precious stone used as a feminine first name.

Sarah or **Sara** a feminine first name meaning 'princess' (*Hebrew*). In the Old Testament Sarah was the wife of ABRAHAM and mother of ISAAC. She appeared to be barren but then gave birth to Isaac when she was in her sixties. Diminutive forms are Sadie, Sal, Sally.

Saraid (pronounced *sarr-ad*) an Irish feminine first name meaning 'best one'. In legend, it is the name of the daughter of King Conn of the Hundred Battles, possessed of mystic skills.

Sasha a feminine variant form of Sacha.

Saul a masculine first name meaning 'asked for by God' (*Hebrew*). In the Old Testament Saul became the first king of the Israel when the tribes to unite under a king. He at first defeated the Philistines but became mad and committed suicide. He was succeeded by DAVID. In the New Testament Saul was the original name of PAUL.

Savanna a form of the Spanish word for an open grassland used as a feminine first name.

Saveur the French masculine form of SALVADOR.

Saxon a masculine first name meaning 'people of the short swords' (*Germanic*).

Scarlett a variation of the word 'scarlet', a bright red colour, used as a feminine first name by Margaret Mitchell (1900–1949) in her novel *Gone with the Wind*.

Scáthach (pronounced *ska-hach*) an Irish feminine first name and that of the warrior woman of the Isle of Skye who taught the arts of battle to CUCHULAINN and FERDIA. The source of the name is not clear, but it is not related to that of Skye itself, which comes from Old Norse. It is of historical interest in displaying close links between Scotland (Alba) and Ireland (Erin) long before the emigration of the Scots.

Scota an Old Gaelic feminine first name whose derivation is not clear. It is a generalised Latin name for an Irishwoman; but was borne as a personal name by two significant women of Gaelic legend, both said to be daughters of a pharaoh. The older Scota is said to be the grandmother of Iber, founder of the Gaels; the younger was the second wife of Míl Espáine (*see* MILES).

Scott the surname of a Scottish Border clan, used as a very popular and widely used first name for boys. F. Scott Fitzgerald (1896–1940) was an American writer, whose best-known novel is *The Great Gatsby* (1925). Scott Glenn is an American film actor. The name was, perhaps, spread even further in the later twentieth century by television's *Star Trek*. The diminutive form is Scotty or Scottie.

Scottie or **Scotty** the masculine diminutive form of SCOTT.

Scoular a south Scottish surname, meaning 'schoolmaster', literally 'schooler', sometimes used as a masculine first name.

Seachlainn *see* MALACHY.

Sealey a masculine variant form of SEELEY.

Seamas or **Seamus** Irish Gaelic masculine forms of JAMES. Seamus Heaney is an eminent Irish poet.

Sean (pronounced *shawn*) an Irish Gaelic masculine form of JOHN. Sean Connery is a Scottish-born film actor. Anglicised forms are Shaun, Shawn, Shane. It has also been used as a feminine form. Sean Young is an American film actress.

Searle a surname, meaning 'armed warrior', used as a surname (*Germanic*).

Seaton a place name and surname, meaning 'farmstead at the sea' (*Old English*), used as a masculine first name. A variant form is Seton.

Sebastian a masculine first name meaning 'august, majestic' (*Greek*). St Sebastian (died *c*.288) was a Roman soldier who became an early Christian martyr. He was shot with arrows and then beaten to death. William Shakespeare (1654–1616) used the name in two plays: for the brother of Viola in his comedy *As You Like It*, and the brother of the king of Naples in *The Tempest*. He also used the name as JULIA's name in disguise in *The Two Gentlemen of Verona*.

Sebastiano the Italian masculine form of SEBASTIAN.

Sébastien the French masculine form of SEBASTIAN.

Secondo the Italian masculine form of SECUNDUS.

Secundus a masculine first name meaning 'second born' (*Latin*). In the New Testament Secundus was a Christian who accompanied Paul on part of his third missionary journey.

Seeley a surname, meaning 'blessed and happy' (*Old English*), used as a masculine first name. A variant form is Sealey.

Seigneur a masculine variant form of Senior.

Seirian (pronounced *sye-reean*) a Welsh feminine first name meaning 'bright one', a feminine form of Seiriol.

Seiriol a masculine first name meaning 'bright one', from *serennu*, 'sparkle' (*Welsh*). It was the name of a sixth-century saint, preserved in the Welsh name of Priestholm Island, Ynys Seiriol.

Selby a place name and surname, meaning 'place by the willow trees' (*Old English*), used as a masculine first name.

Selden a masculine first name meaning 'from the valley of the willow tree' (*Old English*).

Selena a feminine variant form of Selina.

Selig a masculine first name meaning 'blessed, happy one' (*Yiddish*). A variant form is Zelig.

Selina a feminine first name meaning 'heavenly' (*Greek*). A variant form is Selena. A diminutive form is Lina.

Selma feminine form of Anselm.

Selwyn or **Selwin** a Welsh masculine form of Julian. *See* Sulien.

Semele a feminine first name meaning 'single' (*Greek*). In Greek mythology Semele was the daughter of King Cadmus of Thebes who was tricked by Hera into persuading Zeus, Hera's husband and Semele's lover, to attend her with the same majesty as he approached Hera. When he did, accompanied by lightning and thunder, Semele was instantly consumed by fire but Zeus managed to save their son, Dionysus.

Sencha (pronounced *senn-ha*) an Irish Gaelic masculine first name meaning 'historian'. The *seanachaidh* was the historian and keeper of the traditions of the *tuath* or clan.

Senga (1) a feminine first name meaning 'slender' (*Gaelic*). (2) backward spelling of Agnes.

Senior a surname, meaning 'lord' (*Old French*), used as a masculine first name. A variant form is Seigneur.

Seóbhrach (pronounced *sho-rach*) a Scottish feminine first name from the Gaelic *seóbhrach*, meaning 'primrose'.

Seonag (pronounced *shon-ak*) the Scottish Gaelic feminine form of JOAN.

Seonaid (pronounced *sho-na*) a Scottish Gaelic form of JANET. The anglicised version Shona is often found. *See also* SINEAD.

Seóras a Scottish Gaelic masculine form of GEORGE.

Seosamh (pronounced *sho-sa*) the Irish and Scottish Gaelic form of JOSEPH.

Septima feminine form of SEPTIMUS.

Septimus a masculine first name meaning 'seventh' (*Latin*).

Seraphina or **Serafina** a feminine first name meaning 'of the seraphim, of burning faith' (*Hebrew*).

Serena a feminine first name meaning 'calm, peaceful' (*Latin*).

Serge the French masculine form of SERGIUS.

Sergei the Russian masculine form of SERGIUS.

Sergio the Italian masculine form of SERGIUS.

Sergius a masculine first name, from that of a Roman family, of Etruscan origin and unknown meaning. It was the name adopted by several popes, including St Sergius I (639–701) who came into conflict with Emperor Justinian.

Sesto the Italian masculine form of SEXTUS.

Sétanta an Irish Gaelic masculine first name and the original name of CU-CHULAINN.

Seth a masculine first name meaning 'appointed' (*Hebrew*). In the Old Testament Seth was a third son of Adam and Eve sent to replace the murdered ABEL.

Seton a masculine variant form of SEATON.

Seumas (pronounced *shay-mas*) an Irish Gaelic masculine form of JAMES.

Sewald or **Sewall** or **Sewell** a surname, meaning 'sea powerful' (*Old English*), used as a masculine first name. A variant form is Siwald.

Sexton a surname, meaning 'sacristan' (*Old French*), used as a masculine first name.

Sextus a masculine first name meaning 'sixth' (*Latin*).

Seymour a surname, meaning 'from Saint-Maur in France' (*Old French*), used as a masculine first name.

Shalom a masculine first name meaning 'peace' (*Hebrew*).

Shamus an anglicized masculine form of SEAMUS.

Shane an anglicised masculine form of SEAN.

Shanel or **Shanelle** a feminine variant form of CHANEL.

Shanley a surname, meaning 'son of the hero' (*Irish Gaelic*), used as a masculine first name.

Shannon the Irish river name, perhaps related to Gaelic *sionn*, 'old', has found a new role as an increasingly popular feminine first name, not inaptly as it had its own goddess, named Sinann or Sionan.

Shari a feminine diminutive form of SHARON.

Sharon a Biblical place name mentioned in the Song of Solomon used as a feminine first name (*Hebrew*). Sharon Stone is an American film actress. A diminutive form is Shari.

Shaw a surname, meaning 'small wood or grove' (*Old English*), used as a masculine first name.

Shawn or **Shaun** an anglicised masculine form of SEAN.

Shea a surname, meaning 'stately, dauntless' (*Irish Gaelic*), used as a masculine first name.

Sheana an anglicised feminine form of SÍNE.

Sheba (1) a feminine diminutive form of BATHSHEBA. (2) or **Saba** the name of a former kingdom in the southwest Arabian Peninsula, mentioned in the Bible, used as a feminine first name.

Sheelagh a feminine variant form of SHEILA.

Sheelah (1) a feminine first name meaning 'petition' (*Hebrew*). (2) a feminine variant form of SHEILA.

Sheena an anglicised feminine form of SÍNE.

Sheffield a place name, meaning 'open land by the Sheaf river' (*Old English*), used as a masculine first name.

Sheila or **Shelagh** or **Sheela** an anglicised feminine form of Sile, the Irish and Scottish Gaelic form of CELIA. This name became highly popular in Australia, to the extent that all girls were 'Sheilas'.

Sheldon a surname, meaning 'heathery hill with a shed, flat-topped hill, or steep valley' (*Old English*), used as a masculine first name.

Shelley a surname, meaning 'clearing on a bank' (*Old English*), used as a feminine first name. Shelley Long is an American film actress best known for appearing in the TV sitcom *Cheers*.

Shepard a surname, meaning 'sheep herder, shepherd' (*Old English*), used as a masculine first name.

Sherborne or **Sherbourne** a surname, meaning 'clear stream' (*Old English*), used as a masculine first name.

Sheree or **Sheri** a feminine variant form of CHÉRIE.

Sheridan a surname, meaning 'seeking' (*Irish Gaelic*), used as a masculine first name. Sheridan Morley is an English writer and biographer.

Sherilyn a feminine first name, a combination of SHERRY and LYNN. Sherilyn Fenn is an American film actress

Sherlock a masculine first name meaning 'fair-haired' (*Old English*).

Sherman a surname, meaning 'shearman' (*Old English*), used as a masculine first name.

Sherrie or **Sherry** a feminine variant form of CHERIE.

Sherwin a surname, meaning 'loyal friend or fast-footed' (*Old English*), used as a masculine first name.

Sherwood a place name and surname, meaning 'shore wood' (*Old English*), used as a masculine first name.

Sheryl a feminine variant form of CHERYL.

Shirl a feminine diminutive form of SHIRLEY.

Shirley a surname and place name, meaning 'thin clearing', used as a feminine first name. Its popularity as a feminine name was established by Charlotte Brontë (1816–55) in her novel *Shirley*. A diminutive form is Shirl.

Sholto a masculine first name meaning 'sower, seed-bearing' (*Scottish Gaelic*).

Shona the anglicised feminine form of SEONAID.

Sian (pronounced *shan*) the Welsh feminine form of JANE. It is cognate with Gaelic SÍNE. Sian Phillips is a well-known Welsh actress.

Siarl (pronounced *sharl*) the Welsh masculine form of CHARLES.

Sib a feminine diminutive form of SIBYL.

Sibeal an Irish feminine form of SYBYL.

Sibyl or **Sibylla** a word meaning 'soothsayer' (*Greek*) used as a feminine first name. In Greek mythology they were certain women endowed by Apollo with the gift of prophecy. Their number is variously stated but is generally given as ten. Variant forms are Sybyl, Sybylla. A diminutive form is Sib.

Sid a masculine diminutive form of SIDNEY.

Siddall or **Siddell** a surname, meaning 'broad slope' (*Old English*), used as a masculine first name.

Sidney a surname, meaning 'wide island' (Old English), used as a masculine or feminine first name. A variant form is SYDNEY. A diminutive form is Sid.

Sidonia or **Sidonie** or **Sydony** a feminine first name meaning 'of Sidon' (*Latin*).

Siegfried a masculine first name meaning 'victory peace' (*Germanic*).

Siegmund the German masculine form of SIGMUND.

Siencyn the Welsh masculine form of English Jenkin, literally 'little JOHN'.

Sierra the word for a mountain range used as a feminine first name (*Spanish*).

Sig a masculine diminutive form of SIGMUND.

Sigismond the French masculine form of SIGMUND.

Sigismondo the Italian masculine form of SIGMUND.

Sigiswald a masculine first name meaning 'victorious ruler' (*Germanic*).

Sigmund a masculine first name meaning 'victory protection' (*Germanic*). A diminutive form is Sig.

Sigrid a feminine first name meaning 'fair and victorious' (*Old Norse*). A diminutive form is Siri.

Sigurd a masculine first name meaning 'victorious guardian' (*Old Norse*).

Silas a shortened masculine form of SILVANUS. In the New Testament Silas was an early Christian missionary and prophet and a companion of PAUL on his journeys.

Sile the Gaelic feminine form of CELIA, CECILY, often rendered in English as SHEILA, SHELAGH, etc.

Sileas (pronounced *shee-luss*) the Scottish Gaelic feminine form of JULIA.

Silvain a French masculine form of SILVANUS.

Silvana feminine form of SILVANO.

Silvano the Italian masculine form of SILVANUS.

Silvanus a masculine first name meaning 'of a wood' (*Latin*). In Roman mythology Silvanus was a god of the fields and forests, the Roman counterpart of the Greek Pan. A variant form is SYLVANUS.

Silvester a masculine first name meaning 'of a wood' (*Latin*). A variant form is SYLVESTER. A diminutive form is Sly.

Silvestre a French and Spanish masculine form of SILVESTER.

Silvestro an Italian masculine form of SILVESTER.

Silvia a feminine first name meaning 'of a wood' (*Latin*). William Shakespeare (1654–1616) used the name for the beloved of Valentine in *The Two Gentlemen of Verona*. A variant form is SYLVIA.

Silvie the French feminine form of SILVIA.

Silvio the Italian and Spanish masculine forms of SILVANUS.

Sim (1) a masculine diminutive form of SIMON, SIMEON. (2) a feminine diminutive form of SIMONE.

Sím (pronounced *sheem*) a Scottish Gaelic form of SIMON, virtually a hereditary name among chiefs of the Clan Fraser, who are known as Mac-Sími.

Simeon a masculine variant form of SIMON. In the Old Testament Simeon was the second son of JACOB and LEAH from whom one of the twelve tribes of Israel was descended. In the New Testament Simeon was a Jew who recognised Jesus as the Messiah.

Simmy a masculine diminutive form of SIMON.

Simon a masculine first name meaning 'hearing with acceptance' (*Hebrew*). In the New Testament Simon was the name of two of the apostles of Jesus: the original name of Peter and Simon the Zealot. Simon was also the name of the man in whose house Mary Magdalene anointed Jesus' feet. A variant form is SIMEON, Symeon. Diminutive forms are Sim, Simmy.

Simona feminine form of SIMON. A diminutive form is Sim.

Simone the French feminine form of SIMONA.

Simwnt the Welsh masculine form of SIMON.

Sinann *see* SHANNON.

Sinclair a surname, meaning 'from St Clair in France' (*Old French*), used as a masculine first name. A variant form is St Clair. Sinclair Lewis (1885–1951) was an American writer.

Síne (pronounced *sheena*) an Irish Gaelic feminine form of JANE or JEAN. An anglicised form is found in Sheena and Sheana.

Sinead (pronounced *shin-aid*) the Irish Gaelic feminine form of JANET. Sinead Cusack, the actress, and Sinead O'Connor, the singer, have kept the name prominent.

Siobhán (pronounced *shiv-awn*) the Irish Gaelic feminine form of JOAN, from Old French Jehane. In the latter form it was introduced to Ireland by the Normans in the twelfth century. The actress Siobhán McKenna (1923–86) helped to establish the name in recent times.

Sion the Welsh masculine form of JOHN. The diminutive is Sionyn.

Sionan *see* SHANNON.

Sioned a Welsh feminine form of JANET.

Sionym the Welsh masculine diminutive form of SION.

Sior the Welsh masculine form of GEORGE.

Siri a feminine diminutive form of SIGRID.

Sis a feminine diminutive form of SISLEY.

Sisley a feminine variant form of CECILY. Diminutive forms are Sis, Sissie, Sissy.

Sissie or **Sissy** a feminine diminutive form of SISLEY.

Siwald a masculine variant form of SEWALD.

Skelton a surname, meaning 'farmstead on a hill' (*Old English*), used as first name.

Skerry a masculine first name meaning 'sea rock' (*Old Norse*).

Skip a masculine diminutive form of SKIPPER.

Skipper a nickname and surname, meaning 'jumping' (*Middle English*) or 'ship's captain' (*Dutch*), used as a masculine first name. A diminutive form is Skip.

Skipton a place name and surname, meaning 'sheep farm' (*Old English*), used as a masculine first name.

Slade a surname, meaning 'valley' (*Old English*), used as a masculine first name.

Sly a masculine diminutive form of SILVESTER, SYLVESTER.

Smith a surname, meaning 'blacksmith' (*Old English*), used as a masculine first name.

Snowden or **Snowdon** a surname, meaning 'snowy hill' (*Old English*), used as a masculine first name.

Sofie the French feminine form of SOPHIE.

Sol (1) a masculine first name meaning 'the sun' (*Latin*). In Roman mythology Sol is the god of the sun, the counterpart of the Greek Helios. (2) a masculine diminutive form of SOLOMON.

Soliman an Arabic masculine form of SOLOMON.

Solly a masculine diminutive form of SOLOMON.

Solomon a masculine first name meaning 'peaceable' (*Hebrew*). In the Old Testament Solomon was the son of David and Bathsheba who succeeded his father as king of Israel. He built the temple at Jerusalem and was reputed to be very wise. Arabic forms are Sulayman or Suleiman, Soliman or Solyman. Diminutive forms are Sol, Solly.

Solveig a feminine first name meaning 'house strong' (*Old Norse*).

Solyman an Arabic masculine form of SOLOMON.

Somerled a masculine first name the source of which is *sumar-lioi*, 'summer warrior' (Old Norse), referring to a Viking raider. Its modern Gaelic form is SOMHAIRLE. Somerled, Lord of Argyll (died 1164) was the ancestor of the Lords of the Isles.

Somerset a place name, meaning 'settlers around the summer farmstead' (*Old English*), used as a masculine first name.

Somerton a place name, meaning 'summer farmstead' (*Old English*), used as a masculine first name.

Somhairle a modern Scottish Gaelic masculine form of SOMERLED. It is anglicised as SORLEY and sometimes mistakenly as Samuel.

Somhairlidh (pronounced *sorr-lee*) the Old Scottish Gaelic masculine form of SOMERLED.

Sonya or **Sonia** a Russian feminine diminutive form of SOPHIA.

Sophia a feminine first name meaning 'wisdom' (*Greek*). Diminutive forms are Sophie, Sophy.

Sophie or **Sophy** feminine diminutive forms of SOPHIA, now used independently.

Sophronia a feminine first name meaning 'of a sound mind' (*Greek*).

Sorcha (pronounced *sorr-ha*) a feminine first name meaning 'bright, radiant' (*Irish/Scottish Gaelic*).

Sorley an anglicised masculine form of SOMHAIRLE. Sorley Maclean (1911–96) was a great Gaelic poet of the twentieth century.

Sorrel a masculine first name meaning 'sour' (*Germanic*), the name of a salad plant used as a masculine or feminine first name.

Spencer a surname, meaning 'steward or dispenser' (*Old French*), used as a masculine first name. Spencer Tracy (1900–1967) was an eminent American film actor.

Spring (1) a feminine first name meaning 'desire' (*Sanskrit*). (2) the name of the season between winter and summer used as a feminine first name.

Squire a surname, meaning 'shield bearer' (*Old French*), used as a masculine first name.

Stacey (1) a masculine diminutive form of EUSTACE, now used independently. Stacy is a variant form. (2) or **Stacie,** feminine diminutive forms of EUSTACIA, ANASTASIA, now used independently.

Stacie a feminine variant form of STACEY.

Stacy a masculine variant form of Stacey. Stacy Keach is an American film actor.

Stafford a surname, meaning 'ford by a landing place' (*Old English*), used as a masculine first name.

Stamford a masculine variant form of STANFORD.

Standish a surname, meaning 'stony pasture' (*Old English*), used as a masculine first name.

Stanford a surname, meaning 'stone ford' (*Old English*), used as a masculine first name. A variant form is Stamford.

Stanhope a surname, meaning 'stony hollow' (*Old English*), used as a masculine first name.

Stanislas or **Stanislaus** a masculine first name meaning 'government and glory' (*Slavonic*).

Stanley a surname and place name meaning 'stony field' (*Old English*), used as a masculine first name.

Stanton a surname, meaning 'stony farmstead' (*Old English*), used as first name.

Star or **Starr** an English feminine form of STELLA.

Stasia a feminine diminutive form of ANASTASIA.

Stefan a German masculine form of STEPHEN.

Stefano the Italian masculine form of STEPHEN.

Steffan the Welsh masculine form of STEPHEN.

Steffi or **Steffie** feminine diminutive forms of STEPHANIE.

Stella a feminine first name meaning 'star' (*Latin*).

Stephan a German masculine form of STEPHEN.

Stephanie feminine form of STEPHEN. A diminutive form is Stevie.

Stephen a masculine first name meaning 'crown' (*Greek*). In the New Testament Stephen was the first Christian martyr. Stephen was also the name adopted by several popes. Stephen Fry is an English comedian, writer and actor. A variant form is STEVEN. Diminutive forms are Steve, Stevie.

Sterling a surname, meaning 'little star' (*Old English*), used as a masculine first name. A variant form is Stirling.

Steuart a masculine variant form of STEWART.

Steve a masculine diminutive form of STEPHEN. Steve Martin is an American comedian and film actor.

Steven a masculine variant form of Stephen. Steven Spielberg is an American film director and producer whose films include *Jaws* and *Schindler's List*.

Stevie a feminine diminutive form of STEPHANIE, STEPHEN. Stevie Smith (1902–71) was an important English poet.

Stewart the surname, meaning 'steward', from *stig-ward*, 'housekeeper' (*Old English*), used as a masculine first name. The name is wholly identified with Scotland through its adoption as a surname by the High Stewards of the kingdom. In the fourteenth century the Stewarts became the royal house. The French form Stuart has also been in use since the sixteenth century, and both forms are used as first names. A variant form is Steuart.

Stirling (1) a masculine variant form of STERLING. (2) a place name, meaning 'enclosed land by the stream' (*Scottish Gaelic*), used as a masculine first name. Stirling Moss is an English racing driver.

St John (pronounced *sinjon*) a masculine first name meaning 'Saint John'.

Stockland a surname, meaning 'land of a religious house' (*Old English*), used as a masculine first name.

Stockley a surname, meaning 'cleared meadow of a religious house' (*Old English*), used as a masculine first name.

Stockton a place name and surname, meaning 'outlying farmstead' (*Old English*), used as a masculine first name.

Stoddard a surname, meaning 'horse keeper' (*Old English*), used as a masculine first name.

Stoke a place name and surname, meaning 'outlying farmstead' (*Old English*), used as a masculine first name.

Storm the word for a meteorological condition of violent winds and rain, hail or snow used as a masculine or feminine first name. Storm Jameson (1891–1986) was an English writer.

Stowe a surname, meaning 'holy place' (*Old English*), used as a masculine first name.

Strachan or **Strahan** a surname, meaning 'little valley' (*Scots Gaelic*), used as a masculine first name.

Stratford a place name, meaning 'ford on a Roman road' (*Old English*), used as a masculine first name.

Struan a territorial name from Perthshire, meaning 'streams', from *sruthan* (*Scottish Gaelic*), used as a masculine first name. It is associated with the Clan Robertson, of the same locality.

Stuart the French masculine form of STEWART.

Sue or **Sukey** or **Sukie** feminine diminutive forms of SUSAN.

Sulayman an Arabic masculine form of SOLOMON.

Sulien a Welsh masculine first name meaning 'sun-born'. This name is sometimes confused with Selwyn, 'Julian', and its Breton form Sulian.

Suleiman an Arabic masculine form of SOLOMON.

Sullivan a surname, meaning 'black-eyed' (*Irish Gaelic*), used as a masculine first name.

Summer a feminine first name meaning 'season' (*Sanskrit*), the name of the season between spring and autumn used as a personal name.

Sumner a surname, meaning 'one who summons' (*Old French*), used as a masculine first name.

Susan the English feminine form of SUSANNA. Susan Sarandon is an American film actress. Diminutive forms are Sue, Sukey, Sukie, Susie, Susy.

Susanna or **Susannah** a feminine first name meaning 'lily' (*Hebrew*). In the Old Testament Susanna was a young Jewish woman saved from death by Daniel. In the New Testament Susanna was one of the women who cared for Jesus and his apostles in Galilee. A variant form is SUZANNA.

Susanne a German feminine form of SUSANNA.

Susie or **Susy** feminine diminutive forms of SUSAN.

Sutherland a place name and surname, meaning 'southern land' (*Old Norse*), used as a masculine first name.

Sutton a place name and surname, meaning 'southern farmstead' (*Old English*), used as a masculine first name.

Suzanna a feminine variant form of SUSANNA.

Suzanne a French and German feminine form of SUSAN.

Sven a masculine first name meaning 'lad' (*Old Norse*).

Syb a feminine diminutive form of SYBYL.

Sybille the French feminine form of SYBYL.

Sybyl or **Sybilla** feminine variant forms of SIBYL, SIBYLLA. A diminutive form is Syb.

Sydney a masculine variant form of SIDNEY. Sydney Pollack is an American film director who also acts.

Sylvain a French masculine form of SILVANUS.

Sylvanus a masculine variant form of SILVANUS.

Sylvester a masculine variant form of SILVESTER. Sylvester was the name adopted by several popes, including Sylvester II (*c.*940–1003) who was the first French pope (999–1003). Sylvester Stallone is an American film actor. A diminutive form is Sly.

Sylvia a feminine variant form of SILVIA.

Sylvie the French feminine form of SILVIA.

Symeon a masculine variant form of SIMON. In the New Testament Symeon was (1) an ancestor of Mary, mother of Jesus, and (2) one of the Antioch congregation who chose Paul and Barnabus for missionary work.

T

Tab or **Tabby** feminine diminutive forms of TABITHA.

Tabitha a feminine first name meaning 'gazelle' (*Aramaic*). Diminutive forms are Tab, Tabby.

Tad a masculine diminutive form of THADDEUS, also used independently.

Taddeo the Italian masculine form of THADDEUS.

Tadhg (pronounced *taig*) a masculine first name meaning 'poet', 'bard' (*Irish Gaelic*). It is a frequent name in Old Irish sources, and a tribute to the esteem in which poets were held. Anglicised versions include Thady, Teague.

Taffy Welsh masculine form of DAVID (*Celtic*).

Taggart a surname, meaning 'priest' (*Scots Gaelic*), used as a masculine first name.

Tait a surname, meaning 'cheerful' (*Old Norse*), used as a masculine first name. Variant forms are Tate, Teyte.

Talbot a surname, meaning 'command of the valley' (*Germanic*), used as a masculine first name.

Taliesin (pronounced *tal-ee-sinn*) a masculine first name meaning 'radiant brow' (*Welsh*). This was the name of one of the earliest of the great Old Welsh poets, said to have lived in the kingdom of Strathclyde in the sixth century.

Talitha a feminine first name meaning 'maiden' (*Aramaic*).

Tallulah a place name, meaning 'spring water' (*North American Indian*), used as a feminine first name.

Talorc a masculine variant form of TALORCAN.

Talorcan a masculine first name and that of a Pictish king who defeated the Dalriada Scots in AD 736. It is preserved in the place name Kiltarlity. Variant forms are Talorgan and Talorc or Talorg.

Talorg a masculine variant form of TALORCAN.

Talorgan a masculine variant form of TALORCAN.

Tam a masculine diminutive form of THOMAS (*Scots*).

Tamar a feminine first name meaning 'palm tree' (*Hebrew*). In the Old Testament Tamar was (1) a sister of Absalom who married two of Judah's sons and then Judah himself, and (2) a daughter of Absalom. Diminutive forms are Tammie, Tammy.

Tamara the Russian feminine form of TAMAR. Tamara Karsavina is a Russian ballerina who moved to the United States.

Tammas a Scottish masculine form of THOMAS. The diminutive form is Tam. A further pet form is Tammy, although this has also become a girls' name in its own right, from being an abbreviation of Tamsin or Tamar.

Tammie or **Tammy** (1) a feminine diminutive form of TAMAR, TAMSIN now used as a first name in its own right. (2) a masculine diminutive form of TAMMAS.

Tamsin a Cornish feminine contraction of THOMASINA, now used independently. A diminutive form is Tammie.

Tancred a masculine first name meaning 'thought strong' (*Germanic*). Tancred (died 1112) was a Norman soldier and one of the leaders of the First Crusade who took part in the capture of Jerusalem.

Tancredi or **Tancredo** Italian masculine forms of TANCRED.

Tania or **Tanya** feminine diminutive forms of TATIANA, TITANIA, now used independently.

Tanisha a feminine first name meaning 'born on Monday' (*Hausa*).

Tansy a feminine first name meaning 'immortal' (*Greek*), the name of a medicinal plant bearing yellow flowers used as a feminine first name.

Tara the anglicised form of Temair, the name of the ancient capital of Ireland, used as a feminine first name. It may mean 'mound' and be related to Irish Gaelic *torr*, 'hill', 'tower'.

Tariq a masculine first name meaning 'night star' (*Arabic*).

Tarquin a masculine first name from the Roman family name Tarquinius.

Tate a masculine variant form of TAIT.

Tatiana feminine form of a Roman family name of unknown meaning (*Latin*). Diminutive forms are Tania, Tanya.

Taylor a surname, meaning 'tailor' (*Old French*), used as a masculine first name.

Teague an anglicised masculine form of Irish TADHG.

Tearlach (pronounced *char-lach*) the Scottish Gaelic form of CHARLES.

Tebaldo an Italian masculine form of THEOBALD.

Ted or **Teddie** or **Teddy** masculine diminutive forms of EDWARD, THEODORE, THEODORIC.

Teenie a feminine diminutive form of CHRISTINE.

Tegwen or **Tegan** a feminine first name meaning 'beautiful, fair' (*Welsh*), a feminine version of Tegyn, the name of an early Welsh saint.

Tegyn *see* TEGWEN.

Teilo a masculine first name and that of a sixth-century saint, preserved in Llandeilo and many other places.

Tel a masculine diminutive form of TERENCE.

Teleri a Welsh feminine first name from the River Tyleri in Monmouth.

Temair *see* TARA.

Tempest the word for a violent storm used as a feminine first name.

Tennison or **Tennyson** masculine variant forms of DENISON.

Teobaldo an Italian and Spanish masculine form of THEOBALD.

Teodora an Italian and Spanish feminine form of THEODORA.

Teodorico an Italian masculine form of THEODORIC.

Teodoro an Italian and Spanish masculine form of THEODORE.

Teodosia an Italian feminine form of THEODOSIA.

Terence a masculine first name, from that of a Roman family name of unknown origin (*Latin*). Variant forms are Terrance, Terrence. Diminutive forms are Tel, Terry.

Terencio a Spanish masculine form of TERENCE.

Teresa the Italian and Spanish feminine forms of THERESA. St Teresa of Avila (1515–82) was a Spanish ascetic nun who reformed the Carmelite order. Her works include an autobiography, *The Way to Perfection*. In 1970 she was proclaimed a Doctor of the Roman Catholic Church.

Terese a feminine variant form of THERESA.

Teri a feminine diminutive form of THERESA.

Terrance or **Terrence** masculine variant forms of TERENCE.

Terri a feminine diminutive form of TERESA, THERESA, now used independently.

Terris or **Terriss** a surname, meaning 'son of TERENCE', used as a masculine first name.

Terry (1) a feminine diminutive form of TERESA. (2) a masculine diminutive form of TERENCE.

Tertius a masculine first name meaning 'third' (*Latin*).

Tess or **Tessa** or **Tessie** feminine diminutive forms of ESTHER, TERESA, THERESA. The English novelist and poet Thomas Hardy (1840–1928) used the form Tess for the eponymous heroine of his novel *Tess of the d'Urbervilles* (1891).

Tewdwr a Welsh masculine first name, anglicised as Tudor, and a royal name long associated with Anglesey.

Teyte a masculine variant form of TAIT.

Thad a masculine diminutive form of THADDEUS.

Thaddeus a masculine first name meaning 'gift of God' (*Greek-Aramaic*). In the New Testament Thaddeus was one of the apostles of Jesus. Diminutive forms are Tad, Thad, Thaddy.

Thaddy a masculine diminutive form of THADDEUS.

Thady an anglicised masculine form of Irish TADHG.

Thaine a surname, meaning 'holder of land in return for military service' (*Old English*), used as a masculine first name. A variant form is Thane.

Thalia a feminine first name meaning 'flourishing blossom' (*Greek*). In Greek mythology Thalia was one of the muses, the goddesses who presided over the sciences and arts.

Thane a masculine variant form of THAINE.

Thea a feminine diminutive form of ALTHEA, DOROTHEA, now used independently.

Thecla a feminine first name meaning 'god glory' (*Greek*).

Theda a feminine diminutive form of THEODORA, THEODOSIA.

Thelma feminine first name coined in the 19th century by the English writer Marie Corelli (1855–1924) for her novel *Thelma*, perhaps from 'wish' (*Greek*).

Theo a masculine or feminine diminutive form of THEOBALD, THEODORE, THEODORA.

Theobald a masculine first name meaning 'bold for the people' (*Germanic*). A diminutive form is Theo.

Theodor a Scandinavian and German masculine form of THEODORE.

Theodora feminine form of THEODORE. Diminutive forms are Dora, Theo.

Theodore a masculine first name meaning 'the gift of God' (*Greek*). St Theodore (died 690) was the Greek-born seventh archbishop of Canterbury and the first archbishop of the whole English church. Diminutive forms are Ted, Teddie, Teddy, Theo.

Theodoric or **Theodorick** a masculine first name meaning 'people powerful' (*Germanic*). Diminutive forms are Derek, Derrick, Dirk, Ted, Teddie, Teddy.

Theodorus a Dutch masculine form of THEODORE.

Theodosia a feminine first name meaning 'gift of God' (*Greek*).

Theodosius masculine form of THEODOSIA.

Theophila feminine form of THEOPHILUS.

Theophilus a masculine first name meaning 'lover of God' (*Greek*). In the New Testament Theophilus was the Christian to whom LUKE addressed his gospel and the Acts of Apostles.

Theresa a feminine first name meaning 'carrying ears of corn' (*Greek*). Theresa Russell is an American film actress. Diminutive forms are Teri, Terri, Terry, Tess, Tessa, Tessie, Tracey, Tracie, Tracy.

Thérèse the French feminine form of THERESA. St Thérèse of Lisieux (1873–97) was a French Carmelite nun noted for her spiritual autobiography, *The Story of a Soul*.

Theresia or **Therese** German feminine forms of THERESA.

Theron a masculine first name meaning 'hero' (*Greek*).

Thewlis a surname, meaning 'ill-mannered' (*Old English*), used as a masculine first name.

Thibaut a French masculine form of THEOBALD.

Thierry or **Thiery** a French masculine form of THEODORIC. Thiery d'Ardaine was one of the legendary twelve paladins who attended on Charlemagne.

Thirza a feminine first name meaning 'pleasantness' (*Hebrew*). Variant forms are Thyrza, Tirza.

Thom a masculine diminutive form of THOMAS.

Thomas a masculine first name meaning 'twin' (*Aramaic*). In the New Testament Thomas was one of the apostles of Jesus, 'Doubting Thomas', who could not accept Christ's resurrection until he touched the wounds. St Thomas Aquinas (1224–74) was one of the Doctors of the Roman Catholic Church. Diminutive forms are Tam, Thom, Tom, Tommy.

Thomasina or **Thomasine** feminine forms of THOMAS.

Thor a masculine first name meaning 'thunder' (*Old Norse*), in Norse mythology, the god of thunder. A variant form is Tor.

Thora feminine form of THOR.

Thorburn a surname, meaning 'Thor's warrior or bear' (*Old Norse*), used as a masculine first name.

Thordis a feminine variant form of TORDIS.

Thorketit *see* TORQUIL.

Thorndike or **Thorndyke** a surname, meaning 'thorny ditch' (*Old English*), used as a masculine first name.

Thorne a surname, meaning 'thorn tree or hawthorn' (*Old English*), used as a masculine first name.

Thorold a masculine first name meaning 'THOR rule' (*Old Norse*). A variant form is Torold.

Thorp or **Thorpe** a surname, meaning 'farm village' (*Old English*), used as a masculine first name.

Thorwald a masculine first name meaning 'ruled by THOR' (*Old Norse*). A variant form is Torvald.

Thurstan or **Thurston** a surname, meaning 'THOR stone' (*Old Norse*), used as a masculine first name. Thurstan (1078–1140) was an archbishop of York.

Thyrza a feminine variant form of THIRZA.

Tib or **Tibbie** Scottish feminine diminutive forms of ISABEL, ISABELLA.

Tibold a German masculine form of THEOBALD.

Tiebout a Dutch masculine form of THEOBALD.

Tiernan an anglicised masculine form of TIGHERNAC.

Tierney (1) a feminine first name meaning 'lordly', from Gaelic *tighearna*, 'lord' (*Irish Gaelic*). (2) the anglicised masculine form of TIGHERNAC.

Tiffany a feminine first name meaning 'the manifestation of God, the festival of Epiphany' (*Greek*).

Tighernac (pronounced *tyeer-nah*) a masculine first name meaning 'lordly', from *tighearna*, 'lord' (*Irish Gaelic*). This was the name of a celebrated annalist of events in the Celtic world. It is anglicised as TIERNEY or Tiernan.

Tilda or **Tilde** feminine diminutive forms of MATILDA.

Till a German masculine diminutive form of DIETRICH.

Tilly a feminine diminutive form of MATILDA.

Tim a masculine diminutive form of TIMON, TIMOTHY. Tim Robbins is an American film actor and director.

Timmie or **Timmy** masculine diminutive forms of TIMOTHY.

Timon a masculine first name meaning 'reward' (*Greek*). In the New Testament Timon was one of seven men chosen by the apostles of Jesus to look after the Christian congregation. William Shakespeare (1654–1616) used the name for the eponymous hero of his play *Timon of Athens*.

Timothea feminine form of TIMOTHY.

Timothy a masculine first name meaning 'honouring God' (*Greek*). In the New Testament Timothy was a disciple of PAUL who was the leader of the Christian community at Ephesus. Paul addressed two books to him. Diminutive forms are Tim, Timmie, Timmy.

Tina a feminine diminutive form of CHRISTINA, CHRISTINE, etc, also used independently.

Tiphaine a French feminine form of TIFFANY.

Tiree the name of an island, meaning 'land of corn', used as a feminine first name (*Scots Gaelic*).

Tirza or **Tirzah** feminine variant forms of THIRZA. In the Old Testament Tirzah was the name of (1) a daughter of a contemporary of Moses and Joshua, and (2) the name of a city in Samaria that was captured by Joshua.

Tita feminine form of TITUS. A diminutive form of MARTITA.

Titania a feminine first name meaning 'giant' (*Greek*). In medieval folklore Titania was the wife of Oberon and queen of fairies. William Shakespeare (1654–1616) used the two in his comedy *A Midsummer Night's Dream*. Diminutive forms are Tania, Tanya.

Titian an English masculine form of TITIANUS.

Titianus a Roman name derived from TITUS.

Tito the Italian and Spanish masculine form of TITUS. Tito Gobbi (1915–84) was a famous Italian operatic baritone.

Titus a masculine first name meaning 'protected' (*Latin*). In the New Testament Titus was a disciple of PAUL to whom Paul addressed a book. William Shakespeare (1654–1616) used the name for the eponymous hero of his tragedy *Titus Andronicus*.

Tiziano the Italian masculine form of TITIANUS.

Tobey feminine form of TOBY. A variant form is Tobi.

Tobi (1) a masculine variant form of TOBY. (2) a feminine variant form of TOBEY.

Tobias or **Tobiah** a masculine first name meaning 'Jehovah is good' (*Hebrew*). In the Old Testament Tobiah was an opponent of Nehemiah, the Persian king. In the Apocrypha, Tobias was the son of Tobit who was guided on a journey by Raphael. The Scottish playwright James Bridie (1888–1951) based his play *Tobias and the Angel* (1930) on the story. A diminutive form is Toby.

Toby a masculine diminutive form of Tobias, now used independently. A variant form is Tobi.

Todd a surname, meaning 'fox' (*Old Norse*), used as a masculine first name.

Todhunter a surname, meaning 'foxhunter' (*Old Norse/Old English*), used as a masculine first name.

Toinette a feminine diminutive form of Antoinette.

Tom a masculine diminutive form of Thomas, now used independently. Tom Cruise and Tom Hanks are American film actors.

Tomas the Spanish masculine form of Thomas.

Tomás a Spanish masculine form of Thomas.

Tomasina or **Tomina** feminine forms of Thomas.

Tomaso or **Tommaso** Italian masculine forms of Thomas.

Tommie or **Tommy** masculine diminutive forms of Thomas. Tommy Lee Jones is an American film actor.

Tomos a Welsh masculine form of Thomas.

Toni feminine diminutive forms of Annette, Antoinette, Antonia, now used independently.

Tonia a feminine diminutive form of Antonia.

Tonie feminine diminutive forms of Annette, Antoinette, Antonia, now used independently.

Tony (1) a masculine diminutive form of Antony. (2) a feminine diminutive form of Annette, Antoinette, Antonia.

Topaz the white gemstone used as a feminine first name.

Tor a masculine variant form of Thor.

Torcuil the Scottish Gaelic form of Torquil.

Tordis a feminine first name meaning 'Thor's goddess' (*Old Norse*). A variant form is Thordis.

Torin a Scottish and Irish Gaelic masculine first name, probably from a Norse name incorporating that of Thor, god of thunder and war; 'thunder' in Gaelic is *torrunn*.

Tormod (pronounced *torr-o-mot*) a masculine first name meaning 'Norseman' (*Scottish Gaelic*).

Torold a masculine variant form of Thorold.

Torquil a masculine first name from Lewis in the Western Isles, from Gaelic Torcuil, a form of Old Norse Thorketil, 'vessel of Thor'. Thor was the Norse god of thunder and warfare.

Torr a surname, meaning 'tower (*Old English*) or bull (*Old French*), used as a masculine first name.

Torvald a masculine variant form of THORWALD.

Tory a feminine diminutive form of VICTORIA.

Townsend or **Townshend** a surname, meaning 'end of the village' (*Old English*), used as a masculine first name.

Tracey (1) a masculine variant form of TRACY. (2) a feminine diminutive form of TERESA, THERESA.

Tracie a feminine diminutive form of TERESA, THERESA, now used independently.

Tracy (1) a surname, meaning 'Thracian' (*Old French*), used as a masculine first name. A variant form is Tracey. (2) a feminine diminutive form of TERESA or THERESA, now used independently.

Traherne a surname, meaning 'iron strength' (*Welsh*), used as a masculine first name.

Travers a surname, meaning 'crossing, crossroads' (*Old French*), used as a masculine first name. A variant form is Travis.

Traviata a feminine first name meaning 'lead astray' (*Italian*), the title of the eponymous opera by Giuseppe Verdi (1813–1901) used as a feminine first name.

Travis a masculine variant form of TRAVERS.

Treasa (pronounced *tres-sa*) an Irish Gaelic feminine form of Teresa, inspired particularly by St Teresa of Avila.

Trefor a place name, from *tref*, 'settlement', and *vawr*, 'big' (*Cornish/Welsh*), that has long been in use as a first name. It is anglicised as Trevor.

Tremaine or **Tremayne** a surname, meaning 'homestead on the rock' (*Cornish*), used as a masculine first name.

Trent a river name, meaning 'liable to flood' (*Celtic*), used as a masculine first name.

Trev a masculine diminutive form of TREVOR.

Trevelyan a surname, meaning 'mill farm' (*Cornish*), used as a masculine first name.

Trevor the anglicised masculine form of TREFOR. A diminutive form is Trev.

Tricia a feminine diminutive form of PATRICIA.

Trilby a feminine first name coined in the 19th century by George du Maurier (1834–96) for the heroine of his novel *Trilby*.

Trina the latter part of CATRIONA that is assuming an identity of its own as a Scottish and Irish feminine first name.

Trisha a feminine diminutive form of PATRICIA.

Tristram or **Tristam** or **Tristan** a variant form of TRYSTAN. The German composer Richard Wagner (1813–83) used the form Tristan for his opera *Tristan und Isolde*.

Trix or **Trixie** feminine diminutive forms of BEATRICE.

Troy (1) a surname, meaning 'of Troyes' (*Old French*), used as a masculine first name. (2) the name of the city in Asia Minor besieged by the Greeks used as a masculine first name. Troy Donahue is an American film actor who starred in many films in the 1960s.

Truda or **Trudie** or **Trudy** feminine diminutive forms of GERTRUDE.

True the adjective for the quality of being faithful and loyal used as a masculine first name.

Truelove a surname, meaning 'faithful sweetheart' (*Old English*), used as a masculine first name.

Trueman or **Truman** a surname, meaning 'faithful servant' (*Old English*), used as a masculine first name.

Trystan a Cornish and Welsh masculine first name that has been linked to *triste*, 'sad' (*French*), but this is unlikely. The tragic romance of the Cornish chief Trystan and ISEULT of Ireland was drawn into the fabric of the Arthurian legends. Variants of the name include Tristan, Tristram, Tristam.

Tudor (1) the anglicised Masculine form of TEWDWR. (2) a Welsh masculine form of THEODORE.

Tuesday a feminine first name meaning 'day of Mars', the name of the second day of the week used as a feminine first name (*Old English*). Tuesday Weld is an American film actor.

Tullio the Italian masculine form of TULLIUS.

Tullius a Roman family name of Etruscan origin and uncertain meaning used as a masculine first name.

Tully (1) a surname, meaning 'flood' (*Irish Gaelic*), used as a masculine first name. (2) an English form of TULLIUS.

Turner a surname, meaning 'worker on a lathe' (*Old French*), used as a masculine first name.

Turpin a surname, meaning 'THOR the Finn' (*Old Norse*), used as a masculine first name.

Twyford a surname, meaning 'double ford' (*Old English*), used as a masculine first name.

Ty a masculine diminutive form of TYBALT, TYLER, TYRONE, TYSON.

Tybalt a masculine variant form of THEOBALD. In *Romeo and Juliet* by William Shakespeare (1564–1616), Tybalt is a cousin of Juliet and enemy of Romeo, who kills him. A diminutive form is Ty.

Tye a surname, meaning 'enclosure' (*Old English*), used as a masculine first name.

Tyler a surname, meaning 'tile-maker' (*Old English*), used as a masculine first name. A diminutive form is Ty.

Tyrone a territorial name, from the ancient kingdom Tir Eógain, 'land of Eogan', still a county in Ireland, made popular as a first name in the twentieth century by the film star Tyrone Power and the drama producer Tyrone Guthrie. A diminutive form is Ty.

Tyson a surname, meaning 'firebrand' (*Old French*), used as a masculine first name. A diminutive form is Ty.

U

Uberto an Italian masculine form of HUBERT.

Uda feminine form of UDO.

Udall or **Udell** a surname, meaning 'yew-tree valley' (*Old English*), used as a masculine first name.

Udo a masculine first name meaning 'prosperous' (*Germanic*).

Ughes *see* UISDEAN.

Ugo or **Ugolino** or **Ugone** Italian masculine forms of HUGH.

Uilleam (pronounced *eel-yam*) the Scottish Gaelic masculine form of WILLIAM. *See* LIAM.

Uisdean (pronounced *oosh-tyan*) a Scottish Gaelic form of Ugues, Norman-French HUGH.

Ulises a Spanish masculine form of ULYSSES.

Ulisse an Italian masculine form of ULYSSES.

Ulmar or **Ulmer** a masculine first name meaning 'wolf' (*Old English*).

Ulric or **Ulrick** a masculine first name meaning 'wolf power' (*Old English*); the English form of ULRICH.

Ulrica an English feminine form of ULRIKE.

Ulrich a masculine first name meaning 'fortune and power' (*Germanic*).

Ulrike feminine form of ULRICH.

Ulysses the Roman form of the name of the Greek god Odysseus, whose name means 'wrathful' (*Greek*), used as a first name. He is the hero of Homer's *Odyssey* and a prominent character in the Iliad. He married PENELOPE and took part in the Trojan War. He was restored to Penelope at Ithaca after twenty years' wanderings. He appears in the play *Troilus and Cressida* by William Shakespeare (1564–1616), and the Irish-born author James Joyce (1882–1941) reincarnated him as Leopold Bloom in his novel *Ulysses* (1922). A diminutive form is LYSS.

Uma a feminine first name recorded by Robert Louis Stevenson (1850–94) in his story 'The Beach of Falesá'. Uma Thurman is an American film actor.

Umar a masculine variant form of OMAR.

Umberto the Italian masculine form of HUMBERT.

Una (1) an anglicised feminine form of OONAGH. (2) feminine form of 'one' (*Latin*) used by Edmund Spenser (*c*.1552–99) in *The Faerie Queene*.

Unity the quality of harmony or concord used as a feminine first name.

Unwin a surname, meaning 'not a friend' (*Old English*), used as a masculine first name.

Upton a surname, meaning 'upper farmstead' (*Old English*), used as a masculine first name.

Urania a feminine first name meaning 'heavenly' (*Greek*) and in Greek mythology the name of one of the muses.

Urbaine the French masculine form of URBAN.

Urban a masculine first name meaning 'town-dweller' (*Latin*). It was the name adopted by several popes.

Urbano the Italian masculine form of URBAN.

Uri a masculine first name meaning 'light' (*Hebrew*).

Uriah a masculine first name meaning 'fire of the Lord' (*Hebrew*). In the Old Testament Uriah was a Hittite soldier in King David's army and husband of Bathsheba. He was killed in battle on David's instructions so that David could marry Bathsheba. Charles Dickens (1812–70) used the name for the character of Uriah Heep, the ''umble' hypocrite, in his novel *David Copperfield* (1849–50).

Urian a masculine first name meaning 'a husbandman' (*Danish*).

Uriel a masculine first name meaning 'light of God' (*Hebrew*). In Judaism Uriel was one of the four chief angels in apocryphal writings.

Urien a Welsh masculine first name and that of a fifth-century king of the land of Rheged, in what is now southern Scotland. He was incorporated into the Arthurian legends, sometimes as the husband of the witch-queen MORGAN le Fay.

Ursula a feminine first name meaning 'she-bear' (*Latin*). St Ursula was a fourth-century virgin martyr. William Shakespeare (1654–1616) used the name for an attendant of Hero's in his comedy *Much Ado About Nothing*.

Ursule the French feminine form of URSULA.

Uther a masculine first name from *uthr*, 'terrible' (*Welsh*). Uther Pendragon, 'head leader', was the second husband of IGRAINE and the father of King ARTHUR.

Uzziah

Uzziah a masculine first name meaning 'Jehovah is strength' (*Hebrew*). In the Old Testament Uzziah was a king of Judah in whose reign Judah reached the height of its power.

Uzziel a masculine first name meaning 'God is strength' (*Hebrew*). In the Old Testament Uzziel was (1) a grandson of Levi and uncle of Moses and Aaron, and (2) a musician in the service of David.

V

Vachel a masculine first name meaning 'little calf' (*Old French*).

Vail a surname, meaning 'valley' (*Old English*), used as a masculine first name.

Val (1) a masculine diminutive form of VALENTINE. Val Kilmer is an American film actor. (2) a feminine diminutive form of VALENTINA, VALERIE.

Valborga a feminine first name meaning 'protecting ruler' (*Germanic*). Diminutive forms are Walburga, Walborga, Valburga.

Valburga a masculine diminutive form of VALBORGA.

Valda a feminine first name meaning 'flower', from a Cornish word cognate with Welsh *blodyn*, 'flower'.

Valdemar a masculine variant form of WALDEMAR.

Valdemaro an Italian masculine form of WALDEMAR.

Valentin a French, German and Scandinavian masculine form of VALENTINE.

Valentina feminine form of VALENTINE. A diminutive form is Val.

Valentine a masculine or feminine first name meaning 'strong; healthy; powerful' (*Latin*). St Valentine was a third-century Christian martyr whose name as become associated with the practice of sending gifts or cards to loved ones on 14 February, St Valentine's Day, a that seems to have been associated with the mating time of birds. William Shakespeare (1654–1616) used the name in two of his comedies: for a gentleman attending the duke in *Twelfth Night* and as one of the two gentlemen in *The Two Gentlemen of Verona*. A diminutive form is Val.

Valentino an Italian masculine form of VALENTINE.

Valeria the feminine form of VALERIO. William Shakespeare (1654–1616) used the name in his play *Coriolanus*.

Valerian masculine form of VALERIE.

Valeriano an Italian masculine form of VALERIAN.

Valerie a feminine first name meaning 'strong' (*Latin*). A diminutive form is Val.

Valerio an Italian masculine form of VALERIA.

Valéry a masculine first name meaning 'foreign power' (*Germanic*).

Valmai a feminine first name meaning perhaps 'mayflower', from *blodyn*, 'flower', and *mai*, 'May' (*Cornish/Welsh*).

Van a masculine first name meaning 'from, of', a prefix in Dutch surnames now used independently as an English-language first name.

Vance a masculine first name meaning 'young' (*Old English*).

Vanessa a feminine first name invented by Jonathan Swift (1667–1745) for his friend Esther Vanhomrigh, created from the prefix of her surname plus the suffix -essa. A diminutive form is Nessa.

Vasili or **Vassily** Russian masculine forms of BASIL.

Vaughan or **Vaughn** a surname, meaning 'small one' (*Welsh*), used as a masculine first name.

Velvet the English name of a rich, soft cloth used as a feminine first name.

Venetia (pronounced *veneesha*) the Italian name of the region around Venice in northern Italy used as a feminine first name.

Venus the name of the Roman goddess of love, especially sensual love, the equivalent of the Greek Aphrodite. William Shakespeare (1654–1616) wrote a poem, *Venus and Adonis* (1593), that tells of the passion of Venus for the youthful Adonis and the killing of the latter by a wild boar.

Vera (1) a feminine first name meaning 'faith' (*Russian*). (2) a feminine first name meaning 'true' (*Latin*).

Vere a surname, meaning 'from Ver in France' (*Old French*), used as a masculine first name.

Vergil a masculine variant form of VIRGIL.

Verity a feminine first name meaning 'truth' (*Latin*).

Verne or **Verna** feminine diminutive forms of LAVERNE.

Vernon a surname, meaning 'alder tree' (*Old French*), used as a masculine first name.

Verona a feminine variant form of VERONICA.

Veronica a feminine first name meaning 'true image' (*Latin*). St Veronica was a woman of Jerusalem who gave Jesus her veil so that he could wipe the sweat from his brown on the way to Calvary. The veil bore a miraculous imprint of his face. A variant form is Verona. Diminutive forms are Ronnie, Ronny.

Veronika a Scandinavian feminine form of VERONICA.

Veronike a German feminine form of VERONICA.

Véronique a French feminine form of VERONICA.

Veryan *see* BURYAN.

Vesta a feminine first name of uncertain meaning. In Roman mythology, Vesta was the goddess of the hearth, the equivalent of the Greek Hestia. Her public sanctuary was in the Forum in Rome where a sacred fire was kept constantly burning by the Vestal Virgins, her priestesses.

Vi a feminine diminutive form of VIOLA, VIOLET.

Vic a masculine diminutive form of VICTOR.

Vicente a Spanish masculine form of VINCENT.

Vicki or **Vickie** or **Vicky** a feminine diminutive form of VICTORIA, now used independently.

Victoire a French feminine form of VICTORIA.

Victor a masculine first name meaning 'conqueror' (*Latin*). The name was adopted by several popes. A diminutive form is Vic.

Victoria a feminine first name meaning 'victory' (*Latin*). Queen Victoria (1819–1901) was queen of the United Kingdom (1837–1901) in an expansionist period and lent her name to describe the period. Diminutive forms are Tory, Vickie, Vicky, Vita.

Vida a feminine diminutive form of DAVIDA.

Vidal a Spanish masculine form of *vitalis* (*Latin*), 'living, vital'. Vidal Sassoon is an English hairdresser who established a chain of shops.

Vilhelm a Swedish masculine form of WILLIAM.

Vilhelmina a Swedish feminine form of WILHELMINA.

Vilma a feminine diminutive form of VILHELMINA.

Vina a feminine diminutive form of DAVINA, ALVINA.

Vince a masculine diminutive form of VINCENT.

Vincent a masculine first name meaning 'conquering; victorious' (*Latin*). St Vincent de Paul (*c*.1581–1660) was a French priest who founded two charitable orders. Diminutive forms are Vince, Vinnie, Vinny.

Vincente an Italian masculine form of VINCENT.

Vincentia a feminine form of VINCENT.

Vincentio an Italian masculine form of VINCENT. William Shakespeare (1654–1616) used the name for characters in two of his plays, *The Taming of the Shrew* and *Measure for Measure*.

Vincenz a German masculine form of VINCENT.

Vinnie or **Vinny** a masculine diminutive form of VINCENT.

Vinson a surname form of VINCENT used as a masculine first name.

Viola or **Violet** a feminine first name meaning 'a violet' (*Latin*). William Shakespeare (1654–1616) used the form Viola for the heroine of his comedy *Twelfth Night* who is required to pretend to be a boy. A diminutive form is Vi.

Violetta the Italian feminine form of VIOLA, VIOLET.

Virgil a masculine first name meaning 'staff bearer' (*Latin*), the name of the Roman poet of the first century BC. A variant form is Vergil.

Virgilia a feminine form of VIRGILIO. William Shakespeare (1654–1616) used the name for the wife of Coriolanus in his eponymous play.

Virgilio the Italian and Spanish masculine form of VIRGIL.

Virginia a feminine first name meaning 'virginal' (*Latin*). Virginia Woolf (1882–1941) was a noted English novelist, critic and essayist whose works include the novels *To the Lighthouse* (1927) and *Orlando* (1928). A diminutive form is Ginnie.

Virginie a Dutch and French feminine form of VIRGINIA.

Vita (1) feminine form of VITO. (2) a feminine diminutive form of VICTORIA. Vita Sackville-West (1892–1962) was an English writer and noted gardener.

Vitale an Italian masculine form of *vitalis* (*Latin*), 'living, vital'.

Vito the Italian masculine form of VITUS.

Vitore an Italian masculine form of VICTOR.

Vitoria a Spanish feminine form of VICTORIA.

Vitorio the Spanish masculine form of VICTOR.

Vittorio an Italian masculine form of VICTOR.

Vitus a masculine first name meaning 'life' (*Latin*).

Viv a feminine diminutive form of VIVIEN.

Vivian or **Vyvian** a masculine first name meaning 'full of life' from *vivere*, 'to live' (*Latin*). A variant form is Vyvian. *See also* BÉIBHINN.

Vivien or **Vivienne** feminine form of VIVIAN. A diminutive form is Viv.

Vladimir a masculine first name meaning 'royally famous', 'a renowned monarch' (*Slavic*). St Vladimir (*c*.956–1015) was a Viking pagan who became the ruler of Kiev in Russia. He converted to Christianity, married Anna, sister of the Byzantine Emperor Basil II, and became the first Christian ruler of Russia.

Vladislav a masculine first name meaning 'great ruler' (*Slavonic*).

Vyvian a masculine variant form of VIVIAN.

W

Wade a surname, meaning 'to go, or at the ford' (*Old English*), used as a masculine first name.

Wadsworth a surname, meaning 'WADE's homestead' (*Old English*), used as a masculine first name. A variant form is Wordsworth.

Wainwright a surname, meaning 'maker of carts' (*Old English*), used as a masculine first name.

Wake a surname, meaning 'alert, watchful' (*Old English*), used as a masculine first name.

Walburga or **Walborga** feminine diminutive forms of VALBORGA.

Waldemar a masculine first name meaning 'noted ruler' (*Germanic*). A variant form is VALDEMAR.

Waldo a masculine first name meaning 'ruler' (*Germanic*).

Walker a surname, meaning 'a fuller' (*Old English*), used as a masculine first name.

Wallace or **Wallas** a masculine first name that is cognate with 'Welsh' and means an inhabitant of the originally Brythonic kingdom of Strathclyde, which existed up to the end of the tenth century. It was the surname of the great defender of Scotland's liberty in the thirteenth/fourteenth century Wars of Independence, William Wallace, it became a popular first name in the twentieth century. A variant form is WALLIS. The diminutive form is Wally.

Wallis a variant form of WALLACE, used as a masculine or feminine first name. Wallis Simpson (1896–1986) was an American divorcée for whom King Edward VIII (1894–1972) gave up the throne of the United Kingdom. A diminutive form is Wally.

Wally a masculine diminutive form of WALLACE, WALLAS, WALLIS.

Walt a masculine diminutive form of WALTER, WALTON.

Walter a masculine first name meaning 'ruler of army, people' (*Germanic*). Diminutive forms are Walt, Wat, Watty.

Walther a German masculine form of WALTER.

Walton a surname, meaning 'farmstead of the Britons' (*Old English*), used as a masculine first name. A diminutive form is Walt.

Wanda a feminine variant form of WENDA.

Ward a surname, meaning 'watchman, guard' (*Old English*), used as a masculine first name.

Warfield a surname, meaning 'field of the stream of the wrens' (*Old English*), used as a masculine first name.

Warne a surname, meaning 'alder wood' (*Cornish*), used as a masculine first name.

Warner a surname, meaning 'protecting army' (*Germanic*), used as a masculine first name.

Warren a surname, meaning 'wasteland' or 'game park' (*Old French*), used as a masculine first name. Warren Beatty is an American actor and husband of Annette Bening.

Warwick a place name and surname, meaning 'dwellings by the weir' (*Old English*), used as a masculine first name.

Washington a place name and surname, meaning 'Wassa's estate' (*Old English*), used as a masculine first name. Washington Irving (1783–1859) was an American writer whose stories include *The Legend of Sleepy Hollow* and *Rip van Winkle*.

Wat a masculine diminutive form of WALTER.

Watkin a masculine diminutive form of WALTER, literally 'little Walter'.

Watty a masculine diminutive form of WALTER.

Waverley a place name, meaning 'meadow or clearing by the swampy ground' (*Old English*), used as a masculine first name.

Wayne a surname, meaning 'a carter', used as a masculine first name.

Webb a surname, meaning 'weaver' (*Old English*), used as a masculine first name.

Webster a surname, meaning 'woman weaver' (*Old English*), used as a masculine first name.

Wellington a place name and surname, meaning 'Weola's farmstead' (*Old English*), used as a masculine first name.

Wenceslas or **Wenceslaus** a masculine first name meaning 'wreathed with glory' (*Slavonic*). St Wenceslas (*c*.907–929), famed in the Christmas carol, was a duke of Bohemia (*c*.925–929) who attempted to Christianise his people but was assassinated by his brother. Wenceslaus

(1361–1419) was king of Bohemia (1378–1419) and Holy Roman Emperor (1378–1400).

Wenda feminine form of WENDEL. A variant form is Wanda.

Wendel or **Wendell** a masculine first name meaning 'of the Wend people' (*Germanic*).

Wendy a feminine first name invented by Sir J. M. Barrie (1860–1937) for the main female character in his play *Peter Pan* (1904). It gained popularity quite quickly.

Wentworth a surname, meaning 'winter enclosure' (*Old English*), used as a masculine first name.

Werner a German masculine form of WARNER.

Wes a masculine diminutive form of WESLEY.

Wesley a surname, meaning 'west wood' (*Old English*), made famous by the Methodists John Wesley (1703–91) and Charles Wesley (1707–88), used as a masculine first name. Wesley Snipes is an American film actor. A diminutive form is Wes.

Whitaker a surname, meaning 'white acre' (*Old English*), used as a masculine first name. A variant form is Whittaker.

Whitman a surname, meaning 'white- or fair-haired' (*Old English*), used as a masculine first name.

Whitney a surname and place name, meaning 'white island or Witta's island' (*Old English*), used as a masculine or feminine first name. Whitney Houston is an American singer.

Whittaker a masculine variant form of WHITAKER.

Wilbert a masculine first name meaning 'well-born' (*Old English*).

Wilbur a masculine first name meaning 'wild boar' (*Old English*).

Wilf a masculine diminutive form of WILFRID.

Wilfrid or **Wilfred** a masculine first name meaning 'will peace' (*Germanic*). A diminutive form is Wilf.

Wilfrida or **Wilfreda** feminine form of WILFRID.

Wilhelm the German masculine form of WILLIAM. A diminutive form is Wim.

Wilhelmina or **Wilhelmine** feminine form of WILHELM. Diminutive forms are Elma, Minna, Minnie, Wilma.

Will a masculine diminutive form of WILLIAM.

Willa a feminine form of WILL, WILLIAM.

Willard a surname, meaning 'bold resolve' (*Old English*), used as a masculine first name. Willard White is a Jamaican-born opera singer.

Willemot a masculine first name meaning 'resolute in spirit' (*Germanic*).

William a masculine first name meaning 'resolute helmet' (*Germanic*). Diminutive forms are Bill, Will.

Williamina feminine form of WILLIAM.

Willie a masculine diminutive form of WILLIAM.

Willoughby a surname, meaning 'farm by the willows' (*Old Norse/Old English*), used as a masculine first name.

Willson a masculine variant form of WILSON.

Willy a masculine diminutive form of WILLIAM.

Wilma a feminine diminutive form of WILHELMINA; feminine form of WILLIAM.

Wilmer (1) a masculine first name meaning 'famous will or desire' (*Old English*). (2) a masculine form of WILMA.

Wilmot a diminutive surname form of WILLIAM used as a masculine first name.

Wilson a surname, meaning 'son of WILL' (*Old English*), used as a masculine first name. A variant form is Willson.

Wilton a place name and surname, meaning 'floodable place' (*Old English*), used as a masculine first name.

Wim a contraction of WILHELM.

Win a feminine diminutive form of WINIFRED.

Windham a masculine variant form of WYNDHAM.

Windsor a place name and surname, meaning 'slope with a windlass' (*Old English*), used as a masculine first name.

Winifred a feminine first name meaning 'joy and peace' (*Old English*). Diminutive forms are Freda, Win, Winnie, Wynn, Wynne.

Winnie a feminine diminutive form of WINIFRED.

Winona a place name, in Minnesota, USA, used as a first name. Winona Ryder is an American film actress.

Winslow a place name and surname, meaning 'Wine's burial mound' (*Old English*), used as a masculine first name.

Winston a place name and surname, meaning 'friend's place or farm' (*Old English*), used as a masculine first name.

Winter the name for the cold season of the year used as a masculine first name.

Winthrop a surname, meaning 'friend's farm village' (*Old English*), used as a masculine first name.

Winton a surname, meaning 'friend's farm' (*Old English*), used as a masculine first name.

Wolf or **Wolfe** a masculine first name meaning 'wolf' (*Old English*).

Wolfgang a masculine first name meaning 'bold wolf' (*Germanic*).

Wolfram a masculine first name meaning 'wolf raven' (*Germanic*).

Woodrow a surname, meaning 'row (of houses) in a wood' (*Old English*), used as a masculine first name. A diminutive form is WOODY.

Woodward a surname, meaning 'forest guardian' (*Old English*), used as a masculine first name.

Woody a masculine diminutive form of WOODROW, now used independently. Woody Guthrie (1912–67) was an American folksinger and songwriter. Woody Allen is the adopted name of the American actor, writer and film director.

Wordsworth a masculine variant form of WADSWORTH.

Worth a surname, meaning 'farmstead' (*Old English*), used as a masculine first name.

Wyman a surname, meaning 'battle protector' (*Old English*), used as a masculine first name.

Wyn a masculine first name from *gwyn*, 'white, pure' (*Welsh*). A variant form is Wynn.

Wyndham a surname, meaning 'homestead of WYMAN' (*Old English*), used as a masculine first name. A variant form is Windham.

Wynn or **Wynne** (1) a surname, meaning 'friend' (*Old English*), used as a masculine or feminine first name. (2) a masculine variant form of WYN. (3) a feminine diminutive form of WINIFRED.

X

Xanthe a feminine first name meaning 'yellow' (*Greek*).

Xavier a place name, meaning 'new house owner' (*Spanish/Basque*), used as a masculine first name.

Xaviera feminine form of XAVIER.

Xena or **Xene** or **Xenia** a feminine first name meaning 'hospitality' (*Greek*).

Xenos a masculine first name meaning 'stranger' (*Greek*).

Xerxes a masculine first name meaning 'royal' (*Persian*).

Y

Yahya the Arabic form of John. In the Koran Yahya is the counterpart of John the Baptist.

Yale a surname, meaning 'fertile upland' (*Welsh*), used as a masculine first name.

Yann the Breton masculine form of JOHN.

Yasmin or **Yasmine** feminine variant forms of JASMINE.

Yehuda a feminine variant form of JEHUDA.

Yehudi a masculine first name meaning 'a Jew' (*Hebrew*).

Ygraine and **Yguerne** feminine variant forms of IGRAINE.

Yolanda or **Yolande** a feminine variant form of VIOLA.

Yorath a Welsh masculine form of IORWETH, usually found as a surname.

York or **Yorke** a place name and surname, meaning 'estate of Eburos or of the yew trees' (*Celtic/Latin/Old English*), used as a masculine first name.

Yseult a feminine variant form of ISEULT.

Yunus the Arabic form of Jonah.

Yuri a Russian masculine form of GEORGE.

Yusuf the Arabic form of Joseph.

Yves a masculine first name meaning 'yew tree' (*French-Germanic*).

Yvette a feminine diminutive form of YVES.

Yvonne feminine form of YVES.

Z

Zabdiel a masculine first name meaning 'gift of God' (*Hebrew*).

Zabrina a feminine variant form of SABRINA.

Zaccheus a masculine first name meaning 'innocent, pure' (*Hebrew*). In the New Testament Zaccheus was a tax collector in Jericho met Jesus on his visit to Jericho and was his host.

Zach a masculine diminutive form of ZACHARY.

Zachary or **Zachariah** or **Zacharias** or **Zecheriah** a masculine first name meaning 'Jehovah has remembered' (*Hebrew*). In the New Testament Zachary was the father of St John the Baptist. St Zacharias (died 752) was a Greek-born pope (741–752). Diminutive forms are Zach, Zack, Zak.

Zack a masculine diminutive form of ZACHARY.

Zadok a masculine first name meaning 'righteous' (*Hebrew*). In the Old Testament Zadok was a priest who worked closely with King David. 'Zadok the Priest' was the first of four anthems composed by George Handel (1685–1759) for the coronation of George II (1727). It is still performed at British coronations.

Zak a masculine diminutive form of ZACHARY.

Zara a feminine first name meaning 'flower' (*Arabic*).

Zeb a masculine diminutive form of ZEBADIAH, ZEBEDEE, ZEBULON, ZEBULUN.

Zebadiah or **Zebedee** a masculine first name meaning 'gift of the Lord' (*Hebrew*). In the New Testament Zebedee was a fisherman on the Sea of Galilee and the father of James the Great and John, two of the apostles of Jesus.

Zebulon or **Zebulun** a masculine first name meaning 'elevation' (*Hebrew*). In the Old Testament Zebulun was the sixth son of Jacob and Leah and founder of one of the twelve tribes of Israel. Diminutive forms are Lonny, Zeb.

Zed a masculine diminutive form of ZEDEKIAH.

Zedekiah a masculine first name meaning 'justice of the Lord' (*Hebrew*). In the Old Testament Zedekiah was the last king of Judah whose reign ended with the deportation of the Jews to Babylon. A diminutive form is Zed.

Zeke a masculine diminutive form of Ezekiel.

Zelda a feminine diminutive form of Grizelda also used independently. Zelda Sayre was the wife of the American writer F. Scott Fitzgerald.

Zelig a masculine variant form of Selig.

Zelma a feminine variant form of Selma.

Zenas a masculine first name meaning 'gift of Zeus' (*Greek*). In the New Testament Zenas was friend of Paul.

Zenobia a feminine first name meaning 'having life from Zeus' (*Greek*).

Zeph a masculine diminutive form of Zephaniah.

Zephaniah a masculine first name meaning 'hid of the Lord' (*Hebrew*). In the Old Testament Zephaniah was a Hebrew prophet and author of the Book of Zephaniah. A diminutive form is Zeph.

Zinnia the name of a plant with brightly coloured flowers used as a feminine first name, named after the German botanist JG Zinn.

Zoë or **Zoe** a feminine first name meaning 'life' (*Greek*).

PRENTICE-HALL INDUSTRIAL RELATIONS AND PERSONNEL SERIES

DALE YODER, *Editor*

BELCHER—*Wage and Salary Administration, 2nd ed.*

BELLOWS—*Creative Leadership*

BELLOWS—*Psychology of Personnel in Business and Industry, 3rd ed.*

BELLOWS, GILSON, AND ODIORNE—*Executive Skills*

BRINKER—*Social Security*

DANKERT—*Contemporary Unionism in the United States*

DANKERT—*Introduction to Labor*

DAVEY—*Contemporary Collective Bargaining, 2nd ed.*

DUBIN—*Human Relations in Administration, 2nd ed.*

DUBIN—*Working Union-Management Relations*

ECKER, MACRAE, OUELLETTE, AND TELFORD—*Handbook for Supervisors*

GOMBERG—*A Trade Union Analysis of Time Study, 2nd ed.*

LINDBERG—*Cases in Personnel Administration*

MAHONEY—*Building the Executive Team*

OTIS AND LEUKERT—*Job Evaluation, 2nd ed.*

PFIFFNER AND FELS—*The Supervision of Personnel, 3rd ed.*

SHARTLE—*Executive Performance and Leadership*

SHARTLE—*Occupational Information, 3rd ed.*

SHOSTAK AND GOMBERG—*Blue-Collar World*

STONE AND KENDALL—*Effective Personnel Selection Procedures*

THOMPSON—*Personnel Management for Supervisors, 2nd ed.*

TOLLES—*Origins of Modern Wage Theories*

YODER—*Personnel Management and Industrial Relations, 5th ed.*

YODER—*Personnel Principles and Policies, 2nd ed.*

Origins of

Modern Wage Theories

Origins of

Modern Wage Theories

$$HD4975$$
$$.T65\Theta$$

N. ARNOLD TOLLES

New York State School
of Industrial and Labor Relations
Cornell University, Ithaca, New York

Prentice-Hall, Inc.   Englewood Cliffs, New Jersey

Library of Congress Catalog Card No.: 64-17872
PRINTED IN THE UNITED STATES OF AMERICA
[64268-C]

PRENTICE-HALL INTERNATIONAL, INC., *London*
PRENTICE-HALL OF AUSTRALIA, PTY., LTD., *Sydney*
PRENTICE-HALL OF CANADA, LTD., *Toronto*
PRENTICE-HALL OF INDIA (PRIVATE) LTD., *New Delhi*
PRENTICE-HALL OF JAPAN, INC., *Tokyo*
PRENTICE-HALL DE MEXICO, S.A., *Mexico City*

Foreword

Professor Tolles has written a good book. He has surveyed the historical development of wage theory in a scholarly and open-minded manner. In the process he has shown the complex forces involved in the determination of wage levels and the dangers of excessive dogmatism. He thoroughly understands the marginal productivity theory of wages, as developed by John Bates Clark and his followers, and whereas he does not emphasize this as strongly as some might do, he does clearly portray its strengths and its limitations. I personally believe that this is one of the growing points of economics and favor a thorough mathematical and statistical attempt at quantitative verification and the establishment of productivity and supply schedules of labor and capital. But the other factors that operate upon the labor market need to be recognized and sympathetically appraised. This is perhaps Professor Tolles' major contribution.

I especially like his chapter on the three so-called institutional economists, namely, the mordant genius Thorstein Veblen, the painstaking statistician, Wesley Mitchell, and lovable John R. Commons of Wisconsin who developed more good economists than any teacher of his generation. The whole book is readable, eclectic, humane, and in no sense dogmatic. Professor Tolles writes clearly and with real charm, and it is a pleasure to see this fine scholar and devoted teacher bring forth as a by-product of his distinguished career so valuable and worthwhile a book.

SENATOR PAUL H. DOUGLAS

Preface

"Theory" is popularly thought of as the obscure specialty of a few academic pundits—a specialty far removed from the practical concerns of daily life. A study of wage theory may indeed prove obscure and meaningless if conducted in a vacuum. On the other hand, a study of wages, like any other study, can be stultifying if limited to memorizing facts without reference to theory.

A central purpose of this essay is to put today's general public and the wage theorists on speaking terms with each other. Rather than another book on wage theory, what is needed now is an account of how questions about wages have changed and developed in the United States during the last half century. Hence this book recounts highlights of American social history of the twentieth century and relates them to the questions people are asking about wages today. The presentation is in simple English and avoids the unexplained use of the technical jargon of economics. Nevertheless, the issues raised will be worth the attention of advanced students as well as the beginner.

In one sense, this is a purely personal essay, the direct incentive for which was provided in 1954 when the author was a visiting lecturer, under a Fulbright fellowship, at the University of Munich. It represents a condensed version of many private drafts written at different times during the last ten years. In another sense, this is so highly collaborative a work that it is impossible even to list, let alone express appreciation to, the many persons to whom the author is indebted. At one end of the chain is Senator Douglas, the author's first inspiring university teacher. At the other end is Mrs. Joan Monson, an efficient and loyal secretary, who was most insistent that the author "quit fussing and finish something." In between are the dozens of superiors, colleagues, assistants, students, relatives, and friends—at the University of Chicago, the London School of Economics, Mount Holyoke College, Smith College, the United States Department of Labor, the University of California, the American University, Columbia University, and the New York State School of Industrial and Labor Relations at Cornell University —who made possible and rewarding the author's study and teaching.

N. ARNOLD TOLLES

vii

Contents

Origins of

Modern Wage Theories

CHAPTER I

A Defense of Theory

Wage problems and wage policies are more widely studied and debated in the United States of the mid-twentieth century than ever before. On the other hand, wage theory seems, at first sight, to have fallen into disrepute.

In popular speech, the very word *theory* is frequently used as a symbol of contempt. Thus we are often told that "in theory" wages would be such and such but that "in actual practice" wages are quite different from those which the theorists have falsely led us to expect. Some of the textbooks which deal with wages merely describe particular wage problems without mentioning a theory of wages at all. Other textbooks dutifully outline some of the former wage theories but then proceed to ignore them when practical wage problems are treated, or else go on to show that these past theories are wrong. Many professional articles and monographs do attempt to construct theories of wages, but their readers are usually confused by the apparent clash between these different theories. The man on the street and the college student share a general distrust of wage theory because they feel it is difficult to understand or misleading if not actually false.

But has the importance of the theory of wages actually declined during the past half century? We may take our cue from John Maynard Keynes, who wrote the following eloquent passage in the year 1935, as part of the concluding portion of his *General Theory of Employment, Interest and Money:*

> . . . the ideas of the economists and political philosophers, both when they are right and when they are wrong, are more powerful

1

than is commonly understood. Indeed the World is ruled by little else. Practical men, who believe themselves to be quite exempt from intellectual influences, are usually the slaves of some defunct economist. Madmen in authority, who hear voices in the air, are distilling their frenzy from some academic scribbler of a few years back.[1]

The theme of the present essay is that wage theory is in the process of developing into a richer and more realistic tool of wage analysis than was the accepted wage theory at the beginning of the twentieth century. There is no longer any single, simple, all-purpose theory of wages. But this development of specialized wage theories is similar to the development of theory in all areas of human knowledge. To put the subject of wage theory in perspective, it may be helpful to consider at the outset the meaning of the word *theory* in its general sense and to examine the relation between theory and observed facts, theory and practice, and theory in relation to the changing and conflicting doctrines of mankind.

MEANING OF THE WORD, THEORY: RELATION TO OBSERVED FACTS

As used in this essay, the word theory refers to any logical statement of an expected relationship, expressed or implied. Thus the theory (or *law*) of gravity relates the speed of a falling object to its mass. A theory of wages relates wages themselves to the factors which influence the remuneration for human effort and skill or, alternatively, the theory deals with the influence of wages on any of the related factors such as, for example, the volume of employment.

Theory underlies and is essential to all types of systematic knowledge. Lacking a theory, all we have is the observation that something has occurred. Will it ever occur again? If so, why? If not, why not? As soon as we try to answer such questions, we are beginning to build a theory.

Consider, for example, the familiar matter of sunrise and sunset. On a clear day, anyone may observe the appearance of the sun in the east and its disappearance in the west. We observe that the sun rises and sets every day, but at different times in different seasons. Why? When will the sun rise and set? Only after thousands of years of observation and conjecture were men able to answer these seemingly simple questions. Many tentative theories—hypotheses—were advanced before the modern theory of the rotation of the earth on its axis and the earth's rotation around the sun were worked out and

---

[1] John Maynard Keynes, *The General Theory of Employment Interest and and Money* (New York: Harcourt, Brace & World, Inc., 1936), p. 383.

verified. The verified theory then made it possible to predict accurately the time of sunrise and sunset on any future day at any point on the surface of the earth.

The precise kind of theory that is needed depends on the kind of question that is asked. Thus a theory which allows us to predict the time of sunrise is inadequate if we wish to predict the weather on any particular day. The position of the earth in relation to the sun does give us a starting point for the prediction of the temperature of the atmosphere at any given time and place. But an accurate forecast of temperature, wind, and precipitation requires a theory which takes account of many factors besides the rotation of the earth, including (as we now know) conditions in outer space. As we extend our theories we can reduce the chance of error and the extent of that error as against a mere guess based on observations that have not been analyzed in terms of a systematic theory. Similarly, as we shall see in this essay, a theory which helps us to answer one question about wages may be quite inadequate in the face of a different kind of wage problem.

A theory may be either very general or very specialized in its application. Philosophers have always sought for the very general theories or *laws* which would explain all man's universe and all human conduct. On the other hand, storytellers (including many latter-day novelists and investigators of particular cases) have sought to suggest some logic or relationships without attempting to say just when, why, or how often the described experience would be repeated. Both the philosophers and the storytellers have helped to enrich man's knowledge of his universe—the philosophers by helping men to see their situation as a whole, and the storytellers by challenging the accepted generalizations of their time, thus suggesting the need for revised theories. Historically, all types of theory have tended to develop from a few simple and very general statements of relationship to a large number of complex theories which can provide a more exact basis for prediction in particular circumstances. In the physical sciences we are accustomed to the continuous development of complex and specialized theories. We call this *progress*. In the social sciences, however, a similar enrichment of theory too often is taken to mean that all theory has broken down and may now be disregarded.

PRACTICE AND THEORY

Once we understand what is meant by a theory as here defined, it becomes absurd to say that any given statement is right in theory but wrong in practice. If a given theory is adequate and applicable to the problem at hand, then a contrary practice is a bad practice. If the practice is well conceived to advance the objective in question, then any contrary theory needs to be revised. This necessity that theory and practice be brought into harmony is more evident in the well-established physical sciences than it is in the social sciences. No one would say that while the theory of the tensile strength of metals is correct, it is to be ignored in the practice of building a bridge. Yet it is frequently said that a theory of wages is correct but that it should be ignored when one is considering the results of actual wage policies. What is usually meant when the false theory-practice dilemma is raised is that some particular theory is not adequate to explain the particular situation in question. What is needed, then, is either a re-examination of the old theory or a reconsideration of the conflicting practice.

The apparent conflict between theory and practice does exist in the physical as well as the social sciences. One way of dealing with the problem is to treat a theory as providing only a first approximation, useful as a rough guide to practice. An engineer designing a bridge begins with the theory of the subject; but in drawing up the practical design of a bridge, he may make a 50 per cent allowance for unpredictable stresses. The factors involved in dealing with a wage problem may be even more varied and unpredictable than those involved in designing a bridge. A theory of wages may provide only a crude approximation to the results which we seek to predict. Thus the proponents of the marginal productivity theory of wages often say that wages *tend* to conform to the predictions suggested by that theory, which is an admission that wages in some actual situations may deviate considerably from the predicted wages.

Facts which differ to an important extent from the theoretical predictions provide a stimulus for the development of new theories or at least the revision of older theories. The technique of making allowances for unknown influences becomes unsatisfactory when the allowances are large ones relative to the predicated results. When the early jet aircraft began to explode in mid-air, it became clear that some revision was needed in the theory of the fatigue of metals. Similarly, when the accepted theory of wages of the early twentieth century became seriously defective as a basis for predicating wages in particular cases, students of wage problems were forced to re-examine the theory of wages itself. In this connection, it is important to notice that it is the known fact—rather than the unknown fact—which provides the stimulus for the revision of theories. The facts regarding the fatigue of metals were the same before the explosion of jet aircraft as they were after this experience, but it was the new experience which forced an extension of the theories involved. Similarly the growth in the extent and accuracy of knowledge pertaining to actual wages has provided one part of the challenge to the wage theories of the nineteenth century. The nineteenth-century wage theorists had only a scanty knowledge of actual wages as compared with the knowledge we have today. Their generalizations about wages were necessarily restricted by the limited body of facts which they had been able to perceive. Twentieth-century wage theories have emerged in part as a reaction to the challenge of new facts and to our improved perception of the facts.

DOCTRINES AND THEORIES

Changing doctrines provide an even more powerful stimulus to the development of theory than do changing perceptions of the facts. Indeed, doctrine and theory are so closely related that the two concepts are often confused with each other. Still, a distinction needs to be made. A *doctrine,* as the word is used in this essay, represents what someone believes to be a desirable objective of action, while a *theory,* as we have seen, consists of a logic which permits a prediction of the outcome of a line of action.

Some physical scientists like to believe that human doctrines have nothing to do with the pure theory of their subjects of study. It is true that sheer curiosity has a part in spurring the work of the mathematician and the chemist. Yet the objectives and policies of men have impelled, at the beginning, most of the discoveries in the physical sciences. The doctrine that Europe would be enriched by transportation over a shorter route to India led to confirmation of the theory that the earth is round. The doctrine that human health was worth preserving impelled the important advances in medicine and in the biological theories which underlie the practice of medicine. The current doctrine that it is important to conquer outer space is leading to important advances in the theory of the operation of our physical universe.

In the social sciences, even more than in the physical sciences, the clash of conflicting doctrines provides a motive power for the advance of theory. This is so because the subject matter of the social sciences is man himself, with all of man's changing and conflicting doctrines as to desirable human conduct. For example, as long as men accepted the doctrine that each worker should be kept and supported in the class into which he was born, there was little need for any theory of worker remuneration. The breakdown of mediaeval doctrines based on custom forced men to develop some kind of theory of wages. In the body of this essay we shall see how the changing objectives of wage policy (conflicting wage doctrines) during the last half century have led to a re-examination and further development of wage theories.

When doctrines are in conflict, each doctrinal group proceeds to defend its position by an argument based on some kind of logic or theory. The purpose of the argument is to justify the respective positions of each set of the interest groups involved. The eventual outcome of the conflicting arguments is a revised and enriched theory. Doctrines are formulated to support the policies and practices which each group believes to be desirable. Hence doctrines usually develop after practices but in advance of new theories. Wage theory cannot be static. New wage theories continually develop out of the clash of changing wage doctrines as well as out of the clash of accepted doctrines and newly perceived facts.

The essay which follows begins with a sketch of the development of wage theory during the nineteenth century in Great Britain and North America. This theory developed gradually in response to the changing facts and doctrines during the period from Adam Smith to Alfred Marshall and John Bates Clark. By the beginning of the twentieth century what is called *neoclassical* theory had become generally accepted and taught by the leading economists on both sides of the North Atlantic. Thus the material presented briefly in Chapter II provides a convenient starting point for the consideration of the uprooting and re-examination of wage theory during the more recent period.

The wage theory considered orthodox in the year 1900 has been challenged by the sweeping changes of both fact and doctrine which have taken place in the United States and Britain during the past half century. Ten of these major influences on wage theories are described in Chapters III to XII of this essay. This major portion of the essay really consists of a brief social history of the United States as that history has affected current theories of wages. The influences described range from the social work movement of the early twentieth century to the current concern with the problems introduced by price inflation. The selected influences are presented in about the order of their respective appearance. All of them affect present-day thinking about wage problems.

No single, integrated theory of wages has yet appeared to take the place of the orthodox theory of half a century ago. The explanation is that questions which are now asked about the remuneration of human effort are much more varied and specialized than they used to be. The twentieth century has not yet produced anyone of the stature of Alfred Marshall to weave together the bewildering strands of fact and doctrine of our own time into a single fabric. Nevertheless, some degree of consistency of logic in the analysis of wage problems is beginning to appear. In the last chapter of this essay the author emphasizes the need for a distinction between the problem of the general level of wages over long periods of time and the problem of the structure of individual wages at particular moments of time. Around these two general but distinctive problems the new theories of wages are beginning to emerge and crystallize.

CHAPTER II

Development of the Accepted
Wage Theory as of 1900

By the beginning of the twentieth century, the theory of wages seemed to have been settled at last. After a debate among economists which ran through the nineteenth century, a "correct" or "orthodox" theory emerged which any professor could teach with confidence. Anyone who understood this theory was considered to be a master of what was then called "the wages question."

In later chapters, an attempt will be made to show the origins of the changes in wage theory which have occurred during the first half of the twentieth century. But we can best appreciate these changes if we know what it was that was changed. Hence there is need for a brief review of the kind of wage theory which had developed by the year 1900. Attention will be focused here as well as later, not on the technical details of wage theories, but on the practical questions men asked about wages and, therefore, on the broad nature of the theory they developed to help in answering these questions.

First of all, what is the popular understanding of orthodox wage theory? A one-sentence statement of the matter is that wages are determined by the so-called law of supply and demand. This statement does not do justice to the economists and, taken by itself, does not explain very much. Nevertheless, the statement is important because it does suggest that the reward for every kind of human effort is controlled by some kind of impersonal and irresistible force, similar to the force of gravity.

Among practical men, the law of supply and demand is a magic phrase. It is thought by many to be the answer to every kind of argument about wages. It is especially convenient in popular use

8

because it does not commit a person to any particular wage. Whether wages rise or fall, the existing wage at any time and place can be defended as the right one because wages, it is said, are controlled by the law of supply and demand. To act or argue contrary to such a law is often considered to be futile if not immoral.

The repeated droning of the phrase *supply and demand* by employers has caused reformers and critics of the existing state of things to react against theory in general and against economists in particular. Any parrot can become an economist, it has been said, if one simply teaches him to say the words "supply and demand." Because the reformers of the early twentieth century were being told that their efforts were foredoomed by economic theory, they were inclined to dismiss the economists as prejudiced propagandists for those in power. If this was theory, the reformers would have none of it. The controversy which raged at the beginning of the twentieth century was not really about a theory but about a doctrine. The extreme form of the doctrine was that any employer of labor should be allowed to pay whatever wage he chose, that any worker should be content with any wage he could get, and that government should retreat from the fixing of wages and working conditions. If any such doctrine follows from orthodox theory, the reason why it should follow, and the circumstances in which the doctrine should be applied, are not at all clear. In fact, none of the nineteenth-century economists who developed orthodox wage theory accepted the *laissez faire* ("let alone") doctrine completely. These theorists were interested in determining the factors—and the relationship between the factors—which would help them to solutions of the problems which were then prevalent.

If we are to understand nineteenth-century wage theorists—or any influential theorist for that matter—we must understand the setting in which their theories were created and hence the questions which their theories sought to answer.

SUPPLY OF LABOR

Adam Smith: Philosopher of the Commercial System

In nineteenth-century Britain, for the first time in human experience, the majority of a people came to depend for their livelihood on employment for money wages. These money wages were paid to them by enterprises which, in turn, produced goods or services to sell in the market for the largest return possible. This new commercial system had been developing gradually for several centuries.

Its development was well advanced in 1776, the year Adam Smith, a Scottish professor, published his famous *Wealth of Nations*. Smith rightly foresaw that the new commercial system could greatly increase the total volume of goods and services and that this rise in real national income (as we call it today) could make a nation wealthy and at the same time improve the welfare of the ordinary man. However, in 1776, the dominance of the new commercial system was by no means taken for granted, even in Britain. Production and the buying and selling of both goods and labor were still hedged about by a great number of customs, laws, and regulations. These customs, laws, and regulations had been inherited from the past and had served to preserve a privileged position for owners of land and for a number of other groups, including a small group of skilled craftsmen. Adam Smith was not a defender of things as they were. On the contrary, he was a radical critic of the prevailing economic order. He wanted to get rid of the obstructions to the free play of the new and struggling commercial system so that the lot of the common man could be improved.

But what standard would govern wages in this new commercial order? For hundreds of years prior to Smith workers employed by others had received a livelihood that was systematically regulated to keep each class in its accustomed place in society. If producers of all types were to be freed from inherited customs, laws, and regulations, some new force would have to determine wages. Adam Smith believed that the market forces of supply and demand were generally preferable to custom and regulation—in determining the price of labor as well as in determining the price of goods. But Adam Smith saw the need for many exceptions to his laissez-faire principle. Indeed, Smith never attempted any universal economic theory. Instead, he sprinkled his great work with a series of suggestive observations and partial generalizations. Later generations of scholars have devoted much effort to the question of what Adam Smith's theory of wages really was. By quoting one phrase or another from the *Wealth of Nations* it is possible to claim Smith as a supporter of virtually any theory of wages one wishes to choose. This may be an amusing academic exercise, but it does little to advance the theory of wages. Whatever Adam Smith may have meant, he was very clearly keeping his mind focused on the problems of his own day. To try to solve a special wage problem of the twentieth century by quoting some remark of Adam Smith's is futile. Smith's ideas were related, necessarily, to a different set of problems than those which face us today.

Adam Smith did popularize—even if he did not invent—the idea of supply and demand as forces which could, under some circumstances, control wages as well as all other prices. And thus, Adam Smith's *Wealth of Nations* prompted the development of wage theory in the nineteenth century. But this was the beginning, not the end, of the story. What, in turn, controlled the supply of labor? What controlled the demand for labor? Just how did the supply and the demand for labor interact? Above all, just what question about wages was one trying to answer and in what circumstances? Adam Smith did not try to answer these questions for the eighteenth century, much less for the nineteenth or twentieth centuries.

Thomas R. Malthus: The Importance of Population Pressure

The next important step in the development of the nineteenth-century theory of wages was taken by an English clergyman, Thomas Robert Malthus. Malthus published his first *Essay on the Principles of Population* . . . in 1798 and his considerably revised second edition in 1803. Although Malthus was not the originator of any new theory of wages, his thought is fundamental to the great debate which brought to the center of the stage the basic wage question of the nineteenth century.

To understand Malthus, as to understand any theorist, one must comprehend the problem he was facing. The wage problem at the beginning of the nineteenth century appeared to be the problem of stark destitution in the face of rapid increases in production and employer's profits. Looking back, we can see that this situation was a result of a major overturn in the economic arrangements in Britain, including the mass displacement of labor because of the enclosure movement and the effects of the Napoleonic Wars. Malthus sought to explain the resulting poverty in the midst of plenty. Like a proper child of the eighteenth century, he tried to deal with the problem in universal terms. Partly because he adopted a universal form for his theory of population, Malthus has been both praised and damned by successive generations of reformers and churchmen.

What Malthus observed is the incontestable fact that the human race, like any healthy biological organism, can reproduce itself without limit and rapidly, under favorable conditions. What is the necessary condition for this infinite increase in the numbers of human beings? The minimum condition is enough *subsistence* to allow the population to survive. The next question, therefore, is whether the means of subsistence can be increased as fast as the population. The Malthusian answer is "No." Sooner, or later, the scarcity of food will limit the numbers of people who can survive.

Excessive numbers will then be eliminated by the "natural" checks to population (famine, disease, and war), whereas the discovery of new resources will be followed by an increase in the surviving population until, once more, there is just enough subsistence per person to maintain the larger population.

The pessimism of Malthus was *almost* complete. He saw, of course, that any measure which limited the number of births might check the population increase before everyone reached the starvation level. However, Malthus' own religious principles kept him from advocating deliberate birth control. All that was left to relieve the gloom was the possibility of abstinence from sexual intercourse and the postponement of marriage. But Malthus could not honestly be very hopeful about the adoption of these *preventive* checks to population increase.

David Ricardo: The Iron Law of Wages

The population theory of Malthus was converted into a wage theory by a prosperous businessman turned economist, David Ricardo. What emerged was later called the *iron law of wages.* In effect, Malthus had already foreshadowed this "law," even though he had not stated his proposition in the form of a theory of wages. What Malthus provided was a condition which would govern the supply of labor. The supply of labor, Malthus had supposed, would increase until there was just a bare minimum of subsistence for everyone. This minimum of subsistence was, so to speak, the cost of producing the labor supply. Ricardo simply pulled the population theory of Malthus into his general theory of value under which the price of anything would eventually equal the cost of production of the most expensive unit of the supply that was needed to meet demand. This principle could be applied to labor as well as to goods. A minimum of subsistence was the necessary cost of maintaining a labor supply. Just as more goods would be produced, so more labor would come forth so long as the price was more than the cost. In the end, the price would just equal the cost. As far as labor was concerned, this meant that wages could not remain higher than the amount necessary to buy the goods the worker needed in order to live at a bare minimum of subsistence. This is the iron law of wages.

But what about the demand for labor? Ricardo realized that wages might rise or fall temporarily as the demand for labor increased or decreased in relation to the available supply. But Ricardo, like Malthus, was not interested in any temporary state of the demand for labor. What seemed important to Malthus and Ricardo was that the population would adjust itself eventually to any state of demand in such a way as to bring wages into line with the minimum of subsistence.

Ricardo himself was an earnest inquirer into a wide range of the practical problems of his day. His *Principles of Political Economy*, which he reluctantly published in 1817, was intended as a theoretical defense of the national policies he advocated. Chief among Ricardo's doctrines was that Britain should repeal the so-called corn laws so as to admit without import duty the cheaper foodstuffs from the rich lands of the New World. This policy would have been contrary to the interests of the British landlords because it would have lowered the price of British-grown foodstuffs. To defend the advocated policy, Ricardo worked out the theory of rent that became basic to many different types of economic reasoning.

Wage earners and employers would neither benefit nor suffer from the importation of cheaper food. The workers would in any case, Ricardo thought, receive only wages that would cover the cost of their subsistence. Employers would pay lower money wages if food became cheaper, but as the wage cost of their products declined so would the price of the products they sold. The followers of Ricardo converted his reasoning into a doctrinal defense of a policy of low wages in a way that Ricardo himself had not intended. To Ricardo there could be no choice of wage policy because wages would always gravitate toward just enough to cover the cost of a minimum of subsistence. Ricardo's followers sensed that there could be a policy toward wages, and Ricardo's authority was used to justify payment of the lowest wage at which an employer could obtain the labor supply he wanted. As in numerous other cases, the reformist doctrine of one generation became the reactionary doctrine of the next generation.

Karl Marx: Surplus Value versus Cost of Production

It remained for Karl Marx to turn the wage theory of Ricardo inside out. Wages would inevitably fall to a bare subsistence level, said Marx, as long and only as long as the capitalist system survived. The only hope of the workers, therefore, was to get rid of the capitalist system. Starvation wages were not inevitable but merely the result of a social system that valued everything—including labor—at its minimum cost of production. Once the revolution had overturned the capitalist system, everything would be different. Just how it would be different was never made clear.

On the foundation of Ricardo, Marx built his famous theory of *surplus value*. Under capitalism, as Ricardo had said, wages would always tend to a mere subsistence level. But by means of the capitalist method of production, each unit of labor produced a greater value per worker than the value of mere subsistence. This difference between the economic reward to the worker and the value of what he produced was surplus value. This surplus was pocketed by the capitalist employer, and so it represented a robbery of the workers.

The controversy between the followers of Ricardo and of Marx dominated economic thought during the last half of the nineteenth century and even cast a deep shadow on the wage theories of the twentieth century. How could such opposite conclusions be drawn from what seems to be the same basis for reasoning? Part of the answer is that Ricardo based his wage theory on Malthus and Marx did not. To Ricardo, the iron law of wages was based on an inevitable physical fact—the potential increase in population—whereas to Marx the same law was simply due to social arrangements that caused labor to be paid merely its minimum cost of production. The second part of the answer is that Ricardo was considering the relative values of the various parts of a given national product, whereas Marx was considering the dynamics of the situation—that is, how one state of things would lead to another.

As we shall see, later theorists have concluded that Ricardo and Marx were both wrong—or at least incomplete—in their reasoning on these matters. The wages of labor do not necessarily tend toward subsistence level under capitalism. And the whole range of wage problems cannot be solved, either by a theory of relative values in a static economy or by a theory of some inevitable progression of events of the Marxian type.

THE WAGE SHARE

The central wage problem of nineteenth-century theory came to be the problem of labor's share of all goods and services produced in a nation. This is, indeed, only one of the many problems which a theory of wages might seek to answer. Ricardo and Marx made it appear to be the most important wage problem, at least in a capitalist system. The remainder of nineteenth-century wage theory can best be understood if one realizes that this over-all wage-share problem was considered the principal wage issue of that period.

John Stuart Mill: Emphasis on Demand

Around 1850 the actual wages of British workers began to improve. Whatever may have been the causes of this improvement, it gave a new turn to the theory of wages. The birth rate, instead of rising in accord with the formula of Malthus, actually fell. In Britain at that time there was no evidence of any inevitable tendency of wages to sink back toward a minimum subsistence level. By the same token, actual events seemed to belie the Marxian thesis that the capitalist system would inevitably degrade the condition of the workers. These events did not dispose of the "wages problem," but they did suggest the need for a more exact and complete theory of the wage share.

In particular the rise in wages suggested that more attention needed to be given to the demand for labor and to the exact way in which the forces of demand and supply acted to influence prices and wages. These next steps were taken by John Stuart Mill. John Stuart Mill was the son of James Mill, a strict follower of Malthus and Ricardo; but as the younger Mill broke away from his father's influence, he became more and more of a humanitarian reformer. Mill's *Principles of Political Economy,* first published in 1848, became the leading university textbook in economics for the next forty years and was thus an important means of making social reform respectable.

Although John Stuart Mill still considered himself a follower of Malthus and Ricardo, he gave a new twist to their theories. No defender of the established order, Mill bent his chief thought to ways of improving the condition of wage earners. Just as much as Malthus, Mill feared that an increase in the population might drive wages down to a bare subsistence level. But Mill did not believe that such an outcome was inevitable. Deliberate means might be taken to keep the number of births within bounds and so allow a temporary increase in actual wages to be converted into a new and higher minimum level of living. Mill had a much more international outlook than his immediate predecessors. His knowledge of conditions in other countries suggested to him that the habits of living varied from place to place and from time to time and habits and social institutions, therefore, were subject to change and improvement.

If different minimum levels of subsistence were possible, then there could be no single cost of producing the supply of labor. This thought led Mill to treat the supply of labor as a fixed quantity— that is, a quantity which would be regulated by factors quite apart from the wages paid. Hence the important determinant of wages would be the demand for such labor as was available for employment. For the first time since Adam Smith, the nature of the demand for labor began to receive serious attention.

Employers' Willingness to Pay

Before recounting Mill's changing ideas about the demand for labor, some attention should be paid to Mill's treatment of the general "law" of supply and demand. Granted that supply and demand have something to do with a price or wage, no one before Mill had explained precisely how these supply and demand forces really operated. Mill's explanation is essentially the one which is accepted today, at least in the case of a free and unregulated market. According to Mill, the market price will be the price at which the quantity supplied will be equal to the quantity that is demanded. Thus the wages of labor will depend on the price which employers are willing to pay (the state of demand) for the quantity of labor that offers itself for employment. Notice that there is nothing mysterious or righteous about this so-called law. It provides no justification for any existing level of wages. We have given us a certain quantity of labor available for employment. What the wages will be, then, boils down to the nature of the demand for labor, or in simple terms, what employers are willing to pay for the existing quantity of labor.

The Wages Fund Theory

Mill's particular analysis of the demand for labor provides an exciting human interest story because his is a rare case of an economist who admitted publicly that he had been wrong. What first impressed Mill about the demand for labor was that the employer paid his workers out of his accumulated capital. Wage earners needed to consume finished goods every week. Under the prevailing system of employment, they were paid every week the money that permitted them to buy finished goods every week. But the work performed by wage earners did not result in a simultaneous supply of consumable goods. Many months or years would need to pass before the work of an iron miner resulted in the production of the plow that helped to provide the wheat and, later, the bread that the iron miner needed to eat during the week in which he worked. By this kind of reasoning, borrowed from Ricardo and quite consistent with the reasoning of Marx, John Stuart Mill rightly observed that the wages of labor were paid from the accumulated resources of their employers.

At just this point, Mill ventured a leap in the dark. He was groping for an explanation of the nature of the employers' demand for labor. His problem, as he and other economists of his time saw it, was to account for the share of the whole consumable product of a nation going to employed labor. What would be the total amount of wages paid by employers? Because wages were paid out of accumulated resources, Mill at first thought total wages to be equal to the total amount of accumulated capital. By this method of reasoning, Mill suggested that the demand for labor as a whole consisted of the quantity of capital as a whole that had been accumulated by any nation. The accumulated capital was the so-called *wages fund.* Average wages of employed workers seemed to be merely the total wages fund divided by the number of units of labor available.

Further thought caused Mill to modify his simple statement that the total wages consisted simply of the quantity of accumulated capital divided by the number of wage earners. Not all accumulated capital was distributed to wage earners, but only *circulating* (as opposed to *fixed*) capital. And, actually, not all the circulating capital would be distributed to wage earners, but only that part that was, as Mill put it, "destined to the support of the laborers." By making these qualifications, Mill laid himself wide open to attack. What started out to be a theory of the demand for labor had ended up with a statement, in effect, that the wages fund consisted of whatever part of their resources employers would choose to pay in wages! Wages simply were whatever they were.

John Stuart Mill publicly abandoned the wages fund theory in a magazine article of 1869: "The price of labour, instead of being determined by the division of the proceeds between the employer and his labourers, (actually) determines it (the price of labour) . . . the right and wrong of the proceedings of Trade Unions (therefore) becomes a common question of prudence and social duty, not one which is peremptorily decided by unbending necessities of political economy." Curiously, Mill's statements to the effect that the demand for labor consisted of the capital funds destined for the support of laborers, remained in all the editions of his *Principles,* even though the editions of 1871, 1878, and 1885 followed the public repudiation of his wages fund doctrine. By the 1870's Mill was an old man. He had the courage and candor to reconsider his central theory of wages as supposedly determined by the demand for labor, but he no longer had the energy to substitute anything else.

Mill's repudiation of his own wages fund theory left the wages question wide open. On the side of the demand for labor, the ortho- dox wages fund theory had been repudiated by its chief proponent. On the side of the supply of labor, the pre-1850 theories had been undermined. The question remained as to whether, in Marxian terms, existing wages represented robbery of the workers because of surplus value. If wages under the commercial system of production did not represent an exploitation of the employed workers, what, then, was the logic of wages under the existing order of the Western world? The nineteenth-century answer to this question developed as a result of a blend of Austrian, English, Swiss, and American contributions to orthodox theory of value in general.

Karl Marx had pointed out that nothing could be produced without labor and from this obvious truth he reasoned that labor should receive the whole value of what is produced. It was no answer to Marx to say that some payment had to be made for the use of capital, because capital itself was produced by means of labor. Capital was in fact, "jellied labor," to use Marx's own phrase. It was fair enough, admitted Marx, to repay the employer for the wages he had advanced to the workers who made the capital goods, but the surplus value—the profits of the employers—were stolen from the value which labor alone had created. A revised theory of the demand for labor was needed if Marx's theory of exploitation were to be refuted.

THE NATURE OF DEMAND

Before the wage-share problem could be solved, it was necessary to solve a similar problem as to the demand for any kind of goods or service. Why was it that the goods that men found to be most essential to their needs often sold at the lowest prices? The standard answer before 1870 had been to point out a difference between *value in use* and *value in exchange*. That answer merely put the same question in a different form. How could the use value of an item be great while the exchange value remained small? Vaguely, the answer was that the exchange value would be low if a great quantity of the goods were available. True enough, but still there was no explanation of just what the exchange value would be. Mill had said that the value (of goods, but not labor) would settle at the point where the amount supplied and the amount demanded were equal. But what would regulate the amount of a good that would be demanded at any given price?

Marginal Utility

The answer to the above question was devised independently by four economists in four different countries: by Karl Menger, an

Austrian, in 1871; by Stanley Jevons, an Englishman, in the same year; by Leon Walras, a Swiss, in 1874; and by John Bates Clark, an American, in 1881. None of these professors knew of the work of the others at the time each of them solved the century-old problem of the relation of demand to price.

The essence of the answer is that the price anyone will be willing to pay for anything depends upon the last, or final, or *marginal* unit of the item he buys. Furthermore, in a perfectly competitive market, the price paid for the least useful unit of anything will be the price paid for every other similar unit. For example, Mr. Jones might be willing to pay all of his accumulated income for one loaf of bread if he were starving and if only one loaf could be supplied. But if he had already eaten seven loaves of bread during the week, he would not be willing to pay much for an eighth loaf on Saturday night. Yet the producers of bread will depend on the sale of this last loaf—to Mr. Jones and to all the other buyers of their eighth loaves. Since each loaf of bread is like every other (in our example), the price of every loaf will depend on the usefulness (economists call this *utility*) of the last and least useful loaf of the total supply of bread the bakers produced. As a result of this *marginal-utility* logic, a person could at last understand why an only slightly useful item like a one-carat diamond could be sold for hundreds of dollars while a vitally essential item like a one-pound loaf of bread could be sold for only a few cents. The price of a unit of anything must be whatever the buyers are willing to pay for extra or additional units of any total quantity that the sellers want to sell. The buyers would pay a large amount for each unit if only a small number of such units were available. But the buyers would pay only a small sum for each unit of a large quantity of the same kind of goods.

J. B. Clark: Marginal Productivity

All of this might seem to have nothing to do with the theory of wages or with the answer to Karl Marx, but an American, John Bates Clark, clearly saw how marginal utility could be applied to the theory of wages. What is the utility of labor to the employer? Clearly, it is the product the employer gets to sell as a result of engaging the workers. But just as the usefulness of goods is measured by the usefulness of one additional unit of these goods, so the usefulness of labor is measured by what can be produced by one additional unit of labor. The fact that goods cannot be produced without labor has nothing to do with the wages an employer can afford to pay for the services of any one worker. Unless any one worker can produce a value (in addition to what all the others have produced) equal to the value he receives in wages, it will not be worthwhile for the employer to hire that worker. The same is true of each of the other workers, if any one worker can be substituted for any other worker. Hence, the wages per worker at which employers will demand additional labor will be the value of the additional produce obtained by employing an additional worker. This product is the marginal product of labor. (Clark called it the *specific product of labor*.) The theory that the additional product or income obtained by the employment of any one unit of labor will govern the wage paid to any group of workers is known as the *marginal productivity theory* of wages.

At last the orthodox theorists seemed to have a complete answer to the surplus value theory of Karl Marx. If each worker received as wages the value of the marginal product of labor, that was all that could be expected. The marginal product multiplied by the number of workers was the whole product of labor. True, the entire product would be greater than the share labor received. But what Marx had called the "surplus value" was needed to pay the owners of capital for the marginal product contributed by each unit of capital, times the number of units of capital that were used in production.

NEOCLASSICAL WAGE THEORY

The reader will notice that the attention of economists had shifted, since Ricardo, from questions relating to the supply of labor to questions relating to the demand for labor. In place of Ricardo's cost of minimum subsistence, stood Clark's marginal product. In the earlier theory, subsistence was supposed to govern wages by its influence on the supply of labor. By contrast, the marginal productivity principle was now supposed to govern wages through the influence of marginal productivity on the decisions of labor.

Alfred Marshall: The Complexity of Supply and Demand

Supply and demand were both brought back into focus by Alfred Marshall, the Cambridge University professor who dominated economic theory at the close of the nineteenth century and for a long time thereafter. Marshall attempted to show that demand and supply (that is, basically, *utility* and *cost*) were coordinate forces which governed wages as well as other prices. In a famous passage, Marshall wrote:

We might as reasonably dispute whether it is the upper or the under blade of a pair of scissors that cuts a piece of paper, as whether value is governed by utility or cost of production. It is true that when one blade is held still, and the cutting is effected by moving the other, we may say, with careless brevity, that the cutting is done by the second; but the statement is not strictly accurate, and is to be excused only so long as it claims to be merely a popular and not a strictly scientific account of what happens.[2]

And so it is with wages as affected by marginal productivity (*demand*), and by the cost of producing a labor (*supply*). J. B. Clark and the marginal productivity theorists were dealing with a case in which the size of the labor force was fixed, like a scissors blade that is held still. In such a case, with a fixed quantity of labor to be supplied, the remaining wage question is the state of the demand for labor. But if we are interested in a situation where the state of the demand for labor is "held still," we may say, "with careless brevity," that it is the cost of supplying the labor that determines the wage. In both cases, the influence that is supposed to determine the wages does this only in view of the nature of the other influence. Marginal productivity determines wages if one can presume a certain fixed quantity of labor. But the cost determines wages if one presumes a certain fixed state of the demand for labor.

Marshall saw that the effect of costs on the supply of labor, and therefore on wages, is not at all simple. No longer could it be presumed that there is a single and unchanging minimum cost of subsistence for all workers. Instead, there are many different and changeable levels of living for different groups of workers in different places and at different times. Furthermore, costs can influence wages only by changing the quantity of labor that is available for employment. To change the total labor supply in relation to the wages that are anticipated may require thirty or forty years—a whole generation. Moreover, the costs of producing labor—what Marshall called the "efforts and sacrifices" that are required—are not so much undertaken by the worker who receives the wages as by his parents and by the tax payers (government). Finally, what we call the *quantity of labor* is not simply a matter of producing live bodies but also of providing education and training. It is not at all clear that the wages paid must be just enough to repay any particular amount of cost that is involved in making that quantity of labor available.

[2] Alfred Marshall, *Principles of Economics* (London: Macmillan & Co., Ltd., 1890). In the 8th edition (1920) the passage appears in Bk. V, Chap. III, para. 7, p. 348

Orthodox Marginal Productivity Theory

In spite of Marshall's efforts to relate every price to both the state of supply and the state of demand, economists at the beginning of the twentieth century had no general and simple explanation of the supply of labor. Those who sought a general theory of wages embraced, therefore, a theory of the demand for labor—namely the marginal productivity theory. This theory does not mean that the supply of labor is to be ignored, but simply that we begin with a certain total amount of available labor existing in a country at a certain time. The larger the quantity of labor, the lower the wages that can be paid, the smaller the quantity of labor, the higher the wages that can be paid—that is, if all other circumstances are the same. But for any given quantity of labor—say 70 million workers with a certain amount of training and working forty hours a week— the orthodox theory suggests that wages will be equal to the marginal productivity of that labor. If wages were less than this amount, employers would find that they could increase their own earnings by hiring more labor. To do so they would bid against each other for the available labor supply until wages and marginal productivity again were equal to each other.

The orthodox theory of wages, as it had developed by the close of the nineteenth century, was a good bit more subtle and complex than the mere statement "wages are determined by the 'law' of supply and demand"—the statement with which this brief review was begun. It was true that this oft-quoted statement did put into a few words what economists since Adam Smith had been saying. The real meaning of those words, however, had changed during the century as a succession of economists—including many who have not been mentioned—struggled with both the practical issues of their times, with the logic involved in the words supply and demand, and with the relationship between them. What emerged was not so much a law as a statement of normal relationships—that is, the kind of thing one would expect to occur, taking one thing with another, in a whole country and over a period of time long enough for all the adjustments to be made. It always was, and still is, a perversion of orthodox theory to use it as a defense of any particular wage at any particular day. However, this was how theory was actually used by many employers, second-rate teachers, and journalists at the beginning of the twentieth century.

Orthodoxy and Wage Issues

The general idea that the orthodox theory of wages was designed to defend things as they are (the *status quo*) is not correct, but it does contain some grains of truth. Though all of the orthodox wage theorists were reformers, they were not revolutionaries. Once Karl Marx attempted to justify an overthrow of the capitalist system on economic grounds, even the most critical of the orthodox economists were led into the controversy over the moral justification for the partial share that employed workers received of the whole product of a nation. This primary concern with over-all wages as a fraction, or ratio really, of the total national product began with Ricardo and, therefore, through the nineteenth century, was the ordinary meaning of the "wages question." Indeed, after Marx, the general problem of the over-all wage share became the principal concern of all the economists, especially those who followed the theory of John Bates Clark.

As we shall see, the issue of the fractional wage share has given way to much more pressing wage questions in the twentieth century. The more recent development of wage theory is like the nineteenth-century development in one important respect—both developments occurred as a result of changing facts and practical issues. What was once called the wages question is no longer a single question but rather a large and changing group of particular questions. Any useful theory is addressed to a particular question and the more precisely the question is defined the better. American experience in the twentieth century has shown that even the marginal productivity theory does not lead us toward useful solutions to all wage issues.

SUMMARY

The chief question in the minds of the English and American economists of the nineteenth century was the wage-share question. What fraction of a nation's total product would be received by wage earners in a capitalist system? The answers ran in terms of the supply of labor and the demand for labor. During the first half of the century, the most startling labor development was the great increase in the number of wage earners and their abject poverty in comparison with the rising profits of their employers. Reacting to these developments, the leading economists, from Malthus to Marx, put their emphasis on the supply of labor.

During the last half of the nineteenth century, it was evident that the real improvement in average wages could not be explained by either the population theory of Malthus or the surplus value theory of Marx. Hence, from Mill to J. B. Clark, the emphasis shifted to an analysis of the demand for labor. The demand for labor in a capitalist economy evidently depended on the willingness of employers to pay certain wages for certain quantities of labor. What controlled this "willingness"? The answer of the economists at the end of the nineteenth century was that employers would pay the value of the product contributed by any one unit of labor out of the total available for hire. This was the marginal productivity theory of wages.

Once the marginal productivity answer had been worked out, it became the orthodox theory of wages—the theory followed by "right-thinking" people. As usual, the half-educated people clung to the theory more rigidly than the economists themselves and the half-educated were inclined to use the shorthand phrase "supply and demand" without really knowing what lay behind those simple words. The popular impression was that the orthodox theory had been designed to answer all questions about wages. In fact, however, the theory had been worked out to answer one particular question only.

The practical issues of the twentieth century raised many wage questions beyond that of the total wage share. Indeed, the challenge of the twentieth-century wage issues seemed at first to put all wage theory in opposition to the real facts of life. Actually, the rich experience of the twentieth century is gradually leading to many further valuable developments in the theory of wages.

CHAPTER III

Immigration and the Social
Service Workers

Between 1870 and 1914, immigration to the United States represented one of the largest geographical transfers of people in recorded history. A large proportion of these immigrants became wage earners after arrival. Their wages were generally much lower than those of established American workers. This mass of immigrant workers dramatized the plight of the low-wage workers in general and led to a conflict of doctrines about immigration and the general problem of poverty. The distinctive reaction of American social workers to the plight of the immigrants helped to give a number of new directions to the theory of wages.

The accepted wage theory at the beginning of the twentieth century was the marginal productivity theory. As discussed in Chapter II, this theory evolved gradually over a period of more than a century in response to the facts and doctrines of earlier times. By the year 1900, the chief problem to which it addressed itself was what should be the share of wage earners as a whole in the national product as a whole. The facts of immigration and the doctrines of the social workers provided sources of protest against the then generally accepted theory of wages. The older theory might provide a good chain of logic to solve the wage-share problem, but it seemed inadequate to deal with the new facts and doctrines of the twentieth century.

IMMIGRATION—SOME FACTS

Except for native Indians, the entire population of the United States consists of immigrants and their descendants. It may seem strange, then, that immigration after 1870 should have introduced any new elements into the American scene. However, there were

25

three new factors in the situation: (1) the sheer numbers of the new immigrants, (2) the places from which these immigrants came, and (3) the places in the United States to which they migrated.

The number of immigrants to the United States rose from around 50,000 a year in the 1830's, to around 200,000 a year in the middle of the nineteenth century, and to almost 1,000,000 persons a year in the first decade of the twentieth century. Despite the rapid growth of the American economy, this flood of immigration created great problems of adjustment both for the immigrants themselves and for the established workers with whom they competed for jobs.

The place of origin of the new immigrants also changed radically as time went on. The table following suggests this change. The British (English, Welsh, Scotch, and Irish) and the Germans made up the great majority of the older group of immigrants. Increasingly, they gave way to Italians and others from Central and Southern European countries. There were several reasons for this change in countries of origin. Levels of living were rising rapidly in Western Europe after 1870 so that there was no longer as great an incentive for these West-European peoples to emigrate to America. Workers in Southern and Eastern Europe, on the other hand, enjoyed few of the economic advantages of the industrial revolution before 1914. Indeed, serfdom itself was not abolished in Russia until 1861. On balance, then, it became relatively more advantageous for people of Eastern and Southern Europe to migrate to the United States than for the British and Germans to do so. Therefore, immigration followed a general trend that a traditional economist of the time might have predicted. In spite of individual exceptions, most of the immigrants found jobs in the United States without too much difficulty and at higher wages than they could have earned in their home countries.

IMMIGRATION INTO THE UNITED STATES
BY COUNTRY OF ORIGIN, 1871-1920

(Hundreds of thousands of persons per decade)

Years	Immi-grants	Britain	Germany	Central Europe	Russia	Italy & Southern Europe
1871-80	2,812	985	718	73	39	76
1881-90	5,247	1,462	1,453	354	213	332
1891-1900	3,688	660	505	593	504	704
1901-10	8,795	865	341	2,145	1,597	2,311
1911-20	5,736	487	144	902	922	1,460

Source: U. S. Bureau of the Census: *Historical Statistics of the United States, 1789-1945.* (Series B 304-330) Washington, D.C.: U. S. Department of Commerce, 1949.

However, the changed character and the increased volume of the new immigration made the new wage problems difficult to handle. The new immigrants were not only non-English speaking but had cultural traditions much different from those of the dominant peoples of the United States. There had been trouble enough, even in liberty-loving Boston, in assimilating the English-speaking Irish of earlier days. Now came waves of Italians, Bohemians, Russians, Slovaks and many others with unfamiliar languages and cultures. What wage doctrine should be adopted to deal with these "foreigners"?

Wage problems were also complicated by a significant change in the places within the United States to which the masses of new immigrants went. Before 1890 unoccupied farm lands were available in the West where immigrants and others could become farm operators and land owners. After the "passing of the frontier," this opportunity was largely denied to the American labor force. In particular, the rising values of land, as well as the greatly increased capital requirements of industry, were making individual proprietorship impossible for most of the new immigrants. They were largely forced into urban employment as wage earners. The population of New York City multiplied tenfold, from 300,000 in 1840 to more than 3 million by 1900. Chicago, in the same period, had an increase of from 4,000 to 1,700,000. Such cities became the best available places of employment for most of the new immigrants but became, at the same time, the festering sores of American society.

In their homelands, most of these new immigrants had been farm workers. In America, they were added to an increasingly abundant source of wage earners—common laborers—in the cities. One pressing problem, as in Soviet Russia today, was that of housing. The growth of slums raised the indignation of the American social workers. The immigrants had to live in slums because they could not afford better housing out of their incomes as wage earners. Well-intentioned social workers began to wonder what wage doctrine, and thus what wage theory, should be evolved to deal with the insistent problem of the wages of these masses of immigrants who, though obtaining higher incomes than they could have earned in their native lands, were still receiving considerably less than the wages of "native" workers.

THE SOCIAL SERVICE MOVEMENT—SOME DOCTRINES

The mass immigration of 1870 to 1914 forced some rethinking of what position (doctrine) should be adopted toward these immigrants. The chief concern here is with the social workers' position.

By way of contrast, however, three other attitudes toward immigration should be noted briefly.

The dominant attitude until well into the twentieth century was that immigration should be encouraged in order to speed American economic development. This was, of course, the attitude of the American industrial employers. In the United States, labor was scarce in relation to natural resources and the demand for labor expanded as technology advanced. Hence, from this viewpoint, the more immigrant laborers, the better.

A second, slightly different, attitude was that immigration should be encouraged in the interest of the peoples of foreign countries. The symbol of this attitude was the Statue of Liberty in New York harbor, welcoming Europe's "teeming millions" to a land of freedom and opportunity. In economic terms, this was a very orthodox position for anyone who considered himself a citizen of the world. Immigration, it was thought, would tend to raise the levels of living of workers throughout the world. Beyond economics, this world-minded group of humanitarians wanted America to become a haven for the politically and socially oppressed in every country and thus to demonstrate to the world the superiority of American ideals. This second viewpoint was actually close to that of the American employers of the time—though not to the point of supporting positive employer recruitment of labor from abroad. For a different reason than that of the employers, the internationally minded humanitarians welcomed the free entry of immigrants.

A third attitude toward mass immigration was directly contrary to the two we have mentioned. This was the position of established American wage earners. To them, the flood of immigrant labor was a competitive menace in the labor market. Here, too, the economic logic was entirely orthodox, although the objective differed from that of traditional economists. From the viewpoint of American workers, immigration increased the quantity of available labor and thus decreased the marginal product of any one unit of labor.

The social workers' viewpoint differed from all of the viewpoints just outlined. Generally, the social workers accepted the incursion of immigrant families as a fact, neither to be promoted nor resisted. They were concerned with what could be done to improve the level of living of the poorest of the people in any given community.

The inspiration, and hence the doctrine, of the social workers was a religious one—the feeling of responsibility of the more fortunate of God's creatures for the less fortunate of them. There were parallel and reinforcing developments of this social gospel of the British and

American churches. In the United States, the earlier social gospel, roughly from 1840 to 1870, had been devoted to the liberating of the Negro slaves. After the supposed victory of Negro emancipation, the religious devotion to the plight of the common man was directed to immigrant European families in the United States.

For Roman Catholic and Jewish organizations, the turn of the century was a period of great expansion. The mass of the new immigrants were mostly from one or the other of these two religious faiths, and their churches and synagogues provided them with a tie to their homelands and a sense of security in an unfamiliar country. It is not surprising then that the Roman Catholic churches and the Jewish synagogues in America became focal points for expressing the economic interests of their constituents, the increasing masses of relatively poor immigrant families. It was partly the experience of the Catholic churches with their immigrant members, reflected in the influence of the American Cardinal, Cardinal Gibbons, that led Pope Leo XIII to issue in 1891 the famous encyclical, *Rerum Novarum.*

For the Protestant churches the development of concern for the lot of immigrant families represented a real change in attitude. Members of the important Protestant churches were largely of the middle class. They represented the employers of the immigrant workers and generally they lived in different sections of their respective cities than did the immigrants. Considerable turmoil occurred within these churches. The doctrines of such ministers as Washington Gladden (whose *Applied Christianity* was widely read), Lyman Abbot, and Josiah Strong often conflicted with the supposed interest of the men from whom the churches were getting their chief financial support. Nevertheless, the urge to do something about the conditions of the poor continued to gain strength. Christianity, it was felt, could no longer be purely a matter of religious doctrine—it had to be applied as a social doctrine as well.

At first the new Christian conscience took the form of sporadic charitable gifts. Then the effort took on "institutional" features—that is, the systematic organization of philanthropic and educational work. The Salvation Army and the Young Men's Christian Association, in ministering to the poorer classes, not only preached religion but also maintained cheap lodgings, acted as employment agencies, and rescued distressed individuals and families. Then came the social settlements, which might be called the purest flowering of the social service movement. Jane Addams, with her Hull House in the Chicago slums, was the most famous and controversial of the social settlement leaders. Others like Julia Lathrop, Lilian Wald, Florence Kelley, and Robert A. Woods did excellent and influential work among the poorest families.

There was much talk around the turn of the century about America, the "melting pot." The usual implication was that the diverse nationalities, races, and creeds were being assimilated into the American culture. Actually, there was a double kind of assimilation. As the immigrants were assisted to understand American ways of life, the social workers began to appreciate more fully the economic problems of the poorer wage earners.

The social workers began to sense the limitations of voluntary social work, even where this charitable activity was well organized. True, something could be accomplished by helping immigrant wives to plan family budgets, but such measures were insignificant where the family earnings were too small to support a "decent" level of living. More general social action seemed to be needed. The direct experience of the social workers with the problems of the poor gradually led them to press for broad social reforms. Unlike the communists or socialists, the social workers had no idea of remaking society. They just wanted to do something about the economic and other problems of the disadvantaged immigrant families in America.

In pressing for social and economic reforms, the social workers were aided by a growing group of critics of American society. Newspapers, magazines, and book writers in large numbers believed that something was wrong with American political, social, and economic affairs. President Theodore Roosevelt dubbed these critics "muckrakers," for they were raking up the muck of American life—the muck including, mainly, the inferior economic condition of the new immigrant wage earners and the subverting of local, state, and national governments by industrial leaders seeking to exploit these gullible people and the cheap labor they represented. Prominent in this muckraking movement are the names of Jacob Riis, Ida Tarbell, and Upton Sinclair.

In pressing for general social reforms, the social workers joined forces with others who criticized the notion that the private market for labor would automatically provide the right wages for every individual. Free-lance writers and even college professors joined in the protest against the conditions of the ill-paid wage earners. Organizations such as the National Consumer's League, the New York Child Labor Committee, the National Conference of Social Work, and the American Association for Labor Legislation sprang into being. In their different ways these organizations pressed for measures to improve the situation of the lowest-paid wage earners.

The social workers, with their intimate knowledge of the conditions of the lowest-paid wage earners, made particularly telling contributions to the increasing pressure for government action.

Eventually the social workers and their reformist allies came to advocate such measures as a liberalized plan of poor relief, workmen's compensation, limitation of child labor, limitation on the hours of work, and Government determination of minimum wages. Each of these suggested measures implied a theory of wages that contrasted sharply to the accepted theory of the nineteenth-century economists. This theory had, in general, accepted the nature and condition of the labor supply as a fact. Thus the earnings of any man or woman were governed by his or her marginal productivity. If the State should seek to alter any of the conditions of work by measures such as those listed above, the alterations would only undermine the real interests of the working classes.

IMPACT ON WAGE THEORY

The social workers did not think of themselves as economic theorists. They did not write comprehensive academic books on wage theory. Indeed the social workers, faced with problems of relative poverty—especially the poverty of the immigrants—seemed to take an antitheoretical position. Hence there arose the popular misconception that anyone interested in raising the incomes of the poor had to be opposed to all theory, as if theory were necessarily reactionary. Any teacher of economics will find this attitude, even today, among the reformist members of his class.

Actually any program of action (doctrine) implies a theory whether or not that theory is explicitly stated. The various social reforms advocated by the social workers implied a different set of economic theories regarding labor than those that dominated academic circles around the turn of the century. That did not mean that the former theory was wrong, but rather that the former theory was relevant to a different set of perceived facts and was constructed in relation to a different set of social objectives than those of the social workers.

Although the social workers failed to enunciate any new theories of wages, their thinking and the thinking of persons in touch with them sparked explosions through the crust of previous wage theory. Present-day labor economists have accepted some of the theoretical implications of the social workers' approach and are still struggling to classify and formulate appropriate theories of wages to explain and predict what will happen in diverse, particular situations. At least four of these new ways of thinking about wage theories can be discerned.

Individual Wages versus the Wage Share

As we have seen in Chapter II, the marginal productivity theory was constructed primarily to explain the share of wages, as a whole, in any given real national product. The social workers, and their reformist allies, raised quite a different question—namely, what could be done to raise the wages of the lowest-paid workers in the labor force. Strict marginal productivity theorists—of 1900 and a few even today—have sometimes applied marginal productivity theory as if it stated the conditions that govern, not only the broad, long-run determination of "labor's Share," but also the conditions affecting any worker at any point in time. This application of the marginal productivity theory involves what logicians call the "fallacy of composition."

In modern labor markets, at least in the short run, it simply is not true that the tendencies that may be operative generally in the whole economy must also determine the wages of a particular worker in a particular factory. In their efforts to improve the earnings of the poorest industrial laborers, the social workers would not be defeated by any such nonsense. Their observations and their faith convinced them that the wages of the lowest-paid workers could be raised without curtailing employment. Later economists have, indeed, specified the conditions under which this may be done. All this is part of modern wage theory, thanks to the stimulating perceptions and doctrines of the social workers.

Units of Labor

For purposes of simplicity, Ricardo (1817) started with the assumption that each person equalled one unit of labor. Qualifications were introduced by Mill and Marshall, but the old simplifying assumption was retained in most of the wage-share theorizing. One could count the work of a common laborer as one labor unit and that of a machinist as perhaps two labor units, but comparatively little attention was given, in the United States before 1900, to the vital question of how many labor units a given employed worker could provide. This matter of labor units per worker may make the whole difference between a poverty-stricken group of workers and a well-paid group, even under the most rigid of marginal productivity principles. The social workers perceived that the number of units of labor provided by a given worker (and thus the wage an employer could afford to pay him) would be increased by well-administered charitable relief, by social services (such as government financed education, recreational facilities, etc.), by restrictions on such child labor as interfered with the children's development, by workmen's compensation, and by restriction of working hours. Such measures can make possible a higher quality of labor from each worker and, even under the strictest application of marginal utility principles, would ultimately provide greater real earnings for the poorest workers.

Atomistic Competition

The currently accepted theory which faced the social workers assumed pure competition—not only as between the workers, but also as between the employers of labor. In observing the plight of immigrant workers, however, the social workers were among the first to perceive the reality of what came to be called monopsony (the market power of a single buyer, or at most a few buyers, of labor). The immigrant workers, being generally unorganized, competed fiercely with each other; but their employers, as buyers of labor, often did not need to compete with each other. Moreover, in some cases (as in meat packing), these same employers also exercised semi-monopoly (oligopolistic) market power as sellers of their products.

More recently, economists have constructed theories of wages that take account of the results that are likely when employers are monopsonists and when the sellers of products enjoy, in varying degrees, a monopoly position. The social workers themselves did not provide any such formal logic; but the facts they faced, and the ambitions they held for the poor, stimulated the more technical of the economists to work out the vital differences that exist as between pure atomistic competition and the various deviations from it. Eventually it became possible to show just how the wages of the lowest-paid workers could in fact be raised above the levels that had prevailed when workers competed but employers enjoyed non-competitive or partially noncompetitive positions in labor markets or in product markets or both.

Real National Product

The most orthodox of the nineteeth-century economists agreed that the poorest wage earners could be provided with increased earnings if their net revenue product were increased. To many employers of the period prior to World War I this meant, simply, that any worker who needed more earnings should work harder. The social workers sensed that there was something wrong with this prescription. Most of these employees were already working as hard as they could. The wage earnings of the immigrant workers could be increased if management improved its methods of selecting, training, and using its hired labor. From this viewpoint, the reforms advocated by the social workers were expected to make increased labor productivity more profitable to employers and thus make higher wages possible. Herein lie the seeds of the later "scientific management" movement (see Chapter VI).

Historical Viewpoint

The marginal productivity economists viewed wages as those which would exist under equilibrium market conditions in a static economic state. It seems ironic that the nineteenth-century economists took this approach. The fact is they had been writing in a period of the most dynamic economic changes that had been experienced up to that time.

The social workers saw the facts of workers' earnings to be largely the result of historical forces. They included among the historical forces the clash between the factors that impelled mass immigration and the historically derived standards of the native population. To the social workers, the wages of the poorest workers were not to be explained by the existing marginal productivity formula but by the historical facts in any given situation. Thus the social workers paved the way for the approach of the institutional economists (see Chapter V). The institutionalists emphasized the need for an understanding of the origins of existing beliefs (e.g. Thorstein Veblen), as well as the searching for facts which characterized the work of the social service workers in the realm of wages for the poorer workers.

SUMMARY

Mass immigration to the United States, 1870-1914, provided a new set of facts for American wage theorists. The social workers' programs for meeting the relative poverty of the immigrant industrial laborers gave fresh directions to the development of wage theories. The impact of the social-work viewpoint still exerts a powerful influence on American wage doctrines and thus continues to be a factor in setting the problems for more modern theories of wages and employment.

The developments here described provide an illustration of the relationship between facts, doctrines, and theories. The social workers, nontheorists themselves, developed doctrines to cope with the economic results of immigration. Their programs stimulated later economists to develop some of the important, modern theories of the labor market.

CHAPTER IV

Labor Unions, 1890-1920

The most influential trade union leaders, practical men, were protesting against any orthodox theory of wages. Actually some union policies were quite consistent with orthodox theory even though union leaders were not aware they were practicing what professors were teaching. In other respects, however, trade union leaders viewed wage problems from a different angle than the academic theorists of the time. Thus union practices and doctrines raised new problems and stimulated the development of new wage theories.

A brief review of a segment of American labor history may help us to understand the influence of the trade union in the formulation of wage doctrines that developed during the three decades, 1890-1920.

TRADE UNIONS IN THE UNITED STATES

The first group of organized workers in the United States appeared even before the American Revolution. These early unions consisted of small local groups of wage earners who sought, by collective action, to preserve the customary levels of living of each craft—this in the face of the competitive market pressures by merchant capitalists. In this respect the goals of the first labor unions were similar to those of the craft guilds of the Middle Ages.

Early Developments

The years 1827 to 1860 were characterized by increasing demand for political and social reform both in Britain and the United States.

From this period sprang the movement for suffrage (male) without property qualification, for free public education, and for the emancipation of negro slaves. Because the interests of organized labor were to improve the lot of citizens who owned little or no property, organized groups of workers pushed toward a more truly democratic society than had been possible at the time of the American Revolution. Furthermore, labor wanted these privileges for all citizens whether or not they were wage earners.

After the Civil War, the Knights of Labor became the focus of labor organization in the United States. Organized originally as a secret society in 1869, the Knights grew slowly. Its leaders favored "education" and producers' cooperation in a vague attempt both to protect the wage earners and to replace the capitalist system. An upsurge in membership began after 1878 when the Knights threw off the veil of secrecy and became involved in an ever-widening series of strikes over wage issues. By 1886 the Knights claimed some 700,000 members. However, after a second strike against Jay Gould's Wabash railroad line, a strike as unsuccessful as an earlier one had been successful, the membership of the Knights declined rapidly. The membership shrank to about 200,000 by 1888. The Knights had little influence thereafter. This spectacular collapse was the result, in part, of a conflict of personalities and an inefficient organization; but the principal reason for the collapse was confusion about the aims of the Knights as a labor organization.

The medieval strand in the aims of the Knights of Labor is suggested by the word *Knights*. It reflected what was in fact a respectable organization to maintain accustomed levels of living for accepted and separate groups in the society. It was to achieve these ends that the Knights organized. Originally the organization was built along fraternal lines with much secrecy and ceremony. In this initial period the secrecy and ceremony were the cause of some trouble with the Roman Catholic Church. The Knights also sought to control the labor market on behalf of particular labor groups. This goal compelled the Knights to consider possible restrictions in union membership and, of even greater significance, the practicability of using the strike as a weapon against employers.

The very different aim of Karl Marx, that of overthrowing the "capitalist" system, had a distinct influence on some factions within the Knights of Labor. The leaders of the Knights were generally opposed to Marxian doctrines. They supported instead a wide variety of moderate social reform measures. Nevertheless, the Knights were blamed for the Haymarket Square Riots of 1886 and were charged with trying to foment a revolution. The Knights were vulnerable to such a charge because they did agitate against the "wage system." The confused leaders of the Knights of Labor could never quite decide whether they were leading a revolutionary cause, a collective bargaining front against existing (and accepted) employers, or a pressure group for general social reforms (such as the stimulation of producers' cooperatives).

The American Federation of Labor

Samuel Gompers was an immigrant cigar-maker in New York City. As a young man, he was an ardent believer in the revolutionary-socialist doctrines of Karl Marx. However, in the 1870's Gompers became the leader of the anti-socialist craft-union faction of the Knights of Labor. The craft unions within the Knights became increasingly restive under a centralized leadership which tried ineffectually to guide an amorphous mixture of businessmen, farmers, intellectuals, skilled workers, and unskilled laborers. In the 1880's, Gompers and his craft-union associates led a group in opposition to the Knights. This opposition group of labor unions, of which Gompers became president, was called the American Federation of Labor. With the exception of one year, Gompers held that office from the beginning of the AFL in 1886 until his death in 1924.

The American Federation of Labor resolved to protect and advance the economic welfare of those limited groups of workers who could and would stay united in the face of adversity. This policy meant union power needed to be centered in individual, national craft unions, such as those in the building trades, along with a few national industrial unions, such as the Mineworkers. The great masses of unskilled workers and miscellaneous groups of intellectual reformers were largely ignored, or opposed, by the Gompers' leadership. The American Federation of Labor itself was a loose alliance of those particular unions which could best maintain themselves as close-knit organizations of wage earners to support specific wage demands. Gone was the objective of overthrowing the capitalist system.

Gompers and his associates sought to salvage what they could of the labor movement following the debacles of the 1880's. The task was not an easy one. The collapse of the Knights of Labor in 1887 cut total union membership from nearly 1,000,000 to less than 500,000. Falling prices, effective employer opposition, and popular antipathy to "radicalism" added to the woes of organizers of labor unions of all kinds. However, the AFL unions did grow, even though economic conditions were adverse to them, so that by 1896 they had doubled their initial membership of 138,000. During these years Samuel Gompers did a heroic job of holding together and promoting a "respectable" labor organization in the United States.

After 1896 the economic climate for union organization improved and the membership of the AFL unions mounted more rapidly than before. By 1904 the AFL could claim 1,676,000 members. There were also some 400,000 unionists outside the Federation, mainly those in the Railroad Brotherhoods, who held principles similar to those of the AFL; if anything, they were even more conservative and exclusive than the unions allied to the Federation. However, despite the gains of the AFL in this period, there were indications of a hard fight ahead. The defeat of the steel union at Homestead in 1892 had shown that employers could and would present determined resistance, even to the relatively moderate unionism of the AFL. This opposition increased in the years that followed and, coupled with the help employers received from the courts, prevented the unions from using their most efficient methods of coercion. Employer opposition existed not only because it was thought that higher wages would reduce profits, but also because employers, as a class, firmly believed in an extreme form of the nineteenth-century, laissez-faire doctrine. They genuinely believed that unions were depriving workers of freedom of contract, their greatest birthright. A majority of the State and Federal courts held similar views. Thus, in *Adair* v. *U.S.* (1908), the Supreme Court invalidated a section of the Erdman Act which sought to give workers protection from dismissal because of union membership. Mr. Justice Harlan said, "In our opinion that section is an invasion of personal liberty as well as of the right of property, guaranteed by (the fifth) Amendment."

There were also attacks on the AFL from the left. The socialists, both inside and outside the Federation, wanted the AFL to take a more active interest in the political process and thus become more like the European trade unions. At the extreme left, meanwhile, some of those elements of the labor movement that desired more positive, militant action, joined together in 1905 to form the Industrial Workers of the World. This organization, by reason of its irresponsibility, provided employers with a stick with which to belabor all unions, even though it was a rival of the AFL.

The AFL, however, continued to pursue its course of antigovernment "voluntarism," steering a narrow course between the perils of revolutionary unionism and company opposition. But membership in AFL unions did not increase to any appreciable extent during the decade before the First World War, reaching only 1,946,000 in 1915.

The War brought a great upsurge of membership as rising prices made workers more anxious to protect themselves. At the same time, the Wilson administration maintained a favorable attitude toward labor organization. For example, in 1914 Congress passed the Clayton Act which Gompers called the Magna Carta of labor. Also, during World War I, labor leaders were appointed to a variety of administrative boards thus investing the labor movement with a symbol of official recognition and approval.

By 1920, the boom year following World War I, total union membership had risen to more than 5,000,000. Four-fifths of this membership was in unions affiliated with the AFL. However, in spite of this increase, employers were not yet disposed to accept unionism, and their continued opposition to the pro-union policies of the Wilson administration suggested that the labor movement would continue to have difficulties.

NEW DOCTRINES AND OLD THEORY

In the twentieth century, American labor organizations demonstrated their ability to survive and grow under the capitalist system of wage employment, in spite of the prevailing economic and social philosophy of the period. The wage doctrines of the major labor unions of 1890-1920 were quite different from those of the revolutionary minority and of the reformers. These dominant union doctrines also stood in sharp contrast to those of most academic economists of the time. Thus the American labor movement of the period forced academic theorists to reconsider the reasoning they had formerly used to explain wages. These changes in wage theory will be evident to anyone who compares a college textbook in economics of 1900 with a similar textbook of recent years.

On the surface, Gompers and his AFL associates seemed to be sharply opposed to the prevailing academic wage theory. Academic theory attempted to explain how labor, like any other factor of production, would automatically receive—in wages—the value of labor's marginal product. If that proposition were universally true, there would be no need for collective action by labor unions. Obviously the union leaders opposed this doctrine. Gompers, in his now famous testimony before a congressional committee, voiced the AFL union philosophy of pressing continually for "more, and more, here and now."[1] To the extent the previously accepted wage theory

[1] Cf Louis Reed, *The Labor Philosophy of Samuel Gompers* (New York: Columbia University Press, 1930), p. 12.

predicted that labor would automatically receive its "just" share of the product, to that extent Gompers was violently opposed to it. Hence the unfortunate idea arose that a friend of labor must be opposed to any wage theory and, by extension, to any theory at all.

Some of the trade union doctrines did, indeed, challenge the logic of the accepted marginal productivity theory as we shall see. Ironically, however, those union policies which aimed at restricting the supply of labor were perfectly consistent with the orthodox wage theory. Union doctrines stood in stark contrast to the doctrines of most academic economists of the time, but the logic of a restricted labor supply was actually the same logic as that of the marginal productivity of wages.

Restriction of Immigration

The AFL leaders, unlike the leaders of the defunct Knights of Labor and unlike the internationally minded reformers of the time, were ardent advocates of restriction of immigration to the United States. During the period of mass immigration, 1900-1914, union leaders pressed for the enactment of restrictionist immigration laws. Even when immigration was largely shut off by the events of World War I and the restrictionist laws of 1921 and 1924, some union leaders continued to argue for still more drastic restrictions.

The immigration issue was one of doctrine, not theory. Orthodox wage theory had already forecast that the larger the labor supply (with any given capital investment and state of the arts), the smaller would be the marginal product of the individual laborer, and hence, the smaller would be his wage. The doctrine of AFL leaders was that the wage of their members should and could be raised by collective action. The policy of restricting the numbers of the competing immigrant laborers was strictly in line with the accepted theory of the time. The practical union leaders were, in effect, using the marginal productivity logic for their own purposes. They were seeking to limit the over-all quantity of labor to increase labor's marginal product and thus to increase the wage earners' share in the national product.

Restriction of Domestic Labor Supplies

In the period 1890-1920, the AFL trade union leaders also attempted, by collective bargaining and by proposed laws, to restrict the supply of labor in the various particular crafts and industries in which union members were seeking employment. This domestic restrictionist aim was, like restriction of immigration, considered to be antitheoretical. Again the problem was one of doctrine, not logic. Academic economists had generally agreed on the doctrine that all resources, including labor, should be used to produce the maximum national output and thus, indirectly, to increase the real wages of labor as a whole. The trade union leaders subscribed to a different doctrine. They were not much concerned with over-all economic development which, in any case, was proceeding rapidly. Nor were the dominant union leaders particularly concerned with the material welfare of *all* workers. The dominant union leaders sought, primarily, to improve the economic welfare of their own union members. This membership consisted largely of limited groups of relatively skilled workers.

To limit the competing labor supplies in particular areas of employment, the unions used a variety of methods. In some situations they induced local authorities to require tests of ability for entry into certain trades. In other situations the local or international unions required high initiation fees or high dues; this, too, served to restrict the available supply of labor. Still other unions refused to admit nonwhites to membership. These various restrictions on the supply of labor were bolstered by the closed-shop and union-shop provisions of many union-management agreements.

Domestic restrictions on the supplies of particular types of labor that the unions advocated and used were bitterly opposed by most of the academic wage theorists of the time; in turn, union leaders seemed bitterly opposed to the doctrinal views of the academic theorists. Actually, however, these restrictions on the supplies of labor were based on the conventional wage theory. The marginal productivity theory was the basis for predicting that the smaller the quantity of labor in any trade and locality, the higher would be the wages per unit of labor. The orthodox theory assumed, however, that all available labor would be fully employed. The craft unions of the time were not really interested in full employment of all labor but, rather, in the highest possible wages for the restricted numbers of workers they represented. In advocating restrictions of the labor supply, AFL union leaders were unwittingly applying the most orthodox wage theory for their own purposes.

NEW DOCTRINES AND NEW THEORIES

So far we have been considering union policies which were actually based on the orthodox wage theory of the academic economists, in spite of the antitheoretical position of the union leaders.

We now turn to several of the effects of those labor-union doctrines which opened the way to more modern amendments and extensions of the theory of wages.

Marginal Product in Competitive Situations

The nineteenth-century theory of wages assumed nearly perfect competition between producers of a product, between employers of labor, and between workers seeking employment. The garment trades, hand cigar-making, and a few other fields of employment in which the AFL unions sought to organize, were highly competitive both in their product and in their labor markets. In such fields of employment, the accepted wage theory of 1900 would have forecast a nearly perfect equality of the value of the marginal product of labor and the equivalent wages of the employed worker.

It was precisely in these most competitive industries that labor-union leaders asserted most strongly that labor was being exploited. It seemed that in those very situations where the neoclassical assumptions were most accurate, the wage results were most unsatisfactory. One part of the difficulty was the large increase in the number of immigrant workers who brought with them relatively low standards of living. But much more was involved in this particular wage problem. Labor unions sensed that wages would be beaten down whenever a large number of competitors in the product market and a large number of workers in the labor market had unrestricted opportunities to "bargain" individually. In such highly competitive product and labor-market situations, wages would settle at the lowest level acceptable to workers.

Sidney and Beatrice Webb, in their famous chapter on "The Higgling of the Market,"[2] formulated a theory of wages that was an alternative both to the Marxian theory of labor exploitation and to the laissez-faire notion of the supposed exact and just determination of wages under competitive conditions. The Webbs advanced the idea that at each successive stage of production, pressure was put on those engaged in the next stage of the process. Thus factory employers squeezed the wages of defenseless workers because employers were, in turn, being squeezed by wholesalers, wholesalers by retailers, and retailers by consumers. The consumers were thought to have the most choice and the wage earners the least choice. The problem then was that the workers—because they were many in number and in active competition with each other—were in such a

[2] Sidney and Beatrice Webb, *Industrial Democracy* (London: Longmans, Green & Co., Ltd., 1897), Part III, Chap. II.

weak bargaining position that they were squeezed by all other groups, even under supposedly competitive conditions. Those AFL leaders who brought workers (in highly competitive industries such as apparel and cigar-making) together, to bargain collectively, strengthened the bargaining position of the workers and, thus, posed new questions for academic wage theorists. The labor leaders were, in effect, counteracting the ultimate pressure from employers for lower wages (as put forward by the Webbs). The unions challenged the orthodox thesis that intense competition in the product and labor markets would, automatically, result in the highest possible wage for each worker. They felt that bargaining power, rather than calculations of marginal product, was the force that determined wages.

Marginal Product in Noncompetitive Situations

Only a minority of the members of the AFL unions were employed in highly competitive industries. Most of the workers represented by unions in 1890-1920 were employed by a limited number of firms which were something less than competitive as buyers of labor and as sellers of products. Building construction, where the bulk of the craft-union members of the period were employed, provided an example of local labor markets and local product markets where competition was limited in scope. Railroads, steel, coal, and metalworking (although serving wide product markets) also provided examples of concerted managerial policies. "Exploitation" of labor was, in such cases, neither that depicted by Karl Marx nor that depicted by the Webbs. The workers, when lacking collective action, were not being "robbed" because of an interest deduction from the net product (Marx) nor because of consumer pressure on employers and workers (Webbs). Workers were being exploited, most union leaders believed, by the noncompetitive position of business enterprises both as buyers of labor and as sellers of products. In trade union doctrine it followed, therefore, that the wages of union members could be increased by collective bargaining pressure in noncompetitive as well as in highly competitive situations. By the strike or the threat to strike, employers could be forced to pay higher wages.

The union belief that collective action could raise the wages of union members above those that would otherwise prevail was a "practical" doctrine, based on empirical successes rather than on theoretical premises. The union leaders did not pretend to be wage theorists. They simply saw from experience that collective action would force payment of higher wages than would have been paid under the "ideal" conditions of perfect competition among workers and the less than perfect competition among employers, whether in the market for labor or the market for products.

Because the then accepted wage theory was based on assumptions of perfect competition among buyers of labor and among sellers of product, the practical methods of the unions had to be presented as if they were antitheoretical. "In theory," it was frequently said, "unions cannot benefit their members. But in practice, they have done so." Here, again, the false impression is created that theory is something that is not true.

The efforts of organized labor to improve wages, and to seek and improve other benefits, gave a new push to the revision of wage theory. The loose and formless substitute for the academic marginal productivity theory was the so-called bargaining power theory of wages. The bargaining power theory had the merit of sticking more closely to the actual power balance of a situation than did nineteenth-century abstractions. A weakness of the bargaining power theory was, and still is, the difficulty of measuring "bargaining power" in generalized and objective terms. "Bargaining power" is at least as nebulous a concept as "marginal productivity." When a union scores a victory, one may conclude—after the fact—that the union had superior bargaining power. But such a conclusion hardly provides a theory. The theory involved may be based on superior oratory, on more effective "goon squads," on government persuasion or intervention, or on one of a number of other variables in the particular situation.

In the "monopoly" sector of industry, as in the area of intense product-market competition, the workers found themselves at odds with the old theory. The individual worker had no idea what he was worth to the employer. This uncertainty obstructed the free mobility of labor, another prime prerequisite of the marginal productivity analysis. In such a situation, the worker, faced with a rise of living costs, joined his fellows in an effort to extract higher wages from his employer because collective action was the only pressure available to him. On the other hand the employer, who enjoyed some degree of monopoly in his product's market, could often pass higher wage costs on to the consumer in the form of higher prices.

Thus union leaders, because of their practical success in raising the wages of their members, provided a challenge to the former wage theory, based as it had been on the model of perfect competition in labor and product markets. From the practical and supposedly antitheoretical efforts of the unions have grown many of the latter-day theories of monopsony (single buyer), of monopoly (single seller), and of oligopoly (limited numbers of sellers).

The Marginal Product of Individual Workers

Trade unionists believed wages of individual workers could be raised above the wages that the employers would otherwise pay. This belief appeared to conflict with the marginal productivity theory because, according to that theory, employers would already be paying labor the full value of that labor.

Actually, the marginal productivity theory was devised to explain that share of the total national product that labor as a whole would receive. It was one thing to say that labor's over-all fraction of the whole product would *tend* to approximate the marginal product of labor. It was quite a different proposition to say that each individual worker would always be paid exactly what that individual's labor was worth to his employer. It was this extension of the theory to the individual case that the trade unions most strongly opposed.

Trade union experience seemed to show that concerted demands on employers could—and did—yield higher wages for individual union members. This result would have been impossible if the marginal theory correctly explained the exact determination of individual wages, always and everywhere. The trade unionists did not pretend to know what was wrong with the academic theory. They simply sensed, from practical experience, that wages were not neatly and exactly determined the way the professors tried to explain. Once again, the unionists seemed to be taking an anti-theoretical position. They would say, in one form or another, that *theory* says so and so, but in practice the facts are different.

Thus challenged, economists of a later day worked out some of the short-comings of the marginal productivity theory as applied to individual wages at an instant of time and in a specific place. Among other things, the previous theory presumed that both the employer and the worker would know the exact value of the product contributed by each worker. As far as individual workers were concerned, it was clear that such perfect knowledge did not exist. For one thing, the individual employee did not handle his employer's accounts, and could not have understood them if he had. So how could he know the value of what he produced?

The stalwart defenders of traditional theory have frequently contended that it was not necessary for the worker to know the value of his contribution, provided the employer had this knowledge.

If the employer knew how much net revenue each worker contributed, then each employer, competing with other employers in the labor markets, would be forced to pay each worker exactly what the worker added to the employer's net revenue. Thus, all workers would receive wages equivalent to the full value of their marginal contributions to the product of the employer—or so it was supposed.

In some rare instances, it might be possible for employers to know reasonably well what each worker is worth. If the product is highly standardized, if selling prices are highly stable, and if the labor costs are a large part of total cost, then an employer would know approximately how much net revenue he might gain by hiring an additional worker, or how much net revenue he would lose if a worker were separated from his operation. Such situations were hard to find then and are becoming more and more rare in American experience as capital requirements for production increase, production processes became more complex, and product markets become more uncertain.

Objectors to the extended, particularistic use of marginal productivity theory kept pointing out that employers did not, usually, experiment with the results of employing one more or one fewer worker. Instead American employers usually operated a production plant that required certain numbers of workers of each type. A loom, a blast furnace, or a construction project, once put into operation under known techniques, required a certain number of workers to carry out the operation. Once an employer had the required complement of workers, nothing was to be gained in the short run by adding an extra worker; everything might be lost if there were too few workers. Beyond this was the problem that the value of labor to most employers was determined by the manager's estimate of the uncertain future revenue from his productive operation. Every wage agreement, individual or collective, is a "speculation on futures." At the time an individual wage is set, the employer cannot know with any precision what difference in his net revenue will result from the employment of that particular worker. The employer has to guess, of course. If the manager guesses wrong on how many units of product he can sell at a certain price, the employing concern may have less revenue than was expected. If the employing concern is blessed by good fortune and sells more than planned, then the value of an individual's services will be much more than the employer expected when he set the wage rate.

Under such production and marketing conditions, the wise employer will usually set wage rates at as low a level as practicable at the time he has to decide how much to pay each worker. The result-

ing individual wages in "good times" will tend to be well short of
the ultimate contribution of the individual worker to his employer's
net revenue product, though they will tend to be higher than
worker's actual contribution in "bad times."

Marginal Products and Differing Skills

As we have seen, the American labor movement in the period
1890-1920 was dominated by organized groups of skilled, manual
workers. Given this fact, American union leaders adopted policies
to promote the interest of the skilled groups. When a union sought
to restrict the labor supply for a particular craft, it was presuming
that too many skilled workers were already available. Here, reasoning of the short-run variety—at odds with orthodox theory—was in
sharp contrast to the orthodox union reasoning about the long-run
effects of immigration on American wages.

A potent argument for the closed shop, union shop, and other
restrictive practices of unions was that skilled union members were
never sure that unskilled workers might not be substituted for them.
In an age of rapidly changing technology, many men in skilled
handicrafts were being replaced by girls performing such simple
tasks as those of machine operators. Fear of similar developments in
their own trades made skilled union members seek to perpetuate
their jobs by attaching strict conditions on union membership and
on entry into the trade.

Often there was considerable substance to the foregoing arguments. In many cases, the union policies were not, in fact, severely
restrictive. Still the restrictionist motive of the union was quite
apparent. In extreme cases a union would simply refuse to admit
qualified applicants for union membership. Again, when a union
insisted on a period of apprenticeship that was several years longer
than the employers judged to be necessary, it was evident that the
purpose behind the policy was to limit the number of craftsmen.
When a union struck against the employment of qualified workers
who had been denied admission to the union, the restrictionist
policy became the subject of public criticism. Apart from these
extreme examples, it is evident that the craft unions under Gompers'
leadership were deliberately attempting to limit the numbers of
their labor-market competitors. Indeed this matter was a leading
issue in the battles between craft and industrial unions, which
reached a climax in the late 1930's. These controversies over union
practices, aimed to protect the economic position of skilled workers,
raised the general problem of what influences control wage differentials as between various grades of skill.

SUMMARY

By restricting immigration for long-run purposes, and by restricting particular labor supplies for short-run purposes, organized labor was attempting to increase the value of each union member to the employer. An even more important union policy was that of pressing employers for increased wages, backed up by the strike threat. This policy was based on a theory quite different than that supported by most academic economists of the time. The orthodox theory purported to explain that impersonal market forces would force the employer to pay what he could afford to pay each worker. The union theory was that the employer would pay as low a wage as he could "get away with" and that he could "get away with" a wage much below the value of any particular unit of labor by playing one worker against another. Hence the unionist believed that collective action was necessary to force the employer to pay as much as he could afford to pay.

The union perception of the facts of the labor market, coupled with the union objective of raising the wages of union members, forced subsequent generations of economists to revise and enrich the theories of wages. It became evident, on further thought, that there are many different kinds of situations in the labor and product markets and that only rarely did the specific facts of economic life conform to the assumptions that lay behind the competitive model of the nineteenth-century economists. This did not mean that the orthodox theory was logically incorrect. It meant rather that different types of theories were needed to take account of each of a variety of situations. Partly, the actual facts had changed. Partly, it was man's perception of the facts which had changed. The perceptions of wage facts were sharpened by the new doctrines of the labor unionists and by their apparent success, at least in some cases, in raising wages above those that employers would have paid—at least in the short run.

One of the new questions for wage theorists was how to explain, and thus predict for given situations, the relative wages of the various grades of skill. Nineteenth-century economists had taken for granted the differences between the wages of various grades of skill. Adam Smith had tried to explain them on a relative cost-to-labor basis. Smith reasoned that the whole of the advantages and disadvantages of each employment would tend to be equalized (at least in each local community) because labor would move from one employment to the other until equalization was achieved. Some refinements in Smith's theory of wage difference were worked out even before 1890 by Mill, by Cairnes, and by Marshall. However, it was the impact of the craft unions that eventually sparked the revival of this largely dormant part of wage theory. The craft unions believed that they could increase the differential between the wages of skilled and unskilled workers by such policies as we have outlined. The theoretical problem became, not whether the craft unions were right or wrong in the actual series of events, but the broader one of how skill differences in wages are actually influenced (in varying situations) and, therefore, how the result of any given pressure on them may be predicted. Thus was posed the skill-differential aspect of one of the most important current problems of wage theory, the problem of wage structure. Broadly speaking, the wage-structure problem involves the relationship of the reward for any one kind of human effort to the rewards for efforts of all other kinds. Nineteenth-century theory provided no more than a feeble beginning to the solutions for the problems of these wage relationships.

CHAPTER **V**

The Institutionalists

The protests of social workers and labor leaders against orthodox wage theory were nonacademic in nature. These groups of practical people would not accept the implications of orthodox theory, but they offered no substitute wage theory of their own. The institutionalists, on the other hand, were university-trained scholars who were seeking new explanations of wages and of other social arrangements. The theories of the institutionalists were stimulated by the clash of the doctrines of practical men against the accepted wage theory, but now the clash moved within academic halls.

The orthodox theory was based on the premise that every person would and should act in a calculated manner to increase his own material welfare—that is, to increase his pleasure and avoid pain (the so-called "utilitarian" doctrine). On this premise the natural or normal level of wages could be calculated and predicted. The institutionalists, by contrast, contended that orthodox economic theory was woefully inadequate to explain the actions of men. Wages, for example, were not to be explained by any universal law of balance between the forces of supply and demand but by the prevailing institutions under which wages were determined.

The word *institution* was used in a very broad meaning to refer to any pattern of expected or required human behavior. A corporation was obviously an institution, but so was a law, a regulation, a custom, a conventional way of doing things, a belief or any circumstance that moved the actions of mankind. Every institution was believed to have a history, having grown out of the facts and doctrines of some previous time. Yet institutions were subject to change. Conduct that was tolerated or approved at one time and place might be condemned or punished in a different cultural environment. Thus the wages of labor were determined by the prevailing institutions that controlled, in turn, the value to be placed on a unit of labor.

American scholars took the lead during the early twentieth century in developing the institutional approach to economic problems. They borrowed much from the German historical school of economists, sociologists, and philosophers. Throughout the nineteenth century, German scholars had criticized the easy and overgeneralized theories of the British economists and philosophers. After the unification of Germany, following the War of 1870, the energy and the prestige of the German universities increased enormously. Thus the ambitious American scholars who formerly went to Oxford or Cambridge to complete their education now went increasingly to Berlin, Heidelberg, Munich, or one of the other German universities. In Germany, the American students were taught to distrust the British theories and instead to investigate with minute care the historical circumstances that lay behind any social problem. In this way, the ground was prepared for the flowering of institutional economics in the United States.

As might be expected, the institutional approach meant different things to different people. No single man could investigate everything with minute care. Hence the impact of institutionalism is not to be understood completely by a mere definition. It seems best for our purpose to examine the thought of some representative American institutional economists. Thorstein Veblen, Wesley Mitchell, and John R. Commons have been selected for this purpose.

VARIED PROTESTS AGAINST ORTHODOX ECONOMIC THEORY

Veblen, the Critic

Thorstein Veblen (1857-1929) was one of the outstanding American leaders of the protest against the orthodox economic reasoning of his time. He was a prime stimulator of what came to be known as institutional economics. He himself did not provide any specific theory of wages, but he did start a great ferment among the younger economists which, in due course, led to new approaches to the theory of wages.

To understand the influence of Veblen, we need to recall some of the changes in American economic life at the turn of the century. At that time, the United States was being transformed from a nation of farmers to a nation of industrialists. Not only had America copied the best of the British technical methods, but also was herself beginning to pioneer in the advancement of industrial techniques. The working population was expanding, not only because of net increases in the existing population, but also because of a flood of immigrants from other countries. As a result, total national product was increasing rapidly from year to year.

Disturbing social problems went along with this rise toward a position of relative economic superiority. On the one hand, there were great masses of wage earners, especially immigrants, who earned much less than "native" American workers had come to expect. On the other hand, great personal fortunes were being reaped by the successful organizers of the upsurging industrial society, for example, such men as Andrew Carnegie, Jay Gould, John D. Rockefeller, and J. P. Morgan. Such great personal fortunes were bitterly resented by most of the hard-working farmers, small business operators, and mechanics who had dominated American economic life for the previous two centuries. The contrast between the great wealth of the rich and the relative misery of the poor became the great economic issue in the United States during Veblen's lifetime.

Many different solutions (doctrines) were being proposed. The farmers wanted to have the government curtail the economic power of the railroads. The small businessmen, allied with the small farmers, were pressing for action to break up the "trusts" (industrial and financial combinations). The social workers were earnestly trying to find some way of improving the lot of the poor. The socialists were proposing a shift from private to government management of production. The extremist followers of Karl Marx believed that the socialistic goal could only be achieved by a sudden revolution. Orthodox, academic economists proposed that all combinations of workers or employers be dissolved. If this could be accomplished, both wages and profits would be determined by a "natural law." Many of the orthodox economists also thought that both high profits and low wages were a necessary part of the increasing material progress of mankind.

Veblen held up to scorn both orthodox and Marxian interpretations of high profits and low wages. To Veblen there was nothing "natural" about either profits or wages. Moreover, to Veblen, there was no assurance of economic progress. Progress, if any, would depend on the development of the required social arrangements (institutions).

The basic economic problem, as Veblen saw it, arose from a clash between the interests of the profit-directed businessmen and those of the production-minded groups in the nation. Veblen's view of the facts, then, would seem to have been very similar to the views of the social workers, the trade unionists, and, indeed, the Marxists. However, when it came to doctrine—what should be done about it— Veblen differed sharply from each of these groups, as well as from those who advocated letting nature take its course.

Veblen's doctrines are somewhat difficult to unearth. In the many books he wrote, one finds few specific prescriptions, but rather a wealth of historical observation designed to expose the ignorance of nearly everyone else. Running through Veblen's books, however, was the idea that there was always a clash between the interests of productive and unproductive people. Veblen's doctrine really was that the interests of the businessmen should be suppressed and the interests of scientists, engineers, and craftsmen should be supported. Just how this was to be done Veblen never explained in any detail, but he clearly had a bitter zeal for reforming existing social arrangements.

To support his doctrine, Veblen developed a new kind of logic (theory) to explain why people acted as they did. The former economic theory was based on physical mechanics. According to orthodox theory wages, prices, and profits always tend to sink to a natural balance—like the balance of a stone, on a string, which is being pulled toward earth by the physical force of gravitation. Veblen's theory, quite different, was based on biology and history. Men acted as they did, not because they balanced pleasure against pain in a calculated way, but because of their basic instincts and the changes in their social habits (institutions). Men's instincts were both constructive and destructive. The constructive instincts led men to do things for the joy of getting things done. The destructive instincts led men to destroy their fellow men. Hence wages were not so much determined by individual calculations as by social institutions.

One of Veblen's most famous phrases was "instinct of workmanship," the title of one of his best books. By the instinct of workmanship, Veblen meant the built-in desires of people to accomplish something for the pure joy of achievement. Why does a wife cook a good dinner, a husband maintain a comfortable house, an engineer design an efficient bridge, or a worker do a good job in running a machine? Material reward is part of the reason, and Veblen never denied that. But Veblen contended that a more important reason for these constructive actions was that people find pleasure in getting good things done, regardless of the "pain."

Veblen was a critic and a cynic rather than a theorist. As a critic he opposed the notion that existing wages were appropriate wages. Changing institutions—rather than automatic, mechanical laws— determine wages. What form institutions should take, Veblen never said. Nevertheless, he was a powerful influence in the development of new theories of wages. He shook loose the presumptions of the economists. He fostered more strongly than before the idea that wages, like anything else in economic affairs, could be determined by social arrangements and by general sentiments (institutions) rather than by gain-seeking individual calculations of pleasure and pain (utilitarianism).

Veblen seldom thought in terms of physical quantities. However, he roused the academic community by making a mockery of the pretenses of the former economic reasoning. Veblen created no new school of economists, but stimulated groups of passionate followers among economists, historians, and sociologists of his time by his irony and his ability to puncture the pretenses of the self-righteous. Thus a new group was encouraged to take a fresh look at the subject of wages.

Veblen's influence endures in that modern theorists usually attack a wage problem from the standpoint of desires ("instincts") and social habits ("institutions"). Seldom do today's labor economists think of wages as being determined exclusively by "natural law." This change in the approach to wage theory was greatly stimulated by the influence of Thorstein Veblen.

Mitchell, the Statistician

Wesley Mitchell (1874-1948) was probably the most important of the institutionalist leaders during the first thirty years of the twentieth century. More than any other single person, he drove a wedge between the British and the American approaches to economic problems. It was he who led the statistical wing of the institutionalist movement.

Mitchell's work clearly illustrates the growth of a theory from the recognition of new facts and the clash of new and old doctrines. The set of facts which most concerned Mitchell were those associated with business booms and depressions. These facts, he believed, could not be explained by the orthodox notion of normal equilibrium. Mitchell's doctrine was that maximum production and maximum income could and should be attained by wiser public policy and by a better understanding of the facts by businessmen. Mitchell's theory was that economic events were to be explained and predicted as a *cumulative* process, rather than as an approximation to some imagined normal equilibrium. Instead of reasoning about some ideal state of mechanical balance in economic affairs, Mitchell proposed to dig out the facts of any given situation so as to reveal how any state of affairs grew out of the preceding series of events.

Mitchell began his study of economics under J. Laurence Laughlin, a rigid exponent of orthodox economic theory. However, Mitchell's study also began in the stimulating early days of the new University of Chicago. Laughlin was chairman of the Department of Economics at Chicago, but the faculty included as well such nonconformist scholars as Veblen (Economics), Dewey (Philosophy), and McDougall (Psychology) to all of whose views the young Mitchell was also exposed.

Laughlin encouraged Mitchell to write his doctoral thesis, "A History of the Greenbacks," the paper currency used by the Union government to help finance the cost of the Civil War. Mitchell found that there was, in this case, no such thing as a normal "equilibrium." Wages, profits, and production were all affected profoundly by government fiscal policies. Laughlin had hoped that Mitchell would buttress Laughlin's own "gold standard" doctrine. In a sense, Mitchell did this. "A History of the Greenbacks" certainly did reveal unforeseen economic problems encountered by the Union as a result of its departure from the gold standard. But much more was involved in the thesis than either Laughlin or Mitchell realized at the outset of the work. By his painstaking study of the currency inflation of the 1860's and 1870's, Mitchell gave a new direction to economic investigation of all kinds. Accepted economic theories now had to take second place to the discovery of economic facts. The new method for the discovery of economic facts, according to Mitchell and his many followers, was the method of statistics. Wesley Mitchell was one of the first scholars in America to demonstrate the use of statistical methods to interpret a mass of conflicting and diverse information. Compared with the mathematical economists of the 1960's, Mitchell was an amateur. Still he did write the *Making of Index Numbers* in 1938, a bulletin which became a sort of statistical bible for the Bureau of Labor Statistics in the United States Department of Labor.

Mitchell's early study of the greenbacks led to his later study of what he called "business cycles." Looking back the economists of the 1960's cannot honestly say that Mitchell was directly able, as he had hoped, to mitigate business cycles by means of his great collection of facts. However, these facts, collected and analyzed through the efforts of the National Bureau of Economic Research which Mitchell directed, did add much to our knowledge of incomes and production. They also stimulated the remarkable development in the measurement of national income, wage and other shares in that total income, and the flow of money.

Mitchell himself was not particularly interested in wage theory. He did little to outline a logic by which any particular wage could be explained or predicted. Even so, the influence of Mitchell on labor economists in America has been a powerful one. Mitchell, as much as anyone else, cut the economists from their former bonds of "normative" wage theory and thus encouraged those interested in the situation of any particular group of workers to investigate that specific situation rather than to rely on easy generalization. But Mitchell did more than that. His work demonstrated the usefulness of statistical methods. Fifty years ago wage theories were based on random observations fitted into some logical generalization. Because of the influence of Mitchell and his co-workers, the mid-twentieth century approach to wages has been reversed. Any theory is now suspect until it is supported by a statistical analysis of the relevant facts.

Mitchell did eventually develop a theory with respect to his favorite subject, "business cycles." It did not turn out to be a very good theory despite the gargantuan statistical work involved. Mitchell was politically minded, but his great statistical researches provided no clue to the Hoover Administration (1928-1932) on how to reverse the economic trend of the 1920's, which lay behind the great depression of the 1930's. If anything, the findings of Mitchell's Bureau of Economic Research suggested that business depression would correct itself, given enough time. It was J. M. Keynes, the British economist, rather than Mitchell, who shed a really new light on business and depressions. But it was Mitchell who led the movement for the factual investigation of wages (and other economic facts), and thus it was Mitchell who promoted the present-day analysis of wage problems in terms of statistical measurement rather than in terms of broad generalizations.

Commons, the Historian

John R. Commons (1862-1945) represents a third group of institutional economists. More than Veblen or Mitchell, Commons devoted himself directly to worker-employer relations. He mobilized his graduate students of the University of Wisconsin to write, with him, *The History of Labour in the United States,* a classic which presently appears in four volumes. Thus Commons did for the United States what Sidney and Beatrice Webb did for Britain. By painstaking historical research, Commons and the Webbs traced the development of the modern labor movement.

Unlike the Webbs in Britain, Commons never considered himself a socialist and, indeed, students of Commons, notably Selig Perlman, became outstanding critics of the Webbs and of socialism generally. Unlike Veblen, Commons never indulged in satire. He was interested in the historical and legal developments that determined the wages and working conditions of laborers at particular times and in particular circumstances.

The problem of wages, as it appeared to Commons, was not one of a "normal" wage, like that seen by the British economists of the nineteenth century. Wages, in Commons' view of the matter, were determined by the pressures of groups of people—that is by social institutions. Commons was not the first to use the word *institution* in this context, but he was the person who helped most to spell out the meaning of "institutional approach" as applied to wage problems.

The doctrines of Commons were undoubtedly radical for his time. He was, like many other influential economists from Adam Smith onwards, a social reformer. Commons believed that the plight of wage earners could be improved by changes in the institutions that determined wages. One of those institutions was, of course, the trade union. Commons believed that collective organizations of workers could and should operate as institutions to improve the economic position of workers. Real wages, he thought, were not determined by "natural law" but rather by what workers could do for themselves through collective bargaining and by what could be done for them by the government.

The doctrines of Commons and the many persons he influenced, such as John B. Andrews and Robert LaFollette, led to the establishment of the American Association for Labor Legislation. Commons, more than any other economist, realized the valuable part that government could play in the industrial relations process. This was one of the evidences of his radicalism inasmuch as government intervention had been anathema to most of the nineteenth-century economists. Commons realized that unions by themselves could not achieve the optimum conditions of work, although he was in favor of giving them freedom wherever possible. His work with Governor (later Senator) LaFollette in Wisconsin made that state the foremost exponent of labor legislation in the nation. Many of its executive and administrative practices were later copied on a nationwide basis by the New Deal of the 1930's. Commons also looked beyond the money wage and realized that good working conditions were just as important a part of the factory worker's life as the money he received.

From a new view of the facts and from a revised doctrine a new theory arises. So it was in the case of Commons and his followers. The new facts were historical in nature. The new doctrine was that the economic position of American workers should be improved by changes in the American laws. The new theory was that wages could be raised if social arrangements were changed.

The influence of Commons on theories of wages is a subtle one despite the fact that he was most interested in the conditions facing the working people. At the worst, the "institutional economics" that Commons promoted has dissolved, through the pens of other writers, into a description, without generalized meaning, of particular circumstances. At best, the Commons type of institutionalism has led to a more realistic basis for the prediction of particular wages. The notion of patterns of wage determination based on factual and historical circumstances, rather than on a "normal wage," is an idea that Commons helped to introduce into the present-day analysis of wages.

THE INFLUENCE ON WAGE THEORY

Veblen, Mitchell, and Commons provide three leading examples of American economists who challenged the accepted wage theory in the early twentieth century. All three have been called "institutionalists," yet, as we have seen, their approaches were quite different from one another. Veblen, Mitchell, and Commons were followed by thousands of students of wages, and of economic affairs generally, and these followers introduced an even greater variety into the study of industrial and labor problems.

At first sight, these institutionalists seem to have undermined orthodox wage theory, leaving only chaos in its place. Institutionalists, as well as "practical" men, have often given the impression that a theory of any kind is false. Moreover, some of the institutionalist attempts at new approaches proved unfortunate. Nevertheless, institutionalism has had a profound effect on modern wage analysis. When thoughtfully used, the institutional approach has contributed to fresh and more realistic approaches to wage problems.

Wage Reforms—The Dynamics of Change

The important economists of the nineteenth century were all reformers in their various ways, and most of them wanted to improve the lot of the workers. However, they had very restricted theories as to how improvement might be achieved. Basic to the nineteenth-century reasoning was the idea of balance or equilibrium. It was reasoned that whatever might be done to raise wages, each wage would settle in the long run to its "normal level." In the analogy used by Alfred Marshall, the situation was like that of whirling a stone on the end of a string. As soon as the whirling stopped, the force of gravity (like the long-run forces in economic life) would pull the stone to its position of rest, perpendicular to the earth.

The institutional economists used instead an analogy from biology —that is, one change was thought of as leading to another change as part of a continuing process of growth or decay. Social habits and expectations inherited from the past would control the wages paid in the present. These institutions themselves would change under the impact of evolving circumstances. Thus wages would rise or fall in response to changes in the institutions that controlled them. This approach to wage problems is illustrated in the book by Hamilton and May on *The Control of Wages* (1928). The authors presented the many changes in social policy that could be used to raise wages instead of explaining why wages could not be raised above their "normal" level. This new institutional approach grew up as an academic response to social workers and labor leaders who demanded that the wage position of the workers be improved.

This institutionalist approach to wage problems was not entirely new nor was it free from certain weaknesses. John Stuart Mill and Alfred Marshall had seen that limitations on population, improved education, improved production techniques, and increased quality of productive capital goods would make possible a rise in per capita wages. As economists, however, the nineteenth-century theorists were not as concerned as the institutionalists with the processes by which these changes would (or could) be brought about. Present-day emphasis on the economics of development is an outgrowth of the institutionalist movement. It must be admitted that the theory of economic development—and hence the theory of a nation's overall capacity to raise wages—is still controversial. More generally, the theory of the process of social change is far from being a completed theory. However, the institutionalists did stimulate the drive to reason out the sequence of events involved in social change. This is quite a different matter than that of casting overboard all attempts at logic.

Probably the most serious weakness of many of the followers of the institutionalists was that they believed all economic forces can be ignored when one is interested in change rather than equilibrium.

This attitude is a perversion of the thought of the best of the institutionalists. It is often true, for example, that a $2-an-hour wage may be raised to, say $2.05 and, over a period of time, to $2.50, to the advantage of the workers and of the economy generally. But this is not to say that such a change is always possible, nor that the wage in question might just as well be $10 an hour. Economic limits to a desired wage increase still exist, even when employers understandably contend that these limits are more restrictive than is actually the case. The institutionalists did not supplement orthodox wage theory. Rather they enriched that theory by drawing attention to many opportunities for wage reform, through institutional changes, that slavish followers of orthodox wage theory had ignored or denied.

Relationships Between Disciplines

Adam Smith was a professor of moral philosophy, a subject which embraced ethics, psychology, law, history, commerce, government, and economics as those disciplines were understood in the eighteenth century. During the nineteenth century the social sciences—like the physical and biological sciences—grew and became more specialized. Moral philosophy became political economy, a more specialized subject but one which still combined the study of politics with that of economics. By the year 1900, the orthodox economists were writing as if the study of economics could be a self-contained and self-sufficient discipline. Did one wish to understand the subject of wages, for example? Then it was thought sufficient to master the theory of marginal productivity. To be sure, economists often expounded their doctrines as to social policy, but the process by which social policy was formed and changed was largely left to the other social disciplines or shifted to another part of the textbook than that which dealt with economic theory itself.

The institutionalists saw that a problem like that of wages could not be understod merely by means of the insights of a single, specialized discipline. Suppose, for example, that a labor union is attempting to raise the wages of its members. Why was the union formed? Why do the union leaders believe that a wage demand can be won? How seriously must the employer regard the demand? What will be the reaction to the bargaining and to the result of it—by the local community, by the sellers of materials to the employer, by the buyers of the product, and by the government? What will be the effect, in the short run and in the long run, of a wage increase of varying amounts. Adequate answers to such questions, and hence predictions of the result, require contributions from the disciplines of history, sociology, law, political science, business administration, psychology, statistics, and economics. The example just cited is a very restricted one. Throughout the broad area of wage and other economic problems, it was the institutionalists who emphasized that human action is governed by a variety of influences and not merely by the gain-seeking calculations of an individual "economic man." This discovery did not abolish economic theory, as was sometimes supposed, but it did much to force economists to broaden the range of their logic. Modern wage theories need to be based on the findings and the methods of analysis of a variety of specialized disciplines. The best training in labor problems, including wage problems, is now given by universities that make use of the talents of scholars in each of the specialized social sciences. This *inter-disciplinary* approach to labor problems, somewhat like that of Adam Smith in his day, has grown out of the work of the institutionalists.

The attempted integration of economics with a variety of other disciplines involves some dangers as well as advantages. Few if any scholars are able to master the learning of all the specialized social sciences, not to say the relevant physical sciences. The so-called survey course in the colleges is always in danger of being too superficial to be useful. As for research, the interdisciplinary approach is often time-consuming and confusing. Not all labor problems, and certainly not all wage problems, require the use of all the social disciplines. Much is to be gained, therefore, through the use of a single, precise discipline in the planning and execution of a particular research investigation. Even so, the practitioners of one discipline need to learn from the others. Sociologists, psychologists, anthropologists, and historians may teach economists much about why men act as they do. The economists should be able to predict the material consequences of the resulting patterns of action.

Facts: Their Role and Measurement

Obviously, any study of economic life is concerned with the facts of human experience. What is not obvious is how facts can best be related to doctrines and theories, and how the facts themselves can best be collected and analyzed. The institutionalists gave a new emphasis to the importance of facts and stimulated the development of new methods of dealing with masses of facts.

Prior to the twentieth century, observed facts were principally used by the British economists in defense of their doctrines and as illustrations of their theories. Thus the low-wage doctrines of the mercantilists were buttressed by the meager facts of what was then called "political arithmetic." Adam Smith obtained some clues from his wide reading and personal observations of facts, but he used the observations chiefly to enliven the presentation of his anti-mercantilist doctrine that wages would rise under a policy of freedom of trade. Observed facts played a very minor role in Ricardo's *Principles* because Ricardo sought to reduce economics to an abstract science. The facts used by Ricardo were largely those of common knowledge or else they were taken from those previously presented by Adam Smith. Ricardo's numerical illustrations were used to illustrate his theories much as a present-day mathematical economist might assign arbitrary values to the symbols in his equation.

The beginning of new trends in the use of factual observation can be seen in the works of John Stuart Mill and Karl Marx. As a student of logic, Mill was keenly aware of the difference between deductive and inductive methods of reasoning. He sought to use both methods in his *Principles of Economics.* Like his predecessors, Mill often used observed facts to illustrate his deductive reasoning, but Mill also sought to derive his theoretical principles by deductive methods, or at least to modify the earlier propositions. For example, Mill saw the significance of observed differences in social habits as between different countries and periods of time. These observations prevented Mill from assuming that there was a single, fixed standard of living and thus allowed him to modify Ricardo's iron law of wages.

Marx has been called the father of the historical school of economics. He regarded subsistence wages, not as the result of external economic forces, but as the result of the cultural characteristics of the particular system of capitalism. Marx went far beyond his predecessors in attempting to work out a theoretical scheme showing the evolution of one set of economic institutions out of the clashes of fact and doctrine within the preceding stages of economic development. Thus capitalism was considered to be the inevitable result of the breakdown of the medieval economic order. Wages under capitalism, Marx predicted, would inevitably fall until the capitalist system was overthrown as the result of its inherent contradictions. To support his theory, Marx presented an enormous volume of historical facts. Subsequent events have belied many of Marx's predictions, but his use of historical facts did inspire the work of such institutionalists as Veblen and Commons.

The twentieth-century institutionalists were not the first economists to be concerned with the facts of economic life. Yet their emphasis on facts, rather than accepted theory, was a distinctive one. They took obvious delight in confuting both orthodox and Marxian principles by mobilizing the contrary facts of observed experience. Furthermore, they regarded any set of facts as part of a sequence of events rather than a deviation from a position of equilibrium. Finally, the institutionalists were perpetually dissatisfied with the existing quantity and quality of available facts.

The modern American attack on wage problems has been profoundly altered by the insistence of the institutionalists on the prime importance of facts. Half a century ago, a typical student tackled a wage problem by applying the accepted wage theory. This method of attack usually resulted in a justification of the wages being paid, because it assumed that existing wages were determined by the forces controlling the supply and demand of labor as the orthodox theorists portrayed these forces. Today a typical economist tackles a wage problem by seeking facts about the specific situation. Once the facts are established, the modern student of wages may attempt a logical set of reasons for existing wages and perhaps a prediction of the future trend of the wages he is examining. If this inductive process is completed successfully, a new or modified theory emerges to account for the level and trend of the wages in question.

This latter-day emphasis on facts led the institutionalists into the modern use of statistical techniques. In this respect, Wesley Mitchell was an outstanding leader. Once modern students of wage problems went beyond the mere use of facts as illustrations or as clues to new lines of reasoning, they were confronted by masses of facts in apparent contradiction. One worker might be paid $20 a week, for instance, while other workers earned $12, $15, $18, $22.50, $30, $50 and so forth. What was *the* wage? Again, wages changed over time. How much and why did they change? Was there any real improvement in wages over time? Furthermore, wages were different at different places and they changed over time at different rates. How much did wages differ and change? Modern wage analysts want precise, quantitive answers to such questions—not merely isolated illustrations of general principles.

In the field of wage problems, as in other fields, the modern emphasis on facts has forced students to develop and apply the methods of the statistician. These involve the careful collection of large masses of data, the techniques of sampling, the classification of data, the computation of the degree of reliability of the data, the correlation of one set of data with other sets, and the computation of trends. The modern student is not satisfied with a conclusion that a proposition is true. He wants to know how frequently it is true. Nineteenth-century wage theorists lack both the masses of facts and the statistical methods that are now available to students of wage theory. This development arose out of the institutional approach to wage and other social problems.

So great has been the twentieth-century emphasis on the collection and analysis of facts that modern students of wage problems often lose sight of any objective in their grubbing for facts. A student is frequently honored because he has compiled some facts, whether the facts have any significance or not. The wage policies of employers and labor unions are often based on some collections of alleged facts without much attention to any logic or reasoning that might give meaning to the facts. There is a widespread tendency to assemble facts *about* some wage problem without any clear notion as to what conclusion (theory), if any, would be obtained if the facts showed one thing or another. All of us are deluged with facts we cannot use. We often lack the particular facts which would make a difference in our thinking and policies. There is a danger that we shall keep on "knowing more and more about less and less."

These are the defects of an over-emphasis on facts as such. What is needed in dealing with wage problems, as well as other problems, is a carefully stated, tentative theory (hypothesis) in each case and then the mobilizing of facts to test the hypothesis. Isolated facts—indeed even perceptive works of fiction—often provide essential challenges to previously accepted theories. The development of new or modified theories requires the testing of the proposed new theory by means of the careful use of statistical techniques. The tested wage theories that emerge are certain to be more limited in scope than the sweeping generalizations of the nineteenth-century economists, but they are theories nevertheless and more useful than the theories they replace.

SUMMARY

The movement called "institutionalism" represented an intellectual protest against the sweeping generalizations of orthodox wage theory. The movement developed out of the clash between the previously accepted wage theory against the facts of economic life and the doctrines of such practical people as the social workers and the labor leaders of the early twentieth century. The institutionalists emphasized the possibilities of raising wages by changing the environment under which men acted. They insisted that wage problems could not be understood by the narrow assumptions of the calculating "economic man" but instead needed to be studied from the view of a variety of social disciplines. They emphasized the importance of facts in place of accepted generalizations and thus stimulated the use of modern statistical methods in analyzing information on wages and factors related to wages. So pervasive has been the influence of institutionalism that extremists have the impression that wage theory has been replaced by facts. Actually any effective use of facts must be made within the framework of theory. Institutionalism opened the way for new wage theories, supported by representative facts and carefully limited to the specific wage problem to which such facts applied.

CHAPTER VI

The Influence of Scientific
Management on Wage Theory

Thus far we have examined the protests made against classical wage theory by the social workers, the trade unionists, and the institutionalists. Each of these groups attacked the premises of the marginal productivity theory of wages. Each group, in its own way, saw the facts of wages differently than had the nineteenth-century economists, and each had objectives (doctrines) which differed from those of the nineteenth-century economists.

A fourth group which influenced modern wage theory consisted of the leaders of "scientific management." These were industrial engineers, usually serving as technical consultants to American employers. This group did not attack the premises of marginal productivity theory. Rather, they sought to improve the practical application of the classical wage theory by making it possible for employers to increase production and to measure more exactly the product of each worker. Nevertheless, as we shall see, scientific management had a considerable influence in modifying the theory of wages. Its followers had their own views of employed labor and their own doctrines as to what should be done about the relationship between workers and employers.

THE NEW FACTS

Like all reformers, the advocates of scientific management saw the facts of life differently than their predecessors and proceeded to develop a new doctrine which, in turn, led to changes in theory—in this case the theory of wages. Frederick Winslow Taylor and his followers saw, and were inspired by, the great advance of science as applied to American production. They saw, and wished to promote, the breaking up of the craft system of employing labor. They saw, and wished to eliminate, the bitter conflict between employers and labor unions.

Science and the Mechanical Engineer

Toward the end of the nineteenth century, the methods of science were acclaimed by almost everyone in the western world. Scientific methods had, of course, begun to change the world even before Columbus discovered America. A simple form of science had sparked the Industrial Revolution in England during the late eighteenth century. The scientific approach to problems of production continued to grow during the nineteenth century, especially in the United States, France, and Germany. By 1890, the Americans, the French, and the Germans had not only borrowed the advanced production techniques of England but had also begun to develop methods of their own, often more advanced than those being used by the British. German and American engineers were among those leading the way in applying the scientific method to problems of obtaining maximum production.

For Taylor and his adherents, the American advance in the application of the scientific method to production was an observed fact. In the United States, mechanical engineers were greatly increasing the production of many enterprises by application of the scientific method. Hence arose the great reputation of the mechanical engineer. The *fact* that engineering applications of science had been so productive led the scientific-management people to a new view of how labor should be managed and how wages should be determined.

As applied by the mechanical engineer, the scientific method required that any production problem be split up into its small, component parts. Each of these parts was then analyzed to determine the most efficient use of materials and power so as to get the greatest amount of product with the least expenditure. The engineer then combined all the small parts into an integrated whole, regardless of any previous "rule of thumb" as to how the work should be done. These procedures proved to be amazingly successful in areas of material equipment such as the design of machines, the composition of metals, the speed of cutting tools, and the layout of successive steps in the production process. The bottleneck obstructing the upsurge of production seemed to lie at the point where labor was involved. It was natural, then, that the enthusiastic mechanical engineers of the time—having seen their accomplishments in improving the use of material things—should turn their attention to similar methods for managing the use of labor.

Development of New Jobs

A second set of facts that encouraged the scientific-management movement was the rapid spread of new techniques of production that changed the nature of the demand for labor in the United States. This change was especially evident in the metal and metal-working industries around the beginning of the twentieth century. New machinery created new kinds of jobs. To an increasing extent, production was carried on by complex power-driven machinery such as mechanical conveyors, hoists, lathes, shapers, grinders, drills, punch presses, and polishers. Skilled labor was required, of course, for the making, installing, adjusting, and repairing of the new machinery. However, the operators of the new machinery now comprised the bulk of the labor force. The machine operators and assemblers of parts were semiskilled workers. They needed brief instruction as to the motions to be made to do their specialized jobs, but they did not need to be able to understand the machines or to perform any great variety of tasks.

The growing part of factory operation consisted of jobs that were new to everyone. The nature of the new machinery and processes largely dictated the specific kinds of labor that were required. No longer did a trained craftsman perform all the varied operations from raw material to finished product. Instead a succession of speicalized workers were needed to convey the materials from one machine to another, to place the materials or parts in each machine, to operate the levers of the machine, to put together the parts of the product, to inspect the results of each operation, and to pack the finished product for shipment. There were few precedents to guide the operations on these new jobs. The workers adopted such methods of work as they knew or were taught by their foremen. The foremen were usually workers who had been promoted from ordinary jobs in the shop. They were not necessarily familiar with the new processes nor expert in instructing others. Consequently many operations were performed inefficiently as Taylor and other industrial engineers duly observed.

Abundance of Unskilled Labor

This urge to manage the use of labor "scientifically" was spurred on in the United States by the fact that the American labor supply around 1900 consisted increasingly of unskilled immigrants. In earlier times, a traditional method of operation had been taught to a craftsman during his period of apprenticeship. Hence when an employer hired a carpenter or machinist, he could be sure of obtaining a skilled worker. But at the end of the nineteenth century in America, the majority of industrial workers were no longer skilled craftsmen who had learned their trade during years of apprenticeship. Instead the mass of unskilled and semiskilled workers in the growing industries in America were farm workers from Europe who had had no apprenticeship training in any industrial craft. An employer hiring such a worker could not depend on the worker to know how a particular job was to be done.

The difficulty of the employer in using the labor of immigrants was increased because often the immigrants did not read or speak English. The employing company had to have foremen who could give instructions in the worker's native tongue. This task of talking to employees in their own language became an important part of the foreman's job of supervising immigrant workers. Thus the industrial foreman had become a key man in assigning unfamiliar operations and in setting wage rates for each worker. The need for special instruction of the untrained labor force became increasingly evident.

The Rise of Unionism

The threat of labor unions also played a part in stimulating new management methods. The leaders of scientific management were, originally, on the staffs of industrial enterprises. Their own pay checks came from employers. As adherents of employers they shared the employers' fear of the growing and chaotic attempts of labor groups to contest the exclusive authority of the employer to set wage rates. To combat the union's demands for joint bargaining, the leaders of scientific management were encouraged to find a scientific basis for determining wage rates. They hoped to establish a principle for the settlement of wage questions which would make labor unions unnecessary. Thus the clash of employer and union doctrines became one of the facts with which the leaders of scientific management had to deal. Given the worker-management contest about wage rates and working conditions, they came to believe that their task was to come up with a wage formula which would defeat the challenge of the labor unions.

PIONEERS AND THEIR DOCTRINES

The origins of scientific management can best be understood by glancing briefly at the contributions of five men: Taylor, Gantt,

Barth, Halsey, and Gilbreth. These five men made their principal contribution in the period between 1900 and World War I. They were the evangelists of a new doctrine for the management and remuneration of employed labor.

Frederick Taylor

The father of scientific management in the United States was Frederick Winslow Taylor (1856-1915). Taylor was, indeed, a self-made man. After an apprenticeship, he became an ordinary laborer in 1878 at the Midvale Steel Company. After two months, the Midvale company promoted him to "gang boss," a foreman of a group of unskilled laborers. By studying at night, Taylor earned a mechanical engineering degree from Stevens Institute. One of his early successes was the invention of a new steam hammer. This he accomplished after a prolonged study of the other types of steam hammers then in use throughout the world.

As gang boss, Taylor saw that efficiency depended on the wise use of labor and, in turn, on labor's proper use of materials and machinery. He believed that the workers he managed were not doing their work efficiently. Sometimes this inefficiency was because of "soldiering" due either to an inherent laziness or the deliberate withholding of effort due to resentment against the employer. Taylor believed that at other times workers failed to turn out as much as they could because of sheer ignorance about how a specific job might be done with the least effort.

Thus, starting with Taylor, was born the idea of time and motion study—an application of engineering methods to the use of labor. A leading authority described it this way:

> Time and motion study is the accurate, scientific method by which the great mass of laws groverning the best and easiest and most productive movements of men are investigated. . . . They substitute exact knowledge for prejudiced opinion and force in determining all the conditions of work and pay.[1]

The general doctrine of Taylor and his followers was that it was the business of management to manage—a responsibility which management had neglected. Business management had failed to train workers to do their jobs. In view of rapidly changing tech-

---

[1] Robert Franklin Hoxie, *Scientific Management and Labor* (New York: Appleton-Century-Crofts, Inc., 1918), p. 147. Taylor himself reviewed the quoted statement.

niques, there could be no traditional method. Time and motion study was to be used to provide a scientific method for determining what each worker should do during each second of his working time.

Prior to 1900, Taylor and his followers had not been much concerned about wages. However, the time-and-motion-study approach to the instruction of a worker led Taylor and his disciples to consider what wages should be paid for each of the new and sharply defined tasks. Taylor's approach to a doctrine of wages was that the wage system should make the workers realize that the best results for each worker would come from a rigid adherence to the "one best way" of doing each task. That "one best way" would be discovered by time and motion studies of the mechanical engineers. After that discovery, the wage problem would be merely a matter of inducing the individual worker to perform in the "one best way." There thus arose the notion of a bonus payment for the individual worker's conformance to the "one best way."

Taylor objected strongly, not only to pay by the hour but also to uniform pay by the piece. An hourly rate, he believed, gave the worker no incentive to increase his output. Even a straight piece rate provided insufficient incentive because it allowed him to double his earnings by doubling his output, while still working less efficiently than the "one best way." Taylor's *differential piece-rate system* provided a low piece rate for a worker who failed to meet his production quota and a much higher piece rate when the worker met or exceeded this quota. The earnings of the inefficient worker would be so small as to induce him to quit voluntarily.

Taylor's Disciples

Taylor inspired a number of close followers who helped promote scientific management. Four of them will be mentioned individually. Significantly, Taylor did not trust most factory managers of his time to apply his methods. Therefore these followers were important to him because they, at least, understood what he was trying to do. Like religious disciples, they honored their master; but they also made contributions of their own and on several points came to differ with Taylor himself. Dozens of different wage-incentive plans were ultimately devised, each one being called "scientific" by its sponsor. Common to all of the plans of Taylor's immediate followers was the aim to give the individual worker a powerful wage incentive to perform his task according to the precise instructions of the time-study expert.

Henry L. Gantt (1861-1919) went to Midvale Steel in 1887 where he met Taylor. Later Taylor went to Bethlehem Steel where, in 1899, he had Gantt join him. Gantt soon became the respected associate of Taylor and was more influential in this field than anyone except Taylor himself. His chief contribution to the movement was a modification of Taylor's way of paying wages. Taylor's system produced large differences in rewards for fairly small differences in efficiency. His system was especially hard on workers who did not quite meet the quota. To protect the less efficient worker (for whom Taylor had little sympathy), Gantt's *task and bonus plan* provided a guaranteed minimum hourly rate, regardless of his output. The worker who just achieved his standard output quota was paid a premium rate for all hours worked—the premium ranging from 25 to 40 per cent over the minimum hourly rate, depending on the particular case. The worker who exceeded his standard quota was paid a further bonus for the time he saved, as compared with the standard time for the task. Thus slow workers were paid more than under Taylor's formula, although less than under prevailing hourly rates. The fastest workers earned somewhat less than under Taylor's formula and much less than under straight piece rates.

Carl Barth (1860-1916) was an immigrant Norwegian. He first came into contact with Taylor at Bethlehem in 1899 when Taylor wanted solutions to various mathematical problems concerned with the art of cutting metals. By reconciling numerous variables on a special slide rule which he invented, Barth achieved a major breakthrough for scientific management. An adaptation of his slide rule proved applicable to time and motion studies for the determination of workers' tasks as well. Thus Barth had a strong influence in the determination of wages to be paid to workers even though his main interests were technical rather than economic. Barth's own *empirical formula premium plan* for wage payment was seldom used because its complexity made it difficult for the employer to compute payrolls and practically impossible for the worker to understand.

Frederick A. Halsey (1865-1935) was not a close associate of Taylor's; his ideas were parallel to, rather than built upon, Taylor's ideas. He gained a considerable influence on wage policy as the result of a paper—read before the American Society of Mechanical Engineers in 1891—entitled "The Premium Plan of Paying for Labor." Halsey proposed a piece-rate system under which it would never be necessary to cut the rate. The threat of rate-cutting, as he was well aware, was one of the main reasons for the workers' dislike of the piece-rate system. Halsey's plan involved paying a bonus on top of the guaranteed base wage, this bonus to start at a fairly low level of production. Thereafter, however, the employer would get the lion's share of the income from increased production so that the employer would not be tempted to cut the piece rate when the workers' earnings rose.

Frank Gilbreth (1868-1924) had applied scientific methods to industry independently, notably in the form of a new method of bricklaying; but he, unlike Halsey, later became a close disciple of Taylor's. He became interested chiefly in what he called the psychology of management—teaching men to think and act in terms of the most efficient motions. On the subject of wages he largely followed Taylor. One very interesting reflection on wages, however, comes from Gilbreth's *Primer of Scientific Management* (1914).

> *Question:* If the worker produces three times more output under Scientific Management than he does under the traditional plan, why does he not get three times as much wages?
>
> *Answer* (in part): If all of the saving by the use of Scientific Management were given to the worker, management could not afford to maintain the corps of investigators and teachers who are necessary under Scientific Management.[2]

Gilbreth's statement suggests why both management and workers were slow to accept scientific-management methods in their entirety. Employers often found the system too costly. Workers believed that they should obtain in wages the whole of the value of the increased product, as they would under a piece-rate system if the piece rates were not cut.

REACTIONS TO SCIENTIFIC MANAGEMENT

The modern American practice of personnel administration has been profoundly influenced by the doctrines of Frederick Taylor and his disciples. As might have been expected, the doctrines of the original disciples of Taylor have been modified and interpreted in a variety of ways by those who think of themselves as "practitioners" of scientific management. The leading adherents to the movement have included such men as Horace Hathaway, Sanford Thompson, Henry Kendall, and Morris L. Cooke, but almost all of the thousands of technical advisors to American employers have claimed that they were basing their advice on the principles of scientific management. Among the hundreds of thousands of employing companies in the United States, all have been affected, to a greater or lesser degree,

[2] Frank B. Gilbreth, *Primer of Scientific Management,* 2nd Ed. (New York: D. Van Nostrand Co., Inc., 1914), p. 89.

by the scientific-management movement; but none of these companies has adopted all of the prescriptions of the pioneers of the movement. The majority of employers who operate small plants, shops, stores, or service establishments have not been able to afford the elaborate study of each job and each wage rate that the enthusiastic pioneers of the movement advocated, nor have these small employers felt the need for such formal and extensive methods. The larger employers have been able to afford, and usually have felt the need for establishing, uniform assignments of tasks and wage rates and for introducing some kind of wage incentive into their wage-and-salary structures. However, it has usually been easier for management to set up a piece rate or bonus system than to undertake the kind of job analysis which Taylor recommended.

Two of the most lasting, although indirect, effects of the scientific-management movement have been the establishment of personnel departments and the more careful attention by employers to the selection and training of employees. These reforms have helped to define and standardize each unit of labor for which a wage was paid. As for wage rates themselves, American emloyers still use a great variety of payment plans and even use different methods for different classes of workers within the same establishment.

Personnel Departments

Taylor and his adherents eventually convinced the larger businesses in the United States of the need for a staff of specialists in the job of managing persons. This work had been the responsibility of the foreman. But Taylor and his devotees were convinced that personnel management was a separate and specialized part of the organization of any large enterprise.

In the early days of the scientific-management movement, a recognition of the personnel function began by dividing the foreman's authority. One out of each group of foremen was to deal with a separate aspect of a worker's employment. This idea of "functional foremen" proved to be quite impractical. From the worker's view, it was bad enough to have one "boss." It was worse to have several bosses. From management's view, responsibility for results was dispersed.

Large scale American business did not, in the end, adopt the "functional foremen" plan. Instead it created personnel departments. One of the duties of any such personnel department is, in most cases, to determine the wage rate or the permitted range of wage rates to be paid each worker.

Since 1900, personnel departments have had an up-and-down history in American industry. They were very popular among the larger employers during World War I when labor supplies were scarce, but many business concerns liquidated their personnel staffs during the brief business depression of 1921. However, during the prosperous years of 1922-1929, business management again realized the usefulness of personnel departments. It is to this revival of interest that we owe the popularity of courses in personnel administration in the leading universities and colleges in the United States. However, in the 1930's, employers once again cut their personnel staffs, because the overhead cost was not believed to be justified when workers were knocking on the factory gates.

Today personnel departments appear to be here to stay, at least in business enterprises employing 500 or more workers. The rise of personnel managers is an outgrowth of the facts of industrial life and is due in good part to the doctrines Taylor and his followers advocated with respect to what an employer should do about wages. Thus it has come about that the wages of American workers in large business firms are determined more and more by the findings and beliefs of personnel administrators rather than by the freewheeling experimentation of competitors in the markets for products and for labor or the whims of individual foremen.

Selection and Training

Part of the reason for the increased output under scientific management was that only the best employees were used. Taylor himself remarked that of the seventy-five men who constituted the original pig-iron-handling gang at the Bethlehem Steel Works before Taylor arrived, only one in eight was physically capable of maintaining the pace set by scientific methods. It may be presumed that these men were not weaklings. The jobs were strenuous under any conditions. The answer is that the original form of scientific management was extremely exacting in its requirements.

What did Taylor think of the second-class man in view of his own high standards? Taylor's answer was: "I believe the only man who does not come under 'first-class' as I have defined it is the man who can work and won't. I have tried to make it clear that for each type of workman some job can be found at which he is first-class, with the exception of those who are perfectly well able to do the job but won't do it."[3]

[3] Frank Barkley Copley, *Frederick W. Taylor* (New York: Harper & Row, Publishers, 1923), Vol. I, p. 180.

Thus, for Taylor, the management problem included that of finding the man for which the job was best fitted. Yet in Taylor's day there was little to distinguish the scientific-management shops from others as regards methods of selecting and hiring employees. Training consisted of teaching the worker to do exactly what he was told, and to do it faster than before. This did not mean that Taylor did not consider fatigue. By time and motion study, Taylor purports to have discovered a working pace which would create no strain, yet result in more output. Rests at given intervals were mandatory and part of the training consisted of learning how to rest properly.

The present-day attention to the selection and training of workers would have surprised Taylor and his immediate disciples. Every sizable American enterprise now requires work histories of job applicants; most of the larger plants use tests of various kinds to screen the fitness of each applicant for the job openings. Taylor had been content to let workers select themselves and then proceed to weed themselves out by the high or low wages they earned as a result of conforming, or not conforming, to the performance standards. Promotions of employees within a plant are also the subject of much more formal attention than the Taylor group was wont to give. Labor union pressure and other factors have made years of service a more important element in promotion decisions than Taylor would have advocated.

The extent of employee training is also greater than Taylor could have foreseen. The minority of employers who make elaborate time and motion studies of each task conduct employee training along lines which Taylor would have advocated; but employee training programs are now applied to a much wider range of jobs than in Taylor's day. Whether the job is paid by the hour, by the piece, or under a bonus system, formal training for the job is generally undertaken by the larger companies, usually by the personnel department. Moreover, modern training programs go beyond instruction in the correct motions. Modern training seeks to get each worker, from machine operator to company executive, to understand the problems of his job, the problems of working in the particular shop, and the problems of cooperating with fellow workers. On the whole, the timing of the worker's motions are given less attention than the Taylor group gave to them; much more attention is given to training as a means of welding a more effective working team.

Modern methods of selection and training do aim at the objectives of scientific management however much the scope and particular methods may have changed. The basic purpose is still that of improving and standardizing each unit of labor for which the employer pays a wage.

Methods of Wage Payment

The promoters of scientific management did convince the mass of American employers that the worker's wage should be based on the worker's output. Yet if Frederick Taylor were alive today, his greatest disappointment would probably be the failure of American management to adopt his bonus formula for paying wages. Indeed, less than 30 per cent of *factory* labor is paid on the basis of a wage-incentive system, although incentive wages are more readily adaptable to factories than to the larger nonmanufacturing parts of the economy. At that, most of the so-called incentive wages consist of wage payments by the piece rather than by any of the bonus systems.

Part of the reason for the failure of bonus systems to gain universal acceptance can be charged to the great variety of bonus systems which have been advocated. Even among Taylor's immediate disciples, as has been noted, there were differences of opinion as to what particular kind of bonus plan should be adopted. In more recent years, management consultants by the hundreds have attempted to convince managements that their particular incentive plans provided the only "scientific" solution to the employer's wage-setting problem. When experts disagree so widely, it is difficult to believe that their prescriptions are truly scientific.

Another obstacle to the application of bonus systems has been the opposition of labor unions, of which more will be said presently. As unions have grown in strength—especially in the manufacturing industries where incentive wage plans are easiest to install—managements have been pressed to abandon even such bonus systems as they had already installed. The automobile manufacturing industry provides a spectacular case in point. Piece work is accepted and even favored by some labor unions, notably those in the garment trades; but unions are almost unanimous in their bitter opposition to bonus systems.

Apart from union opposition, a fundamental obstacle to the Taylor type of bonus system has been the unwillingness or inability of managements to undertake the detailed time-and-motion studies which Taylor thought a prerequisite to the installation of a bonus scale of wages. The effort and expense required to study each of thousands of tasks is truly prodigious. The problem is intensified by the rapid changes of tasks in modern industry. Ideally, a new study is needed every time a worker's task is altered. Even where the machine operators tasks are stable and standardized, the tasks of the skilled workers may be highly variable from week to week. A scientific wage payment, based on a detailed recording of the minutes spent on each of the many different tasks of a pattern-maker, might well cost more than the wages paid for the performance of the task itself. Hence, even in "bonus shops," the incentive-wage system rarely covers all of the wage earners.

A further difficulty faced by bonus systems is that the factors which govern the output of an individual worker may be very numerous and complex. The aim of a bonus system is to pay each worker according to his performance. But his output per unit of time will depend not only on his individual competence and effort but also on the quality and flow of materials, his familiarity with the task, the cooperation he gets from fellow workers, and a host of factors which are under management rather than worker control. Where the factors affecting worker output are complex, a scientific bonus formula also needs to be complex. In that case, however, the worker is unable to understand what does govern the amount of his weekly paycheck. For example, under the Bedaux system, once very popular with management but now largely abandoned, only a small group of management experts could understand the operation of the wage formula. The workers looked on their paychecks as a gamble and generally believed that management was playing tricks with them. In such a case, employee morale suffered and the whole purpose of the incentive wage was defeated.

The scientific-management consultants failed to provide any universal formula for the determination of individual wages, even though they did convince the managers of large enterprises that good performance should be rewarded. What did result was the much more careful definition of tasks and measurement of results, plus attention by management to the factors affecting output, which management rather than the workers alone could control and improve. These techniques of "engineering the job," Taylor considered an essential part of the scientific-management approach.

Union Opposition

When Frederick Taylor began his time-and-motion studies, he seemed to have no opinion about labor unions one way or the other. At that time there was little effective union organization in the steel industry. Even so, Taylor did run up against opposition to his methods by individual workers. When he did, he proceeded to get the malcontents discharged. As time went on, union opposition to efficiency experts grew bitter and became sustained. The very phrases "scientific management" and "efficiency expert" were used in union circles as terms of abuse.

Union opposition to scientific management genuinely puzzled the industrial engineers, management, and a good part of the public. How could the workers be opposed to efforts to increase their earnings, especially if the methods were "scientific?"

The union leaders, for their part, objected on the grounds which have just been outlined: the multiplicity of bonus systems, the failure of management to make truly scientific studies of the jobs they put under incentive pay, and the obscurity of the factors which governed the worker's paycheck. Union leaders went further. They interpreted time studies and bonus systems as management devices to drive the workers to inhuman efforts for the profit of management and as deliberate management schemes to fight unionism.

There was some truth to these allegations. The efficiency experts were more used to communicating with each other and with business executives than they were in communicating with workers. Moreover, the bonus systems, although typically raising the wage incomes of the workers who stayed on the job, did not raise these incomes in proportion to the increased output as did ordinary piece rates. Workers were not impressed with claims that scientific-management methods created an expense for which employers should be rewarded—especially when the more shoddy incentive plans could be installed without great expense.

Behind these arguments, however, lay a more fundamental union objection. Whatever the intentions of Taylor and his followers, scientific management was popular with many employers because employers wished to avoid union interference with the operations of their plants. For a time, especially during the 1920's, incentive wage plans were effective as antiunion devices. This was so because workers under most incentive plans were earning more than the workers who were represented by unions. Production bonuses worked to undermine unions in a more subtle way. Under such systems, each worker was pitted against his fellows. The unions were hard put to promote or even retain that sense of common interest among the workers upon which labor organization depends. Bonus systems presented much more of a problem for union leaders than did straight piece-rates systems. A union might negotiate the level of piece rates so that the workers would feel that the union had accomplished something for them. By contrast, most of the bonus systems were worked out by management, with their consultants, and were presented as "scientific" results and so not negotiable.

Looking back, it is clear that antiunion employers eventually failed to stem the tide of labor unionism in those very manufacturing plants where scientific-management techniques had been used most frequently. Eventually, even the industrial engineers had to conclude that labor unions were here to stay. Morris L. Cooke, one of the leading industrial engineers of the 1920's and 1930's, declared that it was essential to "coordinate the efficiency ideal of individual leadership with the democratic conception of group control." Increasingly, union representatives have been allowed to participate in formulating work standards, the basis for promotion, and the terms of incentive pay. In turn, some of the labor unions have shown increasing interest in promoting increasing efficiency of both labor and management, as a means of making wage increases possible. As William Gomberg pointed out from the union side:

> This sort of thinking (that only management is competent to conduct a time study) is somewhat at variance with the scientific objectivity to which advocates of time-study technique aspire. To argue over who shall participate in the making of an objective measurement of a task makes as much sense in industrial relations as a demand by a public utility that its customers not be permitted to read the gas or electric meter—such secrecy would breed suspicion in either case.[4]

The Human Needs of Workers

The efficiency experts were generally mechanical engineers. They thought of an employee as another piece of the machinery. The worker was to be constructed so that he would do his task in the "one best way," as figured out by his employer. Then the worker's wages were to be set according to his compliance with this "one best way" of doing any particular job.

What was missing was an appreciation of workers as human beings. Immigrant workers might submit to the "scientific" way of setting their wages; they had little choice in any case. Established American workers, however, took a different view of the efficiency expert's way of setting wages.

A self-respecting worker wants security and assurance for his entire life. His employer, quite naturally, wants to get the largest

[4] William Gomberg, *A Trade Union Analysis of Time Study* (Chicago: Science Research Associates, 1948), p. 13.

possible product per dollar spent on wages. But to gain the lowest labor cost, something more is needed than pay by time and motion. As a human, the employee is concerned with his life as a whole—his security, his responsibility to those close to him, his varied pleasures, and his belief that someone cares about him. The mechanical engineers never quite appreciated the human problem. The employee would resist the machine-like system of setting wages.

During the 1920's, employers of labor began to feel the limitations of the scientific method of setting wage rates. On their own initiative, a number of the larger employers began to establish welfare plans designed to foster in the employee a sense of security and "togetherness." This required some major changes in the cost of employing labor and thus in the logic of wages. These changes in employer attitudes are part of the story of "welfare capitalism," the subject of the next chapter.

WAGE THEORY AND SCIENTIFIC MANAGEMENT

Frederick Taylor and his disciples believed that they had a doctrine (they called it a "philosophy") which would settle the wage question "scientifically," once and for all. Most of them believed that if management would follow their prescriptions, labor unions would be unnecessary, wage controversies would be eliminated, and problems of worker morale would take care of themselves. These high hopes were not realized and, indeed, the application of the various scientific wage formulas stirred up more controversies than they settled. Nevertheless, the scientific-management movement did have an important impact on American reasoning about wages. Directly, the movement helped to sharpen the theoretical distinction between wage income and labor cost; it helped to substitute the concept of wages paid for the performance of a specific task for the concept of occupational wages; it stimulated attempts to provide more precise measures of the worth of a worker than had been defined by the theory of marginal productivity. Indirectly, the very clashes of doctrine which resulted from the practice of scientific management served to stimulate contrary developments of wage theory.

Wage Income versus Labor Cost

David Ricardo and his followers assumed that, given the available natural resources (e.g. "land"), an hour of labor would result in some definite amount of product for sale by the employer. Following Ricardo, the British wage theorists of the early nineteenth century largely ignored both technical improvements in production and the differing skills and efforts of different employers and wage earners. Doubtless they were aware of these important modifying factors, but they chose to put them to one side so as to develop a general and comprehensive theory. For the purposes of this classical theory, wage income and labor costs were treated as if they were the same thing. John Stuart Mill in 1848, and Alfred Marshall in 1890, modified this simple theory somewhat. The quality of management was recognized as a factor which helped to determine the employer's individual profits, and it was acknowledged that some workers were worth more to the employers than were other workers. Yet for the purposes of a general wage theory both the quality of management and the quality of labor were taken for granted in the marginal productivity theory of a scholar such as John Bates Clark (1899). In this static type of wage theory, the higher the worker's income, the higher would be the labor cost per unit of product.

As a result of technical progress and a rising real wage, it gradually became clear that output per worker had to be introduced as a variable factor in any theory of wages which dealt with extended periods of time. Prior to the time of Frederick Taylor, the American economist Frances Walker had advanced the residual theory of wages (*The Wages Question*, 1876). According to Walker's theory, the shares of landowners, investors, and management were determined by certain laws. Labor would receive as wages all that was left of the national product (the residual share) after the shares of rent, interest, and profits were deducted. The residual theory was a theory of long-run determination of shares in line with the limited nineteenth-century tradition and was ultimately rejected by most economists. Yet Walker's wage theory represented a step toward the recognition that output per man was subject to change and thus constituted a vital factor in the determination of wages.

The scientific management type of thinking made worker output the key factor in the *immediate* determination of the wages of each individual worker. According to Taylor's doctrine, it was the responsibility of management to discover the one best way of performing each task and to pay a wage bonus to those workers who conformed successfully to the prescribed method of operation. The worker was regarded as a largely passive factor in production, but still his wages would rise somewhat as his output rose. At the same time, the labor cost to management of each unit of product would fall as part of the very process by which wage income rose. Profits would rise as a reward to the employer who practiced scientific management because not all of the value of the increased output per hour of labor time would be paid to labor as a bonus.

The particular bonus systems advocated by industrial engineers were subject to much criticism. Nevertheless, the doctrine of Taylor and his disciples did sharpen the distinction between wage income and labor cost. Wage theory has been split into two major parts. One part of the theory deals with the factors which may decrease labor cost per unit of output. The other (quite different) part of wage theory deals with the factors which may increase the real wage income of labor. The later labor-cost and wage-income theories tend to deal with relatively limited groups of cases over short periods of time, rather than with long-run tendencies of wages as a whole. Both theories attempt to deal with factors responsible for *change,* rather than with factors of *equilibrium,* such as were represented by the marginal productivity theory of wages.

Task versus Occupation

During the long era of craftsmanship which preceeded the industrial revolution, the income of an individual worker depended largely on his occupation. Within any given mediaeval town there was one level of income for apprentices, another for journeymen, and still another for master craftsmen. For each of these status groups, each trade also had its customary standard of income. Thus the shoemakers earned less than the goldsmiths but more than the weavers, and so forth. These classified standards of income were protected by the local guilds' regulations of apprenticeship, of manufacturing processes, and of the quality and the prices of the products.

The commercial revolution broke up the local market monopolies of the guilds and hence undermined their power to regulate the income of guild members. The agricultural and industrial revolutions converted the mass of workers into wage earners and undercut the sources of livelihood of most of the craft workers. In spite of these developments, the ideal occupational wages—that is, wages paid to workers according to their respective lifetime vocations—remained. Even Adam Smith, who opposed the remnants of guild and legal regulation of wages of his time, accepted the concept of an occupation which was supposedly chosen by each youth, into which he would be trained as an all-round practitioner, and in which he would be engaged throughout his working life. Upon this occupational concept, Smith built his famous theory of the relative levels of wages. In place of the customary or regulated wage, Adam Smith proposed to rely on the workers' own choices of occupation. The wage income of the workers in each occupation (if all interferences were abolished) would be governed by the workers' calculations of the relative advantages and disadvantages of each kind of established type of work. Thus, the levels of wages in the various occupations would be determined by the various qualities of labor supplied in the free labor market as a result of the workers' individual occupational choices.

By the time Frederick Taylor started the scientific-management movement in the early twentieth century, this concept of stable, lifetime occupations no longer represented reality for the majority of American factory workers. True, the miners, the skilled building trade workers, the printers, and the minority of the skilled factory workers still were craftsmen who were closely attached to their respective crafts and trained for all-round competence in their respective occupations. But most of the factory workers were employed on jobs which were new to them. If they received any training at all, it was from their foremen or their fellow workers. In this situation, the wage rate of an individual worker tended to be a *personal* rate. The determination of individual wage rates in the larger plants, as well as the assignment of tasks, was largely left to the foremen. For the unskilled and semiskilled factory workers, there was no uniform occupational rate such as Adam Smith had pictured. Indeed there was often no uniform wage rate, even within a single factory, for employees who did the same work. The rate determined by the foremen was supposed to take account of differences in the performance of different individuals, but the foremen, in the days before personnel departments were established, had no uniform standards for judging the performance or capacity of individual workmen. The prevailing system encouraged gross discrimination between individual workers on the part of foremen. In the hiring, the setting of rates, and the assignment of work, foremen tended to favor individuals they liked personally or else favored those who were hired at a time when labor was hard to obtain. Taylor and his disciples approved of the breakdown of the traditional craft groups and, indeed, wished to push this development further. But the scientific-management advocates wished to establish a uniform and impersonal rate for each distinctive set of specialized operations. Thus Taylor and his followers substituted the concept of the specialized task, as engineered by management, for the concept of an occupation. A worker's earnings were to depend, not on personal favoritism, nor rule of thumb, nor the traditional notions of the appropriate earnings of an all-round craftsman, but rather on his performance of the specific task which management had "scientifically" laid out for him.

Understandably, the labor unions protested bitterly against the breakup of occupations into narrow tasks. In the place of group control of the methods of work, it was proposed that management should direct every motion the worker should make. In place of the variety of tasks which trained craftsmen performed, it was proposed that each workman be trained to do a narrowly defined task. In place of a wage which took account of the most skilled and most difficult part of a worker's duties, it was proposed that the rate for each worker should be based on the single, routine task to which he was assigned. In place of the income security which was enjoyed by worker-group control of the occupational wage rate and which was enhanced by the craftsman's ability to shift from one task to another, it was proposed that workers should accept management's scientific determination of the wage rate for each of the specialized operations which were required from time to time.

Apart from the labor union objections to separate wage rates for each specialized task, it must be said that the Taylor group never devised a truly rational basis for a structure of wage rates. A bonus system might be devised to reward the worker who performed his task in the "one best way." But what were to be the differentials in earnings as between the workers who performed different tasks? The early scientific management group appear to have used the much abhored "rule of thumb" in setting the basis for the relative earnings of workers who performed different tasks. They seemed to have started with the previous earnings of the different groups of workers and then proceeded to apply some arbitrary bonus above those previous earnings for workers who did each task in the approved manner. This procedure left unanswered the question whether the previous wage differentials had been appropriate ones. The problem was made more difficult because occupations were being split into tasks for which there were no established wage standards. To meet this problem of relative wages for different tasks, later industrial engineers and personnel managers have devised various systems of "job evaluation." Through job evaluation, some consistency of rates could be obtained within a plant, but the question then remained as to whose judgment was to be followed concerning the relative worth of the different jobs. The latter-day labor unions have objected to the job evaluation plans of management unless the unions were allowed to participate in setting up the standards of evaluation to be used and to bring grievances when the union believed that the standards had been wrongly applied.

In spite of these and other objections, and in spite of unsolved problems, the scientific-management movement did focus attention on paying wages for the task rather than on the customary occupations to which workers were presumed to be permanently attached. In stressing task wages in place of occupation wages, the scientific-management leaders were in part recognizing developments of their time and in part promoting the doctrine that wage labor should be split into narrowly defined tasks with a wage scale for each task. Like all evangelists, these leaders tended to exaggerate the practical possibilities of the doctrine they were promoting. Occupations did not wholly disappear. Indeed, their importance may now be returning under automated systems of production which require less manual operation and more work of trained professional workers. Yet the influence on wage theory of payment for the specific task has been very great. This influence is reflected in the kinds of wage statistics used in bargaining over wage rates and in the kinds of wage statistics collected by government agencies such as the Bureau of Labor Statistics of the U. S. Department of Labor. It is no longer sufficient to report the wages of machinists, lathe operators, punch press operators, and so forth. For purposes of meaningful comparison, it is necessary to subdivide each of such former occupations into several groups of more specific sets of tasks (Machinists, Grade I, II, and III etc.). Here again can be seen the trend of modern wage reasoning in the direction of more and more specialized types of theories. Where it is true that wages are paid for the performance of specialized tasks, the forces which govern wages are somewhat different than where workers are paid for their all-round competence in an established occupation or profession.

Measurement

The marginal productivity theory of wages, in its extreme form, had pretended to explain the monetary worth of each wage earner to his employer. Logically this worth was to be tested by seeing what would happen to the employer's net revenues if he employed one more or one less worker—that is, a marginal unit of labor. A persistent objection to this theory has been that the presumed result is seldom subject to measurement. It has been said frequently that in practice employers do not experiment with the size of their labor force in the way which the formerly accepted theory described. Once an employer has installed a certain kind of lathe, he needs one lathe operator and not two. More broadly, once the employer has decided on the numbers and types of products he plans to make during a given period of time, he has already decided (given the productive techniques he is using) the number and types of labor he needs. He does not, it is contended, experiment with using one more or one fewer employee so as to test the effect on his net revenue. If management does not know the marginal revenue it obtains from its labor force, it has been asked, how can the marginal productivity of labor determine the wages paid to that labor? What was needed was a wage theory that could be verified by some measurable tests of the results.

The scientific-management advisors proposed to employers a system of measurement of both the exact task of a worker and the exact wage payment for the individual's performance of that specified task. Quantitative measurement was to be substituted for habit or guesswork in determining the wages to be paid. Although few of the industrial engineers were acquainted with the previously accepted wage theory, it can be said that, in effect, they were proposing a system of wage payment which they believed would automatically insure that the wages paid would correspond to the marginal worth to the employer of each individual worker's effort.

For a number of reasons, the particular wage payment plans of the scientific-management groups failed to solve the problem of the worth to an employer of a unit of labor. First of all, individual bonus plans failed to take account of the group contribution of workers to the eventual output. The eventual output, as industrial sociologists have pointed out, is something more (or less) than the sum of the individual worker's efforts. Later advocates of incentive wage problems have tried to answer this problem by establishing various kinds of group bonus or group incentive plans of wage payment.

Secondly, scientific-management wage-payment plans failed to take account of conditions in the employers product and labor markets. The money value of a worker's effort depends on more than the number of physical operations he performs within a given period of time. The effect of the worker's performance on an employer's revenue depends on the price at which the employer can sell the ultimate product or service. Likewise the wage that an employer needs to pay for a task may well depend on the alternative opportunities which workers have to obtain employment in the labor market generally. Even the latter-day plans for setting wage rates on the basis of job evaluation have run into these problems of the changing state of the employer's product and labor markets. The money wage rate—whether a time rate or an incentive rate—may be too high if the employer's product market deteriorates or if comparable workers can be obtained at a lower rate. The established rate may be too low if the product market improves or if an adequate supply of comparable workers cannot be obtained.

Thirdly, scientific wage plans did not solve the problem of the sharing of revenues between the workers, employers, and investors. Indeed most of the wage bonus plans gave the workers less out of any increased output resulting from the worker's improved effort than did straight piece-work plans. This is so because the additional wage payment was less than proportionate to the additional output.

The specific-wage plans of would-be scientists did not, as was claimed, solve the problem of the worth of an employee to his employer. Nevertheless, the scientific-management movement, like the institutionalist movement of the time (see Chapter V), did direct the attention of theorists to the formulation of wage theories which contain factors that can be measured in quantitative terms so that the degree of validity of the theory can be tested in specific cases.

SUMMARY

No account of the origins of recent wage theories would be complete without recognition of the movement called scientific management. The leaders of this movement, beginning with Frederick Taylor, were mechanical engineers. They observed certain facts characteristic of the beginning of the twentieth century: the effectiveness of mechanical engineers in increasing production, the new jobs produced by the progress of the industrial revolution, and the inefficient performance of tasks by the mass of untrained workers. These reformers proposed to apply to the management of labor the methods which had proved so successful in the management of materials and machinery.

The scientific-management leaders proposed that each job should be reduced to the simplest and most efficient set of motions which the operator needed to make. They believed that once the engineer had determined the one best way of doing a job, management should pay wages under a system which would increase the income of those workers who did each task exactly as instructed and which would eliminate those workers who did not follow these precise instructions.

The approval of so-called scientific management has greatly influenced the thinking of present-day employers of labor, notably in the development of personnel departments and of management attention to selection and training of their employees. At the same time the movement brought a bitter reaction by labor unions and, in the end, did not make unions unnecessary as many managements had hoped and expected. One of the weaknesses of the so-called "scientific" approach to wages and personnel problems was its neglect of the fact that wage earners are human beings and so respond differently than machines to control of their operation by impersonal methods.

As for wages specifically, the various bonus plans advocated by industrial engineers did not provide any universal and simple solution, nor did they aid directly in prediction of the course of wages. However, the scientific-management approach did help to teach wage theorists the importance of the difference between wages paid for a specialized task and wages paid for competence in an all-round lifetime occupation. In addition it taught wage theorists the importance of the difference between wage income and labor costs. Finally, scientific management helped to induce economists to use in their theories of wage determination factors which could be measured and tested.

the use of revolutionary methods (such as Karl Marx later advocated). Out of his practical experience as an employer, Robert Owen began to dream of a new kind of industrial society which employers could put into practice. Owen was both a humanitarian and an autocrat. He made a notable success of his business in spite of the doubts of his partners. In his later years, however, Owen's ideas of reform became increasingly vague and thus his "utopian socialism" became the slogan by which his opponents—both Marxist and conservative—ridiculed his impracticality. Nevertheless, Owen as an employer was well ahead of his time and eventually helped to stimulate sentiments favoring the employer's social responsibility.

Similar ideas of welfare were expressed in the United States long before the decade of the roaring 1920's. In addition to numerous self-sufficient communities begun in the New World, profit-making American enterprises began to apply some of Owen's ideas in the cotton mill towns of Massachusetts. Thus, around 1830, the textile employers in such places as Lowell and Waltham began to think they had some positive responsibility for the over-all welfare of the workers they hired. The factory girls in Waltham were treated with a benevolent paternalism reflecting the employers' acceptance of a moral obligation to "take care" of their employees. The Massachusetts employers came to believe they had a moral obligation to protect, supervise, and improve the *whole* life of workers. This approach to labor management was at first profitable. It was not long, however, before the pressures of increased market competition led to a breakdown of this early American system of paternalism.

A later American example of welfare capitalism, still before the 1920's, was that conducted by George M. Pullman, the creator of the American sleeping car system. Pullman, likewise a paternal kind of employer, cared for his employees on the basis of his own ideas on the subject. He constructed a model village on the outskirts of Chicago where he, as employer, attempted to provide for every human need of his employees, as he saw these needs. However beneficent Pullman pretended to be, his actual operations—like those of many mining companies—resulted in rather crude economic pressures on his employees. This autocratic effort of Pullman's got mixed up with the case of Eugene Debs and the great strike of 1894 of the American Railway Workers Union. The Pullman case is an extreme example of the clash between the welfare motives and the profit motives of employers. Pullman expected a 6 per cent return from an investment he made in employee housing. His "benevolence" took the form finally of a reduction of wages but not of rents so that the typical Pullman employee who had to live in a Pullman house was left with perhaps fifty cents a week (say $1.50 in current dollars) after his rent deduction.

Two other American employers who practiced welfare capitalism before World War I were Andrew Carnegie and John D. Rockefeller, Jr. Carnegie believed that rich employers owed an obligation to their employees, and to the nation generally, to spend their riches for the public goods. John D. Rockefeller, Jr. inherited the fortune of his famous father. One part of this fortune consisted of mining properties in Colorado. There, in 1913, occurred the tragic Ludlow massacre, a result of the strike of employees against the Colorado Fuel and Iron Company. Several women and children were killed by company-hired thugs. This tragedy made a deep impression on young Rockefeller and persuaded him, with the advice of Canada's William McKenzie King, to establish the Colorado Industrial Plan to provide employee representation under employer sponsorship. Rockefeller's plan was one of the earliest models of the company union. The intention was humanitarian. The guidance of the plan, however, was kept entirely in the hands of the employing company.

METHODS AND EXTENT

Welfare practices, such as outlined below, were never universal in American industry. As we have seen, the movement of welfare capitalism had its roots in the paternalism of Robert Owen and of the Massachusetts textile operators during the nineteenth century. In the 1920's, the movement became a fairly general one in the United States. Today, in spite of government regulation of the conditions of employing labor, voluntary welfare benefits to workers are still an important part of the over-all remuneration of wage earners and salaried employees.

Activities of Paternalistic Employers

Examples of welfare capitalism have been many and varied. A common element of welfare plans has been the effort of employers to provide employees with something more than cash wages. To illustrate the range and variety of company welfare plans, we refer to seven major groups of such attitudes as compiled by Pigors and Myers.[1]

(1) *Recreation* has been promoted by employers to bring the

[1] Paul Pigors and Charles A. Myers, *Personnel Administration* (New York: McGraw-Hill, Inc., 1947), pp. 503-510.

worker relief from boredom, to provide relaxation, and to generate group spirit. Examples of such recreational plans are many, ranging from athletic teams to glee clubs and dramatic clubs. By the year 1926, a majority of large American companies were making substantial contributions toward the recreation of their employees. Of 430 large companies surveyed in that year, 319 assisted with athletic teams and 235, or more than half, provided such facilities as clubhouses, recreation rooms, gymnasiums, bowling alleys, or game rooms. Some of these activities were costly, but generally efforts to provide recreation for employees had not added greatly to the overall cost of labor. By the year 1926, though companies continued to bear the cost of recreational activities, employers permitted employees to form committees to organize and plan the activities, thus increasing the participation, and presumably the satisfaction, of employees.[2]

(2) *Health and safety* measures of employers comprise a second broad group of welfare measures. Under this heading come physical examinations, first aid, guards on machines, safety instructions, and medical advice and treatment in cases of accidents and sickness on the job. For some years past, the employers surveyed in 1926 had provided some kind of medical service to their employees. The care was primarily first aid at the beginning, but in the decade preceding 1926 the quality of the service had improved so that by 1926 about three-fourths of the 430 companies studied were employing trained nurses and doctors and/or surgeons. This was one of the more important and lasting of the welfare activities of employers. Some went so far as to provide company-owned and managed dispensaries or hospitals. These were usually linked to situations of isolated employment in areas without public facilities.

(3) The area of *Education and Information* has afforded many opportunities for the offering of employee benefits. Among the more popular services of this type have been company-sponsored educational programs, company-financed scholarship funds, the provision of technical libraries for the employees, and the sponsorship of a variety of discussion groups. In 1916 the provision of education for employees was so insignificant that there appears to be no record of any such activity. By 1926, however, 150 of 430 companies reported offering some educational benefits. Company libraries were provided by 127 of the 430 companies, and some 48 were assisting employees with their outside education.

(4) Provisions to increase *Economic Security* has been one of the

[2] Sources of statistical data used in this chapter are included in the appendix ("Bibliographical Notes").

most costly types of welfare benefits. This type of activity can range from thrift clubs, credit unions, or stock-purchases plans to life, accident, or health insurance plans. In some cases, notably life insurance, the cost has often been borne exclusively by the employer. Today private pension and retirement funds are probably the more notable examples of economic security measures, financed partly or wholly by the employer.

The idea of having employees own shares of stock in the company they work for was, undoubtedly, one of the great enthusiasms of the 1920's. Between 1921 and 1925 some 162 stock-ownership plans were started. In 1927 an estimated one million wage and salary workers owned or had subscribed to over one billion dollars in the shares of the various companies employing them. These employees, like other stockholders, lost heavily during the stockmarket crash of 1929. Since then these plans have lost much of their popularity.

Pension plans present quite a different story. This kind of plan began around the year 1884 and grew slowly at first. By 1916 some 116 pension plans were reported by the U. S. Department of Labor (Bureau of Labor Statistics). The two periods of most rapid growth were the years 1916-1920 and 1929-1932. During the latter period, however, pension plans were being abandoned almost as often as they were being established. By the end of 1932 there were 145 pension plans in effect, covering 1,394,000 workers.

Paid vacations, group insurance plans, and sick leave plans are for the most part developments of the 1920's. There were instances of such benefits being offered as early as 1916, but these were exceptions to the rule. By 1926 these benefits were becoming generally accepted among the large companies; by 1960 they were nearly universal, the only exceptions being the very small employer.

In some instances the employer met the entire cost of these economic security plans. However, payment by the employer of the total cost smacked of company domination and paternalism; today employees are often required to help meet the cost.

(5) *Conveniences* for employees have included a wide variety of little things. Most elemental has been the provision of adequate toilets and washrooms. Other instances include the provision of locker rooms, rest rooms, lunch rooms, and lunch wagons. In 1916 only about half of the larger companies operated lunch rooms, whereas by 1926 nearly 70 per cent of the companies had them.

(6) The *Personal and Family Problems* of employees have received the attention of many companies. Measures have included emergency financial assistance to the employee, vocational guidance, and advice on problems of health and family finances. In the study

of 430 companies by the U. S. Department of Labor (Bureau of
Labor Statistics) in 1926, 72 companies were found to be making
loans to their employees, and 196 were supporting savings funds for
their employees. Cooperative stores were supported by 21 companies and legal advice was offered by a few of the larger companies.

(7) Company support to *Community Interests* is the most diverse of the welfare activities among those which have been summarized by Pigors and Myers. Some forms of "community-interest"
activities are quite simple—such as paying for time not worked while
the employee is voting, serving on a jury, or appearing as a witness.
Other employer costs are incurred when an effective union is
established—such as payment for time not worked while an employee is carrying out union duties. Where plant operations are
located in isolated areas, employers have sometimes developed the
basis for the physical and social structures of the whole community
by providing company housing for their employees and their families. For example, in 1916 the Bureau of Labor Statistics compiled
a list of 1,700 firms which provided housing for their employees. In
213 firms, having 423 establishments or plants and employing
466,991 men, 34 per cent of the male employees were living in company houses. This particular type of employee benefit was used
extensively in the textile, steel, and coal-mining industries.

(8) *Employee Representation Plans* were key programs sponsored
by the larger American companies.[3] These provided collective
representation of employees as an alternative to independent labor
unions. The largest companies started their employee representation
plans during the 1920's. Yet this method of providing an employer-
sponsored substitute for labor unions began long before the 1920's,
and was most prominent in the 1930's. The first employee representation plans were called "works councils." Later they were called
shop committees and then employee representation plans. When the
suspicion grew that these devices were being used to combat
independent labor unions, they came to be called company unions.

Company unions sometimes provided a valuable outlet for the
real or fancied grievances of employees. Thus they were an important part of attempts of the larger companies to pay attention
to the whole man, rather than to regard man as a mere tool in the
hands of the industrial engineer. However, as Paul H. Douglas
pointed out in 1921, the employee representation plans did not give
a group of workers the independence in bargaining for wages and
other benefits, that the power of a labor union did. Company unions
have been largely displaced since the 1930's. In fact, under the

[3] Not included by Pigors and Myers in their category of welfare plans.

Taft-Hartley Act of 1947, they can be illegal if the majority of employees vote for an independent union. However, they provided a keystone of welfare capitalism in the 1920's and 1930's.

Recent Developments

Since the decade of the 1920's, welfare capitalism has undergone a transformation. Employee benefits (other than cash wages) have been greatly extended. On the other hand, the movement has lost much of its voluntary character, due both to the increasing requirements on employers by governments and to the increasing pressures on employers by labor unions. The over-all stress has been on economic security measures rather than on those parts of welfare programs which were prominent in the 1920's. The new phrase for the welfare activities of employers—whether voluntary or compulsory—is "fringe benefits."

Employers have now become much more conscious of the large costs of these fringe benefits and realize that these additions to cash wages should be counted as part of the cost to the company of employing its labor. Reflecting this concern, the Chamber of Commerce of the United States has been conducting biennial surveys, since 1947, of the cost of fringe benefits. These surveys show the steadily increasing cost of fringe benefits between 1947 and 1959 until, in the latter year, the average cost of fringe benefits to the 1064 companies surveyed reached 22.8 per cent of ordinary payrolls. The costs varied greatly from company to company, being less than 6 per cent in a few cases and as much as 60 per cent of payroll in a few other cases. However, the greatest number of companies were found to have fringe-benefit costs which added from 16 to 30 per cent to payrolls.

It is worth noticing, first of all, that no specific costs were reported in the Chamber of Commerce studies for the items of *Recreation, Education and Information,* or *Community Services.* These omissions may have been due to any one of several reasons. The most probable reason is that, in 1959, the average costs of these particular welfare activities were too small to be worth reporting separately. Another possible reason may be that the reporting companies consider such activities to be part of the general cost of doing business rather than as additions to the specific cost of employing labor. It may also be that the Chamber did not regard such activities as "fringe benefits" and thus did not question the reporting companies about these particular costs.

The most striking feature of the Chamber's findings is that the cost of these security measures, by themselves, represent an addition to payrolls of an average of 14 per cent or nearly two-thirds of the total costs of all reported fringe benefits. The principle items of economic security were those of pensions and paid vacations and holidays. A minor item was the cost of nongovernment unemployment benefits. Government requirements accounted for nearly all of the relatively small amount of the cost of unemployment benefits whereas pensions, vacations, and holidays involved major costs. The government did not directly require payment of wages during employee vacations or holidays. As for pensions, the cost of meeting government requirements was only about one-third of the total cost of pensions which the employers faced. It is, at present, not possible to find how much of these major costs of pensions, vacations, and paid holidays are the result of employer initiative as compared with labor union pressure, either directly as a result of union demands or indirectly as a result of the need of other employers to meet the negotiated standards.

THE NEW FACTS

The larger American employers of labor in the 1920's began to see some of the limitations of the scientific-management approach to the problems of wages. Thus the welfare capitalism approach to wages came to serve as a supplement to the mechanistic and impersonal view of employees held by the scientific-management experts.

Changes in Supply and Demand for Labor

Welfare capitalism was based on several decisive changes in both labor and product markets between 1910 and 1920. Perhaps the most important of these changes was the reduction in the annual supplies of raw, untrained immigrant workers. The scientific-management advisors to American employers had, in part, based their time-and-motion schemes for paying wages on the abundant supplies of untrained immigrants who needed to be taught the motions needed to carry out a specific task and who were to be paid according to their compliance with the experts' instructions. (See Chapter VI.) Welfare capitalism, at its peak, represented an employer reaction to a different kind of labor supply than that which had been available when the scientific-management movement began.

World War I and later restrictions on immigration reduced the supply of untrained, non-English speaking and compliant labor forces. The industrial employees of the 1920's and thereafter were no longer the "hunkies" the American industrial employers had hired around 1910. The employees of the 1920's had to be treated as individual human beings.

Just when the supply of new immigrant labor dried up, the demand for labor was increased—first, by government expenditures during World War I and then by the relative prosperity of 1922-1929. A rich harvest of profits was available to American manufacturers who could obtain and hold on to the relatively scarce supplies of labor. No longer was it easy to replace a worker by drawing on a great supply of new applicants for employment. An example of the employer reaction to the changes in American supplies of labor was that employers began to appreciate the costliness of "labor turnover." The costs of labor turnover were first importantly measured and analyzed by Sumner Slichter in 1919. Slichter pointed out that an employer faced serious losses when he replaced one worker with another. First there were the costs of recruitment; next, there were the costs of training the new employee; and beyond this, there were the costs of damaged materials caused by the new and untrained worker. Finally, Slichter anticipated modern students of "human relations" in industry when he called to the employers' attention the cost importance of a stable and effective working team in any factory—a relationship which was torn asunder when one worker was replaced by another.

Successes of Unions, 1917-1920

Another hard fact which American industrial employers had to face between 1917 and 1920 was the increasing success of labor unions during World War I (Chapter IV). This labor union success was, as we have seen, greatly increased by the relatively tight labor markets during World War I and by government recognition of labor unions by President Wilson. The effective power of labor unions was also increased as of 1917, because they had become "business unions"—free of some of their nineteenth-century desires to change the world and insisting instead on negotiating wages. During the period 1917-1929, American employers were confronted for the first time with a challenge to the traditional employer's one-sided decision as to whether, say, Joe Johnson should be paid $10 or $30 a week. The leaders of the scientific-management movement had a too simple answer to this wage puzzle. Management, they said, should be responsible for instructing every worker as to what motions each worker should make during every minute of his paid employment. The welfare capitalists of 1917-1929 began to see that the time-and-motion approach to wages was inadequate. The larger manufacturers proceeded to invent some new ways of paying wages in the form of benefits for loyal attachment to the employing organization. In doing so, the employers added some new dimensions to wage theory.

WAGE DOCTRINES OF WELFARE CAPITALISM

The most simple example of the difference between nineteenth and twentieth-century management thinking on wages is provided by asking what the employer should do about the comfort of his employees. At one extreme there is the example of the horrible condition of workers in the British coal mines in the early 1800's. To improve such work-and-wage conditions, some simple changes were necessary. One such change was for the employer to provide adequate and decent toilets at the place of work. From this idea it was but a short step for the employer to think about such things as providing seats for sales clerks, guards for machinery, and elimination of fire hazards. In these changes public opinion played a large part inasmuch as progressivism had altered the social conceptions of industrial conditions.

These simple changes in the method of paying wages began to pave the way for some drastic changes in thinking about wages. These changes, like social changes generally, came about gradually. Something had been done in Britain by 1850 to improve the human conditions of employment. Economists such as John Stuart Mill and Alfred Marshall had pointed out, long before 1900, the advantages to the employer himself of treating his workers as human beings rather than as bits of equipment. Even so, the larger American employers of labor from 1917-1929 pushed forward a somewhat new management view which said that there was more to the problem of wages than the payment of the least possible amount for the performance of the detailed motions which might be prescribed by a foreman or even by an industrial efficiency expert.

Both social pressure and employer initiative were involved in the varied welfare plans of the American employers. Minimum wage laws, workmen's compensation laws, and government inspection and safety regulations were all threatening to put pressure on employers to improve their standards of employing labor. On the other hand, American employers took some initiative during the 1920's in developing schemes for making their employees happier and more productive. Some of these welfare plans sprang from genuine humanitarian motives. The notion began to spread that an employer had some kind of social responsibility for the over-all welfare and happiness of his employees regardless of legislation and outside pressures. Employers hoped, too, of course, that their new welfare plans would "pay off" in terms of greater production, lower labor costs, and greater company profits. In addition, employers were being pushed from behind by legislation, by the general spirit of Wilson's "new freedom," and by the threat of independent labor unions. Whatever the causes, the wealthier American employers of the 1920's exerted themselves to make life more tolerable for their employees. The management aim of making profits was not abandoned but management psychology did gradually change. To impel workers to operate more efficiently, more emphasis was given the carrot, rather than the stick.

What, then, was the wage doctrine of the welfare capitalists? Simply stated, the new doctrine was that an employer needed to spend money—quite beyond the cost of the worker's paycheck—to meet the human needs of that worker and, in some cases, to fight off the antimanagement operations of independent worker organizations. This new concept of wages, largely a result of the conditions in the United States during 1917-1929, changed the thinking of both businessmen and economists as to the theory of wages. In the year 1500, for example, a craftsman was entitled to his customary pay as decided by law or custom. Around 1800, in Britain and North America, a worker's wages were supposed to be set by the impersonal action of labor markets, with the employer paying the lowest wage he could to get the supply of labor he needed. By the 1920's, the larger American employers had adopted a new wage doctrine—the doctrine that an employer needed to pay much more than the weekly paycheck so as to get the lowest wage costs per unit of product from a harmonious, loyal, and competent labor force.

LIMITATIONS AND FAILINGS

New facts produce new doctrines and new theories. However, theorists are human and are often unable to predict future developments accurately. The proponents of Welfare Capitalism were no exception. They failed to consider the relatively high cost of welfare plans to small employers or to foresee the phenomenal growth of labor unions and government regulations that occurred during the 1930's in spite of the paternalistic and voluntary efforts of employers to retain unqualified control of their business operations.

Prohibitive Cost to Small Employers

By the end of the 1920's most of the larger American employers had installed some kind of welfare plan. However, such plans were not often to be found among the smaller employers. The reason for this contrast seems to be that welfare plans were too costly for small companies to take on at their own expense. For example, a single, small employer would seldom have a sufficient number of employees to spread the risk of a pension plan. Also, many types of welfare plans required a considerable minimum cost (recreational and eating facilities, for example). A small company could not spread such overhead costs among many employees. Hence, the cost per worker tended to be prohibitively high.

Another reason for the lack of welfare plans among the smaller employers was the factor of product-market competition. Of course smaller size does not automatically mean that the various individual companies are always highly competitive. Still, each enterprise in an industry of perhaps 200 companies, is much more likely to be competitive in the markets for its products than is an enterprise in an industry with only a handful of large companies. The larger company is more likely to enjoy some slack between its selling prices and its costs, a margin which may be used to pay for the cost of a welfare plan. By contrast, the smaller and highly competitive company is likely to be selling its products for but little more than its costs per unit of product. Thus the smaller and more competitive companies were likely to feel that they could not afford the extra costs of welfare benefits for employees.

Had the smaller employers acted together to agree on some scale of welfare benefits, they might have passed along to the consumer a goodly portion of the costs in the form of higher prices for their products. However, such an agreement was not easy to achieve in an industry of many small producers unless a union (as in the garment industry) pressed all the competing employers to grant the same welfare benefits. Likewise, the costs of welfare benefits might have been equalized, and thus partly passed on to the buyers in the form of higher prices, if the government financed the cost by a tax on all the employers. Both the union method and the tax method of providing welfare benefits have been widely practiced since the 1930's. But neither of these methods was typical of the welfare capitalists of the 1920's. The essence of welfare capitalism at that time, as we have seen, was that of voluntary action by the individual employer to provide something more than cash wages for his employees.

Thus one limitation of welfare capitalism was that its methods were not so easily applied by small companies as they were by the larger companies.

Union Successes After the 1920's

It seems clear that one of the chief motives of the companies which devoted energy and money to welfare plans was to provide a company-sponsored alternative to any labor union which would be independent of the individual employing company. This objective of the welfare capitalists was well achieved in the decade of the 1920's, but was largely frustrated thereafter.

Whatever the forms of welfare benefits, the employer who provided the benefits was seeking to convince the workers that the company was paying attention to the "whole man" better than any union could do. Under welfare capitalism, the initiative remained with the employer. Employees might be invited to form advisory committees on matters of recreation, health and safety, insurance, convenience, etc., but the decisions were those of the company, free from interference by any union. Employers sought to demonstrate to their employees and to the public that they could provide better over-all treatment of their workers than those workers could hope to attain by joining an outside union. This antiunion objective of welfare capitalism is most easily seen in the development of employee representation plans which, as we have noted, spread most rapidly in the early 1930's when the challenge of outside unions began to be widespread. These company-sponsored representation plans offered the employees some apparent means of collective representation for the redress of grievances and, therefore, provided a partial answer to the challenge of the "outside" union.

During the decade of the 1920's, the welfare capitalists were notably successful in defeating the efforts of the outside unions to organize and bargain for the workers. By 1929, there were actually fewer union members than in 1920, despite the considerable growth of the economy during that period. Of course, there were other reasons for this union stagnation, notably the employers' effective use of the courts and some weaknesses of union leadership. However, the methods of welfare capitalism played a part in the suppression of outside unionism, as is suggested by the trends in union membership in each of the several broad classes of industry. Labor unions in the 1920's did best in the construction industry—an industry which consisted mainly of small-sized employers who offered little in the way of welfare benefits.

IMPACT OF WELFARE CAPITALISM ON WAGE THEORY

The facts of wage employment and the practices (doctrines) of the industrial leaders of welfare capitalism stimulated some new trends in modern wage history. None of the leaders of welfare capitalism would have thought of himself as a wage theorist. Still the ambition and the experiments of the welfare-minded industrial managers helped to spark changes in the wage theories of the beginning of the twentieth century.

Labor Costs Redefined

In the nineteenth century, British and American economists had reasoned about wages as if the pay envelope was the entire cost to the employer of the workers he hired. There were exceptions, to be sure, but it was all too easy to think of labor costs as measured by the hourly or weekly wages the employer paid to the worker.

The welfare-capitalist leaders of the twentieth century introduced some new factors into the economists' thinking about wages and labor costs. Labor cost, per unit of product, turned out to be a more complex and interesting concept than that of merely dividing the units of product by the number of manhours at so much per hour. Even in the self-interest of the employing company (apart from any humanitarian motives), it was seen that much more was involved in labor costs than the paycheck and the product. To be specific, an extra dollar a week per employee, when devoted to some employee benefits, could result in greater product and thus lower cost per unit of product than an extra dollar in the weekly pay envelope.

The labor cost for any employer is the money he spends on labor per unit of the product he is able to sell. What the welfare capitalists discovered was that the money to be spent on employer services to workers could be more important in reducing labor costs per unit of product than the same money spent in raising the direct weekly pay. What is called "labor cost" thus came to include what is now called "fringe benefits." A variety of government measures have increased the labor costs of these "fringe benefits." Nevertheless, it was the larger employers in the United States who first suggested the theory that money spent on welfare plans for employees might lower, rather than raise, the labor costs per unit of product. The new reasoning required a wage theory which took into account not only direct wage payments, but also a range of employee benefits and their effect in attaining the lowest possible labor cost per unit of product.

Labor Income Redefined

To the conventional economist of the nineteenth century, the word "wages" stood for both the cost to the employer and for the income of the employee. However, both "labor cost" and "labor income" have turned out to be much more complicated than the earlier economists had imagined them to be. We have just suggested how the activities of the leading American employers raised theoretical questions about labor costs. Equally, the welfare capitalists raised questions about labor income.

For hundreds of years before the industrial revolution, what we now think of as the income of a worker had consisted of specific goods or rights to obtain specific goods. A similar view of labor income was prevalent on the American frontier where a worker tilled his own land and exchanged his produce for that of others. He was not a wage earner in the sense that we know such a worker to be today. With the rise of the commercially-hired worker, quite the opposite assumptions were made about the income of labor. Economists around the year 1900 generally reasoned as if the only thing available to Bill Smith, a laborer, was the money he received at the end of the week.

The welfare capitalists changed such reasoning. The actual (*real*) income of the worker turned out to be much more than his paycheck. A worker's total income, as Adam Smith had emphasized in 1776, consists of the "*whole* of the advantages and disadvantages of employment." An employer might well decrease the disadvantages by providing more comfortable working conditions. An employer might well increase the advantages of employment by providing baseball uniforms and the organization of a baseball team, by establishing a pension plan, by improving the lighting in the shop, or by installing an improved system for the hearing of worker grievances against management. Any one of these revisions in employment conditions changed his over-all real income quite apart from any difference in his paycheck. How much these particular welfare-capitalism methods really did increase a worker's over-all income is not the question at the moment. That question is buried deep in the details of modern surveys of workers' attitudes. What is important is that welfare capitalism pushed the theory of wages both backward and forward—backward to Adam Smith's theory and for-

ward to a more realistic consideration of what was the over-all income
of a worker in particular circumstances.

The Human Relations Approach

The accepted theory of wages around the year 1900 pictured the
worker as a calculating machine which computed the difference
between the pain of work and the pleasures to be obtained by receiving wages. The balance between pleasure and pain was supposed
to be struck by both workers and employers operating in the market
for labor. The scientific-management movement attempted to refine
this arithmetic by proposing that each worker be paid for performing each motion in the "one best way" as determined by the industrial
engineer.

The leaders of welfare capitalism took a different view. By example, rather than as a result of any neat theory, the business
humanitarians of the 1920's began to regard the individual worker
as a person instead of just another machine. Gradually, it became
accepted that an employer should take responsibility for the over-all
needs and emotions of workers. Employers had to satisfy the over-
all human needs of the worker.

Welfare capitalism thus provided a complement to scientific management. In some respects, welfare capitalism worked with a
contrasting logic to that of scientific management. However, many
large companies used the logic of both scientific management and
welfare in dealing with employees. Frequently a large company
would put wage determination in the hands of a time-study man
and put the social activities of the employees, and perhaps their
pension plans, in the hands of other company officials.

SUMMARY

The practices of welfare capitalism laid the foundation for what
is now the "human relations" approach to employment and wages.
After forty years, there is still no settled general theory as to just
what incentives will get a worker to act in a manner that will prove
most profitable to his employer. The only generalization possible is
that each case depends on the circumstances of that case. However,
the lack of a general theory does not mean that there is no theory
at all. As in other aspects of the wage question, the welfare-minded
companies of the 1920's added some new dimensions to the problem
of the determination of wages and to the problem of how any

particular employer could obtain the best advantage for the company by effort beyond the paycheck—by giving the worker, for example, a feeling of security, harmony, and personal regard. The point for wage theory is that all these efforts are costly. What needs to be estimated, in each case, is the expected results in product per manhour, as against the cost of the welfare activities to the employer.

CHAPTER **VIII**

National Minimum Wages—NRA
and the Wage-Hour Law

This chapter and the two that follow deal with the impact on wage theories of the Great Depression of the 1930's and its New Deal aftermath. The economic upheaval of the 1930's drove men to new experiments in many areas of economic and social life. Everywhere doctrines seemed to be contradicted by actual experience. The new, experimental policies were based either on a combination of new doctrines or on doctrines that had been previously discarded in the United States. The clash between old doctrines and the experience of the Great Depression—and the clash between old and new doctrines—led men to re-examine their reasoning (theories); and the experience with new policies helped to provide some tests of the relative usefulness of both new and old theories.

The general subject of this chapter is the policy of requiring by law that private employers throughout the nation pay certain minimum wages. Before 1933, such a policy had been practiced widely outside the United States but, within the United States, only on a very limited scale by several states. But the individual state experiments had been struck down by the courts, and the prosperous 1920's seemed to support the orthodox wage theory that stood in opposition to any such tampering with private economic freedom. It took the shattering experience of the Great Depression to bring about the enactment of minimum wages on a national scale, first by the National Industrial Recovery Act of 1933 and then by the Fair Labor Standards Act of 1938.

ESTABLISHMENT OF EFFECTIVE MINIMUM WAGE
REGULATIONS IN THE UNITED STATES

Orthodox Wage Doctrine and Economic Trends, 1920-1933

At no place or time has orthodox, nineteenth-century wage theory seemed to fit actual experience as well as in the United States of the 1920's. After the short-lived business depression of 1921, total U. S. physical production climbed steadily until it became nearly twice as great in 1929 as it had been in 1921.[1] The profits of the larger manufacturing enterprises increased more rapidly than production and the market value of the shares in these enterprises rose even more rapidly than company earnings. By the late 1920's it appeared that almost anyone could become wealthly merely by borrowing money to buy stocks. There were some dark spots in the picture to be sure, notably those in agriculture and coal mining. However, progress was real throughout the major fields of manufacture, utilities, trade, service, and finance. In particular, factory output per worker increased at an average rate of 4 per cent a year in the decade, 1919-1929. This was considerably faster than during the previous two decades and, indeed, faster than during subsequent peace-time decades. Factory wages rose without any overall rise in prices although the rise in wages was at a lower rate than the rise in output per worker.

All this took place under conditions of largely uninhibited private enterprise. Welfare capitalism (Chapter VII) had, for the time, largely stilled the protests of the social workers (Chapter III) and the institutionalists (Chapter V). Labor unions (Chapter IV) had been reduced to a very minor role in the economy after the depression of 1921. Government policy was to promote private enterprise and to accept and put in force whatever measures were desired by the leading industrialists and financiers. The prevailing wage theory was that wage rates, as well as other prices, settle at levels that both reflect and make possible continued prosperity and growth if they are simply left to the influence of market competition and the enlightened self-interest of business leaders.

The stock market crash, beginning in September 1929, shook the self-confidence of American business leaders. At first, President Hoover and many leading economists of the time argued that the

---

[1] Sources of the statistical data used in this chapter are included in the appendix ("Bibliographical Notes").

drop in security prices was a healthy development. They reasoned that once stock prices were adjusted downward to be realistically in line with expected business earnings, renewed prosperity for everyone would be "right around the corner." However, a general business depression ensued and continued without important interruption through the weary years 1930, 1931, and 1932. By 1932, total national product had sunk to hardly more than half that of 1929 or to about as much as in the depression year 1921. At least one-quarter of the available workers were totally unemployed and many more were being paid for only a few hours of work a week. In view of the increased population, there was actually less real income available per person in 1932 than in the depression year 1921.

As the depression deepened, President Hoover continued to rely on private initiative, but began to invoke a collective sense of business responsibility in place of mere individual self-interest. Hoover appealed to employers to maintain the former levels of wage rates, to retain as many workers as possible, and to return former employees to their previous jobs. During 1930, wage rates were generally maintained, but employment decreased by 6 per cent and, as hours of work were cut, total wages paid by private industry decreased by 10 per cent. During 1931 and 1932 it became impossible even to maintain wage rates—as the volume of sales and prices of goods continued to fall—until finally the whole of private industry was operating at a net loss. By 1932 the hourly wages of factory workers had fallen 17 per cent below their 1929 average, employment had fallen 24 per cent below 1929, and total wage income had been cut to barely half that of 1929.

The National Industrial Recovery Act—A New Doctrine

President Hoover remained hopeful to the end of his term in office, but in March 1933, when Franklin Roosevelt became President, there was still no clear sign that private business could escape the deflationary spiral without direct, government intervention. It seemed clear to Roosevelt that the total amount of money being spent was far too small to purchase even the drastically restricted quantity of goods being produced, even at the drastically reduced level of prices. Under these conditions, private spending for investment in plant, equipment, and inventories had sunk virtually to zero. Accordingly, the new President abandoned the hope that business recovery would occur automatically at some new balance of free-market prices and wages. Instead, President Roosevelt experimented with a large number of new laws, regulations, and policies, using the powers of government to reverse the downward trends of prices and purchasing power. Among these many, sometimes contradictory, measures, the one that most sharply challenged the orthodox theory of wages was the National Industrial Recovery Act of June 16, 1933. The National Recovery Administration (NRA) was established to put this new law into operation. NRA sought to make use of the idea of collective business responsibility advocated by Hoover but with this important difference: the force of law was to support the standards that business leaders collectively devised for themselves. In each industry, a trade association was to propose a "code of fair competition," including standards of wages, hours, selling prices, and trade practices in general. Once an industry code had been approved by NRA, the government would penalize anyone who departed from the prescribed standards of his industry.

The purpose of these "codes of fair competition" was not merely to stabilize the existing conditions of trade but to raise wage rates and reduce the standard hours of work. Instead of sharing the previously limited hours of work at existing rates of pay, the government attempted to get each employer group to pay as much as, or more than, before for a reduced number of standard working hours. Instead of allowing each individual employer to cut the price of his products in an attempt to restore his own volume of sales—a process of competition that led other employers to retaliate with even lower prices and wages—it was now proposed that all competitors in an industry be compelled to sell their products at a single set of uniform prices and specifications. The increased wages under the agreed codes would, it was contended, provide the increased purchasing power with which workers could buy the increased volume of industrial products. Thus, the *laissez-faire* doctrine was replaced, for a time, by the doctrine of collective planning. Legally enforced minimum wages were to provide a keystone for the structure of industrial "self-government" that would eliminate the unfair competition of "chiselers." By these means it was contended that increased production as well as higher wages could be made profitable for private industry.

Wages and Economic Trends, 1933-37

Any conclusions as to the effects of the NRA codes of fair competition are beclouded because the experiment lasted for less than two years, and was only one of many new measures being tried out at the same time. Nevertheless, some account needs to be given of the experience during and immediately following this drastic change in wage policy if only as a prelude to the wage regulation, the Fair Labor Standards Act of 1938, that followed.

NRA itself was brought to an end by the refusal of the U. S. Supreme Court to sanction the enforcement of one of the sanitary provisions of an NRA code. This was accomplished in the famous "sick chicken" case decided on May 27, 1935. (*Schecter Poultry Corp.* et al. v. *U.S.*, 295 US 495 or 55 US Ct 837.) This case involved only a minor code provision and did not deal with wages directly at all. However, noncompliance with code provisions had been an increasing problem for some time prior to the Schecter decision, and thus the whole NRA structure collapsed as soon as it became evident that this type of government control of private business was regarded by a majority of the Supreme Court as contrary to the U. S. Constitution.

The downward spiral of prices gave way to a "reflation" in the Spring of 1933, even before NRA officially took effect. Wholesale prices, which had fallen by 32 per cent in the years 1929-1932, rose again by 20 per cent in the years 1933-1935; then, after a pause in 1936 following the demise of NRA, rose an additional 7 per cent in the single year 1937. This upswing in average prices was both a cause and a consequence of renewed business confidence. Given business confidence, the upswing might have occurred without NRA. However, the mere prospect of NRA gave assurance that the downward spiral of prices would be arrested. Once in operation the NRA system, which encouraged sellers to agree on their selling prices, brought about further price increases as the business leaders who formulated the codes set prices at levels to insure profits. The collapse of NRA halted the prive-level rise temporarily, but by 1937 prices soared again in the absence of an official price-fixing mechanism.

Business activity certainly did begin to recover at the time the new law was first proposed; but that recovery proceeded at least as rapidly during the two years after NRA than during the two years of its existence. Employment, for example, increased by 3½ million persons between 1933 and 1935 and by an additional 3⅘ millions between 1935 and 1937. However, the business recovery was far from complete. The unemployment rate, which was probably about 3 per cent in 1929 and at least 25 per cent in 1933, was still 15 per cent of the larger labor force in 1937.

Money wages per hour of the increasing numbers at work rose under NRA as it was intended they should. For a short period during the latter months of 1933, hourly wages rose faster than did consumer prices. This resulted in a net gain in purchasing power for those who merely continued in employment as well as a much larger gain in total purchasing power for the increasing numbers who were just then becoming employed. The rise in money wages per hour was, indeed, greater than the rise in output per hour of work and the resulting increase in money costs per unit of product contributed to the rise in the prices of goods. But the "purchasing power theory" of recovery required a faster rise in wage incomes than in prices. However, the NRA codes not only raised wage rates but also reduced weekly hours of work. As a result, average weekly earnings at the end of 1934 were only 7 per cent above those of mid-1933. By that time consumer prices had risen more than 7 per cent. Thus the *employed* workers were not able to buy as much with their weekly earnings at the end of 1934 as they had before the NRA took effect. The total money income of all the workers did increase greatly as a result of the increased numbers employed. This increased the total purchasing power, which, in turn, helped to raise sales, production, and employment still further. But the parts of the NRA codes that raised wage rates did not increase the purchasing power of the three-quarters of the workers who were already employed.

During the first year after the collapse of NRA (1935-36), average *hourly* wages did not fall appreciably, as had been feared, and average *weekly* earnings even rose a little because the end of NRA restraints permitted some increase in weekly hours of work. During the second year following NRA (1936-37), *hourly* wages rose by 8 per cent, and in 1937 (as working hours continued to increase) average money earnings *per week* rose by 10 per cent. Even after allowing for the rise in consumer prices (chiefly a 4 per cent rise in 1936), there was still a real gain in the purchasing power of continuously employed workers during the two years after NRA— a slight gain per hour and a greater gain per week.

These post-NRA gains in wages, as well as the concurrent gains in employment, were largely lost again in the single recession year, 1938, as we shall presently see.

The Fair Labor Standards Act—A Replacement for NRA

The doctrine that government should enforce a minimum wage on private employers did not die with the collapse of NRA in 1935. Rather, that doctrine led to a more clear-cut re-enactment of Federal minimum wage legislation three years later and to the acceptance in the United States of government wage policies that ran sharply contrary to the orthodox wage theory of the nineteenth century.

The "sick chicken" decision that ended NRA was one of a series of court decisions that overturned key items of New Deal legislation. A bitter clash ensued between the *laissez-faire* doctrine of the majority of the Supreme Court and New Deal doctrines calling for the intervention of government in the operation of private enterprises. In the course of the struggle, President Roosevelt went so far as to propose the "court-packing bill," which would have allowed him to dilute the influence of the "nine old men" on the Supreme Court by appointing additional members of that court (and others). Roosevelt, as was often said later, "lost the battle but won the war." Congress refused to pass the "court-packing bill," but within two years the court majorities shifted their ground and proceeded to pass favorably on one piece of New Deal legislation after the other.

In spite of his bitter protests against the courts, Roosevelt never attempted to revive the "employer self-government" or the price-fixing features of the NRA. Instead, he began talking about the need for a "floor under wages and a ceiling over hours" to be established by the government itself with some participation by employers, among others, but not by means of industry-by-industry decisions of the employers alone. The need for such legislation was emphasized by the recession of 1938. The enforceability of such legislation was made possible by a dramatic Supreme Court reversal.

The business revival of 1933-1937 was brought to a halt by a sharp and unexpected setback in 1938 when, in a single year, industrial production dropped 31 per cent, employment declined by 3 million persons, wholesale prices fell by an average of 9 per cent, and even the normally sluggish consumer prices fell slightly. Hourly wages continued to rise slightly in 1938, but the curtailment of working hours—not by government order but because of reduced sales—resulted in a 7 per cent decrease in factory workers' average weekly earnings. Neither the boomlet of 1937 nor the recession of 1938 was wholly due to the lack of a legal minimum wage; but the recession began to cast doubt on the ability of private business to sustain recovery and to resist a competitive undercutting of wages should the recession persist. Under these conditions, Congress was more receptive than before to enactment of some new form of minimum wage legislation.

As for the constitutionality of minimum wage legislation, a Supreme Court decision in 1937 reversed the long-standing legal precedent. As far back as 1923, by a 5 to 4 vote, the Supreme Court had declared a minimum wage law of the District of Columbia to be in conflict with its interpretation of freedom of private contract as guaranteed by the Federal Constitution (*Adkins* v. *Childrens Hos-*

pital, 261 US 525). The same stricture presumably applied to any direct control of minimum wages by the Federal Government itself. As recently as 1936, the Supreme Court had again denied a state the power to enforce a minimum wage law (*Morehouse* v. *People, ex re Tipaldo,* 298 US 387). Then in 1937 Justice Roberts switched his vote and a changed majority of the same Supreme Court upheld the power of the State of Washington to enforce a minimum wage— at least for women workers. (*West Coast Hotel Co.* v. *Parrish,* 300 US 379.) "Liberty," said the new majority's opinion, "implies an absence of arbitrary restraint, not immunity from reasonable regulation . . . in the interests of the community." The Federal Government, as well as several of the states, hastened to act on the revised doctrine. By the end of 1938, the Congress had passed the Fair Labor Standards Act, generally called the "wage-hour law." By 1941, in the first case that came before it, the Supreme Court upheld the constitutionality of direct and general minimum wage regulation by the Federal Government. (*US* v. *Darby,* 312 US 100, 657.)

Scope and Basic Provisions of Federal Minimum Wage Laws

The right of the American Government to fix the wages and working conditions of *its own* employees has never been questioned. A slight extension of this government power has been the requirement that private firms having government contracts must meet certain labor standards for employees who perform work in fulfilling those contracts. In 1931, as wage rates began to fall during the Great Depression, the Walsh-Healy Act authorized the Federal Government to set minimum wages under its *building construction* contracts. In 1936, the Bacon-Davis Act extended this wage-setting power to almost all Federal contracts for procurement of government materials. Under these public contract laws, the minimum wage is defined as the "prevailing wage" in the locality where the contract work is performed. In practice, this "prevailing wage" has generally meant the labor union wage scale. Only a fraction of American workers have been directly affected by these public contract laws, but the minimums thus established may have influenced the wages that private employers pay on nongovernmental work. Such was the hope, at least, of the labor unions that pushed for the enactment of these laws, as it was also the fear of those employers who opposed them.

Since 1938, the Federal Government has prescribed minimum wages for industries that employ the great majority of American wage earners. The Fair Labor Standards Act and its various amendments apply to practically all nonfarming employers who are engaged in interstate commerce, whether these employers have contracts with the Federal Government or not. The constitutional phrase, "commerce between the States," has been interpreted to include processes of manufacture and services and not merely the shipment of goods from one state to another. Indeed, an employer may be required to pay the specified minimum wages even if the enterprise sells its products or services entirely within a single state provided that it receives materials, parts, or products from across a state border. An amendment to the Fair Labor Standards Act in 1961 brought under the Federal law for the first time the relatively large-size retail and service enterprises, even when their sales were confined within a single state. Because of the great variety of actual wage levels in the United States, a minimum that seems high for one locality might be absurdly low in another locality. The solution to this problem was to set the initial Federal minimum at a low level and then to raise that minimum, step by step over a period of time. During the first year of the new Act (1939), the national minimum was set by statute at 25 cents per hour—to be raised automatically to 30 cents in the second year and to 40 cents after seven years. Meanwhile the Administrator of the Act was authorized to appoint "industry committees" composed equally of representatives of employers, workers, and the public. A large number of these industry committees were appointed in the period 1939 to 1941, and they proceeded to recommend various minimum rates between 30 and 40 cents an hour that were put into effect after public hearings on each industry recommendation. By the year 1941, however, the war-stimulated inflation of prices and wages had raised most actual wage rates above the highest authorized level of 40 cents an hour.

During World War II, the government was more concerned with setting maximum limits on wages than with raising minimum wage rates. In the post-war period the industry-by-industry approach was abandoned, except for the special low-wage area of Puerto Rico, and the nationwide standard was raised progressively to 75 cents in 1950, to $1 in 1956, to $1.15 in 1961, and to $1.25 as of September 1963. Meanwhile, as we have seen, the amendments of 1961 attempted to extend the coverage of the Federal law to "interstate" or large-size establishments in retail trade, transit, construction, and gasoline service-station industries. For these newly covered workers the Federal minimum was to rise more slowly: from $1 in 1961, to $1.15 in 1964, and to $1.25 in 1965.

From 1938 to 1956 the Act and its amendments all required the employer to pay 1½ times the regular rate (whether the rate was at the minimum or not) for employee hours of more than forty per week. For the industries that were covered in 1961 for the first time, the overtime requirement was eased temporarily so that penalty overtime rates would not be required until 1963 and then only for hours of more than forty-four per week. The schedule for these newly covered industries provided for overtime premium rates after forty-two hours beginning in 1964 and then after forty hours in 1965.

Every attempt to raise minimum rates or to extend coverage of the minimum wage laws has evoked protest by the employers affected whereas labor unions since the 1930's (unlike their predecessors under Samuel Gompers) have continually demanded higher rates and universal coverage. Once established, the standards have been accepted by the employers affected with little continuing protest. There is practically no demand that minimum wages be left to the operation of market forces alone. Indeed, some employers believe minimum wage regulations are a valuable protection against the extremes of low-wage competition.

INFLUENCES OF MINIMUM WAGE REGULATION ON WAGE THEORY

From the earliest times down to the eighteenth century it was generally expected that either custom or law would regulate the remuneration of all types of labor. Indeed, the doctrine that wages should be fixed by the state still prevails in most of the world today. By contrast, the orthodox doctrine of the nineteenth century came to be that wages, like other prices, should be regulated by the forces of supply and demand in the market and, thus, that wages should be kept free from government interference. In the twentieth century, this *laissez-faire* doctrine has been challenged by a variety of social reformers, ranging from those who aim to improve the lot of individual groups of workers to those who contend that the whole economy benefits from the use of government power to control the minimum wages that an employer pays. This clash of doctrines, springing from—and partially tested by—experience has influenced wage theory in several different ways. For convenience, we may classify those influences into two groups: (1) those which relate to the over-all level of wages, and (2) those which are concerned with the wages of particular groups of workers.

General Wage Level Theories

Marxian Theory. The Great Depression of the 1930's seemed for a time to give support to the "surplus value" theory of Karl Marx. This theory asserted that real wages under capitalism would, in the long run, be no more than the amount necessary for the workers' subsistence. But capitalist investment would, at the same time, allow the workers generally to produce much more than was necessary to their collective subsistence—a surplus value. Consequently the workers as a group would not be able to buy back the whole of the output they could produce and the capitalist employers would find insufficient markets for their products. It was for this reason, according to Marxian theory, that a free-enterprise economy would be faced with increasingly periodic gluts of goods, cutbacks of production, and mass unemployment of the labor force. The predicted result was derived from the theory that wages under capitalism could not, for an extended period of time, rise above the subsistence level. The eventual solution was expected to be a revolution by the workers that would overthrow the capitalist order and establish a communistic order. Ever since 1848 communists have been interpreting each period of business depression as a proof that capitalism was about to perish as a result of its own contradictions—helped along, of course, by communist agitation of the workers. To the communists, the severe, prolonged depression of the 1930's seemed to provide decisive proof, at last, that the day of revolution was at hand.

Communist reasoning has never explained satisfactorily the fact of business revival after a depression. It is true that the wage *share* of national income tends to rise during a depression, but the *total* real wage income declines, nevertheless, because of unemployment and short-time work. Total wages rise only as the business revival itself brings renewed employment. Wage *rates* do not usually rise until after the revival is well advanced. Where then do the workers get the purchasing power to make possible the increased sales, production, and employment that occur in the revival and prosperity phases of the business cycle? The answer is not to be found in the works of Marx or his followers but in the works of Mitchell (Chapter V), Keynes (Chapter X), and their followers.

Purchasing-Power Theory. The NRA of 1933-35 represented a deliberate attempt to bring about a revival of business by raising wage rates. From Marxian theory was borrowed the idea that the prolonged business depression was due to insufficient total wage income. Rejected, however, was the Marxian solution of a worker revolution. Rejected also was the theory that employers would raise worker incomes, if only they were urged to do so, because the depressed conditions of the product markets made it impossible for employers, acting individually, either to increase employment or raise wage rates. Instead, the theory behind the NRA was that if employers acted in concert they could stabilize and raise wage rates and thus provide the needed increase in total purchasing power. Through NRA the government was to encourage this concerted action and to enforce the new minimum wages as against any individual employer who might seek to pay lower wages than the minimum set forth in the NRA codes.

The short-lived NRA was only partially successful in bringing about business recovery. Indeed, such recovery as did occur during the life of NRA might well be attributed to New Deal measures quite apart from NRA itself. The fact that after NRA employers could no longer expect wage rates to *fall* did help to end the deflationary spiral of 1929-1933 and did release deferred business expenditures. However, wages represent costs to the employers as well as incomes to the employed workers. Only for the first few months of NRA did wage rates, generally, rise faster than product prices. Thereafter workers as a whole began to lose from rising prices more than they gained from rising wage rates. To pay the increased labor costs resulting from rising wage rates and still make a satisfactory profit, employers needed to raise prices. They were able to do so through the concerted action that the NRA procedures encouraged and abetted. Total purchasing power did continue to rise from 1933 to 1937 and again from 1938 to 1939, but this increase in money income came much more from the increased volume of employment than from higher wage rates per unit of employment.

In spite of the NRA experience, the rate-raising theory for providing increased consumption has persisted. The purchasing-power theory by no means died with the "sick chicken" decision which ended the NRA. To some extent this theory was used to justify the re-establishment of nationwide minimum wage rates under the Fair Labor Standards Act of 1938. Once more, the purchasing-power theorists hoped to reduce unemployment by using government power to enforce a gradually rising level of minimum wage rates. This time the government did not encourage, nor even allow, employers to act together to raise product prices. However, the levels of Federal minimum rates since 1938 have been too low to affect directly the majority of the nation's wage earners. Hence, even if it were possible to raise total purchasing power by forcing a general rise in wage rates, the actual Federal scales of minimum wage rates have provided no real test of the theory. As for the minimum wage laws of the individual states, not only have these rates been generally lower than those of the Federal law but also the state laws, taken together, have applied to only a tiny fraction of the whole wage earning population.

Marginal Productivity Theory. The marginal productivity theory was originally intended as an explanation of the distribution of the entire national product between labor, as a whole, and the other factors of production. As such this theory provided a good general answer to the Marxists who contended that under capitalism labor, as a whole, did not receive the whole value of the national output that labor produced. The orthodox theory proceeded to demonstrate that the value that labor produced was, in fact, labor's marginal, but only partial, contribution to the whole product and that, under the assumption of the theory, labor would actually receive the whole of this, its own, contribution. The theory, then, became a justification of the doctrine that there was no exploitation of labor under capitalism.

The raising of minimum wages by law provided an apparent challenge to the orthodox theory of the level of real wages. If the government could force wages up, then, presumably, the wage share was not fixed by impersonal market forces but by government policy. Actually, however, the minimum wage experience of the United States has provided no satisfactory test of the marginal theory in its original and general meaning. The NRA experiment was too short-lived and the subsequent FLSA minimum rates were too low to change significantly the over-all labor share in the national product. It should be remembered in this connection that the marginal theory referred to real wages, not merely to money wages. Only by raising money wages as a whole more than the rise in prices can the percentage share of wages be increased. No procedure like that of NRA, which permits the concerted raising of both money wage rates and money prices generally, is likely to alter the distribution of the total national income to the benefit of wage earners. In spite of the experiment with NRA, and with other government policy changes since the New Deal period, the marginal productivity theory has proven a reasonably good instrument of prediction of the *over-all* wage share of national income. But this is only one of the questions about wages that theory has attempted to answer.

Theories of Particular Wages

When minimum wage laws were being proposed in the United States a half century ago, many leading economic theorists were predicting that such legislation would not improve the economic position of even the lowest paid workers. For example, John Bates Clark said that real wages were determined by the "specific product of labor" (his phrase for what we now call the marginal product). Any "arbitrary" action to require an employer to pay more than this specific product would merely result in the disemployment of the workers whose wages were to be raised. By contrast, forty years of experience with minimum wage requirements has shown, again and again, that it is possible to raise the wages of particular workers by government action. What, then, was wrong in the contrasting predictions of the orthodox economists? What was wrong, in part at least, was a failure to distinguish between the macro and the micro aspects of economic problems—that is, between the result in the large and the result in the particular cases. It may be true that average wage levels adjust themselves so that labor as a whole tends to receive a share in the national output that corresponds to labor's marginal product (times the number of units of labor employed). Quite different is the extreme micro proposition that any required increase in a particular wage will cause each and every worker receiving such increase to be displaced. The latter theory must suppose that *every* employer is already paying to *each* worker the maximum he can afford to pay—namely, the value of that individual's marginal contribution to the employer's revenue. In fact, most employers cannot know the separate and specific marginal contribution of each individual worker, at least not over short periods of time. Thus some parts of the national labor force may well be paid more and some less than their true marginal products, even though labor as a whole obtains a wage share that corresponds fairly well to the marginal contributions to production of the whole labor force. The rigid, extreme, and particularistic interpretation of the orthodox theory also assumed that all the factors that influence production, sales, and employers' incomes are perfectly in balance and will remain so after any law requires the payment of an increased wage. The fact is that an employer's situation is nearly always a changing one. When the law (or a labor union) compels an employer to pay higher wages, a number of other changes may occur—some the result of the increased wage and some entirely independent of the new requirement.

In considering any such general appraisal, account must be taken of the fact that the standards set since 1938 have been modest ones, considerably below those followed by the vast majority of employers in advance of any given legal requirement. Also, whether because of, in spite of, or unrelated to minimum wage regulations, the United States has escaped from any severe and prolonged business depression since the 1930's. Thus actual business conditions have not yet put the legal minimum standards under general and extreme economic pressure. Government interference, which once was regarded as economic heresy, has become a generally accepted part of the economic structure of the United States. A fringe of the more rigid followers of nineteenth-century economic theory are much more opposed to government regulations of minimum wages than are present-day American businessmen actually subject to these minimum wage orders.

The theoretical controversy has shifted to much more detailed and refined questions than that of the wisdom or iniquity of government wage control. These questions refer to the precise effect of wage regulation on the health of the economy, on the employers affected, on the employment and income of those workers, if any, whose wage rates are raised, on the prices of goods and services, and on the efficiency of management and of workers. Some observations on these questions will be made in the following sections dealing with the impact of minimum wage regulation on wage theory. Experience under the wage regulations of the various states, as well as the Federal Government, will be drawn upon in reaching these further conclusions.

Theories of Employer Adjustments to Increased Wage Rates. Doctrinaire advocates of raising minimum wages by law have argued as if wages could be set at any level the government might decree without any consequence except the desired one of increasing the incomes of the workers affected. Doctrinaire opponents of minimum wage legislation (or of raising previously established legal minimum rates) have argued, as we have seen, that employers would necessarily have to discharge all the workers whose wage rates would otherwise be raised. Out of this clash of doctrines has gradually emerged a much more careful and refined theory of employers' adjustments to an increased minimum wage.

When seeking to learn and, hence, to predict the effects of raising a wage rate, obviously one should limit himself to situations where a wage law or order actually sets a wage above the wage previously paid. It is not enough to say, as minimum wage advocates frequently do, that new wage orders have been put into effect without causing "substantial unemployment" or other adverse consequences. In the United States most of the minimum wage scales have been set, quite deliberately, below the actual wages being paid by most employers to nearly all of their employees. Such a "below-actual" legal minimum may be very useful in preventing a continuing downward spiral of wages and of expected labor costs under competitive pressures or during times of depressed markets. The question faced by every legislature or wage board, however, is the effect of a compulsory wage increase of a certain size on those parts of an industry and those employees whose actual situation would be changed by the new requirement.

In the relatively few American analyzed cases from among those where previous wages have been raised by law, the employers affected have actually made one or more of the following kinds of adjustment:

1. Absorbed the increased labor cost
2. Raised product prices
3. Improved management efficiency
4. Improved labor efficiency
5. Substituted capital for labor
6. Reduced employment

The mere recognition of these varied possibilities represents a notable advance in the theory of particular wages. What remains is to work out a logic that relates the probability of each type of adjustment to each class of situation that may surround the employer when a wage increase is compelled by law and to test that logic against actual experience. As these steps are taken, theory may be used as an instrument of prediction and thus replace the conflicting doctrines of self-interested parties that still dominate particular minimum wage decisions.

Of the six types of employer adjustments to a required increase in minimum wages, the only one with which the orthodox wage theory was concerned was the reduction in employment. It is, indeed, clear that a sufficiently sudden and drastic rise in the required minimum will bring about some curtailment of employment—and hence of wage income—at the point where wages are forced up. The problem is, how much curtailment of employment will there be in relation to how great an increase in the minimum wage. In technical language it is the problem of discovering the "elasticity" of the demand for labor. This concept of elasticity was used by economists long before minimum wage laws were proposed in the United States. It is nevertheless a central concept in predicting the net effect on employment—and thus on wage income—of the employers' many possible reactions to minimum wage laws. Because minimum wage laws in the United States have seldom imposed any sudden and drastic increase in actual wages, the practical question is not that of the effect on employment of a change such as a doubling of wages. Rather the question is what percentage reduction in employment will result from prospective small increases in the wages of the lowest paid groups of workers, assuming that the employers' adjustments take this form rather than the other forms that have been listed. This is the real problem of prediction faced by any body that is considering whether a legal minimum should be raised and, if so, by how much. Thus experience with the minimum wage movement is impelling economic theorists to refine their theories of the elasticity of the demand for labor, to develop the factors governing elasticity, and to test these relationships against actual experience under conditions where the governing factors can be known and measured.

Wage Structure

American experience with minimum wage laws has added considerably to the theory of wage structures, which is still the least developed part of wage theory. When the wages of the lowest paid workers are raised by law, what will be the effect on the wages of workers who have already been earning more than the newly imposed minimum? Is there an inevitable relation between the wages of workers in different occupations, industries, localities, and social strata, or can such wages be changed without repercussion?

When the legal minimum wage was first proposed, it was often argued that "the minimum would become the maximum." The idea behind this phrase was that an employer had just so much to spend for wages. If the lowest wages were raised, the higher wages would be lowered. This reasoning was a carry-over from the nineteenth-century "wages fund" theory under which it was presumed that some definite sums of money (or goods) were "destined for the support of laborers" as a whole. The more for some, the less there would be for others. This kind of theory implied that there was no such thing as separate structures for different kinds of wages. American experience has discredited this antistructure theory of wages. There are no important cases where skilled workers (or those in favored industries or localities) suffered a wage cut as a result of the increased wages of the lowest paid workers.

At the other extreme, employers have often contended that every kind of worker must have a wage increase of as much as the wage increase of the lowest paid workers. The most extreme contention is that every worker must have as great a percentage wage increase as that granted to the lowest paid worker. Thus if Sally has her wages raised from twenty to thirty cents an hour, this represents an increase of 50 per cent. Extremists among the employers objecting to legal minimum wages have often contended that, in such a case, the wage rates of all workers would have to be raised by 50 per cent. Such a doctrine implies a theory of absolutely rigid wage differentials.

Experience has supported neither the "wages fund" nor the rigid wage differential positions. It appears, instead, that the first result of a required increase in minimum wages will be that wage differences will be decreased. Employers will not raise the wages of everyone by as much as they are required to raise the wages of their lowest paid workers. However, over a period of time, the wages of the higher paid workers usually are increased somewhat. Wage differences between different kinds of employees are found to be necessary to the operation of business. There is, after all, a set of wage structures in our economic society. The wage structures are not rigid. Changing conditions of the many different kinds of demands for different kinds of labor skills and changing conditions of the supplies of different kinds of labor will alter the spread of wages between the lowest paid and the highest paid members of the labor force.

What the American minimum wage experience has shown is that differences in wages can be changed considerably over short periods of time. This experience has also shown that established wage differentials do exist and cannot be ignored over a long period of time. Both of these propositions are still very indefinite ones. However, experience is encouraging new developments in the theory of the relation of one wage to another wage, as well as in the other aspects of wage theory that have been discussed.

CHAPTER IX

Government Spending
and Tax Policies

The events of the Great Depression and of World War II challenged some of the formerly accepted doctrines relating to government spending and increased the importance to the nation of government tax policies. This chapter reviews the separate but related uses of deficit spending and the graduated income tax. Neither of these two policies are customarily treated in relation to the theory of wages. Yet, as we shall see, the volume of government spending may greatly affect the total volume of employment and, hence, the total wage income. Likewise, the form of taxation may modify the final distribution of personal income and hence may help to determine the level of living of the dominant group in our society, those who are paid wages or salaries.

DEFICIT SPENDING

For centuries governments of all kinds have been tempted to spend more than they collected in tax revenues. To meet the resulting deficits government bodies have resorted to new forms of taxes, to conquest, to plunder, to borrowing, to devaluing or otherwise debasing the currency, and to printing additional supplies of currency citizens were forced to accept as legal tender in settlement of debts. To combat these evils, the majority of experts on public finance, for at least the past four centuries, have insisted on the doctrine of the balanced budget. The field of public finance was indeed the first of the broad areas of economics to be developed by the economic theorists. Supporting the doctrine of the balanced budget has been the orthodox theory of currency inflation. The gist of this theory is that government spending in excess of revenue must result in a decline in the value of the currency—that is, a rise in the average level of prices when stated in the terms of the inflated volume of money. A distinction is to be made, it is insisted, between the money price of anything—labor, for example—and its true or "real" value. Workers are bound to suffer a decline in "real" wages if the government spends more than it collects in revenues, for then the price of what the workers buy rises faster than the money wages they receive.

The orthodox economists of the nineteenth century, both in Europe and America, supported a further doctrine in opposition to government spending, whether government deficits were involved or not. This was the laissez-faire doctrine of the less government the better. The theory behind this doctrine is that private buyers (who freely choose the goods and services they buy) and private sellers (who bear the costs of supplying these services) are the best judge of what should be produced and hence of how a nation's scarce resources are best allocated. Subject to what used to be a few grudging exceptions to the rule (such as public spending for national defense, maintenance of public order, and the enforcement of contracts), the orthodox position used to be that government operations were bound to be inefficient, wasteful, and graft-ridden as compared with operations conducted for private profit in free, unregulated markets.

These propositions, and something of the theory which lay behind them, will be found in any elementary textbook in economics—the more prominently displayed, the more elementary the textbook. By these standards the American Government of the 1920's was a nearly ideal government in the area of public finance. In 1929, on the eve of the Great Depression, the budgeted expenditures of the Federal Government amounted to only 2½ per cent of the value of the gross national product.[1] These Federal expenditures were a billion dollars a year *less* than Federal tax collections. To fill out the national fiscal picture one needs, of course, to take account of the operations of the various state and local governments. State and local government expenditures, taken as a whole, were about twice as great as the Federal expenditures in 1929 and their combined budgets (on the net) were approximately in balance. Thus governments at all levels, taken together, were showing an over-all annual surplus of about one billion dollars. The budget surplus and the modest scope of

[1] Sources of the statistical data used in this chapter are included in the appendix ("Bibliographical Notes").

government spending represented what was then considered a good "business-like management" of the nation's fiscal affairs.

Unintended Government Deficits, 1930-1932

As the Great Depression set in, governments at all levels and in all countries began to run large deficits contrary to their intentions. The existing set of tax rates necessarily yielded smaller revenues as the money values of private incomes and properties began to fall. To balance government budgets would have required higher and higher rates of taxation, because the revenue yield of any given tax rate was declining. At the same time there were increasing pressures on government to increase expenditure so as to furnish relief for the growing number of destitute and to provide support in time of stress for such politically influential groups as war veterans and farmers. State and local budgets felt the first impact of the increased welfare expenditures and so began running combined deficits of about one billion dollars yearly during the years 1930 and 1931. Under the traditional political doctrine that relief was primarily a local matter, the Federal Government managed to hold budgeted expenditures almost unchanged between 1929 and 1930; but its former surplus was almost wiped out during the very first year of the depression by a decline in revenues of nearly a billion dollars ($0.9 billion). By 1931, even Federal expenditures had increased by $1.4 billion, while Federal revenues dropped another billion dollars. By 1932, the third year of the depression, there was a frantic effort to bring government budgets back to balance in spite of the rising clamor for relief. The Federal and the local governments cut their combined spending by nearly 2 billion dollars. This strenuous effort to balance government budgets failed, however, because revenues continued to fall. The combined Federal, state, and local deficits in 1932 amounted to 1.7 billions in contrast with the one billion dollar surplus of 1929. Orthodox attempts to balance the budget could not cope with a 30 per cent drop in the money value of the national product—from 104 billions in 1929 to 59 billions in 1932. Deficit spending was a fact, however much the government intended otherwise.

New Deal Policies

The administration of Franklin D. Roosevelt, which began in March 1933, was widely and sharply criticized at the time by orthodox businessmen, financiers, and economists for its supposed policy of deficit spending. During the first years of the New Deal, however, deficit spending was more nearly the result of Roosevelt's diverse experiments to deal with the depression than the deliberate adoption of any new fiscal doctrine. Indeed, as a presidential candidate, Roosevelt had promised both a balanced budget and more adequate relief for the victims of the depression. Presumably, Roosevelt expected that banking reform and new legislation, to help farmers and to restore business confidence, would serve to bring about a business revival. The resulting rise in tax revenues would then cover the cost of relief. All this was to be achieved within the confines of a balanced budget. However, by the time Roosevelt was inaugurated, the need for relief expenditures was immediate and budget balancing was put aside to await the expected business upturn.

Between 1932 and 1936, Federal spending as budgeted nearly tripled (3.2 to 8.5 billions annually); and, in spite of some rise of Federal revenues resulting from the partial business recovery, the annual budget deficit in 1936 was still about 3 billions—nearly twice as great as in 1932. This Federal deficit was partly offset in 1936 by a surplus in the combined state and local budgets of half a billion dollars, but on the net all governments together were still spending some 2½ billions a year more than they were collecting in revenues.

As of 1936, even the free-spending Roosevelt was not yet convinced that deficit spending was desirable. Accordingly the Federal Government slashed its relief expenditures in 1937 by one billion dollars, even as its revenues were rising by 2.5 billions. At last, the Federal budget was almost in balance, while the state and local budgets of 1937 were actually showing a slight surplus. Roosevelt believed that business recovery was sufficiently advanced so that private enterprise could restore normal conditions without further deficit spending by the government.

The events of 1938 destroyed these bright hopes. Private business expenditures on plant, equipment, and inventories were only half as great in 1938 as they had been in 1937, and the combined total of business and consumer expenditures dropped by 2.5 billion dollars. The balanced budget had been quickly followed by a renewed business recession, even though recovery from the Great Depression had been far from complete when this slump began.

The business setback in 1938 finally led President Roosevelt to embrace deficit spending as a deliberate antidepression policy. In the face of declining revenues, Federal expenditures for 1938 were budgeted at a billion dollars more than in 1937, and in 1939 revenues and expenditures each rose by another half billion. By 1939, the Federal Government was still running a budgeted deficit of 2.3 billions while the combined state and local budgets were once again approximately in balance. Private business revived again in 1939, although the recovery from the Great Depression was still very incomplete. Unemployment had declined from about 25 per cent of the labor force as of March 1933 to an average of 17 per cent in 1939; but this latter result compared with an unemployment rate of only about 5 per cent in 1929, the last year of full business prosperity. The new doctrine of government spending to combat recession seemed to require further budget deficits, even after New Deal "pump priming" in five of the six preceding years.

Deficit Spending during World War II

Budget deficits, which had been widely condemned by business-men and economists during the 1930's, came to be accepted without question and on an unprecedented scale during World War II. Each year, from 1939 to the peak of defense spending in 1944, the gap between revenue collections and the skyrocketing rates of Federal spending was widened. By 1944, the Federal Government was budgeting a deficit of 52 billions a year—twenty times as much as the average deficits of the 1930's. Now the direct objective was not so much to create full employment as to assist America's hard-pressed allies and, after 1941, to win the war. Whatever the slogan, one economic effect of wartime deficit spending was virtually to eliminate unemployment and, indeed, to raise the total money demand for labor so high as to create acute labor shortages. The unemployment rate fell to less than 1 per cent during the War. The average weekly hours of factory workers in private industry rose from 38.1 in 1940 to 45.2 in 1944 in spite of the fact that most employers were required to pay 1½ times the established wage rate to each employee who worked more than forty hours per week. This extraordinary demand for labor resulted in a wartime redistribution of income in favor of the employed workers. While the money value of the national product was increasing by 73 per cent between 1941 and 1946, total employee compensation increased by 90 per cent in spite of the government's direct efforts to restrain price inflation by restricting wage-rate increases.

The government deficits during World War II, geared as they were to overriding defense needs, were many times greater than were needed to create a condition of business prosperity and full employment. Price inflation ensued just as any orthodox economist would have predicted. (See Chapter XIV.) However, the nation was treated to a dramatic demonstration of the influence of the govern-

ment's spending-revenue ratio on the prosperity of private enterprises. Indeed the vast war production of the United States was
accomplished without any over-all decline in the average real level
of living of the civilian population. The difference between full
employment and the 17 per cent rate of unemployment after the
partial recovery up to 1939 (along with the use of previously idle
nonlabor resources) provided the nation with enough additional real
product of military goods and services to make it possible to mount
the largest war effort in history without any over-all reduction in
civilian consumption. Having once tasted the fruits of full employment, in sharp contrast to the distress of the Great Depression, the
American people were not likely to be satisfied with a doctrine of
budget balancing in any future period of mass unemployment. The
new fiscal doctrine was that the government should gear its total
spending and tax collection to promote the fullest possible use of
the nation's available labor and resources. This doctrine meant that
budget deficits were to be deliberately incurred during depression
periods, either by increased government spending, by reduced tax
collection, or by both. The new doctrine was reflected in the
Employment Act of 1946 which, although not committing the
government to any specific measures, did proclaim the objective of
full employment (along with the objective of stable prices). It also
set up the Council of Economic Advisors to analyze the over-all
business situation and to make recommendations to the President
and the Congress as to appropriate remedies.

The new full employment doctrine is still bitterly opposed by
those who cling to fiscal standards that were orthodox in the nineteenth century. Out of this conflict of doctrines has grown a new
type of economic theory to the effect that the total real wage income
derived from the private sector of the economy is determined, to an
important extent, by the relationship between government's expenditures and government's revenue collections. This theory of aggregate demand and aggregate wage income will be outlined in a
subsequent section of the present chapter.

Some Criticisms of the Deficit Spending Doctrine

A first and most orthodox objection to deficit spending is one we
have already mentioned. This objection is based on picturing government as simply another kind of business enterprise. A private business, it is often contended, should not spend more than it receives
unless its borrowing makes possible the obtaining of income-earning
assets. Governments, it is thought, do not obtain income-earning

assets by means of deficit spending and borrowing. Thus deficit spending by governments is opposed by those who wish to see the government conform to the rules of the game applying to private business.

A second objection to deficit spending is that it increases the Federal debt. (The government debt is increased by the excess of expenditures above revenues.) Thus the total government debt in the United States (Federal, state, and local) rose from 16 billion dollars in 1929 to 48 billion dollars in 1939. That increase in government debt was, however, very small compared to wartime government debts. By 1944, when wartime expenditures reached their peak, the debt of the Federal Government alone had risen to 279 billion dollars. In the 1930's, the Federal Government incurred some 20 billion dollars of debt. During the first half of the 1940's alone, the Federal Government incurred a further 179 billions of debt. Although there was severe criticism of the debt-increasing policies of the 1930's, there was virtually no criticism of ten times as great an increase in the government debt during the wartime period.

Debts are, without doubt, a nuisance to any government. Revenues have to be raised to pay the interest on the debt and to pay off private bond and noteholders who do not accept refunding of government obligations that become due from year to year. A large government debt thus restricts the maneuverability of the debtor government. However, the most important question to be asked about any government debt is just how does the debt compare with the revenue-raising capacity of the government. Government revenues depend, at any given level of tax rates, on the total money value of private incomes. Thus if a government by incurring debt succeeds in raising private incomes, it has actually produced for itself some income-earning assets.

A third criticism of deficit spending is that it leads to an inflation of the over-all level of prices. This problem of price inflation will be dealt with in Chapter XII. This criticism, as far as it applies to fiscal policy, presumes that deficit spending will continue during years of full employment as well as during years of mass unemployment. During the 1930's, when mass unemployment persisted, there was no general rise in average prices even though government deficits were running at the rate of 2 to 3 billion dollars a year. The 2 to 3 billion-dollar deficit spending of the 1930's was too small to produce anything like full employment. The 50 billion dollar deficits of the 1940's, not only produced full (indeed, super-full) employment, but also helped to produce real inflationary pressures during World War II and also during much of the post-war period.

GRADUATED INCOME TAXES

The volume of employment, and hence the total wage income, is affected by the over-all balance between total expenditures and total revenues of government as has just been seen. Taxation, by which government revenues are obtained, also affects the final incomes that wage earners are able to retain and spend.

The most important change in American tax policy during the past half century has been the shift to graduated personal income taxes as a chief source of government revenues. Under a graduated income tax, not only is the tax liability of a person determined by the size of his annual income but, also, the larger the income, the higher the tax rate per dollar. These "progressive" tax rates not only help to obtain government revenues, but they also may help to redistribute final incomes—away from those with large incomes toward those such as the mass of wage or salary workers, who have low incomes.

Growth of the American Income Tax System

Prior to the year 1913, attempts to levy any kind of an income tax in the United States were frustrated by both administrative and legal difficulties. Ten of the American states had experimented with income taxes before 1861, but these taxes were both extremely unpopular and largely unsuccessful in raising revenue. The financial necessities of the Civil War drove both the North and the South to seek new sources of revenue. Income taxes were tried by the Federal Government for the first time during the period 1861 to 1872. Graduated tax rates were used, but the maximum rate was only 5 per cent (except for a 10 per cent maximum rate during the single year, 1864-1865). The outright exemption of incomes below $600 a year left nearly all the wage earners of the time outside the scope of this tax; but the law was so full of loopholes that the rich also were largely able to avoid the tax. Again, as in the earlier experiments of the states, this income tax proved unpopular and a poor source of government revenue. In 1894 a new attempt was made to levy income tax at the Federal level, but the U.S. Supreme Court found the law unconstitutional before it could be put into effect (*Pollock* v. *Farmers Loan and Trust Co.*, 158 US 601 (1894)). The U. S. Constitution specified that the revenues from any "direct tax" had to be apportioned between the states in the ratio of their respective populations, a requirement which made a graduated income tax impractical in view of the contrasts in per capita incomes as between the states. Tax reformers persisted and finally, in 1913, they obtained a ratification of the sixteenth amendment to the Constitution which gave the U. S. Congress explicit power to levy an income tax without state apportionment of the resulting revenues. Income taxes (including corporate income taxes, not discussed herein) have provided the major source of Federal revenues ever since World War I, thus displacing in importance the customs duties and excise taxes which had furnished 90 per cent of the Federal revenues at the beginning of the twentieth century. Two-thirds of the states and several hundred local governments also levy some form of income tax.

The practical importance of income tax was enormously increased by the Federal Government's pressing need for revenues during the two world wars. In the 1920's, after the end of World War I, income tax rates were reduced because the fiscal needs of the U. S. Treasury were then modest and also because the business-minded administrations of the 1920's were opposed to the levying of heavy taxes on the rich. By 1928, the Federal personal income tax not only still exempted almost all wage earners, but the rates on large incomes were very low by present-day standards. After generous exemptions and deductions, the rates in 1928 ranged from a mere ½ of 1 per cent on the first $4000 to 24 per cent on that part of a person's income which exceeded $100,000 per year. With the New Deal, fiscal needs increased and there was a greater disposition to tax the rich with the result that the tax rates were raised and made more steeply progressive. However, it was the fiscal needs arising from World War II that brought income tax to its present position of importance. Since the close of World War II, the high rates and broad scope of personal income tax have been retained. By the year 1959, some tax was levied on 43 per cent of all personal incomes, whereas in 1939 only 10 per cent of total personal incomes had been taxed. Since 1959 the Federal tax rates have ranged from 20 per cent on the first $4000 (after exemptions and deductions) to 91 per cent of taxable personal income in excess of $400,000 per year. In 1959 and more recently, over half of the total Federal revenue has been obtained from the personal income tax alone.

Beginning with World War II, the practical coverage of the income tax was enormously extended by requiring employers to withhold each employee's estimated tax and to remit these amounts to the Treasury at quarterly intervals. This system represented an extension of the scheme of withholding the worker's share of social security taxes (see Chapter IX below), which had been copied, in turn, from the much earlier labor union policy of having the employer "check off" union dues. The practice of withholding a substantial part of wages and salaries introduced an important new dimension to the concept of "wages" itself, the concept of "take-home" pay. While the employer's total labor cost obviously includes the whole of the workers' gross earnings (plus the cost of fringe benefits), the workers' themselves usually think of their wages as being limited to the much smaller net paychecks (after deductions) they take home.

Development of the Graduated Income Tax Doctrine

The doctrine that larger personal incomes should be taxed at a higher rate per dollar than smaller incomes can be traced back to the classical theory of rent expounded by David Ricardo in 1817. In Ricardo's time, as in many previous centuries, the larger British incomes were obtained from the rents of farm lands. Ricardo's doctrine was that the British government should repeal the "Corn Laws." These laws taxed the imports of cheap grain from abroad and thus, by restricting imports, served to enhance the rental income of the British landlords. To justify his antilandlord doctrine, Ricardo drew up a general economic theory of the contrast between costs and rents. According to this theory, the price of reproducible goods (such as wheat) had to cover the costs (such as the subsistence wage of labor) per unit of the goods as produced under the most unfavorable conditions among those which had to be used to obtain a given national supply of these goods (e.g., grain raised on the poorest land in production). Rents, by contrast, consisted of surplus incomes obtained by the lucky owners of the scarce supplies of the more productive lands. The landlords, as owners, did nothing to produce the grain. Hence the government should act to abolish or reduce the incomes from rents by abolishing the tariff duties on competitive grain from the more productive farm lands of other countries. Thereby Britain would obtain cheaper food for the workers, lower labor costs for the employers and, hence, lower prices and increased production of manufactured goods. The large incomes of the landlords would be reduced but, because these rents were not a necessary cost of production, the actual working farmers would produce as much grain as was economically justified by the market demand. Eventually, Britain not only repealed the "Corn Laws" but proceeded, in the twentieth century, to levy heavy taxes on rents and on large personal incomes of all kinds.

Ricardo had confined his tax reform doctrine to the most pressing practical issue of income distribution in his time, namely, the large incomes derived from the economically unnecessary rents of farm land. It remained for a San Francisco newspaperman, Henry George, to use Ricardo's theory of rent as the logical basis for his own attempted reform, the "single tax" (1879). Henry George observed the growth of large personal fortunes by owners of both urban and rural land. He saw the general growth of the country give these lands a scarcity value. George called rent from any kind of land an "unearned" income. His proposed new reform was to have government meet all of its expenses out of revenues obtained from a "single tax" on the rent of land. The "single tax" was to have the deliberate purpose of redistributing personal incomes by taxing away incomes from rents and by raising the after-tax real wages of labor (including, as real wages, the social services that workers would obtain without cost from the government). In spite of widespread agitation for the "single tax," this particular form was never adopted extensively. One reason was that the "single taxers" never found a practical way of separating "pure" rent from the value accruing to land due to investments (costs, which ideally were to be freed from tax). Moreover, it gradually became evident that the revenues to be obtained from a single tax on land would fall short of those needed to meet the growing expenses of government (see the Deficit Spending section of this chapter, page 126).

However impractical the specific "single tax" proposal, the social reformers of the early twentieth century continued to be shocked by the contrast between the pitifully small incomes of the lowest paid wage earners and the self-indulgent, "conspicuous consumption" of the millionaire tycoons of the time (Cf. Chapter III). The comprehensive figures on the distribution of personal incomes, which became available after the income tax was ended, served to confirm the earlier impressions of the tax reformers. Thus, in 1918, the 5 per cent with the smallest incomes (under $500) obtained only 1 per cent of total personal incomes, while the richest 5 per cent (with annual incomes of $8,000 or more apiece) enjoyed 14 per cent of all personal incomes. Again, the lowest-paid 42 per cent, including nearly all the wage earners, received only 18 per cent of total income while a group half as large in number (the 20 per cent with incomes of $1,800 or more) received nearly half of the total incomes. The reformers did not believe that such income contrasts were merited or economically necessary. They demanded that incomes be redistributed by means of "progressive" income taxes.

The economic theory used to support the progressive income tax doctrine was worked out more comprehensively by the great English economist, Alfred Marshall, as an extension of Ricardo's theory of rent (1890). In the short run, Marshall reasoned, a surplus income (income above the necessary cost of production) would be obtained by the fortunate possessor of *any* factor of production which could not be quickly increased in quantity. Marshall called this surplus income a "quasi-rent," that is, a rent-like income. The owner of a particular machine, which was needed to make a product in great demand, would, for instance, get a rent-like income far above the ordinary interest on his investment. Even a person without property would receive an income above that which was strictly necessary to compensate him for his contribution to production if his particular skill, training, or social connections kept him out of competition with the mass of unskilled wage earners.

In the United States of the early 1900's, John A. Hobson was one of the "radical" economists who supported "progressive" income taxes on theoretical grounds. Following the lead of Marshall, Hobson reasoned that the greater part of a person's superior ability to contribute to production, and thus earn a large income, was the result of advantages that had been given to him by other producers and by society as a whole. They were not the result of his own efforts and sacrifices. Thus the government, representing society, had the right to tax a part of the large income and to devote the resulting revenue to benefits for less fortunate wage earners.

The accumulation of facts concerning disparities in personal incomes helped to inspire new doctrines by social reformers in Britain and America. In response to this clash of fact and doctrine, an economic theory was slowly evolved in support of the graduated income tax. The basic elements of this theory, developed over the century prior to the enactment of effective income tax legislation in the U. S., appear in the reasoning of Ricardo, George, Marshall, and Hobson.

Limitations on the Tax Redistribution of Income

Levying nationwide taxes on the basis of personal income is now seldom questioned in the United States. But there remain many detailed administrative and legal problems. For example, how should "income" be defined for tax purposes? How much of the government's revenue should be raised by personal income taxes as opposed to taxes on corporate income, sales, imports, property, franchises, etc.? When income taxes are used by a state or local government, additional problems arise as to the location of the source of income that should, and legally can, be taxed by any particular government authority. On all of these problems, different groups of taxpayers naturally seek to promote tax doctrines which will reduce their particular tax burdens. The many detailed problems of tax policy may be set to one side, however. The issue which most affects wages is the issue of the over-all redistribution of incomes by means of graduated rates of income tax.

The following tabulation presents a general picture of the distribution of personal incomes (1) before taxes in the year 1918 and (2) before and after taxes in the year 1955:

PERCENTAGES OF TOTAL PERSONAL INCOME

Per cent of all persons, by size of income	Before Taxes		Disposable Income After Taxes
	1918	1955	1955
Lowest 20	6	4	4
Second 20	12	11	11
Third 20	14	17	18
Fourth 20	21	23	24
Highest 20	47	45	43
Total	100	100	100

Source: *Federal Reserve Bulletin*, June 1956, p. 569, Supplementary Table 6.

In 1918, only five years after effective Federal income taxes were started, the coverage and the rates of the personal income tax were too limited to have any significant effect on the over-all distribution of personal income. Thus the comparison for that year of incomes after taxes has been omitted from the simplified table as here shown. Comparing the first two columns of the table, we see that incomes before taxes were distributed very much the same in 1955 as they were 37 years earlier. Indeed, the lowest income group lost some ground between 1918 and 1955. The income share of this group (one-fifth of the total) fell from 6 to 4 per cent of the total before taxes. The highest income group also lost ground. The share of this contrasting group (also one-fifth of the total) fell from 47 to 45 per cent before taxes. Wage earners are to be found, both in 1918 and 1955, almost entirely within the three lowest income groups. The relative before-tax income of this group was unchanged over the thirty-seven year period. Both in 1918 and in 1955, 60 per cent of the persons received only 32 per cent of the total personal income before taxes.

To what extent did graduated tax rates actually redistribute income in 1955? It may come as a surprise that the redistribution of income was so very slight. In 1955 the lowest income group was relatively no better off after taxes than before. The highest income group did experience a slight reduction in their after-tax share of total disposable income, but only from 45 per cent before taxes to 43 per cent after taxes. The share of the groups represented chiefly by wage earners was hardly changed at all by the income tax. The 60 per cent with the lowest incomes retained only 33 per cent of the total after-tax disposable income as compared with 32 per cent of the before-tax income.

As for the personal income tax itself, the most interesting question as far as the distribution of income is concerned is whether the graduated rates are an illusion or whether there is some inner law of the economic system which preserves the contrasts between personal incomes, whatever the system of taxes. The evidence seems to support the thesis that Federal income taxes have been "graduated" hardly at all in their net effect, in spite of the sharp differences in tax rates. The fact is that the *lower* the individual income the *higher* the proportion of taxable income under existing laws. For example, in 1956 persons with incomes of less than $3,000 paid Federal income taxes on almost their entire income, at a tax rate of 20 per cent. By contrast, those with incomes of $1,000,000 or more, although having a top tax rate of 91 per cent and averaged, scheduled rates of 88 per cent, actually paid Federal income taxes on only 39 per cent of their whole income. Similar results are to be found from bottom to top of the whole income scale. The explanation seems to be that tax "loopholes" are much more available to high-income than to low-income taxpayers. Examples of these "loopholes" include deductions from taxable income for depreciation, depletion, and money expenses—including expenses for entertaining customers. In addition, the capital gain in the value of most property is taxed only when the property is sold and then at a much lower and ungraduated rate than the rate on ordinary income. Wage earners are seldom involved in major business transactions which would allow them to reduce the taxable part of their incomes and, in any case, wage earners can seldom afford the services of expert accountants and lawyers to help them take advantage of the technicalities of the tax laws. Thus it appears that income tax laws in the United States to date have done little to redistribute personal income. If such are the facts, then it must be concluded that the United States has not yet provided an effective test of the economic effect of any wholesale equalization of incomes by means of taxation.

IMPACT ON WAGE THEORY

Twentieth-century changes in spending and taxing policies of government have given two new directions to the theory of wage incomes: (1) They have stimulated a new theory of total employment; and (2) They have revived, on a broader scale, an old theory which stresses the rent element in the income of labor and the other factors of production.

The Theory of Employment as a Determinant of Wage Income

Unfortunately, workers who obtain their incomes from wages or salaries cannot count on stable employment. In fact, personal and family incomes of wage or salary workers are likely to depend more on the volume of available employment than on the wage or salary rate. Part of the worker's problem is his relative immobility and, hence, his inability to take advantage of the constantly shifting, specific demands for labor. But even a perfect mobility of labor would not guarantee steady incomes at times of massive unemployment. Therefore, the theory of wage income needs to include a theory of the total volume of available employment.

A modern theory of the volume of employment was put into systematic form by an Englishman, John Maynard Keynes. Keynes developed this logic as a result of his reflections on the mass unemployment of labor in Britain during the 1920's and the worldwide condition of mass unemployment during the 1930's. In the United States, neither the Hoover nor the Roosevelt administration policies of the 1930's were deliberately based on the theories of this professor. Indeed, Keynes himself was quite critical of the inconsistencies of Roosevelt's New Deal program. As so often happens, policy under the New Deal went ahead of systematic logic. Nevertheless, it was Keynes who developed a systematic theory to justify deficit spending by governments in times of severe business depression. Other economic theorists and statisticians have refined and modified parts of the Keynesian theory. The basic logic remains intact, however, and has now become an essential part of the theory of total wage income.

Keynes began by rejecting the conventional proposition—based on marginal productivity reasoning—that a general wage-rate reduction would help to solve the problem of mass unemployment. He rejected equally the NRA type of proposition that mass unemployment was to be cured by a general raising of wage rates. To cut wages across the board would undermine the bulk of consumer purchasing power. To raise money wage rates faster than the price of labor's output would increase production costs.

Keynes cut through the argument about lowering wage rates (employer inspired) or raising wage rates (labor union inspired) by focusing attention on the total of actual spending—the "effective demand" for goods and services as a whole. What was lacking in a period of general business depression and mass unemployment was a large enough volume of money spending. Who does this spending? Millions of different people and organizations. For simplicity, Keynes divided all these spending agencies into three groups: consumers, businessmen, and governments. Each of these spending groups have different sources of income and different reasons for spending or not spending.

The consumers consist largely of wage and salary workers. In the United States, for example, about two-thirds of all money incomes are derived from wages or salaries. These numerous but relatively low-paid persons spend, in any given period of time, about nine-tenths of the income they receive. Thus the chief factor in determining the money spending of private households is the total amount of income they receive.

The businessmen—the chief organizers of production—have different reasons for spending or nonspending. Their reasons for spending depend, not on current income received, but on the estimated prospect of a net profit (what Keynes called the "marginal efficiency of capital").

Governments act differently than either private households or private business organizations. The volume of government spending is determined by social purposes: not like private households, by income received, nor like businessmen, by estimated net profit. Hence, it is government spending in excess of current government revenues which is most likely to pull a nation out of a condition of mass unemployment.

One might think that the lift given to the economy by deficit spending would be in proportion to the amount of deficit spending. Actually, there is a much greater effect. Suppose, for instance, that the whole national product is valued at 500 billion dollars. Now suppose that the government spends 5 billion dollars more than it collects in taxes. What will be the new value of the national product if deficit spending is the only change in the situation? A quick answer would be 505 billion dollars (500 plus 5). This reply would be incorrect. Actually, the national income will rise by several times the 5 billion dollar amount of deficit spending.

The reason is to be found in what Keynes calls the "multiplier effect." The expenditures of government become the incomes of private firms and households. What will those who receive the extra income do with it? Mostly they will spend it. When they do, these new spendings become the incomes of still other people. If those who receive the extra income spend nine-tenths of it (saving one-tenth), then the 5 billion dollars of extra government spending will result in a 50 billion dollar increase in total money spending. Thus, when there is a large mass of unemployed labor and equipment, the effect of deficit spending will be to increase employment and total wage income by several times the amount of the increased deficit spending. That is not all. As this increased total money spending increases the sales of private organizations, the estimates of future profits will improve and total business spending will rise. Finally, the increased spending of households and business organizations will raise the tax-paying capacity and thus increase government revenues arising from any given set of tax rates. Thus government budgets can eventually be balanced under conditions of high-wage income. This would be in contrast to a balanced budget with a meager level of wage income, resulting from the waste of available, but unused, resources.

Keynes did not advocate deficit spending under all circumstances. The Keynesian prescriptions for curing mass unemployment were quite different from his prescriptions for curing a condition of general price inflation (see Chapter XIII). His logic, indeed, suggests the use of completely opposite policies, depending on whether the problem is that of widespread unemployment (hence low wage incomes) or whether the problem is that of an over-all rise in average prices.

The Theory of Rent and the Tax Redistribution of Income

The logic of the early nineteenth-century wage theory was that a free market would insure that each worker would be paid what his contribution to production was worth. The facts regarding disparities in incomes challenged this theory. The social desires (doctrines) of a series of reformers led them to seek ways of reducing the differences in personal incomes. One of the suggested methods for equalizing personal incomes was that of the graduated income tax. By this device it was hoped that the government might overcome some of the differences in incomes as between wage earners, on the one hand, and the fortunate enterprisers and owners of property on the other hand.

Government Spending and Tax Policies

The problem here raised for the theory of wages is whether a government can achieve an effective redistribution of income in favor of wage earners. More significantly, the problem is that of locating and measuring the factors which control wage incomes of individuals. The controversy over the graduated personal income tax will continue to force latter-day theorists to reconsider the formerly-accepted logic of the determination of differences in wage income. Is it rigidly determined by labor market forces or can a government—without peril to the volume of production—redistribute net incomes in favor of the relatively poor wage earners?

Incomes *before* taxes are broadly distributed in about the way that the marginal productivity theory would lead one to expect. In the more developed countries, for example, where enterprises and capital are abundant as compared to labor, incomes are more equal than in the rapidly developing countries where the supply of labor is abundant and the other factors of production are relatively scarce.

Net incomes of wage earners *after* taxes present a different problem. The orthodox logic sets out the factors which govern the income earning capacity of each individual. Thus it has been presumed that no form of taxation could change the relative net incomes of wage earners. The low-paid wage earner, according to this logic, would remain as low paid after taxes as he was before taxes. The highly "productive" enterprisers and property owners would obtain high net incomes, whatever the tax rates.

The newer logic of wage incomes is that net incomes are at least partially determined by the collective human decisions of the society. Within a wide range of market values of labor, it is now reasoned that taxation (along with union pressures) can improve the relative net incomes of wage earners. In particular, it may be possible to mitigate the extremes of income distribution by taxing away the surplus or rent-like elements of income, to the relative advantage of low-income wage earners.

Unfortunately, as we have seen, the American experience with graduated income taxes has not provided any test of the usefulness of either the older or newer theories of relative wage income. The Federal income tax is graduated in appearance, but not in fact. Even after a century of experience, we do not know how much the wage earner's net income can be improved by graduated tax rates. We do know, as did economists a century ago, that governments may well impose a tax on the "windfall" incomes of lucky enterprisers and property owners, without adverse results. Even so, we still do not know how much improvement in the lower net wage incomes can be achieved by graduated income taxes.

function so that poor relief ("welfare") payments have long been a normal expenditure of local governments. Nevertheless, the prevailing American doctrine prior to the Great Depression was that each worker should provide out of his own earnings for the protection of himself and his family against the risks of unemployment, ill-health, and old age.

This individualistic doctrine was typical of British thought at the time the classical wage theory was formulated. Continental Europe never completely accepted this doctrine of individual self-reliance. Accordingly, as the industrial revolution cut workers loose from personal ties to family and employer, continental Europeans were the first to place responsibility on government for the care of the unemployed. Bismarck used the continental doctrine of the responsibility of government to counteract the agitation of the socialists. Accordingly, compulsory social insurance against the risks of sickness, accidents, and old age was made part of the law of the new German State in the 1880's. By the end of the nineteenth century, most of the countries of continental Europe had followed the German example. In Britain the individualistic tradition survived longer but did in time change. By 1908 Britain had a national system of old-age pensions and had adopted by 1911 a national compulsory system of sickness insurance. Even more startling, Britain became the pioneer in adopting compulsory unemployment insurance. The British National Insurance Act of 1911 introduced unemployment insurance experimentally in six major manufacturing and construction industries. In 1920 the British unemployment insurance system was extended to cover all industries.

The United States clung to its frontier tradition of rugged individualism and resisted all forms of compulsory social insurance—except that against industrial accidents (workmen's compensation)—right through the prosperous 1920's. The doctrines of the social workers (see Chapter III)—aided by the labor unions (Chapter IV)—had helped to bring about workmen's compensation legislation in most of the heavily industrialized states even earlier than the 1920's. Similarly, the doctrines of welfare capitalism (Chapter VII) had, by the 1920's, induced many of the larger employers in the United States to provide pensions, group life insurance, and paid sick leave for their employees. However, except for meager savings or charitable relief, the American worker prior to the 1930's had virtually no protection against the three greatest causes of loss of income: the lack of any available job, old age, and ill-health.

Peculiarities of the American labor union and of the U. S. political structure help explain the tardy development of social insurance in the United States. Under the influence of the doctrines of Samuel Gompers, major American labor unions were opposed in principle to the government's protection of the wage earner during the entire period 1881-1930, the period when social insurance was developing in other countries. (See Chapter IV.) Union leaders believed that the worker should look to his union, rather than to government, for the protection he needed. This union doctrine prevailed even though only a fraction of American workers were union members and few of the existing unions were financially able to provide benefits to members. Government action, furthermore, was blocked by the constitutional structure of the American political system. Jurisdiction over industrial and labor matters had not been delegated to the central government by the Constitution. Thus each of the 48 states had to act to secure nationwide protection. Comprehensive social insurance, being expensive, required some form of major taxation. The burden of such taxes, when adopted by any one state, would have put employers in that state at a competitive disadvantage in national markets. Moreover, there was grave doubt whether the U.S. Supreme Court would have allowed a state to compel employers to meet the costs of social insurance. The Court had, after all, forbidden the District of Columbia to compel an employer to pay a minimum wage to a worker. (*Adkins* v. *Childrens Hospital,* see Chapter VII.) How could the courts be expected, then, to sanction any law which attempted to compel an employer to remunerate a person who was not even currently employed by him?

Behind these obstacles, and probably of greater significance in explaining the lag in social insurance, was the prevailing American tradition of self-reliance. During the prosperous 1920's particularly, the need for anything beyond individual self-reliance was difficult to see. The rising tide of prosperity, including the rise in average real wages during the 1920's, suggested that the American system of individualism was operating without serious flaw. If there were any problems, they were obscured. There were, for example, no comprehensive statistics on the numbers of unemployed or poverty-stricken aged workers, the nearest approximations being estimates derived from local rosters of those regarded as eligible for charitable relief for any reason. The resulting ignorance allowed Americans to feel smugly superior to countries like Britain which had adopted social insurance programs. Many Americans saw a cause and effect relationship between the social insurance program and the unemployment problem in Britain. In the 1920's in Britain, 10 per cent or more of the workers were unemployed. The American view was that in Britain they "paid a man not to work!"

Against this background, the change in American attitudes toward social security between 1929 and 1935 was truly revolutionary. The reality of the Great Depression clashed violently with the doctrine of individual self-reliance. Even affluent middle-income groups came to know joblessness and financial ruin during the early 1930's as a result of the debacle in the security markets, the collapse of agricultural prices, the bank and business failures, and the drastic layoffs in the executive staffs of the surviving concerns. Thus the dogma of automatic and universal prosperity for all who were willing to work and save was eroded by actual experience. As for the wage earners, reliable information on unemployment and poverty did not exist. But the mounting load of poor relief could not be ignored. In 1929 the welfare and the then minor social security expenditures of all government agencies, taken together, amounted to only 4 per cent of the nation's gross national product.[1] At the time of the passage of the Social Security Act in 1935, these welfare costs had risen to 10 per cent of the smaller national product. It was evident as early as 1930 that millions of formerly employed workers were being forced to live on some form of charity. Some measure of collective responsibility for relief of the unemployed came to be accepted. How this social responsibility was to be discharged became the overriding issue.

Voluntary private charity was an early casualty of the mounting relief load—in spite of the frenzied efforts of social workers—because the financial means of the well-to-do supporters of private charities were themselves sharply curtailed. Public relief had been almost exclusively the responsibility of local governments, but these resources also proved inadequate. (Cf. Chapter IX.) Local tax revenues declined as the depression deepened and many localities and states were unable even to borrow the relief funds. The Federal Government under President Hoover was reluctant to depart from the tradition of the local community's responsibility for the care of its impoverished residents; but the needs of the unemployed could not be met without recourse to the broader borrowing capacity of the U. S. Treasury. Thus, to preserve the appearance of local autonomy, the Reconstruction Finance Corporation, a Federal agency, lent relief money to the states. The states, in turn, lent money to cities, towns, and counties which, in turn, distributed the doles.

With the advent of the Roosevelt administration in 1933, the Federal Government embarked on a massive and unprecedented

[1] Sources of the statistical data used in this chapter are included in the appendix ("Bibliographical Notes").

direct relief system of its own, administered at first by the Federal Emergency Relief Administration (FERA). This temporary agency met the worst of the relief emergency, but it proved a very unsatisfactory solution. The vast new system was difficult to administer. It was subject to frauds and was very expensive. Gradually the Federal Government substituted for FERA the Works Progress Administration (WPA) and the Civilian Conservation Corps (CCC). These agencies required that recipients prove that they were destitute (pass the "means test") and, also, if able bodied, engage in some assigned work ("work relief"). The work relief system helped to eliminate fraud, but was widely criticized for not being useful or for competing unfairly with private enterprise. Moreover, the per capita expense of work projects was even greater than direct relief. In addition, like direct relief, available funds depended on annual appropriations from an increasingly restive Congress and were thus uncertain. Finally, it was especially difficult to justify any particular scale of work relief payments. If prevailing wage rates were not paid, the system was in danger of undermining established wage scales. If prevailing rates were paid, the appropriate rates had to be determined separately for each locality and the payments might prove too great in relation to the useful work accomplished. Yet because the recovery of private business was slow and incomplete throughout the 1930's and because the financial capacities of state and local governments remained inadequate, the Federal Government could not escape this new responsibility. Even after the partial recovery of 1933-1935, the Federal Government was spending almost as much for the relief of the destitute as all the state and local governments combined. This was in sharp contrast to Federal expenditures in 1929 which were only 15 per cent of the total (mainly in the form of farm and veteran's benefits).

This account of social security in the twentieth century depicts one of the major changes in the determinants of the income of wage earners. Speaking broadly, the Social Security Act of 1935 established for those able to work a national system of compulsory insurance against the risks of unemployment, loss of income due to advancing age, and loss of income to survivors resulting from the death of the wage earner. The original legislation has been amended many times since 1935, but almost without exception the changes have been in the direction of extending the scope of coverage and of liberalizing the benefits provided. Abandonment of the system has never been seriously contemplated. Earlier state unemployment compensation laws had provided some guaranteed protection against disability arising from accidents occurring on the job. The major income loss for which the American wage earner still lacks guaranteed protection is that caused by ill-health— except, of course, for the relatively few instances of ill-health arising from industrial accidents.

Social security benefits, unlike public or private charity, are provided as a legal right of the worker without the degrading necessity of proving destitution. Eligibility to receive social security benefits is established by the fact of previous paid employment. The amount and duration of benefits is governed to a considerable extent by the amount of the worker's previous wages and the duration of his previous employment. Thus the American social security system has become an integral part of the wage system itself.

The compulsory aspect of the social security system takes the form of a Federal tax on payrolls. The Federal tax to support unemployment benefits is a legal obligation of the employers alone. The tax to support the old age and survivors' benefits is divided equally between employees and employers. The employer must remit to the government the whole of the old age tax, as well as the unemployment tax, but the employer is entitled to deduct the worker's portion of the old age tax from the worker's paycheck. The combined social security contribution rates have risen from 5 per cent of payrolls in 1937 to 10 per cent of payrolls in 1963. They are scheduled (as of 1964) to rise to a total of 12 per cent by 1969. The annual proceeds of these taxes exceed 10 billion dollars. Unlike European social security systems, the United States system is financed by means of the special payroll taxes without a direct contribution by the Federal treasury. Thus the payment of benefits is independent of legislative appropriations and, indeed, neither the collected revenues nor the benefit expenditures appear anywhere in the Federal budget statements. In most years, social security revenues have exceeded benefit payments by a wide margin. On the other hand, the automatic increase in future claims—due to the lack of previous lifetime coverage for the present population and to the increase in the average age of the population, together with successive liberalization of the benefits—make even the vast present social security reserves inadequate to meet the estimated cost of the presently stipulated old age benefits.

Social security benefits fall far short of compensating American workers in full for the loss of income during unemployment and after retirement. In addition, they have provided no protection against the major risk of disabling sickness. Severe limitations are imposed on the duration of unemployment benefits, on the portion of past wages the worker may receive as unemployment or old age benefits, and most important, on the maximum dollar amounts of the benefits. These and other limitations are not pertinent to our present discussion, however. The impact of social security on theories of wages arises primarily from income losses which are compensated rather than from those which are not.

IMPACT ON WAGE THEORY

Eventually, the theory of wages must take account of the changes introduced by social insurance as well as the public policy choices involved in different social security programs. So far, remarkably little has been done to integrate consequences of social insurance with the theory of wages, considering that social security has existed in Germany for more than 80 years, in Britain for more than 50 years, and in the United States for more than 25 years. Indeed, social insurance seems to have been given more attention by historians and political scientists than by economists. Instruction in labor economics often does include descriptive material on the risks faced by the modern worker and the measures proposed to help him cope with these risks. However, the wage theories presented or implied usually ignore social insurance completely. The following comments are limited, therefore, to some tentative suggestions as to the impact of social insurance on wage theory. No well-rounded theoretical statement can be offered at this time.

Worker Freedom and Economic Welfare

The individualistic wage theory of the nineteenth century depicted the worker as maximizing his economic welfare by making a free choice between work and leisure and between alternative employment opportunities. The uncertainty of a worker's income was treated no differently than the risks faced by a merchant or manufacturer. Presumably the more risky the employment, the higher the current income to be obtained in a free market. Moreover, the individual was considered the best judge of the risks he might face and was expected to meet these risks. He might choose to be self-insured by setting up his own reserve. (i.e., saving); or he might buy insurance and thus pay others to bear the risks for him. From this individualistic reasoning, it followed that any kind of compulsory social insurance would reduce the economic welfare of the worker by curtailing his freedom of choice.

The modern wage earner's lack of knowledge, lack of foresight, and lack of means may make such reasoning seem absurd to some. Yet this reasoning is the substance of one of the still current, historic arguments against compulsory social insurance. Unemployment insurance was opposed partly because it was felt that those workers who were subject to unusually irregular employment were compensated by higher wage rates on irregular work. Compulsory old-age pension and survivor-benefit proposals were opposed partly because it was believed better for the individual worker to save to provide for his own old age and, if necessary, to buy annuities or life insurance from private companies to fit his individual needs. Compulsory health insurance is currently being opposed in the United States partly because it is felt that individual needs for hospital and medical care differ widely and are best judged by the worker-buyer and his personal physician-seller, and because private health and hospitalization policies are available to anyone who wishes to protect himself against uncertain future costs of illness.

The contrasting views of the adherents of social insurance doctrines are too well known to require repetition in this place. However, the clash between the doctrines of individualism and of the welfare state will not be resolved until the logic of wage theory considers the consequences of each in precisely defined circumstances. As this is done, the choices of policy will be seen to involve variations in degree, rather than categorical choices between the extremes of freedom and compulsion. If it is absurd to assume that complete individual freedom will automatically provide maximum lifetime welfare for the worker, it does not follow that the greatest workers welfare would be obtained by substituting complete government services for the worker's money wage.

Payroll Taxes and the Demand for Labor

Social security programs in the United States, unlike those in most other countries, have been financed entirely by means of payroll taxes. Political, rather than economic, considerations seem to have led to this choice. The framers of the American legislation were anxious to avoid "dole from the public treasury," a stigma attached to many relief programs and, in the 1920's, to British unemployment benefits themselves. They believed, perhaps rightly, that social security benefits would be less vulnerable if the costs were paid for in advance and in proportion to the earnings of workers. This would establish the workers' rights to benefits and would avoid having the benefits considered a public charity dependent upon appropriations from the Congress or state legislatures.

Whatever merits payroll-tax financing may have, it is a tax on employment. According to orthodox wage theory such a tax reduces either the amount of labor demanded, or the wages of labor, or both. This conclusion follows from the orthodox demonstration that the wage which any employer can afford to pay will be equal to the marginal contribution to his net revenues of the number of workers engaged. A tax directly related to the amount the employer pays in wages would decrease by the amount of that tax the employer's net revenues and thus either reduce the wages he could afford to pay, or the number of persons he would choose to retain in employment, or perhaps both to some extent. By contrast, if social security benefits were paid for out of general government revenues, the costs would fall on all taxpayers in accordance with the general schedule of taxes. As Federal Government revenues are now raised chiefly by means of progressive income taxes, the additional costs of social security benefits if paid for out of general revenues would have fallen more largely on those with the greatest ability to pay. In any case they would have produced less downward pressure on wage rates or employment than do payroll taxes.

Apart from the political considerations mentioned above, the choice of payroll taxes seems a strange one for an Administration determined to raise wages and to cope with conditions of acute unemployment. The Administration either faced a hard choice or else did not believe the implications of orthodox wage theory.

It might be contended that the original payroll tax of 5 per cent (3 per cent unemployment tax on the employer plus 1 per cent each on employer and employee for the old-age insurance tax) was not large enough to reduce materially the demand for labor. Now that payroll taxes have reached a total of 10 per cent (3 per cent unemployment tax plus 3½ per cent each for old age insurance) and are scheduled to go higher, it may be well for economists to consider whether orthodox wage theory needs to be modified or whether at least a partial substitute needs to be found for the payroll-tax method of financing social security benefits. In this connection, consideration needs to be given to the subsequent discussion of the influence of social security benefits and revenues on the stabilization of the economy.

Experience Rating

Thus far American social security taxes have been discussed as though levied at a uniform rate for all employers. Such is the case outside the United States, when payroll taxes are used, and such is the case with the Federal payroll tax to support the old age and survivors insurance in the United States. However, the unemployment tax is subject to experience rating—that is, employers whose layoffs occasion relatively small claims for unemployment benefits are assessed unemployment taxes at less than the standard 3 per cent rate. At least five different types of experience-rating tax formulas are used in the various states, permissible tax rates ranging from 4 per cent of payrolls down to the Federal minimum of 0.3 per cent.

The avowed purpose of the variable rate is to provide an incentive for the employer to prevent unemployment by stabilizing his own demand for labor. This unique American concept has a curious history. During the 1920's and early 1930's, American courts almost certainly would have invalidated any insurance plan which compelled an employer to pay the costs of benefits to persons who were not under a contract of employment with him. Yet the courts did permit states to enforce workmen's compensation laws which assessed the cost of stipulated benefits against an employer on whose premises an accident to a worker had occurred. The courts sanctioned this exception to the constitutional guarantees of individual property rights partly because accidents are preventable. The logic is that an employer is prompted to prevent accidents if he has to pay benefits to injured employees. John R. Commons (Cf. Chapter V), in seeking a supportable legal basis for unemployment insurance, drew an analogy between workmen's compensation and what he therefore called "unemployment compensation." He reasoned it would be constitutionally valid and socially desirable to compel each employer to pay the stipulated costs of compensation for unemployment he, the employer, caused by his own layoffs. Commons and his followers popularized the concept of the employer's individual responsibility for unemployment, the possibilities of regularizing employment by each employer, and the need for unemployment compensation laws. These measures were advocated —not just to help meet the needs of the unemployed workers—but also to give the employer an incentive to prevent unemployment much as workmen's compensation had stimulated the "safety first" movement.

Prior to the Federal Social Security Act of 1935, Wisconsin was the only state which had passed an unemployment compensation or insurance law (1932). This law followed Commons' prescriptions, originally providing for a separate unemployment reserve fund for each individual employer and limited any worker's benefits to those which could be paid out of the separate fund of his previous employer. An employer's contributions could cease once his reserve had reached the required size. Thus an employer would gain if he avoided layoffs and thus the drain on his reserve fund. Commons' followers were, appropriately, very influential in framing the Federal Social Security Act of 1935. There appeared to be need for a law to build on, rather than overturn, the one existing compulsory unemployment benefit law. As it happened, the change in U.S. Supreme Court opinion following President Roosevelt's unsuccessful "court packing" proposal (Cf. Chapter VIII) made unnecessary any analogy between unemployment compensation and workmen's compensation in testing the Social Security Act of 1935. But the idea that unemployment was preventable by action of the individual employer, if only he were given a financial incentive to stabilize his own demand for labor, became part of the American social security doctrine.

The logic of gearing the unemployment tax to the layoff experience of the individual employer seems to have limited application to the general problem of stabilizing workers' wage incomes. It is true that seasonal swings in production can be ironed out somewhat by producing for stock in off-seasons, by giving off-season discounts to customers, and by shifting the assignments of particular workers. Indeed farsighted employers have found such a course of action profitable as well as humane. But major causes of unemployment are due to industry-wide and economy-wide deficiencies in product demands and, therefore, in labor demands. These are usually beyond the power of any individual employer to control or to offset. If major causes of unemployment were preventable by the individual employer, employers would already have had a more than sufficient incentive to regularize their operations. By regularizing their operations, they would be able to spread overhead costs more completely and avoid much of the cost of labor turnover.

The issue might not be an important one if it were not for the fact that variable unemployment taxes have some positively undesirable effects. Industries with a steady demand (such as banking) are given a higher "merit rating" (a lower tax rate) than those subject to irregular and seasonal demands (such as apparel manufacture); but surely the difference in their layoff experience is not due to any comparable difference in the "merit" of these groups of employers. Moreover, the incentive is to reduce the tax, whether unemployment is prevented or not. Employers seek to get the benefit claims of former employees disallowed in order to keep their taxes down. The various states try to attract new enterprises by using benefit formulas designed to keep their unemployment tax rates low. The result is that reserves to meet depression needs are insufficient.

Benefits, Revenues, and Stabilization of the Economy

The previous discussion of government spending and taxation has touched upon government fiscal operations as determinants of wage income (Chapter IX). That discussion did not include the effects of social security operations because these are handled independently of budgeted government expenditures and revenues.

Taking the quarter century of social security operation in the United States, total tax collections have so greatly exceeded benefit expenditures that reserves of some 30 billion dollars have been accumulated. Even these reserves are inadequate to meet future old-age benefit claims. Further increases in tax rates will be necessary. However, while these reserves are being built up, the social security system has been operating to reduce private incomes through taxation more than it increased them through benefit expenditures. Thus social security has acted generally as an anti-inflationary force and as a depressant on the total demand for labor.

In recession years, however, social security tax collections automatically fall as payrolls decline and expenditures automatically rise as more benefit claims are paid. The greatest variation in benefit claims naturally takes place in the unemployment-benefit segment of the system and, in fact, these benefit payments exceeded unemployment taxes in each of the following readjustment or recession years: 1946, 1949, 1950, 1954, 1955, 1958, and 1960. When the OASI operations are included, the years of net deficit spending are fewer due to the building up of reserves for future old age and survivors claims; but there was still net deficit spending by the combined social security system in 1949, 1957, and 1958.

Social security—and unemployment compensation in particular—is now generally recognized as one of the "automatic stabilizers" of the economy. It is automatic because neither the tax relief nor the additional spending depend on decisions and legislative action at the time of the need. Both are built in to the permanently established system of taxes and expenditures. This consideration is very important because government decisions taken after a recession or an inflationary boom has begun are likely to be delayed too long to have the maximum effect in stabilizing aggregate demand. While statisticians are diagnosing the situation, while congressional committees and congressmen are attempting to arrive at a concensus as to the measures to be taken, and while necessary legislation, regulations, and authorizations are in preparation, the economic situation changes, perhaps for the worst. By contrast, the social security system operates promptly as an offset to both recessions and booms and at an early stage of either dislocation. Even relatively small total amounts of deficit spending or surplus accumulation may be effective if they are timely. From this standpoint, there is more to be said in favor of payroll tax financing than previously appeared in the discussion of the payroll-tax aspect of social security operations. In any case, the theory of total wage incomes needs to be elaborated to take account of the particular operation of social security expenditures and revenues, as well as of general government spending and tax collection.

The Social Minimum and the Labor Supply

Opponents of social insurance have often argued that wage earners would be unwilling to work if they had a right to a minimum income while not working. Experience has proven this extreme contention false. However, it is reasonable to suppose that the scales of assured social security benefits do influence to some extent the minimum price at which labor is available for employment. Thus the payment of social security benefits has helped to stimulate new attention to one of the oldest problems of wage theory—namely, what factors determine the supply of labor and how do they operate.

Nineteenth-century theory never did explain very satisfactorily the relation between wages and the quantity of labor. In the first half of the century, economists were chiefly concerned with the long-run relationship. Malthus, Ricardo, and Marx (speaking of the situation under capitalism) all reasoned that even a wage level which provided incomes just high enough to forestall starvation would result in an infinitely large supply of labor and, hence, that wages could never permanently rise above this starvation level. This thesis came to be known as the "iron law of wages." British experience later in the nineteenth century made it clear that wages could be raised and held very much above this physical starvation minimum, without the necessity of a population explosion. Thereupon the neoclassical economists of the latter half of the nineteenth century explained that social institutions, rather than any physical "iron law," would determine the number and quality of the labor supply. Such reasoning opened up new outlooks, but still did not produce any consistent and coherent theory of labor supply. The end of the century did witness the development of the marginal productivity theory of wages; but this theory, even if adequate, assumed rather than explained the number of workers which would be available for employment and thus was, and is, entirely a theory of labor demand. Even the more recent theories of Keynes and his followers consist of reasoning about the aggregate demand for labor and contribute nothing to account for the size of the labor supply.

The operation of the social security system and the fuller information now available about the size and characteristics of the labor force and of the unemployed have induced economists to think with fresh minds about the relationships between wages and the supply of labor. The new approach to the logic of the supply of labor involves the concept of a social minimum income (in any community and for each type of labor) which is believed to be a key factor in determining the quantity of labor available at any given wage and, conversely, in determining the lowest actual wage required to obtain any given quantity of labor. The scale of social insurance benefits is considered to be one of the elements of this socially determined minimum. Social security benefits are thought of as an important determinant of workers' expectations and thus determinants of the low end of the range of wages which may be paid.

Much more than social insurance benefits are involved in the social minimum, of course. Such factors as the minimum wages legally permissible (see Chapter VIII), the wage standards set by labor unions (see Chapter XI), and the wage-plus-benefit standards of employers (see Chapter VII), all help to make up the social minimum which underpins the wage structure and governs the labor supply.

One of the bolder uses of the social-minimum concept in explaining the total labor supply is that of Clarence D. Long. Until quite recently, Professor Long's researches had led him to the conclusion that there was little, if any, relationship between changes in the average wages of American workers and any changes in the long-run supply of labor. Long's more recent work begins by observing that five-sixths of the unemployment in the United States between 1947 and 1960 was of the kind which prevails even in the years of greatest demand for labor. Hence Long argues that the "creeping unemployment" of our times has not been due to any lack of a total money demand for labor, but rather to a rise in the social minimum which has been out of line with the productivity of the "stragglers" in the labor force. These "stragglers" may be physically able to work, but they are those workers who have not been able to keep up with the improved education and training of the great majority of American workers and who thus have become more or less permanently unemployable at the social minimum levels of wages and performance which have been generally achieved. It would seem to follow that reduction in the relatively high levels of unemployment now prevailing requires either a reduction in the social minimum or a raising of the productive capacity of the "stragglers." Otherwise, according to this analysis, we shall be faced with higher and higher rates of unemployment, regardless of any increase in the total money expenditures on labor (i.e., any increased demand for labor).

Professor Long's thesis has been cited as an example of one of the more challenging new theories of the labor supply and, hence, of the relations between wages, employment, and unemployment. Economists are still far from working out an adequate theory of the overall labor supply, but Long's reasoning illustrates the impact of twentieth-century facts, doctrines, and institutions on the further development of one of the older subjects of wage theory. The conditions relating to the labor supply in modern America are certainly quite different from the semi-starvation conditions in Britain of two centuries ago or, indeed, of most parts of the world today. Modern wage theories are in the process of catching up with the new developments. In some respects, such as the provision of guaranteed minimum pensions, the social security system operates to limit the labor supply by inducing early retirement. In other ways, such as the provision of a guaranteed minimum income during unemployment, the social security system may be operating to hold up the minimum price at which labor can be obtained thus increasing the number of workers who are not employable at the minimum wage the employer must pay. These generalizations are not very meaningful without a more detailed specification yet to be developed of the relevant conditions of the labor markets in which the relationships are presumed to exist. In spite of the great progress during the last thirty years in statistical measurement of the labor force and its characteristics, much remains to be done in defining the factors governing the size, quality, and adaptability of the labor force and thus in gearing statistical measurement to a scheme of logical analysis of labor supply in relation to wages.

CHAPTER XI

Growth of Labor Union Power

In 1920, at the height of the business boom which followed World War I, American labor unions had a combined membership of about 5 million.[1] This was equal to 20 per cent of all the workers seeking employment outside of agriculture (cf. Chapter IV). After the sharp, but short, business depression of 1921, union membership dropped to 4 million. Thereafter, union membership continued to decline during the prosperous 1920's. By 1929 the combined membership was only 3 ½ million, or slightly more than 10 per cent of the increased numbers of nonagricultural workers. Relative to the working population the unions were hardly any stronger in 1929 than they had been in 1910. "Scientific management" and "welfare capitalism" (cf. Chapters VI, VII) seemed to be prevailing over the doctrines of the labor unions. Many observers predicted the eventual demise of unions.

These predictions seemed well supported as the Great Depression of the 1930's continued to sap union strength. By 1933 the unions claimed no more than 3 million members. In view of the drastic decline in the industrial labor force during the early 1930's, the membership total represented 11 ½ per cent of the nonagricultural workers of 1933. However, effective union strength declined much more than is suggested by the figures of claimed membership. A considerable, although unknown, proportion of the 3 million consisted of former members who had ceased to pay union dues and

---

[1] Sources of the statistical data used in this chapter are included in the appendix ("Bibliographical Notes").

who were certainly in no position to exercise collective unfluence over wages or working conditions.

The New Deal period of the 1930's witnessed a dramatic rebirth of American union strength. This unprecedented growth continued throughout World War II. In 1939, on the eve of the War, union membership had reached 9 million, or 29 per cent of all nonagricultural workers. At the end of the War in 1945, there were nearly 15 million union members. This number represented 36 per cent of a civilian labor force that had expanded by one-third during the six war years.

Actually the influence of unions between 1933 and 1945 increased much more than the membership figures suggest. The once powerful United Mine Workers had revived from a state of near collapse. For the first time in history, the unions effectively organized the basic mass-production manufacturing industries of steel, aluminum, auto and aircraft, as well as major branches of other metal-working industries. In these basic industries, including coal mining and railroad and ocean shipping, practically all of the manual workers were union members. Moreover, under the National Labor Relations (Wagner) Act of 1935, a union which proved that it represented a majority in any recognized jurisdiction became legally entitled to bargain with the employer on behalf of all the employees in that jurisdiction. Thus unions with few if any members in some parts of an industry or occupational group were sometimes able, jointly with the employers, to determine effectively the wage levels for the entire industry or occupation. As in the past, labor unions were frequently able to bargain effectively for all of an industry's workers in a locality or a region, even though they were weakly organized in other areas—and such bargaining could effectively determine the area wages if the product or service did not compete closely with those produced elsewhere or if the organized area was in a superior economic position. In this way unions became the locally dominant wage-setting agency in such employments as building, printing, and barbering, in local and regional trucking and taxi service, on the docks, in meat packing, in lumber and nonferrous metals, and in some major branches of the electrical and metal-fabricating industries.

After the close of World War II, labor union strength levelled off. As compared with the 15 million membership in 1945, membership in 1962 was still only about 16 million. This represents only one-third of the expanded working populations, excluding agriculture. Nearly all of the individual unions have maintained about as large a membership as they had in 1945, but only a few have shown any significant further growth. New organization of the previously unorganized and the attainment of recognized bargaining rights in new situations are proving more difficult. This is partly because the earlier wave of unionism had skimmed off those groups most easily organized and partly because new restrictions were placed on unions by the Labor-Management Relations (Taft-Hartley) Act of 1948. The unions have had little success in recruiting new members in the largely unorganized South, in the smaller communities throughout the country, or in the smaller-sized plants and companies. Moreover, unions have had little appeal to the "white collar" groups of clerical, sales, service, administrative, and technical employees, and it is precisely these groups of nonmanual workers which are growing—both in absolute numbers and relative importance. Nevertheless, no one is now predicting, as many did in the 1920's, that labor unions have been outmoded. For the time at least, labor unions have been "contained"; but they show no signs of being routed. Indeed many people feel that unions are still "too powerful" especially in their exercise of so-called monopoly power in the setting of wages.

CONFLICT OF WAGE DOCTRINES

The growth of American unions to a position of national power was no tea party. In the early days of NRA, thousands of workers flocked to join unions faster than the decimated ranks of the leaders could enroll them. Millions of workers became zealous members who had never thought of joining a union before and whose families had no tradition of unionism. In many instances, the rank and file got out of the control of the leadership, were quick to strike, and sometimes took violent action in the new-found belief that collective action could accomplish almost anything. Most of the employers who found themselves face to face with union demands had never dealt with any union before, except perhaps some conservative craft unions. Unionism was almost inconceivable to the management leaders of the great corporations in the basic manufacturing industries, especially to those who had prided themselves on their paternalistic care of their employees. They thought that workers should be as loyal and as grateful to the company as the executives who surrounded them. Right up to the entry of the United States into World War II, strikes were still taking place in major industries because the right of a union to bargain on behalf of workers was still questioned. To a large, if not dominant, segment of management, the mass union movement represented an unconstitutional plot of "that man in the White House." This is not the place to recount even the major incidents in the sometimes violent struggle. What is pertinent is an account of the clash of doctrines that led to further questioning of the accepted theories of wages.

Management Doctrines

Only a minority of American employers were used to bargaining with labor unions prior to the 1930's; these employers were largely in the local building and printing trades or on the then largely noncompetitive railroads. For most other employers, wage negotiations with unions were few and involved no more than a small minority of their more skilled workers. Hence they seldom faced the problem of arriving at a companywide decision, involving the proceeds of the business, in agreement with a union negotiator who could not be discharged by management. The vast majority of employing companies agreed that unions were iniquitous. They defended management doctrines by means of two, apparently inconsistent, theories: the nineteenth-century wage theory of impersonal determination of wages by competitive market forces, and the twentieth-century theory of welfare capitalism that wages were (and should be) determined by the policy decisions of management for the welfare of all.

The first theory, if applicable, would have made unions unnecessary and ineffectual, as most British economists of the first half of the nineteenth century believed them to be. The trouble was that the same theory would have left no room for management decisions on wages. If the price of labor, along with the prices of materials, machinery, power, transportation, and investment funds, and the selling prices of the products or services, were all precisely determined by "the law of supply and demand," and if technical methods were uniform and themselves competitive, then management did nothing but order the indicated resources and fill the orders of customers. Here lay no justification for business profits, except enough to pay off the investors and pay what amounted to a wage to the management personnel who took their reward in the form of profits rather than as a salary. The classical economists, indeed, had forecast just such a minor role for management and profits.

The observed facts of American life belied this theory, at least as applied to the individual business enterprise. Moreover, the results of the competitive theory of wages were inconsistent with the self-image of management personnel. This perhaps exaggerated image was that of highly trained and experienced teams making important decisions on which the fate of industries, and even the nation, depended, not to mention the true welfare of employees. Business concerns made profits, they said, because of the superior decisions which guided them. Businessmen deservedly earned those profits because of the small supply and great demand for the services of such gifted individuals. But if this second theory were applicable, wages were not impersonally determined after all. Rather they resulted from important management decisions. If unions sought to influence those wage decisions, the management answer had to be that businessmen knew their business better than the man in overalls or the outside agitator who sought to represent him.

Union Doctrines

Labor unions, consisting as they do of workers who decide to be represented by a union, show an even greater diversity of wage doctrine than do business managements. In the formative period of the American labor movement, say prior to 1910, almost every kind of social, economic, and political philosophy had been represented by union leaders. By the 1930's, however, only the two extremes of communist and business-union doctrine were of importance.

Communist doctrine was by now different from the disembodied yearning of the Marxists prior to World War I. Now it was led, instructed, financed, trained, and disciplined by agents of Soviet Russia and their knowing or unsuspecting followers. The wage demands of union leaders who fell under this influence consisted of approximately what the Soviet Russian government said they should be at any given time. Apart from tactical shifts in the "party line," the Marxian doctrine was the same as it always had been, namely that all the earnings from production were created by labor, that profits represented exploitation of the workers, and that the welfare of the workers could never be improved permanently until they rose in revolution to dispossess the owners and managers of all private property used for production and sale to others. According to Marxian doctrine, the size of the wage demand mattered less than that the demand itself should be a step in the direction of attaining the "inevitable" destruction of the capitalist economic order. Communist doctrine has never been supported by more than a tiny fraction of the American working men; but it has weakened the effectiveness of the unions, both by causing internal disruption within the labor movement, and by giving opponents of unions damaging grounds for antiunion tactics. A harassed businessman, confronted by the unfamiliar union opposition to his accustomed ways of conducting his affairs, may perhaps be forgiven for sometimes feeling that all unions are communist inspired.

In the 1930's and 1940's, as in the beginning of the century, the vast majority of union leaders and union members accepted the existing economic order and were quite content to leave the basic management of business to the owners of capital or their representatives. They accepted, moreover, part of the second of the two management doctrines—namely that managements do make decisions and that wages are so determined. The clash of doctrine involves the nature of these management decisions on wages and other working conditions. Business-minded unions simply do not believe that a unilateral management decision on the wages to be paid will be in the best interests of the workers who, individually, have little choice except to abide by the decision or quit and be replaced by someone who is less demanding. Thus the great majority of American unions believe that wages will be higher if determined jointly by representatives of management and of the workers, subject to the right of workers as a group to withhold their services (strike) if they are not satisfied with management's response to their demands. Though most American unions have no objection to profits in principle, they believe that profits will be higher than they need to be if management is allowed to buy labor at the lowest price it can get individual workers to accept. In short, union doctrine is that wages can be raised by collective bargaining—at the expense of profits if necessary—and to as high a level as other managements in comparable enterprises have shown they could pay. What would be the resulting wages or increase in wages? Union leaders do not pretend to know. They simply believe that management can be induced to pay more than management would voluntarily pay and that the only way to find out how much more is to test out each situation by presenting demands for higher wages and then by bargaining, like businessmen, to get the best terms possible in each situation.

Up to this point, the union doctrines after 1933 do not seem to be very different from those of the business unions of earlier periods (Chapter III). The conflict with management was more intense than before, but its logic remained much the same. However, the mass unionism of the 1930's added at least three fairly new dimensions to the doctrinal clash: the internal craft versus industrial union conflict, the pretense of unions that pressure on wages was in the public interest, and the public concern over the disruption of production during strikes.[2] These aspects of the conflict became important as unions had now organized a significant segment of the national economy. Each of the new conflicts raised new problems for wage theory.

Craft versus Industrial Union Doctrine

In 1938, after four years of bitter internal conflict, the American labor movement was split wide apart by the secession of a large group of unions under the leadership of John L. Lewis, president of the United Mine Workers and a leading vice president of the American Federation of Labor, to form the rival Congress of Industrial Organizations. Seventeen years later, at the end of 1955, the two groups merged again to form the present AFL-CIO. During those 17 years and for the years immediately preceding them, it was often difficult to determine whether a given union more mistrusted employers or a rival union which was trying to get members and recognition away from it. Union rivalry made matters difficult even for the employer. It greatly complicated the problem of the government in getting worker support for war production. What issues were involved in this rivalry?

The immediate issue centered around the hundreds of thousands of workers who had flocked to join a union as soon as it appeared that the Roosevelt administration would encourage rather than oppose unions. The old AFL had consisted largely, although not entirely, of a federation of unions of the more skilled workers. These were organized by "craft," which usually meant by groups in related occupations, such as carpenters, machinists, garment cutters, or teamsters. Skilled workers had been the easiest to organize and the most steadfast under attack and adversity. The most important exception was Lewis' own United Mine Workers, which organized all workers in and around the coal mines, but which had fallen apart in the late 1920's only to revive spectacularly in the early days of the New Deal. In the great manufacturing industries, thousands of semi-skilled workers wanted to join a union, even when there was no existing craft union for them to join. Such workers were first organized into "federal" locals, attached directly to the central federation rather than to any established national union. The federal local was devised as a temporary organizing unit, pending the issuance of a series of local charters to the various craft unions who would then assume jurisdiction over the appropriate members of the disbanded

[2] A fourth issue, price inflation, is discussed in Chapter XII.

federal local. The majority of the leaders of the AFL wanted to continue this practice in the interest of protecting and strengthening the jurisdictions of their previously chartered national unions. The Lewis group of unions wanted the Federation to charter national unions industry by industry rather than craft by craft. The refusal of the AFL to do so led to the formation of the rival CIO federation.

Behind the acrimonious personal rivalry of union leaders was the bitter history of union ineffectiveness during the prosperous 1920's— and the even more bitter memory of the 1892 Homestead strike in which Andrew Carnegie defeated the craft unions of the time and rid the steel industry of effectual unionism for the next forty years. Lewis and many scholars of the labor movement believed that separate craft unions would be increasingly futile as mass production and the displacement of skilled workers by semiskilled workers spread throughout American manufacturing industry. To the leaders of the majority of established craft unions, the Lewis proposal and the surge of unrecruited, unreliable, and irresponsible unskilled and semiskilled members represented a threat to their established way of life. To Lewis and his followers, it was a holy cause on which hung the fate of unionism in America. The doctrinal difference then was between those who considered unions to be an instrument of the aristocracy of labor, to forward their particular interests, and those who considered unions to be the representative of Labor, with a capital "L," the means by which the mass of the lower-paid workers—and especially the lowest paid—would improve their economic condition.

The issues proved to be overdrawn on both sides. Many of the new industrial unions did not try to organize every worker in an industry. Many of the so-called craft unions were, or shortly became, as industry-wide as a so-called industrial union. Faced by the CIO rivalry the AFL leadership bestirred itself and by 1942 had so far succeeded in organizing the unorganized as to surpass the total CIO membership. After the end of World War II, both union groups faced a Congress and public which were generally less friendly, as is reflected in the restrictions on unions in the Taft-Hartley Act of 1948. Continued rivalry was weakening the public position of both camps. With the death of some of the leaders of the old interunion battle, the new leadership reunited the two groups into one central federation. Even so, there is, apart from particular union organizational forms, a difference of emphasis that has a bearing on the theory of wages. Is the wage outcome any different if union bargaining is in behalf of a minority of the skilled workers than if the bargaining takes place across the board for all employees in an industry; or are the wage differentials by skill determined independent of the type of union bargaining?

The Public Interest Doctrines of Unions and Employers

The leader of even a small group of exceptionally skilled or fortunate workers will likely think of his efforts as advancing the welfare of all workers and the economy as a whole. If other workers earn less, they have only to train themselves and join a union of their own. Meanwhile, a blow struck for any group of workers is in the interest of labor generally. Because the majority of the country these days consists of wage earners and their families, anything done for labor is considered a contribution to the welfare of the nation. Union leaders yield to no one in their intense patriotism!

This doctrine that "my interest is the public interest" reflects a widespread human desire. At root, the union leader's doctrine is the same as that of the millionaire businessman. If society has rewarded the businessman richly he will nearly always contend that it is because he has made some peculiarly great contribution to the national welfare. Would others like to be wealthy? They have merely to work as hard, be as clever, and use methods that will prove as successful.

However, there is still a difference between the role of unions that represent more than a third of the working population—and mostly in great areas of industry—and a minority movement of one-tenth of the wage earners. The actions of the former group are clearly charged with more potential good or bad influences on the country; in the eyes of the union leaders, they simply must be good influences. Thus the powerful unions of the 1940's, 1950's, and 1960's have developed two more or less new types of rationale for their efforts to raise the wages of their members. One public interest doctrine is that by putting wage pressure on managements, the unions help to force all managements to be increasingly efficient, thus raising the national product higher than it would be otherwise. That doctrine is not entirely new, but its truth or falsity now is of greater importance than ever. A second public interest doctrine of unions is the purchasing power doctrine. Union leaders believe, as did Lord Keynes, that workers are unemployed and the economic system functions in low gear because of a deficiency of money demand. Their prescriptions are different from those of Keynes, however. If wages are raised generally, then the wage earners who have the lower incomes will get purchasing power which otherwise would be left with the high-income profitmakers. The receivers of low incomes will spend that income, rather than save it as would high-income receivers, and their money spending will help meet the need for greater demand for the nation's output. Thus the union-induced wage increases serve the public interest.

This kind of reasoning is likely to unnerve a member of management. In his view, it is management which serves the public interest by making profits and investing these profits in improved plant and equipment thus increasing society's productive capacity. In addition, by avoiding undue wage increases, management keeps money costs and sales prices down so that all consumers—not just the organized worker—can purchase a greater volume of goods and services.

An example of this clash of doctrines is provided every time the union-management agreement in the steel industry comes up for renegotiation. Both sides prepare for the showdown by using expensive publicity to demonstrate to the public that the fate of the nation depends, on the one hand, on the winning of a wage increase of so many cents an hour or, alternatively, on management's refusal to give a penny. After much publicity—and perhaps a long strike—both sides eventually compromise their morality and devotion to the public by the acceptance, on labor's part, of something less than the amount requested and by giving, on management's part, something more than nothing. In such circumstances, it might be better if both sides would admit that they are trying to get the best deal they can. If it is true that the wage level of the nation hinges on a few key settlements of this kind, then the public should know what measure of truth there may be in either contention. The attempt to find answers serves to stimulate new thought on the logic of wage bargaining because neither side accepts any longer the application of the orthodox marginal productivity theory of wages to its particular case.

Public Doctrine Regarding Strikes

It is not easy to define "the public," but one segment of the public is certainly comprised of those who, directly or indirectly, consume (use) the products or services of industry. The consuming public has no independent notion of what the wages of any given group of workers should be. However, the public will become annoyed if the supply of a product or service is cut off. Even a small craft union has the power to cut off the supply of a product in some circumstances—for example, by striking a key group of skilled workers whose labor is essential to the operation of an industry. However, so long as organized labor comprised only a small minority of the workers, such cases were rare and occurred mainly where production and consumption were localized. Otherwise, the consumers could be served by plants that were not on strike. However, once the workers in the great basic industries were organized, the failure of management and labor to agree on a new contract might bring a crisis at almost any time. It is easy to exaggerate the importance to the public of a temporary halting of production. Coal miners never could understand the public's concern over a coal strike. The miner knew that he was lucky to get more than two hundred days of work a year in any case. Even if one hundred or so days were spent on strike, the year's work and production would be no less. On the other hand, some strikes can have disastrous effects. For example, a nationwide transportation strike would be crippling after only a few days. The public would be greatly inconvenienced, too, if any entire industry went on strike thus eliminating all source of supply. In wartime, a strike could cripple supply lines and create a real threat to the national defense.

However one assesses the impact of a strike, the power of present-day unions to halt production puts the institution of voluntary collective bargaining under great strain. Neither management nor labor likes to accept an outsider's binding arbitration under compulsion. Yet the public, interested in maintaining continuous service, wants someone to convince the parties to collective bargaining to accept a wage (or other collective-bargaining) decision without a strike. If one could believe that wages are properly determined by impersonal market forces, the need for strikes, at least on wage issues, might be avoided. But the orthodox wage theory does not fit each individual circumstance and, indeed, was not designed for that purpose (see Chapter II). No adequate substitute has been devised. Yet there must be a logic of causes and consequences in wages as in other matters. The growth of labor union power has thus brought about another impetus—this time from the public—for a more adequate theory of wages.

IMPACT ON WAGE THEORY

It would be a gross error to suggest that the clash of doctrines arising from the growth of labor union power as just described has already been resolved by any complete set of theories. Even if that were so, this essay could not adequately describe such theories. What is important is to recognize that this clash of doctrines represents a force which will eventually produce a logic to fit the known facts and resolve the contentions. The clash of doctrines in the controversy over the repeal of the British Corn Laws eventually resulted in Ricardo's theory of economic rent. The clash of doctrines resulting from the thesis of Karl Marx eventually produced the marginal productivity theory of wages. The facts and doctrines arising from mass unionism are compelling economists and other students of industrial relations to test old theories and to devise new ones where necessary. Some progress has been made. It will be convenient to divide the following discussion between theories of the general wage level from theories of wages in particular situations.

The Wage Share and the General Wage Level

The wage theory of Karl Marx supported his prediction that the workers' share in the total national product would decline progressively under capitalism. It suggested that property owners would exploit the workers more and more until finally the workers would revolt and dispossess the capitalists. Orthodox (capitalist) wage theory predicted that the wage share would correspond to the marginal contribution of labor. Thus if the proportions of labor and capital used in production remained the same, the over-all wage share would be constant. The wage theory implied by the doctrines of business unions is that effective collective bargaining will increase the percentage of the national product distributed to labor as wages. How has the orthodox theory stood the test of experience in the United States?

No test was possible when only a few wage earners were organized. Even if collective bargaining was successful in raising the wages of the few organized workers by considerable amounts, there was no noticeable over-all effect when the increase was averaged out as a share of all workers in the entire national product. But with the startling growth in the scope and strength of labor unions during the 1930's and 1940's, one would have expected to find a noticeable increase in the percentage of the national product paid as wages. Was there?

Serious difficulties arise in answering this question. One is a technical problem associated with the use of national income statistics. The available data do not show the income of wage earners separately. They show them as a part of the total of all wages and salaries, including the salaries of business managers and such. Another problem relates to cyclical fluctuations in the income shares. In times of business recession, wages normally account for an increased share in a decreased total national income. The reverse is true when business activity rises. A further, special difficulty arises in evaluating the impact of World War II on the income shares. A conclusive test of marginal productivity theory would require an accurate and independent measurement of the total quantities of labor and capital devoted to the production of consumers' goods. When allowances for the foregoing difficulties are made, this author's current judgment is that the national income amounts do not show any provable change in the wage share of the national product attributable to the growth of labor union power, except in one respect. The national statistics of the distribution of earned income do not take account of the transfer to labor of income in the form of social security payments or in the form of fringe benefits given to workers by employers, either voluntarily or as the result of collective bargaining agreements. Labor's aggregate income share appears to have increased by just about the amount of these transfer payments. Roughly then, there is no evidence that negotiation of wage rates at the bargaining table has resulted in any change in the wage share; but labor's increased power may be considered as partly responsible for the Social Security Act and, especially in the 1950's, for the liberalization of the fringe benefits granted by employers. Thus the evidence so far gives us no reason to doubt the validity of the marginal productivity theory for the purpose for which that theory was primarily devised: to account, not for the money level of earnings nor for the wages paid in any particular situation, but rather for the share of labor as a whole in the total national product.

As everyone knows, both the average money wage per worker and the average real wage (allowing for changes in the price level) have increased tremendously since 1933. This has been made possible by the steady advance in production per worker. Employed workers have received at least their former share of this increased product in the form of higher wages. But whether strong union organization promoted or impeded the increase in output per man and whether wages would have been lower or higher for workers as a whole (organized or not) in the absence of strong labor organization are still highly controversial questions. The theory of wages must be developed further before these questions can be put in a form answerable by the use of statistics.

Theory of Particular Wages and Wage Relationships

More important to most people than either the over-all average wage or the wage share are the wages paid in specific circumstances. Yet it is when orthodox theory is used to explain particular wages that it is most seriously at odds with observed facts. Even if the over-all wage share is what the marginal productivity theory says it should be, it does not follow that even a single worker's wage will be exactly equal to the value of the marginal product of labor. The original theory expressed a tendency to which events, on the whole, approximately conformed. If each wage in a given moment of time is either higher or lower than the value of the marginal product, the average of these wages might still be equal to the marginal product of labor as a whole.

Here are some of the questions brought to the fore by the clash of doctrine surrounding the rise in labor union power:

1. *Union and Non-Union Wage Relationship.* Are the wages paid to workers covered by collective bargaining higher than those of non-union workers all else being equal?

2. *Skill Differentials in Wages.* Has the growth of labor union power been responsible for the narrowing of the differences in wages between workers of different levels of skill? What governs these difficulties, and what may be predicted in the future?

3. *Geographic Differences in Wages.* Have regional or size-of-community wage differences been affected by the growth of union power? What factors govern differences in average wage income and in wages paid for the same work in similar circumstances, except for the circumstance of location of the place of employment?

4. *Inter-Industry Wage Differences.* Has the spread of unionism increased or reduced the differences in wages paid for similar work by different industries? What factors govern differences. How do they operate?

5. *Inter-Plant and Inter-Company Differences.* An important union doctrine is that no company or plant should gain extra profits by paying lower wages than its competitors. Have the increasingly strong unions been able to reduce these wage differences between plants and companies in the same industry or the same area? What factors determine such differences? How do they operate?

6. *Individual Worker Wage Differences.* Different unions have different doctrines on this question. All unions seek to standardize the wage rate—to get rid of management favoritism toward some individuals—but they differ as to the basis for standardizing. Have individual wages for the same work in the same plant become more or less uniform under the influence of strong labor unions? If more uniform, in what way? What factors govern individual wage differences? How do they operate? Certainly the employer does not know the value of the marginal product of each worker. Hence marginal productivity theory cannot furnish the answer.

These six questions all relate to the internal structure of wages— that is, the relationship of one wage to another. There is not a clear and accepted answer to any of these questions at present. The rise of labor union power did not originate these questions, but the social change and the clash of doctrines surrounding the rise of unions did increase the interest in, and urgency of, finding acceptable answers. No mere accumulation of facts can furnish the answers or provide the basis for future predictions. Economists must work out theories applicable to each of the questions. The theories of wage structure are of much greater importance today than the theory of over-all wage share or wage level. A theory appropriate for one set of circumstances is not necessarily useful in resolving a different kind of clash of conflicting doctrines.

CHAPTER XII

Inflation and the Control of Wage Increases

Mass unemployment was the overriding economic problem of the years 1930 to 1939 (cf. Chapter XI). The outbreak of World War II reversed the economic setting. The effects of that War began to be felt in 1940 and 1941, even before the United States became officially involved. The new economic problem became that of slowing up the rise in the average level of money prices.

FROM DEPRESSION TO WARTIME INFLATION

The unemployment of the 1930's was overcome automatically during the war years 1940-1945. Whereas some 17 per cent of the nation's labor force was still unemployed in 1939, the unemployment rate dropped to less than 2 per cent during 1944 and 1945, even though the nation's labor force was greatly expanded by the addition of women, youths, and older persons.

Increased Demand

The reason for this sudden change in the economic climate was clear enough. In 1940 and 1941 American firms received huge war orders from England and France as well as defense orders from the American Government. In 1942-1945, the American Government, now at war, spent from 30 to 50 million dollars more each year than it collected in taxes. At the same time, American firms stepped up their investments in plant, equipment, and inventories. The output of goods increased, of course, but much of the increased output was to be used for destructive purposes rather than to meet consumer demands. The high volume of money spending not only absorbed the unemployed but tended constantly to push up average prices and average wages.

Government Anti-Inflation Policies

The government used both indirect and direct methods to stem the tide of rising prices. One indirect method was to push the sale of U. S. Savings Bonds to divert the money used to buy bonds from the consumer markets. The direct methods were those of price and wage controls. Regulations of the Office of Price Administration made it illegal to raise prices without government permission. The War Labor Board at first attempted to enforce a prohibition on increases in wage rates beyond an initial increase of 15 per cent above the level of January 1941. This was the so-called Little Steel formula, named after the wage dispute case in which this precedent was established. By 1944 the Little Steel formula began to break down because both the labor unions and each employer really desired higher money wages. Employers as a group supported the wage limitations; but individual employers found ways to raise wages in their own plants, hoping to get and retain a labor force which would help them to reap the assured profits from wartime contracts and wartime consumer spending. Workers and their union representatives wanted higher money wages, especially since consumer costs were still rising—this in spite of the efforts of the Office of Price Administration. Ultimately, the War Labor Board took on the difficult task of establishing and enforcing thousands of "wage brackets" for the key occupations in each major labor market in the United States. Even if they agreed to do so, unions and employers were not supposed to be able to raise wage rates above those already prevailing (the top of each bracket) for each of the key occupations in each labor market.

Disputed Facts

The facts as to the rise of money prices and money wages during World War II were bitterly disputed at the time. These facts are still a matter of some contention among economists. The official figures show that average wholesale prices rose by 37 per cent between 1939 and 1945, and that average consumer-goods prices rose by 29 per cent.[1] Both of these measures are subject to a margin of error. The

[1] Sources of the statistical data used in this chapter are included in the appendix ("Bibliographical Notes").

stated prices of goods and of labor referred to inferior goods and inferior labor as the war continued. Thus it is clear that the official measures of prices and wage rates did not show the full extent of the rise in either of them. Consumers were getting inferior shirts, for example, at the officially established price for a shirt. Many consumer items were not available at all. Because of the demand for labor, many workers were suddenly upgraded (from lathe operator to machinist, for example). They thus earned a higher wage for no more skill than before. And, of course, wage earnings were being raised because of full employment and premium rates of pay for overtime work. As a result, wage incomes rose much faster than wage rates.

The official measures of prices and wages did understate somewhat the actual increases. Nevertheless, the broad picture is reasonably clear. Between 1939 and 1945, while average consumer prices were rising by about 29 per cent, average straight-time hourly rates of urban workers rose by about 62 per cent, and average weekly earnings of factory workers rose by about 86 per cent. Considering the powerful pull of excessive money demand during the war, these price and wage increases were remarkably small. The surprising fact is that the United States was able to engage in the giant war effort without reducing the average real level of living of its civilian population. Absorption of the unemployed, plus overtime work, and the recruitment of additional people to the labor force served to turn out the necessary war material without a cutback in the average level of living of American households.

POST WORLD WAR II INFLATION

By the year 1946, government regulation of prices and wages was breaking down. Once the war was over, employers, workers, and consumers all wanted to be rid of the limiting affects of government controls. The whole apparatus of the direct control of prices and wages was quickly dismantled. Business interests had expected prices to fall when price controls were lifted. Instead the inflationary pressures continued. Consumers made purchases of goods, household equipment, and automobiles—items which had been unavailable during the war. Businessmen spent vast amounts of money to gear their production to the peacetime markets. The government, meanwhile, was unwilling to cut deficit spending enough to offset the spending by private citizens. Hence the results of wartime deficit spending really had their chief effect in the postwar period.

Between 1945 and 1948, average wholesale prices rose by 52 per cent, average prices of consumer goods rose by 34 per cent, and average hourly earnings of employed workers rose by 22 per cent. The Korean War brought another surge of deficit spending, amounting to 18 billion dollars during the years 1952 to 1954. Once again the U. S. Government tried to limit the resulting rise in average prices by imposing direct controls on prices and wage rates. Again actual prices and wages rose. Between 1949 and 1952, average wholesale prices rose by 13 per cent, average prices of consumer goods and services by 11 per cent, and average hourly earnings by 19 per cent.

The price inflation, 1939 to 1952, is now generally conceded to have been due to the "demand pull" resulting from wartime deficit spending by the government. At the time, however, many blamed union wage demands. During the war periods of 1940-1945 and 1951-1952, the effects of deficit spending were mitigated by government control over increases in prices and wages. These control measures served principally to defer the inflationary pressures. Most of the increase in prices actually took place in the years following each of the two wars.

The problem of price inflation in the years following 1953 appears to be somewhat different. Deficit spending has not been large in this latter period. Available fixed capital and labor has not been fully used. Unemployment rates, even in the relatively prosperous years of 1953, 1955, 1957, and 1963, rose to 2.9, 4.4, 4.3, and 5.7 per cent respectively. In the recession years of 1954 and 1958, unemployment rose to 5.6 and 6.8 per cent of the labor force. These unemployment rates are not high when compared to the 15 to 25 per cent unemployment during the Great Depression. But they do indicate a condition of considerably less than full employment. Still, prices keep on rising. Between 1952 and 1960, average wholesale prices rose by 2 per cent, average consumer prices rose by 11 per cent, and average hourly earnings rose by 37 per cent. This situation has led economists and policy makers to consider and argue about a number of different doctrines as to the desirability of price inflation and the role of unions in setting the general levels of money wages and costs.

CONFLICTS OF DOCTRINES AND THEORIES

Following World War II, a conflict ensued between two main doctrines relating to the action to be taken regarding the rise in average prices. At the same time, there existed a conflict between two principal theories as to the cause of these price increases. Many people believed the rise in prices to be inherently bad and advocated prevention at all costs. The chief argument in support of this view was that people with fixed or slowly changing incomes were hurt by the rising prices of whatever they purchased. On the other hand, some eminent economists argued that a mild degree of price inflation was essential to the continued rapid growth of the economy. The current rate of growth of the national product was compared unfavorably with the rate of growth of earlier periods, especially World War II, and with that of other countries, especially Soviet Russia. Price inflation was conceded to be bad when the rate of increase became too great; but just what was "too great" was not clear.

The conflict was between what came to be known as the "demand pull" and the "cost push" theories. Many economists reasoned that the price increases were due essentially to the upward pull on prices of too great a volume of spending resulting from the excess purchasing power created during the war years, from the high rate of business spending on plant, equipment, and inventories, and from the failure of the government to restrict its own post-war spending. Others, observing the wage increases resulting from labor negotiations in such industries as steel, reached the opposite conclusion. They believed that the price increases were made necessary by the upward push on the costs of production due to wage increases in excess of the gains in output per worker.

Price Stability and Growth

The first conflict in policies had to do with whether the average level of prices should rise, fall, or remain stable. The self-interest of individuals—whether they are employers or wage earners—is clear enough. Everyone would like to see rising prices in the products or services he has to sell and falling prices in the products and services he has to buy. Individuals equate their problem with the problem of the country as a whole. Everyone likes to believe that what is good for him is good for the country. Personal biases keep creeping into agruments over price inflation. At the higher or more general level of conflict, there are bitter differences of opinion about price level policy. At one extreme are those who believe that average prices should fall. This policy appeals to those whose money incomes are fixed or not subject to much change—widows, orphans, pensioners, and many salaried workers. The argument is that benefits of increased production should be distributed throughout the nation in the form of gradually falling average prices. It is argued that with lower prices any given money income would buy more goods and that, therefore, the money demand for the products of industry would be sustained. This plea for falling average prices was associated with the studies of the Brookings Institution. In recent years however, the facts of the post-war period have made falling average prices an impractical goal.

At the opposite extreme are the economists who favor a gradually increasing level of average prices. Robert Nathan, Alvin Hansen, and Leon Keyserling favor this type of price doctrine. The pro-inflation doctrine naturally appeals to labor union groups and to others who can take the most advantage of rising prices. The inflationary doctrine ought to appeal to businessmen because profits rise faster than other incomes during periods of rising prices. This doctrine does, indeed, appeal to those who deal in common stocks, but the public position of American business leaders generally has been opposed to price inflation policies. Perhaps the reason for business opposition to rising prices is that operating firms generally take for granted their selling prices and are thus mainly concerned with keeping down their money costs.

Those who support policies which lead to rising prices have an argument of their own. The argument is that rising prices stimulate the growth rate of the economy. This group of price inflationists argue that the year-to-year increase in American production has been held down by insufficient total money demand for the output of American production. They do not contend that rising average prices are good in and of themselves, but rather that they are better than stagnation. The late Professor Sumner Slichter, among others, expressed this view. This pro-inflation doctrine is being pushed in part because, in the economic competition between the United States and Soviet Russia, the United States appears to have had a much lower annual rate of growth. Professor Fritz Machlup, on the other hand, has most vigorously denied that rising prices are helpful to long-run economic growth.

In between these deflationary and inflationary doctrines is the position of most economists and probably most citizens. If the levels of prices could be fairly well stabilized, both businessmen and labor leaders would know the kind of economic climate with which they had to deal. Of course some prices would fall and others would rise; but if the average level of prices could be kept reasonably constant, the rise of individual prices would simply reflect the changing conditions of demand and supply in the respective markets.

Cost Push or Demand Pull

Among those who argue for a stable average price level there is still a second conflict of doctrine. This is a sort of "who done it" affair. When prices rise, employers blame the unions and the government. Unions blame the employers and, sometimes, the government. Government officials, depending on their leanings, blame the employers or the unions or both. The doctrine of the National Association of Manufacturers and the U. S. Chamber of Commerce has been that labor unions should be restrained by government because unions, by exercising their superior bargaining power, keep raising wages, and hence money prices. The labor unions argue (when they are not favoring price inflation) that the monopolistic employers should be prevented by the government from raising the prices of their products. Government officials and congressmen sometimes argue that employer conspiracies should be broken up. At other times they argue that unions should be restrained or broken up. At still other times they argue that the government should prohibit wage or price increases or both. Still another government doctrine has been that union and employer representatives should be "statesmen" and voluntarily subordinate their immediate interests to the national welfare by being moderate in their wage-fixing and price-fixing policies. This approach was tried in 1961 when the President's Council of Economic Advisors appealed to unions and managements generally to limit wage increases to 3 per cent a year, which was roughly equal to the estimated rate of increase in output per worker in the country.

These shifting doctrines of government officials bring us to a third type of clash—the clash of doctrines as to the means to be used to prevent or restrain an inflation of average money prices. The followers of J. M. Keynes think they have the perfect doctrine for dealing with either falling or rising prices. This Keynesian doctrine is not, as many suppose, a doctrine which always favors price inflation. It was, and is, a doctrine of total money speinding. According to the followers of Keynes, total money spending is likely to be *either* too small to buy back the products of industry or so large as to cause a rise in the average level of prices. According to the Keynesian doctrine, the government should stimulate an increase in money spending whenever there is mass unemployment of labor and resources. Likewise, a government faced with the threat of rising prices should curtail money spending. Particular wage bargains and the setting of particular product prices are not supposed to have any important effect on the average level of prices. What counts is the total volume of money spending by consumers, businessmen, and government. When consumer and business spending is so great as to force up the average level of prices, the government should either curtail the volume of private spending or itself spend less than it collects in taxes. Government can curtail private spending by forcing up the level of interest rates. It can curtail its own spending by running a budgeted surplus of government receipts over government expenditures. Keynes himself proposed that wartime increases in wages should be paid in the form of government bonds redeemable after the war at a time to be determined by the government (of Britain, in this case) when an increase in total spending was needed. Thus Keynes, contrary to popular impression, was just as much interested in preventing an inflation of prices as he was interested in preventing price deflation and mass unemployment.

Opposed to Keynes and his followers is the doctrine of those who favor direct government control of wage rates and product prices. The advocates of direct and specific government controls over prices and wages do not think that the over-all controls of private borrowing (monetary measures) or of government taxation and spending (fiscal measure) can be effective in preventing a rise in the average level of prices. The anti-Keynesian doctrine is that a government which is faced with a rising level of prices should tackle that problem at the "grass roots," rather than at the level of total spending. Some prices are more important than others, it is contended, and these particular prices should be kept from rising.

Among those who advocate specific and particular government controls, there are further conflicts of policy. Labor unions press for controls over the employers' selling prices, but want no controls over wage increases they may demand. Employers, on the other hand, want the government's help in resisting union demands for increased wages, but want to be free of government control in setting the prices of the products or services they sell.

Now, as during past centuries, these clashes of self-interest have stimulated economists to work out new theories of wages.

Impact on Wage Theory

Nineteenth-century economists, and Keynes also, assumed that wages were controlled by the impersonal forces of supply and demand in the labor markets. According to their reasoning, average levels of wage rates would not be affected very much by the policy decisions of employers or labor unions.

A different theory of wages and prices has resulted from the more recent clash of doctrines about the post-war problem of price inflation. This new theory has reference to the wage-cost push on average prices. The new theory involves assumptions about employer and union monopolies, and the leadership of big unions and big employers in setting the price for the whole economy.

The cost-push theory of price inflation assumes that the sellers of products will set their selling prices at levels high enough to cover costs and insure usual profits. Anything which raises money costs will thus require higher prices. For the country as a whole, most costs are labor costs. Hence it is the rise in labor costs which pushes up prices. Labor unions are supposed to be the chief sinners for it is the union wage demand which raises labor costs. In former times the unions had organized only a small fraction of the American workers. Now that unions are large—and powerful—they can, it is supposed, control the general level of money wages and, hence, the level of prices.

One argument against this theory is that prices during the post-war period have risen most in the industries where unions are weakest. During the 1950's, for example, the average price of consumer *services* rose by 41 per cent. The average price of foods rose by 18 per cent, while the average price of manufactured goods rose by about 14 per cent. Labor unions are generally weak in the service industries, hardly exist at all in farming, but are strong in the manufacturing part of the economy, the segment of the economy which showed the smallest rate of price increase. How then can labor unions be blamed for the price inflation?

The cost-push theorists have an answer to this objection. In the first place the picture is not as clear as the over-all figures suggest. The workers in the transportation and barbering industries are tightly organized, and the prices of transit services and haircuts have risen very fast indeed. The costs of farm products to the consumer consist mainly of the costs of transportation and processing—areas in which labor unions are strong and where wage demands have been unusually great. However, the principal answer of the cost-push theorists rests on the theory of "key bargains." They point out that wage settlements in key areas set the pace for the money wages throughout the whole economy, whether unionized or not. The wage increases obtained by the unions of steel workers, auto workers, and electrical workers are widely known. To meet these wage increases, other employers are compelled to raise wage rates and broaden fringe benefits. If the employers of unorganized workers did not raise wages in line with the pattern set by settlements in key areas, they might lose workers, suffer the effects of the lowered morale and efficiency of their workers, and might, indeed, expose themselves to the threat of unionization. Notice that this "key bargain" theory deals with wage *increases* rather than the absolute level of wage rates. Firms which have paid relatively low wage rates may continue to be low-wage firms. But if everyone is granting about the same wage *increases,* money wages will rise bringing increased labor costs and increased prices. The relative rates of price increase, the cost-push theorists contend, reflect the shifting demands for different kinds of goods and services rather than the relative strength of the cost-push in each sector.

A second objection to the cost-push theory is reflected in the following question: How is it that the employers can get higher profits by raising the price of their products? If that is possible, then why don't the sellers raise their selling prices regardless of any increase in their costs? The answer of the cost-push theorists rests partly on a theory of monopoly, partly on a theory of public relations, and partly on a theory of government policy.

Monopoly of Unions

If sellers of products and services were perfectly competitive, market conditions would set a price on output quite outside of the seller's control. But when there is only one seller, or only a few sellers, each seller has some control over his selling prices. He can then have a price *policy* and decide whether it is more or less profitable to raise his prices. The economic theory involved is most clearly ilustrated by the (rare) case of a single seller of a single product for which there is no practical substitute. In such a case the seller will set a price he believes will give him the greatest money revenue, regardless of his costs. In actual fact the price-policy problem is generally more complicated because there is something less than a complete seller's monopoly. Take steel production as an example.

There are a dozen major American sellers of basic steel products. In addition, for some uses, domestic steel competes with aluminum, copper, and plastic products, as well as with imports of steel products from other nations. Thus, there are some limits on the selling price which any one seller can charge. Even so, the steel companies have a price policy. They decide which prices to change and proceed to administer them with the object of obtaining some target rate of profit on their investment. The producers of steel learned more than half a century ago that it was impractical to undercut each other's prices. So they adopted a "follow the leader" pricing policy. The leader has usually been the U. S. Steel Corporation. Once U. S. Steel publishes its selling prices, item by item, the other steel producers generally follow and quote the same prices. The management aim in steel and other such mass-production industries is to fix the selling prices, on a tacitly agreed basis, so as to allow each of the major companies to survive and to retain its accustomed share of the total sales by the industry.

There are as well so-called labor monopolies. A strong labor union, as in steel and auto manufacturing, can use the strike weapon as a threat to withdraw the supply of labor unless the union's wage and other demands are met by the employers. In some situations, employers can control their selling prices while unions, at the same time, can control the supply of labor. Economists call such a case a "bilateral monopoly." There is not a complete monopoly either by the sellers of the products or by labor but the sellers in this case can gain more than truly competing sellers can gain by agreeing on a price policy. And the workers gain more than they might have otherwise by means of concerted wage demands on their employers. In this type of situation, both the employers and the workers gain by raising money wages. The proposed solution to this logical problem depends on the political ideas of the policy makers. Some persons advocate nationalizing an industry such as steel. Others want to return to something like the nineteenth-century idea of pure competition among all sellers by carving many small producing companies out of the few existing large ones. Still others suggest "cutting the unions down to size" to eliminate so-called union monopolies, even though pure competition among employers is not to be restored.

Public Relations

When an employer raises the price of his products because of a wage-increase demand, a logical question follows. Why didn't the employer raise his prices before the labor union won its wage-increase? If greater profits can be reaped by raising prices, why not raise prices even before costs are increased? The wage-cost-push theory of price inflation assumes that the average level of money prices of goods and services will be determined by the deliberate price-policy decisions of the sellers. But why is the pricing policy of an employer based on the increase of his labor costs?

The explanation may be that the pricing polices of the partly monopolistic industries are influenced by their sense of public relations considerations. The managements of these large and semi-monopolistic firms must be alert to threats of anti-trust actions. Their public relations image, therefore, must be that of a company attempting to hold down increases in the prices of its products. Any price-raising action at the apparent initiative of the company would threaten the company's public position as witness the furor in 1962 when the steel industry attempted a price increase of $6 a ton. The steel industry subsequently withdrew that increase under Presidential pressure. Any union demand for wage increases must also be resisted for reasons of public relations. But once the union demands have been partly granted, after much public screaming by both unions and managements, the employers have a solid public-relations justification for raising their selling prices. Thus the labor unions are often the scapegoats for a pricing policy which may yield the employers higher money profits, in spite of the increase in wage rates, and which exempts the employer from public criticism by putting the blame for increased prices on the labor unions.

Government Policy

The theory of government policy, as used by the more sophisticated cost-push theorists, is that pro-labor governments adapt themselves to the wage settlements of the labor unions. It may be recognized that government might prevent a price inflation if it sufficiently curtailed credit and collected taxes sufficiently in excess of its own expenditures. These measures restrict total spending. If spending were sufficiently restricted, employers could not afford increased wage costs and so, sooner or later, would refuse to grant inflationary wage demands. The trouble, say the cost-push theorists, is that restrictive government policies would cause both widespread strikes and widespread unemployment. The strikes would occur because the labor unions would expect the annual wage increases to which they have become accustomed. The mass unemployment would occur because employers would no longer be able to match their increased costs by raising their selling prices. Whereas a government which was willing to risk the chance of widespread strikes or widespread unemployment might stop the rise in prices, post-war governments have not been willing to take these risks. Thus governments are forced to go along with the levels of money wage costs as set, directly or indirectly, by the powerful labor unions. Postwar American governments, it is reasoned, have had to sustain total spending by making credit easily available and by enough deficit spending to avoid mass unemployment under the wage-cost conditions imposed by the unions.

The government's policy will likely be shaped by the kind of theory held by the policy makers. If they accept the reasoning of the cost-push theorists and want to prevent price inflation, then the government will attempt to weaken the so-called monopoly power of labor unions or control directly the prices of labor and of goods and services. To successfully weaken the bargaining power of the labor unions would be most difficult. To install controlled wages and prices would be even more difficult.

What then is left of either the theory of total money spending or the theory of cost-push inflation? Government control of total money income runs into the problems of strikes and mass unemployment; government control of particular prices and wage rates runs into the problems of setting and enforcing these controlled wage rates and prices. Theory may provide a guide policy, but the problem of application by government is still, in the 1960's, very much subject to the clash of theories about how money wages and money prices are determined and the clash of doctrines about how wages and prices should be regulated. Further refinements are necessary to take account of the varied strategic factors determining wages in different kinds of situations.

CHAPTER **XIII**

The Emerging Theory of Wages

The thesis of this essay has been that the theory of wages, like all useful theories, has evolved out of the conflict of observed current fact with established theory and out of the conflict of doctrines as to which economic policies should be pursued. The marginal productivity theory was shown to have developed out of the changing facts and doctrines of the nineteenth century. Recently that theory has been challenged in the United States by a multiplicity of new facts and new doctrines. The result is frequently interpreted as a breakdown of wage theory. Ten of the major developments in the social history of the United States during the twentieth century have been examined to see what impact each of them had on the orthodox wage theory. The developments examined have ranged from mass immigration around the turn of the century to the rise in average prices after World War II. The doctrines examined have ranged from those of the social workers to the postwar advocates of the curtailment of the "monopoly power" of labor unions. An attempt has been made to assess the significance for wage theory of each cluster of changing fact and conflict of doctrine, whether the issues raised have been satisfactorily dealt with by wage theory or not. The results may, at first sight, seem to confirm the belief that wage theory has indeed broken down and that all that remains is to drift aimlessly in a sea of facts. But before we dismiss wage theory, let us see in what sense, if any, it has developed and grown.

If one means by "wage theory" a single, simple generalization that will serve to answer any question about wages, then indeed twentieth-century experience has demolished any such theory. But a useful theory is one which is relevant to an issue or question. As the wage issues of the twentieth century have changed and multiplied, the need is seen for more and more special, limited, precise, and complex theories to express the logic of the relationships involved in each new question. The twentieth century has yet to produce an Alfred Marshall to knit all these specialized theories into a related and symmetric whole. However, the new and modified partial theories are increasingly representative of the facts and more closely responsive to the issues of doctrine than any single theory of wages yet devised could possibly be.

This is an essay on social history—with wage theory the central focus—rather than a technical treatise on theory. However, a few suggestions about the ways in which the subject of wage theory has developed and about its future development would seem useful. First let us select and define the leading questions that have been asked about wages and then see how well the nineteenth-century theory helps answer these questions, how far any new theories have progressed, and how great the gaps still are in our reasoning about the relationships involved in each question. A broad distinction needs to be made between questions about the general or average level of wages and questions about particular wages and wage relationships. The two questions will be used as a guide in grouping the items of discussion that follow.

THEORIES OF THE GENERAL WAGE LEVEL

The Wage Share

Nothing in twentieth-century American experience has diminished the validity of the orthodox marginal productivity theory as an instrument for explaining and predicting the share of total wage income in the total national product. This was the question precipated by Karl Marx and the question which, after all, the theory was originally devised to answer. It is true that the statistical information used by Paul H. Douglas in his monumental, *Real Wages in the United States, 1890-1926*, was not always perfectly adapted to his empirical test of the theory. It is also true that no such thorough test has been made since. But not even the spectacular growth of labor union power since the 1930's has produced any evidence in conflict with the logical proposition that the over-all share of real wages, as paid to employed labor by private employers, would be governed as that theory suggested. What the twentieth-century experience has suggested is that labor's share might be improved by progressive taxation, by social security transfer payments, and perhaps by the beneficence of employers and the pressure of unions to secure important fringe benefits. It is also now more clear than it would have been at the beginning of the century that during business recessions employed labor's share in the diminished total product will increase and that the reverse will occur as business revives. But all this is at least consistent with the orthodox wage theory even if it does not positively establish its validity.

The Level of Real Wages

Modern interest in the general level of wages has to do with its absolute size, rather than its percentage relationship to the total national product. But if the long-run share of wages tends to remain constant, it follows that the real wages of labor as a whole must move parallel to the movement of real national output per employed worker. Twentieth-century experience also confirms this orthodox conclusion, with one important modification. The upward trend of labor's total claims to goods and services has, indeed, conformed closely to the average rate of increase in output per employed worker. Certainly, nothing has come of organized labor's ambition to increase wages at the expense of business profits, taking the economy as a whole and allowing for differences between prosperous and depressed years. The modification of the orthodox theory must take account of the variable portion of the whole national product which may be used to increase or improve the nation's productive capacity and the variable proportion which a government may divert to war and war preparations. The total of goods and services that wage earners can command cannot be greater than the total amount of goods and services that are made available for consumption, plus or minus changes in inventory stocks of those goods. However, it appears that labor as a whole has more to gain by increases in the output per employed worker than by encroaching on the nonlabor shares of available consumer goods and services. Here, again, twentieth-century experience has, on the whole, tested and confirmed the nineteenth-century orthodoxy.

The Money Wage Level and the Unemployment Rate

If our question has to do with how changes in average or total money wages are related to the proportion of available labor which is unemployed, that is, to the recovery of private business from depression or recession, then we meet for the first time a major defect in nineteenth-century wage theory. The original theory, indeed, had nothing to do with the depression-recovery problem for the simple reason that practically full employment of available labor and resources was assumed as a basis for the theory and, therefore, the condition of less than full employment was not examined. However, the generally accepted inference drawn from the marginal productivity theory prior to J. M. Keynes was that the cure for business depression was a general reduction of money wage rates. This inference involved a confusion of the individual with the general situation. The American experience of 1929 to 1933 suggested, as the earlier British experience had suggested to Keynes, that wage-rate cutting was a self-defeating method for promoting general recovery because wage cuts reduced further the already deficient effective total money demand for the total output.

The NRA experience of 1933-35 showed that some business recovery would result from measures that promoted the belief of employers that money wage rates would not decline further in the future. On the other hand, the NRA experience also indicated that the needed increase in effective demand could not be obtained by a deliberate and over-all increase in money wage rates. This was so because higher wage rates not only increased the purchasing power of the employed workers but also increased the money costs of production and, hence, the money prices of goods (except insofar as output per manhour increased). Subsequent to the practical experience of the NRA, Keynes published his aggregative theory of employment which indicated that recovery depended upon the combination of investment spending by private business and deficit spending by government. The Keynesian theory, although still stoutly resisted by some economists and by many businessmen, is now generally accepted and is being developed further by the younger economists. The income tax method of collecting government revenues—and the social security system of declining tax revenues and increasing benefit expenditures during recession periods—have both helped to insure deficit spending by government in times of business recession. They have provided some of the "automatic stabilizers" of the private economy, and thus have helped to sustain total wage income since the time of the Great Depression.

The Money Wage Level and Price Inflation

The experience during World War II amply demonstrated that a sufficiently large volume of deficit spending by government could produce full and even overfull employment. However, this was accomplished at the expense of a powerful upward pressure on the average level of prices. The immediate effect on prices can be partly damped down by direct controls on increases of output prices and of wage rates, but the result of such controls is to defer part of the inflationary pressure until after the deficit spending has ceased. When the controls are lifted, as they were in 1946, prices and money wages resume their rise. The question for wage theory then becomes how important, if important at all, are increases in money wages in causing price inflation at times when there is but little current deficit spending and when the economy is running at considerably less than full employment levels.

The answer to this question is still unsettled and subject to conflicts between adherents of the "demand pull" versus the "cost push" theories of rising average prices. When wage controls were lifted, those who were suspicious or antagonistic toward labor unions were inclined to place the blame for rising commodity prices on the wage demands of the powerful unions. The same economists now generally concede that the price rise between 1945 and 1952 was due mainly to excessive total money spending; but they do feel that the price inflation since 1952 is largely the result of the upward pressure on costs caused by money wage-rate increases in excess of the increases in manhour output, as a direct or indirect result of union wage demands. Wage theory quite clearly needs further refinement and development before it can deal adequately with the relationship of money-wage increases to increases in average prices—particularly when output prices are partly administered by the sellers rather than being determined by impersonal forces in highly competitive markets. As usual, the need for a more fully developed theory arises because of a conflict of doctrines. In this case the underlying conflict is really over the question of whether labor unions should be encouraged or restricted.

THEORIES OF THE STRUCTURE OF WAGES

Most of the conflicts between doctrines concerning wages during the twentieth century have raised theoretical issues as to the determination of particular wages rather than the general or average level of wages. Accordingly, American economists in the twentieth century have contributed more to the advancement of the theory of particular wages than to the theory of the over-all average of wages. This aspect of wage theory also appears to offer the most attractive area for further theoretical and empirical study.

Each of the ten historical episodes that have been examined raised some problems as to the relation of individual classes of wages to the determining factors of the relation of one class of wage to another, or to the effect of the level of a given kind of wage on the functioning of other parts of the economic system. This was the case even when the problems examined started out to be those of broad policies designed to raise the general level of wages.

The common belief that wage theory has broken down often seems to arise from unsuccessful attempts to use the nineteenth-century theory of the general wage level, without modification, to explain or predict wages of particular kinds in particular situations. This confusion of the general with the particular is like saying that the theory of gravity broke down as soon as the first balloon went up. A special theory may at first be needed to explain the balloon's ascension, but it soon becomes possible to elaborate the theory of gravity itself to take account of the apparently contrary phenomenon of rising, as well as falling, objects.

Similarly, when the social workers tried to improve the welfare of immigrant wage earners in the United States, when the early labor unions tried to raise the wages of the special groups they had organized, and when governments first tried to raise the wages of the lowest-paid workers, the slavish followers of orthodox wage theory contended that none of these changes was possible because wages were determined by the law of the marginal productivity of labor. The fact that these reform efforts met with moderate success quite naturally led their advocates to believe that wage theory was false and to conclude that economists were the enemies of the wage earners. Meanwhile Taylor and his followers in the name of scientific management tried to substitute engineering for economics. Though they showed that individual wages could be raised, they raised as many social problems as they solved. Those industrial leaders we have called the "welfare capitalists" made some use of the methods of scientific management but sought to soften the resulting antagonisms and to raise both wages and their own profits by paternalistic guidance and care for the wage earner. They thus showed that, within limits, it was possible to reconcile increased wage earnings with decreased labor cost per unit of product. Until the beginning of the Great Depression, the general prosperity and the beneficent reputation of the management leaders served to stifle attempts of labor unions to organize the wage earners independently, even though only a minority of employers had the desire or the opportunity to be welfare capitalists. Thereafter wages of various kinds in the United States have been governed by kaleidoscopic combinations of the policies of various labor unions, the administered policies of various kinds of business managements, and the wage and other economic policies of government. Almost everyone would agree that wages are determined by some kind of policy, but we often lose sight of the economic environment which gives rise to some policies, puts limits on others, and in any case, shapes the wage results of any given policy.

Among academic economists it was the institutionalists who showed that there was more to the heaven and hell of economic life than could be explained by the simple mechanics of the balance scale used by the nineteenth-century economists. The institutionalists tended to find the analogy of biologic growth and decay more useful than simple mechanics to explain wages in any selected case and to predict their future development. The institutionalists also fostered respect for the results of empirical investigation—a respect that had been lacking in the followers of orthodox wage theory. Many of these had thought that a few glib generalizations could be substituted for patient research. The weakness of the institutionalists, however, was that they were able to arrive at very few generalizations of their own, even of a limited character. They left behind an approach and a critical spirit that has characterized twentieth-century thought about economic matters. But they did not succeed in replacing the orthodox wage theory. As a result, the institutionalists contributed to the false impression that all wage theory was useless and that all that was needed was to collect facts.

Facts about wages have been collected in greater volume and with greater precision than ever before in human experience. Is it possible now to say anything more than that any wage is what it is? Gradually, it appears that some limited generalizations are possible. We must begin by recognizing that every worker is unique and thus not entirely interchangeable with any other worker. Furthermore, the mobility of workers as between employments is, in the short run, quite limited as compared with the mobility of other factors of production. It follows that the individual wage is to some extent the result of custom and administered decision, rather than the result of a pinpoint balance between the amount demanded and the amount supplied. But this does not mean that a wage level is completely arbitrary. We must introduce, then, the concept of a range between maximum and minimum possibilities. At any moment of time the range may be a wide one, in the sense that the wage might fall anywhere between widely separated maximum and minimum levels without a change in any of the related variable factors in the situation. But as time passes, more choices become available both to the worker and his employer and the range is therefore narrowed. When we group a collection of workers according to common characteristics, we find that exceptions to the rule begin to stand out from the central tendency of the wages of that group. How, then, should the workers be grouped for the purpose of arriving at some limited generalization regarding their wages? The groups whose wages we analyze need to be formed on the basis of empirical experimentation and of logical thought as to characteristics or factors that are likely to make a difference between different wages.

A partial list of factors that have been found to make a difference in the wages actually paid to an individual worker follows:

Employer evaluation of contribution to net revenue
Method of wage payment
Age
Length of service (seniority)
Sex
Ethnic group
Geographic location of the employment
Size of the community where the job is located
Wage policy of the applicable labor union
Size of employing establishment
Size of employing company
Earnings of the employing company—present, past, and expected
Wage policy of the employer
Industry of the employer (type of product)
Occupation or task of the worker

These and perhaps other characteristics of any wage situation are not wholly independent of each other and some are not always discriminating factors. Moreover some of them are "dummy variables" in the sense that they are objective reflections of underlying factors which may actually control the situation. The particular factor or factors used in the analysis of a given wage situation must depend to some extent on the availability of information about that factor. However, we now know from experience that workers and jobs that have one or more of these characteristics are more likely to have similar wages than those with contrasting characteristics. To the extent that the wage situation can be identified according to a combination of several of these wage-related characteristics, we can obtain an increasingly accurate measure of the probable wage and can make increasingly accurate predictions as to a future wage. Each of these characteristics has a logical relationship to the determination of the wage result. But much more remains to be done in defining the precise nature of the relationships and, of course, in establishing the probability that a wage will fall within some stated range.

The range, and the probability that a wage will fall within it, is not static. A theory of the wages of any group of workers needs to take account of the continuing changes in the economic, social, and legal forces which change the incidence of any given factor on the wages paid. That is the major reason why a purely empirical finding at a moment of time is insufficient and why a significant generalization requires a logical analysis of the reasons for the relationship between a characteristic and the observed wage. For example, wage differences according to skill (groups of occupations) have narrowed spectacularly in the United States during the last half century. Why? Until we know the logic of the reasons for changes in this relationship, we lack a good instrument for predicting the effect of future skill differences on wages.

The line of analysis here suggested, following the actual progress of wage analysis in the United States, includes within it many of the common generalizations about particular wages. Thus it is often said that wages depend on the "bargaining power" of the union, rather than on the "theories of economics." But what, precisely, is the bargaining power of a union; and does it, in fact, determine the wage independently and without limit? Clearly it is not sufficient to reason backwards, as is sometimes done, and say that a relatively high wage proves that the union's bargaining power is great. However, the above listed characteristics of the wage situation do help to establish the probable limits of the range within which bargaining may make a difference in the precise wage. Likewise what has been called the "wage policy of the union," when this is expressed in terms of the reasons for that policy, needs also to take account of the way in which the bargaining itself may affect the particular wage or group of wages that would otherwise occur.

When the multiple determinants of particular wages are considered, the futility of applying a mere marginal productivity theory becomes apparent. The marginal productivity theory may express a general tendency governing the wages of all employed workers in the economy, but it fails almost completely to relate the many specific factors which help determine the wage of any individual worker or distinctive group of workers. Likewise, it is absurd to say that particular wages cannot be raised because they are determined by marginal productivity. Wages have been raised repeatedly, both because existing wages in a particular case are not necessarily equal to the value of the marginal product of any worker or partial group of workers (it would be the sheerest accident if this were so), and because the factors on which marginal productivity depends may be changed, as the social workers, the welfare capitalists, and the legal regulations of wages have demonstrated in practice. This is not to say that the marginal productivity theory is wrong, but merely that it is too generalized to express the factors influencing *particular* wages. It needs to be expanded if it is to account for the complex set of forces that influence the wages of a particular group.

This analysis has been rather abstract. It does not pretend to present a particular theory of wages. There is no universally accepted substitute for orthodox theory at present. But the logic of wage determinants and of wage relationships is continually developing in the United States. They develop in response to conflicting doctrines; and the conflicting doctrines reflect the ever-changing factual circumstances of the American economy and the contrast in the ideals of different groups of the American people. As a result, a richer and more realistic theory of wages is in the process of emerging.

Bibliographic Notes

Bibliographic Notes

Chapter I

The author's views toward facts, practices, problems, doctrines, and theories are those he has found necessary for clarity during some thirty years of teaching economics. Specific indebtedness is acknowledged to Alfred Marshall, *Principles of Economics* (Esp. Book I, Chap. III). London: Macmillan & Co., Ltd., 1890; also to John Maynard Keynes, *The General Theory of Employment Interest and Money*. New York: Harcourt, Brace & World, Inc., 1936.

For further reading on the history, philosophy, and methods of science, see:

Columbia Associates in Philosophy, *An Introduction to Reflective Thinking* (Esp. Chap. IV). Boston: Houghton Mifflin Company, 1923.

Conant, James B., *Science and Common Sense* (Esp. Chaps. I and III). New Haven, Conn.: Yale University Press, 1951.

Hobson, E. W., *The Domain of Natural Science* (Esp. Chaps. II and XIX). New York: The Macmillan Company, 1923.

Thornton, Jesse E., ed., *Science and Social Change* (Esp. Part I). Washington, D. C.: The Brookings Institution, 1939.

One of the most extensive syllabi on the history of science is that of Henry Guerlac, *Science in Western Civilization*. New York: The Ronald Press Company, 1952.

Chapter II

The leading works of Smith, Malthus, Ricardo, Mill, and Marshall are documented in the text. The works of economists referred to but not documented are:

Clark, John Bates, *The Distribution of Wealth.* New York: The Macmillan Company, 1889.

————, *The Philosophy of Value.* New York: The Macmillan Company, 1881.

Jevons, W. Stanley, *The Theory of Political Economy.* London: Macmillan & Co., Ltd., 1871.

Marx, Karl, *Das Kapital: Kritik der politischen Ökonomie,* Vol. I. Hamburg: Otto Meissner, 1867.

————, and Friedrich Engels, *Manifesto of the Communist Party,* trans. Samuel Moore. New York: International Publishers, 1932.

Menger, Karl, *Grundsätze der Vollkswirtschaftslehre.* Wien: W. Braunmuller, 1871. (English translation by the London School of Economics and Political Science, 1934.)

Walras, Leon, *Éléments D'Économie Politique Pure.* Lausanne: F. Rouge, 1874.

Some leading general histories of economic thought, all of which deal with nineteenth-century wage theories, are:

Cannan, Edwin, *Review of Economic Theory.* London: P. S. King and Son, Ltd., 1929.

Catlin, Warren B., *The Progress of Economics.* New York: Bookman Associates, 1962.

Gide, Charles, and Charles Rist, *Histoire des Doctrines Économiques.* Paris: Larose et Tenin, 1909. (Trans. R. Richards, *A History of Economic Doctrine.* Boston: D. C. Heath & Company, 1915.)

Gray, Alexander, *Development of Economic Doctrine.* London: Longmans, Green & Company, Ltd., 1931.

Haney, Lewis H., *History of Economic Thought* (Rev. Ed.). New York: The Macmillan Company, 1924.

Neff, Frank A., *Economic Doctrines* (2nd Ed.). New York: McGraw-Hill Book Company, 1950.

Chapter III

Immigration—Some Facts
The most convenient general source of immigration statistics is *Historical Statistics of the United States* (cited in the text). On the changing economic opportunities after 1900, which tended toward concentration of new immigrants into the urban slums, the author relied largely on:

Commons, John R., *Races and Immigrants in America* (Choice of employers and reliance on charity, esp. p. 166). New York: The Macmillan Company, 1907.

Fairchild, Henry Pratt, *Immigration: A World Movement and Its American Significance* (Importance of languages and cultural factors, esp. p. 230). New York: The Macmillan Company, 1913.

Goodrich, Carter, and Sol Davison, "The Wage Earner and the West-ward Movement" (Minimum effect of westward migration in im-proving the economic situation of eastern industrial workers, esp. p. 115). *Political Science Quarterly*, LI (1936).

Handlin, O., *The Uprooted* (Growth—New York City and Chicago, 1840–1900, esp. p. 145). Boston: Little, Brown & Co., 1951.

Hofstader, R., *The Age of Reform* (New farms in relation to immi-grants, 1890–1919, esp. p. 52). New York: Alfred A. Knopf, Inc., 1955.

Hourwich, I. A., *Immigration and Labor* (Unemployment of immi-grants at point of entry, esp. p. 126, 129). New York: G. P. Putnam's Sons, 1912.

Schultz, Theodore, *Agriculture in an Unstable Economy* (New land put into use after the "passing of the frontier" in the "golden age of American agriculture," pp. 114ff.). New York: McGraw-Hill Book Company, 1945.

Turner, Frederick Jackson, *The Frontier in American History* (The work which popularized the concept of the "passing of the frontier"). New York: Holt, Rinehart & Winston, Inc., 1920.

The most extensive source of information on the wages of the foreign-born as compared with native-born workers was collected by the U. S. Immigration Commission of 1907–1910. Fairchild, *Immigration: A World Movement and Its American Significance* (Esp. p. 229), quotes some of the major findings. John A. Ryan compared earnings of adult urban in-dustrial workers (largely immigrants) around the year 1900 with his living wage of $12 a week: *A Living Wage* (Esp. p. 155). New York: The Macmillan Company, 1906.

The Social Service Movement—Some Doctrines
The religious roots of the social service movement are treated exten-sively in:

Gladden, Washington, *Applied Christianity*. Boston: Houghton Mifflin Company, 1891.

May, Henry R., *Protestant Churches and Industrial America*. New York: Harper & Row, Publishers, 1949.

Ryan, John R., *A Living Wage* (See p. 33 re *Rerum Novarum*).

Schlesinger, A. M., *Political and Social Growth of the American People*. New York: The Macmillan Company, 1914.

The developing relationship of social service work to the urban, immi-grant workers and to the growing demands for reform are portrayed in:

Addams, Jane, *Twenty Years at Hull House*. New York: The Macmillan Company, 1910.

Goldmark, Josephine, *Impatient Crusader: Florence Kelley's Life Story*. Urbana, Ill.: University of Illinois Press, 1953.

Ryan, John R., *A Living Wage*.

Schlesinger, A. M., *Political and Social Growth of the American People*.
Woods, Robert A., and A. J. Kennedy, *The Settlement Horizon*. New
York: Russell Sage Foundation, 1922.
The publications of the "muckrakers" referred to in the text were:
Riis, Jacob, *How the Other Half Lives*. New York: Charles Scribner's
Sons, 1890; Sagamore Press, Inc., 1957.
Sinclair, Upton, *The Jungle*. New York: Doubleday & Company, Inc.,
1906; Harper & Row, Publishers, 1951.
Tarbell, Ida, *History of the Standard Oil Company*. New York: The
Macmillan Company, 1925.
Impact on Theory
Lees-Smith, Hastings Bernard, "Economic Theory and Proposals for
a Legal Minimum Wage" (A British economist's elaboration of an
orthodox theorist's objections). *Economic Journal* (1907) XII.
Individual Wages versus the Wage Share
Hamilton, Walter, and Stacey May, *The Control of Wages* (Esp. p.
105). Garden City, N. Y.: Doubleday & Company, Inc., 1923.
Atomistic Competition
The general significance of varying degrees of monoply and monopsony
as compared with atomistic competition was first developed intensively
by Robinson in England and Chamberlin in the United States:
Chamberlin, Edward, *The Theory of Monopolistic Competition*. Cam-
bridge, Mass.: Harvard University Press, 1946.
Robinson, Joan, *The Economics of Imperfect Competition*. London:
Macmillan & Co., Ltd., 1933.
The specified implications for wage theory of the absence of atomistic
competition were developed by Paul H. Douglas:
Douglas, Paul H., "Wage Theory and Wage Policy", *International
Labour Review*. Geneva: March, 1939, pp. 319–60.
————, *The Theory of Wages*, (Esp. Chap. III). New York: The
Macmillan Company, 1957.
Historical Viewpoint
John Bates Clark presented marginal productivity theory in its most
inflexible form (*The Distribution of Wealth*, cited in Chap. II). Yet at
the end of the *Distribution* (Chaps. XXV and XXVI) Clark himself fore-
cast the need for an equally important "dynamic" or historical approach
to economic problems.

Chapter IV

The original and most detailed general history of American workers'
unions was that of John R. Commons and Associates, *A History of Labour
in the United States* (Vols. I and II). New York: The Macmillan Company, 1918. A condensed version of this work was Selig Perlman's *A*

History of Trade Unionism in the United States. New York: The Mac-
millan Company, 1922. A more analytic and later summary history
through the 1930's is that of Professor Montgomery in Chaps. I–V of
Harry A. Millis and Royal E. Montgomery, Organized Labor, Vol. III of
Economics of Labor. New York: McGraw-Hill Book Company, 1945.
An excellent brief history of more recent date is Foster Rhea Dulles,
Labor in America. New York: Thomas Y. Crowell Company, 1949.

The original general history of British labor organizations was Sidney
and Beatrice Webb's The History of Trade Unionism. London: Longmans,
Green & Company, Ltd., 1894. A much later work was that of G. D. H.
Cole, A Short History of the British Working Class Movement. London:
George Allen & Unwin, Ltd., 1923. In Chapter I, Cole (like the author,
but unlike the Webbs) stressed the similarity of the goals of the early
labor unions to those of the medieval craft guilds.

Early Developments

Commons, John R., and Associates, A History of Labour in the United
States (Esp. Vol. I, Part II, and pp. 619–20 for labor goals before
1860; Vol. II, Part VI, Chaps. VII–XII on the period of the Knights
of Labor).

Millis, Harry A., and Royal E. Montgomery, Organized Labor (Esp.
pp. 12–45 on unions before 1860).

Ware, Norman J., The Industrial Worker, 1840–1860. Boston: Houghton Mifflin Company, 1924.

————, The Labor Movement in the United States 1860–1895 (Esp.
Chaps. XI and XII for radical unionism in contrast to the American
Federation of Labor). Boston: D. C. Heath & Company, 1935.

Wolman, Leo, The Growth of American Trade Unions. New York:
National Bureau of Economic Research, 1924.

The American Federation of Labor

Special sources, in addition to those cited above, are:

Cox, Archibald, Cases on Labor Law, No. 3 (Page 75 provides a convenient source for the opinion in Adair vs. U. S., cited in the text).
Brooklyn: Foundation Press, 1958.

Reed, Louis, The Labor Philosophy of Samuel Gompers. New York:
Columbia University Press, 1930.

Taft, Philip, The AFL in the Time of Gompers. New York: Harper &
Row, Publishers, 1957.

NEW DOCTRINES AND OLD THEORY

The restrictionist doctrines of AFL unions are well known. Indeed, their
practical importance has often been exaggerated by opponents of unions.
Less well-recognized is the consistency of these doctrines with the ortho-

dox marginal productivity theory of wages. Gompers' famous "more and more" statement, cited in the text, may be found conveniently in Louis Reed, *The Labor Philosophy of Samuel Gompers* (p. 12).

Restrictionist policies toward foreign labor are developed in detail by Sylvie Eriksson, "The Attitude of Organized Labor Toward Restriction of Immigration." Unpublished Master's thesis, Cornell University, 1959.

Restriction of domestic labor supplies is more comprehensively discussed in Millis and Montgomery, *Organized Labor* (Chap. X). On the admission policies of unions, see also Sumner H. Slichter, *Union Policies and Industrial Management* (pp. 63–71). Washington, D. C.: The Brookings Institution, 1941. Restriction of membership to white persons has usually been treated as a problem of the difficulty of organizing nonwhites rather than one of deliberate union restriction. However, an example of such restriction in a union constitution is cited in D. W. Hertel, *History of Brotherhood of Maintenance of Way Employees.* Washington, D. C.: Ransdell Inc., Publishers, 1955. In the 1930's the author found *de facto* discrimination against Negroes by local building-trades unions, even when a union constitution specifically forbade such a practice.

As for restriction of work on the job, present-day newspaper readers are familiar with the "featherbedding" controversy between railroad managements and unions. A penetrating study of the liberalization of on-the-job restrictions is that of Jean Trepp McKelvey, *AFL Attitudes Toward Production, 1900–1932.* Ithaca, New York: Cornell University Press, 1952.

NEW DOCTRINES AND NEW THEORIES

The author's purpose in this chapter, as throughout the book, is to trace the general impact of new facts and doctrines on the changing *problems* of wage theory rather than to explore the new theories in detail. For further detailed reading on the impact of unionism on wage theory, the reader is referred to the illuminating comments and rich source material of Melvin W. Reder, "Wage Determination in Theory and Practice" in Neil W. Chamberlain, Frank C. Pierson, and Theresa Wolfson (eds.), *A Decade of Industrial Relations Research 1946–1956* (Chap. III, esp. pp. 81–84). New York: Harper & Row, Publishers, 1958. George H. Hildebrand's companion chapter, "The Economic Effects of Unionism" (*loc. cit.*, Chap. IV) deals principally with issues raised in Chapters XI and XII of this book.

As regards the relation of the value of the marginal product of workers to the employer's production plan, the best analysis known to the author is that in Lloyd G. Reynolds, *Labor Economics and Labor Relations* (Chap. XIX). Englewood Cliffs, N. J.: Prentice-Hall, Inc., 1959.

Chapter V

Walton H. Hamilton described an "institution" broadly as "a cluster of social usages . . . to which we imperfectly accommodate our lives. . . ." in Edwin R. A. Seligman and Alvin Johnson (eds.), *Encyclopedia of the Social Sciences* (VIII, 84–99). New York: The Macmillan Company, 1937. A recent appraisal of the significance of institutionalism for economic policy is that of Morris A. Copeland in "Institutionalism and Welfare Economics," *American Economic Review* (1958) XLVIII, 1–17.

Veblen, the Critic
Thorstein Veblen's most important works, in order of first publication data, were: *The Theory of the Leisure Class* (1899). New York: Modern Library, Inc., 1934; *The Theory of Business Enterprise* (1904). New York: Charles Scribner's Sons, 1904; *The Instinct of Workmanship and the State of the Industrial Arts* (1914). New York: The Macmillan Company, 1914; *The Engineers and the Price System* (1921). New York: The Viking Press, Inc., 1944.

The definitive biography and the most extensive appraisal of Veblen is Joseph Dorfman, *Thorstein Veblen and His America* (1934). New York: The Viking Press, Inc., 1945. Notable brief appraisals are:

Homan, Paul T., *Contemporary Economic Thought* (Esp. pp. 105–92). New York: Harper & Row, Publishers, 1928.

Johnson, Alvin, "Veblen," *Encyclopedia of the Social Sciences* (XV, 234–35). New York: The Macmillan Company, 1937.

Riesman, David, *Thorstein Veblen, A Critical Interpretation*. New York: Charles Scribner's Sons, 1953.

The natural-balance concept of orthodox theory was perhaps best explained by Alfred Marshall, *Principles of Economics* (Book V, Chap. III). Veblen's objection to this concept was expressed in a characteristic piece of satire, quoted by Riesman, *Thorstein Veblen: A Critical Interpretation* (p. 154):

A gang of Aleutian Islanders slushing around in the wrack and surf with rakes and magical incantations for the capture of shellfish one held, in point of taxonomic reality, to be engaged on a feat of hedonistic equilibrium in rent, wages, and interest.

Mitchell, the Statistician
Wesley C. Mitchell was the sole author of the following major works: *A History of the Greenbacks*. Chicago: University of Chicago Press, 1903; *Gold, Prices, and Wages Under the Greenback Standard*. Berkeley, Calif.: University of California Press, 1908; *Business Cycles*. Berkeley, Calif.: University of California Press, 1913; *Business Cycles: Vol. I, The Problem and Its Setting*. New York: National Bureau of Economic Research,

208   Bibliographic Notes

1927; *The Making and Using of Index Numbers*. U. S. Department of Labor, Bureau of Labor Statistics Bulletin No. 656. Washington, D. C.: Government Printing Office, 1938. Mitchell was a co-author of: *Income in the United States—Its Amount and Distribution*. New York: Harcourt, Brace & World, Inc., 1921; and *Measuring Business Cycles*. New York: *National Bureau of Economic Research*, 1946. He has edited numerous other volumes for the National Bureau of Economic Research.

Mitchell's contributions to economic theory are more explicitly stated in his numerous professional articles and essays than in his books. A collection of some of his shorter works was reprinted in *The Backward Art of Spending Money*. New York: McGraw-Hill Book Company, 1937.

The two chief appraisals of Mitchell's work are:

Homan, Paul T., *Contemporary Economic Thought* (pp. 377–466; see pp. 379–83 for the influence on Mitchell of Laughlin and the University of Chicago scholars of Mitchell's graduate student period).

Mills, Frederick C., "Wesley Clair Mitchell," *American Economic Review* (1949) XXXIX, 730–42.

Commons, the Historian

John R. Commons was the sole author of the following major books which reflect his historical-institutional approach to economic problems: *Trade Unionism and Labor Problems*. Boston: Ginn & Company, 1905, 1921; *Races and Immigrants in America*. New York: The Macmillan Company, 1907; *Legal Foundations of Capitalism*. New York: The Macmillan Company, 1924; *Institutional Economics*. New York: The Macmillan Company, 1934, reprinted Madison, Wis.: University of Wisconsin Press, 1961. More important were the following works, for which Commons was the editor and senior collaborator: "Regulation and Restriction of Output," *Eleventh Special Report of the Commissioner of Labor*, H. R. Document No. 734, 58th Congress, 2nd Session. Washington, D. C.: Government Printing Office, 1904; *A Documentary History of American Industrial Society*, 10 vols. Cleveland: The A. H. Clark Co., 1910–1911; *Principles of Labor Legislation*. New York: The Macmillan Company, 1916, revised 1927; *A History of Labour in the United States*. New York: The Macmillan Company, Vols. I and II, 1918; Vols. III and IV, 1935. Other books and forty-five of Commons' professional articles published between 1895 and 1931 are listed in *Institutional Economics* (pp. 9–12).

No adequate over-all appraisal of Commons' work appears to have been published. Two specialized appraisals are: George D. Blackwood, "Frederick Jackson Turner and John Rogers Commons—Complimentary Thinkers," *Mississippi Valley Historical Review* (1954), XLI, 471–88; and Lafayette G. Harter, *John R. Commons: His Assault on Laissez Faire*. Eugene, Ore.: Oregon State University Press, 1962. Unusually informative was the unpublished "Resolution of the Faculty of the University of Wisconsin on the Death of Emeritus Professor Commons," drafted by John M. Gauss, Kenneth H. Parsons, and Selig Perlman; also an autobiography of John R. Commons, *Myself*. New York: The Macmillan Company, 1934, reprinted Madison, Wis.: University of Wisconsin Press, 1963.

Chapter VI

THE NEW FACTS

Science and the Mechanical Engineer
The central role of scientific invention and engineering applications in the original Industrial Revolution is treated in every economic history of Great Britain. One of the brief treatments is in Edward P. Cheyney's *An Introduction to the Industrial and Social History of England* (Chap. VIII). New York: The Macmillan Company, 1901. Much fuller treatment is that of Witt Bowden's *Industrial Society of England Towards the End of the Eighteenth Century* (Chaps. I–III). New York: The Macmillan Company, 1925.

The spread of engineering methods of production to continental Europe is depicted by J. H. Clapham, *The Economic Development of France and Germany, 1815–1913* (Esp. Chaps. III, IV, VII, and IX). Cambridge, Mass.: Cambridge University Press, 1921. The impact of scientific methods on the American industrial economy, and thereby the stimulation of these developments to scientific management, is described by Edward C. Kirkland in *A History of American Economic Life*, 3rd Ed. (Chaps. IX and XII; also pp. 664–66). New York: Appleton-Century-Crofts, Inc., 1951. An excellent general interpretation of the significance of "The Coming of the Machine" is that of John H. Randall, Jr., *Our Changing Civilization* (Chap. VIII). New York: Stokes, 1934; reprinted in Thornton (ed), *Science and Social Change*. Washington, D. C.: The Brookings Institution, 1939.

Development of New Jobs
A classic generalized treatment of the decline of handicraft production was that of Carl Buecher, *Industrial Evolution* (Esp. pp. 191–209). New York: Holt, Rinehart & Winston, Inc., 1901. Characteristic of the industries most adaptable to machine production were summarized in J. A. Hobson, *The Evolution of Modern Capitalism* (pp. 90–92). London: The Walter Scott Publishing Co., Ltd., 1912. These two sources were adapted for use in L. C. Marshall (ed.), *Readings in Industrial Society* (pp. 640–46, and 434–36 respectively). Chicago: University of Chicago Press, 1918. The basic sources of occupational information are the decennial census of population (U. S. Bureau of the Census, after 1913 a bureau of the U. S. Department of Commerce). New occupational titles appear in the successive censuses with increasing frequency after 1880.

Abundance of Unskilled Labor
See Chapter III of this text and the bibliographical notes thereto. The essentially unskilled groups of farm laborers, common laborers, and those reporting no occupation, taken together, comprised 72 per cent of the 7.2

million immigrants to the United States (excluding Hebrews) during the decade 1899–1909. The results of the original classification by the U. S. Commissioner General of Immigration were compiled by the U. S. Immigration Commission (1910), summarized by Jeremiah W. Jenks and W. Jett Lauck, *The Immigration Problem*. New York: Funk & Wagnalls Co., 1922, and adapted by Paul H. Douglas, Curtice E. Hitchcock, and Willard E. Atkins, *The Worker in Modern Economic Society* (p. 192). Chicago: University of Chicago Press, 1923. The author's figures above combine the "old" and the "new" immigration of the 1899–1909 period. If those who reported themselves on arrival as "servants" (24 per cent) were to be considered as unskilled, the remaining group (professional workers, skilled laborers, and miscellaneous) would represent less than 4 per cent of the immigrants, as compared with about 41 per cent of such skilled workers in the U. S. total population as of 1910. Cf. Gladys L. Palmer and Ann R. Miller, "The Occupational and Industrial Distribution of Employment, 1910–50," in William Haber (ed.), *Manpower in the United States* (p. 87, Table VI–1). New York: Harper & Row, Publishers, 1954.

The Rise of Unionism
See Chapter IV of this text and bibliographical notes thereto.

PIONEERS AND THEIR DOCTRINES

Frederick Taylor
The three most important works of Frederick Winslow Taylor, in order of first appearance, were:
"Shop Management," *Transactions of the American Society of Mechanical Engineers* (1903), XXIV, reprinted as *Shop Management* by Harper & Row, Publishers, in 1911.
"On the Art of Cutting Metals," *Transactions of the American Society of Mechanical Engineers* (1906), XXVIII.
The Principles of Scientific Management. New York: Harper & Row, Publishers, 1911.
"Shop Management" and the *Principles*, together with Taylor's testimony before the Special Committee of the House of Representatives to Investigate the Taylor and Other Systems of Management [H. R. 90 (1912) III, 1377–1508], were reprinted as Frederick Winslow Taylor, *Scientific Management*. New York: Harper & Row, Publishers, 1947.
Although uniformly laudatory, the most detailed and informative biography of Taylor is that of Frank Barkley Copley, *Frederick W. Taylor, Father of Scientific Management*, 2 Vols. New York: Harper & Row, Publishers, 1923. Taylor's role in relation to his immediate predecessors and followers is presented succinctly and critically by Horace B. Drury, *Scientific Management*. New York: Columbia University Press, 1915; 3rd. Ed., 1922.

Taylor's Disciples

A good summary of the lives and contributions of Taylor's immediate disciples is that of Drury, *Scientific Management* (Chap. VI). Gilbreth and his talented wife have been the subjects of two biographies: (1) An intimate family portrait by two of his children, adapted for a popular motion picture: Frank B. Gilbreth, Jr. and Ernestine Gilbreth Carey, *Cheaper By the Dozen.* New York: Thomas Y. Crowell Co., 1949. (2) A more objective, although still somewhat sentimental, treatment by Edna Yost, *Frank and Lillian Gilbreth.* New Brunswick, N. J.: Rutgers University Press, 1949.

Descriptions of the different types of incentive wage-payment plans, including those of Taylor's disciples as well as earlier and later variants, may be found in almost any American textbook on personnel administration. A good example is that of William W. Waite, *Personnel Administration* (pp. 298–308). New York: The Ronald Press Company, 1952. A later treatment, in the context of a fuller consideration of employee compensation from the modern employer viewpoint, is that of David W. Belcher, *Wage and Salary Administration* (pp. 386–403). Englewood Cliffs, N. J.: Prentice-Hall, Inc., 1962.

REACTIONS TO SCIENTIFIC MANAGEMENT

The specific contributions of Hathaway, Thompson, Kendall, and Cooke are described by Drury, *Scientific Management* (pp. 42n, 114–17, 129–43, 183). The Taylor Society Bulletins (1916 *et seq.*) provide major source material on the developing ideas of Taylor's most devoted followers. Clarence Bertrand Thompson (ed.), *Scientific Management* (Cambridge, Mass.: Harvard University Press, 1914) provides a valuable "collection of the more significant articles describing the Taylor system of management"; this Thompson collection constituted Volume I of the *Harvard Business Studies;* it includes a review of scientific management literature to 1913 by Thompson himself (pp. 3–48) and articles by Taylor, Thompson (two), and Frank T. Carlton which deal with wages and the workers' relation to scientific management (pp. 636–733).

Two governmental hearings provided extensive and important testimony by advocates of a group led by Louis B. Brandeis with regard to a proposed raise in rates by the Eastern railroads. Interstate Commerce Commission, *Reports*, Vol. XX. Washington, D. C.: Government Printing Office, 1912. Another hearing grew out of organized labor's protests against the use of Taylor's methods at the government's Watertown arsenal. U. S. Congress, *Hearings Before Special Committee of the House of Representatives to Investigate the Taylor and Other Systems of Shop Management,* 3 Vols. Washington, D. C.: Government Printing Office, 1912. A later "exposition of scientific management" which conspicuously omitted any treatment of the wage aspects was published by the Taylor

Society as H. H. Person (ed.), *Scientific Management in American Industry*. New York: Harper & Row, Publishers, 1929.

Personnel Departments—Selection and Training

The shift in emphasis of the scientific management movement "away from the idea of making men work harder to the idea of making their work more effective" is described in the introduction to the third edition of Drury, *Scientific Management* (pp. 7–28). Two of the pioneer books which advocated specialized personnel departments—especially to implement selection, training, and a systematic "labor audit"—were:

Scott, Walter Dill, and Robert C. Clothier, *Personnel Management*. Chicago: A. W. Shaw Company, 1923.

Tead, Ordway, and H. C. Metcalf, *Personnel Administration*. New York: McGraw-Hill Book Company, 1926.

Methods of Wage Payment

The finding of the U. S. Bureau of Labor Statistics that about 27 per cent of factory employees were under incentive pay systems in 1958 and that this proportion had changed little since the end of World War II was reported by Lewis L. Earl, "Extent of Incentive Pay in Manufacturing," *Monthly Labor Review* (1960), LXXIII, 461, 463.

Changing management attitudes toward incentive wage payments are described from two different viewpoints by:

Barkin, Solomon, "Management's Attitude Toward Wage Incentives," *Industrial and Labor Relations Review* (1951) V, 92–107.

Crandall, Richard E., "De-Emphasized Wage Incentives," *Harvard Business Review* (1962) XL, 113–16.

See also "Taylor's Disciples" in the above notes and "Welfare Capitalism" in the notes for Chap. VII.

Union Opposition

The most penetrating single analysis of labor attitudes toward scientific management—indeed of scientific management as a whole—was that of Robert Franklin Hoxie, *Scentific Management and Labor*. New York: Appleton-Century-Crofts, Inc., 1918. Valuable contributions to the understanding of labor's changing attitudes since the 1930's include:

Barkin, Solomon, "Labor's Attitude Toward Wage Incentives," *Industrial and Labor Relations Review* (1948), I, 553–72.

Cooke, Morris L., and Philip Murray, *Organized Labor and Production*. New York: Harper & Row, Publishers, 1940.

Gomberg, William, *A Trade Union Analysis of Time Study*. Chicago: Science Research Associates, 1948. The direct quotation from Gomberg is from p. 13. Gomberg's book also contains a valuable bibliography (pp. 205–34).

Kennedy, Van Dusen, *Union Policy and Incentive Wage Methods*. New York: Columbia University Press, 1945.

The Human Needs of Workers

See "Welfare Capitalism" (notes for Chap. VII). Also, see Barkin, "Management's Attitude Toward Wage Incentives," and Crandall, "De-Emphasized Wage Incentives."

William Foot Whyte and Associates, *Money and Motivation* (New York: Harper & Row, Publishers, 1955) interpret their field-study results as showing the deficiencies of individual incentive-wage systems due to a failure to recognize motivation as involving intergroup relations. Whyte thus lays the groundwork for the human relations approach, both to the rise of labor unions (see notes above for Chap. IV) and to the most recent phase of welfare capitalism (see notes for Chap. VII below).

Chapter VII

Pioneers of Welfare Capitalism
One of the better brief accounts of Robert Owen's proposed reforms is that of G. D. H. Cole, *A Short History of the British Working Class Movement* (pp. 112–18). London: George Allen & Unwin, Ltd., 1923. The application of some of Owen's concepts by New England employers is noted in Commons and Associates, *A History of Labour in the United States* (I, 173–74). New York: The Macmillan Company, 1936. The leading biographers of Robert Owen are G. D. H. Cole, *Robert Owen*. London: Ernest Benn, Ltd., 1925; and the earlier Frank Podmore, *Robert Owen, A Biography*. London: Hutchinson & Co., Ltd., 1906. The National Library of Wales has compiled *A Bibliography of Robert Owen, the Socialist, 1771–1858*. London: Oxford University Press, 1925.

The roles of Pullman, Carnegie, and John D. Rockefeller, Jr., are treated at length in: Carroll Rede Harding, *George M. Pullman and the Pullman Company*. New York: The Newcomen Society in North America, 1951; Andrew Carnegie, *Autobiography*. Boston: Houghton Mifflin Company, 1920; Burton J. Hendrick, *The Life of Andrew Carnegie*. Garden City, N. Y.: Doubleday & Company, Inc., 1932; and Raymond Blaine Fosdick, *John D. Rockefeller, Jr., A Portrait* (Esp. Chaps. VIII and IX). New York: Harper & Row, Publishers, 1956.

Activities of Paternalistic Employers
Two of the influential books in the 1920's which advocated extensive attention to human relations by employers were:

Price, C. W., *Working Conditions, Wages and Profits* (Esp. Part I). Chicago: A. W. Shaw and Co., 1920.

Tead, Ordway, and Henry C. Metcalf, *Personnel Administration* (Esp. pp. 317–20). New York: McGraw-Hill Book Company, 1920.

Following are the sources of specific statistical data cited in the text, under the indicated subheadings:

Recreation: *Health and Recreational Activities in Industrial Establishments, 1926*. U. S. Department of Labor, Bureau of Labor Statistics Bulletin No. 458. Washington, D. C.: Government Printing Office, 1928.

Education and Information: *Monthly Labor Review* (1928), XXVI, 14, 19.

Economic Security: *Monthly Labor Review* (1928), XXVII, No. 2. *Care of Aged Persons in the United States*. U. S. Department of Labor,

Bureau of Labor Statistics Bulletin No. 489. Washington, D. C.: Government Printing Office, 1929; *Monthly Labor Review* (1928), XXVI, 20.

Conveniences: *Monthly Labor Review* (1928), XXVI, 14, 17.

Personal and Family Problems: *Monthly Labor Review* (1928), XXVI, 20.

Community Interests (Company Housing): *Monthly Labor Review* (1917), V, 35–60; also (1936), XLII, No. 6, 1492.

Employee Representation Plans: Douglas, Paul H., "Shop Committees: Substitute for, or Supplement to, Trade Unions," *Journal of Political Economy* (1921), XXIX, 89–107.

Recent Developments

The only comprehensive and continuous surveys of the types and costs of fringe benefits in the United States since World War II have been the annual surveys of the U. S. Chamber of Commerce—*Fringe Benefits*. Washington, D. C.: U. S. Chamber of Commerce, 1948 ff. The edition cited in the text was that of 1960, covering the Chamber's survey for 1959. The results have an upward bias if they are to be used as characteristic of all United States employers, because an undue proportion of the questionnaire responses were obtained from the larger companies, which tend to have more elaborate and costlier fringe-benefit plans. However, the data probably reflect the *trend* of over-all fringe-benefit costs and the *relative* costs of the various types of fringe benefits. Moreover, the over-all percentages themselves are probably indicative of the importance of fringe benefits among the larger firms which have always been the ones most able to follow the methods of welfare capitalism.

THE NEW FACTS

The pioneering study of the costs of labor turnover was that of Sumner H. Slichter, *The Turnover of Factory Labor*. New York: Appleton-Century-Crofts, Inc., 1921. (Data relate to the year 1919.)

The definitive study of labor-union membership was that of Leo Wolman, *Ebb and Flow in Trade Unionism*. New York: National Bureau of Economic Research, 1939. Later data on union membership have been obtained from page 195 of *Statistical Abstract of the United States, 1952* (73rd Ed.). U. S. Department of Commerce, Bureau of the Census. Washington, D. C.: Government Printing Office, 1953.

WAGE DOCTRINES OF WELFARE CAPITALISM

Some account of the abject conditions of British wage earners during the first half of the nineteenth century is now contained in nearly every economic history of the period. The most horrible examples were provided by the coal mines, whose workers were not protected by governmental regulation, labor organization, or the consciences of the absentee employers. The official documents which first exposed the conditions of coal miners in a comprehensive way were those of the Commission of Enquiry into the Employment of Children and Young Persons in the Mines—*First Report*. London: His Majesty's Stationery Office, 1841; and *Second Report*. *Idem*, 1843. Much of this material, together with new data from the textile industry, was used by Friedrich Engels (the collaborator of Karl Marx) in his *The Condition of the Working Class in England* (For data on coal mines, see pp. 134–87, 241–60). London: George Allen & Unwin, Ltd., 1892. The limited improvements made by British employers themselves were recognized by Beatrice Webb in her *The Case for the Factory Acts*. London: Grant Richards, Ltd., 1901— even though Mrs. Webb insisted that the voluntary efforts of employers needed to be buttressed by compulsory factory regulations. The economists' case for improved treatment of workers in the interests of the employers themselves was made by Mill, *Principles* (Esp. Chap. VII), and Marshall, *Principles of Economics* (Esp. Book IV, Chaps. I, V, and VI; also Book VI, Chap. II).

Chapter VIII

The sources of statistical data used are listed under each of the following sections in the order of the first treatment of each subject in the text.

Orthodox Wage Doctrine and Economic Trends, 1920–1933
  Production and Employment:
    Fabricant, Solomon, *Labor Savings in American Industry, 1899–1939* (pp. 43–50). New York: National Bureau of Economic Research, 1945.
    Stigler, George J., *Trends in Output and Employment* (pp. 57–59). New York: National Bureau of Economic Research, 1947.
  The findings of both Fabricant and Stigler are summarized in W. S. Woytinsky and Associates, *Employment and Wages in the United States* (p. 569). New York: The Twentieth Century Fund, 1953.
  Market Value of Shares:
    Leffler, George L., *The Stock Market* (p. 521). New York: The Ronald Press Company, 1951.
  Wages and Earnings:
    Employment and Earnings. U. S. Department of Labor, Bureau of Labor Statistics Bulletin No. 852. Washington, D. C.: Government Printing Office, 1945.
    Lebergott, Stanley, "Earnings of Nonfarm Employees in the United States," *Journal of the American Statistical Association* (March 1948).
  Both of the above sources are adapted by Woytinsky, *op. cit.* (p. 584).

Prices:

Consumer Prices (formerly called Cost of Living Index) and *Wholesale Prices* have been adapted by Woytinsky, *op. cit.* (p. 585) from bulletins of the U. S. Department of Labor, Bureau of Labor Statistics.

President Hoover's Economic Policies:

Schlesinger, Arthur M., Jr., *The Crisis of the Old Order* (Esp. pp. 155–65). Boston: Houghton Mifflin Company, 1957.

National Product and National Income Per Capita: Index of Manufacturing Production from Fabricant, *Labor Savings in American Industry, 1899–1939,* adapted by Woytinsky (p. 570). National income, total and per capita, at current prices and adjusted to cost of living and to the general price level has been adapted by Woytinsky (p. 571) from Robert F. Martin, *National Income in the United States, 1799–1938.* New York: National Industrial Conference Board, 1939.

Unemployment:

Fichandler, T. C., "Unemployment: Its Composition and Measurement," in Woytinsky (p. 398); see also Table 93 in Woytinsky (p. 716).

Hours of Work:

Wolman, Leo, *Hours of Work in American Industry* (Esp. pp. 17–19). New York: National Bureau of Economic Research Bulletin No. 71, 1938.

Wage Rates:

Douglas, Paul H., *Real Wages in the United States,* 1890–1926. Boston: Houghton Mifflin Company, 1930.

Employment and Earnings. U. S. Department of Labor, Bureau of Labor Statistics Bulletin No. 852. Washington, D. C.: Government Printing Office, 1945.

Both of the above are adapted by Woytinsky (p. 584). Wage rates (as distinct from hourly earnings) are for the building trades, where rates fell less rapidly than in other industries in the 1930's.

Employment:

Survey of Current Business: National Income Supplement, 1951. U. S. Department of Commerce. Washington, D. C.: Government Printing Office, 1952. Adapted by Woytinsky (p. 678).

Wage Income and Share in National Income:

Kuznets, Simon, *National Income and Its Composition, 1919–1938* (Esp. pp. 216–18). New York: National Bureau of Economic Research, 1941. Adapted by Woytinsky (p. 575).

Corporate Profits (Losses):

Surveys of Current Business. Idem (p. 150). Adapted by Woytinsky (p. 579).

The National Industrial Recovery Act—A New Doctrine
Variety of Roosevelt Recovery Measures: Major actions of the Federal Government intended to promote business recovery included: (1) Devaluation of the dollar, (2) Reciprocal trade agreements, (3) Federal relief projects, (4) Public works projects, (5) Social Security measures. See Arthur M. Schlesinger, Jr., *The Coming of the New Deal*. Boston: Houghton Mifflin Company, 1955.

Codes of Fair Competition:
Lyon, Leverett, et al., *The National Recovery Administration* (pp. 48–52, 916–33). Washington, D. C.: The Brookings Institution, 1935.

Industrial "Self-Government": The problem of what role, if any, was to be played by the public, labor, and government in this industrial "self-government" is treated in Lyon, *The National Recovery Administration* (pp. 15–26, 210–14, 272–74, 528).

Wages and Economic Trends, 1933–1937
For price trends during N. R. A. see Lyon, *The National Recovery Administration* (pp. 785–93). After 1934, see the U. S. Department of Labor, Bureau of Labor Statistics Price Indexes, summarized by Woytinsky (p. 585).

Employment:
Lyon, *The National Recovery Administration* (pp. 830–44) and Woytinsky (p. 678).

Unemployment:
Handbook of Labor Statistics, 1947. U. S. Department of Labor, Bureau of Labor Statistics Bulletin No. 916. Washington, D. C.: Government Printing Office, 1948. Quoted by Woytinsky, (p. 398, Table 169).
Woytinsky (p. 716, Table 93).

Purchasing-Power Theory:
Lyon, *The National Recovery Administration* (pp. 756–75).

Wages, Hours, and Purchasing Power: (1) During the NRA period, Lyon, *The National Recovery Administration* (pp. 796–807, 845–52). (2) Basic sources for Employment and Earnings, and also for Cost of Living, are the U. S. Department of Labor, Bureau of Labor Statistics bulletins, *passim*. Alternatively, see the *Monthly Labor Review, passim*. Calculations are the author's.

The Fair Labor Standards Act—A Replacement for NRA
The detailed and definitive history and analysis of state minimum wage laws prior to 1938 is Harry A. Millis and Royal E. Montgomery, *Labor's Progress and Some Basic Economic Problems* (Chap. VI). New York: McGraw-Hill Book Company, 1938. Pages 328-42 give an economic criticism of the decision in *Adkins vs. Children's Hospital.*

The most informative brief treatment of federal and New York state minimum wage laws and regulations is that of Donald E. Cullen, *Minimum Wage Laws*, New York State School of Industrial and Labor Relations Bulletin No. 43. Ithaca, N. Y.: Cornell University, 1961. The author's treatment of the subject appeared as N. Arnold Tolles, "American Minimum Wage Laws: Their Purposes and Effects," in *Industrial Relations Research Association: Proceedings of Twelfth Annual Meeting, Washington, D. C., December 28–29, 1959* (pp. 116–33). Madison, Wis.: Industrial Relations Research Association, 1960. Also see the discussion by Peter Henle and John M. Peterson, *loc. cit.* (pp. 134–43). The most important recent references dealing with the issues raised by minimum wage laws were cited either by Cullen, *Minimum Wage Laws*, or by Tolles, "American Minimum Wage Laws: Their Purposes and Effects."

Among the unpublished sources of special merit are two graduate theses in the Library of the New York State School of Industrial and Labor Relations. A critical analysis of the literature on minimum-wage regulation prior to 1953 is contained in Jean Alice Wells, "Effects of Minimum Wage Laws in the United States." Unpublished Master's thesis, Cornell University, 1953. The results of a superior field study of actual employer adjustments to an increased legal minimum wage are reported in Marian Stever McNulty, "The Consequences of the New York State Minimum Wage Order 7–b for the Retail Trade Industry on Sample Establishments in Syracuse and Auburn, New York." Unpublished Doctoral dissertation, Cornell University, 1962.

Chapter IX

DEFICIT SPENDING

Receipts and expenditures of the federal government and of the state and local governments for the years 1929–1954 are those shown in the U. S. Department of Commerce *Survey of Current Business, National Income Supplement, 1954* (pp. 170–73). Washington, D. C.: Government Printing Office, 1954.

Gross national product and the combined net receipts and expenditures of federal, state, and local governments for the years 1929–1959 are those shown in U. S. Board of Economic Advisors, *The Economic Report of the President, January, 1960* (p. 163). Washington, D. C.: Government Printing Office, 1960.

Private business expenditures on plant, equipment, and inventories, and the total of business and consumer expenditures for 1937 and 1938 are shown in *National Income Supplement, 1947* (p. 19). Washington, D. C.: Government Printing Office, 1947.

For the estimated unemployment percentage in March of 1933, see the above notes for Chapter VIII. Unemployment percentages in other years are those from the Bureau of the Census Report on the Labor Force, as compiled in the *Historical Statistics of the United States from Colonial Times to 1957* (p. 73), U. S. Department of Commerce, Bureau of the Census. Washington, D. C.: Government Printing Office, 1960.

Average weekly hours, hourly earnings, and weekly earnings of factory workers are those of the U. S. Bureau of Labor Statistics, as compiled in *Historical Statistics* (p. 92).

Employee compensation and gross national product for 1941–1946 is shown in *National Income Supplement, 1959* (pp. 6–9). Washington, D. C.: Government Printing Office, 1959.

The fact that civilian consumption in the United States during World War II was undiminished—indeed, increased 15 per cent—was determined by the special combined committee set up by the Combined Production and Resources Board, *The Impact of War on Civilian Consumption in the United Kingdom, United States, and Canada*. Washington, D. C.: Government Printing Office, 1945. Morris Copeland of Cornell University, chairman of the indicated committee, kindly furnished this citation.

The gross and net federal government debt and the net state and local government debt for the years 1929–1959 is shown in *Economic Report of the President, January 1960* (pp. 210–11).

Average wholesale prices for the years 1929–1940 are those of the U. S. Department of Labor, Bureau of Labor Statistics, as compiled in *Historical Statistics* (pp. 116–17).

GRADUATED INCOME TAXES

The growth of the American income tax system, including representative tax rates, percentages of federal government receipts obtained from income taxes, percentages of personal incomes taxed, and avoidance of tax liability, are described in:

Copeland, Morris A., *Trends in Government Financing* (Esp. Chap. III). New York: National Bureau of Economic Research, 1960.

Dewhurst, J. Frederic, and Associates, *America's Needs and Resources* (Chap. XVIII, esp. pp. 583–86). New York: Twentieth Century Fund, 1955.

Groves, Harold M., *Financing Government*, 5th Ed. (Esp. pp. 200–204). New York: Holt, Rinehart & Winston, Inc., 1958.

Kahn, C. Harry, *Personal Deductions in the Federal Income Tax* (Esp. pp. 6–9). New York: National Bureau of Economic Research, 1960.

Kendrick, M. Slade, *Public Finance* (Esp. pp. 127–63). Boston: Houghton Mifflin Company, 1951.

The works of Ricardo and Marshall cited in the sketch of the development of income-tax doctrine are those listed in the above notes for Chapter II. Additional citations are:

George, Henry, *Progress and Poverty*. New York: H. George and Co., 1879.

Hobson, John Atkinson, *The Economics of Distribution* (Esp. Chap. X, pp. 295–361). New York: The Macmillan Company, 1900.

The most relevant portions of Marshall's *Principles* relating to "quasi-rent" are Book II, Chap. IV, Secs. 2 and 3; Book V, Chap. IX, Secs. 1, 2, and 3; and Book X, Chaps. 2 and 3. On the single tax movement and its relation to classical doctrines, see: (1) Gide and Rist, *Histoire des Doctrines Économiques* (pp. 545–70); and (2) Broadus Mitchell, "Single Tax," *Encyclopedia of the Social Sciences* (XIV, 64–66). New York: The Macmillan Company, 1937.

IMPACT ON WAGE THEORY

The text on the theory of employment as a determinant of wage income consists of the author's simplified explanation of the part of Keynes' *General Theory*, which bears on total wage income. The reader may more easily understand Dudley Dillard, *The Economics of John Maynard Keynes*. Englewood Cliffs, N. J.: Prentice-Hall, Inc., 1948. An enormous body of professional literature on the aggregative theory has appeared since 1940, when Keynes' theory finally became accepted as "orthodox." Unfortunately, the theory of employment generally has been considered as a separate study rather than as a necessary part of any complete theory of wages.

The theory of rent as applied to the tax redistribution of income is not new, but again there is a general failure to appreciate its importance to the theory of wages—at least in the important sense of a theory of the real spendable income which is obtained from the rewards of human effort.

The proposition that "income before taxes is broadly distributed in about the way that marginal productivity theory would lead one to expect" was that of Paul H. Douglas, *The Theory of Wages*. New York: The Macmillan Company, 1934. Recent confirmation of this proposition as it applies to countries in different stages of development has been furnished by Irving B. Kravis, "International Differences in the Distribution of Income," *Review of Economics and Statistics* (1960) XLII, 408–16. Some doubts as to its validity have arisen recently by reason of the apparent showing that the labor share of the U. S. national income has risen since the 1930's. See, for example, Irving B. Kravis, "Relative Income Shares in Fact and Theory," *American Economic Review* (1959), XLIX, No. 5, 914–49. However, the permanence of the increase in the labor share, in the author's opinion, is still subject to doubt; and, in any case, even a slight rise in the over-all share needs to be tested carefully against the changed relative quantities and qualities of the productive factors. See John W. Kendrick, *Productivity Trends in the United States*. National Bureau of Economic Research No. 71, General Series. Princeton, N. J.: Princeton University Press, 1961. Note esp. Chap. V and the comment therein by Stanley R. Ruttenberg (pp. 224–27).

For the view that the wage share depends not on physical relationships but on the decisions of capitalists, and that unions are essentially unable to increase the aggregate share of labor, see Kenneth E. Boulding, "Wages as a Share in the National Income," in David McCord Wright, *The Impact of the Union* (pp. 123–48). New York: Harcourt, Brace & World, Inc., 1951.

Chapter X

HISTORY OF SOCIAL INSURANCE DOCTRINES

The most adequate single source of analyzed information on the development of social insurance prior to World War II is Harry A. Millis and Royal E. Montgomery, *Labor's Risks and Social Insurance*. New York: McGraw-Hill Book Company, 1938. The detailed indexing of Millis and Montgomery makes unnecessary any specific citations from it in support of the historical sketch presented in the text. The additional citations below provide a guide to other sources of particular items of information.

Origins of modern social insurance on the European continent were first adequately sketched in the English language by I. M. Rubinow, *Social Insurance* (Esp. Chaps. I and II). New York: Holt, Rinehart & Winston, Inc., 1916. Greater detail on individual plans had been given in the *Twenty-Fourth Annual Report* of the U. S. Commissioner of Labor. Washington, D. C.: Government Printing Office, 1910.

The basic document on social insurance in Great Britain, including a historical appendix and recommendations for its extension, was entitled (in the American edition) Interdepartmental Committee on Social Insurance, *The Beveridge Report*. New York: The Macmillan Company, 1942.

The most adequate of the available surveys of American employers' voluntary adoption of both group insurance and pension and unemployment insurance plans just prior to the Social Security Act of 1935 were: (1) *Recent Developments in Industrial Group Insurance*. New York: National Industrial Conference Board, 1934; (2) Latimer, Murray, *Industrial Pension Systems in the United States and Canada*. New York: Industrial Relations Counsellors, Inc., 1933; (3) Brown, J. Douglas, "Company Plans for Unemployment Compensation," *American Labor Legislation Review*, December, 1934.

Provisions made by American labor unions prior to the Social Security Act to protect their members against the risks of sickness, death, old age, and unemployment were summarized in the following: (1) *Beneficial Activities of American Trade Unions,* U. S. Department of Labor, Bureau of Labor Statistics Bulletin No. 465. Washington, D. C.: Government Printing Office, 1928; (2) *Care of Aged Persons in the United States,* U. S. Department of Labor, Bureau of Labor Statistics Bulletin No. 489. Washington, D. C.: Government Printing Office, 1930; (3) Stewart, Bryce M., *Unemployment Benefits in the United States.* New York: Industrial Relations Counselors, Inc., 1930; (4) Kiehel, Constance A., "Security of Job Tenure and Trade Union Out-of-Work Benefits, 1926–1929 and 1930–1933," *American Economic Review* (1937), XXVII, 452–67.

The report which provided the basis for the American Social Security Act of 1935 was the *Report to the President of the Committee on Economic Security.* Washington, D. C.: Government Printing Office, 1935. The background of this report and of the Congressional debates on the original Social Security Act is most adequately explained in Paul H. Douglas, *Social Security in the United States* (Esp. Chaps. I–IV). New York: McGraw-Hill Book Company, 1936. The most comprehensive study and criticism of the operation of the Social Security Act as of 1950 is Eveline M. Burns, *The American Social Security System.* Boston: Houghton Mifflin Company, 1950. The most recent general treatment of both private and public measures against economic insecurity in America is John G. Turnbull, C. Arthur Williams, Jr., and Earl F. Cheit, *Economic and Social Security.* New York: The Ronald Press Company, 1962.

Significant recent studies of particular segments of the American social security problem include: (1) Corson, John J., and John W. McConnell, *The Economic Needs of Older People.* New York: The Twentieth Century Fund, 1956; (2) Sommers, Anne R., and Herman M. Sommers, *Doctors, Patients and Health Insurance.* Washington, D. C.: The Brookings Institution, 1961; (3) MacIntyre, Duncan M., *Voluntary Health Insurance and Rate Making.* Ithaca, N. Y.: Cornell University Press, 1962; and (4) McConnell, John W., and Robert F. Risley, *Economic Security: A Study in Community Needs and Resources,* New York State School of Industrial and Labor Relations Bulletin No. 18. Ithaca, N. Y.: Cornell University, 1951.

IMPACT ON WAGE THEORY

This part of the chapter chiefly consists of reasoning which is based on sources already cited. The following supplementary citations relate to certain specific points, as indicated.

Worker Freedom and Economic Welfare

Eveline M. Burns, among others, has noted the change in American attitudes toward compulsory social insurance occasioned by the gross inadequacy of individual provision for loss of income (as revealed by the depression of the 1930's). See Eveline M. Burns, *The American Social*

Security System (Chap. I and pp. 36–39), and *Social Security and Public Policy* (pp. 77, 269–80). New York: McGraw-Hill Book Company, 1956.

Payroll Taxes and the Demand for Labor

The debate over alternative methods of financing social security benefits and the considerations which led to the adoption of payroll taxes are revealed by Douglas, *The Theory of Wages* (pp. 23, 31, 44–50, 62–68).

The effects of payroll taxes on the demand for labor have been explored most intensively by Seymour E. Harris, *Economics of Social Security* (Chaps. IV, XIII–XV). New York: McGraw-Hill Book Company, 1941.

Experience Rating

The strongest reasoned support for experience rating has been offered by Herman Feldman and Donald M. Smith, *The Case for Experience Rating in Unemployment Compensation.* New York: Industrial Relations Counsellors, Inc., 1939. Qualified support was also given by Millis and Montgomery, *Labor's Risks and Social Insurance* (pp. 167, 176), and much later by Charles A. Myers, "Experience Rating in Unemployment Compensation," *American Economic Review* (1945), XXXV, No. 3, 337–54.

Experience rating was criticized by Harris (pp. 355-60). Its adverse effects have been strongly emphasized by Richard A. Lester in "Financing Unemployment Compensation," *Industrial and Labor Relations Review* (1960), XIV, 52–67. Turnbull, Williams, and Cheit, *Economic and Social Security* (pp. 416–20) attempt a judicious summary of the conflicting arguments. See also Eveline M. Burns, *Social Security and Public Policy* (pp. 165–71).

Benefits, Revenues, and Stabilization of the Economy

Data on total benefit payments and tax collections under the unemployment compensation and old-age-and-survivors provisions of the Social Security Act was obtained from *Historical Statistics of the United States, passim,* U. S. Department of Commerce, Bureau of the Census. Washington, D. C.: Government Printing Office; and also from *Social Security Bulletin, Annual Statistical Supplement, passim,* U. S. Department of Health, Education, and Welfare. Washington, D. C.: Government Printing Office.

Most of the analysis of social-security financing, including Seymour Harris, have been more concerned with reserves versus pay-as-you-go financing (as these alternatives may influence economic growth or stagnation) than with the short-run stabilization of economic activity. Also, any stabilizing effect of social security usually has been attributed to the unemployment compensation system alone, ignoring the influence in the same direction of the OASI system (albeit obscured by the building up of OASI reserves).

The best general statement regarding stabilizing effects of the operation of social security as a whole is that of Ida C. Merriam, "Social Security Programs and Economic Stability," in *Policies to Combat De-*

pression, National Bureau of Economic Research Special Conference, Series No. 7 (pp. 205–35). Princeton, N. J.: Princeton University Press, 1956. Two later statements by Lester follow Merriam's reasoning but are confined to unemployment compensation and stress the limitations of the stabilizing influence under present arrangements. See Lester, "Financing Unemployment Compensation," and the "Economic Significance of Unemployment Compensation, 1950–1959," *Review of Economics and Statistics* (1960), LXII, No. 4, 349–72. See also Eveline M. Burns, *Social Security and Public Policy* (Chaps. IX and X). Arthur F. Burns, in his AEA presidential address, gave to social security a major credit for "Progress Towards Economic Stability," *American Economic Review* (1960), L, No. 1, 4–6.

Chapter XI

HISTORY

For the years prior to 1935, the basic source of union membership data is Leo Wolman, *The Ebb and Flow of Trade Unionism.* New York: National Bureau of Economic Research, 1961. For later years, the basic source is the U. S. Department of Labor, Bureau of Labor Statistics, Division of Industrial Relations; for example, see *idem, Directory of National and International Unions,* Bulletin No. 1267. Washington, D. C.: Government Printing Office. The BLS data, including ratios of union membership to the U. S. labor force and to nonagricultural employment, are reprinted annually in *Statistical Abstract of the United States* (See 84th Ed., p. 250), U. S. Department of Commerce, Bureau of the Census. Washington, D. C.: Government Printing Office, 1963. For a summary analysis of trends during the years 1930–1955, see William Paschall, "Structure and Membership of the Labor Movement," *Monthly Labor Review* (1955), LXXVIII, 1231–39.

Ratios of union membership to the "organizable" group of nonagricultural manual workers plus nonsupervisory white-collar workers are provided by Benjamin Solomon, "Dimensions of Union Growth, 1900–1950," *Industrial and Labor Relations Review* (1956), IX, 544–61. Influences on union membership since World War II are discussed by: (1) Bernstein, Irving, *The Growth of American Unions,* Institute of Industrial Relations, Reprint No. 44. Los Angeles: University of California, 1954; and Kassalow, Everett, M., "Organization of White-Collar Workers," *Monthly Labor Review* (1961), LXXXIV, 234–38.

General histories of labor unions which cover the period since 1935 (surprisingly few considering the impact of the events) include: (1) Dulles, Foster Rhea, *Labor in America.* New York: Thomas Y. Crowell Company, 1949; and (2) Rayback, Joseph G., *A History of American Labor.* New York: The Macmillan Company, 1959.

An excellent brief description of the development of American unions from the 1930's to the early 1960's is contained in Everett Johnson Burtt, Jr., *Labor Markets, Unions and Government Policies* (Chap. VIII, pp. 137–60). New York: St. Martin's Press, 1963. A vivid account of the political and personal factors involved in the growth and subsequent stabilization of union power is provided by John Herling, "Record of Collective Bargaining in the Last Twenty-Five Years" *Industrial Relations Research Association: Proceedings of the Fifteenth Annual Meeting, December 1962* (Esp. pp. 186–201). Madison, Wis.: Industrial Relations Research Association, 1963. A brief but authoritative appraisal of the economic, political, and social strengths and weaknesses of post-World-War-II unions was that of Sumner H. Slichter, "The Position of Trade Unions in the American Economy," in Harrington and Jacobs, eds., *Labor in a Free Society* (pp. 17–44). Berkeley and Los Angeles: University of California Press, 1959.

CONFLICT OF DOCTRINES

The operation of communist doctrine within unions, the varieties of business-union leadership, and the rivalries among unions are aptly described by Jack Barbash, *The Practice of Unionism* (Chaps. VI, XIV, and XV). New York: Harper & Row, Publishers, 1956. See also Arthur M. Ross, "Changing Patterns of Industrial Conflict," *Monthly Labor Review* (1960), LXXXIII, 229–37.

The superior recent books which deal with collective bargaining as a whole are: (1) Beal, Edwin, and Edward D. Wickersham, *The Practice of Collective Bargaining*. Homewood, Ill.: Richard D. Irwin, Inc., 1959; and (2) Davey, Harold W., *Contemporary Collective Bargaining*. Englewood Cliffs, N. J.: Prentice-Hall, Inc., 1959.

The management doctrine that wages are determined by impersonal forces lies behind many arguments to the effect that unions are unnecessary and supposedly impotent. Assuming that management policy is involved, the rationale of the management position has been variously worked out by: (1) Daugherty, Carroll, B., and John B. Parrish, *The Labor Problems of American Society* (p. 52ff). Boston: Houghton Mifflin Company, 1952; (2) Lester, Richard A., *Labor and Industrial Relations* (pp. 215ff). New York: The Macmillan Company, 1951; and originally by (3) Reynolds, Lloyd G., *Labor Economics and Labor Relations*, 2nd Ed. (pp. 551–57). Englewood Cliffs, N. J.: Prentice-Hall, Inc., 1954.

Union wage-bargaining doctrines in the post-World-War-II period were interpreted: (1) by an academic scholar in Arthur M. Ross, *Trade Union Wage Policy*. Berkeley: University of California Press, 1948; (2) by an economic theorist in John T. Dunlop, *Wage Determination Under Trade Unions*. New York: The Macmillan Company, 1944; and (3) by two union economists in Nathaniel Goldfinger and Everett M. Kassalow,

"Trade Union Behavior in Wage Bargaining." George W. Taylor and
Frank C. Pierson, eds., *New Concepts in Wage Determination* (pp. 51–
82). New York: McGraw-Hill Book Company, 1957. The development
of a logical basis for bargaining-power doctrines from Jenkins (1868) to
Joan Robinson (1933) was reviewed by Paul A. Samuelson, "Economic
Theory and Wages" in Wright, David McCord, ed., *The Impact of the
Union* (pp. 320–26). See also "Wage Theories and Bargaining Power"
in Eric Strauss, 'The Wage Revolt of 1955 in West Germany—A Test of
Bargaining Power Theory (pp. 2–9). Unpublished Master's Thesis, Cornell University, 1963.

The doctrine that union (or legal) pressure serves to spur management to increased efficiency (based on "shock" theory) has been variously
stated, implied, or confirmed by: (1) Douglas, Paul H., *Real Wages in
the United States* (pp. 562–64). Boston: Houghton Mifflin Company,
1930; (2) Denison, Edward F., "Measurement of Labor Input," in *Output, Input, and Productivity Measurement: Studies in Income and
Wealth*, Vol. XXV (pp. 353–54), by the Conference on Research in Income and Wealth, National Bureau of Economic Research. Princeton,
N. J.: Princeton University Press, 1961. (3) Reynolds, Lloyd G., *Labor
Economics and Labor Relations*, 3rd Ed. (pp. 521–22). Englewood Cliffs,
N. J.: Prentice-Hall, Inc., 1959; and (4) the author, in citing the findings
of Marian Stever McNulty, *Industrial Relations Research Association,
Proceedings of Twelfth Annual Meeting, December 1959* (See above
notes for Chap. VIII).

The union purchasing-power doctrine has found its theoretical support
in one interpretation of the principle of aggregate effective demand of
Keynes' *General Theory* (See above notes for Chap. II). The doctrine
was strikingly applied on behalf of union wage policy by Robert B.
Nathan, *A National Economic Policy for 1949*. Washington, D. C.: Congress of Industrial Organizations, 1949. The union contention that wage-
rate increases would increase total purchasing power has been criticized
by many economists, notably in 1949 by Sumner H. Slichter, "Comments
on the Steel Report," in *Potentials of the American Economy, Selected
Essays of Sumner H. Slichter* (pp. 406–15), John T. Dunlop, ed. Cambridge, Mass.: Harvard University Press, 1961. After a decade of price
inflation, however, Slichter himself contended (in 1959) that unions
were, indeed, "income-creating institutions" (*loc. cit.*, pp. 420–27, 430–
32). The diverse policy implications of purchasing-power theories were
examined by Samuelson in *Impact of the Union* (pp. 332–41).

IMPACT ON THEORY

The Wage Share and the General Wage Level

The recent literature on the theoretical problem as to whether unions
do or can increase the over-all share of labor in the whole national product
has been brilliantly reviewed by George H. Hildebrand, "The Economic
Effects of Unionism," in Neil W. Chamberlain, Frank C. Pierson, and

Theresa Wolfson, eds., *A Decade of Industrial Relations Research, 1946–1956* (pp. 99–106). New York: Harper & Row, Publishers, 1958. Nineteen references were discussed in this portion of Hildebrand's analysis. A supplementary bibliography covering nine additional references on this topic has been prepared by the author.

Theory of Particular Wages and Wage Relationships.

Hildebrand, in *A Decade of Industrial Relations Research* (pp. 115–27), has reviewed a total of thirty-nine recent contributions to this part of the developing theory of wages. A supplementary bibliography covering thirty-nine additional references has been prepared by the author. The combined bibliography of seventy-eight references has been arranged to show separately the major recent contributions to the study of each of the following types of wage relationships: (1) Union-Nonunion; (2) Skill (including occupations and occupational groups; (3) Geographic; (4–A) Interindustry; (4–B) Interplant and Intercompany; (5) Individual Worker. As regards subjects (2) — (4); the author's bibliography also distinguishes between contributions which deal with the impact of unions on each of these wage differentials and those which involve a general understanding of each differential, regardless of any impact of union influences.

Chapter XII

SOURCES OF STATISTICAL DATA CITED

The percentages of unemployment for various periods during the years 1939–1963 relate to the civilian labor force and are shown in various issues of *Employment and Earnings* (e.g. IX, No. 12, 1), U. S. Department of Labor, Bureau of Labor Statistics. Washington, D. C.: Government Printing Office.

The data on government receipts, expenditures, surplus and "excess spending," "deficit spending," or deficit for various years beginning in 1941 relate to the U. S. federal government and the combined totals for the state and local governments, as shown in annual issues of the U. S. Department of Commerce *Survey of Current Business, National Income Supplement.* Washington, D. C.: Government Printing Office. More accurate measures of the impact of fiscal operations for 1936–1942 are given in Morris A. Copeland, *A Study of Moneyflows in the United States* (Tables 19, 20, pp. 116–99, esp. "Net Money Obtained thru Financing"). New York: National Bureau of Economic Research, Inc., 1952.

Wholesale price movements for the years 1913–1956 are measured in *Wholesale Price Indexes, 1954–1956.* U. S. Department of Labor, Bureau of Labor Statistics, Bulletin No. 1214. Washington, D. C.: Government Printing Office, 1957.

Movements of average consumer prices (formerly called "cost of living") are those of the "all items" index of the Bureau of Labor Statistics, as reproduced in the *Statistical Abstract of the United States, 1963* (Table

228 Bibliographic Notes

473, p. 356), U. S. Department of Commerce, Bureau of the Census. Washington, D. C.: Government Printing Office, 1963.

"Straight-time" earnings consist of average hourly earnings excluding overtime pay, as shown for manufacturing industries, 1941 ff. in *Employment and Earnings Statistics for the United States, 1909–1962*, U. S. Department of Labor, Bureau of Labor Statistics, Bulletin No. 1312–1. Washington, D. C.: Government Printing Office, 1963.

Average weekly earnings refer to the gross earnings of production workers in manufacturing industries, as shown in *Employment and Earnings*.

Movements of the average prices of "goods" and "manufactured goods" and "all commodities except farm products and foods," are as shown in *Wholesale Price Indexes, loc. cit.* Prices of "service" refer to a subdivision of the indexes of consumer prices as set forth in *Business Statistics for 1963*, Biennial Edition (p. 38), U. S. Department of Commerce, Office of Business Economics. Washington, D. C.: Government Printing Office, 1963.

DEPRESSION TO WARTIME INFLATION

Basic official documents which help to explain the origins of price inflation and the attempts made to control it during World War II were among those prepared under the general title of "Historical Reports on War Administration:" (1) *The United States at War*, Bureau of the Budget. Washington, D. C.: Government Printing Office, 1946; (2) *A Short History of OPA*, Office of Price Administration, *idem*, 1947; (3) *Termination Report*, War Labor Board, idem, 1947; and (4) *Industrial Mobilization for War*, War Production Board, *idem*, 1947. Major independent analyses of wartime price inflation include: Jules Bachman, *The Economics Of Armament Inflation*. New York: Holt, Rinehart & Winston, Inc., 1951; A. J. Brown, *The Great Inflation, 1939–1951*. London: Oxford University Press, 1954; and Lester V. Chandler, *Inflation in the United States, 1940–1948*. New York: Harper & Row, Publishers, 1951.

The wartime expansion of the labor force was definitively described by Gertrude Bancroft, *The American Labor Force, Its Growth and Changing Composition*. New York: John Wiley & Sons, Inc., 1958.

The role of savings bonds and other forms of federal bond sales to finance the war effort was described in Henry C. Murphy, *The National Debt in War and Transition*. New York: McGraw-Hill Book Company, 1950.

The importance of British, French, and domestic defense spending in the period prior to the United States entry into the war is explained in *The United States at War* (pp. 10–14, 17–29), and in *Industrial Mobilization for War* (pp. 39–40).

The inflationary effects of war expenditures are explained in general terms by Brown, *The Great Inflation, 1939–1951* (pp. 56–78), and specifically for the United States by Chandler, *Inflation in the United States, 1940–1948* (pp. 15–45, 61–82).

On the deterioration of quality, black markets, and the resulting understatement of the rise in commodity prices under price controls, see Bachman, *The Economics of Armament Inflation* (pp. 98–100, 117–19). Compare the official view of the enforcement of wartime price controls in *A Short History of OPA* (pp. 269–70).

On the upgrading of labor and other reasons for the rise of wages in spite of war controls, see Robert J. Myers, Harry Ober, and Lily Mary David, "Wartime Wage Movements and Urban Wage-Rate Changes," *Monthly Labor Review* (1944), LIX, No. 4, 684–704.

Two general assessments of the role of direct controls of prices and wages are contained in Brown, *The Great Inflation, 1939–1951* (pp. 137–71), and in Chandler, *Inflation in the United States, 1940–1948* (pp. 203–15).

POST-WORLD-WAR-II INFLATION

The postwar termination of price and wage controls is briefly described and evaluated in: (1) *A Short History of OPA* (pp. 81–101, 132–36, 191–97); (2) A. J. Brown, *The Great Inflation, 1939–1951* (pp. 164–65); and (3) Chandler, *Inflation in the United States, 1940–1948* (pp. 214–19).

Price inflation in the United States between World War II and the Korean War was comprehensively analyzed by Chandler, *op. cit.* (pp. 216–52). The insufficient curtailment of government expenditure in this period is analyzed in more detail by Chandler, *op. cit.* (pp. 253–73). The diverse views, as of 1947 and 1948, of the reasons and appropriate remedies for the postwar inflation were presented at two congressional hearings: (1) *Hearing on Economic Stabilization Aids,* U. S. Congress, House Committee on Banking and Currency. Washington, D. C.: Government Printing Office, 1947. (2) *Hearings on the Control of Inflation,* U. S. Congress, Senate Committee on Banking and Currency. Washington, D. C.: Government Printing Office, 1948.

The price inflation connected with the Korean War was described in its world perspective by A. J. Brown, *op. cit.* (pp. 45–49). The nature of the price and wage controls of 1950 and 1951 were outlined by Bachman, *The Economics of Armament Inflation* (pp. 100–16).

A comprehensive analysis of price inflation between 1952 and 1958 is contained in Willard L. Thorp and Richard E. Quandt, *The New Inflation.* New York: McGraw-Hill Book Company, 1959.

CONFLICTS OF DOCTRINES AND IMPACT ON THEORY

The most extensive collection of diverse doctrines and of analyses of facts regarding recent inflation in the United States was that of the Joint Economic Committee of the Eighty-Fifth Congress, at its hearings May

230   Bibliographic Notes

12–22 and December 15–18, 1958, dealing with *Relationship of Prices to Economic Stability and Growth*. A *Compendium of Papers, Commentaries*, and two sets of *Hearings* may be obtained from the Government Printing Office, Washington, D. C.

The most recent comprehensive record of the doctrines and theories of an international group of economists is to be found in D. C. Hague, ed., Inflation: *Proceedings of a Conference Held by the International Economic Association, 1959*. London: Macmillan & Co., Ltd., 1962. A very useful review of the proceedings of this conference is that of D. J. Robertson, *Economic Journal* (1963), LX, No. 290, 281–84. A more limited group of six "independent experts" from five countries, under the auspices of the Organization for European Economic Cooperation, attempted to reach agreement on both the analysis of and recommendations for dealing with the problem of inflation; see William Fellner, et al., *The Problem of Rising Prices*. Organization for European Economic Cooperation document C (61) 12, multilithed, May 1961.

For conflicting views on the importance of growth and the relation between growth and changes in price levels see, among others: (1) *Hearings on Amending the Employment Act of 1946*. U. S. Congress, House Committee on Government Operations (Esp. the testimony of Seymour Harris, p. 77, and Leon Keyserling, pp. 23–24). Washington, D. C.: Government Printing Office, 1958; (2) *Hearings on Employment, Growth and Price Levels*, U. S. Congress, Joint Committee on the Economic Report (Esp. the testimony of Fritz Machlup, pp. 2819–44). Washington, D. C.: Government Printing Office, 1959; (3) G. Maynard, *Economic Development and the Price Level*. London: Macmillan & Co., Ltd., 1962, reviewed by Joan Robinson in the *Economic Journal* (1963), LX, No. 290, 299–300; (4) *The Promise of Economic Growth*, The Chamber of Commerce of the United States (Esp. pp. 2–5, 39–42). Washington, D. C.: Chamber of Commerce of the United States, 1959. (5) Thorp and Quandt, *The New Inflation* (pp. 99–129).

On the relative importance of demand-pull and wage-cost-push inflation in recent years, the doctrines as to the appropriate solutions to the problem, and the associated wage-price theories, see: (1) Bowen, William G., *The Wage-Price Issue*. Princeton, N. J.: Princeton University Press, 1960; (2) Fellner, et al, *The Problem of Rising Prices* (Esp. pp. 35–64); (3) Machlup testimony before the Joint Committee, *op. cit.* (pp. 2819–44); (4) Selden, Richard T., "Cost-Push versus Demand-Pull Inflation, 1955–57," *Journal of Political Economy* (1959), LXVIII, No. 1, 1–20; (5) Thorp and Quandt, *op. cit.* (pp. 76–98, 218–88); (6) Walker, Franklin V., *Growth, Employment and the Price Level* (Esp. pp. 278–79). Englewood Cliffs, N. J.: Prentice-Hall, Inc., 1963.

On the issue of the alleged inflationary influence of unionism, a discriminating analysis of eighteen professional articles besides those just cited has been provided by George H. Hildebrand, "The Economic Effects of Unionism," in Chamberlain, Pierson, and Wolfson, *A Decade of Industrial Relations Research, 1946–1956* (pp. 106–15). New York: Harper & Row, Publishers, 1958.

Chapter XIII

These notes are confined to some contributions to wage theory not previously listed in connection with Chapter I–XII above.

Recent appraisals of the general state of wage theory and the more immediate gaps which need to be filled are to be found in: (1) Cartter, Allan M., *Theory of Wages and Employment* (pp. 1–41). Homewood, Ill.: Richard D. Irwin, Inc., 1959; (2) Dunlop, John, "The Task of Contemporary Wage Theory," earlier statement in John Dunlop, ed., *The Theory of Wage Determination* (pp. 3–27). London: Macmillan & Co., Ltd., 1957. (3) *Ibid* (a different statement) in George Taylor and Frank Pierson, eds., *New Concepts in Wage Determination* (pp. 117–39). New York: McGraw-Hill Company, Inc., 1957. (4) Hague, D. C. "Report on the Proceedings of the 1954 Conference of the International Economic Association," in Taylor and Pierson, *op. cit.* (pp. 337–430); (5) Lester, Richard A., "Results and Implications of Some Recent Wage Studies," in Richard A. Lester and Joseph Shister, eds., *Insights in Labor Issues* (pp. 197–225). New York: The Macmillan Company, 1948; (6) Pierson, Frank C., "An Evaluation of Wage Theory," in Taylor and Pierson, *op. cit.* (pp. 3–31); (7) Reynolds, Lloyd G., "Economics of Labor," in Howard S. Ellis, ed., *A Survey of Contemporary Economics* (pp. 255–87). Philadelphia: The Blakiston Company, 1948.

No single book has included all of the diverse twentieth-century developments of wage theories. The more ambitious attempts, subsequent to the works of Douglas and Pigou, have been: (1) Cartter, *loc. cit.;* (2) Dobb, Maurice, *Wages.* Cambridge, Mass.: Cambridge University Press, 1956; (3) Hicks, J. R., *The Theory of Wages.* London: Macmillan & Co., Ltd., 1932; reprinted New York: Peter Smith, 1948; (4) Robertson, D. J., *The Economics of Wages.* New York: St. Martin's Press, 1961; (5) Rothschild, K. W., *The Theory of Wages.* Oxford: Basil Blackwell, 1954.

Recent treatments of theories of the general wage level include: (1) Gasparini, I., "Approaches to the Determination of the General Level of Wage Rates," in Dunlop, ed., *The Theory of Wage Determination* (pp. 39–47); (2) Johnson, H. G., "The Determination of the General Level of Wage Rates," in Dunlop (pp. 31–38); (3) Krelle, W., "Wage Rates in a Model of the System," in Dunlop (pp. 91–104); (4) Phelps-Brown, E. H., "The Long-Term Movement of Real Wages," in Dunlop (pp. 39–47); (5) Kerr, Clark, "Labor's Income Share and the Labor Movement," in Taylor and Pierson (pp. 260–98); (6) Reynolds, Lloyd G., "The General Level of Wages," in Taylor and Pierson (pp. 239–59); (7) Weintraub, Sidney, *An Approach to the Theory of Income Distribution* (Esp. Chaps. I and VI). Philadelphia: Chilton Books, Publishers, 1958; (8) Weintraub, Sidney, *Some Aspects of Wage Theory and Policy.* Philadelphia: Chilton Books, Publishers, 1963.

The outstanding critical review of the recent literature on theories of wage structure is that of Melvin W. Reder, "Wage Determination in

Theory and Practice," in Neil W. Chamberlain, Frank C. Pierson, and Theresa Wolfson, eds., *A Decade of Industrial Relations Research, 1946–1956* (pp. 64–97). New York: Harper & Row, Publishers, 1958. A good example of the application of modern theories of monopoly and monopsony to wage determination at the plant level is that of Joe S. Bain, *Pricing, Distribution, and Employment* (Esp. Chap. XIII). New York: Holt, Rinehart & Winston, Inc.

The following are some of the more important recent contributions to theories of particular wages and wage relationships, in addition to those directly or indirectly referred to in connection with previous chapters: (1) Demaria, Giovanni, "Aggregate and Particular Labour Supply Curves," in Dunlop, *The Theory of Wage Determination* (pp. 327–33) (2) Lester, Richard A., "A Range Theory of Wage Differentials," *Industrial and Labor Relations Review* (1952), V, No. 4, 483–500; (3) Livernash, E. Robert, "The Internal Wage Structure," in Taylor and Pierson, *op. cit.,* (pp. 140–72); (4) Pierson, Frank C., *Community Wage Patterns.* Berkeley and Los Angeles: University of California Press, 1953; (5) Reynolds, Lloyd G. and Cynthia Taft, *The Evolution of Wage Structure* (Esp. Chap. XIII). New Haven, Conn.: Yale University Press, 1955. (6) Reynolds, Lloyd G., *The Structure of Labor Markets.* New York: Harper & Row, Publishers, 1951; (7) Ross, Arthur M., "The External Wage Structure," in Taylor and Pierson, *op. cit.* (pp. 173–205); and (8) Rottier, G., "The Evolution of Wage Differentials: A Study of the British Data," in Dunlop, *The Theory of Wage Determination.*

Index

Index

235

GAYLORD RG